Readings and Cases in International Human Resource Management

The new edition of *Readings and Cases in International Human Resource Management* examines the interactions between people, cultures, and human resource systems in a wide variety of regions throughout the world.

Taking account of recent developments in the international human resources management (IHRM) field, the sixth edition will enable students to meet the international challenges they will face in the workforce, and sensitize them to the complexity of human resource issues in the era of globalization.

Features include:

- New readings and case studies that account for recent changes in the field, positioned alongside "tried and true" material.
- An increased focus on cross-cultural diversity and tools to bridge "social distance" between team members.
- Supplemental material and teaching notes, available for download, to enhance instructors' abilities to use the readings and cases with their students.

With well-known contributors and field experts, this is the ideal accompaniment for any class in international human resource management, organizational studies, or international business.

B. Sebastian Reiche is an Associate Professor of Managing People in Organizations at IESE Business School, Spain.

Günter K. Stahl is Professor of International Management at WU Vienna, Austria.

Mark E. Mendenhall is the J. Burton Frierson Chair of Excellence in Business Leadership at the University of Tennessee-Chattanooga, USA.

Gary R. Oddou is Professor Emeritus of International Management and former Director of the Global Business Management program at California State University in San Marcos, USA.

Readings and Cases in International Human Resource Management

Sixth Edition

Edited by

B. Sebastian Reiche,
Günter K. Stahl,
Mark E. Mendenhall, and
Gary R. Oddou

Routledge
Taylor & Francis Group

NEW YORK AND LONDON

Please visit the eResource at
www.routledge.com/9781138950528

First published 2017
by Routledge
711 Third Avenue, New York, NY 10017

and by Routledge
2 Park Square, Milton Park, Abingdon, Oxon OX14 4RN

Routledge is an imprint of the Taylor & Francis Group, an informa business

Library of Congress Cataloging in Publication Data
A catalog record for this book has been requested

ISBN: 978-1-138-95049-8 (hbk)
ISBN: 978-1-138-95052-8 (pbk)
ISBN: 978-1-31566-870-3 (ebk)

Typeset in Bell Gothic
by Sunrise Setting Ltd, Brixham, UK

Contents

List of Illustrations ix

B. Sebastian Reiche, Günter K. Stahl,
Mark E. Mendenhall, and Gary R. Oddou
PREFACE: THE WHITE WATER RAPIDS OF INTERNATIONAL
HUMAN RESOURCE MANAGEMENT: ROBIN EARL'S DILEMMA xiv

Acknowledgments xxii
List of Contributors xxiii

PART I
The Context of IHRM: Challenges, Strategies,
and External Forces **1**

Readings

1.1 Paul Evans, Vladimir Pucik, and Ingmar Björkman
PUTTING THE CHALLENGES OF INTERNATIONAL HUMAN
RESOURCE MANAGEMENT INTO PERSPECTIVE 3

1.2 Randall S. Schuler, Susan E. Jackson,
and Ibraiz Tarique
MANAGING GLOBAL TALENT CHALLENGES WITH GLOBAL
TALENT MANAGEMENT INITIATIVES 24

1.3 Wes Harry and David G. Collings
LOCALISATION: SOCIETIES, ORGANISATIONS
AND EMPLOYEES 44

Cases

1.1 Ingmar Björkman
PETER HANSEN: BUILDING A WORLD-CLASS PRODUCT
DEVELOPMENT CENTRE FOR HI TECH SYSTEMS IN CHINA 61

1.2 Evalde Mutabazi and C. Brooklyn Derr
SOCOMETAL: REWARDING AFRICAN WORKERS 70

1.3 Roger Hallowell, David Bowen,
and Carin-Isabel Knoop
FOUR SEASONS GOES TO PARIS   73

PART II
Cross-Cultural and Diversity Management   **103**

Readings

2.1 David A. Thomas
DIVERSITY AS STRATEGY   105

2.2 Mansour Javidan, Peter W. Dorfman, Mary
Sully de Luque, and Robert J. House
IN THE EYE OF THE BEHOLDER: CROSS-CULTURAL LESSONS
IN LEADERSHIP FROM PROJECT GLOBE   119

2.3 Stacey R. Fitzsimmons, Christof Miska, and
Günter K. Stahl
MULTICULTURAL INDIVIDUALS: WHAT CAN THEY BRING
TO GLOBAL ORGANIZATIONS?   155

Cases

2.1 Mark E. Mendenhall
OLIVIA FRANCIS   172

2.2 Joseph J. DiStefano
JOHANNES VAN DEN BOSCH SENDS AN EMAIL   175

2.3 B. Sebastian Reiche and Yih-teen Lee
UWA ODE: A CULTURAL CHAMELEON OR STRANDED
BETWEEN CULTURAL CHAIRS?   177

PART III
Global Staffing and Management of Global
Mobility   **187**

Readings

3.1 David G. Collings, Anthony McDonnell,
and Amy McCarter
TYPES OF INTERNATIONAL ASSIGNEES   189

3.2 Gary R. Oddou and Mark E. Mendenhall
EXPATRIATE PERFORMANCE APPRAISAL: PROBLEMS
AND SOLUTIONS   208

3.3 Jaime Bonache and Luigi Stirpe
COMPENSATING GLOBAL EMPLOYEES   218

Cases

3.1 J. Stewart Black
FRED BAILEY: AN INNOCENT ABROAD   236

3.2 Paula Caligiuri and Henry W. Lane
SELECTING A COUNTRY MANAGER FOR DELTA
BEVERAGES INDIA   243

3.3 Günter K. Stahl and Mark E. Mendenhall
ANDREAS WEBER'S REWARD FOR SUCCESS IN AN INTERNATIONAL
ASSIGNMENT: A RETURN TO AN UNCERTAIN FUTURE   249

PART IV
People Issues in Global Teams, Alliances,
Mergers, and Acquisitions   255

Readings

4.1 Tsedal Neeley
GLOBAL TEAMS THAT WORK: A FRAMEWORK FOR BRIDGING
SOCIAL DISTANCE   257

4.2 Vladimir Pucik, Paul Evans, and Ingmar Björkman
MANAGING ALLIANCES AND JOINT VENTURES   266

4.3 Satu Teerikangas, Günter K. Stahl, Ingmar
Björkman, and Mark E. Mendenhall
IHRM ISSUES IN MERGERS AND ACQUISITIONS   316

Cases

4.1 Carlos Sánchez-Runde, Yih-teen Lee, and
B. Sebastian Reiche
HAILING A NEW ERA: HAIER IN JAPAN   356

4.2 Kathrin Köster and Günter K. Stahl
LENOVO–IBM: BRIDGING CULTURES, LANGUAGES,
AND TIME ZONES   373

4.3 Ingmar Björkman and Ming Zeng
GUANGDONG ELECTRONICS   388

PART V
Responsible Leadership in a Global and
Cross-Cultural Context   401

Readings

5.1 Thomas Donaldson
VALUES IN TENSION: ETHICS AWAY FROM HOME   403

5.2 Günter K. Stahl, Christof Miska, Laura J. Noval, and Verena J. Patock
THE CHALLENGE OF RESPONSIBLE GLOBAL LEADERSHIP   416

5.3 Ina Aust and Marie-Thérèse Claes
GLOBAL LEADERSHIP FOR SUSTAINABLE DEVELOPMENT   438

Cases

5.1 Charlotte Butler and Henri-Claude de Bettignies
CHANGMAI CORPORATION   458

5.2 Nicola Pless and Thomas Maak
LEVI STRAUSS & CO.: ADDRESSING CHILD LABOUR
IN BANGLADESH   466

5.3 Barbara Coudenhove-Kalergi and Christian Seelos
EVN IN BULGARIA: ENGAGING THE ROMA COMMUNITY   477

Index   496

Illustrations

FIGURES

Reading 1.2

Figure 1	Framework for global talent challenges and management	26

Reading 2.2

Figure 1	US versus Brazil	132
Figure 2	US versus France	135
Figure 3	US versus Egypt	138
Figure 4	US versus China	141

Reading 2.3

Figure 1	Managing a multicultural workforce: the organizational implications pyramid	167

Reading 4.1

Figure 1	Views from a dispersed team	259
Figure 2	Rules of engagement for team meetings	262

Reading 4.2

Figure 1	Classification of strategic alliances	271
Figure 2	A strategic framework for understanding international alliances	272

Reading 4.3

Figure 1	Model of the antecedents and consequences of trust in M&As	322
Figure 2	HR's involvement in M&As—four scenarios	343
Figure 3	Situating HR's and management's roles in dealing with human dimensions of M&A activity	344

Reading 5.2

Figure 1   Multiple levels and factors influencing responsible
            global leadership   419

Figure 2   Three prototypical CSR approaches   428

EXHIBITS

Reading 1.2

Exhibit 1   Country assessments for location management decisions   34

Reading 2.1

Exhibit 1   The vital few issues: employees' biggest
            diversity concerns   110

Case 2.3

Exhibit 1   Geopolitical map of Nigeria   185

Case 3.2

Exhibit 1   Ranking of expatriate selection criteria   245

Case 4.1

Exhibit 1   The rules introduced by Zhang in 1984   358
Exhibit 2   ZZJYT and the inverted-triangular
            organizational structure   361
Exhibit 3   Negative entropy and positive feedback loops   364
Exhibit 4   Commitment of the sales team to the
            JPY35 billion target   369

Case 4.2

Exhibit 1   Timeline for the Lenovo–IBM merger   374
Exhibit 2   "New" Lenovo's executive team   383
Exhibit 3   Lenovo's market share, 2005   386

Case 4.3

Exhibit 1   The Guangdong Electronics organization in early 1997 390
Exhibit 2   The ISO 9000 series of quality standards   394
Exhibit 3   The Guangdong Electronics organization
            in November 1998   399
Exhibit 4   Summary of the report made by the quality audit
            group in October 1998   400

Reading 5.1

Exhibit 1	The culture and ethics of software piracy	405
Exhibit 2	What do these values have in common?	408
Exhibit 3	The problem with bribery	413

Reading 5.3

Exhibit 1	Global leaders' challenges	440
Exhibit 2	Millennium development goals	443
Exhibit 3	The Enron case	446
Exhibit 4	The Ogoni versus Shell	448
Exhibit 5	Good leadership in Thailand	448
Exhibit 6	Pepsi bottling champions diversity despite hard times	449
Exhibit 7	Mindfulness	453

Case 5.3

Exhibit 1	Hidden costs in the energy sector	481
Exhibit 2	Formal and informal sector employment	483
Exhibit 3	Risky customers/potentials	489
Exhibit 4	Risky neighborhoods: opportunity overview	491

TABLES

Case 1.3

| Table 1 | Employees-to-room ratios at selected Four Seasons properties | 89 |

Reading 2.2

Table 1	Cultural clusters classified on societal culture practices (as is) scores	124
Table 2	CLT scores for societal clusters	129
Table 3	Summary of comparisons for CLT leadership dimensions	130
Table 4	Cultural views of leadership effectiveness	131

Reading 2.3

| Table 1 | Multicultural types | 164 |

Reading 3.1

| Table 1 | Summary of alternative global mobility types | 203 |

Reading 3.3

Table 1   Compensation approaches and their impact on
            compensation objectives   221

Table 2   The use of different compensation components for global
            assignees (% of companies)   224

Reading 4.2

Table 1   The HR alliance strategy plan   277

Table 2   Alliance manager versus venture manager: roles and
            responsibilities   280

Table 3   Obstacles to organizational learning in international
            strategic alliances   298

Table 4   Core principles for alliance learning   301

Reading 5.2

Table 1   Examples of moral disengagement   422

Table 2   Components of the moral intensity of the ethical issue   425

Table 3   Competencies required to support different
            CSR approaches   430

Reading 5.3

Table 1   Global leadership challenges, roles and competences   452

Case 5.3

Table 1   Source of income   482

APPENDICES

Case 1.3

Appendix 1 Sample core standards   96

Appendix 2 Four seasons goals, beliefs, and principles   98

Appendix 3 Comparative data on Parisian palaces   100

Appendix 4 Predictable patterns of monochronic and
             polychronic cultures   101

Case 2.2

Appendix 1 Country scores on cultural practices   147

Case 5.2

Appendix 1 Memo by the President and CEO John Anderson
accompanying the Worldwide Code of Business Conduct   468

Appendix 2 Levi Strauss & Co. fact sheet   469

Appendix 3 Global Sourcing and Operating Guidelines   472

Appendix 4 Bangladesh: Shetra's Story: the life of a sexually
exploited child in Bangladesh   475

B. Sebastian Reiche, Günter K. Stahl, Mark E. Mendenhall, and Gary R. Oddou

PREFACE: THE WHITE WATER RAPIDS OF INTERNATIONAL HUMAN RESOURCE MANAGEMENT: ROBIN EARL'S DILEMMA

WELCOME TO THE SIXTH EDITION of *Readings and Cases in International Human Resource Management.* If you are a long-time user of this text, we would like to take a moment to thank you for using the book in your teaching or consulting endeavors. We originally put this book together because we couldn't find one ourselves, and we wanted such a book to use in our classes. Since then, with your help, the book has evolved and become a standby for teachers of international management/HRM/OB.

We think the best way to introduce the textbook is with an introductory reading/case. It sets the tone of the book, and, if you like, also makes an excellent reading assignment to begin class with. We call it "The White Water Rapids of Robin Earl."

READING AND CASE: THE WHITE WATER RAPIDS OF ROBIN EARL

Business leaders of the present—let alone the future—need to possess international business skills par excellence in order to survive the chaotic world of international business. It also goes without saying that human resource managers will face new, unforeseen obstacles. Peter Vaill uses the metaphor of "permanent white water" to describe the unpredictable, dynamic nature of doing business in the latter part of the twentieth and twenty-first century.

> Most managers are taught to think of themselves as paddling their canoes on calm, still, lakes ... They're led to believe that they should be pretty

much able to go where they want, when they want, using the means that are under their control. Sure there will be temporary disruptions during changes of various sorts—periods when they will have to shoot the rapids in their canoes—but the disruptions will be temporary, and when things settle back down, they'll be back in a calm, still lake mode. But it has been my experience

... that you never get out of the rapids! No sooner do you begin to digest one change than another one comes along to keep things unstuck. In fact, there are usually lots of changes going on at once. The feeling is one of continuous upset and chaos.[1]

This metaphor aptly illustrates the world of international business. As Vaill notes, in the world of international business, "things are only very partially under control, yet the effective navigator of the rapids is not behaving randomly or aimlessly. Intelligence, experience, and skill are being exercised, albeit in ways that we hardly know how to perceive, let alone describe" (p. 2). This book deals with the challenges that human resource managers will face in the twenty-first century. What will be the general nature of those challenges? Perhaps an example of a firm or individual would help illustrate these challenges. Let us consider the case of Robin Earl. Note that Robin Earl is a North American human resource manager in a North American company. However, she could just as easily be a manager in any medium-sized European, Asian, South or Central American, Australian or New Zealand, or African company. The issue is not her gender, her nationality, or the nationality of her firm, but rather the challenges she faces due to globalization.

ROBIN EARL'S "WHITE WATER RAPIDS"

Robin Earl is Director of Human Resources for BCN, a firm that, among other things, manufactures a line of semiconductors. BCN has been very successful in the last ten years. Sales have increased at an annual rate of 7 percent and profits have correspondingly grown.

BCN has had overseas sales offices for the last seven years, exporting its products from its local manufacturing operations to South America and Southeast Asia. Recently, BCN's top management has been mulling over the possibility of developing manufacturing and distribution capabilities in South America and Asia—and possibly even in Europe. Doing so would allow BCN to take advantage of cheaper labor rates in some of these countries and to avoid export barriers in others. In addition, it could be more responsive to local demand for its products, and in the age of globalization, move toward being a truly global firm.

Robin was asked by the firm's CEO to prepare an analysis (due on his desk in two weeks) of the human resource impact such moves would have on the firm. As Robin sat down at her desk, she began to jot down ideas. She found herself somewhat baffled by this global angle of HRM, as she had no experience or training in managing human resources internationally. The following are some of her thoughts as she attempted to create an outline for her report.

I. How Will International Assignments Fit into BCN's Business Strategy to Become a Truly Global Firm?

Do we have a clearly focused business strategy for becoming a multinational firm? She made a mental note to call John Fukumoto, the VP of Finance, to see how far the thinking of the top management team had progressed on that front. *How will the development of BCN's human resources fit into such a plan? I wonder why I am not on that planning team?* Robin wondered how she could insert herself into that process without being suspected of having ulterior motives.

What kind of perspective and experience should BCN's future top management have if they will be leading a true multinational firm? How will that experience be best obtained—through international assignments or by the use of consultants? Am I going to be responsible for educating management regarding international issues? If so, it's the blind leading the blind, she thought, for she would not even be sure how to evaluate the validity of an external consultant's proposals. *I could always hire experts to evaluate the bid proposals of consulting firms,* she thought, *but that would run into serious budget squeezes for my department.*

Who should we send—our high potentials that are destined to lead the company in the next 10 years or our non-designated personnel? How important will it be to have a global perspective at the top versus having one throughout the levels of the company?

Robin began to think about dual-career couple issues as well. *Just how hard will it be to attract our best people to go to a foreign country if their spouse has a good career here,* she wondered. She had heard about some firms that have formed a consortium in the foreign country to help provide employment for spouses of the repatriate. Working together, they had more flexibility than if they were trying to go it alone.

Will local managers—if we use local managers—desire to be promoted to US headquarters? Will top management desire that? Fifteen years from now what will, and what should, BCN's top management look like: an Asian managing a South American plant and a mixture of South Americans, Asians, Europeans, and Americans at headquarters? The cost of hiring the numbers of new workers—not to mention well-qualified managers—is not going to be loose change. I hope they aren't ignoring the cost of hiring well-qualified managers and retaining them in their financial analyses, Robin thought. *How will we retain the best and the brightest? What do Asians want in rewards? What do South Americans want? Is a good salary enough or are other factors involved?*

II. Which Countries Have Cultures that Best Fit BCN's Needs?

Robin remembered reading a newspaper article that mentioned that one of the factors important to Japanese firms locating in the US was finding compatible regional cultural norms. The Japanese liked the Southern US culture because of its regard for interpersonal relations in business settings, tradition, and respect for elders and persons in positions of authority. *Which countries have educational systems that would best support the knowledge base that our personnel will need? Which countries have social systems that favor unions more than management? Which cultures within these regions are most favorable to American expatriates and their families? Most importantly, which cultures promote a strong work ethic?*

Which countries have governments that are stable and are not likely to change and upset the equilibrium of our workers' and managers' work schedules? What about the possibility of terrorism? Will I have to devise a terrorism-prevention training program? Which countries are friendly to us, not just business-wise but in their perceptions of Americans and their right to manage the local residents? I wonder how much kidnap insurance costs? Robin's mind began to wander. She envisioned herself in a small, box-like hole covered with rusty iron bars. When would her kidnappers give her water? Her reverie was broken by a more practical concern that flashed across her mind.

III. Should We Send Our Own Personnel Overseas or Hire Locally?

Which countries in Asia, South America, or Europe have qualified personnel to staff manufacturing operations from top to bottom? Do some countries have laws that require hiring a certain percentage of local workers? Robin remembered meeting a man once at a professional convention who had worked for a mining company in Africa. He reported having had to hire local workers for all positions below middle management level, with the promise to phase out all Americans within ten years.

Can or should the subsidiary management come from BCN headquarters? If not, where would we find local managers to hire? The universities? Robin recalled reading once that, in France, the norm was to hire managers from the "Grand Écoles" and not from the universities. *If we send our personnel, who should go? How long should their assignments be? How expensive will it be to house an American family at their accustomed standard of living in the new country? How should we select the Americans to send? Should we base our decisions on experience in the company, adaptability potential, or desire to relocate? What if nobody wants to go?*

IV. How Will We Train Employees for Such Assignments?

How much training will they need before they go? How in depth will it need to be? Do they need language training or is English good enough? Robin thought that most business people around the world speak English, so maybe this was not really an issue. *Will the firm budget my department the resources necessary to do quality training or will I be left with a budget that will allow nothing more than bringing in a few local professors for a couple of hours each to do area briefings? Who can I call on to do the training?*

Robin felt somewhat relieved when she remembered reading about some cross-cultural training firms in the ad section of an HRM newsletter she reads. But her Confidence ebbed when the following thought occurred to her: *How will I know if the training these external consultants provide is valid and helpful or just a dog and pony show? Can I, with my staff, develop my own training program? What kind of time and money will such an endeavor require?* As Robin began mentally planning a strategy to develop training programs with her staff, her mind switched to yet another problem.

V. What Are the Career Implications of Foreign Assignments?

Should the assignments be developmental or should slots simply be filled as they open up, regardless of whether or not the move will develop the employee? Robin was vaguely aware that companies such as IBM, Ciba-Geigy, and Philips view international assignments as an integral part of their management development for senior posts. *If the assignment is developmental, what will we do when the employee returns?* Robin wondered if the company would give her authority to dictate what position returning managers should receive . . . She doubted they would give her that authority. *But what would happen to these experienced internationalists if they didn't have a clear career path for them when they returned? How will we reintegrate these employees into BCN's home operations? We'll lose them*, Robin thought to herself, *if we can't offer them a good position when they return. How will the HRM department keep informed of the needs, concerns, performance, and evaluation of the overseas employees? By phone? Email? Teleconferencing? Site visits?* Robin wondered whether she could justify trips to the Far East as site visits. They may be necessary, but might be viewed by others as a new perk for the HRM department.

The re-entry part kept bothering Robin. Not only is there the position transition issue to plan for, but she wondered how they might best capture their learning about the foreign operations. *This could be really valuable*, she thought. *It could help us coordinate our efforts better, understand the challenges of our foreign operations, etc.*

VI. How Productive Will the Cheap Labor Be?

If we do opt to set up in a country where the labor rates are inexpensive, can we introduce our management systems into the manufacturing plants? Will those systems be in harmony with the work culture of that country? I wonder if we will run into transfer of technology problems? Probably. Okay, so, how do we train local workers to understand how we do things at BCN? Will I have to design those training programs too?

I wonder if our managers will have to develop unique incentive systems to get their subordinates to work. No, probably not . . . well, then again, maybe. After all, the people under me have different buttons that make them work harder—those buttons are not the same for everyone here in the US. Is it possible, Robin wondered, *for some cultures to have work norms that are antithetical to promotion and pay inducements? I think those would be universal motivators! Maybe this won't be a major problem. Maybe it will be more of a fine-tuning issue in terms of adapting our job design, incentive systems, and motivational techniques to the country where we decide to set up shop.* Then the thought occurred to her, *What about motivating and evaluating the Americans overseas?*

VII. How Should We Do Performance Evaluation?

Can we just use the same forms, procedures and, criteria, or is there something unique about a foreign assignment that requires unique performance evaluation systems? When should we evaluate people? Robin remembered reading in a professional newsletter that expatriate employees require at least six months to settle into their overseas assignments. *Would it be fair to evaluate employees before six months? When would it be valid? After eight, ten, or twelve months? This is getting very messy,* Robin sighed.

Should the criteria by which to judge performance in Asia and other places be relative to the country in question, or should we use the same evaluation criteria everywhere? The last thing Robin felt like doing was overseeing the development of a new performance evaluation system! *We can get by with our current one,* she mentally noted. *Who should do the evaluating? Headquarters, the regional subsidiary superiors, peers, or a mixture of superiors and subordinates? Should the criteria revolve around bottom-line figures or personnel objectives? If financial-type performance criteria are emphasized, what happens if the dollar depreciates significantly against the local currency and wipes out the expatriate manager's cost savings and profits? How can the expatriate manager be evaluated, motivated, and rewarded under such conditions?*

What about nationality differences in performance evaluation? If an American manager is being evaluated by a Peruvian subsidiary manager, will the evaluation be fair or is there potential for some sort of cultural bias? What if the American manager is a woman? Will we be able to put together an attractive, but not too costly, compensation package for our expatriates? I wonder what such a package would look like. We need to offer something good to entice the employee to go, especially if the employee might lose the spouse's income, yet if there's too great a difference in the package between the repatriate and local personnel, which will create "we–them" problems.

VIII. Will the Unions Be Trouble?

Robin's thoughts were now racing between problems. *I remember reading somewhere,* she mused, *that in order to shut down a manufacturing facility in France (or was it Germany or Sweden?), management had to give the workers a full year's notice, retrain them, and then find them new jobs!* She knew the top management of her firm would find such a contingency troubling at best. *Well, maybe the Asian labor markets are less unionized and won't be as problematic.* Then Robin recalled meeting a public relations spokeswoman for a toy firm at a party, and the nightmare she had described.

It seems that the U.S. management of her company had pressured the contract manufacturers in Hong Kong and the PRC to increase production dramatically in order to fill unforeseen demands during the Christmas season. The press had gotten hold of cases where female workers were working sixteen-hour days with no breaks; if the employees complained, they were terminated on the spot. Also, some of the women had miscarried. It was a public relations nightmare. *Maybe dealing with unions wouldn't be all bad . . . maybe unions would protect us from questionable ethical nightmares,* Robin thought. But then she thought of codetermination laws in coun- tries such as Germany and worker's representatives sitting on the local boards of directors—that would not be easy for American managers to stomach. *And what about managing people from other cultures? We have a hard enough time in our California and Texas plants, let alone overseas!* As Robin put down her pen, the obvious complexity of the report loomed before her. She had just scratched the surface of the basic human resources issues associated with "globalization" and there seemed to be no end to the potential permutations around each problem. *This will be no easy task,* she concluded. As she left her office and made her way to the parking garage, she wondered, *Where can I go for help?*

BCN's situation closely parallels the initial path on which virtually all companies must have had to tread in reaction to the issues, challenges, and opportunities associated with the globalization of business. Within the globalization context of business operations, many business decisions become critical. While some of those decisions pertain to a firm's financial or physical resources, the most neglected and perhaps most important decisions to be made concern the management of the firm's international human resources. One of the greatest problems is the lack of a global perspective on the part of a firm's managerial cadre. As a member of one culture, the manager tends to see life from that perspective, to judge events from that perspective, and to make decisions based on that perspective. In an increasingly global business environment, such a perspective breeds failure.

Our principal objective for this book is to sensitize the reader to the complex human resource issues that exist in the global business environment. With this primary objective in mind, as stated previously, we have attempted to represent many regions of the world balanced by the quality of information and discussion potential of the reading or case.

Most publishing companies are turning to online creation of packets of readings and cases. Although a good idea in theory, it requires a great deal of research in case repositories and online journal systems to design a supplemental text of one's own. Most instructors are too busy with other obligations to spend the time necessary to design and create supplemental texts online, particularly if there is a good alternative, and we believe a book such as this one is just that alternative. We believe there is a need for books to be published of "tried and true" cases and readings that provide stimulating and intellectually challenging material, yet written in ways that engage both the student and the instructor. If you are a new adopter of the book, we would like to thank you, and we look forward to your comments concerning your experience in using the book. Feel free to contact us with your feedback.

In this new edition of our book, we have kept the best cases from the previous editions and added new readings and cases that have the same type of "feel" as the old, "tried and true" ones. The format of the book has changed somewhat, as have the conceptual groupings of each major section of the book. We were reluctant to tamper with a conceptual format that so many people liked, but our field is dynamic, and in order to be current we have updated many of the readings and some of the cases. However, a few of these readings and cases seemed to us to be classics. That is, the issues they address seem to transcend time (and copyright date)! We chose to keep these in the book, since we like to teach from them, and we know that most of you do as well.

This book can be used in a variety of ways in human resource manage- ment, management, and organizational behavior courses. It can stand alone, if the instructor's preference is to teach predominately a case course. It can be used in tandem with other textbooks that have an IHRM, management, or organizational behavior focus, or as a supplement to them. Or the book can be used as a main text in human resource management or other related courses, and supplemented with other readings and texts with which the instructor is comfortable.

The instructor's manual is available on this book's website at Routledge. Contained in the instructor's manual are teaching notes for the cases, class discussion notes and guidelines for the readings, and in-class and out-of-class assignments for the cases and readings. It also contains a few additional cases from previous editions that have been replaced by newer material in the book, but that some of you may want to continue to use in your courses. Our goal is to support you as an instructor in all of your needs.

As stated earlier, our main objective for the book is simply this: to sensitize the reader to the complex human resource issues that exist in the global business environment. With this objective in mind, we have attempted to represent many regions of the world in terms of the locations in which the readings and cases are based: Bangladesh, Bulgaria, Canada, China, Egypt, France, Germany, India, Japan, Malaysia, Mexico, the Netherlands, Nigeria, Senegal, Sweden, the UK, and the US.

Additionally, our readings and cases involve cross-cultural interaction between people and cultures and human resource systems in the following combinations: US–India, US–Japan, Senegal–France, China–Japan, Germany–US, Austria–Bulgaria, the Netherlands–Mexico, Canada–France, Sweden–China, China–US, Bangladesh–US, and Germany–China.

However, in providing for this diversity of location and interaction, we chose not to "force fit" something into the book for the sake of regional or geographic representation. We included what we felt were quality readings and cases in the field of international human resource management. We do not view this book as a North American HR text nor a European HR text. Our goal was to create a book of readings and cases that would focus on the points of confluence between cultures, human resource systems, and people in this era of globalization.

NOTE

1   Peter Vaill, *Managing as a Performing Art: New Ideas for a World of Chaotic Change* (San Francisco, CA: Jossey-Bass, 1989) p. 2.

Acknowledgments

WE WOULD LIKE TO THANK all those who have contributed to this book. Many of the authors willingly sent us cases, articles, manuscripts in progress, and bibliographies that they had developed over the years. We regret that we could not include all the sources offered to us.

We would like to express our gratitude to three people, for without their assistance and support this new edition of the book would not have occurred: our editor at Routledge, Sharon Golan, for her determined support and belief in this edition of the book and for her patience and flexibility in working with our needs; Sharon's editorial assistant, Erin Arata, who was instrumental in navigating us through the project; and Eren Akkan, who conducted an extensive search of the literature to help us identify new articles and cases that we believe are must-reads for those interested in international human resource management and who liaised with several publishers to make their inclusion happen.

A special thanks goes to our wives, Megan, Dorit, Janet, and Jane, and our families for their unwavering support of us over the years as we have pursued our fascination with "things international"—they make all we accomplish possible and our gratitude to them is eternal.

B. SEBASTIAN REICHE
Barcelona, Spain

GÜNTER K. STAHL
Vienna, Austria

MARK E. MENDENHALL
Signal Mountain, Tennessee

GARY R. ODDOU
Oceanside, California

Contributors

Ina Aust (formerly Ehnert)
Louvain School of Management

Ingmar Björkman
Aalto University
School of Business

J. Stewart Black
INSEAD

Jaime Bonache Pérez
Universidad Carlos III de Madrid
Faculty of Social Sciences
 and Law

David Bowen
Thunderbird School of Global
 Management, Arizona State
 University

Charlotte Butler
INSEAD

Paula Caligiuri
Northeastern University

Marie-Thérèse Claes
Louvain School of Management

David G. Collings
Dublin City University
Business School

Barbara Coudenhove-Kalergi
Center for Responsible
 Management

Henri-Claude de Bettignies
INSEAD, France and Singapore

C. Brooklyn Derr
Emeritus Professor
The Marriott School of Management,
 BYU

Joseph J. DiStefano
International Institute for
 Management Development
 (IMD)

Thomas Donaldson
The Wharton School
University of Pennsylvania

Peter W. Dorfman
New Mexico State University

Paul Evans
INSEAD

Stacey R. Fitzsimmons
University of Victoria

Roger Hallowell
HEC Paris

Wes Harry
Bradford University School of
    Management

Robert J. House
The Wharton School
University of Pennsylvania

Susan E. Jackson
Rutgers University
School of Management and Labor
    Relations

Mansour Javidan
Thunderbird School of Global Manage-
    ment, Arizona State University

Carin-Isabel Knoop
Global Research Group
Harvard Business School

Kathrin Köster
Hochschule Heilbronn

Henry W. Lane
Northeastern University

Yih-teen Lee
IESE Business School
People Management Department

Thomas Maak
University of South Australia Business
    School

Amy McCarter
National University of Ireland, Galway

Anthony McDonnell
Queen's Management School
Queen's University

Mark E. Mendenhall
College of Business, University of
    Tennessee

Christof Miska
Vienna University of Economics and
    Business

Evalde Mutabazi
EM Lyon Business School

Tsedal Neeley
Harvard Business School

Laura J. Noval
Vienna University of Economics and
    Business

Gary R. Oddou
California State University San
    Marcos

Verena Patock
Vienna University of Economics and
    Business

Nicola Pless
University of South Australia Business
    School

Vladimir Pucik
CEIBS and Hong Kong University of
    Science and Technology

B. Sebastian Reiche
IESE Business School
People Management Department

Carlos Sánchez-Runde
IESE Business School
People Management Department

Randall S. Schuler
Rutgers University
School of Management and Labor
    Relations

Christian Seelos
KU Leuven

Günter K. Stahl
Vienna University of Economics and
    Business

Luigi Stirpe
Universidad Carlos III de Madrid
Faculty of Social Sciences and Law

Mary Sully de Luque
Thunderbird School of Global Manage-
    ment, Arizona State University

Ibraiz Tarique
Pace University

Satu Teerikangas
University College London

David A. Thomas
Harvard Business School

Ming Zeng
Alibaba.com

PART I

The Context of IHRM: Challenges, Strategies, and External Forces

Readings

- Paul Evans, Vladimir Pucik, and Ingmar Björkman
  PUTTING THE CHALLENGES OF INTERNATIONAL HUMAN RESOURCE
  MANAGEMENT INTO PERSPECTIVE

- Randal S. Schuler, Susan E. Jackson, and Ibraiz Tarique
  MANAGING GLOBAL TALENT CHALLENGES WITH GLOBAL TALENT
  MANAGEMENT INITIATIVES

- Wes Harry and David G. Collings
  LOCALISATION: SOCIETIES, ORGANIZATIONS AND EMPLOYEES

Cases

- Ingmar Björkman
  PETER HANSON: BUILDING A WORLD-CLASS PRODUCT DEVELOPMENT
  CENTRE FOR HI TECH SYSTEMS IN CHINA

- Evalde Mutabazi and C. Brooklyn Derr
  SOCOMETAL: REWARDING AFRICAN WORKERS

- Roger Hallowell, David Bowen, and Carin-Isabel Knoop
  FOUR SEASONS GOES TO PARIS

Paul Evans, Vladimir Pucik, and Ingmar Björkman

PUTTING THE CHALLENGES OF INTERNATIONAL HUMAN RESOURCE MANAGEMENT INTO PERSPECTIVE*

L IKE MANY OTHER COMPANIES, the Swedish-Swiss corporation ABB that was born out of a merger in 1988 wanted to be a fast-growing firm with a wide international presence. Percy Barnevik, its Swedish CEO, is notable for recognizing the dilemmas that this involved, adopting the now well-known corporate mantra of "acting local but thinking global." His vision was to create an international company that was able to deal effectively with three internal contradictions: being global and local, big and small, and radically decentralized with centralized reporting and control.[1] The key principle was local entrepreneurship, so most of the decision-making was to be done at the lowest possible level, in the 5,000 independent profit centers, the business units that became the foundation of the ABB organization.

Influential country managers controlled operations in countries within a matrix structure of regions and business segments. ABB also established business-steering committees and functional councils to coordinate the different units, exploit synergies, and help transfer knowledge and best practices across the network of local units. The firm developed a management information system called ABACUS that contained data on the performance of the profit centers. Barnevik and his team of top managers traveled extensively to ensure communication and knowledge-sharing across units, while international assignments helped instill all units with the corporate ethos that Barnevik was pursuing: initiative, action, and risk-taking.

However, after becoming one of the most admired companies in the world during its first 10 years, ABB encountered significant problems in its second decade. Hit by the economic downturn in Europe, limitations in the firm's management started to emerge. While flexible and responsive to local contexts, ABB had failed to achieve sufficient global synergies and efficiency. Conflicts between business areas and national units meant that many managers felt that decision-making was unclear. The local profit centers continued to operate their own human resources management (HRM) systems, which were, at best, aligned at national levels but not at regional or global levels.

Barnevik's successors between 1997 and 2005 tried to impose more clarity and discipline by eliminating the country managers and regions, giving more power to global businesses, also introducing centralized corporate processes to improve global control, coordination, and efficiency. However, these top-down initiatives further increased the complexity of the firm, and without country managers in place to coordinate local operations, the company verged on paralysis. Country managers were reintroduced, the structure was simplified by selling all businesses except for two (power and automation), and a new global ABB People Strategy was launched, aimed at linking HRM with the business. By 2005, ABB was profitable once again but had shrunk from 213,000 employees (in 1997) to 102,000. A new CEO, Fred Kindle, found a firm with a high degree of local entrepreneurship and innovation, but with limited coordination and still unsatisfactory global efficiency. Barnevik's contra-dictions were still on the table.

In this reading, we examine the challenges facing ABB from the historic perspective of internationalization of the firm and the concomitant evolution of HRM. The dilemmas faced by ABB have always existed. What has changed is the nature and speed of communication between a company's headquarters and its subsidiaries around the world. But the essential problems of being flexible and responsive to local market needs while promoting global efficiency, avoiding duplication, and coordinating and controlling diverse units and people remain.

As we will discuss, some modern firms have adopted a *multidomestic* strategy, with autonomous local operations that can respond readily to local needs, while others pursue a centralized *meganational* strategy to prevent duplication and make global operations more efficient. Their approach to human resource management is radically different.

However, both of these strategies have limitations, leading to the idea that con-temporary global corporations have many contradictions, as ABB recognized. They have to be simultaneously local and global in scope, centralized and decentralized, capable of delivering short-term results while developing future assets, managing multiple alliances without full control, and responding to market pressures to do things better *and* cheaper *and* faster. In light of this, we examine the concept of the *transnational organization*, at the heart of which is the notion of contradiction,[2] and we explore the implications for people management.

EARLY INTERNATIONALIZATION

International business is not a recent phenomenon, nor is international HRM a product of the twentieth or twenty-first century. The Assyrians, Phoenicians, Greeks, and Romans all engaged in extensive cross-border trade. Roman organizations spanning Asia, Africa, and Europe are often heralded as the first global companies, in that they covered the whole of the known world.

The pioneers of international business were the sixteenth- and seventeenth-century trading companies—the English and Dutch East India companies, the Muscovy Company, the Hudson's Bay Company, and the Royal African Company.[3] They exchanged merchandise and services across continents and had a geographical spread to rival today's multinational firms. They signed on crews and chartered ships, and engaged the services of experts with skills in trade negotiations and foreign languages, capable of assessing the quality of goods and determining how they should be handled and loaded. These companies were obliged to delegate considerable responsibility to local representatives running their operations in far-away countries, which created a new challenge: how could local managers be encouraged to use their discretionary powers to the best advantage of the company? The trading companies had to develop control structures and systems to monitor the behavior of their scattered agents.

Formal rules and procedures were one way of exercising control, but this did not eliminate the temptations of opportunistic behavior for those far from the center. Other control measures were therefore developed, such as employment con-tracts stipulating that managers would work hard and in the interests of the company. Failure to do so could lead to reprimand or dismissal. Setting performance measures was the next step. These included the ratio of capital to tonnage, the amount of outstanding credit on advance contracts, whether ships sailed on time, and the care taken in loading mixed cargoes. There were also generous financial incentives, such as remuneration packages comprising a fixed cash component and a sizeable bonus. Such a mix of control approaches was not far off contemporary methods used to evaluate and reward managerial performance in large multinationals.

The Impact of Industrialization

The Industrial Revolution originated in Britain in the late eighteenth century. The emergence of the factory system in Europe and the US had a dramatic impact both on international business and on the management of people. The spread of industrialization in Europe and the US provided growing markets for minerals and foodstuffs and prompted a global search for sources of supply.

Cross-border manufacturing began to emerge by the mid-nineteenth century. But it was difficult to exercise real control over distant operations. The rare manufacturing firms that ventured abroad often used family members to manage their international operations. For example, when Siemens set up its St Petersburg factory in 1855, a brother of the founder was put in charge. In 1863, another brother established a factory to produce sea cables in Britain. Keeping it in the family was the best guarantee that those in distant subsidiaries could be trusted not to act opportunistically.

The international spread of rail networks and the advent of steamships in the 1850s and 1860s brought new speed and reliability to international travel, while the invention of the telegraph uncoupled long-distance communication from transportation. It became possible for firms to manufacture in large batches and to seek volume distribution in mass markets. The rapid growth in firm size provided a domestic platform from which to expand abroad, paving the way for a surge in international business activity in the last decades of the nineteenth century.[4]

The late nineteenth and early twentieth centuries saw a number of developments in international business and people-management practices. In parallel with developments in transport and communication, industrialization was having a significant impact on the organization of firms. They were being reshaped by new manufacturing techniques, by the increased specialization and division of labor, and by a change in the composition of the workforce from skilled tradesmen to unskilled workers, previously agrarian, who were unaccustomed to industry requirements such as punctuality, regular attendance, supervision, and the mechanical pacing of work effort— similar to the situation in labor-intensive industries in China during the last 30 years. Early personnel management practices were shaped in factories experiencing discipline and motivation problems, where entrepreneurs such as Robert Owen in Scotland (often referred to as the father of modern personnel management) began to pay more attention to working conditions and the welfare of employees.

The growth in international manufacturing sustained a flourishing service sector, which provided the global infrastructure—finance, insurance, transport—to permit the international flow of goods. All this led to a degree of internationalization that the world would not see again until it had fully recovered from the damage to the global economy created by two world wars. It was a golden age for multinationals, with foreign direct investment accounting for around 9 percent of world output.[5]

War and Economic Depression

The outbreak of World War I, followed by a period of economic depression and then World War II, transformed management practices and multinational activity in very different ways, stimulating the development of people-management practices but suppressing international trade.

The sudden influx of inexperienced workers (many of them women) into factories in 1915 to service war needs increased the pressure on managers to find ways to improve productivity rapidly. Tasks had to be simplified and redesigned for novices. To contain labor unrest, more attention had to be paid to working conditions and employee demands, which also meant training first-line supervisors. These initiatives centralized many of the aspects of employment relations previously discharged by individual line managers. In some progressive firms, employees began to be viewed as resources, and the alignment of interest between the firm and workers was emphasized. The 1920s also saw the development of teaching and research, journals, and consulting firms in personnel management.[6]

However, the Great Depression was the start of a bifurcation in employment practices in the US and Japan, the latter having gone through a period of rapid industrialization and economic growth. Leading firms in both the US and Japan were experimenting with corporate welfarism in the 1920s.[7] However, the depth of the Depression in the US in the 1930s meant that many firms had no option except to make lay-offs and repudiate the welfare arrangements that had been established in many non-unionized firms. They turned instead to a path of explicit and instrumental contracts between employee and employer, with wages and employment conditions often determined through collective bargaining.[8] Because of the militarization of the Japanese economy, the impact of the Depression was much less severe on that side of the Pacific. Under legislation fostering "social peace" in the name of national unity, large firms maintained these welfare experiments, leading step-by-step to an HRM orientation built around implicit contracts (lifetime employment, corporate responsibility for the development of staff, and low emphasis on formalized performance evaluation). Endorsed by the strong labor unions that emerged in post-war Japan, these practices became institutionalized, reinforcing and reinforced by Japanese societal values.

In the West, World War II intensified interest in the systematic recruitment, testing, and assigning of new employees in order to leverage their full potential. Psychological testing used by the military spilled over into private industry.[9] In addition, the desire to avoid wartime strikes led the US government to support collective bargaining, strengthening the role of the personnel function as a result.

If these external shocks had some salutary consequences for the development of personnel practices, they had quite the opposite effect on multinational activities. The adverse conditions during the interwar years encouraged firms to enter cross-border cartels rather than risk foreign investments. By the late 1920s, a considerable proportion of world manufacturing was controlled by these cartels—the most notorious being the "seven sisters" controlling the oil industry.[10]

World War II dealt a crushing blow to these cartels, and after the war, the US brought in aggressive antitrust legislation to dismantle those that remained. While US firms emerged from the war in excellent shape, European competition was devastated, and Japanese corporations (known as *zaibatsu*) had been dismembered. The war had stimulated technological innovation and American corporations had no desire to confine their activities to the home market. A new era of international business had begun.

THE MODERN MULTINATIONAL

Although Europe had a long tradition in international commerce, it was the global drive of US firms after World War II that gave birth to the multinationals as we know them today. American firms that had hardly ventured beyond their home markets before the war now began to flex their muscles abroad, and by the early 1960s, US companies had built an unprecedented lead in the world economy.

American firms also found faster ways of entering new markets. Many moved abroad through acquisitions, followed by investment in the acquired subsidiary in order to benefit more fully from economies of scale and scope.[11] This was the approach taken by Procter & Gamble (P&G), who established a presence in Continental Europe by acquiring an ailing French detergent plant in 1954. An alternative strategy was to join forces with a local partner, as in the case of Xerox, which entered global markets through two joint ventures, with the English motion picture firm the Rank Organisation in 1956, and with Fuji Photo Film in Japan in 1962.

In professional services, McKinsey and Arthur Andersen scrambled to open their own offices in foreign countries through the 1950s and 1960s. Others, such as Price Waterhouse and Coopers & Lybrand, built their international presence through mergers with established national practices in other countries. For most others, the route was via informal federations or networks of otherwise independent firms.

Advances in transport and communications—the introduction of commercial jet travel, the first transatlantic telephone link in 1956, then the development of the telex—facilitated this rapid internationalization. More significant still was the emergence of computers. By the mid-1970s, computers had become key elements in the control and information systems of industrial concerns, paving the way for later complex integration strategies. Taken together, the jet plane, the new telecommunications technology, and the computer contributed to a "spectacular shrinkage of space."[12]

Alongside these technological drivers of internationalization, powerful economic and political forces were at work. Barriers to trade and investment were progressively dismantled with successive General Agreement on Tariffs and Trades (GATT) treaties. Exchange rates were stabilized following the Bretton Woods Agreement (July 1944), and banks started to play an international role as facilitators of international business. The 1957 Treaty of Rome established the European Community. US firms, many of which already perceived Europe as a single entity, were the first to exploit the regional integration. European companies were spurred by "the American challenge" (the title of a best-selling call-to-arms book by the French journalist and politician Jean-Jacques Servan-Schreiber in 1967), encouraging them to expand beyond their own borders.

Staffing for International Growth

In the decades following World War II, virtually all medium- and large-sized firms had personnel departments, typically with responsibility for industrial (union) relations and for the operational aspects of employment, including staffing subsidiaries abroad.[13] The newly created international personnel units focused on expatriation, sending home-country managers to foreign locations.

The largest 180 US multinationals opened an average of six foreign subsidiaries each year during the 1960s.[14] This rapid international expansion opened up new job possibilities, including foreign postings. While US firms in the immediate post-war period had been "flush with veterans who had recently returned from the four corners of the globe [and who] provided a pool of eager expatriates,"[15] more managers were now urgently needed. People had to be persuaded to move abroad, both those with much-needed technical skills and managers to exercise control over these expanding foreign subsidiaries. In most companies at the time, this meant paying people generously as an incentive to move abroad.

In the late 1970s, horror stories of expatriate failure gained wide circulation — the technically capable executive sent out to run a foreign subsidiary being brought back prematurely as a borderline alcoholic, with a ruined marriage, and having run the affiliate into the ground. Academic studies seemed to confirm this problem,[16] which for some companies became a major handicap to international growth. It was no longer just a question of persuading people to move abroad, it was a question of "how can we help them to be successful?" While the reluctance to move abroad was increasing, often for family reasons but also because of the mismanagement of re-entry to the home country, concern over the rising costs of expatriation was growing.

International business also became a subject of academic study during this period. In the early 1980s, the challenges of expatriation started to attract the attention of researchers, reinforced by the new-found legitimacy of HR, and the concern of senior managers anxious about growth prospects abroad. While it was too early to talk of an international HRM field, international growth was leading to new challenges beyond expatriation that were to shape this emerging domain.

Organizing for International Growth

Rapid international growth brought with it the problems of controlling and coordinating increasingly complex global organizations—where control refers to visible and hierarchical processes and structures while coordination signifies tools that facilitate alignment through lateral interactions such as cross-boundary project teams and informal social networks. The awareness that international HRM is crucial not just for international staffing but also for building corporate cohesion and inter-unit collaboration grew and matured between the 1960s and 1990s. It was becoming increasingly apparent that the traditional structures were not sufficient to cope with the growing complexities of managing international business.

Many firms selling a wide range of products abroad opted for a structure of worldwide product divisions, whereas those with few products but operating in many countries would typically organize themselves around geographic area divisions, as did IBM.[17] The tricky question was how to organize when the firm had many different products sold in many different geographic markets. It was not at all clear how companies should deal with this zone of maximum complexity.

In practice, two responses emerged. Some firms implemented matrix organizations involving both product and geographic reporting lines, others increased the number of headquarters staff in coordinating roles. Both of these routes were ultimately to show their limitations, but the two paths gave rise to a growing understanding of the potential role of HRM in dealing with the fundamental problems of cross-border coordination and control.

The Matrix Structure Route

By the early 1970s, several US and British companies (Citibank, Corning, Dow, Exxon, and Shell, among others) had adopted the idea of matrix as a guiding principle for their worldwide organization. Right from the start, some management scholars urged caution, pointing out that matrix is much more complex than reporting lines and structural coordination.[18] Matrix had to be built into leadership development, control and performance appraisal systems, teamwork, conflict resolution mechanisms, relationships, and attitudes, anticipating the later insight that matrix has more to do with HRM than it has to do with structure.[19] Few of the companies that opted for the matrix solution had such supporting elements in place.

A focus on *reporting lines*, the first dimension of coordination, was not sufficient. Attention also had to be paid to the second dimension of coordination, *social architecture*—the conscious design of a social environment that encourages a pattern of thinking and behavior supporting organizational goals. This includes interpersonal relationships and inter-unit networks, the values, beliefs, and norms shared by members of the organization, and the mindsets that people hold. ABB's Percy Barnevik was conscious of the importance of the social elements of the international firm, and thus the need for extensive communication, travel, and relocation of people across units.

Common management processes are a third element of coordination, including processes for managing talent (including recruitment, selection, development, and retention of key personnel), performance and compensation management, and knowledge management and innovation. As ABB's problems compounded, it became increasingly obvious to executives that they had to develop and implement global management processes, although it was less clear how to do this.

Many companies found matrix structures difficult. They led to power struggles, ambiguity over resource allocation, buck-passing, and abdication of responsibility. In theory, a manager reported to two bosses, and conflicts between them would be reconciled at the apex one level higher up. However, it was not unusual to find companies where managers were reporting to four or five bosses, so that reconciliation or arbitration could only happen at a very senior level. While matrix might ensure the consultation necessary for sound decision-making, it was painfully slow. By the time the firm had decided, for example, to build a new chemical plant in Asia, nimbler competitors were already up and running. By the early 1980s, many firms reverted to structures where accountability lay clearly with the product divisions, although some (such as ABB) retained a structure with many matrix features.[20]

But if matrix structures were gradually going out of fashion, the matrix problem of organization was more alive than ever. Practitioners and researchers argued that the traditional hierarchic tools of control (rules, standard operating procedures, hierarchical referral, and planning) could not manage the growing complexity of information processing.[21] Organizations required strong capabilities in two areas: first in information processing and second in coordination and teamwork. There was an explosion of interest in how to improve coordination while keeping the reporting relationships as clear and simple as possible.[22]

Gradually, it became clear that the matrix challenges of coordination in complex multinational firms were essentially issues of people and information technology (IT) management. Matrix, as two leading strategy scholars were later to say, is a "frame of mind" nurtured more than anything else by careful human resource management.[23]

The Headquarters Coordination Route

Most organizations took the well-trodden path of keeping control of international activities with central staff. This was particularly true for German and Japanese companies, but was also the dominant organizing pattern in Anglo-Saxon firms. As with matrix, this approach was initially successful but eventually led to inefficiencies and paralysis. Again, speed was shown to be the Achilles heel.

It took a long time to work through decisions in German *Zentralebereiche* (central staff departments), and particularly in Japanese *nemawashi*[24] (negotiation) processes of middle-up consultative decision-making. However, multinationals from both of these countries were largely export-oriented with sales subsidiaries abroad, and the disadvantages were initially outweighed by the quality of decision-making and commitment to implementation that accompanied the consensus-oriented decision-making. The complex consultative processes worked reasonably well as long as everyone involved was German or Japanese.[25]

The strains of staff bureaucracy began to show in the US in the early 1980s as companies started to localize, acquiring or building integrated subsidiaries abroad. With localization of the management of foreign units, the coordination of decision-making by central staff became more difficult, slowing down the process at a time when speed was becoming more important. Local managers in lead countries argued for more autonomy and clearer accountability, while the costly overhead of the heavy staff structures associated with central coordination contributed to the erosion of competitiveness.

Faced with the second oil shock and recession in the late 1970s, American firms were the first to begin the process of downsizing and de-layering staff bureaucracies, followed by Europeans in Nordic and Anglo-Saxon countries. The Japanese and Germans followed more slowly. After decades of post-war international growth, attention in HRM shifted to the painful new challenges of dealing with organizational streamlining and job redesign, lay-offs, and managing change under crisis.

Firms that had pursued the headquarters-coordination route came to the same conclusion as firms that had invested in a matrix structure: they had to develop non-bureaucratic coordination and control mechanisms by building lateral relationships facilitated by human resource management. The control and coordination problem became another important strand in the development of international HRM.

HRM Goes International

During the 1980s, the idea that HRM might be of strategic importance gained ground. The insight that strategy is implemented through structure had taken hold — and it was then logical to argue that strategy is also implemented through changes in selection criteria, reward systems, and other HR policies and practices. In turn, this challenged the notion that there might be a "best" approach to HRM—the approach would depend on the strategy.

Perhaps appropriate HRM practice also depends on cultural context? This question was prompted by the difficulties that expatriates had experienced in trans-planting management practices abroad, and was supported by growing research on cultural differences, pioneered by Geert Hofstede's study based on the global IBM opinion survey. This showed significant differences in the understanding of management and organization.[26]

The emergence of "the Japanese challenge" in the 1980s as both threat and icon further highlighted the issue of cultural differences, as well as the strategic importance of soft issues such as HRM. Numerous studies attempted to explain how the Japanese, whose country was destroyed and occupied after World War II, had managed to rebound with such vigor, successfully taking away America's market share in industries such as automobiles and consumer electronics. How had they managed to pull this off with no natural resources apart from people? A large part of the answer seemed to lie in distinctive HRM practices that helped to provide high levels of skill, motivation, and collective entrepreneurship, as well as collaboration between organizational units.[27] This was a shock for Western managers, who suddenly realized that other approaches to management could be equally or even more successful.

New international human resource challenges were emerging. Many governments began to apply pressure on foreign firms to hire and develop local employees. Given the cost of expatriation, this persuaded some multinational firms to start aggressively recruiting local executives to run their foreign subsidiaries. This often required extensive training and development, but as one observer pointed out, "The cost must be weighed against the cost of sending an American family to the area."[28] At Unilever, for example, the proportion of expatriates in foreign management positions dropped from 50 percent to 10 percent between 1950 and 1970.[29]

However, there was a catch-22 in localizing key positions in foreign units: the greater the talent of local people, the more likely they were to be poached by other firms seeking local skills. Consequently, localization was a priority for only a minority of multinational firms until well into the 1990s, except for operations in highly developed regions such as North America, Europe, and Japan.[30]

Some firms used expatriate assignments for developmental reasons rather than just to solve an immediate job need. In these corporations, high-potential executives would be transferred abroad in order to expose them to international responsibilities. The assumption was that with growing internationalization, *all* senior executives needed international experience, even those in domestic positions. For example, the vice president of P&G had already pointed out in 1963: "We never appoint a man simply because of his nationality. A Canadian runs our French company, a Dutchman runs the Belgian company, and a Briton runs our Italian company. In West Germany, an American is in charge: in Mexico, a Canadian."[31] This meant that P&G was able to attract the very best local talent, quickly developing an outstanding reputation around the globe for the quality of its management. For local firms in France, Singapore, Australia, and Brazil, P&G was the management benchmark, and not only in the fast-moving consumer goods sector. Other firms started to adopt the P&G approach, although this created new challenges for international HRM. How does one manage the identification, development, transfer, and repatriation of talent spread out across the globe?

The link between international management development and the problems of coordination and control was established by the landmark research of Edström and Galbraith. They studied the expatriation policies of four multinationals of comparable size and geographic coverage in the mid-1970s, including Shell.[32] The research showed that these companies had quite different levels and patterns of international personnel transfer.[33] There were three motives for transferring managers abroad. The first and most common was to meet an immediate need for particular skills in a foreign subsidiary. The second was to develop managers through challenging international experience. However, the study of Shell revealed a third motive for international transfers—as a mechanism for control and coordination. The managers sent abroad were steeped in the policies and style of the organization, so they could be relied on to act appropriately in diverse situations. Moreover, frequent assignments abroad developed a network of personal relationships that facilitated coordination.

It appeared that Shell was able to maintain a high degree of control and coordination while at the same time having a more decentralized organization than other firms. This suggested that appropriate HRM practices could allow a firm to be globally coordinated and relatively decentralized at the same time, avoiding the matrix and corporate staff traps. Global control and coordination, it appeared, could be provided through socialization, minimizing the necessity for centralized headquarters control or bureaucratic procedures.

These findings drew attention to expatriation, mobility, and management development as a vital part of the answer to the matrix/bureaucracy problem of coordination. In truth, the concept was not entirely new—the Romans had adopted a similar approach to the decentralization dilemma two millennia before, staffing far flung regions with trusted governors socialized to safeguard the interests of the Empire.

By the mid-1990s, with globalization deepening, surveys consistently showed that global leadership development was one of the top three HRM priorities in major US corporations.[34] In some companies in Europe and the US, international management development was seen to be so critical that this department was separated from the corporate HR function, and reported directly to the CEO.

ENTER GLOBALIZATION

By the end of the 1980s, the traditional distinction between domestic and multinational companies had started to become blurred. International competition was no longer the preserve of industrial giants; it was affecting everybody's business. Statistics from the 1960s show that only 6 percent of the US economy was exposed to international competition. By the late 1980s, the corresponding figure was over 70 percent and climbing fast.[35]

Globalization surfaced as the new buzzword at the beginning of the 1990s, though it has different meaning for different people, sometimes with strong negative overtones. Viewed as interdependence and interconnectedness, many of the ingredients of globalization had actually been around for several decades. The steady dismantling of trade barriers in Western Europe and in North and South America, the increasing availability of global capital, advances in computing and communications technology, the progressive convergence of consumer tastes, and, in particular, the universal demand for industrial products had all been underway for some time. What made a difference was that these trends now reached a threshold where they became mutually reinforcing.

Widespread deregulation and privatization opened new opportunities for international business in both developing and developed countries. The multinational domain, long associated with the industrial company, was shifting to the service sector, which by the mid-1990s represented over half of total world foreign direct investment. Problems of distance and time zones were further smoothed away as communication by fax gave way to email and fixed phone networks to wireless mobile technology. Globalization was further stimulated by the fall of communism in Russia and Eastern Europe. Together with China's adoption of market-oriented policies, huge new opportunities were opened to international business as most of the world was drawn into the integrated global economy.

Multinationals increasingly located different elements of their value-adding activities in different parts of the world. Formerly hierarchical companies with clean-cut boundaries were giving way to complex arrangements and configurations, often fluctuating over time. The new buzzword from GE was "the boundaryless organization."[36] With increasing cross-border project work and mobility, the image of an organization as a network was rapidly becoming as accurate as that of hierarchy. For example, a European pharmaceutical corporation could have international R&D partnerships with competitors in the US, and manufacturing joint ventures with local partners in China, where it also outsourced local sales of generic products to a firm strong in distribution.

Traditionally, the only resources that multinationals sought abroad were raw materials or cheap labor. Everything else was at home: sources of leading-edge technology and finance, world-class suppliers, pressure-cooker competition, the most sophisticated customers, and the best intelligence on future trends.[37] Global competition was now dispersing some of these capabilities around the world. India, for example, developed its software industry using a low-cost strategy as a means of entry, but then quickly climbed the value chain, just as Japan had done previously in the automobile industry. The implication of such developments was that multinational firms could no longer assume that all the capabilities deemed strategic were available close to home.

With the erosion of traditional sources of competitive advantage, multinationals needed to change their perspective. To compete successfully, they had to do more than exploit scale economies or arbitrage imperfections in the world's markets for goods, labor, and capital. Toward the end of the 1980s, a new way of thinking about the multinational corporation came out of studies of how organizations were responding to these challenges. The concept of the transnational organization was born.

The Road Map for Managing Globalization

If there is a single perspective that has shaped the context for our understanding of the multinational corporation and its HRM implications, it is Bartlett and Ghoshal's research on the transnational organization.[38] To this we can add Hedlund's related concept of heterarchy and Doz and Prahalad's studies on the multi-focal organization, all of which have origins in Perlmutter's geocentric organization.[39] These strategy and management researchers grew to believe that people management is perhaps the single most critical domain for the multinational firm. None of them had any interest in HRM by virtue of their training, but all were drawn to the HRM field by findings from their research.

Doz and Prahalad began to link the fields of multinational strategy and HRM when researching the patterns of strategic control in multinational companies.[40] As they saw it, multinational firms faced a central problem: responding to a variety of national demands while maintaining a clear and consistent global business strategy. This tension between strong opposing forces, dubbed local responsiveness and global integration, served as a platform for much subsequent research on multinational enterprises, and it was captured by Sony's "think global, act local" aphorism, also adopted by ABB as its guiding motto.

Bartlett and Ghoshal developed these concepts further in their study of nine firms in three industries (consumer electronics, branded packaged goods, and telephone switching) and three regions (North America, Europe, and Japan).[41] They discovered that these companies seemed to have followed one of three internationalization paths, which they called "administrative heritage":

- One path emphasized responsiveness to local conditions, leading to what they called a "multinational enterprise" and which we prefer to call multidomestic. This led to a decentralized federation of local firms led by entrepreneurs who enjoyed a high degree of strategic freedom and organizational autonomy. The strength of the multidomestic approach was local responsiveness to customers and infrastructure. Some European firms, such as Unilever and Philips, and ITT in the US, embodied this approach.

- A second path to internationalization was that of the "global" firm, typified by US corporations such as Ford and Japanese enterprises such as Matsushita and NEC. Since the term global is today applied like the term multinational to any large firm operating on a worldwide basis, we prefer to call such a firm the meganational firm. Here, worldwide facilities are typically centralized in the parent country, products are standardized, and overseas operations are considered as delivery pipelines to access international markets. The global hub maintains tight control over strategic decisions, resources, and information. The competitive strength of the meganational firm comes from efficiencies of scale and cost.

- Some companies appeared to have taken a third route, a variant on the meganational path. Like the meganational, their facilities were located at the center. But the competitive strength of these "international" firms was their ability to transfer expertise to less advanced overseas environments, while allowing local units more discretion in adapting products and services. They were also capable of capturing learning from such local initiatives and then transferring it back to the central R&D and marketing departments. The "international" enterprise was thus a tightly coordinated federation of local firms. Some American and European firms, such as Ericsson, fitted this pattern, heralding the growing concern with global knowledge management.

It was apparent to Bartlett and Ghoshal that specific firms were doing well because their internationalization paths matched the requirements of their industry.

Consumer products required local responsiveness, so Unilever had been thriving with its multidomestic approach, while Kao in Japan—centralized and meganational in heritage—had hardly been able to move outside its Japanese borders. The situation was different in consumer electronics, where the centralized meganational heritage of Matsushita (Panasonic and other brands) seemed to fit better than the more localized approaches of Philips and GE's consumer electronics business. And in telecommunications switching, the international learning and transfer ability of Ericsson led its "international" strategy to dominate the multidomestic and meganational strategies of its competitors.

Perhaps the most significant of Bartlett and Ghoshal's observations was that accelerating global competition was changing the stakes. In all three industries, it was clear that the leading firms had to become more transnational in their orientation — more locally responsive *and* more globally integrated *and* better at sharing learning between headquarters and subsidiaries. What has been driving this change? Increasing competition was shifting the competitive positioning of these firms from *either/or* to and. The challenge for Unilever (like ABB in the opening story) was to maintain its local responsiveness, but at the same time to increase its global efficiency by eliminating duplication and integrating manufacturing. Conversely, the challenge for Matsushita was to keep the economies of centralized product development and manufacturing, but to become more local and responsive to differentiated niches in markets around the world.

The Transnational Solution

The defining characteristic of the transnational enterprise is its capacity to steer between the contradictions that it confronts. As Ghoshal and Bartlett put it:

> managers in most worldwide companies recognize the need for simultaneously achieving global efficiency, national responsiveness, and the ability to develop and exploit knowledge on a worldwide basis. Some, however, regard the goal as inherently unattainable. Perceiving irreconcilable contradictions among the three objectives, they opt to focus on one of them, at least temporarily. The transnational company is one that overcomes these contradictions.[42]

However, it is not clear that all multinational firms are destined to move in a transnational direction. While all companies are forced to contend with the dimensions of responsiveness, efficiency, and learning, and intensified competition heightens the contradictory pressures, these features are not equally salient in all industries. Moreover, the pressures do not apply equally to all parts of a firm. One subsidiary may be more local in orientation, whereas another may be tightly integrated. Even within a particular function, such as marketing, pricing may be a local matter, whereas distribution may be controlled from the center. In HR, performance management systems may be more globally standardized, whereas reward systems for workers may be left to local discretion. Indeed, this differentiation is another aspect of the complexity of the transnational—one size does not fit all.

In many ways, the transnational concept drew its inspiration from the concept of matrix. But transnational is neither a particular organizational form nor a specific strategic posture. Rather, it is an "organizational model," a "management mentality," and a "philosophy."[43] The transnational challenge is therefore to create balanced perspectives[44] or a "matrix in the mind of managers."[45] The challenge for senior management is to build a common sense of purpose that will guide local strategic initiatives, to coordinate through a portfolio of processes rather than via hierarchic structure, and to shape people's attitudes across the globe.[46]

This leads international HRM researchers to examine the local—global tension in multinationals.[47] On the one hand there are pressures for HRM policies and practices to be adapted to fit local institutional rules, regulations, and norms, as well as the cultural context. Yet if the multinational decentralizes the responsibility for HRM to local units, this can result in duplication, excessive cost, and lack of regional or global-scale advantages within the HR function. Even more importantly, this may handicap inter-unit learning within the corporation while handicapping coordination. For example, a failure to address issues related to corporate social responsibility in a globally consistent manner can cost the company dear. Siemens experienced this when a corruption scandal erupted in 2007, as did Nike, severely criticized for not having tightly supervised labor practices across their global network of suppliers.

Capabilities and Knowledge as Sources of Competitiveness

Today, management, strategy, and international business scholars are increasingly focused on capabilities and knowledge as drivers of competitive advantage. A core organizational capability is a firm-specific bundling of technical systems, people skills, and cultural values.[48] To the extent that they are firm specific, such organizational capabilities are difficult to imitate because of the complex configuration of the various elements. The capabilities can therefore be a major source of competitive advantage (although their very success can also create dangerous rigidities).

The distinguishing feature of a capability is the integration of skills, technologies, systems, managerial behaviors, and work values. For example, FedEx has a core competence in package routing and delivery. This rests on the integration of barcode technology, mobile communications, systems using linear programming, network management, and other skills.[49] The capability of INSEAD or IMD in executive education depends on faculty know-how integrated with program design skills, marketing, relationships with clients, the competence and attitude of support staff, reward systems, and a host of other interwoven factors that have evolved over the years.

Another crucial source of competitive advantage comes from the firm's ability to create, transfer, and integrate knowledge.[50] At the heart of the surge of academic and corporate interest in management of knowledge lies the distinction between explicit and tacit knowledge. The former is knowledge that you know that you have, and in organizations explicit knowledge is often codified in texts and manuals. The latter is personal, built on intuition acquired through years of experience, and hard to formalize and communicate to others. One of the main approaches to knowledge management is to build collections of explicit knowledge (customer contacts, presentation overheads, etc.) using software systems, and to make that knowledge available via an intranet. Another approach is to focus on building connections or contacts between people in the organization that can be used to transfer tacit knowledge.[51] Many professional firms have gone down this route, for instance by creating yellow-page directories that allow consultants to find individuals who have relevant experience and encouraging the development of informal relationships among people interested in a certain topic area. In a world where the retention of people is more difficult, it is particularly important to retain and transfer their knowledge.

These ideas about the source of competitive advantage are related to the *resource-based perspective* of the firm, which views it as a bundle of tangible and intangible resources. If such resources are valuable to the customer, rare, difficult to purchase or imitate, and effectively exploited, then they can provide a basis for superior economic performance that may be sustained over time. This view quickly attracted the attention of HRM scholars because its broad definition of resources could be applied to HRM-related capabilities, such as training and development, teamwork, and culture. Resource-based theory helped to reinforce the interrelationship between HRM and strategy. It provided a direct conceptual link between an organization's more behavioral and social attributes and its ability to gain a competitive advantage. This influential view, based largely on research on multinational corporations, has continued to play an important role in current strategy and HRM thinking.

THE EVOLUTION OF INTERNATIONAL HRM

As we have seen, the challenges of foreign assignments, adapting people management practices to foreign situations, and coordinating and controlling distant operations have existed since antiquity. It is only during the last 50 years that specialized personnel managers have begun to assume a responsibility for these tasks. With the acceleration of globalization, these and other international HRM issues have developed into a central competitive challenge for corporations. As Floris Maljers, former co-chairman of Unilever, put it: "Limited human resources—not unreliable or inadequate sources of capital—has become the biggest constraint in most globalization efforts."[52] Many scholars studying the multinational firm would agree.

The centrality of these HRM issues has increased over time. For example, as the bottom-line consequences became more visible, concern over expatriation broadened to include the understanding that it was not just about sending managers abroad but also about helping expatriates to be successful in their roles and future careers. The scope of expatriation has changed—today, expatriates come not only from the multinational's home country but also from other, third countries. Localization of staff in foreign units became a new imperative, leading to the complex task of tracking and developing a global talent pool. As globalization started to have an impact on local operations, for example in China, it also became clear that even local executives needed to have international experience. Globalization has raised awareness of the pivotal role played by managerial talent in implementing global strategies, and multinationals from different parts of the world are increasingly competing for talent from the same global talent pools.

As we enter the second decade of the twenty-first century, multinationals from high-growth emerging markets have become major global investors. Large international acquisitions by firms such as Tata Steel from India and CEMEX from Mexico, the world's largest building material company, have transformed industries that were traditionally dominated by firms from developed countries. The shift away from countries such as the US and Japan dominating lists of the world's largest companies is clear. Out of the world's 500 largest corporations, the US lost 26 of its 177 spots between 1999 and 2008, and Japan no less than 55 of its 81. The winners were emerging countries such as China (from 10 to 29), South Korea (12 to 14), India (1 to 7), Taiwan (1 to 6), Mexico (2 to 5), Brazil (3 to 5), and Russia (2 to 5).[53] Even Western scholars increasingly look to these emerging markets for new lessons in human resource management and building capabilities.[54]

As the ABB story illustrated, the failure of structural solutions to address the problems of coordination and control led to an increased focus on how HR practices might assist in providing cohesion to the multinational firm. HRM and strategy came together in the transnational concept, which helped to dissolve many of the traditional boundaries in organizational thinking. Today, the strategic importance of international HRM is widely recognized.

The increasing centrality of international HRM issues has blurred the boundaries between this domain of academic study and others. Once no more than an appendix to the field of personnel/HR management, international HRM has become a lens for the study of the multinational enterprise, the form of organization that dominates the world economy. Understanding the complex challenges facing today's global organizations calls for interdisciplinary work with scholars of strategy, institutional economics, organization, cross-cultural management, leadership, change management, organizational culture, and others.

NOTES

* Many of the observations in this reading are drawn from our recent book (Evans et al., 2011).

1. Barham and Heimer, 1998.
2. Bartlett and Ghoshal, 1989.
3. Carlos and Nicholas, 1988. On the other side of the world, southern Chinese clans spread their hold across Southeast Asia in the fourteenth and fifteenth centuries.
4. Wilkins, 1970.
5. Even by the early 1990s, foreign direct investment had only rallied to around 8.5 percent of world output (Jones, 1996). Recent data show the stock of FDI to be 22.4 percent of global GDP in 2007 (World Investment Report 2008, UNCTAD—available at www.unctad.org/Templates/WebFlyer.asp?intItemID=4700&lang=1).
6. Kaufman, 2007.
7. Moriguchi, 2000.
8. Kaufman, 2007.
9. Jacoby, 1985.
10. Sampson, 1975; Vernon et al., 1997. Similarly, in pharmaceuticals, electric light bulbs, steel, and engineering industries, elaborate arrangements were established among national

champions, allowing them to focus on their home markets and to suppress international competition.

11.   Chandler, 1990.
12.   Vernon, 1977.
13.   Kaufman, 2007.
14.   Vaupel and Curhan, 1973.
15.   Hays, 1974.
16.   Tung, 1982.
17.   Stopford and Wells, 1972.
18.   Argyris, 1967.
19.   Davis and Lawrence, 1977.
20.   It would be misleading to say that matrix structure is dead. Some organizations introduced matrix organizations in the late 1980s and 1990s. The matrix structure that ABB employed until 1998 is perhaps the most well known example. Research suggests that matrix structure can be appropriate as a transition organization, facilitating the development of a "matrix culture," leading to different forms of multidimensional organization, facilitated by coordination mechanisms that the matrix introduced (Ford and Randolph, 1992; Galbraith, 2008).
21.   Ford and Randolph, 1992; Galbraith, 1977.
22.   Martinez and Jarillo, 1989.
23.   Bartlett and Ghoshal, 1990.
24.   The *nemawashi* process in Japanese firms is an informal process of consultation, typically undertaken by a high potential individual, involving talking with people and gathering support for an important decision or project.
25.   Many German international firms had an unusual structure abroad, where the sales subsidiary was run jointly by a local general manager with a German commercial manager on a *primus inter pares* basis, facilitating this consensual approach.
26.   Hofstede, 1980.
27.   See Pucik and Hatvany, 1981 and Pucik, 1984. The success of Japan threw the spotlight on HR ingredients such as long-term employment, intensive socialization, team-based appraisal and rewards, slow promotion, and job rotation. Distinctive features of Japanese management that received attention in the West included continuous improvement, commitment to learning, quality management practices, customer-focused production systems, and consultative decision-making.
28.   Oxley, 1961.
29.   Kuin, 1972.
30.   Even today, localization (how to develop the talent of local staff) remains one of the most neglected areas of international human resource management.
31.   "Multinational companies: Special report," *BusinessWeek*, April 20, 1963, p. 76.
32.   Edström and Galbraith, 1977.
33.   "Three times the number of managers were transferred in Europe at [one company rather than the other], despite their being of the same size, in the same industry, and having nearly identical organization charts" (Edström and Galbraith, 1977, p. 255).
34.   See the SOTA (State of the Art) surveys run annually since 1995 by the Human Resource Planning Society, reported each year in the journal *Human Resource Planning*; see also a survey undertaken in Fortune 500 firms by Gregersen et al., 1998.
35.   Prescott et al., 1999.
36.   Ashkenas et al., 1995.
37.   Such clusters of critical factors helped particular nations to develop a competitive advantage in certain fields—such as German firms in chemicals or luxury cars, Swiss firms in pharmaceuticals, and US firms in personal computers, software, and movies.
38.   Bartlett and Ghoshal, 1989.
39.   See Hedlund, 1986; Prahalad and Doz, 1987; and Perlmutter, 1969.

40. Doz et al., 1981; Doz and Prahalad, 1984, 1986.
41. Bartlett and Ghoshal, 1989.
42. Ghoshal and Bartlett, 1998, p. 65.
43. Bartlett and Ghoshal, 1989.
44. Doz and Prahalad, 1986.
45. Bartlett and Ghoshal, 1989.
46. Ghoshal and Bartlett, 1997.
47. Rosenzweig and Nohria, 1994; Björkman and Lu, 2001.
48. Hamel and Prahalad, 1994; Leonard, 1995.
49. This example is taken from Hamel and Prahalad, 1994, who provide a more complete definition, emphasizing that core competences should be gateways to the future.
50. Kogut and Zander, 1992.
51. Polanyi, 1966; Nonaka and Takeuchi, 1995.
52. Cited by Bartlett and Ghoshal, 1992.
53. See http://money.cnn.com/magazines/fortune/global500/2008/full_list/.
54. For example, Cappelli et al., 2010 examine the lessons of business leaders in India.

REFERENCES

Argyris, C. (1967). "Today's problems with tomorrow's organizations." *Journal of Management Studies* 4(1): 31–55.

Ashkenas, R.N., D. Ulrich, T. Jick, and S. Kerr (1995). *The boundaryless organization: Breaking the chains of organizational structure.* San Francisco, CA: Jossey-Bass.

Barham, K., and C. Heimer (1998). *ABB: The dancing giant.* London: Financial Times/Pitman.

Bartlett, C.A., and S. Ghoshal (1989). *Managing across borders: The transnational solution.* Cambridge, MA: Harvard Business School Press.

Bartlett, C.A., and S. Ghoshal (1990). "Matrix management: Not a structure, a frame of mind." *Harvard Business Review* (July–August): 138–45.

Bartlett, C.A., and S. Ghoshal (1992). "What is a global manager?" *Harvard Business Review* (September–October): 124–32.

Björkman, I., and Y. Lu (2001). "Institutionalization and bargaining power explanations of HRM practices in international joint ventures: The case of Chinese — Western joint ventures." *Organization Studies* 22(3): 491–512.

Cappelli, P., H. Singh, J. Singh, and M. Useem (2010). *The India way: How India's top business leaders are revolutionizing management.* Boston, MA: Harvard Business School Publishing.

Carlos, A.M., and S. Nicholas (1988). "Giants of an earlier capitalism: The chartered trading companies as modern multinationals." *Business History Review* 62 (Autumn): 398–419.

Chandler, A.D. (1990). *Scale and scope: The dynamics of industrial capitalism.* Cambridge, MA: Harvard University Press.

Davis, S.M., and P.R. Lawrence (1977). *Matrix.* Reading, MA: Addison-Wesley.

Doz, Y., and C.K. Prahalad (1984). "Patterns of strategic control within multinational corporations." *Journal of International Business Studies* 15(2): 55–72.

Doz, Y., and C.K. Prahalad (1986). "Controlled variety: A challenge for human resource management in the MNC." *Human Resource Management* 25(1): 55–71.

Doz, Y., C.A. Bartlett, and C.K. Prahalad (1981). "Global competitive pressures and host country demands." *California Management Review* 23(3): 63–74.

Edström, A., and J.R. Galbraith (1977). "Transfer of managers as a coordination and control strategy in multinational organizations." *Administrative Science Quarterly* 22(2): 248–63.

Evans, P., V. Pucik, and I. Björkman (2011). *The global challenge: International human resource management.* Boston, MA: McGraw-Hill.

Ford, R., and W. Randolph (1992). "Cross-functional structures: A review and integration of matrix organization and project management." *Journal of Management* 18(2): 267–94.

Galbraith, J.R. (1977). *Organization design. Reading*, MA: Addison-Wesley.

Galbraith, J. (2008). *Designing matrix organizations that actually work: How IBM, Proctor & Gamble, and others design for success*. San Francisco, CA: Jossey-Bass.

Ghoshal, S., and C.A. Bartlett (1997). *The individualized corporation*. New York: Harper-Business.

Ghoshal, S., and C.A. Bartlett (1998). *Managing across borders: The transnational solution*, 2nd ed. London: Random House.

Gregersen, H.B., A.J. Morrison, and S. Black (1998). "Developing leaders for the global frontier." *MIT Sloan Management Review* 40(1): 2–32.

Hamel, G., and C.K. Prahalad (1994). *Competing for the future*. Boston, MA: Harvard Business School Press.

Hays, R.D. (1974). "Expatriate selection: Insuring success and avoiding failure." *Journal of International Business Studies* 5(1): 25–37.

Hedlund, G. (1986). "The hypermodern MNC: A heterarchy?" *Human Resource Management* (Spring): 9–35.

Hofstede, G. (1980). *Culture's consequences. Comparing values, behaviors, institutions, and organizations across nations*. Beverly Hills, CA and London:Sage.

Jacoby, S.M. (1985). *Employing bureaucracy: Managers, unions and the transformation of work in American industry*, 1900–1945. New York: Columbia University Press.

Jones, G. (1996). *The evolution of international business*. London: Routledge.

Kaufman, B. (2007). "The development of HRM in historical and international perspective." In *The Oxford handbook of human resource management*, Eds. P. Boxall, J. Purcell, and P. Wright. New York: Oxford University Press.

Kogut, B., and U. Zander (1992). "Knowledge of the firm, combinative capabilities, and the replication of technology." *Organization Science* 3(3): 383–97.

Kuin, P. (1972). "The magic of multinational management." *Harvard Business Review* (November–December): 89–97.

Leonard, D. (1995). *Wellsprings of knowledge: Building and sustaining the sources of innovation*. Boston, MA: Harvard Business School Press.

Martinez, J.I., and J.C. Jarillo (1989). "The evolution of research on coordination mechanisms in multinational corporations." *Journal of International Business Studies* 20(3): 489–514.

Moriguchi, C. (2000). "Implicit contracts, the Great Depression, and institutional change: The evolution of employment relations in US and Japanese manufacturing firms, 1910–1940." Working paper. Harvard Business School, Boston.

Nonaka, I., and H. Takeuchi (1995). *The knowledge-creating company: How Japanese companies create the dynamics of innovation*. New York: Oxford University Press.

Oxley, G.M. (1961). "The personnel manager for international operations." *Personnel* 38(6): 52–8.

Perlmutter, H.V. (1969). "The tortuous evolution of the multinational corporation." *Columbia Journal of World Business* 4: 9–18.

Polanyi, M. (1966). *The tacit dimension*. London: Routledge & Kegan Paul.

Prahalad, C.K., and Y. Doz (1987). *The multinational mission: Balancing local demands and global vision*. New York: Free Press.

Prescott, R.K., W.J. Rothwell, and M. Taylor (1999). "Global HR: Transforming HR into a global powerhouse." *HR Focus* 76(3): 7–8.

Pucik, V. (1984). "White-collar human resource management in large Japanese manufacturing firms." *Human Resource Management* 23(3): 257–76.

Pucik, V., and N. Hatvany (1981). "An integrated management system: Lessons from the Japanese experience." *Academy of Management Review* 6(3): 469–80.

Rosenzweig, P.M., and N. Nohria (1994). "Influences on human resource management practices in multinational corporations." *Journal of International Business Studies* 25(2): 229–51.

Sampson, A. (1975). *The seven sisters: The great oil companies and the world they made*. London: Hodder & Stoughton.

Stopford, J.M., and L.T. Wells (1972). *Managing the multinational enterprise*. London: Longman.

Tung, R.L. (1982). "Selection and training procedures of US, European, and Japanese multinationals." *California Management Review* 25(1): 57–71.

Vaupel, J.W., and J.P. Curhan (1973). *The world's largest multinational enterprises*. Cambridge, MA: Harvard University Press.

Vernon, R. (1977). *Storm over the multinationals: The real issues*. Cambridge, MA: Harvard University Press.

Vernon, R., L.T. Wells, and S. Rangan (1997). *The manager in the international economy*. Englewood Cliffs, NJ: Prentice Hall.

Wilkins, M. (1970). *The emergence of multinational enterprise*. Cambridge, MA: Harvard University Press.

Randall S. Schuler, Susan E. Jackson, and Ibraiz Tarique

MANAGING GLOBAL TALENT CHALLENGES WITH GLOBAL TALENT MANAGEMENT INITIATIVES*

INTRODUCTION

BEGINNING IN THE LATE 1990S, firms around the world were confronted with a major threat to doing business: a demand for talented employees that far surpassed the supply (*McKinsey Quarterly*, 2008; Michaels et al., 2001). "Talent" and "talent retaining and talent management" became key expressions in global business. Firms faced many challenges, including having the right number of competent employees at the right place and at the right time. Increasingly, they also faced the challenges of needing to reduce the costs of operations, thus moving operations abroad, paying lower wages, and then having to find competent employees to staff the facility. Collectively, these challenges, because of their significant human capital issues, came to be known as "global talent challenges" and were dealt with through "global talent management" initiatives. These were composed of various HR actions depending upon the nature of the global talent challenge.

This reading describes these global talent challenges and global talent management initiatives. Some of our discussion reflects conditions that were present during recent economic and financial boom times (i.e. the years leading up to 2008), when worker shortages were a primary concern. Economic expansion is likely to return eventually, so labor shortages are likely to be of continuing concern. Nevertheless, in the near term, this concern may subside somewhat. Regardless of the size of the gap between the available and desired pool of talent globally, relocation and cost reduction through lower compensation levels are likely to remain major global talent challenges for the next several years.

GLOBAL TALENT CHALLENGES AND GLOBAL TALENT MANAGEMENT

In today's rapidly moving, extremely uncertain, and highly competitive global environment, firms worldwide are encountering numerous global talent challenges. *Global talent challenges (GTCs) are significant human capital issues that focus on managing a firm to ensure just the right amount of the right talent and motivation, at the right place, at the right price, during all economic and financial ups and downs in a very competitive world for the purposes of balancing the workforce with the needs of the firm in the short term, and positioning the firm to have the workforce needed in the long term* (Schuler et al., 2010).

To successfully address global talent challenges, firms of all sizes can and must take advantage of a wide variety of human resource management (HR) actions, which include the development of human resource policies and the design and implementation of specific HR practices (see Jackson et al., 2009). Conceptualized broadly, *global talent management (GTM) refers to the systematic use of HR actions (policies and practices) to manage the several global talent challenges that a firm confronts.* These can include HR policies and practices related to planning and forecasting, obtaining, selecting, motivating, developing, evaluating, retaining, and removing employees consistent with a firm's strategic directions, while taking into account the evolving concerns of the workforce and regulatory requirements (Schuler et al., 2010).

MAJOR FORCES AND SHAPERS OF THE GLOBAL TALENT CHALLENGES

Global talent management is carried out in the context of a dynamic environment. Among the many factors that shape the specific challenges and responses of particular firms are several major drivers, which include: (a) globalization, (b) changing demographics, (c) demand for workers with needed competencies and motivation, and (d) the supply of those needed competencies and motivation. Figure 1 depicts the linkage between these drivers and several HR actions used to manage global talent. We describe these drivers in more detail in the following paragraphs.

Globalization: World Trade, Competition, Customers, Individuals

Globalization is a concept that people use when referring to many different phenomena. Of particular relevance to our discussion are: expansion of world trade, intensified competition among firms, the potential to reach many more customers around the world, and the array of individuals worldwide who now comprise a global labor market.

World Trade

The value of world trade expanded from $89 billion in 1953 to more than $10 trillion in 2008. Although the contraction that occurred in 2009 may slow the rate of future

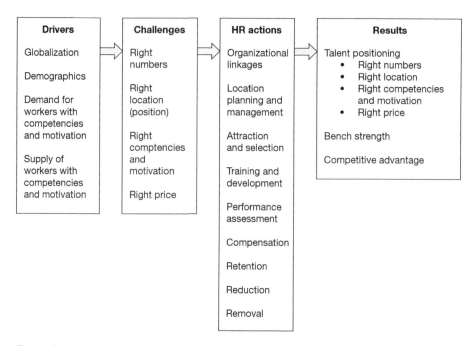

Drivers	Challenges	HR actions	Results
Globalization	Right numbers	Organizational linkages	Talent positioning • Right numbers • Right location • Right competencies and motivation • Right price
Demographics	Right location (position)	Location planning and management	
Demand for workers with competencies and motivation	Right comptencies and motivation	Attraction and selection	Bench strength
Supply of workers with competencies and motivation	Right price	Training and development	Competitive advantage
		Performance assessment	
		Compensation	
		Retention	
		Reduction	
		Removal	

Figure 1. Framework for global talent challenges and management

expansion in the near term, the value of world trade may nevertheless reach $27 trillion by 2030. Foreign direct investment (FDI) went from $59 billion in 1982 to more than $1 trillion in 2008. The formal labor market expanded from 2 billion workers in 1990 to more than 3.5 billion in 2008. The global economy is projected to expand to $75 trillion by 2030, up from $10 trillion in 1970 and $40 trillion in 2008 (Kearney, 2008; Stephenson and Pandit, 2008). While such forecasts of specific values are only best estimates, most observers agree that the long-term trend is for continued expansion of world trade. Thus, while forecasts made early in 2009 pointed to a significant slowdown in FDI and world GDP that year (*The Economist*, February 21, 2009), by the end of the same year, forecasts for 2010 were projecting a modest upturn globally.

Competition

Competition has never been this intense and so multifaceted: it is fast developing, complex, extremely widespread, but also subject to the current global economic and financial crises (The *Economist*, February 21, 2009; Zakaria, 2008; Cairns and Sliwa, 2008; IBM, 2008; Hill, 2007). Global competition has forced many firms to improve quality and strive for innovation (often based on rapidly developed and more sophisticated technology), and increasingly global competition means that enhanced quality and innovation must be achieved while also keeping cost low. Thus, small and larger firms in almost every country are being forced to adapt and quickly respond as they compete with firms worldwide to gain and sustain global competitive advantage (*The Economist*, March 14, 2009; Engardio and Weintraub, 2008; Porter, 1985;

IBM, 2008; Stephenson and Pandit, 2008; Palmisano, 2007; Schuler and Tarique, 2007; Gupta and Govindarajan, 2001). Globalization requires multinational companies to seek economies of scale and scope, find and take advantage of optimal locations while anticipating future relocations, adapt to local differences, learn continuously, and transfer knowledge more effectively than their competitors (Ghemawat and Hout, 2007; Porter, 1985; Krugman, 1979, 1981; Gupta and Govindarajan, 2001). A global competitive advantage awaits those firms that succeed in meeting these challenges (Daniels et al., 2007).

Customers

Customers in virtually all industries are demanding more, and often for less. The telecom industry is migrating rapidly from traditional fixed-line phone service to mobile smartphones. Companies such as BT are selling "experiences" more than telephone "hardware." Customers are demanding innovation and BT is responding by focusing on services and providing a social networking capability (Werdigier, 2008). And this applies to customers the world over, with some differences reflecting unique characteristics of the countries (Zakaria, 2008). Thus, for the typical company today, it is important to think and act global (IBM, 2008; Mendenhall et al., 2008; Dickmann and Baruch, 2010), which includes being where the customers are. Increasingly, companies such as Nokia, IBM, Tata, Caterpillar, and BT find that the growing customer base is in the BRIC countries (Brazil, Russia, India, and China) and in emerging economies throughout Asia, Latin America, and Eastern Europe.

Individuals

Individuals have been entering into the labor market in increased numbers over the past 15 years (Zakaria, 2008; Friedman, 2005). It has been estimated that more than 1.5 billion people have entered the global formal labor market during the past 15 years. Friedman (2005) argued that the development and spread of inexpensive technologies has flattened the world and facilitated the entry of all these workers into the workforce. One major consequence is the ability of firms to employ workers in the developing economies of the world at much lower wages than is possible in the developed economies of the world. Weekly wages in the developed economies are equivalent to monthly and even yearly wages in developing economies (US Department of Labor, 2008; Gomez-Mejia and Werner, 2008). The movement of work to an array of dispersed locations that may include both developed and developing economies is most likely to succeed when all employees have the needed competencies and motivations to do the work, when the work of dispersed employees is effectively coordinated, and when a firm's HR actions are consistent with the full array of relevant employment regulations in every location (Porter, 1985; Hill, 2007; World Bank, 2008; Palmisano, 2007). In addition to meeting these challenges, as multinational firms make decisions about workforce location and relocation, they also must address the challenges of developing an appropriate customer base, identifying and outmaneuvering competitors, managing transportation costs, reducing the possible consequences of political instability, protecting their intellectual property and rights, and so on (Porter, 1985; Daniels et al., 2007; World Bank, 2008; Palmisano, 2007).

Demographics

Worldwide demographics are another major driver of global talent management. In North America, Western Europe, Japan, and Australia, the age of retirement is being ushered in by the baby boomer generation. While this may be a relatively short-term phenomenon in North America (due to current birth and immigration rates), population shrinkage is a longer-term event in Western Europe and Japan (Strack et al., 2008). The long term-term outlook is grim: by 2025 the number of people aged 15–64 is projected to fall by 7 percent in Germany, 9 percent in Italy, and 14 percent in Japan (Wooldridge, 2007; *The Economist*, 2006).

"If you take into consideration the 70 million Baby Boomers expected to retire over the next 15 years (in the U.S.) and only 40 million workers expected to enter the workforce in the same period, you can plainly see that a shortage of workers is imminent" (Adecco, 2008: 9). "By 2010, it is expected the U.S. will face a shortage of more than 10 million workers" (Adecco, 2008: 10). And, according to Stephen Hitch, a human resource manager at Caterpillar in Peoria, Illinois: "We've got a global problem and it's only going to continue to get worse" (Coy and Ewing, 2007: 28). Of course, these pre-2008 projections are now being adjusted somewhat with more baby boomers extending their retirement dates due to significant depletions of their retirement savings as a consequence of the current economic and financial crises (Hansen, 2009a).

While the populations of many developed economies are aging and shrinking in size, the populations of developing and emerging economies are expanding and getting younger (Strack et al., 2008). Thus, there are major variations in demographic characteristics by age and by region that multinational firms need to know and consider in locating and relocating their operations internationally.

Demand for Workers with Competencies and Motivation

Although the pace of globalization has diminished greatly, new *jobs* are still being created that require higher levels of competencies, which are broadly defined as "basic and advanced skills, knowledge and abilities," or the "right know-how" (Daniels et al., 2007; Palmisano, 2007). For existing jobs, there is a growing need for employees who are willing to do the job under new and changing conditions that require the development of additional competencies (motivation). For skilled jobs, for example, there is a need for increased competencies to operate more sophisticated machinery, to interact with more demanding customers, and to use more advanced technology to perform the functions of the traditional skilled jobs (National Commission on Adult Literacy, 2008). And it appears that these increased competencies are being associated with almost all jobs traditionally performed in multinational firms around the world today (Price and Turnbull, 2007).

In addition to the increased need for basic skills and advanced skill levels for basic entry-level, front-line and skilled jobs, there are a rising number of jobs that involve "knowledge work" and thus there is increasing demand for "knowledge workers." This is true around the world, be it in China, India, Europe, or North America. By one estimate, 48 million of the 137 million workers in the US alone can be classified as knowledge workers. Knowledge work often requires competencies that are developed through extensive education and training, and it is generally work that is capable of having a significant impact on the success of the company (Jackson et al., 2003). Knowledge workers include managers, leaders, technicians, researchers, accountants, information specialists, consultants, and medical and pharmaceutical professionals. In multinational firms, knowledge workers such as these often work together in teams that cross cultural and geographic borders: "In the 21st century knowledge creation, integration and the leveraging of such 'new' knowledge are considered the *raison d'etre* of multinational firms" (Brannen, 2008). "The growing need for talented managers in China represents by far the biggest management challenge facing multinationals and locally owned businesses alike" (Lane and Pollner, 2008). Even if demand for managers and other knowledge workers has slowed significantly recently, the need for highly motivated and talented knowledge workers is likely to remain strong well into the future (Roach, 2009).

Just before the economic and financial crises began in 2008, the most prevalent question was: "Where are all the workers?" Although this is not the prevalent question today, it is likely to return sooner than later:

> Whether you can hear it or not, a time bomb is ticking in C-suites worldwide. Its shock waves will resonate for decades ... Surveys conducted by the firm I work for (Egon Zehnder International) indicate that the number of managers in the right age bracket for leadership roles will drop by 30% in just six years. Factor in even modest growth rates, and the average corporation will be left with half the critical talent it needs by 2015.
>
> (Fernández-Aráoz, 2009: 72)

Just as the global economy began to slow in 2008, a study conducted by the global staffing agency Manpower Inc. found that nearly 40 percent of 37,000 companies across 27 countries were finding it a challenge to hire the people they needed (Manpower Inc., 2008a). A 2007 survey of more than 1,300 senior managers around the world found that the most significant trend expected to affect their business over the next 5 years was greater competition for talent worldwide (Price and Turnbull, 2007). More specifically, CEOs are searching for industry, technical, and particularly management skills to support geographic expansion. Many CEOs consider insufficient talent to be a significant barrier to global integration, surpassing the importance of regulatory and budgetary hurdles (IBM, 2008). In other words, most companies worldwide, regardless of size, are confronting and/or will soon confront their global talent challenge of talent shortage that, if ignored, will impact their global business strategies (Dunning, 2000; Manpower Inc., 2008b).

This global talent challenge appears to be a concern across many countries/companies, and especially in India, China, and Brazil. According to a recent survey in China "88% of the Chinese executives said their globalization efforts were hindered by the scarcity of people with real cross-cultural knowledge or experience managing foreign talent; ninety-three percent said that Chinese companies would not achieve their global aspirations unless they developed suitable leaders more aggressively" (Dietz et al., 2008). For entry-level corporate positions, there seems to be a mismatch between the skills found among many Chinese graduates and the types of skills that are needed by local, regional, and multinational companies (Lane and Pollner, 2008).

The most frequently cited reasons for candidates being under-qualified include: poor English skills (which are needed to conduct international business), lack of experience working in teams, and a reluctance to assume leadership roles (*McKinsey Quarterly*, 2008). So while the graduation numbers of countries such as India, China, and Brazil are very impressive, those who are qualified to begin working in many companies are significantly less. For example, in India, the percentage of engineering graduates deemed qualified enough to hire is estimated to be 25 percent; in China the estimated portion is 10 percent; and in Brazil it is 13 percent (*McKinsey Quarterly*, 2008). McKinsey predicted that India would face a shortage of 500,000 staff capable of doing work for multinationals (Engardio, 2007). Clearly, the skills gap is threatening the technology boom in India (Sengupta, 2006). According to Jose Sergio Gabrielli, President of Petrobras, the state-run oil company in Brazil, "The lack of availability of technical ability may be a constraint on growth, no doubt about it" (Downie, 2008: C1, C5). The supply situation in other major countries around the world is largely the same as in India, China, and Brazil.

Supply of Workers with Competencies and Motivation

In developed economies such as North America, Western Europe, and Japan, there is also an expected shortage of competencies. According to a report from the US National Commission on Adult Literacy (2008), between 80 and 90 million American adults do not have the basic communication (also called people or "soft") skills to function well in the global economy or to earn family-sustaining wages. Unique among other advanced industrial countries, American 25 to 35 year olds are not as well educated as their parents. This same reality is also being found in Arab nations, where the younger generation sees that connections rather than education are often the route to career success (Harry, 2007). According to the US National Commission on Adult Literacy (2008), declining educational achievement now puts the US at a competitive disadvantage. The lack of technical knowledge workers continues to drive companies such as Microsoft, Cisco, and Wipro to plead with the US Congress to expand the number of H-1B visa permits granted each year (Preston, 2008; Herbst, 2009; Wadhwa, 2009).

Today the situation related to worker "shortages" is substantially different from the pre-economic and financial crises period described above, the period of time when "global talent management" became popular (The *Economist*, February 21, 2009). By late 2008, a majority of companies that had already begun to downsize were planning to continue making more cuts that year (McGregor, 2009). So, while the shortages described above are likely to return eventually, in the near term firms may find that there is a surplus of workers at all levels of competency and motivation worldwide. As the economic slowdown continues, it will result in reduced demand for goods and services worldwide, creating excess capacity in most firms and putting downward pressure on prices. The pressure for cost reduction may become intense and the use of workforce cost reduction may become irresistible (Mohn, 2009; *The Economist*, February 21, 2009). An increase in recent mergers and acquisitions to reduce capacity and costs suggests that workforce reductions are likely to continue in the next few years (The *Economist*, March 14, 2009). Competition among workers and countries is likely to result in more wage competition and more governmental support to encourage firms to bring jobs to their country.

Because these conditions will be with us for the near term, it seems appropriate to include them in our discussion and framework of global talent management (GTM). That is, we recognize that managing global talent is difficult in times of both talent shortages and talent surpluses. Because labor market conditions are always in flux, global talent management requires firms to stay focused on how actions they take in the near term might influence their ability to adapt to changing conditions in the longer term. Furthermore, we include the talent characteristics of location and price (wage level) in our treatment of GTM. For a more complete treatment of this approach and a review of the academic GTM literature, see Tarique and Schuler (2010).

Global Talent Challenges: Summary

Thus there are several global talent challenges that firms need to manage as effectively as possible, including:

- too little talent is available now when it is needed;
- too much talent is available now and it is not needed;
- the needed talent is available in the wrong place (or position); and
- the needed talent is available at the wrong price.

As a consequence of such conditions, firms may need to: (a) reduce/add workers and positions in their home country; (b) move to another country and establish new operations at lower cost levels; or (c) reduce/add workers, even in other countries. In addition, they may need to train and develop existing staff rather than hire new staff from the outside. They may also need to improve their performance management and compensation systems to ensure that the workers they have are as productive as they can be. In some situations, firms may need to reduce and remove workers from multiple locations. In other words, there are many HR actions that can be taken by firms, both to manage through the current environment of economic and financial crises, and to position themselves for the period of recovery after the crises. Appropriate HR actions taken to address the challenges of global talent management can enable a multinational firm to gain and sustain a global competitive advantage (Lane and Pollner, 2008; Porter, 1985; Stephenson and Pandit, 2008; Palmisano, 2007).

HR ACTIONS TO ADDRESS GLOBAL TALENT CHALLENGES

Due in part to the existence of many drivers of the global talent challenges, there are many possible HR actions that firms can use in their global talent management initiatives (Beechler and Woodward, 2009). Matching an accurate diagnosis of a company's talent management situation with possible HR actions is a first step in gaining and sustaining a global competitive advantage that may result from the successful implementation of the correct action. Several categories of possible HR actions that can be considered by multinational firms include:

- organizational linkages;
- location planning and management;
- attraction and selection;
- training and development;
- performance assessment;
- compensation;
- retention;
- reduction; and
- removal.

Organizational Linkages

Talent management actions can only gain and sustain a global competitive advantage if they are linked to the actions and strategies of the organization (Nag et al., 2007). Nokia decided to relocate to Cluji, Romania knowing that the labor force there was both competent and willing to work at substantially lower wages than the workforce in Bochum, Germany (Ewing, 2008). This move by Nokia fit well with their business strategy, which was to produce high-quality cell phones in a highly competitive market near a new marketplace. The HR action reflected a tight linkage between the firm's business strategy and its global talent management strategy. This linkage was possible because Nokia gathered extensive labor market information and then used it to make an informed decision about where to (re)locate their operations. The business strategy and talent management strategy development reflected a tight reciprocal linkage (Ewing, 2008).

Location Planning and Management

Multinational firms such as Nokia have been rapidly expanding and (re)locating around the world (Porter, 1985; Hill, 2007; Daniels et al., 2007; Ewing, 2008). In a period of the past 3 years, IBM hired more than 90,000 people in Brazil, China, and India (Hamm, 2008). In 2001, Accenture had 250 employees in India; by 2007 it had more than 35,000 employees in India (Engardio, 2007). As a consequence of firms moving rapidly to India, India's seemingly unlimited skilled labor supply was nearly fully employed by 2008. Now, companies thinking about moving operations to India need to develop new talent management strategies in order to attract workers away from their existing employers, and then retain these same individuals. As the available supply of workers shrinks, decisions must be made about whether to locate elsewhere or perhaps develop training programs to train for the competencies that are needed, as Microsoft has done in China and Nokia did in Romania (Chen and Hoskin, 2007; McGregor and Hamm, 2008). To help ensure a supply of dependable labor at the right price when Chinese companies locate abroad, they also send many of their own employees (Wong, 2009).

Multinational firms that are now thinking of expanding or relocating operations confront a large number of questions that are the essence of location planning and management, including:

- Why go? Why move at all from where we are right now? Should we rather just outsource part of our existing operations, or offshore part of our existing operations?
- Where go? What locations should we move to? Have we done country assessments on the country locations on such issues as: compensation levels, workforce skills availability, employment legislation, and culture compatibility?

An extensive list of items composing "country assessments for location management decisions for IHRM" is shown in Exhibit 1:

- How go? Shall we expand our operations by ourselves? Should we outsource some of our existing operations to others? Should we enter into a joint venture with a local partner? Should we use a merger or acquisition?
- When go? Do we need to go within a year? Do we have time to develop an image in a new country that will enable us to attract the best applicants (i.e. be perceived as "One of the Best Companies to Work for")? If we enter another country, will we need to develop new ways of managing the workforce? Will we have to change our practices of recruiting and training, for example, for the local employees? Will we want to create a common set of HR policies and practices for all our locations?
- How link? How do we link employees in multiple international locations with each other so as to gain efficiencies and transfer knowledge effectively?

Besides addressing these questions, multinational firms will likely need to also engage in more traditional human resource planning and forecasting (i.e. making estimates of the numbers of individuals and skills that will be needed in their various locations) using existing attrition and retirement data of the current employees in conjunction with the business plans of the firm. Of course, even traditional planning tools may benefit from modifications that take into account the fact that the past is not always a good predictor of the future, especially in these more uncertain and dynamic times (Cappelli, 2008). Under conditions of great uncertainty, scenario planning might be more prudent than the use of more traditional forecasting techniques (Courtney, 2008; Dye et al., 2009; *The Economist*, February 28, 2009).

EXHIBIT 1. Country assessments for location management decisions

Topic	Content	Example Websites
General facts about country	Size, location, population, infrastructure, country culture, customs, business etiquette, political systems, societal concerns, natural resources, educational system	• odci.gov/cia/publications/factbook • getcustoms.com; cyborlink.com • economist.com/countries • //news.bbc.co.uk/2/hi/country_profiles/default.stm • geert-hofstede.com • foreignpolicy.com • bsr.org • export.gov/marketresearch.html
Attractiveness of country to business	Familiarity of country; government support; favorable labor conditions; economic and political stability	• economist.com • doingbusiness.org • sustainability.org • bsr.com • //news.bbc.co.uk2/hi/business/5313146.stm • kpmg.com • orcworldwide.com
Competitiveness factors	Familiarity of country; government support; favorable labor conditions; economic and political stability	• economist.com • doingbusiness.org • sustainability.org • bsr.com • //news.bbc.co.uk2/hi/business/5313146.stm • kpmg.com • orcworldwide.com
FDI flows/levels	Amount of foreign direct investment coming into a country by other countries and companies establishing operations or buying operations	• economist.com • census.gov/foreign-trade/balance
Labor market	Regulations, size, competencies, ease of hiring/firing, costs, unemployment rates	• doingbusiness.org • manpower.com • adecco.com • atkearney.com • wfpma.org • pwc.com • mckinsey.com • ilo.org/public/English/employment/index.htm
HR policies (actual/likely)	Wage levels for several job classes; talent management; human resource planning; union qualities; T&D support; safety and health	• dol.gov; ilo.org • atkearney.com • economist.com/countries • businessweek.com • ft.com • iht.com • bcg.com • mckinsey.com • //jobzing.com

Note: Selected websites provided to access data on topics of interest.

© Randall S. Schuler, 2010, Rutgers University.

Attraction and Selection

Today organizations are finding that they are having a much more challenging time finding the workers with the competencies they need to perform a wide variety of jobs, regardless of worldwide location (Scullion and Collings, 2006). In essence, workers at every level are more important than ever to multinationals that hope to be competitive, both globally and locally (Guthridge et al., 2008; Huselid et al., 2009). How firms navigate this challenge reflects assumptions they make about workforce management. Two philosophically distinct approaches to attracting and selecting talent are evident in the current literature. One approach assumes that some of a firm's employees are more valuable than others. Huselid et al. (2009) capture this approach with the use of alpha terminology, (e.g. Type "A" players, Type "B" players, and Type "C" players). They also assign these same letters to the positions in the firm. For positions, "A" indicates the most significant impact on the firm's strategy and its key constituencies and positions that offer the greatest variability in performance. For players (the employees), "A" indicates those employees who perform at the highest level of performance variability. The result of this categorization is that firms then would devote the most, but certainly not all, of their resources in their global talent management efforts to "A"–"A" combinations.

In contrast to what Huselid et al. (2009) refer to as their "differentiated workforce approach," companies such as the UK insurance company Aviva have developed a global talent management strategy that focuses on managing the "vital many" rather than risk alienating the bulk of its workforce by focusing exclusively on "highfliers" (the "A"–"A" combinations) (Guthridge et al., 2008).

From the premise that all employees are equally valuable (versus the differen-tiated approach in which some are treated as more important than others) flows a number of actions that help confront the talent management challenge. Rather than differentiate the workforce based on their value to the firm, the alternative approach leads a firm to create differentiated value propositions to attract and retain the full diversity of applicants and employees available in the labor market. For example, the UK retailer Tesco develops separate recruiting and selection tactics for applicants for frontline clerks depending upon whether they are straight from school, are working part-time, or are graduates wanting full-time work. There is a separate website whose materials and language are tailored to that group (*McKinsey Quarterly*, 2008). Tactics used for different groups are based on what the firm thinks will be most effective and valued by the applicants, not on the firm's view that some applicants are more valuable than others.

Although we have presented these two competing philosophies as if firms must choose one or the other, this is overly simplistic. Indeed, a better approach to thinking about who is included as "talent" may be to recognize that firms vary in their degree of inclusiveness, going from including everyone (high inclusiveness) to only the top 5 percent or so (low inclusiveness).

Training and Development

In locations where competencies fall short of what firms need, training and development programs can be used to improve the quality of talent available and at the same time increase a firm's appeal as an employer. In China, Microsoft uses development and recognition programs that appeal to first-time programmers. Development programs include a rotation to the US and recognition programs include being selected as a Silk Road Scholar (Chen and Hoskin, 2007).

Multinational firms such as Microsoft and Schlumberger also offer attractive career management opportunities. Schlumberger makes it possible for engineers to achieve recognition and compensation equivalent to managers while remaining on their engineering career track (*Schlumberger Annual Reports*, 2007, 2008). Applying this more broadly, multinational firms can be expected to emphasize internal markets even more (allowing employees to move around from job to job more freely), with rapid promotion for the superstars (Wooldridge, 2007).

To address the need for leaders and managers with a global mindset that is broader than knowledge about the details of local country operations, many Chinese companies have begun sending their best managers to intensive management-training programs, such as those offered through a corporate university or business school (Dietz et al., 2008).

Performance Assessment

Performance assessment is a key ingredient in successful global talent management (Varma et al., 2008). The performance assessment system at Novartis is central to its global talent management efforts (Siegel, 2008). At the heart of it is a system that grades employees on (a) business results (the "what") and (b) values and behaviors (the "how"). While the business results are unique to each business area, the values and behaviors (ten in all) are common across the entire firm. Combining these two performance dimensions results in a nine-box matrix for assessing employee performance. This assessment process takes place within the context of the business performance cycle, which begins with the strategic plan for the firm and cascades down to define "what" each business unit is expected to accomplish. Novartis employees receive quarterly performance feedback, participate in self-assessments, and engage in development planning and career discussions. Together, these practices are aimed at improving competencies, motivating talent, determining training needs, and establishing a basis for performance-based pay (Siegel, 2008).

Compensation

Compensation rates around the world reflect today's dynamic economic and competitive business conditions (US Department of Labor, 2008; Gomez-Mejia and Werner, 2008). In response to multinationals locating in their countries, local companies in China and India often must pay Western-level salaries (Wooldridge, 2007; Banai and Harry, 2005). Demands for compensation increases by workers in China caused some multinationals to move and/or consider moving operations to Vietnam and Bangladesh, in addition to keeping some of their operations in China, producing what is often referred to as "China plus one strategy" (Bradsher, 2008).

The recent global economic slowdown put more pressure on firms to move to lower-wage nations, and this trend may continue as global demand contacts and industries find themselves with excess capacity. Nevertheless, as long as the supply of qualified managers is limited in emerging economy nations, firms that wish to expand into those markets will need to offer high salaries in order to secure the talent they need.

At Novartis, pay-for-performance is an important component of their global talent management effort (Siegel, 2008). Using the results of an employee's performance assessment in the nine-box performance matrix, a bonus payout is calculated that recognizes both the individual's performance and the performance of their business unit. Because the market for employees such as those in research and development is global, firms such as Novartis set compensation rates at levels that reflect the global environment, even when that means paying salaries that are above the norm in some countries (Siegel, 2008). To help manage compensation costs, however, firms in this situation may locate their operations to second-tier (lower-cost) cities. Another tactic is to recruit talent that is currently under-employed (e.g. engineers who are temporarily working as taxi drivers because they have lost their jobs during the economic downturn).

Retention

Retaining talent is one of the biggest talent management challenges for global accountancy firms. Historically, annual turnover rates at these firms have been between 15 and 20 percent. In these accountancy firms, a variety of factors contribute to high turnover rates among early-career employees, including long hours, pressure to study during off-hours in order to pass professional certification exams, and an "up or out" partnership model (Harry, 2008). Jim Wall, the managing director of human resources at Deloitte, estimated that every percentage-point drop in annual turnover rates equated to a saving of $400–$500 million for the firm (The *Economist*, July 21, 2007). To stem the turnover tide among early-career accountants, some firms have attempted to increase long-term commitment by providing data to employees, showing that employees who stay at least 6 years with their first employer are likely to earn higher pay at other firms when they do eventually leave (The *Economist*, July 21, 2007). More likely to be effective are retention strategies that include characteristics such as: (a) top management making a strong commitment that talent management is a priority for all employees; (b) assessing the efficacy of current recruiting sources; (c) expanding the list of recruiting sources; (d) sourcing talent globally; (e) constantly monitoring labor markets worldwide; (f) establishing diversity programs; (g) establishing accountability among managers for retention goals; and (h) rewarding managers for improving talent retention (Guthridge and Komm, 2008; Caye and Marten, 2008; Holland, 2008).

Reduction and Removal

If global economic and financial conditions continue to deteriorate, unemployment will likely spread dramatically (*The Economist*, January 31, 2009; *The Economist*, March 14, 2009; Powell, 2009). The ILO estimated that more than 50 million jobs would be lost globally in 2009, and again in 2010. Because hiring usually lags behind economic recovery, low employment levels are expected to persist until at least 2012. Thus, the challenge of managing under conditions of surplus talent is likely to be with us for the next few years. Accordingly, "reduction and removal" HR actions are likely to dominate the global talent management agenda of many firms.

Reduction can involve the reduction of work hours, days, overtime, pay levels, pay increases, benefits, new hires and holidays, and also the increased use of attrition, unpaid leave, assignment for local volunteer work, sabbaticals, and contract employees and outsourcing (Mirza, 2008; Boyle, 2009). From these activities, firms can reduce their costs and existing employees can retain their jobs. In contrast, removal refers to the use of layoffs or other measures that result in permanent job loss (Hansen, 2009b). Firms have a great deal of choice in how they shrink their workforces, but their choices are not unlimited. For multinationals, decisions about which HR actions to use must reflect the concerns of various unions, governmental regulations, cultural norms, and corporate values.

INTEGRATED AND FLEXIBLE SYSTEMS OF HR ACTIONS FOR GLOBAL TALENT MANAGEMENT

As this brief summary of possible HR actions suggests, multinational firms must make an array of decisions about how to manage their global talent. Ideally, the HR actions they select reflect both the specific challenges facing the firm currently and consideration of the future challenges that are likely to arise as economic conditions change over time. Although the recent economic downturn has slowed business glob-ally, firms still need to hire and manage their talent in anticipation of their future needs. Furthermore, the selection of particular HR actions is likely to be most effec-tive in firms that adopt a systemic approach to global talent management. That is, HR actions need to be mutually supportive and internally consistent with each other, while also fitting firm characteristics such as top management leadership, vision, values, strategy, size, culture, and industry.

In a study entitled *The War for Talent* (Michaels et al., 2001), it was found that HR professionals spent a great deal of their time formulating and managing the traditional HR policies and practices such as recruiting, selecting, training, perfor-mance appraisal, and compensation. While these are important for addressing talent management challenges, their effectiveness results from being linked with the firm's strategies and directions, and this linkage was found to be lacking. "HR under-performs in companies where its capabilities, competencies, and focus are not tightly aligned with the critical business priorities" (Rawlinson et al., 2008: 23). Additionally, the study concluded that most HR professionals need to do a better job of measuring the impact of HR actions using metrics that are aligned with business strategies. Thus, for example, a firm might track the performance records of employees who have participated in global management training programs and compare them to those who have developed global skills on the job and/or compare them to people with no global exposure, using performance metrics that reflect desired strategic business outcomes such as revenue, profit targets, or retention of direct reports.

RESULTS OF EFFECTIVE GLOBAL TALENT MANAGEMENT

As shown in Figure 1, there are several potential results that are likely to follow from HR actions that successfully address a firm's global talent challenges. In particular, we have argued that addressing the challenge of global talent management improves the firm's success in having the right people at the right place at the right time with the needed competencies and motivation and at the right price at all levels and all locations (positions) of the firms (Lane and Pollner, 2008; Guthridge et al., 2008). In time, these effects accumulate and deepen the firm's bench strength (or future positioning) for all positions in the company, both anticipated and unanticipated, in all current and future locations around the world (Rawlinson et al., 2008).

In the short term, successful HR actions may provide a firm with a temporary advantage over competitors. In the long term, as the firm's global talent management system matures and as learning about how to management global talent becomes embedded in organizational systems, it may be possible for the firm to establish a sustainable global competitive advantage. Sustainability of competitive advantage is never assured, because the drivers of global talent management are likely to change continually (Porter, 1985; Daniels et al., 2007). Nevertheless, as firms gain experience and begin to develop the competencies needed for global success, they simultaneously position themselves to adapt as changing conditions require in the future. The development of such a virtuous cycle of effects seems more likely to occur in firms that take actions specifically designed to train and develop the firms' leaders and HR managers (Caye and Martin, 2008; Guthridge et al., 2008).

BARRIERS TO GLOBAL TALENT MANAGEMENT

It seems apparent that multinational firms have good reason to invest considerable resources in meeting the global talent challenges they face, but success in this endeavor remains elusive. Based on the responses of more than 1,300 executives worldwide, Guthridge et al. (2008) identified several barriers to the use of HR actions for global talent management. Many of these barriers to successful talent management exist for domestic firms, but they become more complex and difficult to overcome in global firms. The barriers include:

- the fact that senior managers do not spend enough time on talent management, perhaps thinking that there are other more pressing things to be concerned with;
- organizational structures, whether based regions, products, or functions, that inhibit collaboration and the sharing of resources across boundaries;
- middle- and front-line managers who are not sufficiently involved in or responsible for employees' careers, perhaps because they see these activities as less important than managing the business, and/or because they require such a long-term perspective;
- managers are uncomfortable and/or unwilling to acknowledge performance differences among employees—a step that is required in order to take actions to improve performance;

- managers at all levels who are not sufficiently involved in the formulation of the firm's talent management strategy, and therefore have a limited sense of ownership and understanding of actions designed to help manage the firm's global talent; and
- HR departments that lack the competencies needed to address the global talent challenge effectively, and/or lack the respect of other executives whose cooperation is needed to implement appropriate HR actions.

While there are many barriers to overcome, multinational firms such as IBM, Toyota, Procter & Gamble, Novartis, ThyssenKrupp, and Schlumberger have shown that success is possible with the commitment, leadership, and involvement of the top management (Farndale et al., 2010; Takeuchi et al., 2008; Lane and Pollner, 2008; Palmisano, 2007).

CONCLUSION

Many of the most pressing challenges facing global firms today are directly related to human capital challenges, and more specifically global talent challenges (Rawlinson et al., 2008; Adecco, 2008; Walker, 2007; Scott et al., 2007; Price and Turnbull, 2007; Scullion and Collings, 2006). These global talent challenges arise due to the ever-changing characteristics of the environment. In particular, among the major drivers are: enhanced globalization, evolving demographics, the need for more competencies and motivation, and the growing shortage/surplus of needed competencies and motivation. For firms throughout the world, the changing environment— particularly during volatile economic and financial periods of boom-and-bust such as those experienced in recent years—presents both global talent challenges and an opportunity to gain a sustainable global competitive advantage (Porter, 1985; Cairns and Sliwa, 2008). In this reading, we sought to provide a brief overview of possible HR actions that can be used to build an integrated and flexible system for global talent management, and described some of the barriers to success in this endeavor. The greatest challenge may simply be the need for firms to be relentless in their efforts to effectively manage global talent, for even when success is achieved in the near term, new HR actions will soon be required simply to stay one step ahead of competitors. For the HR profession, an immediate challenge is to develop the supply of HR talent with the competencies and motivations required to understand the drivers that create global talent management challenges, develop systems that are tailored to address a particular firm's specific global talent needs, and work in partnership with the senior management team to ensure a close linkage between HR actions programs and the strategic objectives of the firm.

NOTE

* The authors wish to express thanks for preparatory comments and suggestions to Clemens Brugger, Dave Collings, Paul Sparrow, Mark Saxer, Hugh Scullion, Ken Smith, Rosalie Tung and Nadia Wicki. Supported by a grant from the School of Management and Labor Relations,

Rutgers University. Adapted from our chapter in H. Scullion and D. Collings (Eds.), *Global Talent Management* (London: Routledge, 2010).

REFERENCES

Adecco (2008) *The next decade's talent war* (Geneva: Adecco).

Banai, M. and Harry, W. (2005). Transnational managers: A different expatriate experience. *International Studies of Management and Organization,* 34 (3): 96–120.

Beechler, S. and Woodward, I.C. (2009). Global talent management. *Journal of International Management* 15: 273–285.

Boyle, M. (2009). Cutting costs without cutting jobs, *Business Week,* March 9: 55.

Bradsher, K. (2008). Investors seek Asian options to costly china, *The New York Times,* June 18: A20.

Brannen, M.Y. (2008). What would it take for Japanese managers to be globally agile? Pressing concerns for Japanese talent management. Paper presented at the Academy of Management Annual Conference, August 9–13, Anaheim, CA.

Cairns, G. and Sliwa, M. (2008). *A very short, fairly interesting and reasonably cheap book about international business* (London: Sage).

Cappelli, P. (2008). *Talent on demand* (Boston, MA: Harvard Business School).

Caye, J-M. and Marten, I. (2008). *Talent management.* (Boston, MA: The Boston Consulting Group).

Chen, W. and Hoskin, J. (2007). Multinational corporations in China: Finding and keeping talent, *SHRM,* October: 1–4.

Coy, P. and Ewing, E. (2007). Where are all the workers? *Business Week,* April 9: 28–31.

Courtney, H. (2008). A fresh look at strategy under uncertainty: An interview, *McKinsey Quarterly,* December.

Daniels, J.D., Radebaugh, L.H., and Sullivan, D.P. (2007). *International business: Environment and operations* (Upper Saddle River, NJ: Pearson/Prentice-Hall).

Dickmann, M. and Baruch, Y. (2010). *Global career management* (London: Routledge).

Dietz, M.C., Orr, G., and Xing, J. (2008). How Chinese companies can succeed abroad, *McKinsey Quarterly,* May.

Downie, A. (2008). Wanted: Skilled workers for a growing economy in Brazil, *The New York Times*: C1, C5.

Dunning, J. (2000). The eclectic paradigm as an envelope for economic and business theories of MNE activity, *International Business Review,* 9: 163–190.

Dye, R., Sibony, O., and Viguerie, S.P. (2009). Strategic planning: Three tips for 2009, *McKinsey Quarterly,* April.

The Economist (2006) The battle for brainpower, *The Economist*: October 5.

The Economist (2007) Accounting for good people, *The Economist,* July 21: 68–70.

The Economist (2009) Swinging the axe, *The Economist,* January 31: 69–70.

The Economist (2009) Turning their backs on the world, *The Economist,* February 21: 59–61.

The Economist (2009) Managing in a fog, *The Economist,* February 28: 67–68.

The Economist (2009) When jobs disappear, *The Economist,* March 14: 71–73.

The Economist Intelligence Unit (2006) The CEO's role in talent management: How top executives from ten countries are nurturing the leaders of tomorrow. *The Economist* (London: The Economist Intelligence Unit).

Engardio, P. (2007). India's talent gets loads of TLC, *Business Week,* August 20 and 27: 52–53.

Engardio, P. and Weubtraub, A. (2008). Outsourcing the drug industry, *Business Week,* September 15: 49–53.

Ewing, E. (2008). Nokia's new home in Romania, *Business Week,* January.

Farndale, E., Scullion, H., and Sparrow, P. (2010). The role of the corporate HR function in global talent management, *Journal of World Business,* 46 (2).

Fernández-Aráoz, C. (2009). The coming fight for executive talent, *Business Week,* December.

Friedman, T.L. (2005). *The world is flat* (New York: Farrar, Straus & Giroux).

Ghemawat, P. and Hout, T. (2007). *Redefining global strategy* (Boston, MA: Harvard Business School Press).

Gomez-Mejia, L. and Werner, S. (2008). *Global compensation* (London: Routledge).

Gupta, A. and Govindarajan, V. (2001). Converting global presence into global competitive advantage, *Academy of Management Executive,*15: 45–58.

Guthridge, M. and Komm, A.B. (2008). Why multinationals struggle to manage talent, *McKinsey Quarterly*, May: 1–5.

Guthridge, M., Komm, A.B., and Lawson, E. (2008). Making talent management a strategic priority, *McKinsey Quarterly*, January: 49–59.

Hamm, S. (2008). International isn't just IBM's first name, *Business Week*, January.

Harry, W. (2007). Employment creation and localization-the crucial human resources issues for the GCC, *International Journal of Human Resource Management,* 18 (1): 132–146.

Harry, W. (2008). Personal communication, October 1, 2008.

Hansen, F. (2009a). Downturn dilemma, *Workforce Management,* February 16: 29–30.

Hansen, F. (2009b). HR in the downturn, *Workforce Management,* February 16: 16.

Herbst, M. (2009). A narrowing window for foreign workers? *Business Week,* March 16: 50.

Huselid, M.A., Beatty, R.W., and Becker, B. (2009). *The differentiated workforce* (Boston, MA: Harvard Business School Press).

Hill, C.W.L. (2007). *International Business: Competing in the global marketplace,* 6th ed. (New York: McGraw-Hill/Irwin).

Holland, K. (2008). Working all corners in a global talent hunt, *The New York Times,* February 24: 17.

IBM (2008). *The enterprise of the future* (New York: IBM).

Jackson, S.E., Hitt, M.A., and DeNisi, A. (2003). *Managing knowledge for sustained competitive advantage* (San Francisco, CA: Jossey-Bass).

Jackson, S.E., Schuler, R.S. and Werner, S. (2009). *Managing human resources,* 10th ed. (Mason, OH: Cengage, Southwestern Publishing Company).

Kearney, A.T. (2008) *Globalization 3.0* (Boston, MA: A.T. Kearney).

Krugman, P. (1979). A model of innovation, technology transfer, and the world distribution of income, *The Journal of Political Economy,* 87 (2): 253–266.

Krugman, P. (1981). Intraindustry specialization and the gains from trade, *The Journal of Political Economy,* 89 (4): 959–973.

Lane, K. and Pollner, F. (2008). How to address China's growing talent shortage, *McKinsey Quarterly,* 3: 33–40.

McGregor, J. (2009). A pink-slip pandemic, *Business Week,* March 23 and 30: 14.

McGregor, J. and Hamm, S. (2008). Managing the global workforce, *Business Week,* January 28: 36–51.

McKinsey Quarterly (2008) The war for talent, *McKinsey Quarterly,* 10 January.

Manpower Inc. (2008a) Borderless workforce survey, *Manpower White Paper.*

Manpower Inc. (2008b) Confronting the talent crunch, *Manpower White Paper.*

Mendenhall, M.E., Osland, J.S., Bird, A., Oddou, G.R., and Mazevski, M.L.G. (2008). *Global leadership: Research, practice and development* (London: Routledge).

Michaels, E., Handfield-Jones, H. and Axelrod, B. (2001). *The war for talent* (Boston, MA: Harvard Business School Press).

Mirza, B. (2008). Look at alternatives to layoffs, *SHRM On-line,* December 29.

Mohn, T. (2009). The long trip home, *The New York Times,* March 10: D1, D5.

Nag, R., Hambrick, D.C., and Chen, M-J. (2007). What is strategic management, really? Inductive derivation of a consensus definition of the field, Strategic Management Journal, 28: 935–955.

National Commission on Adult Literacy (2008) *Reach higher America: Overcoming crisis in the U.S. workforce* (Washington, DC: National Commission on Adult Literacy), June.

Palmisano, S. (2007). The globally integrated enterprise, *Foreign Affairs*, 85 (3): 127–136.

Porter, M. (1985). *Competitive advantage: Creating and sustaining superior performance* (New York: Free Press).

Powell, B. (2009). *China's hard landing, Fortune*, March 16: 114–120.

Preston, J. (2008). Visa application period opens for highly skilled workers, *The New York Times*, April 1: A5.

Price, C. and Turnbull, D. (2007). The organizational challenges of global trends: A McKinsey global survey, *McKinsey Quarterly*, May.

Rawlinson, R., McFarland, W., and Post, L. (2008). A talent for talent, *Strategy + Business*, Autumn: 21–24.

Roach, S. (2009). Testimony before the Chinese American Committee on Economic and Security, February 17.

Schlumberger Annual Reports (2007, 2008).

Schuler, R.S. and Tarique, I. (2007). International HRM: A North America perspective, a thematic update and suggestions for future research, *International Journal of Human Resource Management*, May: 15–43.

Scott, V., Schultze, A., Huseby, T., and Dekhane, N. (2007). *Where have all the workers gone?* (Chicago, IL: A.T. Kearney).

Scullion, H. and Collings, D. (2006). *Global staffing systems* (London: Routledge).

Sengupta, S. (2006). Skills gap threatens technology boom in India, *The New York Times*, October 17: A1, A6.

Siegel, J. (2008). Global talent management at Novartis, *Harvard Business School* (Case #9–708–486).

Stephenson, E. and Pandit, A. (2008). How companies act on global trends: A McKinsey global survey (Boston, MA: McKinsey).

Strack, R., Baier, J., and Fahlander, A. (2008). Managing demographic risk, *Harvard Business Review*, February: 2–11.

Tarique, I. and Schuler, R.S. (2010). Framework and review of global talent management and suggestions for future research, *Journal of World Business*, H. Scullion and D. Collings (special guest editors), 46 (2).

Takeuchi, H., Osono, E., and Shimizu, N. (2008). The contradictions that drive Toyota's success. *Harvard Business Review*, June: 96–104.

US Department of Labor (2008). *International comparisons of hourly compensation costs in manufacturing, 2006* (Washington, DC: Bureau of Labor Statistics).

Varma, A., Budhwar, P., and DeNisi, A. (2008). *Performance management systems* (London: Routledge).

Wadhwa, V. (2009). America's immigrant brain drain, *Business Week*, March 16: 68.

Walker, M. (2007). *Globalization 3.0* (Wilson Quarterly and reprinted by A.T. Kearney, 2008).

Werdigier, J. (2008). Retooling for a changing telecom landscape, *The New York Times*, March 8: C2.

Wong, E. (2009). China's export of labor faces growing scorn, *The New York Times*, December 21: A1–A9.

Wooldridge, A. (2007) The battle for the best, *The Economist: The World in 2007*, p. 104.

World Bank (2008). See the six indicators the World Bank uses to describe the extent of employment regulations in countries at www.doingbusiness.org.

Zakaria, F. (2008). *The post-American world* (New York: Norton).

Wes Harry and David G. Collings

LOCALISATION: SOCIETIES, ORGANISATIONS AND EMPLOYEES

INTRODUCTION

LOCALISATION HAS EMERGED as a key issue in the management of multinational corporations (MNCs). The concept is, however, often used in generic terms without specific definition. In this regard, Hideo Sugiura, the former vice chairman of Honda, distinguished between four types of localisation: localisation of products, profit, production and people (cited in Evans et al., 2002). Although the primary focus of this reading will be on people, we will also touch on some of the other concepts in setting the context for our later discussions. In this regard, a key debate centres on the extent to which MNCs' 'foreign affiliates (or subsidiaries) act and behave as local firms versus the extent to which their practices resemble those of the parent corporation or some other global standard' (Rosenzweig and Nohria, 1994: 229). Indeed, based on their work on patterns of strategic control in multinationals, Doz and Prahalad (1986) have argued that responding to a variety of national demands while maintaining a coherent strategy is a key strategic challenge facing MNCs. In a similar vein, Bartlett and Ghoshal (1998) call for organisations to maintain a 'dynamic balance' between globalisation (implementing globally standard practices) and localisation (adapting practices to account for the host environment) if they are to become truly transnational. The staffing orientations pursued by MNCs in their foreign affiliates are generally a key indicator of the firm's orientation in this regard. Specifically, firms that pursue an ethnocentric orientation are likely to fill key positions in subsidiary operations with parent country nationals or employees from the home country of the MNC. In contrast, MNCs that pursue a polycentric approach are significantly more likely to fill key positions at subsidiary level with host country nationals or employees from the country in which the subsidiary is located.

Localisation of labour (sometimes called labour nationalisation, host country national development or indigenisation) is defined as: 'the extent to which jobs originally filled by expatriates are filled by local employees who are competent to perform the job' (Selmer, 2004: 1094) and it is often considered one of the crucial drivers of the employment policies of many nation-states. It also influences the state's relationships with foreign organisations seeking to operate within their national boundaries. Evans *et al.* (2002) see localisation as systematic investment in the recruitment, development and retention of local employees, which is an important element in the globalisation strategy of multinationals. However, they also point to the differences between the rhetoric and the reality of many localisation strategies and the barriers to the implementation of localisation strategies will be considered below.

Demographics and cost concerns are often key drivers of localisation, particularly in the Gulf Cooperation Council countries (Bahrain, Kuwait, Oman, Qatar, Saudi Arabia and United Arab Emirates) and failure to solve the problems of ineffective localisation may have wide-ranging and long-term consequences (Yamani 2000). Debates around localisation are not restricted to managerial employees however, and also concern the employment of HCNs at lower levels in the organisational hierarchy. In this regard it might seem easy to create jobs for locals but in practice the creation of worthwhile productive jobs depends on an appropriate education system, suitable work ethic within the host population and willingness on the part of employers to make a sustained and genuine effort to support and transfer skills, attitudes and behaviours. As should be apparent from the proceeding introduction the localisation of human resources at managerial and staff levels is important not only in the context of developing the human resources of the host economy but also in building mutually beneficial, long-term relationships between the employing organisation and the host society. Further, lower profit margins in developing countries and a growing unwillingness among governments in poorer countries to allow key positions in foreign MNCs to be occupied indefinitely by expatriates are forcing more and more organisations to examine alternatives to traditional expatriate staffing methods (Sparrow *et al.*, 2004). In this reading we will first outline the key forces driving local responsiveness in international business. We then consider the business advantages and disadvantages of local responsiveness. Our discussion then focuses more specifically on the localisation of human resources and again the advantages and disadvantages of this will be outlined. After exploring the nature of localisation in practice, finally we consider the role of expatriates in the localisation process.

THE CHANGING MEANING OF LOCAL RESPONSIVENESS IN INTERNATIONAL BUSINESS

At one time organisations from developed countries could virtually afford to ignore local needs and wishes in servicing foreign markets, particularly those in developing countries. They generally had a monopoly, or near monopoly, of goods and services and so could impose on local markets whatever they wanted to sell. Some imposed, or tried to impose, their business practices and cultures in foreign operations (cf. Hertz, 2001). Some international organisations could even impose their will on sovereign states. The power of the companies was generally applied and monitored by expatriates, usually nationals of the parent country of their employer.

The imposition of products, services and people was resented, particularly for the colonialist attitudes which came with the imposition. Further, citizens from developing countries continue to resent expatriates holding high paid jobs, which they considered could be done by HCNs, and they often commented on the lack of commitment of expatriates to the local operations (Brewster, 1991). Since the 1960s, the desire to build nation-states and national economies has led to a strong move for nationalisation, local partnerships or at least significant investment within the host country (Sparrow *et al.*, 2004). In the following section we consider the business advantages and disadvantages of localisation.

THE BUSINESS ADVANTAGES AND DISADVANTAGES OF LOCALISATION

There are many sound economic and ethical reasons for MNCs to develop a localisation strategy. Such developments are not without some difficulties and disadvantages however and these are discussed below.

Advantages

There are four main advantages in developing localisation policies. First, localisation of human resources may improve relations between foreign investors and host country governments. Selmer (2004) has argued that this is the case in the Chinese context as the government favours the development of local employees. Indeed Lasserre and Ching (1997) have shown that central and provincial authorities there may view localisation to be an indication of foreign firms' commitment to the country. Thus from the MNC's point of view a localisation strategy may help to ensure foreign operations operate with minimum levels of conflict with the host authorities. Further it may assist the firm in gaining lucrative contracts or tenders with public sector organisations.

Second, localisation of human resources may improve communication, and, ultimately business performance in the host country. This is because communication local to local is usually more effective than foreigner to local. Human nature tends to favour the familiar rather than the strange. In this regard customers generally want to be served by those who understand their needs and it is most often fellow nationals and long-term residents who understand what these needs are. Successful organisations recognise that a shared language, with the local nuances, helps in communications and understanding. Further, HCNs may provide a valuable resource in developing local contacts in the host environment. While expatriate managers may have greater access to higher level institutional contacts, local employees will generally be in a better position to develop business relationships with lower levels of organisational and government hierarchies (Lasserre and Ching, 1997; Selmer, 2004). This is particularly important in some societies such as China where guanxi is vital for developing business contacts and opportunities.

Third, host country labour is generally a more reliable resource than temporary workers, who even if they work in the country for a long time, have divided loyalty

(Black and Gregerson, 1992) and certainly see their ultimate destination as a different location. The loyalty of the foreign labour is purchased at a price that, with few exceptions, is more expensive than local labour. Harry and Banai (2005) have described the motivation of many senior expatriates and the costs of employing them – at rates much higher than most host country nationals. In a similar vein, it has been shown that expatriates operating in a Chinese context can be paid five times more than HCN comparators in total compensation (Economist Intelligence Unit, 1997; Selmer, 2004). Ruhs and Godfrey (2002) have shown that even for 'cheap' foreign labour, the costs, over the long term, are greater than most societies would willingly bear.

Finally, from an economic perspective, by responding to local needs, especially through investing capital and employing local labour, the organisation increases the wealth of the local population and so increases their ability to buy products and services sold by local businesses. Even if the market is small and poor, there can be good potential for growth and long-term profit (Prahalad, 2004). MNCs can create the capacity to consume by paying reasonable wages, training and developing staff and treating them well should be able to reap advantages from increased markets in the host country. Those organisations that develop local markets may gain a dominant market position, which latecomers will find hard to overturn.

Disadvantages

There are four main disadvantages in developing localisation policies. First, understanding local markets takes time and effort. Sometimes local management can make costly mistakes or events can occur outside their direct control that will cost the parent company heavily in financial terms, as companies such as Union Carbide in Bhopal India or Shell in Nigeria have found. The cost of educating customers who might not be familiar with a product or service, even those intended to meet apparent local needs, can be very high. So too can be the cost of adjusting the product or service to meet these local needs, for example smaller packets for those customers who cannot afford to buy enough to hold a stock of an item (Das, 1993) or different coloured materials to meet local preferences. On the basis of a cost-benefit analysis, organisations may feel that the costs associated with the adaptation of products to account for the local context may outweigh the benefits associated with such an action (Shenkar and Luo, 2004). Further, organisations may, on the basis of a user/need analysis of consumer needs, even decide not to introduce a popular product or service into a particular market (Shenkar and Luo, 2004: 419–20).

Second, there are disadvantages in having to make changes in the ways of working to meet local conditions. For example, the work patterns might be different from those expected or preferred, such as split shifts giving a long break at midday, or twelve-hour, six-day working with long vacations. Indeed, it has been argued (Nash, 2004) that the traditional Spanish siesta is coming under threat from globalisation as a growing number of MNCs are increasingly persuading executives that they cannot be absent from their desks for hours during the middle of the day. This indicates that these MNCs consider the siesta to be impractical in the modern globalised business environment. Thus, they are not prepared to sacrifice their traditional working time arrangements for what they consider to be an impractical and unworkable tradition that is at odds with their ideology for how the business enterprise should be run.

Third, managing without expatriates involves looser coordination from an HQ perspective and potentially greater problems in communicating with HQ from a subsidiary perspective. Indeed, empirical research has shown that the staffing decisions with regard to key executive appointments (with expatriates or locals) significantly impacted on the parent company's operational control of the host operations (Child and Yan, 1999). While more indirect methods of control have been effectively used to monitor subsidiary performance, a direct link with the subsidiary through a parent country national may aid in ensuring that communication lines between the HQ and the subsidiary are open and efficient. Without this link, the HQ may not have an accurate picture of how the subsidiary is performing. Specifically, while more indirect control methods such as financial reporting can provide HQ with a quantitative overview of subsidiary performance, some of the nuances of the subsidiary operation may be lost in the figures. For example, in some situations profit levels in the local market may not meet international levels or expectations but nonetheless they can still make a steady and potentially increasing contribution to the organisation's portfolio. Likewise, inefficiencies or financial problems could potentially be hidden in financial statements or other reporting procedures.

Fourth, a major concern of senior HQ managers with respect to localisation strategy is the fear of losing intellectual property rights, particularly in the emerging markets where the perception is that everything can be copied. Selmer (2004) describes this as an 'agency problem' and argues that expatriate presence may help to guard against local managers pursuing their personal self-interest in managing the subsidiary or making decisions that are incongruent with the organisation's global strategy. In this vein, Boisot and Child (1999) have noted that due to concerns over embezzlement in the Chinese context, many foreign firms have reserved the option of appointing their chief financial officers from within the organisation.

Having examined the advantages and disadvantages of local responsiveness in international management in a broader sense, we will now focus specifically on the localisation of human resources.

LOCALISATION OF HUMAN RESOURCES

In this section, we will consider the localisation of non-managerial staff in foreign subsidiaries. This is significant, as the number of non-managerial staff employed in subsidiaries is generally far in excess of those in managerial roles. This cohort of employees is generally neglected in the extant literature, however.

While globalisation appears to offer many advantages to international organisations, it does have the potential disadvantage that these organisations are judged not just as economic entities but as social creations that are expected, not least by customers and domestic pressure groups, to behave in a responsible and ethical manner – wherever they operate. Thus, localisation is not as straightforward a proposition as it may immediately appear. Hence, in this context a key ethical decision for international HR managers to consider is what to do when an employment practice that is illegal or even viewed as morally suspect in the home country is legal and acceptable in the host country (Briscoe and Schuler, 2004). Major international companies such as Shell, Union Carbine and Nike have found that their 'local' practices are judged by 'home' country ethical standards with the potential harm that does to reputation and sales (Litvin, 2003). Take, for example, the criticism Nike has received in recent years due to the conditions prevailing in its outsourced productions facilities in lower wage-cost countries (cf. Morris and Lawrence, 2003). In this regard, there are sound ethical reasons for developing local human resources (Hailey, 1999). These reasons include human rights in terms of employment and training opportunities not being linked to race and nationality but to capability, and with meeting the reasonable requirements of the whole stakeholder community and contributing to the greater human development.

It might seem straightforward to develop the skills required to localise many of the tasks required in large-scale industrialised operations and complex administrative services, but in the context of developing countries, it is important to note that the skills, attitudes, behaviours and methods of learning necessary in rural and small-scale industrial activities are not easily transferable to the large-scale and complex activities that characterise multinational investment. As most employees (and customers) will have little exposure to the requirements of industrialised and complex operations, it will take time, much training and expenditure to develop the workers to meet the organisation's needs.

We will now examine the benefits and barriers of localising human resources.

THE BENEFITS OF LOCALISING HUMAN RESOURCES

There are many benefits that arise from utilising local people rather than expatriates to fill key positions within foreign operations. Often these benefits are underestimated, particularly for senior positions, for reasons that are often based on racial or national stereotypes (Banai, 1992).

We have discussed above the advantages of provider and customer sharing a common language as well as common cultural communications and expectations. The impact of this sharing cannot be underestimated. As noted above, HCNs may provide a valuable resource in developing local contacts in the host environment. Specifically, we pointed to the fact that while expatriate managers may have greater access to higher level institutional contacts, local employees will generally be in a better position to develop business relationships with lower levels of organisational and government hierarchies (Lasserre and Ching, 1997; Selmer, 2004).

The cost of local employees is generally lower than that of expatriates. Expatriate costs are usually a multiple of the national employee, and expatriates are among the most expensive employees, even in home country terms (e.g. Brewster, 1991; Harry and Banai, 2005; Scullion and Brewster, 2001). Even the cost of administering the expatriate employees' conditions of service can be high, compared with that of the administration of host country nationals, with HR staff engaged in carrying out cost of living comparison studies, developing tax equalisation formulae and managing international careers (Dowling and Welch, 2004).

The lower costs of the host country staff and their longer-term employment means that the return on investment in recruiting and training these staff may be higher than for expatriates. Organisations that encourage the development and promotion of local staff are likely to see improved morale and greater retention rates of their best staff. These staff will stay for longer, ensuring that valuable knowledge and capability are retained within the organisation and thus making a potentially more valuable return from the investment in their recruitment and development than investing in expatriate staff. The long-term relationship between the local operation and the host population often means that the company is no longer seen as foreign but local. For example, Ford of Dagenham is now generally considered British and not American, and the Wellcome stores are generally considered a Hong Kong 'belonger' there.

As discussed earlier, the localisation of human resources may also have a positive political impact. Host country governments may view the localisation process as an indication of attachment or commitment to the host country and thus may aid or at least not greatly hinder the operation of the MNC in the host country. Even if there are no short-term political benefits, there are certainly long-term benefits, as Hailey (1999) and Litvin (2003) have shown, for taking an ethical stance not to exploit foreigners. In this regard, Sparrow et al. (2004: 133) posit: 'regulators and governments look at the behaviour of a company against local legal, socio-cultural and environmental norms'. Thus, ethical decisions in this regard are particularly complex, as not only must MNCs be cognisant of host norms in this regard, but also they are constrained by home norms and beliefs as discussed above. A final advantage of using local managers to run the foreign subsidiary is that this staffing approach allows the MNC to adopt a lower profile in sensitive political conditions than would be the case with expatriates in charge (Scullion, 1992).

The Barriers to Localising Human Resources

While it might seem to make economic, financial and ethical sense to localise human resources, there are many barriers that may mean the continued use of expatriates is more practical and sometimes preferable. In this section, we will outline some of the key challenges in this regard.

Most resistance to localising human resources is from the private sector organisations (national and international) where short-term costs are emphasised to the detriment of long-term benefits. In this section, we will outline the key challenges to the localisation of human resources with a particular focus on non-managerial employees. Specifically, we focus on: education and the workplace, jobs on offer that do not appeal, inappropriate selection methods, training and costs.

Education and the Workplace

Intelligence and potential are evenly spread in the human population, and no race or nationality lacks the ability to develop necessary skills, attitudes or behaviours required by modern organisations. However, whereas most developed countries have built up their skilled workforces and managerial systems, along with the educational support systems over many decades, in developing areas such as the Gulf Cooperation Council, China and Eastern Europe the pace of development has been very rapid. The pace has been so rapid that insufficient members of the host population have been educated to develop the capability needed by employers. For example, Warner (1985) noted that two in three Chinese managers had no qualifications beyond middle school in the mid-1980s. Further, their knowledge and skills in areas such as auditing, cost accounting, marketing and personnel were relatively weak. In a similar vein, Micklethwait (1996) posited that China was producing only 300 MBA graduates annually in 1995, when foreign joint ventures alone could have absorbed 240,000 of them.

The education systems in most developing countries are different from those in industrialised countries of the West. For most countries, education has focused on basic literacy (if that) and learning from an older generation how to undertake agricultural, small-scale repair or retail tasks. Even in Eastern Europe and states of the former Soviet Union, where the standards of education were high in terms of technical knowledge, there were considerable differences in terms of attitudes towards work and behaviour at work. Indeed, Kiriazov et al. (2000) posit that management training in Eastern European countries has traditionally focused on rote learning as opposed to action learning, thus limiting the potential contribution of these management graduates. Recently, organisations such as the Open University have begun to operate in these countries and Bennett (1996) reports some 7,000 annual enrolments in their courses in Russia alone. In many countries, little money has been spent on education in general and in education for the workplace in particular. In commenting on this issue in less developed international economies, a senior banking official commented: 'In countries like Vietnam and China, people are very keen to work for foreign multinational companies. The problem isn't getting people to come to work, the difficulty is with the government relations, *the language skills and standards of education*. You've got to support the employees with a lot of training' (quoted in Solomon, 1995: 64, emphasis added).

In these countries, significant resources have gone into educating the elite in tertiary education establishments at home or abroad and little spent on basic education for the mass of the population. For example, within Saudi Arabia the dropout rate after primary schooling is 30 per cent. In this regard, Yamani (2000) has demonstrated the wide gap between the expectations of the generation entering the workforce in Saudi Arabia and the reality of the workplace. Fewer than half of the 100,000 Saudis entering the employment market each year find a job (*The Economist*, 2002).

In the GCC, and many other countries, the emphasis in education is often on cultural or nation building rather than on ensuring employability in the workplace. In most countries, including in the developed world, technical subjects are shunned in favour of social sciences and other fields that might be useful in developing 'thinking skills' but are not immediately applicable in most work situations.

Jobs on Offer Do Not Appeal

In some countries, such as those of the GCC, even when young people are well educated and qualified, they may be reluctant to work in the type of jobs that are available. The socio-political elites who have access to the best education institutions are more likely to want to work in government or be entrepreneurs than to work for someone else. This is especially the case if the potential employer is a foreign organisation, although the prestige of a period in a well-known international organisation may be attractive at the beginning of a career.

Jobs that are not attractive to most HCNs, when they are wealthy enough to have a choice, include heavy manual work, domestic service and, in some parts of the Middle East, cash handling jobs including bank teller and jobs that involve providing direct service to a customer. Even poorly educated people will try to avoid such jobs. Thus, employers have a choice of bringing foreigners from poorer countries or of harnessing technology to change the nature of the manual work, or make changes in task design to make the job more attractive to HCNs. This is illustrated in many studies of the fast food sector where organisations such as McDonald's and Burger King regularly rely on cheap imported labour to fill jobs that are generally unattractive to large cohorts of the host population (see the various contributions in Royle and Towers, 2002).

Likewise, Kiriazov et al. (2000) argue that in Eastern European countries the move from the command economy towards capitalism poses serious challenges to many employees. Many of these employees were attached to the characteristics of the old command economy such as job security, guaranteed pay and highly structured jobs, as well as traditions such as nepotism and elements of the black economy that characterised the command economy (Kiriazov et al., 2000). For these reasons, combined with the fact that these employees would have witnessed a high number of business failures among inward-investing MNCs, local employees may not want to work for these MNCs and they may exhibit low levels of motivation if they are employed (ibid.).

In countries such as China, sometimes it is not the job but the supervision that makes locals reluctant to accept the work. The potential recruit may prefer not to work for a foreign supervisor, especially if from a country that is not well regarded by the hosts, or if there is a female supervisor of a male, or a younger supervisor of an older worker, or a supervisor from a different tribe or region. In this regard, Gamble et al. (2003) provide some useful illustrations of reluctance to work under the supervision of Japanese expatriates in the retail sector.

Inappropriate Selection Methods

Even where there is a pool of available candidates seeking employment, MNCs may use inappropriate selection methods to select appropriate employees (Briscoe and Schuler, 2004; Sparrow, 1999). Selection methods utilised by the MNC may have been chosen based on their suitability in other cultures or are based upon the methods used for expatriates or other parent country nationals. Further, schools and other educational establishments generally fail to adequately prepare students for the methods used in selection and recruitment. Indeed, the concept of being interviewed is a challenge in many cultures. Paper-and-pencil tests might also be unfamiliar to many candidates. It is considered, in some societies, immodest to outline achievements and shameful to ask for a job. In the past, it is likely that a father or uncle would provide the employment and no application or selection was necessary.

This reliance on others to help find a job continues to be widely practised. The 'old school tie' may no longer work in the West but the network built up in business school, golf club or other gathering still helps executives find jobs. Weir and Hutchings (2006) have demonstrated in the Chinese context the significance of 'Guanxi' (the word 'Wasta' is used in a similar context in the Arab world) as the more usual methods used by local people to get jobs for themselves, their relations and friends. Capability is of much less importance than are connections. For a person with a role in selection, it is fully expected, in many places, that power to appoint will be used to give jobs to 'their' people rather than to 'other' people. So tribal or political affiliation, shared nationality (particularly among expatriates) and connections with customers or suppliers are all seen as crucial criteria when deciding who should be offered a job. While this nepotism may seem inappropriate in the global business context, it is important to note that empirical evidence in the European context has highlighted the importance of informal contexts in the selection of individuals for international assignments (see, for example, Harris and Brewster, 1999).

Training

A lack of appropriate training of HCNs is one of the crucial barriers in promoting successful localisation. As we have mentioned above, there are often gaps in the education system that mean employers have to make greater efforts in training than are necessary in societies where the education system and employment needs have been more closely aligned.

In many countries, the major task is not the issue of skills but rather attitudes and behaviours. The education system of the former Soviet Union, for example, produced people with good technical and professional skills but poor work attitudes, symbolised by the phrase 'Employers pretend to pay the staff and the staff pretend to work' (Harry, 2006). Likewise, Kiriazov et al. (2000) posit that the focus in training is on theory rather than application in Eastern European firms, resulting in poor quality levels and high scrap rates. Other examples are found in the GCC, where, culturally, students do not expect to work hard, and hence often resort to bullying of teachers and invigilators to pass and graduate (cf. Kapiszewski, 2001; Yamani, 2000). Students with these attitudes are poor at attending and concentrating on work and bring with them this undisciplined approach to work, so are unable to work at the standards required by most employers. Expatriates often use the lack of self-discipline on the part of the HCNs as a reason or excuse to resist localisation.

Costs

It is not only with regard to training costs that HCNs can be expensive in the short term, particularly for lower-level jobs. Where the number of capable local staff is lower than the labour market requires, local candidates will often be more expensive to employ than expatriates. Thus, in a country such as many of those in the GCC, which is resource and capital rich but labour poor, the HCN will be more expensive than the expatriates employed in similar jobs. This higher cost is driven by low remuneration rates expected by third country nationals (in this context, expatriates from poor countries) or those from countries with high income taxes, and by host governments providing social payments or alternative undemanding work, which makes working for a foreign employer unattractive unless for very high pay. In time, it can be expected that the high costs of locals in relation to expatriates in these atypical situations will decline as governments place more restrictions on the employment of expatriates and have less ability to offer high social security payments or undemanding jobs. Within the GCC, countries such as Bahrain, Oman and Saudi Arabia will soon reach a stage where local labour will be cheaper than that of the expatriates legally employed within the country.

The case study in Box 1 illustrates some of these points.

LOCALISATION IN PRACTICE

While the implementation of a localisation strategy may seem relatively straightforward, research highlights the complexity of the process in practice.1 Writing in this context, Gamble posits, based on his empirical study, 'localization is likely to proceed at a much slower pace than its main advocates may wish or anticipate, and that there are practical, cultural, and strategic factors which may, and perhaps should inhibit rapid localization' (Gamble 2000: 883).

Thus, in this section, we briefly outline some of the key stages an organisation should follow in designing a strategy for the localisation of human resources. In this regard, it is clear that the first step in implementing a successful localisation programme is the design of an appropriate strategy. At this stage, it is important to first weigh up the costs and benefits of implementing a localisation strategy. If localisation is seen as appropriate, then the MNC should formalise and codify clear localisation objectives (Law et al., 2004; Wong and Law, 1999). In this context, it is important to be cognisant of a number of key points.

BOX 1. Case Study: Oman

Oman is one of the poorest of the Gulf Cooperation Council (GCC) States but has been host to many foreign workers, especially from South Asia. Prior to the 1970s, Omanis had mainly been engaged in agriculture and fishing with some trading. Omanis also worked as expatriates in other GCC States, especially in the military. During the 1980s, the government took a fairly casual attitude to localisation, believing that the employers of expatriate workers were committed to creating work for the growing numbers of Omanis, 44 per cent of whom were under 15 years of age (*The Economist*, 2002).

By the mid-1990s, the government had lost patience with the promise of localisation 'tomorrow'. The attempt at partnership between government and employers had not worked, as the employers had focused on short-term gains and preferred to use cheap and compliant foreign workers rather than the potentially more expensive, and probably less easily bullied, local population for a wide range of jobs. So the government used the legislation and regulation to force employers to create employment for Omanis as a requirement of operating within the country.

The banking sector had to rapidly replace expatriates with Omanis so that, by 2000, 95 per cent of clerical jobs and 75 per cent of senior- and middle-level positions had to be occupied by Omanis. Job categories such as human resource managers, bus drivers and delivery staff were to be reserved for Omanis and not only would no work permits be issued for these jobs but severe penalties would be imposed on those employers who did not comply.

Despite warnings from expatriates and employers' businesses, the picture was not of business failure. The banking sector did not collapse and, although they have been forced to invest more in staff and training, the long-term benefits to the country and to businesses have been considerable.

First, Selmer (2004) posits that implementing a process of localisation for purely cost-cutting reasons may be inadvisable. MNCs would be better to pursue localisation when such programmes fit with the strategic goals of the organisation. Thus, localisation should be driven by the search for strategic advantage as opposed to a forced compromise between home and host regimes (Taylor, 1999). Hence, it is important in completing the cost-benefit analysis of the merits of localisation that the MNC ensures that a localisation strategy is congruent with the company's strategic objectives. Empirical research, while highlighting the importance of supportive HR policies, suggests that the development of objectives and planning for localisation is the key stage in ensuring the success of localisation efforts in MNCs (Law et al., 2004).

The second key step in implementing a localisation programme is the *localising stage* (Wong and Law, 1999). During this stage, specific HR policies that support the localisation process should be adopted. However, while developing localisation policies is relatively easy, implementing them is not as simple, and indeed localisation driven from above is not sufficient because implementation of these policies must account for host conditions and requires the buy-in of both host and expatriate managers (Fryxell et al., 2004). Hence, in designing localisation policies, MNCs must provide opportunities and incentivise host managers to promote their development so that they can assume the roles held by expatriates (Law et al., 2004). In this regard, training of HCNs emerges as key. Indeed, Braun and Warner (2002) have demonstrated the significance of in-house training, assignments abroad and mentoring programmes in developing locals in the Chinese context. Significantly, however, Fryxell et al. (2004: 279) note that managers 'cannot expect simple recipes for successful localization'; rather, they must develop a programme based on a congruent package of policies and practices. Indeed, they argue that successful localisation efforts are driven by an appropriate combination of elements rather than a linear relationship between separate elements of the programme. A further key element of this stage is the development of incentives for managers to implement the localisation programme, and this will be considered in greater detail below.

The final stage in the localisation process is the *consolidation stage*, which occurs when HCNs have the necessary skills and competence to assume roles traditionally held by expatriates (Wong and Law, 1999). During this stage, the repatriation of expatriate managers emerges as a key factor. Specifically, if the MNC fails to adequately manage the repatriation process and offer incumbent expatriates attractive packages on repatriation, the whole localisation effort may be jeopardised (Law et al., 2004). This is because the self-interest of expatriates may dictate that they do not engage with the localisation process and perhaps even attempt to thwart efforts at localisation in an attempt to prevent repatriation and the associated career and personal issues associated with the process.

Thus, it should be apparent from the above discussion that localisation is, in practice, a relatively complex proposition. Nonetheless, empirical research in the Chinese context appears to support the view that MNCs who are truly committed to the localisation process are likely to plan for localisation and support the programme with appropriate human resource management policies and practices. Further, it is unlikely the localisation programmes will have much success without top management commitment, planning and goal setting and the implementation of appropriate HR policies and practices (Fryxell et al., 2004; Law et al., 2004). In the final section, we outline the role of expatriates in the localisation process.

THE ROLE OF EXPATRIATES IN THE LOCALISATION OF HUMAN RESOURCES

It has been argued that 'effective localization commences with the incumbent expatriates' (Selmer, 2004: 1094). Expatriates, perhaps because they can earn more abroad than at home, can also be serious obstacle to effective localisation. Expatriates' willingness and competence in developing competent HCNs as their own replacements is hugely significant in determining the success of the localisation process (Keeley, 1999; Law et al., 2004; Rogers, 1999; Selmer, 2004).

The many roles of expatriate assignments include filling skills gaps where skills are not available among host employees. In this regard, if localisation programmes are to be successful then, expatriate assignees must assume the roles of mentor and coach to host employees (Evans et al., 2002; Law et al., 2004). It is imperative that HCNs benefit from the knowledge and skills of the expatriate manager if they are to grow and develop and ultimately assume the responsibilities once held by the expatriate. This may be problematic for a number of reasons. First, expatriates may consider themselves unable to contribute to the localisation process (Selmer, 2004). Not all expatriates will be born mentors, nor will they necessarily have the skills required for developing their HCN managers (Lynton, 1999; Melvin and Sylvester, 1997). In addition, many expatriates may fail to promote localisation due to the short-term nature of their foreign assignment brief, which may promote the achievement of quantitative performance results such as return on investment or quality levels (Selmer, 2004). Further, there is growing evidence that the expatriate's individual self-interest may also potentially restrain localisation initiatives (Fuller, 2005).

Expatriates may give excuses about the locals not being hard working, not being interested nor capable, not trustworthy or too expensive to train and to employ. Empirical research (Selmer, 2004), however, indicates that unwillingness rather than inability tends to impede localisation. In addition, Furst (1999) found that some expatriates neglect their responsibilities for local staff development as soon as they are faced with the uncertainties associated with the repatriation process (Law et al., 2004).

Thus, the challenge for MNCs deploying expatriates and host country employers of international itinerants (Banai and Harry, 2004) in selecting, training and assigning expatriates with the aim of promoting localisation is to articulate the importance of HCN development, to provide training in mentoring skills to the employees and to design reward packages that recognise and promote the localisation of human resources. For those who are motivated by extrinsic rewards, incentive schemes offering a bonus for handing over to a host country national within a specific period can be effective. The role of intrinsic motivators should also be recognised. Many individuals get satisfaction from passing on skills to others, enjoy learning new skills themselves (such as how to improve capability of others in foreign lands) or have the self-satisfaction of a job well done (Banai and Harry, 2004). Thus, the challenge for the international HR manager is to develop a compensation system that accommodates these various motivators and encourages appropriate behaviours in expatriate employees. Further, as noted above, the significance of appropriate repatriation policies should be considered.

The expatriate's support is crucial to the success of the localisation process. Not only can expatriates transfer skills and knowledge, but they can also set an example and pass on attitudes, behaviours and standards that the locals will emulate. If the expatriate is resistant, cynical or incapable, then effective localisation will fail or be postponed. In contrast, if the expatriate is supportive, the localisation is much more likely to succeed (Selmer, 2004), particularly where there is a climate of trust between expatriate and HCN (Fryxell et al., 2004).

Expatriates may fulfil an important role as conduits in disseminating corporate structure and culture to subsidiary, host country employees (Gamble, 2000). They can be a very effective means of passing on knowledge and can greatly assist the process of localisation – or retard the process. Those expatriates linked to a parent organisation can act as champions for the host country nationals being developed. Independent expatriates find that their career path is boosted by the ability to train, to advise and to be consultants helping with localisation (cf. Banai and Harry, 2004). The most effective expatriates will realise that they are no longer employed as 'doers' but as supporters of those who have taken over as producers.

CONCLUSION

In this reading, we have outlined the key forces driving local responsiveness in international business. We then considered the business advantages and disadvantages of local responsiveness. Our discussion then focused more specifically on the local-isation of human resources, and again the advantages and disadvantages of this were outlined. After exploring the nature of localisation in practice, we considered the role of expatriates in the localisation process. It should be apparent that localisation is not always the appropriate strategy for MNCs and should not be considered a panacea for problems in subsidiary operations. Nonetheless, what should be apparent from our discussions is that localisation is a complex process and that successful localisation begins with appropriate planning and the development of an appropriate strategy. The implementation of this strategy requires top management support and the development of congruent HR policies that fit with the strategy and the host context. If these conditions are met, localisation can represent an important element of an MNC's internationalisation strategy.

NOTE

1. The majority of this literature emanates from a Chinese context and thus this discussion is primarily based in this context. The potential for study on localisation in different economies is ample. In particular, research on localisation in MNCs in more developed countries would be welcome.

REFERENCES

Banai, M. (1992) 'The ethnocentric staffing policy in multinational corporations: a self-fulfilling prophecy', International Journal of Human Resource Management, 3(3): 451–72.

Banai, M. and Harry, W.E. (2004) 'Boundaryless global careers: the international itinerants', International Studies of Management and Organization, 34(3): 96–120.

Bartlett, C.A. and Ghoshal, S. (1998) Managing Across Borders: The Transnational Solution, 2nd edn, Boston, MA: Harvard Business School Press.

Bennett, D.R. (1996) 'The stalled revolution: business education in Eastern Europe', Business Horizons, 39(1): 23–9.

Black, J.S. and Gregerson, H.B. (1992) 'Serving two masters: managing the dual allegiance of expatriate employees', Sloan Management Review, 33(4): 61–71.

Boisot, M. and Child, J. (1999) 'Organizations as adaptive systems in complex environments: the case of China', Organization Science, 10: 237–52.

Braun, W.H. and Warner, M. (2002) 'Strategic human resource management in western multinationals in China: the differentiation of practices across different ownership forms', Personnel Review, 31: 533–79.

Brewster, C. (1991) The Management of Expatriates, London: Kogan Page.

Briscoe, D.R. and Schuler, R.S. (2004) International Human Resource Management, 2nd edn, London: Routledge.

Child, J. and Yan, Y. (2001) 'Investment and control in international joint ventures: the case of China', Journal of World Business, 34: 3–15.

Das, G. (1993) 'Local memoirs of a global manager', Harvard Business Review, 71(2): 38–47.

Dowling, P.J. and Welch, D.E. (2004) International Human Resource Management: Managing People in a Multinational Context, 4th edn, London: Thomson Learning.

Doz, Y. and Prahalad, C.K. (1986) 'Controlled variety: a challenge for human resource management in the MNC', Human Resource Management, 25(1): 55–71.

The Economist (2002) 'People pressure', The Economist, 21 March, www.economisl.com, accessed 23 March 2002.

Economist Intelligence Unit (1997) 'Local Heroes', Business China, 9: 1–3.

Evans, P., Pucik, V. and Barsouxm, J.L. (2002) *The Global Challenge: Frameworks for International Human Resource Management*, Boston, MA: McGraw-Hill.

Fryxell, G.E., Butler, J. and Choi, A. (2004) 'Successful localization in China: an important element in strategy implementation', *Journal of World Business*, 39: 268–82.

Fuller, T. (2005) 'Skilled help hard to find in China', *International Herald Tribune*, Beirut edition, 16 March.

Furst, B. (1999) 'Performance management for localization', in J. Lee (ed.) *Localization in China: Best Practice*, Hong Kong: Euromoney.

Gamble, J. (2000) 'Localizing management in foreign-invested enterprises in China: practical, cultural and strategic perspectives', *International Journal of Human Resource Management*, 11(5): 883–1004.

Gamble, J., Morris, J. and Wilkinson, B. (2003) 'Japanese and Korean multinationals: the replication and integration of their national business systems in China', *Asian Business and Management*, 2(3): 347–69.

Hailey, J. (1999) 'Localization as an ethical response to internationalization', in C. Brewster and H. Harris (eds) *International HRM*, London: Routledge.

Harris, H. and Brewster, C. (1999) 'The coffee-machine system: how international selection really works' *International Journal of Human Resource Management* 10(2): 488–500.

Harry, W.E. (2006) 'History and HRM in Central Asia', *Thunderbird International Business Review*, 48(1).

Harry, W.E. and Banai, M. (2005) 'International itinerants', in M. Michael, N. Heraty and D. Collings (eds) *International HRM and International Assignments*, Basingstoke: Palgrave Macmillan.

Kapiszewski, A. (2001) *Nationals and Expatriates, Reading*, UK: Ithaca Press.

Keeley, S. (1999) 'The theory and practice of localization', in J. Lee (ed.) *Localization in China: Best Practice*, Hong Kong: Euromoney.

Kiriazov, D., Sullivan, S.E. and Tu, H.S. (2000) 'Business success in Eastern Europe: understanding and customising HRM', *Business Horizons*, 43(1): 39–43.

Lasserre, P. and Ching, P-S. (1997) 'Human resources management in China and the localization challenge', *Journal of Asian Business*, 13(4): 85–100.

Law, K.S., Wong, C.S. and Wang, K.D. (2004) 'An empirical test of the model on managing the localisation of human resources in the People's Republic of China', *International Journal of Human Resource Management*, 15: 635–48.

Litvin, D. (2003) *Empires of Profit: Commerce, Conquest and Corporate Responsibility*, New York: Texere.

Lynton, N. (1999) 'Building a unified corporate culture', in J. Lee (ed.) *Localization in China: Best Practice*, Hong Kong: Euromoney.

Melvin, S. and Sylvester, K. (1997) 'Shipping out', *China Business Review*. May–June: 30–4.

Micklethwait, J. (1996) 'The search for the Asian manager', *The Economist*, 338(7956): S3-S5.

Morris, R.J. and Lawrence, A.T. (2003) 'Nike's dispute with the University of Oregon', in D.C. Thomas (ed.) *Readings and Cases in International Management: A Cross-cultural Perspective*, London: Sage.

Nash, E. (2004) 'Spanish suffer lack of sleep as globalisation ends siesta', *The Independent*, 20 December.

Prahalad, C.K. (2004) *The Fortune at the Bottom of the Pyramid: Eradicating Poverty Through Profits*, London: Wharton School Publishing/Pearson.

Rogers, B. (1999) 'The expatriates in China: a dying species?', in J. Lee (ed.) *Localization in China: Best Practice*, Hong Kong: Euromoney.

Rosenzweig, P.M. and Nohria, N. (1994) 'Influences in human resource management practices in multinational corporations', *Journal of International Business Studies*, 25(2): 229–42.

Royle, T. and Towers, B. (eds) (2002) *Labour Relations in the Global Fast-Food Industry*, London: Routledge.

Ruhs, M. and Godfrey, M. (2002) 'Cheaper labour on tap: wage and productivity trends in Kuwait', unpublished paper developed from ILO Migrant project.

Scullion, H. (1992) 'Strategic recruitment and development of the international manager: some European considerations', *Human Resource Management Journal*, 3(1): 57–69.

Scullion, H. and Brewster, C. (2001) 'Managing expatriates: messages from Europe', *Journal of World Business*, 36(4): 346–65.

Selmer, J. (2004) 'Expatriates' hesitation and the localization of Western business operations in China', *International Journal of Human Resource Management*, 15(6): 1094–107.

Shenkar, O. and Luo, Y. (2004) *International Business*, Hoboken, NJ: Wiley.

Solomon, C.M. (1995) 'Learning to manage host-country nationals', *Personnel Journal*, March: 60–7.

Sparrow, P. (1999) 'International recruitment, selection and Assessment,' in P. Joynt and B. Morton (eds) *The Global HR Manager: Creating the Seamless Organization*, London: Institute of Personnel and Development.

Sparrow, P., Brewster, C. and Harris, H. (2004) *Globalizing Human Resource Management*, London: Routledge.

Taylor, B. (1999) 'Patterns of control within Japanese manufacturing plants in China: doubts about Japanization in Asia', *Journal of Management Studies*, 36(6): 853–74.

Warner, M. (1985) 'Training China's managers', *Journal of General Management*, 11(2): 12–26.

Weir, D. and Hutchings, K. (2006) 'Guanxi and Wasta: a review of the traditional ways of networking in China and the Arab world and their implications for international business', *Thunderbird International Business Review*, 48(1).

Wong, C.S. and Law, K.S. (1999) 'Managing localization of human resources in the PRC: a practical model', *Journal of World Business*, 34: 26–40.

Yamani, M. (2000) *Changed Identities*, London: Royal Institute of International Affairs.

Ingmar Björkman

PETER HANSON: BUILDING A WORLD-CLASS
PRODUCT DEVELOPMENT CENTRE FOR
HI TECH SYSTEMS IN CHINA

INTRODUCTION

PETER HANSON, the Head of the Product Development Centre (PDC) of Hi Tech Systems in Shanghai had been in China for five months. He was the first person in the Product Development Centre when he arrived in Shanghai in April 2000. Thinking back at the period he had spent in China so far, he felt that things had gone quite well. The PDC was now up and running and today, on September 12, 2000, Peter welcomed its sixteenth employee.

Nonetheless, Peter still had a number of concerns. The PDC was still rather small and it was possible for him to interact with and influence all employees. As the PDC would grow significantly over the next year, he wanted to make sure to create a healthy and positive atmosphere and orientation towards work. His vision was to create a world-class PDC in Shanghai, but how to do that in a country that mainly was a recipient of technological know-how from abroad, and what measures should be taken to convince other parts of Hi Tech Systems to engage in joint development projects with his PDC? And even if he managed to develop the competencies needed to build a world-class PDC through careful recruitment and selection as well as good investments in training and development, how were they to retain the employees in a market where job hopping was common, money apparently an important reason why people switched jobs, and well-educated people had ample opportunities in other companies? Basically, his question was: would lessons on how to manage human resources obtained in North America and Europe apply also in the People's Republic of China?

PRODUCT DEVELOPMENT IN HI TECH SYSTEMS

Hi Tech Systems was established in Stockholm, Sweden, in 1976. By the late 1980s, it had become known as one of Europe's most innovative firms in its industry. The growth continued in the 1990s, with firm profitability remaining healthy. The company is currently one of the three largest firms in its industry. Hi Tech Systems' global manufacturing comprises six production facilitates in five different countries on three different continents. Approximately 45 percent of sales come from Europe, but Japan, China and, in particular, the United States have become important markets.

Product development is seen as key to the success of Hi Tech Systems. Almost 20 percent of Hi Tech Systems' employees are working in research and development. Hi Tech Systems has Product Development Centres (PDCs) in Sweden, the UK, the US, Japan, Hong Kong (China) and, most recently, mainland China. There is a global PDC management group headed by Johan Lind that consists of all the PDC heads, which convenes once a month. Johan Lind reports to the head of global product development in Hi Tech Systems, Anders Jonsson.

The responsibility for product development programs resides with the global business lines and the "platforms" (such as Japanese user interface). Research programs within the business lines that lead to actual products also draw on the work being done within the platforms. In each PDC, people work on projects related to both Hi Tech Systems business lines and platforms.

A full-grown PDC has some 400–500 employees, a variety of competencies, and is expected to have the capability needed to develop an entire new product. There are several reasons why the company has established a whole portfolio of PDCs. First, different areas differ in terms of technologies and standards relevant for the business. Therefore, it makes sense to locate research and development activities in locations where the technologies reside. Second, by dispersing PDCs to different parts of the world, the company can move product creation activities in response to environmental and market changes. Third, it enables Hi Tech Systems to draw on human resources not available in one location. Hi Tech Systems has traditionally done most of its product creation in Sweden, but as a result of growth there are not enough engineering students in the whole country to satisfy its needs. Fourth, products need to be local-adapted and this is easier to carry out locally than in a distant PDC.

In a typical research program, most of the work on the key components of a new product is done within one single "core" PDC. Within each project, there is a fairly clear distribution of responsibilities across the PDCs involved. Other 'peripheral' PDCs are typically involved in developing locally adapted variances of the product. Most of the work has typically already been done in the core PDC before the other PDCs get involved (although, in order to ensure that the necessary local adaptations of the final product can be made at a later stage, people from each of the geographical regions are involved in steering groups during the conceptualization stage). The knowledge transfer mostly takes place through people from the PDCs who visit the core PDC for 1–3 months to work with the product development people before they return to their own units. At the point when the project has been established in the peripheral PDCs, the focal project leader reports to the global head of the focal product development project and to the head of their own PDC. Heavy emphasis is put on establishing and following up project milestones.

HI TECH SYSTEMS IN CHINA

The People's Republic of China started opening up to the outside world in 1979. In 1992, the Hi Tech Systems group established a representative office in Shanghai and, in 1995, a first joint venture was established. By the beginning of 2000, Hi Tech Systems already had four joint ventures and wholly owned subsidiaries in China. Hi Tech Systems had become a significant player in the rapidly growing Chinese market, where it was competing with other Western, Japanese, and also increasingly strong local competitors. China had become one of Hi Tech Systems' most important markets. Most of the products sold in China were produced in the firm's local factories.

However, Hi Tech Systems had so far no Product Development Centre in China. Towards the end of the 1990s, there was a growing consensus that this neglect had to be rectified. A decision to establish a PDC in Shanghai was made by Hi Tech Systems' management board in January 2000. Peter Hanson was chosen to head the PDC.

PETER HANSON

Peter Hanson was born in California in 1962. After graduating from college with a major in management, his first job was with a major US industrial firm. As a part of his job, in 1989–90 he spent 6 months in Hong Kong. During his assignment in Hong Kong, he fell in love with Asia and China. Since that moment he knew that he was going to return to Asia. Peter also met his future wife, who moved with him to the US. In 19991–93, Peter did an MBA and then started to work in a small start-up company. In late 1997, Peter was persuaded by one of his previous colleagues to join Hi Tech Systems. When joining Hi Tech Systems, Peter was appointed operations manager. After some months, he was asked to head the engineering unit of the new Product Development Centre that was built up in Philadelphia. Peter accepted the job, which meant that he would be responsible for the largest unit of the PDC. Peter and his new boss, Curtis O'Neill, soon became very close, with Peter acting as the second in charge of the PDC. Peter recalls:

> I learnt a lot from Curtis. He was very people-oriented. He would make sure that you get an opportunity to get into an environment where you either learn or you don't. He gave people lots of challenges, lots of learning opportunities, where they could prove themselves. He would also quite directly point to areas of improvement. He also underlined the importance of networking, how to build networks of people that you can draw on.

One of the things that Peter learned soon after joining Hi Tech Systems was the importance of having good personal contacts within the company. The Hi Tech Systems global product development worked, to a significant extent, through informal contacts across units and it was crucial to be well connected. His choice of the five product line managers in his department reflected this view. While people in the Philadelphia unit expected and pressured him to choose local people for the positions, he selected three expatriates and only two local employees:

> People thought I was taking promotions away from Philadelphia. I had my own views in mind – we needed to be connected to the other centers. If you're well connected people trust you to do a good job within a research program, and it is also easier to get technical help if needed. I then used lots of interviews with the candidates to convince people about their capabilities and to get some buy-in from the other managers. I also made sure to tell people that the objective was to fill the positions with local people in two-three years. In fact, the line managers had as an explicit objective to develop a local replacement of themselves.

During the next 18 months, Peter visited Sweden several times. He often took part in the global PDC group meetings as O'Neill's stand-in. The global PDC management also knew that he was interested in returning to Asia, something Peter had mentioned from the outset in his performance management discussions.

ESTABLISHING THE PRODUCT DEVELOPMENT CENTRE

During the summer of 1999, the global PDC management group decided that a feasibility study on the possible creation of a PDC in the People's Republic of China should be carried out. In October 1999, Peter was asked to become involved in the project. His task was to examine the data and write a report on whether or not a PDC should be established and, if so, where in China it should be located. By that time, Peter also knew that he would be the preferred candidate as head of the PDC (if approved). In January 2000, the Hi Tech Systems global management board approved the establishment of a PDC in Shanghai. One of the advantages of Shanghai was that the PDC would be able to use the existing Hi Tech Systems organization in the city. It would be easier to learn from the experiences of Hi Tech Systems' largest Chinese production and its China headquarters, both of which were located in Shanghai. In February, Peter went to China on a pre-visit mainly to meet with people in the Hi Tech Systems organization.

When it became clear that the PDC would be established, Peter started to look for people. There was no established policy for people management within the global product creation organization, but Peter was told to draw on the HR department at the Hi Tech Systems group in China for support. He thought he would initially need approximately ten positions for expatriates, and it would be of crucial importance to find suitable people for the key positions:

> It was networking all the way – the social networks were very important! There were many people who knew that I would do it and some of them contacted me. I contacted and spoke to lots of people in all parts of the Hi Tech Systems organization. I wanted the candidates to have experience in launching Hi Tech Systems products in China. They should know the Chinese

environment and culture. This meant that there were only a very small number of people who fulfilled my criteria. And they had to commit to staying at least two or even three years, which is not usual in Hi Tech Systems. Towards the end of the period they start hunting for another job anyhow.

Peter finally identified four people that he wanted: one Swede, and three persons from the People's Republic of China who had studied and worked for several years abroad (two in the United States, one in Sweden). One of them he already knew in advance, the others he had identified through his networking activities. All the Chinese had a strong educational background, with degrees from top Chinese universities before leaving the country for overseas graduate studies. Everybody had at least some experience in leading their own teams:

> I talked a lot to them. Have they thought about living in China? Were they (the Chinese) conscious about the challenges involved in going back to China? For instance, people may be jealous of them making much more money, travelling abroad and having much higher positions than they themselves had? Have they realized that it's going to be a start-up operation, and that it may be difficult to get things started and people on board?

To persuade the people he wanted to accept relocating to China, Peter tried to create a positive and challenging vision for the PDC. To date, Hi Tech Systems had probably not done enough to meet the needs of the Chinese-speaking countries. Did they want to become a part of the process of creating a world-class PDC in China? The PDC would become responsible for the Chinese user interface platform – did they want to participate in the challenge of its development? Being restricted by the company's expatriate compensation policy, which was built on a standardized job grading system, he was able to offer competitive but not exceptional salaries. He finally managed to persuade all four candidates to accept a job in his PDC. They all knew each other from their previous jobs. During the late spring of 2000, he found some additional people in the global Hi Tech Systems organization who also agreed to taking up jobs in Shanghai:

> A part of my strategy was to get people from different Product Development Centers. By having these people in my organization we are able to easily reach into the other PDCs, which is particularly important in the beginning as we are dependent on doing parts of larger projects in collaboration with other centers. If we have good people who have credibility from each of the other PDCs, we will be recognized and seen as trustworthy.

But Peter did not see technical competence as the only important criterion. In his view:

> 80 percent is attitude. It doesn't matter what you can do, if you lack drive. With drive you can always fill in the gaps ... Perhaps it has something to

do with my own background. I have had to manage without an engineering education in an organization and industry that are extremely technology-intensive.

The PDC was to report to the Global PDC management and to the Hi Tech Systems China country management. As agreed upon with the Global PDC management group, PDC Shanghai would be responsible for product creation in the Chinese language area, including mainland China, Hong Kong, Singapore, and Taiwan. In the beginning, it would mostly do limited parts of larger products in collaboration with other global PDCs, working, for example, on software and on Chinese-specific applications. The long-term vision was eventually to have the competencies to be able to build new products in China.

THE START OF THE PRODUCT DEVELOPMENT CENTRE

Peter and his family finally arrived in Shanghai on April 12, 2000. The next employee arrived from overseas in May, and by September the unit had 16 employees, half of whom had been recruited from abroad. Peter's estimate was that, long term, 15–20 percent of the employees would be from overseas but that it would take 3–4 years to decrease the proportion of expatriates to that level:

> When you build a home, first you build the foundations. You need to make sure that the foundations are in place – the recruitment process, human resources management, finance. Then you need key managers to build the organization around.

In the recruitment of local employees, the PDC was collaborating closely with Hi Tech Systems' human resources (HR) department. After job descriptions and job grade levels had been determined by the PDC, the HR department would announce the position using both advertisements and the Hi Tech System home page, receive CVs, do a first screening of the candidates, and arrange for interviews and assessment of the applicants. The interviews were done by a minimum of two PDC managers, who also acted as observers in the assessment centers organized by the HR department. For the assessment of applicants in China, Hi Tech Systems used "The Space Shuttle." The Space Shuttle was a game where the applicants worked together in a group with the objective of reaching an agreement on how to build a space shuttle. By observing the applicants involved in a problem-solving situation where they also interacted with each other, the observers could draw their own conclusions about the applicants. Recruitment and selection of local employees largely resembled practices used elsewhere in the global Hi Tech Systems organization.

Some other Western firms had apparently made larger adjustments in their selection practices in China. For instance, Peter had heard that Shell had changed its selection practices based on an in-depth study of its existing Chinese managers and entry-level management trainees. Traditionally Shell focused on analytical and problem-solving abilities. However, when, for example, applicants were asked to identify the strengths and weakness of the Chinese educational system and then say what they would do to remedy deficiencies if they were the Minister of Education, if there were any responses at all they tended to be uniformly bland. It was also found that the kind of "Who would you throw out of the airplane?" question commonly used in the West also tended to engender a "learned helplessness effect" on the part of Chinese university graduates, who have excelled at clearly defined tasks in a familiar environment and who had "learnt" to respond to the unfamiliar by simple freezing. Shell's system identified the Chinese education system as the chief culprit. The educational system is hierarchical, extremely competitive and almost exclusively based on examination of rote learning. Problem-oriented interaction among strangers is unnatural and problematic for most Chinese. Therefore, to evaluate the decision-making skills, communication skills, analytical problem-solving abilities, and leadership capabilities of the applicants based on hypothetical cases solved in assessment situations may be very difficult. As a result, Shell's study recommended the use of real case studies rather than hypothetical questions.[1]

Competence development would probably be key to the success of the PDC, both in terms of localizing its operations and in producing good results. By mid-September, the new employees had mostly worked on small projects, such as setting up the IT system. A couple of people had also been sent to Hong Kong to work in the field with experienced engineers for 3 weeks. Formal training would be important, and the PDC would need to collaborate with Hi Tech Systems' HR unit on the course program offered to the PDC employees. To what extent should the Chinese employees receive the same content and delivery as Hi Tech Systems employees elsewhere? In China, the Confucian- and communist-influenced Chinese educational system in which the learner is a mostly passive receiver who is obedient to instructor tends to create linear rather than lateral thinking and precedent-based problem-solving where the focus in on getting the "right" answer.

Nonetheless, hands-on on-the-job coaching would be even more important for the development of the new employees. Most of the responsibility for coaching would obviously be on the experienced Hi Tech Systems employees but also important would be to bring in people from other PDCs for visits in Shanghai. Coaching on the part of the expatriates would be extremely important, Peter thought. He had already been discussing it at length with the managers that he had hired, but he was not sure whether or not that was enough, especially not when the unit would grow over the next couple of years. He certainly would not be able to coach all expatriates by himself.

In Hi Tech Systems' globally standardized performance management system, all employees should carry out performance management discussions with their superiors. Within this system, individual objectives are established and followed up. According to company policy, the individual's objectives must be specific and, if possible, measurable; key activities for how to reach the objectives shall be specified; criteria for how to evaluate the performance agreed upon; and, finally, development plans decided upon. Peter's aim was that every new employee would do their first performance management discussion within a month after they joined the organization. All Hi Tech Systems superiors in China were trained in how to use the system but there was still a question of how the "Western" system would be implemented in the

Chinese culture characterized by respect for hierarchy, face, and harmonious personal relationships.

Peter had also given the question of the relationship between employee competence development and career progress quite a lot of thought. In Hi Tech Systems worldwide, people achieved high status by having excellent technological knowledge and skills rather than having made a successful career as a manager. However:

> In China especially the young people expect to get a new title every year; otherwise they had better start looking for another company. The speed of expected career progression clearly differs from the West. To develop the level of competence required for the next career step will be a challenge. Can they achieve it once a year? I think very few will.

The compensation of employees would follow the Hi Tech Systems policies. Managers and team leaders were compensated based on both business and individual performance. High-level executives and senior managers had a large business performance component in their bonus system, while the compensation of lower-level employees was mostly based on their individual performance. In the Shanghai PDC, individual performance would be evaluated based on 4–5 objectives. Peter required that the objectives had to be measurable on a ten-point scale. For instance, a manager's performance could be evaluated based on the manager's ability to fill positions in his/her group, employee satisfaction (as measured in company-wide surveys), employee turnover, the team's ability to stay within the budget, and some measure of quality (to be determined in discussions between the person and Peter). Each person's performance was evaluated every 6 months, and bonuses paid accordingly. The target bonus was 10 percent of the person's base salary, with 20 percent as maximum. People working on a specific development project were evaluated not every 6 months but the evaluation rather followed the milestones of the project. The bonus element was also somewhat larger for people working on projects than for other PDC members.

Peter believed that the compensation system would work well in China. Having clear objectives and rewards linked with their fulfillment would help send a clear message to the employees: your performance equals what you deliver – not the personal connections, or "*guanxi*," that you have! Nonetheless, at least in the start-up phase of the PDC it might be somewhat difficult to establish feasible objectives for the employees. Additionally, there had been reports from other foreign firms that there was a tendency among local employees to set objectives so that they would be reached by the subordinates.

LOOKING TOWARDS THE FUTURE

Analyzing the start-up phase of PDC, Peter found that many things had gone quite smoothly. For instance, the two Chinese "returnees" who had joined PDC so far (the third was still in Sweden but would relocate next month) seemed to do well. Although China had changed a lot since they left the country some 10 years ago, their interaction with the local employees seemed to go well.

Managing the growth would certainly be a challenge in the next couple of years, Peter thought. For instance, local employees would have to be taught to manage themselves and to take responsibility – behaviors not automatically understood and accepted in the Chinese environment. While the Hi Tech Systems culture was non-hierarchical and meritocratic, the Chinese culture is hierarchical, and the "face" of superiors could be at stake if subordinates made their own initiatives rather than waiting for orders from their superiors. Furthermore, since the communist regime from 1949, the Chinese have been discouraged from engaging in competitive and entrepreneurial behavior. The Chinese proverb "the early bird gets shot" aptly illustrates the reluctance on the part of Chinese employees to engage in the kind of innovative behavior that Peter wanted to see in the PDC. On the other hand, Peter had seen several Chinese changing their behavior significantly abroad. What should they do to promote this behavior also in the Shanghai PDC?

Peter was also looking for somebody to work closely with Hi Tech Systems' HR function. This person would work closely with him and the line managers to define future competence needs and how they could be met. "So far I guess I have fulfilled this role, but I'm afraid that neither me nor line managers will have time enough to pay sufficient attention to this issue in the future."

Finally, Peter was concerned about retention. "I have also been told by [a human resources expert] that a 1 renminbi salary difference may make a person switch job." Peter believed that money would not be key to retaining the employees, though. To create a positive, family-like atmosphere might help. Peter had started a tradition of everyone in his unit meeting for a snack on Monday mornings. He also made a conscious effort to spend time talking to people in the department. Furthermore, he had invited people out for lunch and dinner. To maintain a positive relationship between the foreign and local employees, he tried to coach the expatriates not to mention how much money they made, how they lived, and how cheap they found most things to be in Shanghai (say "reasonable" instead, was his advice). All this had apparently contributed to there starting to circulate rumors that "things are done a bit differently in PDC." He was now thinking of whether to involve the employees' families in some way. Formal team-building exercises should probably also be done.

There were so many things to do ... Peter looked out of his window in one of the many new multi-story buildings in the Pudong area of Shanghai – where should he start?

NOTE

1.   The Economist Intelligence Unit (1998) *China on the Couch.* September 28, 3–4.

Evalde Mutabazi and C. Brooklyn Derr

SOCOMETAL: REWARDING AFRICAN WORKERS

I T WAS A MOST UNUSUAL MEETING at a local cafe in Dakar. Diop, a young Senegalese engineer who was educated at one of Frances's elite engineering *grandes écoles* in Lyon, was meeting with N'Diaye, a model factory worker to whom other workers from his tribe often turned when there were personal or professional difficulties. N'Diaye was a chief's son, but he didn't belong to the union and he was not an official representative of any group within the factory.

Socometal is a metal container and can company. While multinational, this particular plant is a joint venture wherein 52 percent is owned by the French parent company and 48 percent is Senegalese. Over the last 20 years, Socometal has grown in size from 150 to 800 employees and it has returns of about 400 million FCFA (African francs) or $144 million. The firm is often held up as a model in terms of its Africanization of management policies, whereby most managers are now West African with only 8–10 top managers coming from France.

During the meeting, N'Diaye asked Diop if he would accept an agreement to pay each worker for 2 extra hours in exchange for a 30 percent increase in daily production levels. If so, N'Diaye would be the guarantor for this target production level that would enable the company to meet the order in the shortest time period. "If you accept my offer," he said with a smile, "we could even produce more. We are at 12,000 [units] a day, but we've never been confronted with this situation. I would never have made this proposal to Mr. Bernard but, if you agree today, I will see that the 20,000 [unit] level is reached as of tomorrow evening. I'll ask each worker to find ways of going faster, to communicate this to the others and to help each other if they have problems."

Mr. Olivier Bernard, a graduate of Ecole Centrale in Paris (one of France's more prestigious engineering schools), was the French production manager, and Diop was the assistant production manager. Mr. Bernard was about 40 and had not succeeded at climbing the hierarchal ladder in the parent company. Some report that this was due to his tendency to be arrogant, uncommunicative, and negative. His family lived in a very nice neighborhood in Marseille, and it was his practice to come to Dakar, precisely organize the work using various flowcharts, tell Diop exactly what was expected by a certain date, and then return to France for periods of 2–6 weeks. This time he maintained that he had contracted a virus and needed to return for medical treatment.

Shortly before Mr. Bernard fell ill, Socometal agreed to a contract requiring them to reach, in a short time, a volume of production never before achieved. Mr. Bernard, after having done a quick calculation, declared, "We'll never get that from our workers – *c'est impossible!*" After organizing as best he could, he left for Marseille.

Diop pondered what N'Diaye had proposed, and then he sought the opinions of influential people in different departments. Some of the French and Italian expatriates told him they were sure that the workers would not do overtime, but most agreed it was worth a try. Two days after his meeting with N'Diaye, Diop felt confident enough to take the risk. The next morning, N'Diaye and Diop met in front of the factory and Diop gave his agreement on the condition that the 30 percent rise in daily production levels be reached that evening. He and the management would take a final decision on a wage increase only after assessing the results and on evaluating the ability of the workers to maintain this level of production in the long run.

The reasons given by the French and Italian expatriates for why the Senegalese would not perform overtime or speed up their productivity are interesting. One older French logistics manager said, "Africans aren't lazy but they work to live, and once they have enough they refuse to do more. It won't make any sense to them to work harder or longer for more pay." And the Italian human resource manager exclaimed, "We already tried 2 years ago to get them to do more faster. We threatened to fire anyone caught going too slow or missing more than 1 day's work per month, and we told them they would all get bonuses if they reached the production target. We had the sense that they were laughing behind our backs and doing just enough to keep their jobs while maintaining the same production levels."

Four days after their first negotiation, the contract between Diop and N'Diaye went into action. Throughout the day, N'Diaye gave his job on the line to two of his colleagues in order to have enough time and energy to mobilize all the workers. The workers found the agreement an excellent initiative. "This will be a chance to earn a bit more money, but especially to show them [the French management] that we're more capable than they think," declared one of the Senegalese foremen. From its first day of application, the formula worked wonders. Working only 1 extra hour per day, every work unit produced 8 percent more than was forecast by Diop and N'Diaye. Over the next 2 months, the daily production level oscillated between 18,000 and 22,000 units per day – between 38 and 43 percent more than the previous daily production. It was at this production level, never experienced during the history of the company, that Mr. Bernard found things when he returned from his illness.

"I", said Diop, "was very happy to see the workers so proud of their results, so satisfied with their pay raise, and finally really involved in their work … In view of some expatriates' attitudes it was a veritable miracle … But, instead of rejoicing,

Mr. Bernard reproached me for giving 2 hours' pay to the workers, who were only really doing 1 hour more than usual. 'By making this absurd decision,' he said, 'you have put the management in danger of losing its authority over the workers. You have acted against house rules . . . You have created a precedent too costly for our business. Now, we must stop this ridiculous operation as quickly as possible. We must apply work regulations.' And he slammed the door in my face before I had the time to say anything. After all, he has more power than me in this company, which is financed 52 percent by French people. Nevertheless, I thought I would go to see the managing director and explain myself and present my arguments. I owed this action to N'Diaye and his workers, who had trusted me, and I didn't care if it made Bernard any angrier."

In the meantime, the workers decided to maintain the new production level in order to honor their word to N'Diaye and Diop. A foreman and friend of N'Diaye stated, "At least he knows how to listen and speak to us like men."

The foreman indicated, however, that they might return to the former production level if Bernard dealt with them as he did before.

CASE DISCUSSION QUESTIONS

1. What are the underlying cultural assumptions for Mr. Bernard and how are these different from the basic assumptions of N'Diaye and Diop?
2. What would you do if you were Bernard's boss, the managing director?
3. In what ways is a reward system a cultural phenomenon? How might you design an effective reward system for Senegal?

Roger Hallowell, David Bowen, and Carin-Isabel Knoop

FOUR SEASONS GOES TO PARIS

Europe is different from North America, and Paris is very different. I did not say difficult. I said different.

A senior Four Seasons manager

THE LINKAGE BETWEEN SERVICE CULTURE AND COMPETITIVE ADVANTAGE

THE ENDURING SUCCESS of service organizations such as Southwest Airlines, the Walt Disney Company, Wal-Mart, and USAA (among others) is frequently attributed in no small degree to their corporate cultures. These companies have built and maintained organizational cultures in which everyone is focused on delivering high customer value, including service, and individuals behave accordingly. The culture influences how employees behave, which, in turn, shapes the value that customers receive, in part through the thousands of daily encounters between employees and customers.

Corporate culture has been linked to competitive advantage in companies, for better or worse,[1] and in service companies, in particular.[2] Culture is so important in service companies because of its effect on multiple factors affecting customer value, factors as critical as employee behavior and as mundane (but important) as facility cleanliness. These aspects are especially visible to customers, who often co-produce a service with employees. In many services, employee and customer interactions take place continually, in many parts of the organization, so that no realistic amount of supervision can ever exercise sufficient control over employee behavior. Under these circumstances, culture becomes one of management's most effective, if unobtrusive, tools to influence employee thoughts, feelings, and, most importantly, behavior.

UNDERSTANDING CORPORATE CULTURE

Our model of corporate culture, which uses Schein[3] as a point of departure, consists of the following four components: underlying assumptions, values, employee perceptions of management practices, and cultural artifacts.

Underlying Assumptions

These are basic assumptions regarding the workplace, such as the assumption that subordinates should fulfill their job requirements as a condition of employment.

Values

These are those things that are viewed as most important in an organizational setting, such as cost control, customer satisfaction, and teamwork.

Values exist in two forms in organizations. The first is what can be termed "espoused values," which are what senior managers or company publications say the values are.

The second form is "enacted values," which are what employees infer the values to be. Although enacted values, per se, are invisible, employees infer what they are by examining the evidence found in the next two components of culture: management practices and cultural artifacts. These two components are more readily observed than assumptions and values.

Employee Perceptions of Management Practices (Particularly Relating to Human Resources): Policies and Behaviors

Employees' views of practices such as selection, training, performance appraisal, job design, reward systems, supervisory practices, and so on shape their perceptions of what values are actually being enacted in a setting. For example, although customer service may be an espoused value, if job applicants are not carefully screened on service attitude, or if employees who provide great service are not recognized and rewarded, then employees will not believe that management truly values service. In short: culture is what employees perceive that management believes.

Cultural Artifacts

These include heroes, rituals, stories, jargon, and tangibles such as the appearance of employees and facilities. Again, given the espoused value of customer service, if jargon used to characterize customers is usually derogatory, then a strong service culture is unlikely to emerge.

In contrast, if espoused values are enacted – and thus reflected in policies, management behaviors, and cultural artifacts – then a culture may emerge in which senior management and employees share similar service-relevant thoughts, feelings, and patterns of behavior. This behavior has the potential to enhance customer value and contribute to competitive advantage.

EXPORTING CORPORATE CULTURE: CAN CULTURE TRAVEL ACROSS BORDERS?

If a company succeeds in creating a corporate culture that contributes to competitive advantage in its home country, can it successfully "export" that corporate culture to another country – particularly if that country's national culture is strongly distinct, as is the case in France?

The Issue of Flexibility Versus Consistency

Will an organization's *corporate* culture "clash" or "fit" with a different *national* culture? The key consideration here is what components of corporate culture link most tightly to competitive advantage and, as a consequence, must be managed *consistently* across country borders – even if they seem to clash with the culture of the new country. Alternatively, are there components of culture that are not critical to the linkage? If so, *flexibility* may enhance the competitiveness of the corporate culture given the different national culture.[4]

One way to frame this analysis is around whether the potential clash between corporate and national culture is over the corporate values themselves, i.e., *what* they are, or over the manner of their implementation, i.e., *how* they are enacted (specifically, management practices and cultural forms). Is there a clash between core corporate values and core country values? If so, and if those core values are critical to competitive advantage, then perhaps the company cannot be successful in that setting. If the clash is over how values are enacted, then some management practices or cultural forms can be modified in the new setting. However, this requires managers to ask which practices or forms can be modified, enhancing the competitive advantage of the corporate culture, and which practices, if modified, will undermine corporate culture.

In short, all of the elements of corporate culture can be thought of as the threads in a sweater: when a thread sticks out of a sweater, sometimes it is wisely removed, enhancing the overall appearance. However, sometimes removing a thread will unravel the entire sweater. Managers must determine which aspects of their corporate cultures will "stick out" in a new national environment and whether modifying or eliminating them will enhance the organization or weaken it.

FOUR SEASONS HOTELS AND RESORTS: OVERVIEW

In 2002, Four Seasons Hotels and Resorts was arguably the world's leading operator of luxury hotels, managing 53 properties in 24 countries. Being able to replicate "consistently exceptional service" around the world and across cultures was at the heart of the chain's international success and sustained advantage.

For Four Seasons, "consistently exceptional service" meant providing high-quality, truly personalized service to enable guests to *maximize the value of their time*, however guests defined doing so. Corporate culture contributed to the firm's success in two ways. First was through the values that the organization espoused. For Four

Seasons, these were personified in the Golden Rule: "Treat others as you wish they would treat you." Second was the set of behaviors that employees and managers displayed, in effect the enactment of the firm's values. The organizational capability of translating core values into enacted behaviors created competitive advantage at Four Seasons. Doing so required managers to address a central question as they expanded into new countries: what do we need to keep consistent, and what should be flexible, i.e., what should we adapt to the local market?

Performance

Four Seasons generally operated (as opposed to owned) mid-sized luxury hotels and resorts. From 1996 through 2000 (inclusive), Four Seasons increased revenues from $121 million to $347.5 million and earnings from $55.7 million to $125.8 million, a 22.6 percent compounded annual growth rate (CAGR). Operating margins increased from 58.8 percent to 67.9 percent during the same period. Four Seasons' 2001 revenue per room (RevPAR), an important hospitality industry measure, was 32 percent above that of its primary US competitors and 27 percent higher than that of its European competitors. Growth plans were to open five to seven new luxury properties per year, predominantly outside of North America.

Four Seasons entered the French market by renovating and operating the Hotel George V, a historic Parisian landmark. The hotel was renamed the Four Seasons Hotel George V Paris (hereafter, "F. S. George V").

International Structure

Each Four Seasons property was managed by a general manager responsible for supervising the day-to-day operations of a single property. Compensation was, in part, based on the property's performance. Hotel general managers had a target bonus of 30 percent of base compensation. 25 percent of the bonus was based on people measures (employee attitudes), 25 percent on product (service quality), and 50 percent on profit.

Four Seasons' management believed that the firm's regional management structure was a key component of its ability to deliver and maintain the highest and most consistent service standards at each property in a cost-effective manner. General managers reported directly to one of the 13 regional vice presidents or directly to one of the two senior vice presidents, operations. A regional marketing director, an area director of finance, and a regional human resources director completed each support team. The majority of these individuals were full-time employees of a Four Seasons-managed property, with a portion of their time devoted to regional matters, including both routine management and deciding how to customize Four Seasons' operating practice to the region.

Management

Four Seasons' top management team was noted for its longevity, many having been at the firm tor over 25 years. Characteristics that executives attributed to their peers included an international flair, a respect for modesty and compassion, and a "no excuses" mentality.

Italian in Italy, French in France

The firm's top managers were very comfortable in a variety of international settings. Antoine Corinthios, president, Europe, Middle East, and Africa, for example, was said to be "Italian in Italy, French in France." Born and educated in Cairo, Corinthios then spent 20 years in Chicago but described himself as a world citizen. He was as much of a cultural chameleon as he wanted Four Seasons hotels to be. "When I speak the language of the environment I am in, I start to think in the language I am in and adapt to that culture. If you are going global, you cannot be one way," he explained.

No Bragging, No Excuses

Modesty, compassion, and discipline were also important. A manager who stayed with Four Seasons from the prior management of the George V described the Four Seasons due diligence team that came to the property as "very professional and not pretentious; detail oriented; and interested in people. They did not come telling me that all I did was wrong," he remembered, "and showed a lot of compassion. The people are good, but still modest – many people in the industry can be very full of themselves." Importantly, excuses were not tolerated at Four Seasons. "Oh, but we have just been open a year" or "The people here do not understand" were not acceptable statements.

Strong Allegiance to the Firm

Both corporate and field managers often referred to the firm as a "family," complete with rules, traditions, and tough love. There was a strong "one-firm sentiment" on the part of managers in the field; they worked for the firm, not for the individual property to which they were assigned. For example, a general manager explained, "We are happy to let stars go to other properties to help them."

Service Orientation

Customer service extended to all levels in the organization. Managers sometimes assisted in clearing restaurant tables in passing. "If I see that something needs to get done," a manager explained, "I do it."

FOUR SEASONS' APPROACH TO INTERNATIONAL GROWTH

> Today, we have opened enough properties overseas that we can go into any city or town and pull people together to fulfill our mission.
>
> Isadore Sharp, Founder and CEO

Diversity and Singularity

One of the things Four Seasons managers were wary about was being perceived as an "American" company. They found it useful in Europe to position Four Seasons as the Canadian company it was. One noted, "The daughter of a property owner once told us, 'I do not want you to be the way Americans are.' She assumed that Americans say, 'Do it my way or take the highway.' Canadians are seen as more internationally minded and respectful of other value systems."

According to Corinthios, "Our strength is our diversity and our singularity. While the essence of the local culture may vary, the process for opening and operating a hotel is the same everywhere." He continued:

> My goal is to provide an international hotel to the business or luxury leisure traveler looking for comfort and service. The trick is to take it a couple of notches up, or sideways, to adapt to the market you are in. Our standards are universal, e.g., getting your message on time, clean room, good breakfast; being cared for by an engaging, anticipating and responding staff; being able to treat yourself to an exciting and innovative meal – these are global. This is the fundamental value. What changes is that people do it with their own style, grace, and personality; in some cultures you add the strong local temperament. For example, an Italian concierge has his own style and flair. In Turkey or Egypt you experience different hospitality.

As a result, "Each hotel is tailor made" and adapted to its national environment, noted David Crowl, vice president sales and marketing, Europe, Middle East, and Africa:

> Issy Sharp once told me that one of our key strengths is diversity. McDonald's is the same all over. We do not want to be that way. We are not a cookie cutter company. We try to make each property represent its location. In the rooms, we have 40 to 50 square meters to create a cultural destination without being offensive. When you wake up in our hotel in Istanbul, you know that you are in Turkey. People know that they will get 24-hour room service, a custom-made mattress, and a marble bathroom, but they also know that they are going to be part of a local community.

According to David Richey, president of Richey International, a firm Four Seasons and other hotel chains hired to audit service quality, "Four Seasons has done an exceptional job of adapting to local markets. From a design perspective, they are much more clever than other companies. When you sit in the Four Seasons in Bali, you feel that you are in Bali. It does not scream Four Seasons at you."

A manager explained Four Seasons' ability to be somewhat of a cultural chameleon with an analogy to Disney: "Unlike Disney, whose brand name is so strongly associated with the United States, Four Seasons' brand doesn't rigidly define what the product is. The Four Seasons brand is associated with intangibles. Our guests are not looking to stay in a Canadian hotel. Our product has to be 100 percent Four Seasons, but in a style that is appropriate for the country."

According to Crowl, Four Seasons learned from each country and property: "Because we are an international hotel company, we take our learning across borders. In Egypt, we are going to try to incorporate indigenous elements to the spa, but we will still be influenced by the best practices we have identified at our two spas in Bali."

Globally Uniform Standards

The seven Four Seasons "service culture standards" expected of all staff all over the world at all times are:

1. SMILE: Employees will actively greet guests, smile, and speak clearly in a friendly manner.
2. EYE: Employees will make eye contact, even in passing, with an acknowledgment.
3. RECOGNITION: All staff will create a sense of recognition by using the guest's name, when known, in a natural and discreet manner.
4. VOICE: Staff will speak to guests in an attentive, natural, and courteous manner, avoiding pretension, and in a clear voice.
5. INFORMED: All guest contact staff will be well informed about their hotel, their product, will take ownership of simple requests, and will not refer guests elsewhere.
6. CLEAN: Staff will always appear clean, crisp, well-groomed, and well-fitted.
7. EVERYONE: Everyone, everywhere, all the time, show their care for our guests.

In addition to its service culture standards, Four Seasons had 270 core worldwide operating standards (see Appendix 1 for sample standards). Arriving at these standards had not been easy; until 1998, there were 800. With the firm's international growth, this resulted in an overly complex set of rules and exceptions. The standards were set by the firm's senior vice presidents and Wolf Hengst, president, worldwide hotel operations, who explained, "We had a rule about the number of different types of bread rolls to be served at dinner and number of bottles of wine to be opened at lounges. But in countries where no bread is eaten at dinner and no wine is consumed, that's pretty stupid."

"While 270 standards might seem extensive," Richey noted, "if there are only 270, there are thousands of things that are not covered over which the general manager and local management team have a lot of control."

In addition, exceptions to the standards were permitted if they made local sense. For example, one standard stated that the coffee pot should be left on the table at breakfast so that guests could choose to refill their cups. This was perceived as a lack of service in France, so it was amended there. Standards were often written to allow local flexibility. While the standards require an employee's uniform to be immaculate, they do not state what it should look like. In Bali, uniforms were completely different from uniforms in Chicago. Managers underlined the fact that standards set *minimum expectations*. "If you can do something for a client that goes beyond a standard," they told staff, "do it." As a result, stories about a concierge taking a client to the hospital and staying with that person overnight were part of Four Seasons lore, contributing to cultural artifacts.

To evaluate each property's performance against the standards, Four Seasons used both external and internal auditors in its measurement programs. "Our standards are the foundation for all our properties," a senior manager noted. "It is the base on which we build." "When you talk to a Four Seasons person," Richey concluded, "they are so familiar with each of the standards, it is astonishing. With many managers at other firms this is not the case."

"We have been obsessed by the service standards," Hengst concluded. "People who come from the outside are surprised that we take them and the role they play in our culture so seriously. But they are essential. Talk to me about standards and you talk to me about religion." Another manager added, "Over time, the standards help to shape relationships between people, and those relationships contribute to building our culture."

Delivering Intelligent, Anticipatory, and Enthusiastic Service Worldwide

A manager stated, "We decided many years ago that our distinguishing edge would be exceptional, personal service – that's where the value is. In all our research around the world, we have never seen anything that led us to believe that 'just for you' customized service was not the most important element of our success." Another manager added, "Service like this, what I think of as 'intelligent service,' can't be scripted. As a result, we need employees who are as distinguished as our guests – if employees are going to adapt, to be empathetic and anticipate guests' needs, the 'distance' between the employee and the guest has to be small."

There were also tangible elements to Four Seasons' service quality. The product was always comfortable – so much so that at guests' requests, the company made its pillows, bedspreads, and mattresses available for sale. Guests could also count on a spacious bathroom, which was appreciated by the world traveler, especially in Europe where bathrooms tended to be small. "However, there are differences in the perception and definition of luxury," explained Barbara Talbott, executive vice president of marketing. "In the US, our properties have public spaces with a luxurious, but intimate, feeling. In the Far East, our properties have large lobbies enabling guests to see and be seen. People around the world also have different ways of using a hotel – restaurants, for example, are more important in hotels in Asia, so we build space for more restaurants in each property there."

Human Resources and the Golden Rule

Four Seasons' managers believed that human resource management was key to the firm's success. According to one senior manager, "People make the strength of this company. Procedures are not very varied or special. What we do is fairly basic." Human resource management started and ended with "the Golden Rule," which stipulated that one should treat others as one would wish to be treated. Managers saw it as the foundation of the firm's values and thus its culture. "The Golden Rule is the key to the success of the firm, and it's appreciated in every village, town, and city around the world. Basic human needs are the same everywhere," Sharp emphasized. Appendix 2 summarizes the firm's goals, beliefs, and principles.

Kathleen Taylor, president, worldwide business operations, provided an example of how Four Seasons went about enacting the Golden Rule as a core value. "We give employees several uniforms so they can change when they become dirty. That goes to their dignity, but it is uncommon in the hospitality industry. People around the world want to be treated with dignity and respect, and in most organizational cultures that doesn't happen."

Managers acknowledged that many service organizations made similar statements on paper. What differentiated Four Seasons was how the chain operationalized those statements. Crowl noted, "A service culture is about putting what we all believe in into practice. We learn it, we nurture it, and most importantly, we do it."

In 2002, for the fifth year in a row, Four Seasons was among *Fortune* magazine's list of the top 100 best companies to work for in North America. While turnover in the hospitality industry averaged 55 percent, Four Seasons' turnover was half that amount.

GOING TO PARIS

However it developed its approach and philosophy, Four Seasons management knew that entering France would be a challenge.

The George V Opportunity

The six hotels in Paris classified as "Palaces" were grand, historic, and luxurious. Standard room prices at the F. S. George V, for example, ranged from $400 to $700. Most palaces featured award-winning restaurants, private gardens, and expansive common areas. For example, the Hotel de Crillon, a competitor to the F. S. George V, was an eighteenth-century palace commissioned by King Louis XV. The nine-story George V was designed in the 1920s by two famous French art deco architects. The property was located in one of Paris's most fashionable districts. For comparative data on Parisian palaces, please refer to Appendix 3.

Observers of the Paris hotel scene noted that by the 1980s and 1990s, the George V, like some of its peers, was coasting on its reputation. In December 1996, HRH Prince Al Waleed Bin Talal Bin Abdulaziz al Saud purchased the hotel for $170 million. In November 1997, Four Seasons signed a long-term agreement to manage the hotel. "We needed to be in Paris," John Young, executive vice president, human resources, explained, "We had looked at a new development, but gaining planning permission for a new building in Paris is very hard. Since we look for the highest possible quality assets in the best locations, the George V was perfect. It established us very powerfully in the French capital."

In order to transform the George V into a Four Seasons, however, an extensive amount of effort had to be placed into both the tangible and experiential service that the property and its people could deliver.

Physical Renovations

Four Seasons' challenge was to preserve the soul of the legendary, almost mythical, George V Hotel while rebuilding it for contemporary travelers. Four Seasons closed the hotel for what ended up being a two-year, $125 million total renovation. Because the building was a landmark, the facade had to be maintained. The interior of the hotel, however, was gutted. The 300 rooms and suites were reduced to 245 rooms of larger size (including 61 suites). Skilled craftsmen restored the facade's art deco windows and balconies, the extensive wood paneling on the first floor, and the artwork and seventeenth-century Flanders tapestries that had long adorned the hotel's public and private spaces.

The interior designer hired by Four Seasons, Pierre Rochon, noted, "My main objective was to marry functionality with guest comfort, to merge twenty-first-century technology with the hotel's 'French classique' heritage. I would like guests rediscovering the hotel to think that I had not changed a thing – and, at the same time, to notice how much better they feel within its walls."[5] The fact that the designer was French, Talbott pointed out, "signaled to the French that we understood what they meant by luxury."

While Four Seasons decided to build to American life-safety standards, it also had to adhere to local laws, which affected design and work patterns. For example, a hygiene law in France stipulates that food and garbage cannot travel the same routes: food and trash have to he carried down different corridors and up/down different elevators. Another law involved "right to light," stipulating that employees had the right to work near a window for a certain number of hours each day. As a result, employees in the basement spa also worked upstairs in a shop with a window for several hours a day, and as many windows as possible had to be programmed into the design.

The new Four Seasons Hotel George V opened on December 18, 1999 at 100 percent effective occupancy (occupancy of rooms ready for use). Managers credited extensive publicity, the millennium celebration, and the profile of the property for that success. The opening was particularly challenging because Four Seasons only took formal control of operations on December 1, in part due to French regulations. "The French are very particular about, for example, fire regulations, but the fire department would not come in and inspect until everything else was complete," a manager said.

BECOMING A FRENCH EMPLOYER

Entering the French hospitality market meant becoming a French employer, which implied understanding French labor laws, business culture, and national idiosyncrasies.

Rules

France's leaders remained committed to a capitalism that maintained social equity with laws, tax policies, and social spending that reduced income disparity and the impact of free markets on public health and welfare.[6] France's tax burden, 45 percent of GDF in 1998, was three percentage points higher than the European average – and eight points higher than the OECD average. A further burden on employers was the 1999 reduction of the work week to 35 hours. Unemployment and retirement benefits were generous. Importantly, Four Seasons' management was not unfamiliar with labor-oriented government policy. "Canada has many attributes of a welfare state, so our Canadian roots made it easier to deal with such a context," Young explained.

The country was known for its strong unions.[7] "In France, one still finds a certain dose of antagonism between employees and management," a French manager underlined. The political party of the Force Ouvrière, the union that was strongest at the F. S. George V, garnered nearly 10 percent of the votes in the first round of the 2002 French presidential election with the rallying cry, "Employees fight the bosses!"

"If you look at the challenges of operating in France," noted Corinthios, "they have labor laws that are restrictive, but not prohibitive. The laws are not the same as, for example, in Chicago. You just need to be more informed about them." The law did give employers some flexibility, allowing them to work someone a little more during peak business periods and less during a lull. A housekeeper, for example, might work 40-hour weeks in the summer in exchange for a few 30-hour weeks in the late fall. Furthermore, French employers could hire 10 percent to 15 percent of staff on a "temporary," seasonal basis.

A particularly tricky area of labor management in France involved terminations. "Wherever we operate in the world," a Four Seasons manager explained, "we do not fire at will. There is due process. There is no surprise. There is counseling. So, Paris isn't that different, except to have the termination stick is more challenging because you really need a very, very good cause and to document *everything* carefully. If you have one gap in the documentation, you will have to rehire the terminated employee."

National and Organizational Culture

Geert Hofstede's seminal work, *Culture's Consequences*,[8] indicates a great disparity between North American (US and Canadian) national culture and that of France. While Hofstede's work has been criticized for the construction of the dimensions along which cultures differ,[9] there is general agreement with the principle that cultures do differ. Further, Hofstede's work and that of other scholars indicate that the differences between North American and French organizational culture are large. Corinthios identified attitudes surrounding performance evaluation as one difference:

> European and Middle Eastern managers have a hard time sitting across from people they supervise and talking about their weaknesses. The culture

is not confrontational. It is more congenial and positive. It is very important to save face and preserve the dignity of the person being reviewed. Some Four Seasons managers using standard forms might even delete certain sections or questions or reprogram them in different languages.

For Didier Le Calvez, general manager of the F. S. George V and recently appointed regional vice president, another significant difference was the degree to which middle and front-line managers felt accountable. "The greatest challenge in France is to get managers to take accountability for decisions and policies," he said. "In the French hierarchical system there is a strong tendency to refer things to the boss."

Le Calvez was also surprised by managers' poor understanding of human resource issues. In France, when a manager has a problem with an employee, the issue generally gets referred to the human resources department. "We, at Four Seasons, on the other hand, require that operating managers be present, deal with the issue, and lead the discussion."

"Seeing is Believing"

When reflecting on their experiences with employees in France, several Four Seasons managers mentioned Saint Thomas ("doubting Thomas"). "They must see it to believe it," Le Calvez explained. "They do not take things at face value. They also tend to wait on the sidelines once they see that something works, they come out of their shells and follow the movement." A Four Seasons manager continued:

> Most of the workforce in France did not know what Four Seasons was all about. For example, they did not think we were serious about the Golden Rule. They thought it was way too American. Initially, there were some eyebrows raised. Because of this skepticism, when we entered France, we came on our tiptoes, without wanting to give anyone a lecture. I think *how* we came in was almost as important as *what* we did.

More Differences

For several Four Seasons managers, working in France required a "bigger cultural adjustment" than had been necessary in other countries. "In France, I always knew that I would be a foreigner," a manager explained. "It took me a while to adjust to the French way." "There is simply an incredible pride in being French," added another. "The French have a very emotional way to do things," an F. S. George V manager explained. "This can be good and bad. The good side is that they can be very joyous and engaging. On the bad side, sometimes the French temper lashes out."

According to Four Seasons managers, what was referred to in the cultural research literature as the French "logic of honor"[10] was strong. While it would be degrading to be "in the service of" (*au service de*) anybody, especially the boss, it was honorable to "give service" (*rendre service*), with magnanimity, if asked to do so with due ceremony. In this context, management required a great deal of tact and judgment.

Managing differing perceptions of time could also be a challenge for North Americans in France. North Americans have been characterized as having a "monochronic" culture based on a high degree of scheduling and an elaborate code of behavior built around promptness in meeting obligations and appointments.[11] In contrast, the French were "polychronic," valuing human relationships and interactions over arbitrary schedules and appointments. These differences created predictable patterns summarized in Appendix 4.

Specific areas where Four Seasons and French national culture differed often related to either (French) guest expectations of a palace hotel, including its physical structure and tangible amenities, or manager–employee relationships. For example, in France, hotel guests expected a palace hotel to have a world-class gastronomic restaurant. They also expected exquisite floral arrangements and to be wowed by the decor. In contrast, Four Seasons hotels generally have excellent, although not necessarily world-class, restaurants and are known for their understated, subtly elegant look. An example of differences in employee–manager relationships can be found in the French managerial practice of being extremely cautious in providing employee feedback to the degree that, according to Four Seasons' managers, the practice is unusual. In contrast, Four Seasons' management practice involved a great deal of communication, including feedback on an individual employee's performance, which managers believed critical to solving problems and delivering superior service.

Cultural Renovation at the F. S. George V

Awareness and management of French cultural patterns were especially important to Four Seasons managers in Paris because a significant portion of the former operator's management and staff remained. Young explained:

> When we explored options for refashioning the George V into a Four Seasons hotel, we realized that without being able to start from scratch, the task would be Herculean. The existing culture was inconsistent with ours. In a North American environment you can decide whom to keep after an acquisition at a cost you can determine in advance on the basis of case law. In France, the only certainty is that you cannot replace the employees. You are acquiring the entity as a going concern. Unless you do certain things, you simply inherit the employees, including their legal rights based on prior service.

To be able to reduce headcount, by law an enterprise had to plan to be closed for over 18 months. Because the F. S. George V owner wanted the renovation to be complete in 12 months, staff were guaranteed a position with Four Seasons unless they chose to leave.[12] "Many of the best employees easily found other jobs, while the most disruptive were still there when the hotel reopened," Young said. "The number of people we really did not want was somewhere in the region of 40 out of 300 coming back on reopening."

Managers uniformly noted that the cultural renovation necessary to enable Four Seasons to be able to deliver its world-class service was on par with the extent of the physical renovation. Young provided an example. "During the due diligence process, the former general manager went to lunch with one of our senior staff. Even though guests were waiting, the maître d' immediately tried to escort the general manager and his party to the general manager's customary table. At Four Seasons this is seen as an abuse of privilege. For us, 'the guest always comes first.'"

Fortunately, in taking over The Pierre in New York, Four Seasons had been through a somewhat similar process. The scale of change necessary in each situation was enormous, as illustrated by this quotation from a senior Four Seasons manager: "Shortly after we bought The Pierre in 1981, a bell captain lamented that the times of the big steamer trunks were over. The staff had not adjusted to jet travel, despite its prevalence for two decades. This is the same kind of recalibration we had to do at the George V."

Apples and Oranges

Young described the firm's approach to cultural transformation in acquired properties with existing staffing:

> If we can achieve a critical mass of individuals among the workforce who are committed to doing things differently, to meeting our standards, that critical mass overcomes the resistance of what becomes a diminishing old guard. Progressively, that old guard loses some of its power. If one rotten apple can ruin the barrel, then you have to seed the organization with oranges that cannot be spoiled by the apples. As a result, a departing old-guard employee is very carefully replaced. Concurrently, individuals with the right culture and attitude are promoted. That creates a new culture, bit by bit by bit. At the F. S. George V, we also appealed to the national pride of our staff to help us restore a French landmark – to restore the pride of France.

"UN BOSS FRANCO-FRANÇAIS"

To effect this cultural change, Four Seasons picked Le Calvez to be general manager. Le Calvez was described as both demanding and "Franco-Français,"[13] an expression used in France to describe someone or something "unequivocally French." At the same time, Le Calvez brought extensive Four Seasons and North American experience. Prior to opening the Regent Hotel in Singapore, he spent 25 years outside France, including 11 years at The Pierre. "He is very international, yet also very French, very attached to his country and its culture," an executive explained. "He knows everyone and has an unbelievable memory for names and events (what happened to so-and-so's mother-in-law, etc.). He is very visible and accessible to the staff, eating in the staff cafeteria."

An F. S. George V manager noted, "The hotel's culture is embodied in the general manager – he shows a lot of love and respect for others and promotes social and cultural and ethnic integration." In a country where people typically referred to each other as Monsieur and Madame with their last name, Le Calvez encouraged the use of the first name. "It is more direct, relaxed, and straightforward. It represents the kind of relationship I want to have with my staff," he stated.

Young commented on the choice of Le Calvez: "The choice of senior leadership is absolutely critical. Adherence to our values and operational goals has to be extremely strong. Hotel openings require a lot of patience and tolerance because results are likely to be less positive as you manage through periods of major change."

The Task Force – "Culture Carriers"

To help Le Calvez and his team "Four Seasonize" the F. S. George V staff and ensure a smooth opening, Four Seasons assigned a 35-person task force, as it did to every new property. A manager noted:

> The task force helps establish norms. We help people understand how Four Seasons does things. Members listen for problems and innuendoes and communicate the right information to all, and squash rumors, especially when there are cultural sensitivities. The task force also helps physically getting the property up and running. Finally, being part of the task force exposes managers who may one day become general managers to the process of opening a hotel.

The task force, composed of experienced Four Seasons managers and staff, reflected the operating needs of each property. For example, if an experienced room service manager had already transferred to the opening property, those skills would not be brought in via the task force.

"The task force is truly a human resource, as well as a strong symbol," a manager explained. "The approach supports allegiance to the firm and not just one property – because members of the task force are not associated with one hotel. We are excited to participate, even if it means working long hours for weeks away from home." Most task force members, who typically stayed three weeks for an opening, stayed seven to eight weeks at the F. S. George V.

Strong Tides

After working 25 years abroad, Le Calvez admitted that he was hesitant to return to work in France in light of the general tension he sensed between labor and management. However, he was encouraged by what he had seen at The Pierre, where Four Seasons managers noted that they had fostered a dialogue with the New York hospitality industry union. Le Calvez felt he could do the same in Paris:

> When I arrived I told the unions that I did not think that we would need them, but since the law said we had to have them, I said 'Let's work together.'

I do not want social tensions. Of course, this is not unique to me; it is Four Seasons' approach. We have to be pragmatic. So we signaled our commitment to a good environment.

Le Calvez communicated this commitment by openly discussing the 35-hour work week, the Four Seasons retirement plan, and the time and attendance system, designed to make sure that staff would not work more than required.

At the outset of negotiations, in preparation for the reopening, Le Calvez took the representatives of the various unions to lunch. As work progressed, he organized tours of the site so that union representatives could see what was being done and "become excited" about the hotel. He noted that, "Touring the property in hard hats and having to duck under electric wires builds bonds. Witnessing the birth of a hotel is exciting." Managers stated that the unions were not used to such an inclusive approach in France.

Young felt that dealing with unions in France was easier than in New York: "In France, you are dealing with an institution backed by stringent, but predictable, laws. In the United States, you are dealing with individuals in leadership who can be much more volatile and egocentric."

Four Seasons' experience with The Pierre proved invaluable. According to Young:

In New York, we redesigned working spaces, and trained, and trained, and trained staff. But we also burned out a couple of managers. The old culture either wears you down or you wear it down. In an environment with strong labor laws, management sometimes gives up the right to manage. At some point, managers stop swimming against the tide. If that continues long enough, the ability to manage effectively is lost. The precedents in a hotel are those that the prior managers have permitted. If the right to manage has been given up, standards are depressed, productivity decreases, margins decrease, and eventually you have a bad business. Regulars are treated well, but many guests are not. Reversing this process requires enormous management energy. It is very wearing to swim against a strong tide. You are making decisions that you believe reasonable and facing reactions that you believe unreasonable.

The 35-Hour Work Week

Managers believed that Four Seasons' decision to implement the 35-hour work week at the F. S. George V to meet the letter and spirit of French law was a major signal to the unions and workforce about the way the company approached human resource issues. "When we hire staff from other hotels, they are always surprised that we obey the law," an F. S. George V manager noted. "They were working longer hours elsewhere."

A 35-hour work week yielded 1,820 annual workable hours per full-time staff equivalent. But since the French had more holidays and vacation than American employees, French employees provided 1,500 to 1,600 workable hours. This compared

Table 1. Employees-to-room ratios at selected Four Seasons properties

Property	Employees-to-Rooms Ratio
Four Seasons worldwide average	1.6
The Pierre New York	2.3
Four Seasons Hotel New York	1.6
Four Seasons Hotel George V Paris	2.5
Four Seasons Hotel Berlin	0.9
Four Seasons Hotel London	1.2
Four Seasons Hotel Canary Wharf, London	1.4
Four Seasons Hotel Milano	2.2

Source: Four Seasons.

to about 2,050 hours in the US for a full-time equivalent. The manager added, "We did not really understand the impact of the 35-hour work week. Each of our 80 managers has to have two consecutive days off a week, and each of the staff can work 214 days a year. Not 215. Not 213. But 214."

In 2002, 620 staff covered 250 rooms, or 2.5 staff per room. On average, Four Seasons hotels had 1.6 employees per room. Depending on food and banquet operations, that average could rise or fall significantly. Table 1 shows employees-to-room ratios at selected Four Seasons properties.

Young felt that labor laws explained about 15 percent of the need for increased staff ratios in Paris; vacations and holidays, 10 percent; with the rest explained by other factors including some logistics of the operation, e.g., a historic building, all compared to US norms. Corinthios elaborated:

> In Paris, you have six palaces competing for the same clients. It is a more formal operation. Guest expectations are very high, as is the level of leisure business (which requires higher staffing). People stay four to six days and use the concierge extensively. The concierge staffing at the F. S. George V is as big as anything we have in the chain. Then there is more emphasis on food and beverage. We have a fabulous chef and more staff in the kitchen for both the restaurant and room service – expectations of service in the gastronomic restaurant are very high.

RUNNING THE F. S. GEORGE V

Recruitment and Selection

Four Seasons wanted to be recognized as the best employer in each of its locations. In Paris, F. S. George V wages were among the top three for hotels. Salaries were advertised in help wanted ads, a first in the industry in Paris according to F. S. George V managers, who believed doing so would help them attract high-quality staff.

At the F. S. George V, as across the firm, every potential employee was interviewed four times, the last interview with the general manager. According to one executive, "In the selection process, we try to look deep inside the applicant. I learned about the importance of service from my parents – did this potential employee learn it from hers?" "What matters is attitude, attitude, attitude," Corinthios explained. "All around the world it is the same. Without the right attitude, they cannot adapt." Another manager added, "What we need is people who can adapt, either to guests from all over the world, or to operating in a variety of countries." One of his colleagues elaborated on the importance of hiring for attitude, and its challenges:

> You would think that you would have a lot of people with great experience because there are so many palace hotels in Paris. But because we hire for attitude, we rarely hire from the other palaces. We hire individuals who are still "open" and tend to be much younger than usual for palace hotels. Then we bet on training. Of course, it takes much longer to train for skills when people do not have them. We look for people persons, who are welcoming and put others at ease, who want to please, are professional and sincerely friendly, flexible, smiley, and positive. At the F. S. George V, people apply for jobs because they have friends who work here.

To spread the culture and "de-demonize" the US, the new F. S. George V management recruited staff with prior Four Seasons and/or US experience to serve as ambassadors. A manager noted, "Staff with US experience share with other staff what the United States is about and that it is not the terrible place some French people make it out to be." Several managers had international experience. About 40 individuals had prior US experience.

"Anglo-Saxon" Recognition, Measurement, and Benefits

Le Calvez and his team launched an employee-of-the-month and employee-of-the-year program. "This had been controversial at Disney. People said it could not be done in France, but we managed to do it quite successfully. It all depends how it is presented," Le Calvez noted. "We explained that the program would recognize those who perform. Colleagues can tell who is good at their job."

Le Calvez used the same spirit to introduce annual evaluations, uncommon in France:

> People said evaluations would be unpopular, but the system seems to work. We told the staff that it would be an opportunity for open and constructive dialogue so that employees can know at all times where they stand. This allows them to adapt when need be. We wanted to make clear that there would be no favoritism, but rather that this would be a meritocracy. Here your work speaks for itself. The idea that your work is what matters could be construed as very Anglo-Saxon!

In another "Anglo-Saxon" action, a "Plan d'Epargne d'Entreprise" was set up for George V employees. This was a combination tax-deferred savings account and 401(k)-type retirement plan. "This is totally new in France," Le Calvez claimed. Employees could contribute up to 4 percent of their salary, and the hotel would match it with 2 percent, to be raised based on profitability. The unions signed the agreement, although they were opposed to the principle of a non-government-sponsored retirement plan.

IMPLEMENTING THE GOLDEN RULE

The Golden Rule was at work at the F. S. George V, as its human resource director illustrated: "Cooks, before joining Four Seasons, used to have very long days starting in the morning to prepare for lunch, having a break during the afternoon, and coming back to prepare dinner. Today they work on either the morning or afternoon shift, enabling a better organization of their personal lives."

"All these gestures take time to work," Le Calvez summarized. "At first employees do not think we mean it. Some new hires think it's artificial or fake, but after a few months they let their guard down when they realize we mean what we say."

Managers believed that the effect of Four Seasons' human resource practices was reflected in customer satisfaction. Indeed, Le Calvez proudly reported that guest cards often included comments on how friendly and attentive the staff were. "All the other palace hotels in Paris are beautiful, but we believe that we have a special focus on friendly and personable service." He continued, "We offer friendly, very personal service. We have a very young and dynamic brigade with an average age of 26, spanning 46 different nationalities."

Communication

To promote communication and problem-solving, the F. S. George V management implemented a "direct line." Once a month, the general manager met with employees, supervisors, and managers in groups of 30. The groups met for three consecutive months so that issues raised could be addressed, with results reported to the group. Managers believed that the F. S. George V was the only palace hotel in France with such a communication process. It was important to note that the groups met separately – that is, employees met separately from supervisors – because subordinates in France did not feel comfortable speaking up in front of superiors.

French law mandated that a *comité d'entreprise* (staff committee) be established in organizations with more than 50 employees. It represented employees to management on decisions that affected employees (e.g., salaries, work hours). At the F. S. George V, Le Calvez chaired the committee's monthly meeting, which included union representatives. "We would do these things anyway, so it is easy to adjust to these laws," Corinthios said. "We do it in France because it is required by law. But we do the same around the world; it just has a different name."

Every morning, the top management team gathered to go over glitches – things that may have gone wrong the day before and the steps that had been, or were being, taken to address the problem. "Admitting what went wrong is not in the French culture," a French Four Seasons manager explained. "But the meetings are usually very constructive."

Finally, about three times a year, Le Calvez and his team hosted an open-door event, inviting employees and their families to spend some time at the hotel. "This is to break down barriers," he explained. "We take people around the hotel, into the back corridors. Try to remind people of a notion that is unfortunately being lost – that of the '*plaisir du travail*' – or enjoying one's work. Furthermore, we celebrate achievement. Good property rankings, for example, are recognized with special team celebrations."

The property also cultivated external communication with the press in a way that was culturally sensitive. Le Calvez and his team felt that they had been very open and responsive to the press (which they stated was unusual in France) and that as a result, "Not a single negative article had been written about Four Seasons Hotel George V since its opening". A colleague added, "The press appreciated that they were dealing with locals. It was not like Disney where everyone was American."

CULINARY *COUP D'ÉTAT*

In a significant diversion from typical Four Seasons practice, a non-Four Seasons executive chef was hired. "In France, having a serious chef and serious food is important," the F. S. George V food and beverage director noted. "You cannot be a palace hotel without that." "We knew that what mattered in Paris was food and decor," Talbott added. Although only 7 percent of room guests were French, most restaurant patrons were French.

Chef Philippe Legendre from the world-famous Parisian restaurant Taillevent was recruited. "Didier came to me through a common friend," Legendre explained. Legendre accepted Four Seasons' offer because "there was something exciting about being part of opening a hotel." He also liked their language, which he described as "optimistic" and "about creating possibilities."

Legendre felt that Four Seasons' real strength was around relationship management (with clients and among staff), which "is not something that we are that good at in France, or place particular emphasis on. We have a lot to learn in the social domain. Everything at Four Seasons is geared towards the needs of the guest. At first it was hard, especially the training. Perhaps because in France we think we know everything."

He continued, "After three years I might not talk the Four Seasons talk, I might not use the same words, but I have the same view and adhere to the same system."

Despite Legendre's success (earning two Michelin stars), a colleague added that, "bringing in such an executive chef was problematic. The challenge is that with this chef you have someone with extraordinary talent, but who must still adjust to the way service is delivered at Four Seasons." Coexistence was not always easy. Legendre described a situation illustrating miscommunication and cultural differences that required tremendous patience on the part of the restaurant, guests, and management:

Recently a man ordered an omelet and his wife ordered scrambled eggs. The man returned the omelet because he decided he wanted scrambled eggs. We made them. Then he sent them back because they did not meet his expectations. Of course, we realize that our oeufs brouillés are different from scrambled eggs, which don't contain cream. Because we are Four Seasons we cooked the eggs as he wanted them, like American scrambled eggs, and didn't charge for them. But cooking is about emotion – if you want to please someone, you have to do it with your heart. *We live differently in France*.

RESULTS

A Cultural Cocktail

The F. S. George V was, in effect, a cultural cocktail. Le Calvez explained, "The F. S. George V is not *only* a French hotel – it is French, but it is also very international. We want to be different from the other palaces that are oh so very French. We want to project the image of a modern France, one that does not have to be dusty. We want to be a symbol of a France that is in movement, a European France, a France that stands for integration and equality."

The cultural cocktail also contained a number of elements unusual in France. At the time of the opening, journalists asked about the "American" smiling culture, which was referred to in France as "la culture Mickey Mouse." Le Calvez replied, "If you tell me that being American is being friendly and pleasant, that is fine by me. People tell me everyone smiles at the Four Seasons George V."

The spectacular flowers in the lobby of the F. S. George V (a single urn once contained 1,000 roses) were both very French and extremely international. "Paris is a city of fashion and culture, artistic and innovative," Le Calvez explained. "That is why, for example, we have the flowers we do. We can do that here." However, the flowers were designed by a young American. Another departure from French standard was the decision to hire women as concierges and men in housekeeping. These were viewed by managers as revolutionary steps in Paris.

Service Quality

Richey summarized the results of the first F. S. George V service-quality audit in October 2000, identifying some differences between French and North American business culture:

Keep in mind that this occurred less than one year after opening, and it takes at least a year to get things worked out. There were three things we talked to Four Seasons' executives about, mostly related to employee attitude. First, the staff had an inability to apologize or empathize. I think that could be construed as typically European, and especially French. Second, the team had a very tough time doing anything that could be described as selling. This is also typically European. For example: say your glass is empty at the bar. In Paris, they may not ask you if you want another drink. Third, the staff were rules and policy oriented. If something went wrong, they would refer to the manual instead of focusing on satisfying the guest.

Things had changed considerably by Richey's second audit in August 2001, when "they beat the competitive market set." The scores showed a significant improvement, raising the property to the Four Seasons' system average.

More good news came in July 2002 with the results of an Employee Opinion Survey, in which 95 percent of employees participated. The survey yielded an overall rating of 4.02 out of 5. The questions that ranked the highest were: "I am proud to work for Four Seasons Hotels and Resorts" (4.65) and "I would want to work here again" (4.61).

The property also received several industry awards, including Andrew Harper's Hideaway Report 2001 and 2002, World's Best Hotels and Resorts, Travel & Leisure Readers' Choice Awards 2001, #2 Best Hotel in Europe, and #5 World's Best Hotel Spa.

CONCLUSION: CULTURE, CONSISTENCY, AND FLEXIBILITY

The Four Seasons Hotel George V case illustrates how a service firm with a strong, successful organizational culture expanded internationally into a country with a distinct, intense national culture. When Four Seasons entered France, some elements of organizational culture were held constant, while others were treated flexibly. Managers never considered altering their *organizational values*, whether related to the service provided to guests, which had to be engaging, anticipating, and responding; the property, which had to be beautiful, luxurious, and functional; or how managers would treat employees, insisting that employees be treated as managers would like to be treated if they performed those jobs. While these values remained constant despite considerable differences in operating environments, the ways those values were enacted did sometimes change. This required changes in policies, management practices, and the use of cultural artifacts.

The tangible elements of service provide clear evidence of flexibility. Like all Four Seasons properties, the F. S. George V is luxurious. However, in France, the first floor of the hotel is adorned with gilt and seventeenth-century tapestries. No other Four Seasons property is decorated this way. The hotel elected to have a two-Michelin-star restaurant, despite the challenges of working with a famous chef in a country where there may be no more distinguished form of celebrity. More subtly, non-tangible elements of service quality changed, requiring changes in policies. For example, a coffee pot is never left on the table for guests to help themselves. This change enables the hotel to meet the standard for service set by a Four Seasons' organizational value ("anticipatory") as interpreted in France, where one should not have to pour coffee oneself.

Management practices also changed. In order to have an engaging, anticipating, and responding staff, managers relied upon employee selection even more heavily than at other properties. In this way, management practice was intensified in response to a new national culture. However, the goal of those intensified selection efforts was to hire a less experienced staff than typical for other palace hotels and the chain. This was because of underlying, inflexible assumptions that many more experienced workers in France have about employment and how they should treat guests. Less experienced individuals are less set in attitudes and cultural stereotypes contrary to delivering the service for which Four Seasons is renowned. Management therefore focused more sharply on hiring based on attitudes rather than prior work experience. Thus, this management practice changed in France to enable Four Seasons to remain true to its organizational values.

The use of cultural artifacts also changed. While a typical Four Seasons property opening would be accompanied by information to the press on the world-renowned service for which the chain is famous, including legendary service stories, in France this was an afterthought to the glory of the property and the appropriateness of the renovations for a *French* architectural landmark.

Many management practices did not change upon arrival in France. Employee-of-the-month and -year recognition programs, feedback practices, and meetings to discuss problems were implemented despite a general belief that they would be found incompatible with the French environment. Yet, they were successful because of *how* they were implemented – using the words of one manager, "on tiptoes." Their more awkward (from a French perspective) elements were amended, and their purpose was communicated gently, but repeatedly. The individuals carefully selected into the Four Seasons' environment did not object to their use because they understood the intent of the practices, as well as their effect. The practices ultimately contributed to achieving the changes in organizational culture that Four Seasons managers believed were necessary, helping to ensure that the "oranges" (new employees) carefully selected into the property became the dominant culture carriers, overwhelming the leftover "apples" who refused to change, creating an environment in which those apples no longer fit comfortably.

Perhaps the most important element of management practice contributing to Four Seasons' success in France was management discipline. This took two forms, both of which can be viewed as contributing to the enactment of organizational values. First, discipline can be seen in the way Four Seasons managers lived the values they espoused; allowing guests to be seated first in the dining room; treating employees with dignity; and adhering to local labor laws and internal policies designed to protect employees. Second, Four Seasons managers had the discipline to insist that employees deliver outstanding service to guests. This occurred through adherence to the core service-culture standards and 270 operating standards (as occasionally amended). Meeting these standards has resulted in customer loyalty. Thus, discipline acts as a glue, ensuring that organizational values actually *drive* a culture, which in turn *contributes* to competitive advantage.

Managers in widely diverse service industries can benefit from Four Seasons' approach to global management when entering countries with distinct, intense national cultures. To do so, they must understand their own organizational culture: what are their (1) underlying assumptions, (2) values, (3) employee perceptions of management practices (policies and behaviors), and (4) cultural artifacts? Managers must then ask what elements of their culture, are essential to competitive advantage in existing environments, and how the new environment will change that linkage. When there is a change, does the element of culture itself need to change (coffee pot no longer left on the table), or does the way the element is implemented, the way a value is enacted, need to change, such as the implementation "on tiptoes" of an employee-of-the-month recognition program. In general, *values core to the organization's "value proposition" (what customers receive from the firm relative to what they pay for it) will not change, but elements of how they are enacted may.*

While organizations eventually come to understand how to operate in a new national environment, successful organizations cannot afford the type of negative publicity and poor financial performance that accompany blundering into a new national culture, as Disney discovered after opening Euro Disney in France. The Four Seasons case study is a single case, based on a single organization. As such, we do not claim that its findings are necessarily applicable to other firms. However, it illustrates an approach to global management that managers of other services may find useful, but which they must customize to their own organizational and cultural needs.

APPENDIX 1: SAMPLE CORE STANDARDS

Reservations

Mission: To provide crisp, knowledgeable, and friendly service, sensitive to the guest's time, and dedication to finding the most suitable accommodation.

- Phone service will be highly efficient, including: answered before the fourth ring; no hold longer than 15 seconds; or, in case of longer holds, call-backs offered, then provided in less than three minutes.
- After establishing the reason for the guest visit, reservationist automatically describes the guest room colorfully, attempting to have the guests picture themselves in the room.

Hotel Arrival

Mission: To make all guests feel welcome as they approach, and assured that details are well tended; to provide a speedy, discreet, and hassle-free arrival for business travelers; to provide a comforting and luxurious arrival for leisure travelers.

- The doorman (or first contact employee) will actively greet guests, smile, make eye contact, and speak clearly in a friendly manner.
- The staff will be aware of arriving vehicles and will move toward them, opening doors within 30 seconds.
- Guests will be welcomed at the curbside with the words "welcome" and "Four Seasons" (or hotel name), and given directions to the reception desk.
- No guest will wait longer than 60 seconds in line at the reception desk.

Hotel Departure

Mission: To provide a quick and discreet departure, while conveying appreciation and hope for return.

- No guest will wait longer than five minutes for baggage assistance, once the bellman is called (eight minutes in resorts).
- No guest will wait longer than 60 seconds in line at the cashier desk.
- Staff will create a sense of recognition by using the guest's name, when known, in a natural and discreet manner.

Messages and Paging

Mission: To make guests feel that their calls are important, urgent, and require complete accuracy.

- Phone service will be highly efficient, including: answered before the fourth ring; no longer than 15 seconds.
- Callers requesting guest room extensions between 1 am and 6 am will be advised of the local time and offered the option of leaving a message or putting the call through.
- Unanswered guest room phones will be picked up within five rings, or 20 seconds.
- Guests will be offered the option of voice mail: they will not automatically be routed to voice mail OR they will have a clear option to return to the operator.

Incoming Faxes and Packages

Mission: To make guests feel that their communications are important, urgent, and require complete accuracy.

- Faxes and packages will be delivered to the guest room within 30 minutes of receipt.

Wake-Up Calls

Mission: To make certain that guests are awakened exactly on time in a manner that gently reassures them.

- When wake-up calls are requested, the operator will offer a second reminder call.
- Wake-up calls will occur within two minutes of the requested time.

Guest Room Evening Service

Mission: To create a sense of maximum comfort and relaxation. When meeting guests, to provide a sense of respect and discretion.

- Guest clothing that is on the bed or floor will be neatly folded and placed on the bed or chair – guest clothing left on other furniture will be neatly folded and left in place; shoes will be paired.
- Newspapers and periodicals will be neatly stacked and left on a table or table shelf in plain view; guest personal papers will not be disturbed in any way.
- Guest toiletries will be neatly arranged on a clean, flat cloth.

Laundry and Valet

Mission: To provide excellent workmanship and make guests feel completely assured of the timing and quality of our service.

- Laundry service will include same-day service; express four-hour service; and overnight service (seven days per week).
- Dry cleaning service will include same-day service; express four-hour service (seven days per week).
- Pressing service will be available at any time, and returned within one hour; and can be processed on the normal laundry schedule.

Room Service

Mission: To provide a calm, competent, and thorough dining experience, with accurate time estimates and quick delivery.

- Phone service will be highly efficient, including: answered before the fourth ring; no hold longer than 15 seconds; or, in the case of longer holds, call-backs offered, then provided in less than three minutes.
- Service will be prompt and convenient; an estimated delivery time (an hour and minute, such as "nine-fifteen pm") will be specifically mentioned; and the order will be serviced within five minutes (earlier or later) than that time.
- Continental breakfast will be delivered within 20 minutes, other meals within 30 minutes, and drinks-only within 15 minutes.
- Table/tray removal instructions will be provided by a printed card, and tables will be collected within twelve minutes of guest call.

APPENDIX 2: FOUR SEASONS GOALS, BELIEFS, AND PRINCIPLES

Who We Are: We have chosen to specialize within the hospitality industry, by offering only experiences of exceptional quality. Our objective is to be recognized as the company that manages the finest hotels, resorts, residence clubs, and other residential projects wherever we locate. We create properties of enduring value using superior design and finishes, and support them with a deeply instilled ethic of personal service. Doing so allows Four Seasons to satisfy the needs and tastes of our discriminating customers, to maintain our position as the world's premier luxury hospitality company.

What We Believe: Our greatest asset, and the key to our success, is our people. We believe that each of us needs a sense of dignity, pride, and satisfaction in what we do. Because satisfying our guests depends on the united efforts of many, we are most effective when we work together cooperatively, respecting each other's contribution and importance.

How We Behave: We demonstrate our beliefs most meaningfully in the way we treat each other and by the example we set for one another. In all our interactions with our guests, business associates, and colleagues, we seek to deal with others as we would have them deal with us.

How We Succeed: We succeed when every decision is based on a clear understanding of and belief in what we do and when we couple this conviction with sound financial planning. We expect to achieve a fair and reasonable profit to ensure the prosperity of the company, and to offer long-term benefits to our hotel owners, our shareholders, our customers, and our employees.

APPENDIX 3: COMPARATIVE DATA ON PARISIAN PALACES

Property	Construction/Style	Capacity (Rooms and Suites)	Amenities	Price (Dollar/Single Room)	Owner	Lessee/Operator
Bristol	Built in 1829/Louis XV–XVI style	180	1 restaurant: Le Bristol 1 interior garden 1 swimming pool 1 fitness center 1 beauty salon	480–600	Société Oetker[c] (1978)	Independent
Crillon	Built in the 18th century/Louis XV–XVI style	152	2 restaurants: L'Ambassadeur and L'Obélix 1 fitness center Guerlain Beauty Institute	460–550	Groupe Hôtels Concorde[a] (1907)	Groupe Hôtels Concorde[a] (1907)
Four Seasons Hotel George V Paris	Built in 1928/Art Deco style	245	1 restaurant: Le Cinq 1 swimming pool 1 fitness center 1 beauty salon	670	Prince Al Waleed Bin Talal[d] (1996)	Four Seasons Hotels and Resorts (2000)
Meurice	Built in the 18th century/Louis XV–XVI style	161	1 restaurant: Le Meurice 1 fitness center Caudalie Beauty Institute	470–550	The Sultan of Brunei (1997)	The Dorchester Group[b] (2001)
Plaza Athenée	Built in 1889/Belle Epoque style	144	2 restaurants: Le Relais Plaza	490–508	The Sultan of Brunei (1997)	The Dorchester Group[b] (2001)
Ritz	Built in 1898/Louis XV–XVI style	139	1 restaurant: L'Espadon Escoffier-Ritz cooking school 1 fitness center 1 beauty salon 1 swimming pool	From 580	Mohammed Al Fayed (1979)	Independent

[a] Groupe Hôtels Concorde was created in 1973 to regroup the luxury hotels such as the Crillon, the Lutetia, and the Hôtel Concorde Saint-Lazare (all in Paris) owned by La Société du Louvre. [b] The Dorchester Group, a subsidiary of the Brunei Investment Agency, was established in 1996 as an independent United Kingdom registered company to manage luxury hotels, including The Dorchester in London, The Beverly Hills Hotel California and the Hotel Meurice in Paris. [c] The Oetker Group is a German agribusiness group which owns four luxury hotels in addition to the Bristol: the Cap Eden Roc in Antibes, France; the Park Hotel in Vitznau, Switzerland; the Brenner's Park Hotel in Baden-Baden, Germany; and the Château du Domaine Saint-Martin in Vence, France. [d] Al Waleed Bin Talal owns 21.9 percent of Four Seasons' stocks. Investments by Prince Al Waleed in Four Seasons' properties include F. S. George V and Riyadh (100 percent); London (majority); Cairo, Amman, Alexandria, Sharm El Sheikh and Beirut (unspecified); and Aviara (minority).

Source: "Four Seasons Hotels and Resorts," Brian D. Egger et al., Crédit Suisse First Boston, April 5, 2002, page 21. http://meuricehotel.com, www.hotel-bristol.com, www.ritz.com, www.fourseasons.com/paris/vacations/index.html, www.plaza-athenee-paris.com, www.crillon.com. Accessed June 2002.

APPENDIX 4: PREDICTABLE PATTERNS OF MONOCHRONIC AND POLYCHRONIC CULTURES

Monochronic People (Americans)	Polychronic People (French)
Do one thing at a time	Do many things at once
Concentrate on the job	Can be easily distracted and manage interruptions well
Take time commitments (deadlines, schedules) seriously	Consider an objective to be achieved, if possible
Are low-context and need information	Are high-context and already have information
Are committed to the job	Are committed to people and human relationships
Adhere religiously to plans	Change plans often and easily
Are concerned about not disturbing others; follow rules of privacy and consideration	Are more concerned with those who are closely related (family, friends, close business associates) than with privacy
Show great respect for private property; seldom borrow or lend	Borrow and lend things often and easily
Emphasize promptness	Base promptness on the relationship
Are accustomed to short-term relationships	Have strong tendency to build lifetime relationships

Source: Adapted from Edward T. Hall, *Understanding cultural differences, German, French, and Americans*. Yarmouth: Intercultural Press, 1990.

NOTES

1. Kotter, J. P. and Heskett, J. L. 1990. *Corporate culture and performance*. New York: The Free Press.
2. Heskett, J. L., Schlesinger, L. A. and Sasser, W. E., Jr. 1997. *The service profit chain*. New York: The Free Press; Schneider, B. and Bowen, D. E. 1995. *Winning the service game*. Boston, MA: Harvard Business School Press; and Berry, L. L. 1995. *On great service*. New York: The Free Press.
3. Schein, E. H. 1990. Organizational culture. *American Psychologist*, 45(2): 109–19.
4. The theory behind this discussion finds its roots in the contingency work of scholars such as Lawrence and Lorch; see Lawrence, P. and Lorsch, J. 1967. *Organization and environment*. Boston, MA: Harvard Business School Press. Other scholars, including James Heskett, have used the contingency perspective as a starting point for theories of internationalization of services; see Loveman, G. 1993. *The internationalization of services*. Harvard Business School Module Note No. 9–693–103, Boston, MA: Harvard Business School Publishing. Heskett's views have influenced ours considerably. We are indebted to Professor Caren Siehl, Thunderbird, for much of the framework on managing the potential clash between organizational culture and country culture, which she developed for her organizational behavior MBA classes. In turn, Caren always acknowledges an intellectual debt to Professor Joanne Martin, Stanford University.
5. *Interior Design*, March 2000, p. S24.
6. For example, maternity leave for a salaried employee's first child was 6 weeks of prenatal leave and 10 weeks of paid leave after birth; for a third child, it was 8 weeks off before and 18 weeks after birth.

7. Communist-controlled labor union (Confédération Générale du Travail) or CGT, nearly 2.4 million members (claimed); independent labor union or Force Ouvrière, 1 million members (est.); independent white-collar union or Confédération Générale des Cadres, 340,000 members (claimed); Socialist-leaning labor union (Confédération Française Démocratique du Travail) or CFDT, about 800,000 members (est.). Source: www.Cia.gov/cia/publications/factbook/goes/fr.html, accessed June 10, 2002.

8. Hofstede's work was based on a survey conducted by questionnaire with IBM employees in 50 different countries; see Hofstede, G. 1982. *Culture's consequences: international differences in work-related values.* Thousand Oaks, CA: Sage.

9. Hofstede's approach has not been without its critics but, as Hickson comments, Hofstede had "frail data, but robust concepts;" see Hickson, D. 1996. The ASQ years then and now through the eyes of a Euro-Brit. *Administrative Science Quarterly,* 41(2): 217–28.

10. See d'Iribarne, P. 1996/97. The usefulness of an ethnographic approach to the international comparison of organization. *International Studies of Management and Organisation,* 18(4):32.

11. Van der Horst, B. Edward T. Hall – a great-grandfather of NLP, www.cs.ucr.edu/gnick/bvdh/print_edward_t_hall_great_htm, accessed April 20, 2002. The article reviews Hall, E. 1959. *The silent language.* New York: Doubleday.

12. One alternative was to give the staff a significant enough severance package to encourage them to go. However, as Young explained, "The government deplores that approach."

13. Usually used to describe a meal – say a first course of fromage de tête (pig's head set in jelly) or bouillabaisse (fish soup), followed by a main course of blanquette de veau (veal stew with white sauce) and rounded off with a plateau de fromage (cheese platter) or tarte aux pommes (apple tart).

PART II

Cross-Cultural and Diversity Management

Readings

- David A. Thomas
  DIVERSITY AS STRATEGY

- Mansour Javidan, Peter W. Dorfman, Mary Sully de Luque, and Robert J. House
  IN THE EYE OF THE BEHOLDER: CROSS-CULTURAL LESSONS IN LEADERSHIP FROM PROJECT GLOBE

- Stacey R. Fitzsimmons, Christof Miska, and Günter K. Stahl
  MULTICULTURAL INDIVIDUALS: WHAT CAN THEY BRING TO GLOBAL ORGANIZATIONS?

Cases

- Mark E. Mendenhall
  OLIVIA FRANCIS

- Joseph J. DiStefano
  JOHANNES VAN DEN BOSCH SENDS AN EMAIL

- B. Sebastian Reiche and Yih-teen Lee
  UWA ODE: A CULTURAL CHAMELEON OR STRANDED BETWEEN CULTURAL CHAIRS?

David A. Thomas

DIVERSITY AS STRATEGY

W HEN MOST OF US THINK OF LOU GERSTNER and the turnaround of IBM, we see a great business story. A less-told but integral part of that success is a people story—one that has dramatically altered the composition of an already diverse corporation and created millions of dollars in new business.

By the time that Gerstner took the helm in 1993, IBM already had a long history of progressive management when it came to civil rights and equal employment. Indeed, few of the company's executives would have identified workforce diversity as an area of strategic focus. But when Gerstner took a look at his senior executive team, he felt that it did not reflect the diversity of the market for talent or IBM's customers and employees. To rectify the imbalance, in 1995 Gerstner launched a diversity task force initiative that became a cornerstone of IBM's HR strategy. The effort continued through Gerstner's tenure and it remained active under subsequent CEO Sam Palmisano. Rather than attempt to eliminate discrimination by deliberately ignoring differences among employees, IBM created eight task forces, each focused on a different group such as Asian employees, gay and lesbian employees, and women employees. The goal of the initiative was to uncover and understand differences among the groups, and to find ways to appeal to a broader set of employees and customers.

The initiative required a lot of work, and it did not happen overnight—the first task force convened almost two years after Gerstner's arrival. But the IBM of today looks very different from the IBM of 1995. The number of female executives world-wide has increased by 370%. The number of ethnic minority executives born in the United States has increased by 233%. Of IBM's Worldwide Management Council (WMC), the top 52 executives who determine corporate strategy, 52% is composed of women, ethnic minorities born in the United States, and non-US citizens. The organization has seen the number of self-identified gay, lesbian, bisexual, and transgender (GLBT) executives increase by 733% and the number of executives with disabilities more than triple.

But diversity at IBM is about more than expanding the talent pool. When I asked Gerstner what had driven the success of the task forces, he said, "We made diversity a market-based issue... It's about understanding our markets, which are diverse and multicultural." By deliberately seeking ways to more effectively reach a broader range of customers, IBM has seen significant bottom-line results. For example, the work of the women's task force and other constituencies led IBM to establish its Market Development organization, a group focused on growing the market of multicultural and women-owned businesses in the United States. One tactic was partnering with vendors to provide much-needed sales and service support to small and midsize businesses, a niche well populated with minority and female buyers. In 2001, the organization's activities accounted for more than US$300 million in revenue compared with $10 million in 1998. Based on a recommendation from the people with disabilities task force, in October 2001 IBM launched an initiative focused on making all of its products more broadly accessible to take advantage of new legislation—an amendment to the federal Rehabilitation Act requiring that government agencies make accessibility a criterion for awarding federal contracts. IBM executives estimated that this effort would produce more than a billion dollars in revenue during the subsequent five to ten years.

Over the past two years, I have interviewed more than 50 IBM employees—ranging from midlevel managers all the way up to Gerstner and Palmisano—about the task force effort and spent a great deal of time with Ted Childs, formerly IBM's vice president of Global Workforce Diversity and Gerstner's primary partner in guiding this change process. What they described was a significant philosophical shift—from a long tradition of minimizing differences to amplifying them and to seizing on the business opportunities they presented.

CONSTRUCTIVE DISRUPTION

Gerstner knew that he needed to signal that diversity was a strategic goal, and he knew that establishing task forces would make a powerful impression on employees. Early in his tenure, Gerstner had convened various task forces to resolve a range of strategic choices and issues. He used the same structure to refine and achieve IBM's diversity-related objectives.

Gerstner and Childs wanted people to understand that this was truly something new. IBM had a long practice of being blind to differences and gathering demographic information only to ensure that hiring and promotion decisions did not favor any particular group. So this new approach of calling attention to differences, with the hope of learning from them and making improvements to the business, was a radical departure. To effectively deliver the message and signal dramatic change, IBM kicked off the task forces on Bastille Day, July 14, 1995. "We chose Bastille Day...because it's considered to be a historic day of social disruption," Childs told me. "We were looking for some constructive disruption."

Each task force comprised 15–20 senior managers, cutting across the company's business units, each from one of the following demographic employee constituencies: Asian; black (African American and of African descent); GLBT; Hispanic; white male; Native American; disabled; and female. To be eligible, members had to meet two criteria: each had to be of executive rank and a member of the constituency.

(Three of the groups—disabled, Native American, and GLBT employees—did not have enough representation in the executive ranks to fill the task forces, so membership also included mid-level managers.) Members were chosen by Ted Childs and Tom Bouchard, then senior vice president (SVP) of human resources, based on their knowledge of and experiences with the top executive team. In particular, Childs sought executives who had spoken to him or to a colleague in his office about their own experiences and perceptions that diversity was an untapped business resource; he persuaded those individuals to participate by describing the effort as a chance to make a difference and to eliminate some of the roadblocks that they may have faced in their careers.

Each task force also had two or more executive co-chairs who were members of the constituency. For these roles, Childs and Bouchard recruited high-performing, well-respected senior managers and junior executives who were at least at the director level. Each task force was also assigned an executive sponsor from the WMC, who was charged with learning about the relevant constituency's concerns, opportunities, and strategies, and with serving as a liaison to top management. The executive sponsors were senior vice presidents, and most reported directly to Gerstner. They were selected by Bouchard and Childs based on their willingness to support the change process and on the potential for synergies within their given business areas.

The first sponsor of the women's task force, for instance, was the SVP of sales and marketing worldwide. Childs knew that the company's senior executives believed that potential buyers in many countries outside of the United States would not work with female executives and that this could interfere with women's success in international assignments. By connecting this SVP with the women's task force, Bouchard and Childs hoped that these barriers could be better understood—and that opportunities for women to advance in the sales organization might improve. Similarly, the SVP for research and development was asked to sponsor the people with disabilities task force, with the expectation that if he could get closer to the day-to-day experiences of people with disabilities in his own organization, then he would gain new insights into the development of accessible products.

Sponsors were not necessarily constituents of their groups. The sponsor for the white men's task force was a woman; the sponsor for the women's task force was a man. Indeed, there was a certain advantage to having sponsors who did not come from the groups they represented. It meant that they and the task force members would have to learn from their differences. A sponsor would have to dig deep into the issues of the task force to represent its views and interests to other WMC members.

In addition to having a sponsor, co-chairs, and members, each task force was assigned one or two HR employees and a senior HR executive for administrative support, as well as a lawyer for legal guidance. The groups also received logistical and research support from Childs's Global Workforce Diversity unit, which was responsible for all of IBM's equal employment and work/life balance programs.

Once the task forces had been set up and launched, Bouchard sent an e-mail to every US employee detailing the task forces and their missions, and underscoring how important the initiative was to the company. In his message, he acknowledged IBM's heritage of respecting diversity and defined the new effort in business terms. Here is an excerpt from the e-mail:

> To sustain [IBM's recognition for diversity leadership] and strengthen our competitive edge, we have launched eight executive-led task forces representing the following IBM employee constituencies... We selected these communities because collectively they are IBM, and they reflect the diversity of our marketplace.

He also encouraged employees to respond with specific suggestions of how to make IBM a more inclusive environment. Childs then compiled more than 2,000 responses to the e-mail and channeled them to the appropriate task forces. As a result of these suggestions, the task forces focused on the following areas for evaluation and improvement: communications, staffing, employee benefits, workplace flexibility, training and education, advertising and marketplace opportunities, and external relations.

The initial charge of the task forces was to take six months to research and report back to the CEO and the WMC on four questions: "What is necessary for your constituency to feel welcome and valued at IBM?" "What can the corporation do, in partnership with your group, to maximize your constituency's productivity?" "What can the corporation do to influence your constituency's buying decisions, so that IBM is seen as a preferred solution provider?" And "which external organizations should IBM form relationships with to better understand the needs of your constituency?"

At first, skepticism prevailed. Here is what one white male executive told me:

> This whole idea of bringing together people in the workplace and letting them form these groups was really repugnant on its face to a lot of people, and of course IBM had been a nonunion company in the United States for a long, long time. I mean, having groups was like letting them into your living room.

And from a black executive:

> I was somewhat skeptical, and there was a level of reluctance in terms of how successful this would ultimately become in IBM, given some of the complex issues around the topic of diversity.

The groups also faced other challenges. When the women's task force met for the first time, many members were relieved to hear that some of their colleagues were sharing similar struggles to balance work and family; at the same time, some of IBM's women believed strongly that female executives should choose between having children and having a career. The dissenting opinions made it more difficult to present a united front to the rest of senior management and to secure support for the group's initiatives.

Task force members also disagreed on tactics. Some within the black task force, for instance, advocated for a conservative approach, fearing that putting a spotlight on the group would be perceived as asking for unearned preferences and, even worse, might encourage the stereotype that black employees are less capable. But most in the group felt that more aggressive action would be needed to break down the barriers facing black employees at IBM.

In both cases, the members engaged in lengthy dialogue to understand various points of view and, in light of very real deadlines for reporting back, were forced to agree on concrete proposals for accomplishing sometimes competing goals. The women's group concluded that IBM needed to partner with its female employees in making work and family life more compatible. The black group decided it needed to clarify the link between its concerns and those of the company—making it clear that the members were raising business issues and that the task force effort was not intended to favor any group.

During the six months of the initial phase, Childs checked in with each group periodically and held monthly meetings to ensure that each was staying focused. The check-ins were also meant to facilitate information sharing across groups, especially if several were grappling with similar issues. The task forces' work involved collecting data from their constituencies, examining internal archival data to identify personnel trends, and reviewing external data to understand IBM's labor and customer markets. Their most critical task was to interpret the data as a means of identifying solutions and opportunities for IBM. Task forces met several times a month, in subcommittees or in their entirety, and at the end of the research period Childs met with each group to determine its top issues—or the "vital few." (See Exhibit 1 "The Vital Few Issues: Employees' Biggest Diversity Concerns.") These were defined as the issues and concerns that were of greatest importance to the group and which would have the most impact if addressed. Childs and the taskforce co-chairs also realized that not addressing these issues would hamper the credibility of the initiative with frontline employees.

On December 1, 1995, the task forces met to share their initial findings. Again, the date was chosen with the idea of sending a message to employees: it was the 40th anniversary of Rosa Parks's refusal to give up her seat on a bus in Montgomery, Alabama, to a white passenger. That act, of course, led to her arrest, and this ignited the Montgomery bus boycotts that ushered in the modern US civil rights movement. Just as the Bastille Day launch signaled a release from old ways of thinking, the timing of this meeting indicated a desire for a radically new approach to diversity.

Several of the task forces shared many of the same issues, such as development and promotion, senior management's communication of its commitment to diversity, and the need to focus on recruiting a diverse pool of employees, especially in engineering and science-related positions. Other concerns were specific to particular groups, including domestic partner benefits (identified by the GLBT task force) and issues of access to buildings and technology (raised by the people with disabilities task force). Overall, the findings made it clear that workforce diversity was the bridge between the workplace and the marketplace—in other words, greater diversity in the workplace could help IBM attract a more diverse customer set. A focus on diversity was, in short, a major business opportunity.

EXHIBIT 1. The vital few issues: employees' biggest diversity
          concerns

Charged with getting to know their constituencies' needs and concerns, IBM's eight diversity task forces gathered data on personnel trends as well as labor and customer markets for their respective groups. Interpreting that information led to the following list of issues—what IBM called the "vital few," as identified by each of the task forces. The taskforce members then used the vital few to shape their thinking about possible business and development opportunities.

Asian
Stereotyping
Networking and mentoring
Employee development and talent
pipelines
Target advertising and marketing

Black
Representation, retention, and
networking
Education and training
Target advertising and marketing

Employees with Disabilities
Recruiting
Target advertising and marketing
Centralized fund for accommodations
Benefits review
New World HQ building (accessibility)
Online help for self-identification

White Male
Executive accountability
Education and awareness
Aging
Work–life balance

Women
Networking
Career advancement
Succession planning
Work–life balance
Flexibility as a business strategy
Executives' personal commitment to
advancing women
Target advertising and marketing

GLBT
Domestic partner benefits
Education and training
Networking
Target advertising and marketing
Online help for self-identification

Hispanics
Recruiting
Employee development and talent pipelines
Target advertising and marketing

Native American
Recruiting
Community outreach
Networking

All eight task forces recommended that the company create diversity groups beyond those at the executive level. In response, in 1997 IBM formed employee network groups as a way for others in the company to participate. The network groups were to run across constituencies, offering a variety of perspectives on issues that are local or unique to particular units. They were to offer a forum in which employees would interact electronically and in person to discuss issues specific to their constituencies. (For more on these groups, see "Engage Employees.")

Another recommendation, this time put forth by the women's group, aimed to rectify a shortage of women in the talent pipeline in technology, identifying young

ENGAGE EMPLOYEES

IBM's diversity task forces asked that the company allow employees who were not at the executive level to get more involved in the effort. The company did so, and diversity councils and employee network groups were born.

The diversity councils, groups of employees across diverse constituencies, were created specifically to address local or unique diversity issues. Through these 72 councils, IBM sought to ensure that its workforce represented an environment that visibly encouraged and valued the contributions and differences of employees from various backgrounds. The objectives included heightening employee awareness, increasing management sensitivity, and making the most of a diverse workforce. For example, within IBM's research and development and engineering units, specific efforts focused on women and minority retention and development in technology-related jobs.

The network groups came out of a grassroots initiative driven by employees, and they had a broader scope than the task forces or councils. At the time of interviewing, IBM had 160 such groups, in which employees interacted electronically and in person to discuss issues specific to their constituency. The black networks, for instance, were helpful in connecting employees working in areas of the company in which there were few black employees. Those who were part of the networks, especially at facilities located far from urban areas, felt less isolated and reported greater job satisfaction.

While diversity councils and employee network groups were independent from the task forces, all three frequently collaborated. The women's task force started diversity councils and employee network groups globally, all of them in close communication with the task force. One area of focus was the importance of mentoring women globally. IBM regions tailored programs to the needs of women in various locations, the goal being to ensure that they would receive advice, guidance, and support, and share knowledge that relevant to other constituencies. This was accomplished via Web-based mentoring, job shadowing, and group mentoring. Additionally, material was made available on IBM's intranet on effective mentoring relationships, and several Web lectures were been developed on this topic.

girls' tendency to opt out of science and math in school as one of the causes. To encourage girls' interest in these disciplines, in 1999 a group of women engineers and scientists in Endicott, New York, ran a pilot Exploring Interests in Technology and Engineering (EXITE) camp. The program brought together 30 middle-school girls for a week that summer to learn about science and math in a fun, interactive way from female IBM employees. In 2000, the women's task force replicated the program in five other locations throughout the United States, reaching 400 girls, and in 2001 the program expanded internationally. In 2004, IBM was to have a total of 37 EXITE camps worldwide—15 in the United States, one in Canada, eight in Asia-Pacific, six in Europe, and seven in Latin America. After the girls attend camp, they are assigned an IBM female scientist or engineer as a mentor for one year.

Since 1999, IBM has reached 3,000 girls through EXITE camps. In 2003 alone, 900 girls attended, and in 2004, 1,100 will have gone through the program. In collaboration with IBM's technology group, the women's task force also created a steering committee focused not only on retaining women in technology at IBM, but also on attracting female scientists from universities.

As for external initiatives that arose from the task forces, IBM's Market Development (MD) unit came directly out of the groups' responses to the third question: "What can IBM do to influence your constituency's buying decisions, so that the company is seen as a preferred solution provider?" It became clear that IBM was not well positioned in relation to the market's fastest growing entrepreneurial segments — female- and minority-owned businesses. The MD was formed as a unit of the Small and Medium-Sized Business Sales and Marketing division. Initially, the group helped IBM revamp its communications strategy for reaching female- and minority-owned companies. Its role then evolved into identifying and supporting sales and marketing strategies aimed at these important segments.

The MD's efforts have directly translated into hundreds of millions of dollars in new revenue. More important to IBM's senior executives, the MD elevated the company's overall level of cultural competence as it responded to the needs of IBM's diverse customer base. A case in point is advertising, where the MD convened teams from the task forces and the advertising department to create constituency casting guidelines and other communications. These changes helped ensure appropriate representation of constituencies in all aspects of the company's marketing, with the guidelines forming the basis for ongoing discussions about how to reach and relate effectively to IBM's diverse customer base.

In 2001, the people with disabilities (PWD) task force, which initially focused on compliance with accessibility laws, began to think about making the leap from compliance to market initiatives. That same year, Ted Childs arranged for each task force to meet with senior management, including Sam Palmisano, then IBM's president. The PWD taskforce leaders took the opportunity to point out the tremendous market potential in government contracts if IBM were to make its products more accessible. Palmisano agreed, and the PWD task force received the green light it needed to advance its projects.

One reason for the increased focus on accessible technology was that, in June 2001, the US Congress implemented legislation mandating that all new IT equipment and services purchased by federal agencies must be accessible. This legislation — known as "Section 508" — made accessibility a more important decision criterion than price in many bid situations, thus creating an opportunity for accessibility IT leaders to gain market share, charge a price premium, or both, from federal buyers. In addition to legislation, other indicators made it clear that the demand for accessibility was growing: the World Health Organization estimated more than 750 million disabled people across the globe, with a collective buying power of $461 billion, and an increase in the number of aging baby boomers in need of accessible technology.

IBM believed that business opportunities would grow as countries around the world implemented similar legislation. Furthermore, the private-sector opportunity for accessible technology could be far greater than that of the government as companies address a growing aging population. IBM's worldwide Accessibility Centers comprise special teams that evaluate existing or future IBM technologies for their possible use in making products accessible. There are now a total of six IBM Accessibility Centers located in the United States, Europe, and Japan.

PILLARS OF CHANGE

Any major corporate change will succeed only if a few key factors are in place: strong support from company leaders, an employee base that is fully engaged with the initiative, management practices that are integrated and aligned with the effort, and a strong and well-articulated business case for action. IBM's diversity task forces benefited from all four.

Demonstrate Leadership Support

It has become a cliché to say that leadership matters, but the issue merits discussion here because diversity is one of the areas in which executive leadership is often ineffectual. Executives' espoused beliefs are frequently inconsistent with their behavior, and they typically underestimate how much the corporation really needs to change to achieve its diversity goals. This happens because diversity strategies tend to lay out lofty goals without providing the structures to educate senior executives in the specific challenges faced by various constituencies. In addition, these strategies often do not provide models that teach or encourage new behaviors.

IBM took several approaches to helping their executives deepen their awareness and understanding. To begin with, the structure of the task forces—how they operated and who was on them—immersed executive sponsors in the specific challenges faced by the employee constituency groups. The groups were a formal mechanism for learning, endorsed at the highest levels of the company.

Second, the chief diversity officer, Ted Childs, acted as a partner with the CEO, as well as coach and adviser to other executives. In addition to educating them on specific issues, as he did when the company decided to offer domestic partner benefits, Childs also worked to ensure that they behaved in ways that were consistent with the company's diversity strategy. A senior executive described Childs's role as a coach and teacher:

> I know that he's had a number of conversations with very senior people in the company where he's just sat down with them and said, "Listen, you don't get it, and you need to get it. And I care about you, and I care about this company. I care about the people who are affected by the way you're behaving, and so I owe it to you to tell you that. And here's how you don't get it. Here's what you need to do to change.

And third, Gerstner and later Palmisano not only sanctioned the taskforce process, but also actively sought to be role models themselves. A number of the executives that I interviewed were struck by Gerstner's interest and active involvement in the development of high-potential minority and female senior managers and junior executives. He took a personal interest in how they were being mentored and what their next jobs would be. He also challenged assumptions about when people would be ready for general management assignments. In one case, Gerstner and his team were discussing the next job for a high-potential female executive. Most felt that she needed a bigger job in her functional area, but Gerstner felt that the proposed job, while involving more responsibility, would add little to the candidate's development. Instead she was given a general management assignment—and the team got a signal from the CEO about his commitment to diversity. His behavior communicated a sense of appreciation and accountability for people development. Indeed, accountability for results became as critical in this domain as it was for all business goals.

Gerstner also modeled desired behaviors in his interactions with his direct reports. One of them told me this story:

> During a board of directors dinner, I had to go to [my daughter's] "back-to-school night," the one night a year when you meet the teachers. I had been at the board meeting that day. I was going to be at the board meeting the next day. But it was the dinner that posed a problem, and I said, "Lou, I'll do whatever you want, but this is the position I am in," and . . . he didn't even blink. He said, "Go to back-to-school night. That is more important." And then. . .he told the board at dinner why I wasn't there and why it was so important. . .to make it possible for working parents to have very big jobs but still be involved parents. He never told me that he told the board. But the board told me the next day. They . . . said, "You should know that Lou not only said where you were but gave a couple minute talk about how important it was for IBM to act in this way."

CEO leadership and modeling did not stop when Gerstner left. One senior executive who was a more recent arrival to the WMC described how Palmisano communicates the importance of the diversity initiative:

> Executive involvement and buy-in are critical. Sam has played a personal and very important role. He personally asked each task force to come and report its progress and agenda to him. He spent time with the [task force that I sponsor] and had a detailed review of what we are doing on the customer set. What are we focused on internally? How can he help in his role as CEO? He's really made it clear to the senior-level executives that being good at [leading the diversity initiative] is part of our job.

Engage Employees as Partners

While the six-month taskforce effort was consistent with IBM's history of promoting equal opportunity, the use of the taskforce structure to address issues of diversity represented a significant culture shift. IBM was a company that had discouraged employees from organizing around any interest not specifically defined by the requirements of their jobs. The idea of employees organizing to advocate was anathema. One white male executive said, "Does this mean that we can have a communist cell here? Are we going to have hundreds and hundreds of these?" The skepticism reached up to the highest levels. When Childs first proposed the taskforce strategy, Gerstner asked him one question: "Why?"

But, in the end, IBM's taskforce structure paved the way for employee buy-in because executives then had to invite constituent groups to partner with them in addressing the diversity challenge. The partnerships worked because three essential components were in place: mutual expectations, mutual influence, and trust.

When the task forces were commissioned, Childs and Gerstner set expectations and made sure that roles and responsibilities were unambiguous. Initially, the task forces' charters were short, only six months (the groups are still active today), and their mission was clear: to explore the issues, opportunities, and strategies affecting their constituencies and customers. Once this work was done, it fell to the corporation's senior executives to respond and to report to the WMC on the task forces' progress at various junctures. Gerstner and Childs followed up with the taskforce sponsors to ensure that the groups were gathering meaningful information and connecting it to the business.

The task forces' work evolved to focus on more tactical issues, and the organization demonstrated its willingness to be influenced, committing significant resources to efforts suggested by the groups. Trust was also built as the taskforce structure allowed employees more face time with executives—executives they would likely not have had a chance to meet—and provided new opportunities for mentoring. According to one taskforce participant:

> What got me to trust that this was a real commitment by the WMC was when I saw them ask for our advice, engage us in dialogue, and then take action. They didn't just do whatever we said, but the rationale for actions was always shared. It made me feel like our opinions were respected as business-people who bring a particular perspective to business challenges.

The taskforce structure was copied on a smaller scale within specific business units. Even without a mandate from corporate brass, most units created their own diversity councils, offering local support for achieving each unit's specific diversity goals. Here, too, the employee partnership model prevailed.

Integrate Diversity with Management Practices

Sustaining change requires diversity to become an integrated part of the company's management practices. This was a priority for Gerstner, who told me:

> If you were to go back and look at ten years' worth of executive committee discussions, you would find two subjects, and only two, that appeared on

every one of the agendas. One was the financial performance, led by our CFO. The second was a discussion of management changes, promotions, moves, and so on, led by our HR person.

In my interviews, among the most frequently mentioned diversity-related HR practice was the "5-minute drill," which began with Gerstner's top team and cascaded down from the chairman to two levels down from CEO. The drill took place during the discussion of management talent at the corporate and business unit levels. During meetings of the senior team, executives were expected at any moment to be able to discuss any high-potential manager. According to the interviewees, an explicit effort was made to ensure that minorities and females were discussed along with white males. The result was to make the executives more accountable for spotting and grooming high-potential minority managers, both in their own areas and across the business. Once it was made explicit that IBM executives were required to watch for female and minority talent, they became more open to considering and promoting these individuals when looking to fill executive jobs.

Managing diversity was also one of the core competencies used to assess managers' performance, and it was included in the mandatory training and orientation of new managers. As one executive responsible for designing parts of this leadership curriculum commented, "We want people to understand that effectively managing and developing a diverse workforce is an integral part of what it means to manage at IBM."

Both Gerstner and Palmisano were clear that holding managers accountable for diversity-related results was key. Gerstner noted, "We did not set quotas, but we did set goals and made people aware of the people in their units who they needed to be accountable for developing." And Palmisano said:

> I reinforce to our executives that this is not HR's responsibility; it is up to us to make sure that we are developing our talent. There is a problem if, at the end of the day, that pool of talent is not diverse.

Link Diversity Goals to Business Goals

From the beginning, Gerstner and Childs insisted that the taskforce effort create a link between IBM's diversity goals and its business goals—that this would be good business, not good philanthropy. The taskforce efforts led to a series of significant accomplishments.

For instance, IBM's efforts to develop the client base among women-owned businesses quickly expanded to include a focus on Asian, black, Hispanic, mature (senior citizens), and Native American markets. The MD unit grew revenue in the company's Small and Medium-Sized Business Sales and Marketing division from $10 million in 1998 to hundreds of millions of dollars in 2003.

Another result of the task forces' work was to create executive partner programs targeting demographic customer segments. In 2001, IBM began assigning executives to develop relationships with the largest women- and minority-owned businesses in the United States. This was important not only because these business sectors are growing fast, but also because their leaders are often highly visible role models, and their IT needs will grow and become increasingly more sophisticated. At the time of interviewing, these assignments had already yielded impressive revenue streams with several of these companies.

The taskforce effort also affected IBM's approach to supplier diversity. While the company had for decades fostered relationships with minority-owned businesses as well as businesses owned by disabled people, the work of the task forces expanded the focus of IBM's supplier diversity program to a broader set of constituencies and provided new insights on the particular challenges each faced. The purpose of the supplier diversity program was to create a level playing field. It is important to note, though, that procurement contracts were awarded based on the merits of the bid—including price and quality—not on the diversity of the vendor. In 2003, IBM did business worth more than $1.5 billion with more than 500 diverse suppliers, up from $370 million in 1998.

• • •

The cynics came around. One black executive said, "Yes, I think [the initiative] has been extremely effective if you look at where we started back in the mid-nineties. I can tell you that I was somewhat skeptical [at first]." Another commented on the growing acceptance of the effort across IBM: "You can see that support actually changed over time from 'I'm not sure what this is about' to . . . a complete understanding that diversity and the focus on diversity make good business sense."

Perhaps the best evidence of the task forces' success is that the initiative not only continued, but also spread and had lasting impact. In more than one instance, after an executive became a taskforce sponsor, his or her division or business unit made significant progress on its own diversity goals. Leaders of some of the task forces described seeing their sponsors grow in terms of their ability to understand, articulate, and take action on the issues identified by their groups. One executive described how the taskforce sponsor experience had been important for him as a business leader and personally, as well as for IBM:

> There is no doubt that this is critical for how we manage the research organization, because of the need for diverse thought. It has affected me substantially because. . .I became involved with diverse populations outside of IBM that I may well not have been connected with if it hadn't been for my involvement with the task force. I'm on the Gallaudet University [school for the deaf] board. Without the task force, I would have never thought of it. And so this has been a terrific awakening, a personal awakening. . . . Since it's focusing particularly on accessibility, we can help in a lot of ways with technology for accessibility, and Gallaudet turns out to be, for the subset of people who are hearing impaired, a terrific place to prototype solutions in this space.

Such comments were not atypical. In many instances, the sponsorship experience was developmental in important and unexpected ways. Having eight task forces meant that, in a group of 52 top leaders, there was always a critical mass strategically connected to the issues. At the time of interviewing, more than half of the WMC members had been engaged with the in the role of sponsor or leader prior to being promoted to the senior executive level.

For IBM, that makes good business sense. The entire effort was designed to help the company develop deeper insights into its major markets, with a direct tie to two of Gerstner's central dictates: IBM needed to get closer to its customers and become more externally focused; and it needed to focus on talent—attracting, retaining, developing, and promoting the best people. On both measures, the company came a long way.

Mansour Javidan, Peter W. Dorfman, Mary Sully de Luque, and Robert J. House*

IN THE EYE OF THE BEHOLDER: CROSS-CULTURAL LESSONS IN LEADERSHIP FROM PROJECT GLOBE

EXECUTIVE OVERVIEW

G LOBAL LEADERSHIP HAS BEEN identified as a critical success factor for large multinational corporations. While there is much writing on the topic, most seems to be either general advice (i.e. being open minded and respectful of other cultures) or very specific information about a particular country based on a limited case study (do not show the soles of your shoes when seated as a guest in an Arab country). Both kinds of information are certainly useful, but limited from both theoretical and practical viewpoints on how to lead in a foreign country. In this reading, findings from the Global Leadership and Organizational Behavior Effectiveness (GLOBE) research program are used to provide a sound basis for conceptualizing worldwide leadership differences. We use a hypothetical case of an American executive in charge of four similar teams in Brazil, France, Egypt, and China to discuss cultural implications for the American executive. Using the hypothetical case involving five different countries allows us to provide in-depth action-oriented and context-specific advice, congruent with GLOBE findings, for effectively interacting with employees from different cultures. We end the reading with a discussion of the challenges facing global executives and how corporations can develop useful global leadership capabilities.

IMPACT OF GLOBALIZATION

Almost no American corporation is immune from the impact of globalization. The reality for American corporations is that they must increasingly cope with diverse cross-cultural employees, customers, suppliers, competitors, and creditors, a situation well captured by the following quote:

> So I was visiting a businessman in downtown Jakarta the other day and I asked for directions to my next appointment. His exact instructions were: "Go to the building with the Armani Emporium upstairs—you know, just above the Hard Rock Cafe—and then turn right at McDonald's." I just looked at him and laughed, "Where am I?"
>
> Thomas Friedman, *New York Times*, July 14, 1997

Notwithstanding Tom Friedman's astonishment about the global world in Jakarta, the fact is that people are not generally aware of the tremendous impact that national culture has on their vision and interpretation of the world. Because culture colors nearly every aspect of human behavior, a working knowledge of culture and its influences can be useful to executives operating in a multicultural business environment. It is a truism by now that large corporations need executives with global mindsets and cross-cultural leadership abilities. Foreign sales by multinational corporations have exceeded $7 trillion and are growing 20 percent to 30 percent faster than their sales of exports.[1] But while the importance of such business grows, 85 percent of Fortune 500 companies have reported a shortage of global managers with the necessary skills.[2] Some experts have argued that most US companies are not positioned to implement global strategies due to a lack of global leadership capabilities.[3]

How can companies best use the available information for executive development and, moreover, what is the validity and value of such information? US and European executives have plenty of general advice available to them on how to perform in foreign settings. During the past few years, much has been written about global leadership, including several books.[4] Journals are also getting into the global action as seen in *The Human Resource Management Journal*, which recently published a special issue on global leadership.[5] Nevertheless, in a recent review of the literature, Morrison concluded that despite the importance of global leadership, "relatively little research has thus far been carried out on global leadership characteristics, competencies, antecedents, and developmental strategies."[6]

Advice to global managers needs to be specific enough to help them understand how to act in different surroundings. For example, managers with an overseas assignment are frequently exhorted to have an open mind and to show respect for other cultures.[7] They may also be told of the importance of cross-cultural relationship management and communication. Some will wrestle with the idea that they need to develop a global perspective while being responsive to local concerns.[8] Or they may wonder if they have the "cognitive complexity" and psychological maturity to handle life and work in a foreign setting. And they are likely to hear or read that they must "walk in the shoes of people from different cultures" in order to be effective.[9] There is nothing wrong with such advice, and the scholars and writers who proffer it have often been pioneers in the field. But it is insufficient for a manager who is likely to assume, mistakenly, that being open-minded in Atlanta, Helsinki, and Beijing will be perceived identically, or that walking in someone else's shoes will feel the same in

Houston, Jakarta, and Madrid. Because of the lack of scientifically compiled information, businesspeople have not had sufficiently detailed and context-specific suggestions about how to handle these cross-cultural challenges. This is a particular problem for those in leadership positions.

Although there are universal aspects of leadership, information about which will be presented shortly, people in different countries do in fact have different criteria for assessing their leaders.[10] The issue for the American manager is whether the attributes that made him or her successful as a leader in the US will also lead to success overseas, be of no value, or, worst of all, cause harm in the foreign operation. Using the findings from an extensive research effort known as the Global Leadership and Organizational Behavior Effectiveness (GLOBE) Project, this reading provides a few answers to the questions about the universal and culture specific aspects of leadership. We will present specific information about key cultural differences among nations and connect the "dots" on how these differences influence leadership. This information should help a typical global executive better understand the leadership challenges s/he faces while managing operations outside the US. It will also provide suggestions on how to more effectively cope with such challenges.

To make the GLOBE findings come alive, we will follow a hypothetical American executive who has been given two years to lead a project based in four different countries: Brazil, France, Egypt, and China. This hypothetical project involves developing a somewhat similar product for the four different markets. The project team in each country is tasked with the marketing of a new technology in the telecommunications industry. The executive will work with local employees in each location. Success will be determined by two criteria: the executive's ability to produce results and to show effective leadership in different cultures and settings.

The four countries represent different continents and very diverse cultures. Brazil is the most populous and economically important South American country. France is the largest, most populous, and most economically developed Latin European country. Egypt is the largest and most populous Arab country. China is the fast-growing giant economy with unprecedented growth in its economic and diplomatic power in the world. We chose these countries to provide context-specific analysis leading to general recommendations for global executives. Our choice of countries was guided by our efforts to cover a wide range of cultures. Before turning to our hypothetical scenario, we will examine common cultural dimensions that characterize nations and discuss why these dimensions are important for the development of global leaders.

COMMON CULTURAL DIMENSIONS

To be open-minded and to understand the cultures of the different countries, managers need to be able to compare their own cultures with those of other countries. After a review of the available literature, especially the work of Hofstede, Trompenaars, and Kluckhohn and Strodt-beck,[11] GLOBE conceptualized and developed measures of nine cultural dimensions. These are aspects of a country's culture that distinguish one society from another and have important managerial implications. While a few of these dimensions are similar to the work of other researchers, the manner in which we conceptualized and operationalized them was different.[12] We reconceptualized a few existing dimensions and developed a few new dimensions. In all cases, the scales designed to capture and measure these cultural dimensions passed very rigorous psychometric tests. A brief description of each cultural dimension is provided below along with the basic research design of GLOBE. Further details can be found on GLOBE's website, www.thunderbird.edu/wwwfiles/ms/globe/.

It might be noted that the GLOBE Project has been called "the most ambitious study of global leadership."[13] Our worldwide team of scholars proposed and validated an integrated theory of the relationship between culture and societal, organizational, and leadership effectiveness. The 170 researchers worked together for ten years collecting and analyzing data on cultural values and practices and leadership attributes from over 17,000 managers in 62 societal cultures. The participating managers were employed in telecommunications, food, and banking industries. As one output from the project, the 62 cultures were ranked with respect to nine dimensions of their cultures. We studied the effects of these dimensions on expectations of leaders, as well as on organizational practices in each society. The 62 societal cultures were also grouped into a more parsimonious set of ten culture clusters (list provided in the next section). GLOBE studies cultures in terms of their cultural practices (the ways things are) and their cultural values (the way things should be). The nine cultural attributes (hereafter called culture dimensions) are:

- **Performance Orientation.** The degree to which a collective encourages and rewards (and should encourage and reward) group members for performance improvement and excellence. In countries such as the US and Singapore that score high on this cultural practice, businesses are likely to emphasize training and development; in countries that score low, such as Russia and Greece, family and background count for more.
- **Assertiveness.** The degree to which individuals are (and should be) assertive, confrontational, and aggressive in their relationships with others. People in highly assertive countries such as the US and Austria tend to have can-do attitudes and enjoy competition in business; those in less assertive countries such as Sweden and New Zealand prefer harmony in relationships and emphasize loyalty and solidarity.
- **Future Orientation.** The extent to which individuals engage (and should engage) in future-oriented behaviors such as delaying gratification, planning, and investing in the future. Organizations in countries with high future oriented practices such as Singapore and Switzerland tend to have longer-term horizons and more systematic planning processes, but they tend to be averse to risk-taking and opportunistic decision-making. In contrast, corporations in the least future-oriented countries such as Russia and Argentina tend to be less systematic and more opportunistic in their actions.
- **Humane Orientation.** The degree to which a collective encourages and rewards (and should encourage and reward) individuals for being fair, altruistic, generous, caring, and kind to others. Countries such as Egypt and Malaysia rank very high on this cultural practice and countries such as France and Germany rank low.

- **Institutional Collectivism.** The degree to which organizational and societal institutional practices encourage and reward (and should encourage and reward) collective distribution of resources and collective action. Organizations in collectivistic countries such as Singapore and Sweden tend to emphasize group performance and rewards, whereas those in the more individualistic countries such as Greece and Brazil tend to emphasize individual achievement and rewards.
- **In-Group Collectivism.** The degree to which individuals express (and should express) pride, loyalty, and cohesiveness in their organizations or families. Societies such as Egypt and Russia take pride in their families and also take pride in the organizations that employ them.
- **Gender Egalitarianism.** The degree to which a collective minimizes (and should minimize) gender inequality. Not surprisingly, European countries generally had the highest scores on gender egalitarianism practices. Egypt and South Korea were among the most male-dominated societies in GLOBE. Organizations operating in gender egalitarian societies tend to encourage tolerance for diversity of ideas and individuals.
- **Power Distance.** The degree to which members of a collective expect (and should expect) power to be distributed equally. A high power distance score reflects unequal power distribution in a society. Countries that scored high on this cultural practice are more stratified economically, socially, and politically; those in positions of authority expect, and receive, obedience. Firms in high power distance countries such as Thailand, Brazil, and France tend to have hierarchical decision making processes with limited one-way participation and communication.
- **Uncertainty Avoidance.** The extent to which a society, organization, or group relies (and should rely) on social norms, rules, and procedures to alleviate unpredictability of future events. The greater the desire to avoid uncertainty, the more people seek orderliness, consistency, structure, formal procedures, and laws to cover situations in their daily lives. Organizations in high uncertainty avoidance countries such as Singapore and Switzerland tend to establish elaborate processes and procedures and prefer formal detailed strategies. In contrast, firms in low uncertainty avoidance countries such as Russia and Greece tend to prefer simple processes and broadly stated strategies. They are also opportunistic and enjoy risk-taking.

REGIONAL CLUSTERING OF GLOBE NATIONS

GLOBE was able to empirically verify ten culture clusters from the 62-culture sample. These culture clusters were identified as: Latin America, Anglo, Latin Europe (e.g. Italy), Nordic Europe, Germanic Europe, Confucian Asia, Sub-Saharan Africa, Middle East, Southern Asia, and Eastern Europe. Each culture cluster differs with respect to the nine culture dimensions (e.g. performance orientation). Table 1 shows a summary of how the clusters compare in terms of their scores on cultural practices.

The clusters that are relevant to this reading are in bold. For instance, clusters scoring highest in performance orientation were Confucian Asia, Germanic Europe

Table 1. Cultural clusters classified on societal culture practices (as is) scores

Cultural Dimension	High-Score Clusters	Mid-Score Clusters	Low-Score Clusters	Cluster-Average Range
Performance Orientation	**Confucian Asia** Germanic Europe Anglo	Southern Asia Sub-Saharan Africa Latin Europe Nordic Europe Middle East	**Latin America** Eastern Europe	3.73–4.58
Assertiveness	Germanic Europe Eastern Europe	Sub-Saharan Africa **Latin America Anglo** Middle East Confucian Asia Latin Europe Southern Asia	Nordic Europe	3.66–4.55
Future Orientation	Germanic Europe Nordic Europe	**Confucian Asia Anglo** Southern Asia Sub-Saharan Africa Latin Europe	**Middle East Latin America** Eastern Europe	3.38–4.40
Humane Orientation	Southern Asia Sub-Saharan Africa	**Middle East Anglo** Nordic Europe Latin America Confucian Asia Eastern Europe	**Latin Europe** Germanic Europe	3.55–4.71
Institutional Collectivism	Nordic Europ Confucian Asia	**Anglo** Southern Asia Sub-Saharan Africa Middle East Eastern Europe	Germanic Europe Latin Europe **Latin America**	3.86–4.88
In-Group Collectivism	Southern Asia Middle East Eastern Europe Latin America Confucian Asia	Sub-Saharan Africa Latin Europe	**Anglo** Germanic Europe Nordic Europe	3.75–5.87
Gender Egalitarianism	Eastern Europ Nordic Europe	**Latin America Anglo** Latin Europe Sub-Saharan Africa Southern Asia Confucian Asia Germanic Europe	Middle East	2.95–3.84
Power Distance		Southern Asia Latin America Eastern Europe Sub-Saharan Africa Middle East Latin Europe Confucian Asia **Anglo** Germanic Europe	Nordic Europe	4.54–5.39
Uncertainty Avoidance	Nordic Europe Germanic Europe	**Confucian Asia Anglo** Sub-Saharan Africa Latin Europe Southern Asia	**Middle East Latin America** Eastern Europe	3.56–5.19

NOTE: Means of high-score clusters are significantly higher ($p < 0.05$) than the rest, means of low-score clusters are significantly lower ($p < 0.05$) than the rest, and means of mid-score clusters are not significantly different from the rest ($p > 0.05$).

and Anglo (the US and the UK among other English-speaking countries). Clusters scoring lowest in performance orientation were Latin America and Eastern Europe. The Appendix shows the actual country scores for the six clusters in this reading.

MANAGING AND LEADING IN DIFFERENT COUNTRIES

Given the differences found in cultures around the globe, what does an effective American manager need to do differently in different countries? Everything, nothing, or only certain things? From a leadership perspective, we can ask whether the same attributes that lead to successful leadership in the US lead to success in other countries. Or are they irrelevant or, even worse, dysfunctional? In the following sections, we will answer these questions. We will examine some similarities and differences among cultures regarding management and leadership practices. We then assert that many of the leadership differences found among cultures stem from implicit leadership beliefs held by members of different nations.

Expatriate managers working in multinational companies hardly need to be reminded of the wide variety of management practices found around the world. Laurent, and more recently Trompenaars and Briscoe and Schuler,[14] document the astonishing diversity of organizational practices worldwide, many of which are acceptable and considered effective in one country but ineffective in another country. For instance, supervisors are expected to have precise answers to subordinates' questions in Japan, but less so in the US. As another example, the effectiveness of working alone or in a group is perceived very differently around the world; this would certainly influence the quality, aptitude, and fair evaluation of virtual teams found in multinational organizations.[15] An inescapable conclusion is that acceptable management practices found in one country are hardly guaranteed to work in a different country. Titus Lokananta, for example, is an Indonesian Cantonese holding a German passport, managing a Mexican multinational corporation producing Gummy Bears in the Czech Republic.[16] What management style will he be most comfortable with, and will it be successful with Czech workers and Mexican CEOs? How does he effectively manage if a conflict evolves between managing his workers and satisfying his supervisors?

Should we, however, conclude that cultural differences are so vast that common management practices among countries are the exception rather than the rule and will ever remain so? Not necessarily. Companies are forced to share information, resources, and training in a global economy. The best business schools educate managers from all over the world in the latest management techniques. Using academic jargon, the issue of common versus unique business and management practices is framed using contrasting perspectives embodied in the terms *cultural universals* versus *cultural specifics*. The former are thought to be found from the process of cultural convergence whereas the latter from maintaining cultural divergence. Perhaps not surprisingly, empirical research supports both views. For example, in their event management leadership research program Smith and Peterson found both commonalities and differences across cultures in the manner by which managers handled relatively routine events in their work.[17] All managers preferred to rely on their own experience and training if appointing a new subordinate, relative to other influences such as consultation with others or using formal rules and procedures. However, there were major differences in countries in the degree to which managers used formal company rules and procedures in contrast to more informal networks, and these differences co-vary with national cultural values.[18] As another example, Hazucha and colleagues[19] found a good deal of similarity among European countries regarding the importance of core management competencies for a Euromanager. Yet there were significant differences among countries in the perceived attainment of these skills. Javidan and Carl have recently shown important similarities and differences among Canadian, Taiwanese, and Iranian managers in terms of their leadership styles.[20]

Should we also expect that leadership processes, like management practices, are similarly influenced by culture? The answer is yes; substantial empirical evidence indicates that leader attributes, behavior, status, and influence vary considerably as a result of culturally unique forces in the countries or regions in which the leaders function.[21] But, as the colloquial saying goes "the devil is in the details," and current cross-cultural theory is inadequate to clarify and expand on the diverse cultural universals and cultural specifics elucidated in cross-cultural research. Some researchers subscribe to the philosophy that the primary impact of culture depends on the level of analysis used in the research program. That is, some view the basic functions of leadership as having universal importance and applicability, but the specific ways in which leadership functions are enacted are strongly affected by cultural variation.[22] Other researchers, including the contributors to this reading, question this basic assumption, subscribing more to the viewpoint that cultural specifics are real and woe to the leader who ignores them.

DO REQUIRED LEADERSHIP QUALITIES DIFFER AMONG NATIONS?

It has been pointed out that managerial leadership differences (and similarities) among nations may be the result of the citizens' implicit assumptions regarding requisite leadership qualities.[23] According to implicit leadership theory (ILT), individuals hold a set of beliefs about the kinds of attributes, personality characteristics, skills, and behaviors that contribute to or impede outstanding leadership. These belief systems, variously referred to as prototypes, cognitive categories, mental models, schemas, and stereotypes in the broader social cognitive literature, are assumed to affect the extent to which an individual accepts and responds to others as leaders.[24]

GLOBE extended ILT to the cultural level of analysis by arguing that the structure and content of these belief systems will be shared among individuals in common cultures. We refer to this shared cultural level analog of individual implicit leader-ship theory (ILT) as *culturally endorsed implicit leadership theory* (CLT). GLOBE empirically identified universally perceived leadership attributes that are contributors to or inhibitors of outstanding leadership. Project GLOBE's leadership questionnaire items consisted of 112 behavioral and attribute descriptors (e.g. "intelligent") that were hypothesized to either facilitate or impede outstanding leadership. Accompanying each item was a short phrase designed to help interpret the item. Items were rated on a 7-point Likert-type scale that ranged from a low of 1 (this behavior or characteristic greatly inhibits a person from being an outstanding leader) to a high of 7 (this behavior or characteristic contributes greatly to a person being an outstanding leader). Project GLOBE also empirically reduced the huge number of leadership attributes into a much more understandable, comprehensive grouping of 21 primary and then 6 global leadership dimensions. The 6 global leadership dimensions differentiate cultural profiles of desired leadership qualities, hereafter referred to as a CLT profile. Convincing evidence from GLOBE research showed that people within cultural groups agree in their beliefs about leadership; these beliefs are represented by a set of CLT *leadership profiles* developed for each national culture and cluster of cultures. For detailed descriptions of the statistical processes used to form the 21 primary and 6 global leadership dimensions and development of CLT profiles, see House et al.[25] Using the six country scenarios, in the last half of this reading we will show the range of leadership responses that should be effective in each cultural setting. The six dimensions of the CLT leadership profiles are:

1. **Charismatic/Value-Based.** A broadly defined leadership dimension that reflects the ability to inspire, to motivate, and to expect high performance outcomes from others on the basis of firmly held core beliefs. Charismatic/value-based leadership is generally reported to contribute to outstanding leadership. The highest reported score is in the Anglo cluster (6.05); the lowest score in the Middle East cluster (5.35 out of a 7-point scale).

2. **Team-Oriented.** A leadership dimension that emphasizes effective team building and implementation of a common purpose or goal among team members. Team-oriented leadership is generally reported to contribute to outstanding leadership (highest score in Latin American cluster (5.96); lowest score in Middle East cluster (5.47)).

3. **Participative.** A leadership dimension that reflects the degree to which managers involve others in making and implementing decisions. Participative leadership is generally reported to contribute to outstanding leadership, although there are meaningful differences among countries and clusters (highest score in Germanic Europe cluster (5.86); lowest score in Middle East cluster (4.97)).

4. **Humane-Oriented.** A leadership dimension that reflects supportive and considerate leadership but also includes compassion and generosity. Humane-oriented leadership is reported to be almost neutral in some societies and to moderately contribute to outstanding leadership in others (highest score in Southern Asia cluster (5.38); lowest score in Nordic Europe cluster (4.42)).

5. **Autonomous.** This newly defined leadership dimension, which has not previously appeared in the literature, refers to independent and individualistic leadership. Autonomous leadership is reported to range from impeding outstanding leadership to slightly facilitating outstanding leadership (highest score in Eastern Europe cluster (4.20); lowest score in Latin America cluster (3.51)).

6. **Self-Protective.** From a Western perspective, this newly defined leadership dimension focuses on ensuring the safety and security of the individual. It is self-centered and face-saving in its approach. Self-protective leadership is generally reported to impede outstanding leadership (highest score in Southern Asia cluster (3.83); lowest in Nordic Europe cluster (2.72)).

Table 2 presents CLT scores for all 10 clusters. Analysis of Variance (ANOVA) was used to determine if the cultures and clusters differed with respect to their CLT leadership profiles. Results indicate that cultures (i.e. 62 societal cultures) and clusters (i.e. 10 groups consisting of the 62 societal cultures) differed with respect to all six CLT leadership dimensions ($p < .01$).

Table 3 presents summary comparisons among culture clusters to indicate which clusters are most likely to endorse or refute the importance of the six CLT leadership dimensions. Tables 2 and 3 may be used in combination to provide an overall view of how the different cultural clusters compare on the six culturally implicit leadership dimensions.[26]

CROSS-CULTURAL LEADERSHIP IS NOT ONLY ABOUT DIFFERENCES

The global and cross-cultural leadership literature is almost exclusively focused on cultural differences and their implications for managers. There is a basic assumption that leaders operating in different countries will be facing drastically different challenges and requirements. GLOBE surveys show that while different countries do have divergent views on many aspects of leadership effectiveness, they also have convergent views on some other aspects. From the larger group of leader behaviors, we found 22 attributes that were universally deemed to be desirable. Being honest, decisive, motivational, and dynamic are examples of attributes that are believed to facilitate outstanding leadership in all GLOBE countries. Furthermore, we found eight leadership attributes that are universally undesirable. Leaders who are loners, irritable, egocentric, and ruthless are deemed ineffective in all GLOBE countries. Table 4 below shows a few examples of universally desirable, universally undesirable, and culturally contingent leadership attributes.

Identifying universally desirable and undesirable leadership attributes is a critical step in effective cross-cultural leadership. It shows managers that while there are differences among countries, there are also similarities. Such similarities give some degree of comfort and ease to leaders and can be used by them as a foundation to build on. Of course, there may still be differences in how leaders enact such attributes. For example, behaviors that embody dynamic leadership in China may be different from those that denote the same attribute in the US. Current research currently under way by GLOBE team members is focused on this issue.

UNDERSTANDING CULTURALLY CONTINGENT LEADERSHIP

In this section, we will focus on those attributes of leadership that were found to be culturally contingent. These are attributes that may work effectively in one culture but cause harm in others. To provide an action-oriented analysis, we explore differences in effective leadership attributes among the four countries in our hypothetical scenario and discuss specific implications of these differences for our hypothetical American manager. Admittedly, we are being ethnocentric using the American manager as the focal person who finds himself/herself managing in a foreign culture.

Table 2. CLT scores for societal clusters

Societal Cluster	CLT Dimensions					
	Charismatic/ Value-Based	Team Oriented	Participative	Humane Oriented	Autonomous	Self-Protective
Eastern Europe	5.74	5.88	5.08	4.76	4.20	3.67
Latin America	5.99	5.96	5.42	4.85	3.51	3.62
Latin Europe	5.78	5.73	5.37	4.45	3.66	3.19
Confucian Asia	5.63	5.61	4.99	5.04	4.04	3.72
Nordic Europe	5.93	5.77	5.75	4.42	3.94	2.72
Anglo	6.05	5.74	5.73	5.08	3.82	3.08
Sub-Sahara Africa	5.79	5.70	5.31	5.16	3.63	3.55
Southern Asia	5.97	5.86	5.06	5.38	3.99	3.83
Germanic Europe	5.93	5.62	5.86	4.71	4.16	3.03
Middle East	5.35	5.47	4.97	4.80	3.68	3.79

NOTE: CLT leadership scores are absolute scores aggregated to the cluster level.

Table 3. Summary of comparisons for CLT leadership dimensions

Societal Cluster	CLT Leadership Dimensions						
	Charismatic/ Value-Based	Team-Oriented	Participative	Humane Oriented	Autonomous	Self-Protective
Eastern Europe	M	M	L	M	H/H	H
Latin America	H	H	M	M	L	M/H
Latin Europe	M/H	M	M	L	L	M
Confucian Asia	M	M/H	L	M/H	M	H
Nordic Europe	H	M	H	**L**	M	**L**
Anglo	**H**	M	H	H	M	L
Sub-Sahara Africa	M	M	M	H	L	M
Southern Asia	H	M/**H**	L	**H**	M	**H**/H
Germanic Europe	H	M/L	**H**	M	H/**H**	L
Middle East	L	L	L	M	M	H/**H**

NOTES: For letters separated by a "/", the first letter indicates rank with respect to the absolute score, second letter with respect to a response bias corrected score. H = high rank; M = medium rank; L = low rank. H or L (bold) indicates Highest or Lowest cluster score for a specific CLT dimension.

Table 4. Cultural views of leadership effectiveness

The following is a partial list of leadership attributes with the corresponding primary leadership dimension in parentheses:

Universal Facilitators of Leadership Effectiveness
- Being trustworthy, just, and honest (integrity)
- Having foresight and planning ahead (charismatic–visionary)
- Being positive, dynamic, encouraging, motivating, and building confidence (charismatic–inspirational)
- Being communicative, informed, a coordinator, and team integrator (team builder)

Universal Impediments to Leadership Effectiveness
- Being a loner and asocial (self-protective)
- Being non-cooperative and irritable (malevolent)
- Being dictatorial (autocratic)

Culturally Contingent Endorsement of Leader Attributes
- Being individualistic (autonomous)
- Being status conscious (status conscious)
- Being a risk taker (charismatic III: self-sacrificial)

Obviously, expatriate managers are found from virtually all industrialized nations; however, there are over 200,000 US expatriates worldwide.[27] Nevertheless, expatriates from non-American and non-Western countries should be able to identify with cultural differences between their culture and that of the comparison countries. GLOBE cultural data for the five comparison countries can be found in Table 1 and the Appendix. Please note, the US, Brazil, and France are part of the Anglo, Latin American, and Latin European clusters, respectively. Egypt and China are part of the Middle East and Confucian Asia clusters, respectively.

Each section below begins with a summary of how each culture cluster fares with respect to the CLT profile.ß We then show how the countries of interest in this reading compare on specific leadership attributes that are culturally contingent. Next, we examine in detail what these differences mean and what they imply for the hypothetical American executive.

Brazil

Brazil is part of GLOBE's Latin American cluster. Viewing Tables 2 and 3, it is apparent that the CLT leadership dimensions contributing the most to outstanding leadership in this country cluster include charismatic/value-based and team-oriented leadership, followed by the participative and humane-oriented CLT dimensions. Autonomous and self-protective leadership are viewed as slightly negative. Table 3 shows that the Latin America cluster receives the highest rank for the team-oriented dimension, among the highest ranks for charismatic/value-based leadership, and ranks lowest with respect to the autonomous CLT leadership dimension. It occupies the middle ranks for the remaining CLT dimensions.

Figure 1 below contrasts the US and Brazil on the culturally contingent leadership items. Perhaps due to their high in-group collectivism, Brazilian managers intensely dislike the leaders who are individualistic, autonomous, and independent. A Brazilian sales manager working in the petrochemical industry recently reflected this, suggesting, "We do not prefer leaders who take self-governing decisions and act alone without engaging the group. That's part of who we are." While American managers also frown upon these attributes, they do not regard them as negatively as do the Brazilians. An American manager needs to be more cognizant to make sure that his/her actions and decisions are not interpreted as individualistic. He/she needs to ensure that the group or unit feels involved in decision-making and that others' views and reactions are taken into consideration.

On the other hand, Brazilian managers expect their leaders to be class- and status-conscious. They want leaders to be aware of status boundaries and to respect them. A manager in a large company in Brazil noted that blue- and white-collar workers from the same company rarely socialize together within and outside of work. They expect leaders to treat people according to their social and organizational levels. Perhaps due to their high power distance culture, Brazilians believe that people in positions of authority deserve to be treated with respect and deference. They prefer a formal relationship between the leader and followers. The same petrochemical sales manager told how Brazilian subordinates tend to stay outside of the perceived boundaries of their leaders and respect their own decision-making limitations. He added, "It's clear who has the most power in the work environment in Brazil, but in America this is not always the case." Americans tend to frown on status- and class-consciousness. Respect, to an American manager, does not necessarily mean deference but mutual respect and open dialogue. Americans tend to see formality as an obstacle to open

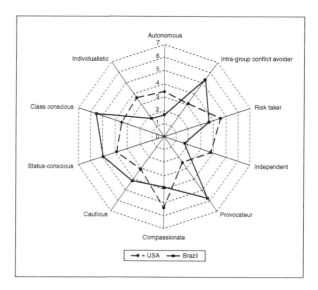

Figure 1. US versus Brazil

debate. But what seems an open debate to an American manager may be viewed as aggressive and unacceptable behavior on the part of the subordinates by a Brazilian manager. So, while Brazilians do not like individualistic leaders, a typical American manager should be cautious using an open style of decision-making. While it may be a good idea in an American organization to directly contact anyone with the right information regardless of their level, such behavior may be seen as a sign of disrespect to those in formal positions in a Brazilian organization.

Another important difference is that American managers prefer a less cautious approach and a greater degree of risk-taking. In contrast, Brazilian managers prefer a somewhat more cautious and risk-averse approach. This is consistent with the finding that US culture is more tolerant of uncertainty than is Brazilian culture. Also, perhaps due to stronger assertiveness and performance orientation in American culture, US managers seem to favor a speedier decision-making process and a higher level of action orientation. Brazilians, on the other hand, may be more sensitive to group harmony and risk avoidance. A Brazilian account manager leading a four-company consortium working on a $200 million US contract with the Federal Department of Roads in Brazil realized this when a conflict occurred among the consortium players. He noted:

> Since our contract was a long-term relationship, we could not focus only on the particular moment. I had to find a way to motivate and to build a trusting environment. The only way to do so was to promote several meetings with all the consortium members trying to find a way to put all the members back together. By doing this, I assumed this was the best action to produce results, no matter how difficult it was or how much time it required.

Still another difference relates to the strong in-group collectivism dimension of the Brazilian culture. They expect their leaders to avoid conflict within the group to protect its harmony, but at the same time they like their leaders to induce conflict with those outside the group. A particularly successful executive working in Brazil told how Brazilians take pride in membership in small groups, especially families. In business, he said that people who are members of the same group expect special treatment (such as price discounts, exclusivity of contracts, etc.). In fact, without these group affiliations, attracting and conducting business can be difficult. American managers seem to dislike both these attributes, perhaps due to their stronger performance-orientation culture. Avoiding internal conflict, simply to maintain group harmony, even at the expense of results, is not a positive attribute to Americans. The typical American view of harmony is reflected in the following quote from the popular book *Execution* by Bossidy and Charan:[28]

> Indeed, harmony—sought out by many leaders who wish to offend no one—can be the enemy of truth. It can squelch critical thinking and drive decision making underground. When harmony prevails, here's how things often get settled: after the key players leave the session, they quietly veto decisions they didn't like but didn't debate on the spot. A good motto to observe is: "Truth over harmony."

Finally, an important and counter-intuitive finding is that American respondents have a much stronger desire for compassion in their leaders. They want their leaders to be empathetic and merciful. The Brazilian respondents, on the other hand, are quite neutral about this attribute. While this seems to go against the conventional stereo-types of Americans and Brazilians, it seems to be rooted in the fact that Brazil is reported to be a less humane culture than is the US. Confirming this finding, one manager stated that this reflects the expectation that people should solve their own problems, relying on help from their family or groups.

When in Brazil...

Here are a few specific ideas on what our hypothetical American manager needs to do when he starts working with his Brazilian team:

Very early on, he needs to spend time meeting with the key executives in the orga-nization, even those who may not be directly relevant to his project. This is an import-ant step because of high power distance and in-group collectivism in that culture. Being a foreigner and a newcomer, it is crucial to show respect to those in positions of power and to start the process of building personal ties and moving into their in-groups. Further, this step helps make sure that the other stakeholders do not view the manag-er's team as being insular, something that is likely to happen in high in-group cultures.

While it is important to work with the individual members of the team, it is also critical to spend as much time as possible with the team as a whole, both in formal work-related occasions and in informal settings. The families of the team members should also be invited to get together on many occasions. They are an important part of the relationships among team members. The high in-group culture facilitates the group working closely together, and the Brazilians' dislike for independent and indi-vidualistic leaders means that the leader is expected to treat the team and their close families as an extended family, spending much time together.

In developing a business strategy for the team's product, it is important to keep in mind Brazil's low scores on performance orientation and future orientation and its high score on power distance. The process of strategy development needs to allow for input from the employees, but the manager needs to be patient and to make an effort to encourage and facilitate the employees' participation. The Brazilian employees will not be as forthcoming with their ideas and input as typical American employees are. At the same time, the manager will need to make the final decision and communicate it. Brazilian employees are not used to strong participation in decision-making, but they also do not like leaders who simply dictate things to them. The strategy should not be seen as too risky or ambitious and should not have a long time horizon. Instead, it should consist of explicit short-term milestones. It should also focus on delivering short-term results to enhance employee understanding and support.

Due to the country's low score on institutional collectivism, employees will not be moved much by grand corporate strategies and visions. Instead, they would be more motivated by their individual and team interests, so the reward system should be based on both individual and team performance, although the team component should have the greater emphasis. The manager should also not be surprised if there are not many clear rules or processes and if the ones in existence are not followed very seriously. These are attributes of a society such as Brazil with low levels of rules orientation. Instead, the manager needs to make it very clear early on which rules and procedures are expected to be followed and why.

France

France is part of the Latin Europe GLOBE country cluster. The most desirable CLT dimensions in this cluster are charismatic/value-based and team-oriented leader-ship. Participative leadership is viewed positively but is not as important as the first two dimensions. Humane-oriented leadership is viewed as slightly positive, whereas autonomous leadership is viewed as slightly negative and self-protective is viewed negatively. Table 3 shows that the Latin Europe cluster is medium/high for charismatic/value-based leadership. It is in the middle rank for the remaining CLT leadership dimensions except the humane-oriented and autonomous dimensions where it ranks among the lowest-scoring clusters.

Figure 2 shows the contrast between French and American leadership on culturally contingent leadership attributes. The French culture is similar to the US on one cultural dimension, in that they both practice moderate levels of uncertainty avoidance. Although both cultures utilize predictable laws and procedures in business and society, characteristic of uncertainty avoidance cultures, France is much better known for its strong labor unions and bureaucratic formality. There are, however, significant differences between the French and American respondents on other cultural dimensions and leadership attributes. Both groups seem to like sincere and enthusiastic leaders who impart positive energy to their group, although American managers have much stronger preferences for these attributes. This may be a reflection of the finding that French culture is not as performance-oriented as US culture.

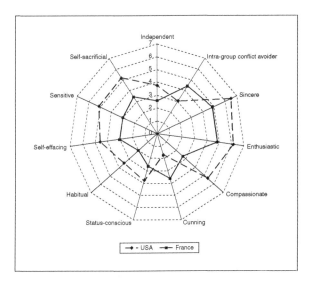

Figure 2. US versus France

Besides their dislike for avoidance of conflict within the group (as discussed earlier), American managers have a clear dislike for cunning and deceitful leaders. The French, on the other hand, are neutral about both attributes. While Americans see these attributes as dysfunctional, the French see them as a part of the job that goes with the position of leadership. Compared to the US, in-group collectivism is more noted in French societies in the form of "favoritism" given to people from similar education, family, social, and even regional backgrounds. This is shown in the general tension that is perceived to exist between labor and management, as well and employees and clients.[29]

American managers seem to have a strong preference for compassionate and sensitive leaders who show empathy towards others. In contrast, French managers seem to have a distinctly negative view towards both these attributes. The CEO of an international audit firm expressed this in a quality audit of a French hotel stating, "The staff had an inability to apologize and empathize. I think that could be construed as typically European, and especially French."[30] These same behaviors would be expected from their leaders. Such a large contrast can perhaps be explained by the fact that the French culture is much less humane-oriented and much more power-oriented. To French managers, people in positions of leadership should not be expected to be sensitive or empathetic, or to worry about another's status because such attributes would weaken a leader's resolve and impede decision-making. Leaders should make decisions without being distracted by other considerations. Indeed, a very successful corporate executive in France noted that a leader should be able to handle change that affects the environment, but at the same time not change his/her characteristics, traits, and skills that put the leader in that position. In other words, they should allow no distractions.

In contrast to Americans, French respondents have a negative view of leaders who are self-sacrificial and self-effacing. They do not like leaders who are modest about their role and forgo their own self-interest. The French executive added, "A leader must be clear about his role and vision. If a leader puts himself in a compromising situation, then doubt will arise in the followers' minds about the leader and that would affect their views of the roles the followers play in the broader picture." To them, the leader has an important role to play and important decisions to make, and s/he should not minimize that. They also do not like leaders who are habitual and tend to routinize everything because that diminishes the importance of their role. They do still prefer their leaders to work with and rely on others to get things done and do not like independent leaders. A French CEO known for his corporate turnaround finesse explained that leaders should not have too much independence from their followers because otherwise this would denote lack of character from the followers. He adds that a leader should guide without having too much power over the followers' thought processes, to ensure diverse thinking critical to conserve several solutions to the leader.

To sum up, a typical American executive taking on a leadership role in a French organization will face a more bureaucratic and formal work environment with higher levels of aggressiveness and lower levels of personal compassion and sensitivity than s/he is used to.

When in France . . .

The American manager in our scenario will face a very different experience with his or her French team. These managers will experience much more formal and impersonal relationships among the team members. The concept of visionary and charismatic leadership that is popular among American managers may not be as desirable to the French. They do not expect their leaders to play heroic acts and, due to their high power distance, have a more bureaucratic view of leaders. So, the American manager, in contrast to his experience in Brazil, needs to tone down the personal side of relationships and be much more business-oriented. The manager also has to be more careful and selective in contacting other executives and stakeholders. Their preference for maintaining high power distance may curb their enthusiasm about meeting with someone if they feel it is a waste of time and of no clear value to them. It is perhaps best for our American manager to make an offer to them and leave it to them to decide. Their low humane-orientation culture may mean that they are not particularly interested in being supportive of others, even in the same organization, especially if they are from separate in-groups.

Due to lower levels of future orientation and performance orientation, grand corporate strategies and visions may be of limited value to a French team. Any strong competitive language may be seen as typical American bravado. The manager needs to develop a process for making strategic decisions about the project and get the team members involved, but he needs to keep in mind that French employees may be best motivated by transactional forms of leadership where they see clear individual benefit in implementing the team's plans. The strategy and action plans need to be simple and well planned. So, the content and process of strategy development for the French team may have many similarities with the Brazilian team, even though they are different on many other dimensions.

Egypt

Egypt is part of the Middle East cluster. There are a number of striking differences in comparison to other clusters. While both charismatic/value-based and team-oriented leadership are viewed as positive, they have the lowest scores and ranks relative to those for all other clusters. Participative leadership is viewed positively, but again scores low compared with other clusters' absolute score and ranks. Humane-oriented leadership is perceived positively, but only about equally to other cluster scores. The self-protective CLT dimension is viewed as an almost neutral factor; however, it has the second-highest score and rank of all clusters.

Figure 3 below shows a contrast of leadership styles in the US and Egypt. The Egyptian culture is distinct by its emphasis on in-group and institutional collectivism, power distance, humane orientation, and male domination. In terms of leadership, American managers dislike autocratic leaders who want to make all the decisions themselves and micromanage their employees. They do not want their leaders to suppress others' ideas, even if they disagree with them. Egyptian managers have a more temperate view of such executives, perhaps due to their strong power distance culture.

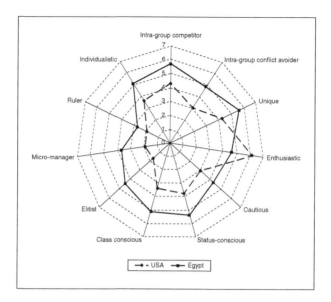

Figure 3. US versus Egypt

A very important difference is the image of leaders in the Egyptian versus the American mind. Egyptian managers seem to have an elitist, transcendent view of their leaders. They view them as a distinct group and a breed apart. They want their leaders to be unique, superior, status- and class-conscious, individualistic, and better than the others in their group. They show strong reverence and deference toward their leaders. Americans, on the other hand, have a more benign and simplistic view toward their leaders. They do not see them as a breed apart or superhuman. They regard them as successful people but not extraordinary ones.

The country of Egypt has been ruled by dictators dating as far back as the time of the Pharaohs. Leaders were expected to lead by portraying a self-assured image. To maintain power, Egyptian leaders need to continuously be involved in making decisions. In the Arabic culture that is very much influenced by Islam, men do not wish to appear weak.

Despite such high level of respect for leaders, Egyptian employees, perhaps due to their very strong in-group collectivism, prefer their leaders to respect group harmony, avoid group conflict, and take caution in decision-making. It is rare to see leaders, especially political leaders, come out publicly and criticize a popular belief. They tend to avoid a conflict when it is not necessary, and they often use this collectivtism to build their influence and popularity.

The importance of family as kinship is the most significant unit of Egyptian society. An individual's social identity is closely linked to his/her status in the network of kin relations. Kinship is essential to the culture. Describing the tendency toward generosity and caring in their society, an Egyptian manager told of how early Islamic authorities imposed a tax on personal property proportionate to one's wealth and distributed the revenues to the needy. This type of government behavior left a certain culture of doing business in Egypt that has a strong emphasis on harmony with the environment, the industry, and the competition.

When in Egypt . . .

Our hypothetical American manager will find that his experience in Egypt will have both similarities and differences with his time in France and Brazil. First, what the manager may regard as a normal informal leadership style in the US may be seen as weak and unworthy of a leader. This manager (typically a male) is expected to act and be seen as distinct from the others on the team and present an image of omnipotence. In the minds of his Egyptian team members, he needs to be seen as deserving of his leadership role and status. Addressing his role as a leader, a project manager from Egypt noted that being a leader brought with it great responsibility. He was in charge of disciplining anyone that did not follow the team rules. He noted, "In order to keep the team spirit up and focused on our goals, we can't afford to have individuals deviating from what we have set out to do." This is almost the opposite of his experience in France.

The American manager will also find that due to very strong in-group collectivism, various groups inside and outside the organization tend to show in-group/out-group phenomena in decision-making; i.e. strong participation by in-group members, little participation by out-group members, strong communication with in-group members, and little communication with out-group members. The extent to which Egyptians take pride in belonging to certain groups is immensely important. Families have endured through difficult times, requiring many of the members to stay together and work together. Family businesses tend to be passed from father to son without too many exceptions. Maintenance of the in-group is paramount in any decision. Leaders build their legitimacy not necessarily by accomplishing high performance but rather by forging loyalty to the group and group values. Furthermore, as a result of reliance on personal relationships, decision-making criteria and processes regarding any aspect of the organization tend to be informal and unclear.

Given such cultural underpinnings, the American manager needs to do even more than he did in Brazil to build and maintain group harmony. Many informal and formal meetings are needed, but there are three important differences compared with the experience in Brazil. First, to Egyptians, the team leader is more than just an executive; he is a paternal figure who will be rather autocratic but benign. He cares about them and their families. The relationship between the boss and employees is much more emotional and personal in Egypt. The Egyptian project manager described how he helped one of his employees who had experienced some personal difficulties. Explaining that the employee's behaviour was unacceptable, the manager added, "At the same time, I tried to understand if there were any personal issues that forced him to behave the way he did. I felt an obligation to try to help him." Second, due to very high humane orientation in Egypt, if the family of an employee has a problem, colleagues and the boss will quickly get involved to help. Taking care of friends in need is a major element of the culture and there is very little demarcation between colleagues and friends. Third, it is easier and more acceptable for the boss in Brazil to get to know the family members and spend time with them during social occasions. It is not, however, a good idea for him to try to do the same with Egyptian families. The contact should only be with and through the employee. Egyptian families tend to be more private and inaccessible to outsiders, possibly due to the intense in-group culture. People tend to stay close to their roots and develop a very strong sense of belonging. In short, even though the American manager will spend time building personal ties and maintaining in-group relationships both in Egypt and Brazil, the nature of his behavior will need to be somewhat different.

Like Brazil, the manager needs to pay his respects and call on the key executives in the Egyptian organization and start the process of building personal relationships. Unlike the French executives, the Egyptian executives will in all likelihood enjoy this approach and respond positively.

In developing a business strategy for the team, several cultural attributes need to be taken into consideration. The team will enjoy providing input but they expect decisions to be made by the leader. Family-related activities are always celebrated and employees are often excused from work to be able to properly plan such occasions. However, leaders also tend to use the friendly environment to maintain their control and build loyalty within their workforce. Egyptian employees expect their leaders to develop and communicate heroic and grand strategies. Due to their high institutional collectivism and performance orientation, it is helpful to design and communicate ambitious strategies and put them into the broader context of the corporation. Employees will resonate to ideas that would help the corporation and the unit achieve prominence in their competitive arenas. They also like strong rhetoric and get excited by the desire to be part of the winning team. In terms of the reward system, individual performance-based financial rewards, while helpful, are not the best motivators. The system should be seen to be humane to all; it should have a strong group-based component, and it should consist of a variety of benefits that are not typically offered in the US. Such benefits should be focused on the families of employees. For example, tuition assistance to employees' children, paid family vacation, and free or subsidized toys or home appliances could be very well received. As with other Middle East countries, although it is important for the individual to be successful, it is the family or group success that is more dominant.

China

China is part of the Confucian Asia cluster. The two CLT dimensions contributing to outstanding leadership are charismatic/value-based and team-oriented leadership, even though these scores are not particularly high. Humane-oriented leadership is viewed favorably, but it is not as important as the first two CLT dimensions. Although participative leadership is also viewed positively, it is about equal to the lowest-scoring clusters. Autonomous leadership is viewed neutrally, and self-protective leadership is seen as a slight impediment to effective leadership. Table 4 shows that compared to other GLOBE countries, the Confucian Asia cluster is ranked relatively low with respect to participative and relatively high with respect to self-protective leadership dimensions.

As shown in the Appendix, the US and Chinese cultures are similar in terms of their performance orientation, humane orientation, and power distance. The Chinese culture seems to be less future oriented, less assertive, more collectivist, both small group and socially, and more rules oriented.

Figure 4 below shows the comparison of culturally contingent leadership attributes between American and Chinese managers. Both American and Chinese managers like excellence-oriented leaders who strive for performance improvement in themselves and their subordinates. This is probably driven by the fact that both cultures share a strong performance orientation, as shown in the Appendix. They also both like leaders who are honest. However, the figure shows that the US scores on both these attributes are higher than the Chinese scores.

Chinese managers seem to like leaders who are fraternal and friendly with their subordinates and who have an indirect approach to communication, using metaphors and parables to communicate their point. American managers have a neutral view of fraternal leadership and a negative view of indirect leadership. The difference can probably be explained by the fact that the US culture is much more assertive and less in-group oriented than that in China (see Appendix). In a less assertive culture such as China, people tend to use nuances and a context-rich language to communicate. They prefer indirect communication to avoid the possibility of hurting someone. Furthermore, in a highly group-oriented culture such as China, group harmony is critical and the leader's role is to strengthen group ties. As a result, leaders are expected to be supportive of their subordinates and act as good friends for them. They are expected to build emotional ties with their groups and their relationships with their subordinates go far beyond what is the norm in a country such as the US. The leader is seen as a paternal figure who should take care of his subordinates and their families.

American managers are not excited about leaders who are status conscious and are negative toward leaders who are elitist. In contrast, Chinese managers like the former type of leadership and are neutral toward the latter. This is reflective of the importance of hierarchy in the Chinese culture. Confucianism's "Three Bonds" — emperor rules the minister, father rules the son, and husband rules the wife—serve as

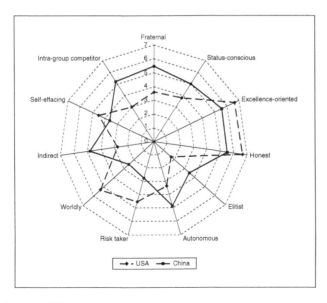

Figure 4. US versus China

the foundation of the Chinese society: "Chinese business structure can be directly linked to the history of patriarchy: the owner or manager plays the father's role, and the subordinates or employees play the son."[31]

Within such a hierarchical structure, the leader tends to be authoritative and expects respect and obedience and tends to make autonomous decisions. That is why Chinese managers do not admire leaders who are self-effacing, because such leaders do not emanate confidence. A group of American managers was recently in China to discuss a possible joint venture with a Chinese company. American managers expected to spend a few days working with their Chinese counterparts to brainstorm ideas and develop action plans. After a few frustrating days, they were told that they needed to find a Chinese agent to help them implement the deal. In conversations with the Chinese agent, they learned that the Chinese counterpart's expectation from the meetings was very different. They learned that the Chinese company wanted to use the meetings to help build personal ties among the Chinese and American managers and was upset that the Americans were asking aggressive questions and were focused solely on business rather than personal matters. They also learned that the top Chinese executive had no interest in sharing decision-making with anyone. Instead, he wanted to use private lunches and dinners with the head of the American delegation to make serious decisions and reach agreements.

Chinese managers are very negative toward worldly leaders who have a global outlook. In contrast, Americans admire such leaders. This could be explained by the fact that the two cultures are very different in terms of in-group collectivism. The Chinese culture is very high on this dimension, which means it is less interested in anything outside of their in-group. Perhaps they view the world as out-group compared to China and view it as less important.

When in China . . .

The Chinese culture is distinct by its high performance orientation, high institutional orientation, and high in-group collectivism. Building personal ties and relationships is reflected in the Chinese concept of "guanxi" whose loose English translation is networking. It is a manifestation of the fact that one's value and importance is embedded in his/her ties and relationships. As a result, "In China, the primary qualities expected in a leader or executive is someone who is good at establishing and nurturing personal relationships, who practices benevolence towards his or her subordinates, who is dignified and aloof but sympathetic, and puts the interests of his or her employees above his or her own."[32]

Much of Chinese life and culture is based on Confucian ideas, which emphasize the importance of relationships and community. Even the word "self" has a negative connotation.[33] Our hypothetical American manager needs to be careful about how his behavior and manners are perceived by the Chinese. Being polite, considerate, and moral are desirable attributes. At the same time, the American manager can get the Chinese employees excited by engaging their high performance culture. Developing an exciting vision is very effective. The relative high score on future orientation can also help the new manager get the employees motivated. But perhaps the most critical key success factor is how the manager goes about building personal ties and relationships with a wide network of individuals and groups. His "guanxi" will be the ultimate test of his success. In building guanxi with his employees, he needs to show high respect to the employees' families, keep them in mind when designing work schedules and reward systems, and make sure that employees see him and the organization as a strong supporter of their own guanxi. Perhaps a big challenge to the American executive is how to make sure his natural American assertiveness does not turn his Chinese employees and counterparts off and does not impede his efforts at building strong relationships.

EMBARKING ON A CROSS-CULTURAL LEADERSHIP JOURNEY

The existing literature on cross-cultural management is more useful at the conceptual level than at the behavioral level. Much of the advice offered to executives tends to be context-free and general such as "understand and respect the other culture." But the problems facing a typical global executive are context-specific; for example, how to understand and respect the Brazilian culture. In behavioral terms, understanding the Brazilian culture may be quite different from understanding and respecting the Egyptian culture because they are very different cultures.

In this reading, we have presented the cultural profiles of four countries based on a rigorous and scientific research project. We have also provided very specific ideas on the managerial implications of the different cultural profiles along with action-oriented advice on how an American manager can "put himself in the other culture's shoes" and be adaptable. Besides the culture specific ideas presented earlier, we propose a two-step process for any executive who is embarking on a new assignment in a new country. Regardless of the host country, these two steps help build a positive pathway towards cultural understanding and adaptability.

First, the executive needs to share information about his own, as well as the host country's, culture. Most of the advice that executives receive is about how they can adapt and adjust to other cultures. We propose a somewhat different approach. When people from different cultures come into contact, they usually have unstated and sometimes false or exaggerated stereotypes about the other side. While it is important that the executive learn about the host culture, it is not sufficient. Executives need to tell the host employees about their own cultures. For example, if these executives are in Egypt, then they should show the employees how the American and Egyptian cultures and leadership attributes compare. They should show both similarities and differences. In this reading, we showed that there is a set of leadership attributes that are universally desirable and universally undesirable. Similarities represent a fertile ground to build mutual understanding. The informed executive can then use the session to discuss their implications. What does integrity mean to a French manager? Or to a Brazilian manager? The executive can also compare the findings about his/her own culture with their perceptions of American culture to dispel any misunderstandings. This exercise in mapping and surfacing cultural attributes can go a long way to build mutual understanding and trust between the players. For example, our findings show that American culture is reported to be more moderate on many cultural dimensions than it is stereotypically believed to be. One of the unique features of GLOBE is that we have taken several steps to ensure that the reports by country managers are not confounded by such things as methodological problems and represent the true broader culture of their societies.

Second, the global manager needs to think about how to bridge the gap between the two cultures. Much of the advice executives receive seems to suggest, explicitly or implicitly, that the executive needs to become more like them. We do not necessarily subscribe to this viewpoint. While it is important to understand the other culture, it does not necessarily mean that one should automatically apply their approach. For example, leaders are seen as benign autocrats in Egypt. If an American manager does not like this approach, then he should educate the employees on his approach to leadership; why it is not dictatorial, and why he prefers it. Managers need to make sure the employees understand that their approach is not a sign of weakness, but a more effective style for the manager and for the team's and organization's success. It is a judgment call to say it is a "more effective" style than what the team is used to, but it is one that they should employ with the team. The global manager needs to tell the employees what managerial functions they are willing to change and what team functions they would like the employees to change so that the team can work from, and succeed on, common ground incorporating both cultures. The manager then needs to seek their help on both approaches; i.e. each culture making changes to accommodate and strengthen the other. Both approaches can take place at the same time and with respect to both cultures, as long as the manager gets the employees involved in the process. In other words, instead of a solitary learning journey for the executive, managers can create a collective learning journey that can be enriching, educational, and productive for both sides.

ATTRIBUTES OF GLOBAL LEADERS

The essence of global leadership is the ability to influence people who are not like the leader and come from different cultural backgrounds. To succeed, global leaders need to have a global mindset, tolerate high levels of ambiguity, and show cultural adaptability and flexibility. This reading provides some examples of these attributes. In contrast to a domestic manager, the hypothetical manager discussed in this reading needs a global mindset because s/he needs to understand a variety of cultural and leadership paradigms, and legal, political, and economic systems, as well as different competitive frameworks.[34] We used GLOBE findings to provide a scientifically based comparison of cultural and leadership paradigms in the five countries. We showed that countries can be different on some cultural dimensions and similar on others. Brazil and Egypt are both high on in-group collectivism, but different on performance orientation. France and the US are both moderate on uncertainty avoidance but differ on power distance. China and the US are both high on performance orientation but very different on in-group collectivism. Furthermore, there are similarities and differences in the countries' leadership profiles. While a leadership attribute such as irritability is universally undesirable, another attribute such as compassion is culturally contingent, i.e. it is much more desirable in the US than in France.

Tolerance of ambiguity is another important attribute of a global leader. Every new country that s/he has to work in represents a new paradigm and new ways of doing things. This is typically an uncomfortable position for many people to be in because it requires learning new ideas quickly and letting go of what has already been learned. Of course, in the four scenarios, we showed that there are things in common across cultures and there are portable aspects of cultural learning. But we also showed that there are differences as well. Figuring out which one is which and what to do represents potentially stressful ambiguity to an expatriate manager.

Cultural adaptability refers to a manager's ability to understand other cultures and behave in a way that helps achieve goals and build strong and positive relations with local citizens. In the country scenarios, we showed that while in France the manager should not emphasize grand and ambitious corporate strategies, he can do this in China. Cultural adaptability refers to the mental and psychological ability to move from one situation and country to another. It means the ability to do a good job of developing personal relationships while in Egypt and then doing it very differently in France. The dexterity to adjust one's behavior is a critical requirement. Not everyone can do this; to many people it may bring into question one's own identity. In some ways, it is reminiscent of acting but the difference is that the global manager, unlike the actor, lives and works among real people and not other actors, so his task is more complicated.

DEVELOPING GLOBAL LEADERS

As mentioned earlier in this reading, a large majority of *Fortune* 500 corporations report a shortage of global leaders. Devising programs that would develop a global mindset in leaders has been called "the biggest challenge that looms in the new millennium for human resource managers."[35] There are a variety of ways that companies can enhance their pool of global leaders. To start with, they can make a large volume of information on cross-cultural and global issues and country-specific reports available to their managers. We have already referred to several books on this topic. In addition to the special issue of the *Human Resource Management Journal* mentioned earlier, there are special issues of other journals.[36] There are also a variety of software packages such as a multimedia package called "Bridging Cultures," a self-training program for those who will be living and working in other cultures. In addition, several services such as CultureGrams (www.culturegram.com) provide useful information about many countries. There are also a few websites providing useful information to managers[37] such as www.contactcga.com, belonging to the Center for Global assignments, the CIA World Fact Book at www.odci.gov/cia/publications/facxtbook/, and Global Dynamics Inc.'s www. globaldynamics.com/expatria.htm.

Formal education and training can also be helpful in developing global leaders. A recent survey showed that a large majority of firms were planning to increase funding for programs that would help globalize their leaders.[38] But despite its prevalence among multinational corporations, there is general consensus among experts that it is not a highly effective source of developing global leaders.[39] It is generally best used as a component of a comprehensive and integrated development program. Work experience and international assignment is by far the most effective source for developing global leadership capabilities.[40] Some experts view long-term international assignments as the "single most powerful experience in shaping the perspective and capabilities of effective global leaders."[41] Increasingly, companies such as GE, Citigroup, Shell, Siemens, and Nokia are using international assignments of high-potential employees as the means to develop their managers' global leadership mindsets and competencies.

APPENDIX 1: COUNTRY SCORES ON CULTURAL PRACTICES

Performance Orientation

Anglo Cultures	Latin Europe	Middle East Cultures	Confucian Asia	Latin America
USA 4.49	France 4.11	Egypt 4.27	China 4.45	Brazil 4.04
Canada 4.49	Israel 4.08	Kuwait 3.95	Hong Kong 4.80	Bolivia 3.61
England 4.08	Italy 3.58	Morocco 3.99	Japan 4.22	Argentina 3.65
Ireland 4.36	Portugal 3.60	Qatar 3.45	Singapore 4.90	Colombia 3.94
New Zealand 4.72	Spain 4.01	Turkey 3.83	South Korea 4.55	Costa Rica 4.12
South Africa (W) 4.11	Swiss (French) 4.25		Taiwan 4.56	Ecuador 4.20
Australia 4.36				El Salvador 3.72
				Guatemala 3.81
				Mexico 4.10
				Venezuela 3.32

Future Orientation

Anglo Cultures	Latin Europe	Middle East Cultures	Confucian Asia	Latin America
USA 4.15	France 3.48	Egypt 3.86	China 3.75	Brazil 3.81
Canada 4.44	Israel 3.85	Kuwait 3.26	Hong Kong 4.03	Bolivia 3.61
England 4.28	Italy 3.25	Morocco 3.26	Japan 4.29	Argentina 3.08
Ireland 3.98	Portugal 3.71	Qatar 3.78	Singapore 5.07	Colombia 3.27
New Zealand 3.47	Spain 3.51	Turkey 3.74	South Korea 3.97	Costa Rica 3.60
South Africa (W) 4.13	Swiss (French) 4.27		Taiwan 3.96	Ecuador 3.74
Australia 4.09				El Salvador 3.80
				Guatemala 3.24
				Mexico 3.87
				Venezuela 3.35

APPENDIX 1—*continued*

Anglo Cultures	*Latin Europe*	*Middle East Cultures*	*Confucian Asia*	*Latin America*

Assertiveness Orientation

Anglo Cultures	*Latin Europe*	*Middle East Cultures*	*Confucian Asia*	*Latin America*
USA 4.55	**France 4.13**	**Egypt 3.91**	**China 3.76**	**Brazil 4.20**
Canada 4.05	Israel 4.23	Kuwait 3.63	Hong Kong 4.67	Bolivia 3.79
England 4.15	Italy 4.07	Morocco 4.52	Japan 3.59	Argentina 4.22
Ireland 3.92	Portugal 3.65	Qatar 4.11	Singapore 4.17	Colombia 4.20
New Zealand 3.42	Spain 4.42	Turkey 4.53	South Korea 4.40	Costa Rica 3.75
South Africa (W) 4.60	Swiss (French) 3.47		Taiwan 3.92	Ecuador 4.09
Australia 4.28				El Salvador 4.62
				Guatemala 3.89
				Mexico 4.45
				Venezuela 4.33

Anglo Cultures	*Latin Europe*	*Middle East Cultures*	*Confucian Asia*	*Latin America*

Societal Collectivism

Anglo Cultures	*Latin Europe*	*Middle East Cultures*	*Confucian Asia*	*Latin America*
USA 4.20	**France 3.93**	**Egypt 4.50**	**China 4.77**	**Brazil 3.83**
Canada 4.38	Israel 4.46	Kuwait 4.49	Hong Kong 4.13	Bolivia 4.04
England 4.27	Italy 3.68	Morocco 3.87	Japan 5.19	Argentina 3.66
Ireland 4.63	Portugal 3.92	Qatar 4.50	Singapore 4.90	Colombia 3.81
New Zealand 4.81	Spain 3.85	Turkey 4.03	South Korea 5.20	Costa Rica 3.93
South Africa (W) 4.62	Swiss (French) 4.22		Taiwan 4.59	Ecuador 3.90
Australia 4.29				El Salvador 3.71
				Guatemala 3.70
				Mexico 4.06
				Venezuela 3.96

APPENDIX 1 — *continued*

In-Group Collectivism

Anglo Cultures	Latin Europe	Middle East Cultures	Confucian Asia	Latin America
USA 4.25	France 4.37	Egypt 5.64	China 5.80	Brazil 5.18
Canada 4.26	Israel 4.70	Kuwait 5.80	Hong Kong 5.32	Bolivia 5.47
England 4.08	Italy 4.94	Morocco 5.87	Japan 4.63	Argentina 5.51
Ireland 5.14	Portugal 5.51	Qatar 4.71	Singapore 5.64	Colombia 5.73
New Zealand 3.67	Spain 5.45	Turkey 5.88	South Korea 5.54	Costa Rica 5.32
South Africa (W) 4.50	Swiss (French) 3.85		Taiwan 5.59	Ecuador 5.81
Australia 4.17				El Salvador 5.35
				Guatemala 5.63
				Mexico 5.71
				Venezuela 5.53

Humane Orientation

Anglo Cultures	Latin Europe	Middle East Cultures	Confucian Asia	Latin America
USA 4.17	France 3.40	Egypt 4.73	China 4.36	Brazil 3.66
Canada 4.49	Israel 4.10	Kuwait 4.52	Hong Kong 3.90	Bolivia 4.05
England 3.72	Italy 3.63	Morocco 4.19	Japan 4.30	Argentina 3.99
Ireland 4.96	Portugal 3.91	Qatar 4.42	Singapore 3.49	Colombia 3.72
New Zealand 4.32	Spain 3.32	Turkey 3.94	South Korea 3.81	Costa Rica 4.39
South Africa (W) 3.49	Swiss (French) 3.93		Taiwan 4.11	Ecuador 4.65
Australia 4.28				El Salvador 3.71
				Guatemala 3.89
				Mexico 3.98
				Venezuela 4.25

APPENDIX 1—*continued*

Anglo Cultures	*Latin Europe*	*Middle East Cultures*	*Confucian Asia*	*Latin America*

Power Distance

Anglo Cultures	*Latin Europe*	*Middle East Cultures*	*Confucian Asia*	*Latin America*
USA 4.88	**France 5.28**	**Egypt 4.92**	**China 5.04**	**Brazil 5.33**
Canada 4.82	Israel 4.73	Kuwait 5.12	Hong Kong 4.96	Bolivia 4.51
England 5.15	Italy 5.43	Morocco 5.80	Japan 5.11	Argentina 5.64
Ireland 5.15	Portugal 5.44	Qatar 4.73	Singapore 4.99	Colombia 5.56
New Zealand 4.89	Spain 5.52	Turkey 5.57	South Korea 5.61	Costa Rica 4.74
South Africa (W) 5.16	Swiss (French) 4.86		Taiwan 5.18	Ecuador 5.60
Australia 4.74				El Salvador 5.68
				Guatemala 5.60
				Mexico 5.22
				Venezuela 5.40

Anglo Cultures	*Latin Europe*	*Middle East Cultures*	*Confucian Asia*	*Latin America*

Gender Egalitarianism

Anglo Cultures	*Latin Europe*	*Middle East Cultures*	*Confucian Asia*	*Latin America*
USA 3.34	**France 3.64**	**Egypt 2.81**	**China 3.05**	**Brazil 3.31**
Canada 3.70	Israel 3.19	Kuwait 2.58	Hong Kong 3.47	Bolivia 3.55
England 3.67	Italy 3.24	Morocco 2.84	Japan 3.19	Argentina 3.49
Ireland 3.21	Portugal 3.66	Qatar 3.63	Singapore 3.70	Colombia 3.67
New Zealand 3.22	Spain 3.01	Turkey 2.89	South Korea 2.50	Costa Rica 3.56
South Africa (W) 3.27	Swiss (French) 3.42		Taiwan 3.18	Ecuador 3.07
Australia 3.40				El Salvador 3.16
				Guatemala 3.02
				Mexico 3.64
				Venezuela 3.62

APPENDIX 1 — *continued*

Anglo Cultures	Latin Europe	Middle East Cultures	Confucian Asia	Latin America
Uncertainty Avoidance				
USA 4.15	**France 4.43**	**Egypt 4.06**	**China 4.94**	**Brazil 3.60**
Canada 4.58	Israel 4.01	Kuwait 4.21	Hong Kong 4.32	Bolivia 3.35
England 4.65	Italy 3.79	Morocco 3.65	Japan 4.07	Argentina 3.65
Ireland 4.30	Portugal 3.91	Qatar 3.99	Singapore 5.31	Colombia 3.57
New Zealand 4.75	Spain 3.97	Turkey 3.63	South Korea 3.55	Costa Rica 3.82
South Africa (W) 4.09	Swiss (French) 4.98		Taiwan 4.34	Ecuador 3.68
Australia 4.39				El Salvador 3.62
				Guatemala 3.30
				Mexico 4.18
				Venezuela 3.44

NOTES

* Mansour Javidan is professor and director of the Garvin Center for the Cultures and Languages of International Management at Thunderbird, The Garvin School of International Management in Arizona. He is on the board of directors of the GLOBE (Global Leadership and Organizational Behavior Effectiveness) research program. Contact: javidanm@t-bird.edu.

Peter W. Dorfman is a full Professor in the Department of Management, New Mexico State University. Contact: pdorfman@nmsu.edu.

Mary Sully de Luque is an Assistant Professor of Management and a Research Fellow at Thunderbird, The Garvin School of International Management. Contact: sullym@t-bird.edu.

Robert J. House holds the Joseph Frank Bernstein endowed chair of Organizational Studies at the Wharton School of the University of Pennsylvania. Contact: house@wharton.upenn.edu.

1.   House, R. J., Hanges, P. J., Ruiz-Quintanilla, S. A., Dorfman, P. W., Javidan, M., Dickson, M., et al. 1999. Cultural influences on leadership and organizations: Project GLOBE. In W. F. Mobley, M. J. Gessner, and V. Arnold (Eds.), *Advances in global leadership* (vol. 1, pp. 171–233). Stamford, CT: JAI Press.

2.   Gregersen, H. B., Morrison, A. J., and Black, J. S. 1998. Developing leaders for the global frontier. *Sloan Management Review*, Fall: 21–32.

3.   Hollenbeck, G. P. and McCall, M. W. 2003. Competence, not competencies: Making global executive development work. In W. Mobley and P. Dorfman (Eds.), *Advances in global leadership* (vol. 3). Oxford: JAI Press.

4.   Black, J. S., Morrison, A. J., and Gergersen, H. B. 1999. *Global explorers: The next generation of leaders*. New York: Routledge; Rhinesmith, S. H. 1996. *A manager's guide to globalization*. Chicago: Irwin; Osland, J. S. 1995. *The adventure of working abroad: Hero tales from the global frontier*. San Francisco, CA: Jossey-Bass; Black, J. S., Gergersen, H. B., Mendenhall, M. E., and Stroh, L. K. 1999. *Globalizing people through international assignments*. Reading, MA: Addison-Wesley; Mobley, W. H. and Dorfman, P. W. 2003. *Advances in global leadership*. In W. H. Mobley and P. W. Dorfman (Eds.), *Advances in global leadership* (vol. 3). Oxford: JAI Press.

5.   Gergerson, H. B., Morrison, A. J., and Mendenhall, M. E. 2000. Guest editors. *Human Resource Management Journal*, 39, 2&3, 113–299.

6.   Morrison, A. J. 2000. Developing a global leadership model. *Human Resource Management Journal*, 39, 2&3, 117–131.

7.   Kiedel, R. W. 1995. *Seeing organizational patterns: A new theory and language of organizational design*. San Francisco, CA: Berrett-Koehler.

8.   Pucik, V. and Saba, T. 1997. Selecting and developing the global versus the expatriate manager: A review of the state of the art. *Human Resource Planning*, 40–54.

9.   Wills, S. 2001. *Developing global leaders*. In P. Kirkbride and K. Ward (Eds.), *Globalization: The internal dynamic*. Chichester: Wiley, 259–284.

10. Bass, B. M. 1997. Does the transactional-transformational leadership paradigm transcend organizational and national boundaries? *American Psychologist*, 52(2), 130–139.

11. Hofstede, G. 1980. *Culture's consequences: International differences in work-related values*. Newbury Park, CA: Sage; Hofstede, G. 2001. *Culture's Consequences: Comparing values, behaviors, institutions, and organizations across nations*, 2nd ed. Thousand Oaks, CA: Sage; Trompenaars, F. and Hamden-Turner, C. 1998. *Riding the waves of culture*, 2nd ed. New York: McGraw-Hill; Kluckhohn, F. R. and Strodtbeck, F. L. 1961. *Variations in value orientations*. New York: Harper & Row.

12. House, R. J., Hanges, P. J., Javidan, M., Dorfman, P. W., and Gupta, V., and GLOBE Associates. 2004. *Leadership, culture and organizations: The globe study of 62 societies*. Thousand Oaks, CA: Sage.

13. Morrison, A. J. 2000. Developing a global leadership model. *Human Resource Management Journal*, 39, 2&3, 117–131.

14. Laurent, A. 1983. The cultural diversity of western conceptions of management. *International Studies of Management and Organization*, 13(2), 75–96; Trompenaars, F. 1993. *Riding the waves of culture: Understanding cultural diversity in business*. London: Breatley; Briscoe, D. R. and Schuler, R. S. 2004. *International human resource management*, 2nd ed. New York: Routledge.

15. Davis, D. D. and Bryant, J. L. 2003. Influence at a distance: Leadership in global virtual teams. In W. H. Mobley and P. W. Dorfman (Eds.), *Advances in global leadership* (vol. 3, pp. 303–340). Oxford: JAI Press.

16. Millman, J. Trade wins: The world's new tiger on the export scene isn't Asian; it's Mexico. *Wall Street Journal*, p. A1. May 9, 2000.

17. Smith, P. B. and Peterson, M. F. 1988. *Leadership, organizations and culture: An event management model*. London: Sage.

18. Smith, P. B. 2003. Leaders' sources of guidance and the challenge of working across cultures. In W. Mobley and P. Dorfman (Eds.), *Advances in global leadership* (vol. 3, pp. 167–182). Oxford: JAI Press; Smith, P. B., Dugan, S., and Trompenaars, F. 1996. National culture and the values of organizational employees: A dimensional analysis across 43 nations. *Journal of Cross-Cultural Psychology*, 27(2), 231–264.

19. Hazucha, J. F., Hezlett, S. A., Bontems-Wackens, S., and Ronnqvist, G. 1999. In search of the Euro-manager: Management competencies in France, Germany, Italy, and the United States. In W.H. Mobley, M.J. Gessner, and V. Arnold (Eds.), *Advances in global leadership* (vol. 1, pp. 267–290). Stamford, CT: JAI Press.

20 Javidan, M. and Carl, D. 2004. East meets West. *Journal of Management Studies*, 41:4, June, 665–691; Javidan, M. and Carl, D. 2005. Leadership across cultures: A study of Canadian and Taiwanese executives, *Management International Review*, 45(1), 23–44.

21 House, R. J., Wright, N. S., and Aditya, R. N. 1997. Cross-cultural research on organizational leadership: A critical analysis and a proposed theory. In P. C. Earley and M. Erez (Eds.), *New perspectives in international industrial/organizational psychology* (pp. 535–625). San Francisco: The New Lexington Press.

22. Chemers, M. M. 1997. *An integrative theory of leadership*. London: Lawrence Erlbaum Associates; Smith, P. B. and Peterson, M. F. 1988. *Leadership, organizations and culture: An event management model*. London: Sage.

23. Shaw, J. B. (1990). A cognitive categorization model for the study of intercultural management. *Academy of Management Review*, 15(4), 626–645.

24. Lord, R. G. and Maher, K. J. 1991. *Leadership and information processing: Linking perceptions and performance* (vol. 1). Cambridge, MA: Unwin Hyman.

25. House, R. J., Hanges, P. J., Ruiz-Quintanilla, S. A., Dorfman, P. W., Javidan, M., Dickson, M., et al. 1999. Cultural influences on leadership and organizations: Project GLOBE. In W. F. Mobley, M. J. Gessner, and V. Arnold (Eds.), *Advances in global leadership* (vol. 1, pp. 171–233). Stamford, CT: JAI Press.

26. In addition to the aggregated raw (i.e. absolute) scores for CLTs provided in Table 2, we also computed a response bias corrected measure as an integral part of the analysis strategy. We referred to this measure as the relative measure because of a unique property attributed to this procedure. These relative CLT scores indicate the relative importance of each CLT leadership dimension within a person, culture, or culture cluster. This procedure not only removed the cultural response biases, but it also had the advantage of illustrating the differences among the cultures and the clusters. Along with ranking the clusters with absolute CLT scores, we used this relative measure to compare the relative importance of each CLT dimension among cultures. Ranking of clusters using both types of scores are presented in Table 3. We should point out that the correlation between the absolute and relative measures is close to perfect—above .90 for all of the CLT leadership dimensions. Computational procedures for this measure are detailed in House et al., 2004.

27. Cullen, J. B. 2002. *Multinational management: A strategic approach* (2nd ed.). Cincinnati, OH: South-Western Thomson Learning.

28.   Bossidy, L. and Charan, R. 2002. *Execution: The discipline of getting things done.* New York: Crown Business Books. p. 103.

29.   Hallowell, R., Bowen, D., and Knoop, C. 2002. Four Seasons goes to Paris, *Academy of Management Executive*, 16(4), 7–24.

30.   Ibid.

31.   Dayal-Gulati, A. 2004. *Kellogg on China: Strategies for success,* Evanston, IL: Northwestern University Press.

32.   De Mente, Boye Lafayette. 2000. *The Chinese have a word for it: The complete guide to Chinese thought and culture. Chicago*: Passport Books.

33.   Rosen, R. *Global Literacies.* Simon & Schuster, 2000.

34.   Black, J. S. and Gergersen, H. B. 2000. High impact training: Forging leaders for the global frontier. *Human Resource Management Journal*, 39 (2&3), 173–184.

35.   Oddou, G., Mendenhall, M.E., and Ritchi, J. B. Leveraging travel as a tool for global leadership development. *Human Resource Management Journal*, 39, 2&3, 159–172.

36.   Dastmalchian, A. and Kabasakal, H. 2001. Guest editors, special issue on the Middle East, *Applied Psychology: An International Review.* vol. 50(4); Javidan, M. and House, R. Spring 2002 Guest editors, special Issue on GLOBE, *Journal of World Business,* Vol. 37, No. 1; Peterson, M. F. and Hunt, J. G. 1997. Overview: International and cross-cultural leadership research (Part II). *Leadership Quarterly*, 8(4), 339–342.

37.   For more information, see Mendenhall, M.E. and Stahl, G. K. Expatriate training and development: Where do we go from here? *Human Resource Management Journal*, 39, 2&3, 251–265.

38.   Black, J. S., Morrison, A. J., and Gergersen, H. B. 1999. *Global explorers: The next generation of leaders.* New York: Routledge.

39.   Dodge, B. 1993. Empowerment and the evolution of learning, *Education and Training*, 35(5), 3–10; Sherman, S. 1995. How tomorrow's best leaders are learning their stuff. *Fortune*, 90–106.

40.   Conner, J. 2000. Developing the global leaders of tomorrow. *Human Resource Management Journal*, 39, 2&3, 147–157.

41.   Black, J. S., Gergersen, H. B., Mendenhall, M. E., and Stroh L. K. 1999. *Globalizing people through international assignments.* Reading, MA: Addison-Wesley.

Stacey R. Fitzsimmons, Christof Miska, and Günter K. Stahl

MULTICULTURAL INDIVIDUALS: WHAT CAN THEY BRING TO GLOBAL ORGANIZATIONS?

GLOBAL BUSINESSES are fast-moving places with technologies that enable people to be more mobile than ever. Not only do individuals travel more frequently and connect with people from societal cultures that are different from their own, but as globalization dissolves geographical barriers, more and more individuals find themselves identifying with not only one culture but with two or even more. Immigration statistics indicate that this demographic is both large and growing. In 2006, 12 percent of the population in OECD countries were foreign-born (OECD, 2009), and multicultural individuals are becoming so important that UNESCO discussed their impact in a recent report (*Investing in Cultural Diversity and Intercultural Dialogue,* 2009).

Indra Nooyi and Carlos Ghosn could be poster children for multiculturalism. Indra Nooyi, CEO and chair of PepsiCo, ranked the #1 most powerful woman by Fortune Magazine from 2006 to 2009 (Fortune, 2009), draws on her multicultural identity to shape PepsiCo as a global company. Nooyi moved to the US to complete her Master's degree at Yale, after degrees at the Indian Institute of Management and Madras Christian College. Under her watch, PepsiCo ramped up its international sales, and she has turned PepsiCo into a corporation that truly appreciates and derives benefit from its diverse employees. She also speaks out – sometimes controversially – in favor of working globally:

> Although I'm a daughter of India, I'm an American businesswoman ...
> Graduates, as you aggressively compete on the international business stage,
> understand that the five major continents and their peoples – the five fingers
> of your hand - each have their own strengths and their own contributions to
> make. Just as each of your fingers must coexist to create a critically import-
> ant tool, each of the five major continents must also coexist to create a world

in balance. You, as an American businessperson, will either contribute to or take away from, this balance.

(Indra Nooyi, as cited in *Business Week,* May 20, 2005)

Carlos Ghosn, another well-known multicultural, is president and CEO of both Renault and Nissan. He speaks five languages, was born in Brazil, spent time in Lebanon as a child, graduated with engineering degrees from Paris, and is a French citizen. When he merged Renault with Nissan, he drew on his Brazilian-Lebanese-French background in order to succeed in Japan, a country that was completely foreign to him at the time.

In contrast to monoculturals, multiculturals possess considerable experience in two or even more cultural settings. Because they take part concurrently in several cultural contexts, multiculturals develop cultural awareness and knowledge about the habits, norms and values of several cultures. They understand and apply the rules of their cultures and are usually fluent in the respective languages, which helps them operate within and between their cultures (David, 2006). In other words, multiculturals have deeply internalized more than one culture (Nguyen and Benet-Martinez, 2007), making them potentially valuable in the world of international business and global organizations, where cultural fluency is both a necessity and a challenge.

Yet, few global organizations are truly aware of multicultural individuals' potential. One reason might be that there is more than one way to be multicultural (Nguyen and Benet-Martinez, 2007), making it challenging for organizations to identify multicultural employees. Alternatively, organizations may not be aware of the particular skills their multicultural employees possess, may be threatened by people of mixed cultural identity or may see them as a source of problems. Even organizations that consider a multicultural workforce an asset may lack the necessary processes to leverage the distinct skills of multiculturals (e.g. selection processes to place them in positions where they can realize their full potential). In order to understand how organizations can best use their multicultural employees' skills, it is important to first understand what multicultural employees contribute to international business.

HOW CAN MULTICULTURAL EMPLOYEES CONTRIBUTE TO GLOBAL BUSINESS?

Next, we explore multiculturals' impact on five international business activities – international teams, intercultural negotiations, international assignments, mergers and acquisitions, global leadership and ethics – illustrated with examples about Indra Nooyi and Carlos Ghosn.

Multiculturals' Impact on Teams

When you have a very diverse team – people of different backgrounds, different culture, different gender, different age, you are going to get a more creative team – probably getting better solutions, and enforcing them in a very innovative way and with a very limited number of preconceived ideas.

(Ghosn, April 11, 2008)

I look at the amazing diversity of our Executive Committee. We have
29 people in the Executive Committee. We have a Sudanese leading Europe,
a North American as a vice chair, an Italian who is leading North American
beverages, a Middle Easterner runs Asia, and I don't even want to talk about
the CEO. That diversity is what keeps our company grounded and helps us
make market-based, sensible decisions.

(Nooyi, 2009)

Indra Nooyi and Carlos Ghosn have both harnessed the power of diverse teams
to drive innovation at PepsiCo and Nissan-Renault. Ghosn, in particular, is known for
using cross-cultural and cross-functional teams whenever possible. "Competing in the
global marketplace requires the contributions of multitalented, multicultural people
working together to achieve success" (Carlos Ghosn, as cited in Rivas-Micoud, 2007).
In the future, Nooyi's list of the cultures represented on her executive committee
might include more hyphenated cultures: Sudanese-French, Italian–American or
Chinese-Canadian. As businesses move from teams where each individual has only one
culture to teams where each individual has two or more cultures, we propose two
ways multicultural individuals might influence team effectiveness: they might act as
bridges across cultural faultlines, and reduce the process time required to tap multiple perspectives.

First, global teams are usually multicultural. Divisions within groups – also
known as faultlines - often develop along cultural lines, promoting disharmony, dissatisfaction and poor performance (Lau and Murnighan, 2005; Polzer et al. 2006).
Faultlines develop along cultural lines when the group's composition emphasizes
cultural divisions. For example, American–Chinese teams often develop faultlines,
because it is obvious who is Chinese and who is American. In order to avoid faultlines and the tendency of culturally diverse teams to divide into *factions based on
nationality,* managers can make subgroup divisions less obvious by including multicultural individuals (e.g. Chinese–Americans) on the team (Gibson and Vermeulen,
2003). When team members straddle the cultural divide, and belong in both groups,
they become bridges across the faultline, reducing its effect (Lau and Murnighan,
2005). Multiculturals can bridge faultlines through language, cultural knowledge
or by explaining the opposing subgroup's behavior. Also, team members are less
likely to categorize multiculturals into specific national or cultural groups (e.g.
"she's typically Chinese"), which reduces "us versus them" thinking, intergroup
hostility and stereotyping. Overall, we predict that when multicultural individuals
are part of teams that cross cultures, those teams will be less likely to develop cultural faultlines and dysfunctional team dynamics than cross-cultural teams using
only monoculturals.

Second, multicultural individuals may benefit teams by speeding up the process
of tapping diverse perspectives in a multicultural team. The most common reason
to purposefully build multicultural teams is to benefit from new ideas drawn from
different cultural perspectives, but the most common drawback is that multicultural teams take longer to perform tasks, because of conflict, misunderstandings or
differences in values (called process time) (DiStefano and Maznevski, 2000;

Schippers et al., 2003). Multicultural individuals may bring new ideas to the team, because they have multiple cultural perspectives, and are able to access more than one simultaneously, but are less likely to produce team conflicts and misunderstandings, because they also share cultures with their teammates. For example, experiments showed that Asian–American multiculturals developed more creative dishes from both Asian and American ingredients, rather than from all Asian or all American ingredients (Cheng et al., 2008). We predict that multicultural employees can contribute the most to internationally focused creative team activities, such as global product development, scenario planning and the design of a locally adapted marketing strategy.

Overall, when teams are made of individuals from multiple cultures, it usually takes longer for those individuals to understand one another than for members of a monocultural team (DiStefano and Maznevski, 2000; Thomas, 1999). When the team's multiculturalism comes from multicultural individuals instead of monoculturals from different cultures, the team may be able to work together faster, because faultlines may be weakened and because multiculturals are more likely to be curious about other cultures, as evidenced by Carlos Ghosn's comments in this reading. Multicultural individuals may be most useful in teams that are expected to perform complex, internationally focused tasks.

Multiculturals' Impact on Intercultural Negotiations

As CEO of PepsiCo, Indra Nooyi negotiates with businesses all over the world. Among her biggest negotiations were the merger with Quaker Oats Company in 2000, and her negotiations with the Indian media and government in 2006 about Pepsi's health standards in India. She was able to draw on her own cultural norms and bargaining strategies in both cases, adding to the ease of negotiations. It is a different situation in China, where she has very little experience, but her experience seeing the world through multiple cultural frames taught her to look for opportunities for integrative deals, based on cultural differences. For example, she took a two-week trip to China because she wanted to get a better feel for the country. "What are its issues? What makes it tick? I didn't want to come here clueless as to what was going on" (Indra Nooyi, as cited in Einhorn, 2009). Her experience demonstrates several ways multicultural negotiators can improve negotiations.

Good negotiators find a balance between maximizing individual objectives and common goals simultaneously. It is therefore important that negotiators understand their counterparts' goals, expectations, and negotiation strategies, which in a cross-cultural setting frequently turn out to be an obstacle. When negotiators share a culture, they usually share common expectations about acceptable negotiation strategies, behavior, and the sequence of the bargaining process. However, when negotiators from different cultures meet, they are often used to different cultural norms and standards (Cohen, 1997). For example, Argentineans, French and Indians prefer top-down approaches, from general to specific principles, whereas Mexicans, Japanese and Brazilians prefer building agreement from bottom up (Salacuse, 2005). Because of these types of differing expectations, same-culture negotiations, such as US–US or

Japanese–Japanese, tend to have better outcomes than cross-cultural bargaining, (Brett and Okumura, 1998). We propose two ways multiculturals may be able to mitigate some of these intercultural negotiation challenges.

First, multicultural negotiators might appreciate differences in perspectives and negotiation strategies more than monoculturals, rather than seeing dissimilarities as obstacles. Multiculturals may develop this skill because they are constantly confronted with diverse or even contradicting realities, so they learn how to deal with such situations and how to make the best of them (Tadmor et al., 2009). Especially if negotiations are complex and require creative solutions, multicultural experience may be an advantage. Galinsky et al. (2008) found that perspective-taking (the ability to consider the world from another person's viewpoint) helped negotiators identify creative bargaining solutions. Multiculturals, because of their multiple cultural backgrounds, are likely to possess good perspective-taking abilities and thus have an advantage in negotiations that require considering different views. In fact, Nooyi identifies this ability as her key negotiating strength: "I always look at things from their point of view as well as mine" (Indra Nooyi, as cited in Hobbs, 2008).

Second, multicultural negotiators may be able to positively influence their negotiation partners' communication experience. Research shows that although cross-cultural negotiations are often fraught with tensions and misunderstandings, international negotiations can produce higher joint gains than same-cultural negotiations when the communication experience is pleasant for both parties (e.g. when both parties feel comfortable and make efforts reciprocating and adapting to the other party's norms and expectations) (Liu et al., 2010). When both partners feel at ease and the negotiation takes place in an atmosphere of trust and respect, intercultural negotiators may be able to leverage their multiple perspectives for increased creativity, creating joint gains. Together, these mechanisms indicate that in international negotiations, multiculturals may be at an advantage because they are better able to take both perspectives and positively influence their negotiation partners' communication experience.

Multiculturals' Impact on Expatriation

As a larger number of organizations become increasingly global, it will become gradually more necessary for employees to move internationally. In fact, international job rotations may be among the most effective talent development tools (Stahl et al., 2009). Yet, international assignments are fraught with failure. Some return home early, while others are merely ineffective; all are costly to the organization. Multicultural individuals may be more successful in international assignments than monoculturals because they possess certain skills and knowledge that help them adjust to a different cultural environment.

Brannen et al. (2009) found that multicultural individuals have higher cultural metacognition than monoculturals, a key aspect of cultural intelligence. This aspect of cultural intelligence is essential in situations where international assignees are not familiar with the host culture, because it facilitates cross-cultural adjustment and cultural learning (Thomas et al., 2008). When Carlos Ghosn took positions in France and Brazil, he identified with the cultures, and knew how to work effectively in both locations. In contrast, when he moved to the US and Japan, he had no prior experience with the cultures, and had to learn how to be effective as he went along. As a multicultural individual, he had the mindset and skills necessary to be effective in cultures he knew well, and in those he did not. As he says in his book, when choosing an expatriate, "I wouldn't pick a person who'd never lived abroad, ... who'd never demonstrated an ability to work in a different culture from his own, and send him into such a situation. I had the 'ideal' background." (Ghosn and Riès, 2005).

However, multiculturalism's impact on expatriation success is not straightforward. Expatriates are not only faced with the challenges associated with adapting to a different culture and work environment, but must also act as liaisons between the foreign subsidiary and the home office. In this capacity, they must demonstrate strong commitment to the head office, and make sure that the company's global policies are carried out locally – a situation that has been termed the *dual allegiance* dilemma (Black and Gregersen, 1992; Vora et al., 2007). Dual allegiance refers to the fact that expatriates are often torn between their allegiance to the home office, and their allegiance to the local subsidiary.

There are four ways expatriates resolve the dual allegiance dilemma: by remaining primarily loyal to their home-country environment *(hearts at home)*; by prioritizing local needs over the needs of head office *(gone native)*; by caring primarily about their own careers, over and above the needs of head office or the local subsidiary *(free agents)*; or by remaining highly committed to both the parent firm and the local subsidiary, and trying to reconcile the often conflicting demands and expectations of both organizations *(dual citizens)* (Black and Gregersen, 1992). Although each of these patterns may have some benefits, the first three patterns tend to be detrimental to the firm: Hearts-at-home expatriates sometimes force head office ideas on to subsidiaries, regardless of their local effectiveness; gone-native expatriates sometimes fight head office to a degree that impedes global coordination; and free agents have lost their allegiance to the parent firm, without making any attempts to adjust to the local environment. By contrast, dual citizens tend to excel at coordinating between head office and the local subsidiary, and they have a higher probability of completing the international assignment successfully (Vora et al., 2007). They are also better than the others at transferring knowledge.

Multicultural individuals may solve the dual allegiance dilemma differently than monoculturals, because they have experience managing two or more sometimes-conflicting identities. People such as Carlos Ghosn are more strongly linked to a global identity, rather than to individual countries, so they may be less likely to take on either the hearts-at-home or gone-native positions, and more likely to become dual citizens. However, a potential danger of a multicultural orientation is that managers may be prone to become "free agents", i.e. they may lack a strong commitment to either the parent firm or the local organization. When Ghosn was working for Michelin, he was willing to travel to any location, with any company. He saw himself as a global citizen, first and foremost, and as such may have had lower loyalty to any one country or organization. This example illustrates a challenge that is unique to multicultural employees.

Multiculturals' Impact on Ethics and Leadership

Indra Nooyi faced a particularly thorny ethical dilemma starting in 2003, when PepsiCo India was accused of allowing pesticides from local groundwater into their soft drinks, and of using up scarce water for an unnecessary commodity. The nation was appalled, protestors defaced ads, several Indian states banned soft drinks altogether and sales crashed. In addition, the government debated imposing strict new standards on soft drink companies. They would bring Indian standards in line with Europe's, but would make it difficult to operate profitably in the country. By 2006, when Nooyi took over as PepsiCo's CEO, things had not improved. Nooyi had to act quickly to convince India that Pepsi's products were safe and that they were protecting India's water supply.

Executives and businesspeople working in the global arena must decide whether to use their own ethical principles, or to adopt the local ethical principles. For example, when working in countries where bribery is common, some managers refuse to take part because bribery is universally wrong, while others accept some level of bribery – such as "facilitation payments" – as normal in that context. These two perspectives are called universalist and relativist ethical perspectives, respectively, and they represent two broad categories of ethical argumentation across cultures (Windsor, 2004). Ethical universalism assumes that the situation does not influence what is ethical; only universal rules determine what is ethical. The most famous example is Kant's categorical imperative, where right and wrong are based on rules that apply at all times, regardless of circumstances or consequences (White and Taft, 2004). In contrast, ethical relativism assumes that each culture has the right to determine its own set of rules about right and wrong. Visitors must respect the local customs and adapt to them (Tasioulas, 1998).

Multicultural employees may be able to reconcile these seemingly conflicting perspectives because they have more complex cognitive schemas associated with ethical decision making – particularly in cross-cultural contexts – and can use their multicultural identities to strike the appropriate balance between global consistency and local sensitivity – what ethics scholars Donaldson and Dunfee have described as "a need to retain local identity with the acknowledgement of values that transcend individual communities" (1999, p. 50). Frame switching gives multiculturals experience seeing the world from more than one perspective, and as a consequence, potentially increases their ability to determine when different is different and when different is simply wrong.

PepsiCo's Indra Nooyi, for example, endorses ethical relativism while at the same time adhering to universal standards and maintaining the ability to make decisions that are in the best interest of the whole organization. Nooyi's response to Pepsi's problems in India was universalist and reflected the company's global commitment to environmental sustainability and safety: "One thing I should have done was appear in India three years ago and say: Cut it out. These products are the safest in the world, bar none. And your tests are wrong." Despite these strong words, she also adopted some relativist behaviors, by reducing water usage to one quarter of previous levels. "We have to invest, too, in educating communities in how to farm better, collect water, and then work with industry to retrofit plants and recycle" (Indra Nooyi, as cited in Brady, 2007).

Multiculturals' ability to balance global consistency and local flexibility in ethical decision making has important implications for multinational corporations. If a company (e.g. from the US) wants to enforce a bribery ban when working abroad, then it might be better served by monocultural employees from the parent country, who are less likely to be responsive to local needs and expectations. If a company wants to recognize that different environmental standards exist across their operations, staffing key positions with local managers who lack a strong global orientation might be the best choice. Companies that have adopted a transnational approach to business ethics, which requires managers to be responsive to both global and local imperatives, might be best served by multicultural employees, whose ability to see complex ethical situations from multiple perspectives should be useful in this context.

Multiculturals' Impact on Cross-Border Alliances, Mergers and Acquisitions

Alliances, mergers and acquisitions are notoriously difficult to implement successfully. In mergers and acquisitions (M&A), special emphasis is usually placed on the strategic and financial goals of the deal, while the cultural and people implications rarely receive as much attention. However, research shows that the failure of M&A that otherwise have a sound strategic and financial fit is often due to problems integrating the different cultures and workforces of the combining firms (Marks and Mirvis, 2001; Pucik et al., 2010). Problems are exacerbated when M&A occur between companies based in different countries. In addition to obstacles created by differences in the institutional environments, cultural chauvinism, differences in management styles and business norms, and the often-unanticipated challenges inherent in communicating across long distances can all undermine the success of M&A. For example, the poor performance of DaimlerChrysler, one of the most talked – about mergers of the past decade, is often attributed to a culture clash that resulted in major integration problems (Vlasic and Stertz, 2000).

Strategic alliances tend to be more successful than mergers, but they are difficult to manage – especially across borders. In 1999, Carlos Ghosn led the alliance between Nissan and Renault. From an outside perspective, the cultural and language barriers seemed insurmountable. Nissan was in a desperate financial situation, and Renault had only recently pulled out of its own slump. Yet, the alliance's success was due, in part, to the fact that neither firm had enough power to control the other. Instead of forcing Nissan to change, Ghosn had to rely on building strong relationships across the organizational and cultural boundaries. In hindsight, this looks like brilliant strategizing, but it was likely also influenced by Ghosn's uniquely multicultural identity. He explains, "It's imperative for each side to preserve its own culture while at the same time making an effort to understand the other's culture and to adapt to it. We've chosen a way based on mutual respect and the acknowledgement of two enterprises and two identities" (Ghosn and Riès, 2005).

In cross-border alliances and M&A, multicultural managers may influence outcomes in several important ways and at different stages of the process. A key asset of multiculturals is their greater cultural empathy, perspective-taking skills and ability to bridge cultural gaps. These skills are important before the alliance or merger takes effect, during the due diligence and negotiation stages. The purpose of cultural due diligence is to evaluate factors that may influence the organizational fit, to understand the future cultural dynamics as the two organizations merge, and to prepare a plan for how cultural issues should be addressed if the deal goes forward. Questions of this nature require the due diligence team to probe into the normative structure, core values and assumptions, and the core philosophy of the company itself in order to understand the company from a holistic cultural perspective. In addition, the culture of the target company or partner reflects the industry, national and regional cultures in which it is embedded (Schneider and Barsoux, 2003). Thus, the cultural due diligence team must understand and assess not only the company itself but also the context in which the company exists, particularly its national culture. Managers with a multicultural background, who have a thorough understanding of both the acquiring firm's and the target's (or partner's) culture, and the environment in which it is embedded, can play a key role in the evaluation of the cultural fit and the development of the integration strategy.

Strategic alliances and M&A require some degree of interdependence and integration, and the integration is always a delicate and complicated process. There will be inevitable culture clashes and questions will arise about which identity will dominate when corporate cultures are combined. Instead of melting everyone together, senior executives must capitalize on the differences in culture. Carlos Ghosn discussed this point as follows:

> People will not give their best efforts if they feel that their identities are being consumed by a greater force. If any partnership or merger is to succeed, it must respect the identities and self-esteem of all the people involved . . . Two goals – making changes and safeguarding identity – could easily come into conflict. Pursuing them both entails a difficult, yet vital balancing act.
>
> (Carlos Ghosn, as cited in Stahl, 2004, p. 5)

To pull off this balancing act, companies are increasingly turning to dedicated integration managers supported by transition teams (Ashkenas and Francis, 2000). It seems likely that individuals who are well versed in both companies' cultures are better able to serve as integration managers or members of transition teams because they understand the vulnerabilities on both sides and are able to come up with culturally appropriate solutions that preserve the identity and dignity of all the people involved.

TYPES OF MULTICULTURAL INDIVIDUALS

This reading has so far focused on potential skills and abilities of multicultural employees as a group, but there is more than one way to be multicultural (Table 1). Each one is associated with its own unique set of benefits and challenges, and it is important for organizations to understand the differences, so they can avoid assuming

Table 1. Multicultural types

Multicultural Type	Description	Example
Marginals	Marginals have more than one culture, but feel disassociated with both or all of them	April Raintree, Métis character in a Native Canadian novel: "It would be better to be a full-blooded Indian or full-blooded Caucasian. But being a half-breed, well, there's just nothing there." (Mosionier, 1999, p. 142; Pucik et al., 2010)
Separated	Separated multiculturals keep their cultural identities apart and identify with one or the other depending on the context	Andrea Jung, CEO of Avon, and Chinese–American: "I've definitely become more assertive . . . It really was critical to have that *Western* versus *Eastern* aspect, and still feel like I never had to change who I am." ("Women@Google: Andrea Jung," 2009)
Integrated	Integrated multiculturals merge their cultures together, resulting in a new, hybrid culture	Eric Liu, former speechwriter for President Clinton, and Chinese–American: "I could never claim to be Chinese at the core. Yet neither would I claim, as if by default, to be merely 'white inside.' I do not want to be white. I only want to be integrated." (Liu, 1998)
Cosmopolitans	Cosmopolitans identify with many cultures, are usually frequent travelers, and have lived in several different countries	Carlos Ghosn, President and CEO of Renault and Nissan, and French–Brazilian–Lebanese: "He is the quintessential global executive." (Najjar, 2008, August) "When you are an outsider and you cannot be categorized into one culture, it makes people feel that you are unlikely to be biased." (Ghosn, 2008, August)

all multiculturals share the same perspective. This is not an exhaustive list of ways to be multicultural, but the following four types are useful when considering how multicultural individuals can contribute to international business activities.

Marginals are people who have more than one culture, but who feel disassociated with both or all of them. Marginalization is psychologically difficult. For example, a survey of 5,366 immigrant adolescents across thirteen countries found that marginalized immigrants fared the worst, both psychologically and socioculturally (Berry et al., 2006). Even though Berry and colleagues' study demonstrates that this pattern is common among multicultural individuals, business people often do not talk openly about feeling marginalized, perhaps because of the negative implications of this pattern. However, there may be some benefits to being marginal. In particular, marginalized individuals may feel free to choose activities that are unconventional to both cultures (Rudmin, 2003). Because they have an in-depth knowledge of, yet are somewhat detached from, the cultures they represent, they may be able to make unpopular or even painful decisions, for example regarding layoffs and pay cuts, in a culturally appropriate manner.

Marginals may be more likely to employ a universalist ethical perspective, because they are less likely to switch cultural frames. Even though marginals have deeply internalized cultures, their cultural frames remain relatively stable, so they may be more likely to see ethics as a relatively stable construct, and may be more likely to endorse ethical universalism as a consequence. With respect to expatriation, and based on similarities with their cultural identity structures, we propose that marginals may be most likely to become free agents. Marginals have weak links to their own cultures, so may be more likely to also see themselves as weakly linked to their organizations.

Cosmopolitans, on the other hand, identify with many cultures (Hannerz, 1990). They are usually frequent travelers, and have lived in several different countries (Thompson and Tambyah, 1999). Cosmopolitans such as Carlos Ghosn tend to do well psychologically, with evidence that they are highly adaptable and are able to think in complex ways (Tadmor et al., 2009). Their multiple identities also make them especially resilient to identity threats (Binning et al., 2009). For example, if a South African-Dutch-German person felt like her Dutch identity was being threatened, she could switch to South African or German identities momentarily, to cope with the threat. This could explain why cosmopolitans tend to have better psychological outcomes than other types of multiculturals.

Both marginals and cosmopolitans may be at risk of becoming free agents during expatriation, and of preferring universalist ethics over relativist ethics. Marginals are only weakly identified with their cultures, while cosmopolitans identify more strongly with a global identity, over their individual countries. As a result, both types may take a similar approach with their organizations, and also see themselves as weakly linked to both parent and local organizations. Marginals and cosmopolitans also have relatively stable cultural frames, so they may be more likely to see ethics as a stable construct, and endorse ethical universalism as a result. Cosmopolitans alone may have an advantage during negotiations, over other types of multiculturals, because they have broader cultural experience than other multiculturals.

Separated and *integrated multiculturals* are related types, because they both identify with two cultures, although they mentally organize those cultures differently (Hong et al., 2000). Separated multiculturals keep their cultural identities apart. They identify with one or the other, depending on the context, resulting in two unique sets of cultural values. Integrated multiculturals merge their cultures together, resulting in a new, hybrid culture.

Research suggests that integrated multiculturals seem to have a lot of benefits, including lower stress, better social integration across cultures, and more creativity than separated individuals (Cheng et al., 2008; Mok et al., 2007). However, separated multiculturals seem to have higher levels of cognitive complexity, perhaps because they spend more time switching back and forth between cultural lenses.

Separated and integrated multiculturals may be more likely to use a relativist ethical perspective, because they switch frames in response to the cultural environment (Cheng et al., 2006). Frame-switching increases their experience seeing the world from more than one perspective, and as a consequence, potentially increases their endorsement of ethical relativism. Separated multiculturals may be most likely to take on either the hearts-at-home or gone-native positions, because they find it difficult to feel strong allegiance to two organizations, especially when their interests are in conflict with each other. For similar reasons, integrated multiculturals should be most likely to become dual citizens, and have bigger creative potential because they are used to combining differences and contradictions. These relationships are likely to hold because individuals take on whichever cultural identity pattern feels most natural to them, indicating that they're more likely to use an organizational identity pattern that reflects their cultural identity pattern. Now that it is clear that multicultural individuals as a group have unique skills to contribute to international business, and that different types of multiculturals may contribute different skills, we suggest how organizations can tap these skills.

MANAGING A MULTICULTURAL WORKFORCE: IMPLICATIONS FOR ORGANIZATIONAL CULTURE DEVELOPMENT AND HUMAN RESOURCE MANAGEMENT

Multicultural employees have the potential to add value in the five key areas described above, but only when organizations implement the procedures necessary to use their skills (for example, selection processes and career development practices to place them in positions where they can be most useful). Given that multinational organizations often fail to take advantage of the knowledge, skills and experiences of their global employees, organizations with the right processes in place have an opportunity to get ahead of their competitors. Ahead, and illustrated in Figure 1, we propose steps organizations can take in order to leverage the distinct skills and abilities of their multicultural employees. Organizations should first develop an organizational culture that encourages diversity of thought and perspectives; next, place value on hiring people with multicultural backgrounds, and place them strategically so they can use their unique skills; and, finally, train and develop multicultural employees to further enhance their skills with respect to the organization's requirements.

Figure 1. Managing a multicultural workforce: the organizational implications pyramid

Organizational Culture Development

Organizations that value multiple cultures are more likely to benefit from cultural diversity (Jackson et al., 2003), because when they don't, they risk suppressing employees' multicultural identities, and suppressing the skills and abilities that emerge from being multicultural as a consequence (Ely and Thomas, 2001). Organizational contexts that suppress multicultural identities could have especially strong organizational cultures, and value one particular way of thinking. They train employees to think, behave and react similarly to one another, resulting in a cohesive workforce, but one that misses out on the unique benefits of its multicultural employees (Jackson et al., 2003). Therefore, organizations should create visible signs that the company values employees with a multicultural background, and that international experience and a cosmopolitan orientation will improve one's career advancement within the organization. For example, leaders could create multicultural role models by promoting multiculturals to top management positions, or by instituting international experiential programs, explained ahead. Ideally, these initiatives should originate from the top-down, in order to stress their strategic importance, and to shift organizational culture. By shaping the organizational culture towards one that values multiculturalism, companies can provide the necessary context to leverage multiculturals' potential. Simply hiring multicultural employees is not enough; it is also essential to set up the conditions that allow their skills to emerge.

Staffing

Companies should develop systems that identify multiculturals' potential for both recruiting and placement. Multiculturals should be placed in positions where they can be most useful, otherwise their unique skills will be wasted. For example, the leadership and ethics section of this reading discussed strategically placing multicultural employees, in order to achieve particular outcomes and ensure global consistency in responsible leadership and ethical decision-making.

According to our analysis, multiculturals are most likely to contribute to the success of diverse teams when they are working on complex tasks requiring creativity. Therefore, organizations should identify tasks and teams with these characteristics, and try to place multicultural employees on those teams. For example, multicultural employees are more likely to benefit an international coordination team, rather than a team focused on coordinating with a stable, local supplier (DiStefano and Maznevski, 2000).

Since it is not practical to measure how much individuals identify with their cultures for recruitment purposes, we recommend hiring people with a wide variety of multicultural backgrounds, and placing them strategically once more is known about their particular skill sets. This approach will also help shift the organizational culture in the right direction.

Training and Development

We recommend using corporate training and development programs to achieve two goals: supporting multiculturals to become more conscious of their skills and abilities, and developing similar skill sets among monocultural employees. On average, monoculturals are not likely to develop these skills to the same degree as multiculturals, even with training, but they can be developed in order to close the gap. Mentorship and coaching are best suited to achieving the first goal, while global experiential programs could achieve both.

For example, Pless et al. (2011) studied a global experiential program at PricewaterhouseCoopers, where high-potential employees work with local partners in developing countries for eight weeks. The program helped managers acquire skills similar to those of multiculturals. Experiencing the heightened ambiguity, competing tensions and challenging ethical dilemmas associated with working in a foreign culture can trigger a transformational experience and produce new mental models in managers. Evidence shows that this program helped participants broaden their horizons, reduce stereotypes and prejudices, learn how to perceive the world through the eyes of people who are different, and work effectively with a diverse range of stakeholders – qualities similar to those of multicultural employees – which are essential for leading responsibly in a global and interconnected world. If a program like this one is not feasible because of cost or time constraints, then organizations could use short-term field experiences to expose employees to sub-cultures within their own countries (for example, by looking after homeless people, working with juvenile delinquents, or living with immigrants seeking asylum) to provide significant cultural immersion experiences and perspective-taking skills (Mendenhall and Stahl, 2000).

Overall, organizations can create visible signs that the company values multicultural employees by hiring and placing employees to maximize their ability to use their skills, mentoring new multicultural employees by senior-level multicultural role models, and developing all employees for multicultural skills, using experiential programs. Together, these steps should create the conditions that allow multicultural employees to shine.

CONCLUSION

Multicultural individuals may contribute valuable skills to teams, negotiations, alliances, mergers and acquisitions, international assignments, ethics and leadership. Although this discussion has focused primarily on multiculturals' overall contributions, their experiences are not universal, and organizations are at risk of alienating their multicultural employees unless they consider the different ways to be multicultural. The next step is for companies to take advantage of the potential in their multicultural employees by staffing, training and leading with these benefits in mind.

REFERENCES

Ashkenas, R. N. and Francis, S. C. (2000). Integration managers: Special leaders for special times. *Harvard Business Review*, 78(6), 108–116.

Berry, J. W., Phinney, J. S., Sam, D. L. and Vedder, P. (2006). Immigrant youth: Acculturation, identity and adaptation. *Applied Psychology: An International Review*, 55, 303–332.

Binning, K. R., Unzueta, M. M., Huo, Y. J. and Molina, L. E. (2009). The interpretation of multiracial status and its relation to social engagement and psychological well-being. *Journal of Social Issues*, 65, 35–49.

Black, J. S. and Gregersen, H. (1992). Serving two masters: Managing the dual allegiance of expatriate employees. *Sloan Management Review*, 33(4), 61–71.

Brady, D. (2007, June 11). Pepsi: Repairing a poisoned reputation in India. *BusinessWeek*.

Brannen, M. Y., Garcia, D. and Thomas, D. C. (2009). *Biculturals as natural bridges for intercultural communication and collaboration*. Paper presented at the International Workshop on Intercultural Collaboration, Palo Alto, CA.

Brett, J. and Okumura, T. (1998). Inter- and intracultural negotiation: U.S. and Japanese negotiatiors. *Academy of Management Journal*, 41, 495–510.

BusinessWeek (May 20, 2005). Indra Nooyi's graduation remarks. *BusinessWeek*, from www.businessweek.com/bwdaily/dnflash/may2005/nf20050520_9852.htm.

Cheng, C.-Y., Lee, F. and Benet-Martínez, V. (2006). Assimilation and contrast effects in cultural frame switching: Bicultural identity integration and valence of cultural cues. *Journal of Cross-Cultural Psychology*, 37, 742–760.

Cheng, C.-Y., Sanchez-Burks, J. and Lee, F. (2008). Connecting the dots within: Creative performance and identity integration. *Psychological Science*, 19, 1178–1184.

Cohen, R. (1997). *Negotiating Across Cultures*. Washington, DC: United States Institute of Peace.

David, E. J. R. (2006). Biculturalism. In Y. Jackson (Ed.), *Encyclopedia of Multicultural Psychology*. Thousand Oaks, CA: Sage.

DiStefano, J. J. and Maznevski, M. L. (2000). Creating value with diverse teams in global management. *Organizational Dynamics*, 29, 45–63.

Donaldson, T. and Dunfee, T. W. (1999). When ethics travel: The promise and peril of global business ethics. *California Management Review*, 41(4), 45–63.

Einhorn, B. (2009, July 2). Pepsi's Indra Nooyi focuses on China. *BusinessWeek*.

Ely, R. J. and Thomas, D. A. (2001). Cultural diversity at work: The effects of diversity perspectives on work group processes and outcomes. *Administrative Science Quarterly, 46,* 229–273.

Fortune. (2009). 50 Most Powerful Women. Retrieved January 22, 2010, from http://money.cnn.com/popups/2006/fortune/mostpowerfulwomen/1.html.

Galinsky, A. D., Maddux, W. W., Gilin, D. and White, J. B. (2008). Why it pays to get inside the head of your opponent: The differential effects of perspective taking and empathy in negotiations. *Psychological Science, 19,* 378–384.

Ghosn, C. (2008, August). Carlos Ghosn tells students to embrace diversity. Retrieved July, 2010, from www.aub.edu.lb/news/archive/preview.php?id=74360.

Ghosn, C. (April 11, 2008). The transcultural leader: Carlos Ghosn, CEO of Renault, Nissan. from http://knowledge.insead.edu/ILSTransculturalLeaderGhosn080501.cfm?vid=45.

Ghosn, C. and Riès, P. (2005). *Shift: Inside Nissan's historic revival* (J. Cullen, trans.). New York: DoubleDay.

Gibson, C. B. and Vermeulen, F. (2003). A healthy divide: Subgroups as a stimulus for team learning behavior. *Administrative Science Quarterly, 48,* 202–239.

Hannerz, U. (1990). Cosmopolitans and locals in world culture. In M. Featherstone (Ed.), *Global culture: Nationalism, globalization and modernity*. London: Sage.

Hobbs, S. (2008, June). Indra Nooyi: Simon Hobbs meets the CEO and chairman of PepsiCo. *CNBC Business*.

Hong, Y.-Y., Morris, M. W., Chiu, C.-Y. and Benet-Martínez, V. (2000). Multicultural minds: A dynamic constructivist approach to culture and cognition. *American Psychologist, 55,* 709–720.

Investing in Cultural Diversity and Intercultural Dialogue (2009). UNESCO (United Nations Educational, Scientific and Cultural Organization).

Jackson, S. E., Joshi, A. and Erhardt, N. L. (2003). Recent research on team and organizational diversity: SWOT Analysis and implications. *Journal of Management, 29,* 801–830.

Lau, D. C. and Murnighan, J. K. (2005). Interactions within groups and subgroups: The effects of demographic faultlines. *Academy of Management Journal, 48,* 645–659.

Liu, E. (1998). *The Accidental Asian*. Toronto: Random House.

Liu, L. A., Chua, C. H. and Stahl, G. K. (2010). Quality of communication experience: Definition, measurement, and implications for intercultural negotiations. *Journal of Applied Psychology, 95*(3), 469–487.

Marks, M. L. and Mirvis, P. H. (2001). Making mergers and acquisitions work: Strategic and psychological preparation. *Academy of Management Executive, 15*(2), 80–92.

Mendenhall, M. and Stahl, G. (2000). Expatriate training and development: Where do we go from here? *Human Resource Management, 39,* 251–265.

Mok, A., Morris, M. W., Benet-Martínez, V. and Karakitapoglu-Augün, Z. (2007). Embracing American culture: Structures of social identity and social networks among first-generation biculturals. *Journal of Cross-Cultural Psychology, 38,* 629–635.

Mosionier, B. C. (1999). *In Search of April Raintree*. Winnipeg, Canada: Portage & Main Press.

Najjar, G. (2008, August). Carlos Ghosn tells students to embrace diversity. Retrieved July, 2010, from www.aub.edu.lb/news/archive/preview.php?id=74360.

Nguyen, A.-M. D. and Benet-Martinez, V. (2007). Biculturalism unpacked: Components, measurement, individual differences, and outcomes. *Social and Personality Psychology Compass, 1,* 101–114.

Nooyi, I. (2009, May 12). Address to the Economic Club of Washington, from www.pepsico.com/Download/IKN_Economic_Club.pdf.

OECD (2009). *Society at a Glance 2009*: OECD Social Indicators. Paris: OECD.

Pless, N., Maak, T. and Stahl, G. (2011). Developing responsible global leaders through International Service Learning Programs: The Ulysses experience. *Academy of Management Learning & Education,* 10, 237–260.

Polzer, J. T., Crisp, C. B., Jarvenpaa, S. L. and Kim, J. W. (2006). Extending the faultline model to geographically dispersed teams: How colocated subgroups can impair group functioning. *Academy of Management Journal, 49*, 679–692.

Pucik, V., Bjorkman, I., Evans, P. and Stahl, G. (2010). Human resource management in cross-border mergers and acquisitions. In A.-W. Harzing and J. van Ruysseveldt (Eds.), *International Human Resource Management* (3rd ed.). London: Sage.

Rivas-Micoud, M. (2007). *The Ghosn Factor: 24 lessons from the world's most dynamic CEO.* New York: McGraw-Hill.

Rudmin, F. W. (2003). Critical history of the acculturation psychology of assimilation, separation, integration, and marginalization. *Review of General Psychology, 7*, 3–37.

Salacuse, J. W. (2005). *Leading Leaders: How to manage smart, talented, rich and powerful people.* New York: AMACOM.

Schippers, M. C., Den Hartog, D. N., Koopman, P. L. and Wienk, J. A. (2003). Diversity and team outcomes: The moderating effects of outcome interdependence and group longevity and the mediating effect of reflexivity. *Journal of Organizational Behavior, 24*, 779–802.

Schneider, S. and Barsoux, J. L. (2003). *Managing Across Cultures.* London: Prentice Hall.

Stahl, G. K. (2004). Getting it together: The leadership challenge of mergers and acquisitions. *Leadership in Action, 24*(5), 3–6.

Stahl, G. K., Chua, C. H., Caligiuri, P., Cerdin, J.-L. and Taniguchi, M. (2009). Predictors of turnover intentions in learning-driven and demand-driven international assignments: The role of repatriation concerns, satisfaction with company support, and perceived career advancement opportunities. *Human Resource Management, 48*, 89–109.

Tadmor, C. T., Tetlock, P. E. and Peng, K. (2009). Acculturation strategies and integrative complexity: The cognitive implications of biculturalism. *Journal of Cross-Cultural Psychology, 40*, 105–139.

Tasioulas, J. (1998). Consequences of ethical relativism. *European Journal of Philosophy, 6*, 172.

Thomas, D. C. (1999). Cultural diversity and work group effectiveness. *Journal of Cross-Cultural Psychology, 30*, 242–263.

Thomas, D. C., Stahl, G., Ravlin, E. C., Poelmans, S., Pekerti, A., Maznevski, M., et al. (2008). Cultural Intelligence: Domain and Assessment. *International Journal of Cross Cultural Management, 8*(2), 123–143.

Thompson, C. J. and Tambyah, S. K. (1999). Trying to be cosmopolitan. *Journal of Consumer Research, 26*, 214–241.

Vlasic, B. and Stertz, B. A. (2000). *Taken for a Ride: How Daimer-Benz drove off with Chrysler.* New York: Wiley.

Vora, D., Kostova, T. and Roth, K. (2007). Roles of subsidiary managers in multinational corporations: The effect of dual organizational identification. *Management International Review, 47*, 595–620.

White, J. and Taft, S. (2004). Frameworks for teaching and learning business ethics within the global context: Background of ethical theories. *Journal of Management Education, 28*, 463–477.

Windsor, D. (2004). The development of international business norms. *Business Ethics Quarterly, 14*, 729–754.

Women@Google: Andrea Jung. (2009). Mountain View, CA: Google.

Mark E. Mendenhall

OLIVIA FRANCIS

J IM MARKHAM DID NOT KNOW what to do. The more he tried to ana-
lyze the problem, the murkier it became. Normally, Jim felt confident in counseling
his students - both past and present – but this time it was different. Olivia Francis had
been one of the best students he had ever taught in the MBA program. She was intelligent and curious, one of those rare students whose thirst for knowledge was uppermost
in her reasons for being in the program.

She had never disclosed much about her family or her past to him, but he knew
from her student file and information sheet, and from bits and pieces of conversations
with her, that she had come from a poor, somewhat impoverished neighborhood in St
Louis and had earned her way through college on academic scholarships and part-
time jobs. Upon graduation from the MBA program, she left the Midwest, taking a job
with a prestigious consulting firm in Denver, and at the time he had felt sure she would
travel far in her career. Perhaps that is why her phone call earlier that morning troubled him so much.

Awaiting him on his arrival to his office was a message on his answering machine
from Olivia. He returned her call and wound up talking to her for an hour. The salient
portions of their conversation began to run through his mind again. What had struck
him initially were the range and the depth of her emotions. Never had he spoken to
anyone before that had seethed with so much rage. After she had vented the rage, like
air slowly being discharged from a balloon, she became almost apathetic, and her
resignation to her situation almost frightened him – her only way out, as far as she
could see, was to find another job. Jim could not recall ever being in a situation where
he felt he had absolutely no control over what happened to him, where his input was
meaningless to the resolution of a problem that he faced.

Olivia had stated that her first performance appraisal had been below average,
and two weeks ago, her second appraisal was only average. She felt that she had
worked hard on her part of the team's projects and believed her work was first rate.
The only reason for the appraisals, as far as she could see, was that she was not White.
She was the only African-American on the team – in the whole office for that matter.

Jim believed her when she said that her work was excellent, for her work had always been excellent as a graduate student and as a research assistant. He had attempted to get her to analyze the situation further, but it was like pulling teeth; she seemed emotionally worn out and just wanted out.

"Surely they gave you more feedback about your performance on the first appraisal than that it was below average?" he remembered asking. All she would say is that they mentioned something about her attitude, not being a team player, that her work was technically exemplary, but that she was part of a team and that working with others was as critical as the nature of the work she did by herself. Olivia, however, stated that she felt that this was a smokescreen for the fact that she had been dumped on the office by a corporate recruiter with a diversity quota to fill, and that they were trying to get rid of her by using subjective criteria that she couldn't really defend herself against. The frustration came back to Jim as he remembered probing her for more information.

"What was the tone of your manager in the feedback session?"

"Condescending, false sincerity; there was a lot of talk on his part of 'my potential.' It was humiliating, actually."

"How do the other people in your team act toward you? Are they friendly, aloof, or what?"

"Oh, they're friendly on the surface – especially the project leader – but that's about as far as it goes."

"Is the project manager the person who gave you this feedback?"

"No, she is under the group manager. He is a long-time company guy. But obviously she gives him her evaluation and impressions of me, so I'm sure that they both pretty much see issues regarding me eye-to-eye."

"Tell me more about the group manager."

"Mr. Bresnan? I don't know much about him to tell you the truth. He oversees five project teams, and each project manager reports to him. He comes in and gives us a pep talk from time to time. Other than that, I've never had occasion to really interact with him. He's always cracking jokes, putting people at ease. Kind of a 'Theory Y' type – at least on the surface."

"Do you ever go to lunch as a group?"

"Yes, they go to lunch a lot and they invite me along, but all they talk about are things I don't find very interesting – they're kind of a shallow bunch."

"What do you mean, 'shallow'?"

"They couldn't care less about real issues – their discussions range from restaurants to social events around town to recent movies they've seen."

"Does the project manager go to these lunches?"

"Yes, she comes and even plans parties after work, too. Her husband is a movie producer. Nothing big, just documentaries and that type of thing, but they put on airs, if you what I mean. She is really gregarious and always wants to be of help to people, but she strikes me as putting on a front, a mask. Obviously she isn't really sincere in wanting to help everyone 'be the best that they can be' – that's one of her little slogans by the way – after all, look what happened to me."

"Why do you think they're prejudiced against you?"

"Well, the poor appraisals for one thing – those are completely unfounded. They do other less obvious things, too. Twice I've overheard some of them from behind cubicles relaxing and telling ethnic jokes.

"Is it just a few of them that do this? I can't believe all of them are racist."

"I don't know! I don't enter the cubicle and say, 'Hi everyone, tell a few more jokes!' But it isn't just one or two of them. Look, I obviously don't fit in, do I? It's lily-white in the office, and I'm not."

"What do they do that is work-related that bothers you?"

"Well, when project deadlines get closer their anxiety level increases. They run around the office, yell at secretaries ... it is like a volcano building up power to explode. They worry and agonize over the presentation to the client and have four or five trial presentation runs that everyone is required to go to. It's all so stupid."

"Why is that?"

"The clients always like what we produce, and with a few relatively small adjustments, our work is acceptable to the clients. So, it's as though all that wasted energy was needless. We could accomplish so much more if they would just settle down and trust their abilities."

"How do you act when they are like this?"

"I do my work. I respond to them rationally. I turn my part of the project in on time, and it is good work, Professor Markham. I guess I try to be the stabilizing force in the team by not acting as they do – I guess I just don't find the work pressures to be all that stressful."

"Why not?"

"Oh, I don't know really. Well maybe I do a little bit. I don't know if you know this or not, but my mother was a single parent with four kids. I was the oldest. She worked three jobs, and I looked after the kids when I came home from school. She worked hard to provide for us, so I would be in charge of the smaller kids sometimes upwards of nine o'clock at night. Doing your homework while taking care of a sick kid with the others listening to the television - that's stressful! These people at work, they don't know what stress is. Most of them are single, or if they are married they don't have any kids. They all seem very self-centered, like the universe revolves around them and their careers."

"What kind of behavior at work seems to get rewarded?"

"I guess doing good work doesn't. What seems to get rewarded is being white, being more or less competent, and being interested in insipid topics. Professor Markham, don't you know of any firms that are more enlightened that I can send my résumé to? I'm looking for a firm that will reward me for the work I do and not for who I am or am not."

* * *

Jim leaned back in his chair, pondering what to do next. He had promised Olivia that he would call her back in a day or two with some advice. He sensed that he didn't quite understand her problem – that there was more to it than what appeared on the surface – but he felt he didn't have enough data to analyze it properly. He decided to go for a walk around the neighborhood to clear his mind. As he opened the front door and gazed down his street, he suddenly realized for the first time that his neighborhood was lily-white.

Joseph J. DiStefano

JOHANNES VAN DEN BOSCH
SENDS AN EMAIL

Professor Joe DiStefano prepared this mini-case as a basis for class discussion rather than to illustrate either effective or ineffective handling of a business situation.

The mini-case reports events as they occurred. The email exchanges in both cases are reported verbatim, except for the names, which have been changed. Professor DiStefano acknowledges with thanks the cooperation of "Johannes van den Bosch" in providing this information and his generous permission to use the material for executive development.

A **FTER HAVING HAD SEVERAL** email exchanges with his Mexican counterpart over several weeks without getting the expected actions and results, Johannes van den Bosch was getting a tongue-lashing from his British MNC client, who was furious at the lack of progress. Van den Bosch, in the Rotterdam office of Big Five Firm, and his colleague in the Mexico City office, Pablo Menendez, were both seasoned veterans, and van den Bosch couldn't understand the lack of responsiveness.

A week earlier, the client, Malcolm Smythe-Jones, had visited his office to express his mounting frustration. But this morning he had called with a stream of verbal abuse. His patience was exhausted.

Feeling angry himself, van den Bosch composed a strongly worded message to Menendez, and then decided to cool off. A half hour later, he edited it to "stick to the facts" while still communicating the appropriate level of urgency. As he clicked to send the message, he hoped that it would finally provoke some action to assuage his client with the reports he had been waiting for.

He reread the email, and as he saved it to the mounting record in Smythe-Jones' file, he thought, "I'm going to be happy when this project is over for another year!"

Message for Pablo Menendez
Subject: IAS 1998 Financial statements
Author: Johannes van den Bosch (Rotterdam)
Date: 10/12/99 1:51 p.m.

Dear Pablo,

This morning I had a conversation with Mr Smythe-Jones (CFO) and Mr Parker (Controller) re: the finalization of certain 1998 financial statements. Mr Smythe-Jones was not in a very good mood.

He told me that he was very unpleased by the fact that the 1998 IAS financial statement of the Mexican subsidiary still has not been finalized. At the moment he holds us responsible for this process. Although he recognizes that local management is responsible for such financial statements, he blames us for not being responsive on this matter and informing him about the process adequately. I believe he also recognizes that we have been instructed by Mr Whyte (CEO) not to do any handholding, but that should not keep us from monitoring the process and inform him about the progress.

He asked me to provide him tomorrow with an update on the status of the IAS report and other reports pending.

Therefore I would like to get the following information from you today:

- What has to be done to finalize the Mexican subsidiary's IAS financials;
- Who has to do it (local management, B&FF Mexico, client headquarters, B&FF Rotterdam);
- A timetable when things have to be done in order to finalize within a couple of weeks or sooner;
- A brief overview why it takes so long to prepare and audit the IAS f/s;
- Are there any other reports for 1998 pending (local gaap, tax), if so the above is also applicable for those reports.

As of today I would like to receive an update of the status every week. If any major problems arise during the finalization process I would like to be informed immediately. The next status update is due January 12, 2000.

Mr Smythe-Jones also indicated that in the future all reports (US GAAP, local GAAP and IAS) should be normally finalized within 60 days after the balance sheet date. He will hold local auditors responsible for monitoring this process.

Best regards and best wishes for 2000,

Johannes

B. Sebastian Reiche and Yih-teen Lee

UWA ODE: A CULTURAL CHAMELEON OR STRANDED BETWEEN CULTURAL CHAIRS?

The instrument had been there all this time, but I never quite understood how to play it. During my travels I learned all that I needed to bring MY music alive.

U WA ODE WAS STANDING on the terrace of a Barcelona-based business school where only moments ago she had graduated from a 17-month long Global Executive MBA program. Still feeling the rush of accomplishment, she had stepped out onto the terrace to enjoy a quiet moment by herself before rejoining her family and fellow graduates for the graduation dinner. As she looked out over the night-lit city, she reflected on the events in her life that had taken her from her country of birth, Nigeria, to England, Northern Ireland, Texas, and finally, Louisiana.

With the MBA program coming to an end, Uwa needed to decide whether she would continue to pursue her current career in an oilfield services company headquartered in the United States. If she wanted to achieve the career success within the company that matched her ambition, then the company would most likely relocate her every two to three years from one country to the next, or sometimes they might relocate her within the same country. Alternatively, Uwa could also make a career change that would allow her to move to a place that she could identify with, that would feel like home, and where she would have the opportunity to finally start building a permanent home. However, Uwa also considered starting her own business to take what she had learned from her international experiences and contribute to the business landscape in Africa by moving back to a continent she had not lived on for almost 17 years. After learning from the many cultures and countries that she had lived in so far, Uwa felt a responsibility to her country of origin and strived to preserve her cultural heritage. This was clearly more than just a sentimental wish, seeing that Africa offered a myriad of business opportunities and a lot of room for economic development. Uwa would be excited to return to the place of her birth and contribute to its development. At the same time, she was under no illusion as to the cultural dilemma that this might pose because she really was not the typical Nigerian that people might expect her to be.

As she was about to rejoin the graduation dinner, she realized that her next personal and professional decisions were looming large on the horizon. The decision was much more complex than simply weighing up the financial benefits or the opportunities to travel and see the world. This decision would be pivotal for Uwa's life and for her future.

A MULTICULTURAL CHILDHOOD

Uwa's parents are both from Edo State in Nigeria (see **Exhibit 1** for a geopolitical map of Nigeria). They both speak English as their first language but because they are from the same ethnic culture, they also share a local language, which they speak with each other. Her parents left Edo State when they were teenagers and moved to Lagos State, which is also in Nigeria. As for their university education, her father studied in England and her mother in France. After several years they returned to Nigeria where her father started his career with a multinational company that relocated him every three years. This gave her family the opportunity to work and live in the Netherlands twice, in England, in the United States, in Singapore and in several different states in Nigeria. Her parents felt that some of those moves caused too much instability for Uwa and her two sisters, so her father would relocate to some of the countries by himself while the rest of the family remained in Nigeria and visited him during vacations.

Uwa's father started his career in Rivers State, which had a different culture from their culture of origin. Uwa had always wondered why, as a family, they did not eat the same food or speak the same Nigerian language as her local friends from Rivers State. The Odes family had one culture at home, and spoke Uwa's parents' language, but Uwa and her siblings played, went to school, and interacted with classmates in a different cultural context. Very early on, Uwa started to feel displaced, not only because her family had relocated from one state to another but also because her parents themselves felt and acted displaced. This had a lasting impact on how Uwa viewed her own cultural heritage. Today, Uwa and her siblings define themselves differently from her parents, in spite of understanding their parents' culture and language. While Uwa and her sister would say that they are from Port Harcourt city (Rivers State) her parents would cite Benin City as their cultural origin. Aside from the relocations themselves, her father's work context also affected the way that Uwa and her family lived. As Uwa recalled:

> During the first 16 years of my life in Nigeria, in between the relocations, we lived in a purpose-built international, multi-racial, inter-racial and cross-cultural environment. All my friends who lived in the camp with me were also displaced from their parents' cultures. We had friends who were non-Nigerians growing up and going to school with us. Going to school we 'camp kids' were always 'odd' compared to the other kids who did not live in our 20-square-mile

camp. The camp was artificially designed to remind everyone from different nationalities of their homes: there were swimming pools, tennis clubs, golf courses, a grocery store, recreational centers, a salon—you get the idea. Once you drove into the camp, it was really like we did not live in Nigeria. So even though we were Nigerian, we were living in our own bubble, separated from our country.

After high school, a month after her 16th birthday in 1996, Uwa relocated to London to join her sister, who had left two years earlier, to start her A levels. She would go on to finish her tertiary education in London as well. The process of adjusting to her new life in London began on the day that she landed. Uwa remembered:

I realized that I didn't understand the jokes or subtle witty comments, and I sounded very different and dressed differently from the people around me. Back in Nigeria, I had graduated as head girl of my school. I was very popular, I had the best grades at my high school, my mum was a known entrepreneur in town... Everyone knew me: the other kids, the teachers, the parents. And now, for the first time in my life the people around me wanted me to explain who I was. They didn't know my personality, my jokes, who my family was, how many siblings I had. In 16 years, I had never been unknown, undefined—and there I was. Worst of all, everyone would ask what country I was from and this immediately separated me in teenage social circles. The Nigerian teenagers were the funniest—the ones who were either born in London or who had moved there many years before me. They would identify with me but their first question was always: 'When did you move to London?' The longer you had been in London the more accepted you were because you sounded like them, understood the culture and could navigate your way around. So I would lie awake wishing for time to go by so I could say that I had been in London for three years, instead of three months.

Uwa's adjustment process involved many different steps that all happened at the same time. In her first year in London, she never referred to the time she had spent in London in terms of months. Instead, she would always say that she had been there almost a year. It gave her a pass to be accepted and hang out with the people she wanted to be friends with. She also realized that she had to change the way she looked and sounded:

The first weekend in London I went shopping with my mum and my older sister who had been going to school in London for the previous two years. That weekend I allowed my older sister to choose every outfit my mum bought for me—after all I was about to start the same school my sister was going to and I didn't want to look different. I also realized my sister's accent had changed. That weekend I spent hours going through teenage magazines looking at how girls my age dressed and I watched television for countless hours trying to fine tune my ears. I would practice the words and repeat my new-found accent over and over again. After a while, when I said that I was from Nigeria people would remark: 'Wow, I never would have guessed except for your name!'

ENTERING THE PROFESSIONAL WORLD

In 2002, after graduating from university with a degree in engineering, Uwa started her first job in London. Like her father, she chose to work in the oil industry and she began her career at a local engineering company. However, she soon started worrying that she would be in London forever if she did not get a job with an international company. Uwa explained:

> I worried that I would stop absorbing other cultures and experiences that the world has to offer. Besides, there were still days when London did not feel like 'home' and I was not going to return to Nigeria—I was too different now. In a way, I was searching for what I had been used to growing up: the promise of the move.

After eight years in London, Uwa joined an international company that offered her exactly what she was looking for. She was immediately relocated to Belfast, Northern Ireland, where she spent about three years living and working. Her time in Belfast also coincided with feelings of being uprooted and this led Uwa to make a pivotal decision: she purchased a house. Uwa felt like she wanted something that was hers. She wanted to be able to go home to something that she owned instead of feeling like nothing was permanent. However, it turned out she could not make Belfast her home so she accepted a move to the United States in 2007 with the same company. With this move came another dance of adaptation and assimilation.

After almost five years in Texas and one year in Louisiana, Uwa finally made a decision that Louisiana would be her last non-permanent move. A year after she moved to Louisiana, Uwa realized that she had a lot of friends but none of them lived near her. She was not married and had no children. Even more importantly, she had not put down any roots, which was the opposite of the life that she had aspired to have. When Uwa was studying in London and her parents were living in Amsterdam, she remembered begging her parents to go home. Her parents replied: "But where do you want to go back to? We are in Amsterdam now and there is nobody in Nigeria." After relocating to Louisiana, Uwa was tired of exploring so many new places that were ultimately only temporary. It occurred to her that she felt quite content for her life to revolve around work, her apartment, and the gym because she was weary of building roots, making friends, and establishing traditions in a place, only to leave again.

During her professional career, her moves had been linked to promotions as opposed to places where she might like to build a life. In those places, most people were expatriates like her, all coming and going with multiple cultural experiences. Now, she wanted to find out where her cultural experiences might be relevant, where she could make long-term friendships, where she could identify with the place and its people, and where she could build a more permanent life, a home, and a family. In fact, an important reason for embarking on her Global Executive MBA was because the program would bring her back to Europe. It would give her enough new experiences and time to explore the world, in addition to providing her with academic fluidity. She hoped to identify where she wanted to live and find the opportunity to relocate to a place that she could call home.

Uwa realized how important this was after her boss offered her a job back in London, which she rejected straight away. Her boss could not understand why because it would mean that she could return to a city where she had lived for many years. As much as Uwa longed to return to Europe, at the time she wondered whether London was really the right place for her. After all, she was many cultures all in one. Her experiences stretched far beyond London and she did not want to just lay to rest the last six years in the United States. What was more, her British accent had given way to American English that now clearly set her apart in the United Kingdom and from her two sisters, who had lived there much longer than she did. She simply wanted to give herself time to decide on a final home.

THE MULTICULTURAL DIVIDEND

In contemplating her next personal and professional steps, Uwa also reflected on the advantages of her multicultural life. She would often describe each of the cultures that she had experienced as a beautifully different and unique song, and her process of living through each one as the art of mastering a new dance. She felt that she would not want to trade her experiences for different ones and that her life had been a truly enriching experience. As Uwa recalled:

> I feel like I have many persons living inside me. It is almost an exciting feeling. I know that I can change accents, the tone of my conversation, my way of thinking, my body language, my emotional intelligence, the interpretation of my surroundings, my point of view and even my jokes if I come across anyone who shares a cultural commonality with any of the places I have lived in. It means I am never afraid of change and I am never without friends. These are some of the many beautiful aspects of moving and experiencing the world the way I have.

Uwa's experiences also benefited her professional career. While working in a multicultural company, she had been able to lead multicultural teams successfully and bring out the best in everyone because of her experiences. In fact, she had often been selected for job promotions because of this very experience and skill. By and large, Uwa felt she had a good understanding of how to make decisions across many cultures to create a win–win result for everyone. For example, her company would often involve her in client negotiations. Most of her company's clients were international, so she would be selected to be part of the contract negotiations as a way of developing relationships and understanding with clients. As yet another sign that her company valued her skills, Uwa had also worked with the executive board on several occasions to redefine company policy. A few times, she had also been selected as part of a team of 20—out of a workforce of over 150,000—to be the voice of the employees and help the company to define effective policies across their global organization.

Further, when engaging with people who did not share the experiences of several cultures, Uwa had learned to quickly bring a new point of view into the discussion, and she was always able to understand several points of view at a time. Uwa also felt privileged to have few prejudices and a high sense of tolerance and empathy. Even when she did not understand another person or a cultural practice, Uwa would ask for clarification rather than making a quick judgment, because it constituted a key learning moment for her. She also tried to instill this cultural understanding in her team:

> In the United States, when an employee is expecting a baby it is common for coworkers to plan a party called a 'baby shower'. I had one non-U.S. employee, though, who did not tell anyone that his wife was pregnant. One day he happily announced that he had just become a father. His coworkers took this badly; they felt deceived and couldn't understand how they could have worked with him for nine months without him mentioning it once. Some went as far as questioning whether they could still trust him if he would keep such a secret. When I heard about this issue, I assembled my team to explain that in some cultures there are superstitions about celebrating, naming a baby, or buying gifts before the baby's safe arrival. They were all shocked because they had not heard of this before. But with the help of Google, everyone came to understand. I then called the employee and asked him to explain his motivations to his teammates. Needless to say, a party was planned after the baby arrived.

THE MULTICULTURAL BAGGAGE

At the same time, Uwa recognized that there was a flipside to her multicultural life. Because Uwa had had to say goodbyes several times, she was constantly accompanied by a fear of loss—whether it was being separated from friends and loved ones or the initial rejection people may face in a new society while they are still different from the people around them. On the positive side, this meant that Uwa was very cautious about never causing the people around her any kind of pain or feelings of rejection. Although Uwa was afraid to lose another set of friends and move again, the bigger question was about where she truly belonged:

> Where is home? Where am I from? Which culture should I identify with? Is home where I work—even though it is not permanent? Or is home where my parents' house is? Because with all this moving I have not put down any roots anywhere, yet. What is the correct response to the first time someone asks: 'Where are you from?' Should I reply that I am Nigerian? But when I say so, the immediate connotations are not true and the last 17 years of my life go missing unless I respond with further detail. Should I say I am English

because of my second citizenship? But you can tell that I obviously have African heritage! Saying I am English also leaves out the first 16 years of my life. Worse yet, I have adopted an American sounding accent and have lost my British accent. Is that even a plausible response? After all, I have a U.K. passport to back up my claim, which isn't the case if I say that I am American just because I might sound it slightly, because I don't have citizenship or a green card. In fact, I'm in the United States on a visa, with the looming reality that it will expire and I will have to move again.

There was also the question of national identity and loyalty. Should Uwa pick a political party in the United States or join a cause? Should she vote in the English elections and contribute to charities that might benefit from her time and skills? Or should she dedicate her national loyalty to Nigeria and the African continent, which was in dire need of foreign-trained Africans like her? In addition, Uwa felt that her many experiences abroad had also changed her personality. When someone told her that she was quiet, Uwa burst out laughing. How could someone perceive her to be quiet when she was such a sociable and approachable person? Even her family did not seem to recognize all of her personality anymore. In 2012, while living in the United States, her sister had told her:

Each time I see you it is as if another part of your personality has gone. Where is the loud laughter [people thought it was too gregarious at that time so Uwa decided to suppress it], where are the jokes [no one seemed to understand her English jokes so Uwa stopped telling them], and where is the fire and the passion in your soul [people seemed to think it was aggressive so Uwa suppressed that too]?

It took her sister a few days to recognize her. As her sister said: "It's like you are able to be multiple people depending on the situation." What had also changed was Uwa's relationship with her base culture. Uwa's experiences during her many moves showed her that the skills that her parents had taught her did not always apply in every new cultural situation, which meant that she had to learn a whole new set of skills in order to excel. In fact, along the way Uwa had learned several better ways of conduct. While her parents were hesitant to accept this deviation from some of their own cultural traditions, they also acknowledged the positive perspectives that this brought to the family's habits and activities.

THE DECISION

While Uwa was fortunate to have experienced so many places, she also felt that this made her next decision all the more difficult. Maybe a move to a new country, coupled with the experiences from the Global Executive MBA, would provide her with fresh inspiration, even if she stayed with her current employer. Uwa knew the excitement that came with always moving. Maybe she was afraid of not moving. Maybe she loved the feeling of living a nomadic life, the thrill of discovering new cultures, and the challenge of reinventing herself in new cultures. Although she sometimes felt rootless, there was also a fair share of restlessness that kept her fixated on moving and avoiding anything permanent that might take away her freedom of packing her bags and starting all over again whenever she needed to. On the other hand, maybe the next move would turn out to be the permanent place she had always been looking for. She also still felt strangely attached to Africa, and Nigeria in particular. Her parents had decided to retire to Nigeria so she had some family there. However, her older sister who had also moved back to Nigeria earlier was unhappy because she felt that the people did not really understand her and she did not share the views of Nigerian society at large. Uwa, by contrast, did not even have many friends back in Nigeria.

One thing was clear. Uwa had not decided to enroll in the Global Executive MBA only to stay in her current job. She had explicitly wanted to give herself the opportunity to make a drastic career change, a career change that would allow her to move to a place that she could call home. Uwa had also wanted to be around people like her, who had colorful cultural backgrounds themselves and who were citizens of the world: people who would understand what it was like to be a citizen of many countries and to possess many different cultural experiences. In a way, Uwa hoped that, given the transience of her past relationships, these people would turn out to be lifelong friends and that they would be part of the permanent future that she was trying to build.

EXHIBIT 1. Geopolitical map of Nigeria

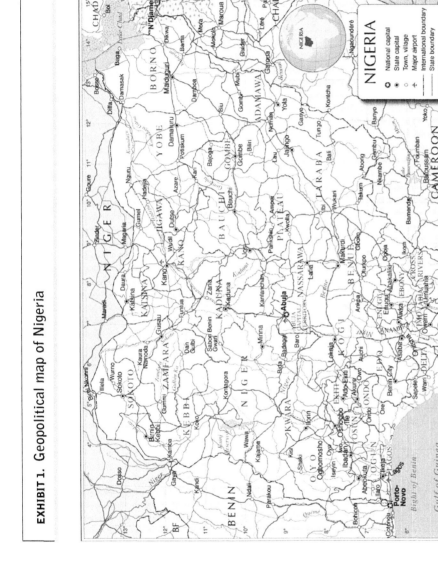

Source: Nations Online Project (www.nationsonline.org).

PART III

Global Staffing and Management of Global Mobility

Readings

- David G. Collings, Anthony McDonnell, and Amy McCarter
  TYPES OF INTERNATIONAL ASSIGNEES

- Gary R. Oddou and Mark E. Mendenhall
  EXPATRIATE PERFORMANCE APPRAISAL: PROBLEMS AND SOLUTIONS

- Jaime Bonache and Luigi Stirpe
  COMPENSATING GLOBAL EMPLOYEES

Cases

- J. Stewart Black
  FRED BAILEY: AN INNOCENT ABROAD

- Paula Caligiuri and Henry W. Lane
  SELECTING A COUNTRY MANAGER FOR DELTA BEVERAGES INDIA

- Günter K. Stahl and Mark E. Mendenhall
  ANDREAS WEBER'S REWARD FOR SUCCESS IN AN INTERNATIONAL
  ASSIGNMENT: A RETURN TO AN UNCERTAIN FUTURE

David G. Collings, Anthony McDonnell, and Amy McCarter

TYPES OF INTERNATIONAL ASSIGNEES

INTRODUCTION

INTERNATIONAL ASSIGNMENTS have long since represented a critical mechanism by which organizations that operate on a global scale can effectively manage and develop their global operations. Such assignments serve multiple purposes including management development, coordination and control, information exchange and succession planning (Black et al., 1999; Edstrom and Galbraith, 1977; Harzing, 2001). For employees, it is claimed that international assignments are "the single most influential force for the development of managers" (Stroh et al., 2005) and can contribute significantly to the development of one's career in the global organization. Much of the research surrounding international assignments has centered on "traditional" international assignments—purpose driven transfers to a foreign location with a duration of between 12 and 36 months (Dowling et al., 2008) and up to 60 months. This is unsurprising because historically such assignments have represented the most dominant form of global staffing arrangement (Collings et al., 2007) and recent indications suggest that assignments of this duration remain prevalent amongst organizations (McDonnell et al., 2011; Brookfield GMAC, 2013).

However, the landscape of global mobility has altered significantly over the past several decades and the topography of global staffing is far more heterogeneous in the contemporary multinational enterprise (MNE) than has previously been the case in the past. This has important implications for the study and practice of international human resource management (IHRM). First, it creates a question as to the utility of academic theories and models based on samples of traditional longer term assignments. Do the findings and recommendations hold true in different modes of international staffing? Second, for IHRM practitioners it demands a wider range of policies and practices to reflect the differing requirements of different staffing types. It is also important to consider the extent to which these differing global staffing options meet the strategic objectives of the sending organization and the individual employees.

This reading begins by considering the role of international assignees in the MNE. The challenges to traditional models of global mobility which relied on longer term assignments are then outlined. Emerging alternatives to global mobility are then introduced, followed by a consideration of the HR challenges and issues emerging from a portfolio approach to global mobility. We conclude with some directions for further study.

EXPATRIATE DEPLOYMENT AND THE MNE

Organizations have physically relocated managers to foreign locations where business operations are based since approximately 1900 BC. Indeed, even at this stage, locals were viewed as inferior and restricted to lower level jobs while parent country nationals (PCNs) or individuals from the headquarters country were afforded superior conditions, similar to modern-day expatriates (Moore and Lewis, 1999: 66–67).

Edstrom and Galbraith (1977) were amongst the first to theorize on the differing objectives of international assignments. Broadly following their conceptualization, literature on international management and IHRM has consistently focused on three core purposes for using international assignments. First, in position filling, where particular knowledge, skills and abilities are not available in the host country, organizations may fill the existing gap with expatriates sourced from other geographic areas. Second, they serve as vehicles for the training and development of current and future international managers. Finally, international assignments may act as a means of organizational development, through knowledge transfer and information sharing amongst subsidiaries as well as the coordination and control of subsidiary units. Others such as Salt and Millar (2006) identify the key drivers of international working as: building new international markets; temporary and short-term access to talent to execute overseas projects; and, to perform boundary spanning roles and facilitate the exchange of knowledge within the firm.

Pucik (1992) further elaborated on the definition of international assignments, categorizing them by "demand" or "learning" driven purposes. Those which are demand driven are identified as serving skill requirements to solve specific problems which arise in the host location. In contrast, leaning driven assignments are characterized as providing a means of developing managerial talent at the individual level as well as for organizational learning. While evidently organizations may use international assignments for an array of motives it should be noted that such are not mutually exclusive and indeed international assignments may serve multiple functions at any one time. Nonetheless, these broad objectives provide a basis for understanding the objectives of global mobility.

The objectives of global mobility have important implications in judging the success or otherwise of international assignments. For example, assignments premised on management development have been shown to result in personal change and role innovation as acclimatizing to the new environment results in the assignee adapting their frame of reference. Alternatively, in control-driven assignments, the emphasis is on locals absorbing the new demands of the expatriate manager and success is considered as locals changing their frames of reference (Shay and Baack, 2004).

The relationship between differing objectives of global mobility and the nature of HR support required by assignees also emerges as an important consideration (see Collings, 2014).

However, the relationship between international assignments and MNEs has been somewhat torturous with some suggesting that there remains a significant underestimation of the complexities which surround them (Dowling and Welch, 2004). Indeed there are a number of challenges which emerge which constrain the potential value which organizations reap from expatriate deployment. While on one hand they have served well for achieving organizational objectives, on the other hand they are fraught with challenges which affect many of the stakeholders involved in the international assignment. This has prompted some debate surrounding the viability of international assignments for organizations. We will now briefly consider some of these challenges before moving on to consider the various alternatives to the traditional international assignment which are common place in the contemporary MNE.

CHALLENGES TO LONG-TERM ASSIGNMENTS

The first key challenge relating to the traditional international assignment emerges in terms of recruitment and selection. Organizations face an increasingly difficult task in attracting employees willing to take on international assignments (Collings et al., 2007). A multiplicity of reasons cited for such difficulties include *inter alia* the rise of dual career couples, growth of difficult assignment locations, less generous expatriate compensation packages, and career concerns.

With the incorporation of women into the labor market within the last half a century, many relationships involve dual careers. Individuals engaged in dual career relationships may be less willing to accept international assignments and, therefore, exclude themselves from the selection phase because of the impact the international phase may have on their partner and their career or the disruption it may cause to personal and family situations (Collings et al., 2007; Forster, 2000). Additionally, the political and cultural constraints of the host countries have been argued to deter employees from accepting international assignments. For example, host countries involved in war, civil unrest, and political instability may be conceived as dangerous to relocate to. Similarly, locations which are culturally distant from the home country and may prove challenging for assignees may be more unattractive when compared to locations which are culturally and perhaps geographically close to the home country. Reflective of these concerns, the Brookfield GMAC (2013) relocations trends study reports cultural difficulties, personal security concerns, language difficulties and the political climate in the host country amongst the top five reasons why such countries are considered challenging. Countries identified as presenting the greatest challenge for organizations in the survey include China, India, Russia, and Brazil, which are particularly worrisome owing to the increasing economic significance of these "BRIC" countries and the requirements of international talent in these markets (Brookfield GMAC, 2013).

An additional challenge emerges when those considering undertaking international assignments reflect on the experiences of previous expatriates through direct communication or through observation. This may influence the decision to accept or decline an international assignment (Tung, 1988). Witnessing the challenges which other expatriates faced on repatriation may result in potential international assignees concluding that an international assignment will hinder rather than benefit their own career should they accept (Black et al., 1992).

Further challenges for organizations relate to costs and expatriate "failure". While the true cost of an international assignment is difficult to measure, traditional international assignments typically incur huge financial costs as well as other costs. Traditional estimates indicate that the average cost of maintaining expatriates abroad was between three and five times the cost of employing them at their home location (Forster, 2000). Indeed, there has been a consistent drive for reducing the costs of global mobility over the past decade or so. Balance sheet compensation packages are regularly being replaced with local-plus packages, or tiered compensation packages which reward based on the strategic function of the individual assignment (see Tornikoski et al., 2015).

Expatriate failure has been a significant and indeed controversial issue within the literature. Expatriate failure is commonly measured as a premature return from an international assignment. Although high expatriate failure rates have been frequently highlighted in literature, of between 20 and 30 percent (Tung, 1981, 1982; Black et al., 1999), such high rates have been challenged by others, suggesting that indicated failure rates are amplified and are not supported by empirical investigation (Harzing, 1995, 2002). However, more recently there have been calls to conceptualize the issue of expatriate failure more broadly (Scullion and Collings, 2006). Such an approach recognizes the potential costs it can lead to – both directly in terms of salaries, relocation expenses, legal issues, and so on, and indirectly through the possibility of market share loss and strained relationships (Collings et al., 2007).

Finally, the retention of expatriate employees after repatriation has become a challenge to the traditional assignment. Arguably repatriation presents the most problematic phase of the international assignment cycle and was identified as the biggest single problem by UK companies over a decade ago (Forster, 2000). Although the expectation may be that repatriation should be relatively straight forward as the expatriate is "coming home" (Stroh et al., 2000), research suggests that this phase is often the most problematic for employees and the sending organization (see Lazarova, 2015). Despite acknowledgement of the fact that retention is a serious problem, there is little evidence to suggest that organizations are developing effective re-entry programs for expatriates returning from international experience. Previous reports suggest that often between 10 and 25 percent of repatriated employees leave their organization within the first year of return (Black et al., 1999; Bonache et al., 2001; Brookfield GMAC, 2013). This is a critical concern for the organization, particularly when the primary purpose of the assignment is learning driven, where it is crucial that organizations proactively plan to reintegrate employees into their organization on return in order to profit from the investment made (Reiche and Harzing, 2011). Causes for high rates of turnover have been connected with feelings of frustration felt by the employee. For the returning expatriate, coming home is often a difficult transition due to assured development of the organization since their departure. However, it is perhaps concerns around career development where repatriated employees feel most of their frustration. Although the academic literature and practitioner reports emphasize the benefits of international assignments for one's career in terms of advancement, empirical evidence to support these claims, at least within the sending organization, is rather scant (Welch, 2003). Furthermore, many empirical accounts report that those who undertook international assignments often experienced negative career implications in terms of missed opportunities while they were abroad or broken promises of promotion when they returned from their assignments and difficulties in finding a suitable position upon return (Stahl and Chua, 2006). In reality many employees find themselves in "holding patterns" upon their return as organizations who fail to effectively plan for their return scour to find suitable positions which merit the newly acquired competencies by the employee (Feldman and Thomas, 1992; Selmer, 1999; Bonache et al., 2001). Furthermore, concerns are raised by repatriates over the under utilization of their newly acquired skills. Many perceive their positions upon re-entry lacking in authority (Lazarova and Cerdin, 2007). Former expatriates perceive that organizations do not value the knowledge experience they acquired while on assignment (Selmer, 1995). Consequently, employees are overcome with feelings of underemployment, and disillusion and leave the organization through frustration with the treatment they have received.

However, Kraimer et al. (2009) found that those who undertook developmental assignments were more likely to progress within the organization upon return than those who accepted assignments which relate to problem solving. Notwithstanding this, developmental driven international assignees are more likely to leave their organization upon return (Dickmann and Doherty, 2010). While international assignments evidently pose complex problems for organizations, they also present a complex challenge for employees. International assignments provide excellent opportunities for skill and knowledge development, general management skill acquisition as well as unique inter-cultural awareness and global leadership development (Black et al., 1999). However, from a more negative perspective, international assignments are often reported to have detrimental career effects. Despite the concerns over the particularly negative implications of international assignments for expatiates and repatriates, some researchers have started to consider why employees continue to accept such postings (Stahl et al., 2002; Lazarova and Cerdin, 2007). However the question remains open as to understanding how individuals weigh up the posited negative implications of international assignments with decisions to undertake international relocations.

CHANGING FORMS OF GLOBAL MOBILITY

The challenges identified above mean that both organizations and individuals alike are re-evaluating their attitudes towards global mobility and indeed the international staffing options available to meet organizational operational objectives and individual career objectives. Indeed, Briscoe and Schuler (2004: 223) concluded a decade ago that the definition of the international employee within the organization has expanded and that the "tradition of referring to all international employees as expatriates ... falls short

of the need for international HR practitioners to understand the options available ...
and fit them to evolving international business strategies." Although there is a
growing literature which focuses on the experiences of self-initiated expatriates,
or those employees who relocate to another country without organizational support
and gain employment in the host country (see Doherty, 2013; Doherty et al.,
2013; Vaiman and Hasleberger, 2013), we focus here on corporate expatriates—
"employees who are temporarily relocated by their organization to another
country ... to complete a specific task or accomplish an organizational goal"[1]
(Shaffer et al., 2012: 1287).

A key point of differentiation between the traditional international assignment
and emerging alternatives is temporal. While international assignments typically
involved sojourns abroad of between one and five years, there is far more variety in
modern forms of international mobility. Evans et al. (2011) argue that the traditional
long-term orientation of international assignments derived from rather ethnocentric
objectives of the traditional assignment. Such assignees predominately acted as corporate agents in establishing control mechanisms in newly established subsidiaries or
by transferring knowledge. Additionally, developmental objectives may have been conceived in more traditional terms as building cross-national, organizational coordination capabilities (see also Collings and Scullion, 2012). However, more recently,
problem solving objectives which are defined by their singular purpose mean that
such long-term sojourns are less necessary. Additionally, it is increasingly recognized
that shorter periods abroad can have beneficial effects on individual's careers. For
example, many international graduate programs now incorporate one or two short
assignments internationally. Such assignments are considered attractive to younger
employees entering the workforce who consider global experience as a key desire in
their early careers. Indeed, a recent consultancy report concluded that the millennial
generation viewed overseas assignments as a rite of passage in their early careers
(PWC, 2010).

The first alternative form of global mobility which we consider is the international business traveller (IBT). The IBT or "frequent flier" is defined as "one for whom
business travel is an essential component of their work" (Welch and Worm, 2006:
284). Employees who take up these international assignments will travel and communicate regularly between the host location and home office; however, they will not
relocate because their roots remain in their home country. While not a new phenomenon in international business, the IBT is increasingly being considered as an alternative to international relocation and, hence, merits discussion. IBTs provide the
advantage of face-to-face interaction in conducting business transactions without the
requirement for physical relocation. By definition, IBTs generally involve relative
short stays in specific locations, the durations of which are dictated by the objective
of the visit. IBTs tend to be utilized for specialized tasks which occur rather irregu-
larly, such as budgeting or production scheduling. Tracking the utilization of IBT as
an alternative to conventional assignments, survey reports have presented the increasingly active position that IBT holds in MNEs. This trend appears to be consistent with
recent survey reports which suggest that international business travel is an increasingly viable alternative option. Over 90 percent of companies surveyed by Cartus

(2012) have either maintained or increased their use of international business travel over the past three years. On the other hand, Boyle and McDonnell (2013) point to the global financial crisis negatively impacting international business travel amongst MNEs operating in Australia. Given the extensive levels of people involved in business travel, it is a significant challenge for MNEs to establish an accurate account of the number of IBTs in their organizations (Welch and Worm, 2006). Clearly the implications of failure to track such assignments from a tax perspective are significant and organizations are increasingly putting extended travel policies in place to accurately track their populations of IBTs (Brookfield GMAC, 2013).

A second alternative form of global mobility is the "commuter assignment." Although a longer term arrangement, commuter assignments generally involve an assignee commuting from their home base to a post in another country, generally on a weekly or bi-weekly basis. Similar to IBTs, commuter assignments involve heavy travel and these assignments are likely to be of a more structured, defined pattern (Stahl et al., 2012). While it is difficult to quantify the extent of usage of such assignments Mayrhofer and Scullion (2002) cite the example of German quality engineers with managerial and technical responsibilities in the clothing industry who travelled frequently to several countries in Eastern Europe, returning regularly for briefings and to spend weekends with their families. In a recent survey of almost 600 MNEs globally, a quarter of the respondents indicated that they use commuter assignments (KPMG, 2013). Indeed, Mayrhofer and Brewster (1997) argue that the geographic situation in Europe means that Euro-commuting and frequent visiting is a viable alternative to expatriate transfers. However, such assignments have profound effects on the lives of the individuals concerned and are frequently incompatible with family life and familiar daily routines, and often do not sustain adequate work life balance. Additionally, individual burnout, fatigue, and tax management are important concerns (Meyskens et al., 2009; Mayrhofer et al., 2008). Such arrangements can be used in a wide range of circumstances where an individual may not wish to relocate their family on taking on a role in a new location.

Third, "rotational assignments" involve an individual working for a set period of time on location in a foreign location followed by a break in the home country. This type of assignment is most common in the oil and gas industries where drilling locations are often incompatible with family life. Again such assignments tend to be longer term arrangement and are often a function of the industries concerned. In a recent world survey amongst 600 multinationals carried out by KPMG (2013), almost 20 per cent of participants indicated that rotational assignments are employed in their organization.

The most common alternative to the traditional assignment is the "short-term" assignment. These assignments are generally viewed as being of a longer duration than a business trip and usually do not last longer than one year (Collings et al., 2007). Similar to previous alternative forms, they generally do not involve relocation of the assignee's spouse or family (Starr and Currie, 2009). Such assignments are suited to organizational, or to a lesser degree individual, development objectives, which could be achieved at a fraction of the costs associated with expatriate assignments (Scullion and Collings, 2006). Indicative of the increasing usage of short-term assignments, 86 percent of firms in the Brookfield GMAC (2013) survey had short-term assignment policies in place. The key advantages of short-term assignments include increased flexibility, simplicity, and cost effectiveness (Tahvanainen et al., 2005: 667–668). Appositely common disadvantages include: (1) taxation issues particularly for assignments over six months duration; (2) potential for side effects such as alcoholism and marital problems; (3) failure to build effective relationships with local colleagues and customers; and (4) work visas and permits (Tahvanainen et al., 2005; Dickmann and Debner, 2011). Short-term assignments have a wide range of applications, from leadership development through to problem solving and project type roles. Empirical evidence suggests that short-term assignments remain the most popular type of alternative assignment amongst organizations. According to the Global Mobility Report Survey, almost a quarter of organizations reported that short-term assignments are most prevalent in their organization (Brookfield GMAC, 2013). Additionally, similar research suggests that these trends are likely to increase, with 94 percent of 122 global organizations stating that their short-term assignment activity is likely to remain the same or increase over the next few years (Cartus, 2012).

The final alternative to the traditional assignment where temporality emerges as a key concern is the "permanent transfer" whereby the individual is permanently transferred to local payroll and local terms and conditions in the host country. Such arrangements are becoming increasingly common and are seen as a cost effective means of transferring staff globally, with some 41 percent of firms having formal policies around permanent transfers (Brookfield GMAC, 2013). This type of mobility has largely been neglected by the academic literature, despite their increasing utilization in practice. Collings et al.'s (2008) study unearthed some evidence of permanent transfers as a staffing option which they traced to operating in low margin industries where the cost constraints of global mobility were particularly significant. However, the findings from Tait et al.'s (2014) exploratory study questioned the cost savings of permanent transfers arguing that the assignment type may be at odds with the MNE's longer term goals regarding talent and knowledge management. However, the area of permanent transfers is largely unresearched and the extent of their usage, the implications on employee outcomes and organization performance all merit further consideration. Permanent transfers have a wide application, although empirical research is required to understand individual employee's motivations to accept such assignments. In terms of utilization levels, 47 percent of organizations indicated that they use permanent transfers as a form of international assignment (KPMG survey, 2013).

We now turn to spatial issues around alternative forms of global mobility with a particular focus on where the assignee and their family are located during the assignment episode. Indeed, a key characteristic of the traditional expatriate assignment was that the assignees and their family generally relocated to the host location for the duration of the assignment. The emergence of these alternative forms of global mobility shift the boundaries of location for the assignees and their families alike. For example, in the case of IBTs and short-term assignees, their base is generally retained in their home country. This means that the assignee's family often remain in the home country, while salary, pension and social security benefits are also handled there

(Peltonen, 2001; Brookfield GMAC, 2013; Tahvanainen et al., 2005). However, where a short-term assignment lasts beyond six months, this can create tax and social security issues and it may not be possible for the assignee to retain tax status in their home country. For similar reasons, commuter and rotational assignees are often classified as resident in their host countries for tax and social security purposes, particularly where they spend in excess of six months of the year in the location. However, their family will remain in the home country. Permanent transfers will, by definition, be located for tax and social security purposes in the host country.

Inpatriation also emerges as a further categorization of alternative international assignee when the location issue is considered. Harvey et al. (2000), define inpatriates as employees from multinational subsidiaries transferred to the headquarters on a permanent or semi-permanent basis. Thus, a key difference between inpatriates and traditional assignees is that inpatriates are located at the headquarters or in the home country of the MNE. As part of a global network, such assignees can act as "linking pins" between foreign subsidiaries and headquarters. Indeed, this boundary spanning role can aid the global competitiveness of the MNE (Harvey et al., 1999). Inpatriation also facilitates the embedding of employees from outside of the MNE's country of origin into the organization, while potentially providing subsidiary talent with defined career paths, and facilitating the learning of organizational cultures, values, and decision making processes (Harvey et al., 2001). Similarly, the return of inpatriates to their home country on completion of their assignment can aid the localization process. Although there is limited empirical evidence on the extent of usage of inpatriate assignments, Collings et al. (2010) concluded that although the absolute number of inpatriate assignees within individual organizations was small they were used in a wide range of MNEs.

HR'S ROLE AND CHALLENGES

The expansion in the variety of assignment types available and utilized by organizations presents certain implications for the HR function. As a starting point for HR, the expansion in the portfolio of assignments will inevitably enlarge the scale of workload for HR as each alternative form of assignment is likely to present its own set of issues similar to, but distinct from, those of traditional assignments. At a basic level this implies an increased administrative burden but there are also high value connotations in terms of organizations adopting a more strategic approach to global staffing, which will mean new policy development and implementation. A key issue across many of the alternative forms of assignment is that they are viewed as outside the remit of the global mobility function owing to many being viewed as non-expatriates, typically seen as more the responsibility of line management (Welch and Worm, 2006). We now turn to considering some of the main HR challenges and implications from alternative types of assignments, which we do in the context of the traditional expatriate cycle that consists of recruitment and selection of assignees, pre-departure preparation, during assignment support, repatriation, and career management.

With respect to recruitment and selection, it appears that formal processes for alternative assignments are especially uncommon, which is not surprising given informal methods also appear to be dominant for long-term expatriates (Brewster, 1991). Tahvanainen et al. (2005) found formal selection in the case of short-term assignments to be an extreme rarity. We would suggest formal selection regarding many of the other forms of alternative assignment to be similarly unusual. Scholarship has shown selection criterion for international assignments to be strongly based on technical skills and a person's track record in their domestic role (Sparrow et al., 2004). While the skills and characteristics that should be incorporated in selection decisions for traditional assignments have been debated and critically discussed, little is known by way of whether there are specific criteria for alternative assignment forms. It seems logical that job descriptions and selection decisions should give due resonance to such issues in the case of roles that will incorporate forms of global mobility (e.g. frequent international business travel). As a result, there needs to be consideration for the skills and capabilities that, if possessed, will increase the likelihood of a successful assignment.

With respect to preparation, Mayerhofer et al.'s (2004) research on "flexpatriate" assignments (defined as individuals that travel away from their home base and across borders for brief assignments) found that the predominant role of the HR function was providing general information on travel, health and safety regulations in the countries in which people were traveling to, taking care of travel insurance, visas and so forth. They note that preparation for the assignment/travel and ongoing support was of secondary importance compared to ensuring the correct travel arrangements had been put in place (typically done by an external travel agency). Of some note was that, despite the lack of organizational support, each interviewee emphasized the importance of informal relationships and networks in assisting them with preparing for an assignment. There was acknowledgement from the organization about the potential importance of cross-cultural skills for flexpatriates but the HR function had not established specific training initiatives for these individuals due to there being some doubt as to whether it would be effective and necessary. Finally, there was no consideration given to preparing flexpatriates for dealing with any stresses that may occur on the different assignments undertaken. The lack of preparation and consideration of the different situations faced by individuals in the different types of assignments undertaken is likely to be only a negative for both organizational and individual outcomes. We see this as a major issue. Issues may be considered as simplistic things like working out the most appropriate accommodation–hotel versus serviced apartment, which may impact health and well-being, to the provision of pre-departure training specific to the assignment being undertaken.

Unsurprisingly, there is little evidence in the research literature that families of individuals undertaking non-traditional expatriate assignments are considered at any point in the assignment cycle. In other words, they are not considered at assignee selection stage nor are they involved in any forms of preparation or ongoing supports. This appears to be an area that HR departments need to consider in a comprehensive manner given the emerging research that shows individuals undertaking alternative types of international work suffer negative quality of work life outcomes and struggle to keep a balance between their work and private/family lives (e.g. DeFrank et al., 2000). There is a multitude of research that has called for MNEs to be more strategic and proactive in their use of expatriate assignments so as to allow for more effective recruitment, selection, preparation, and management. However, the reactivity of alternative assignments such as IBTs and short-term assignments are especially vivid. Mayerhofer et al. (2004) pointed to the case of a HR department holding a second passport for its international staff due to the need for individuals to travel on very short notice. One interviewee recommended having a travel bag ready at all times, both at home and in the office, such was their experience of needing to undertake international travel at short notice. While it is important to acknowledge that much of this may be unavoidable, there needs to be greater appreciation of the impact this may have on the individual and their spouse/family.

Expatriate scholarship has long noted the importance of the provision of support during an assignment (Tung, 1982) but it appears from the limited research undertaken in this area and our own discussions with professionals charged with managing global mobility that no supports are provided in the case of most alternative forms. The case organizations in the Mayerhofer et al.'s (2004) research were very strong in terms of support to expatriates and their families but no recognition was provided to those on shorter/alternative types of global mobility work. We feel that there is a need for consideration of whether HR can involve themselves more in the case of different forms of global mobility to ensure that there are supports available when required. When we consider the earlier point about the short notice often afforded those having to undertake international travel, the provision of supports may have a positive impact. Indeed, the act of considering whether an individual and family can be provided with some useful support by the organization may act as a positive effect in its own right.

A key reasoning behind the emergence and utilization of IBTs, short-term assignments and so forth is that the assignee's family and spouse tend to remain in the home country, meaning that there is a cost-saving benefit for the organization. There has been a significant increase in interest on how to better determine the success and effectiveness of international assignments (see for example, McNulty et al., 2009). While it appears that alternative global mobility forms have, in part, emerged due to being of lower cost than traditional expatriates, they have not been immune to a further drive to lower cost. For example, recent research from Australia has found that reduced international travel was the most common impact of the global financial crisis on MNEs (see Boyle and McDonnell, 2013). Similarly, Salt and Wood (2012) noted that their research found business travel as an area where savings were especially sought when the downturn started to occur. An interviewee (IT consultancy) made the point that, "like most companies, we're now much more careful about who goes on business trips for cost reasons" (Salt and Wood, 2012: 437). However, a key challenge for organizations and the HR function is actually measuring and tracking the level of international travel taking place, as well as other forms of alternative assignments. Anecdotal evidence points to great difficulty in tracking the extent to which alternative international assignments are being used. Consequently, when tracking the numbers is proving difficult it logically points towards there being a very limited appreciation of whether these assignments are effective or successful and of the bottom line cost/benefit to the organization. From both an organizational and individual perspective, there is very little understanding of the returns garnered from the different forms of global mobility. It also points to the additional challenges of measuring the ROI of alternative forms of global mobility.

The nature of careers in organizations and career management has evolved substantially over the last half century. We can note that while careers have traditionally been demonstrated to develop within a single organization, careers developed more recently are most appropriately viewed as complex and unstructured. The way in which individuals think about their career has changed. Traditional careers saw secure lifetime employment with single organizations, largely vertical career progression which was controlled by the organization. Gradual changes in the employment relationship due to the environmental forces at play have generally seen shorter terms of employment, increases in inter-firm mobility and career development managed by the employee to a greater degree (Arthur and Rousseau, 1996). With the emergence of more contemporary theoretical underpinnings, alternative schools of thought have come to the fore offering insights into why employees continue to accept international assignments despite the potential negative implications that may be experienced. Lazarova and Cerdin (2007) propose the notion of the "proactive repatriate." The proactive repatriate is one who is actively engaged with their own personal and professional career development. For such individuals the degree of organizational support which they receive during and at the end of their experience is of secondary importance and instead they use international experience as a tradable asset to advance their careers in the direction which most suitably matches personal needs and values. In this regard Lazarova and Cerdin (2007) suggest that while the issue of turnover upon repatriation may be considered as a consequence of poor organizational support, it may also be stimulated by individuals who proactively seek to advance their careers by seeking opportunities external to the organization which appropriately fit their personal and professional career objectives. These individuals may in fact have had little intention of remaining with the sending organization. Research of this kind has focused on long-term expatriate assignments, meaning that we do not know if individuals feel similarly in respect to undertaking other types of international assignments. The high turnover of repatriates has been noted for some time but whether such an issue exists in the case of shorter assignment methods is unknown. What we can suggest is that there is likely to be little to no consideration of the repatriation process by organizations for assignments of short duration.

MANAGERIAL IMPLICATIONS AND FUTURE RESEARCH

The global mobility landscape is far from homogenous, which has consequences for both practitioners and scholars in the area. HR practitioners need to establish systems of tracking and managing the different mobility portfolios, which we argue will demand a considerable range of policies and practices that are aligned to the different challenges and requirements of different mobility forms. Failing to consider the characteristics and circumstances of different types of international work is likely to fuel negative outcomes, which can be on both an individual and organizational level. For example, at an individual level, organizations cannot continue to turn a blind eye to the issue of work load and traveling time for those undertaking regular international travel. In particular, there is a need for organizations to consider the impact such travel may have on the individual (e.g. jet lag, dietary changes), as well as on their family life (e.g. individual is provided with time-off as a result of the personal/family time taken for travel). There is also a strong case that job descriptions, person specifications, and employment contracts account for the different forms of global mobility that may be encompassed in the role and the additional characteristics or issues that may be involved (Demel and Mayrhofer, 2010). Issues around pay and performance management also emerge as significant factors. For example, the structure of pay for an individual undertaking a short-term assignment is likely to differ to a long-term assignee. With respect to performance management, the question of how a person's performance on assignment is evaluated has emerged. Can an organization adopt the same system to evaluate a person on a long-term assignment, short-term assignment, or IBTs?

The area of global mobility is ripe for theoretical advancement and empirical investigation, with numerous research questions of importance worthy of consideration (see Shaffer et al., 2012). A simplistically worded yet inherently difficult question to answer due to measurement challenges is: what is the actual extent and use of different global mobility types? Brewster et al. (2001) in a UK based study of international assignment types found that approximately one third had no idea of how many staff were frequent fliers, even though they had detailed data on all long-term assignees. Leading on from this there is a key need to understand which types of assignments are most cost effective, and in what cases (e.g. business purpose/situation) are particular types of assignments chosen and why. There has been discussion about the need for expatriate assignments to be used more strategically (Collings et al., 2007) but there is limited understanding of how various types of global mobility are influenced by international organization strategies.

On more HR related points, there is a need for research that examines the HR practices and which supports different forms of global mobility. For example, how do selection, training, rewards, and supports vary with the type of assignment? And, how do differing HR practices relate to key performance outcomes? While the indications suggest that there tends not to be formal processes and supports for flexpatriates (e.g. Mayerhofer et al., 2004), there has been little empirical investigation into this area. Undertaking this type of research is important because, even if there is little being done by the majority of organizations, it may help in identifying best practices that are being used by some pioneering firms with respect to how they manage global mobility. Overall, there is scope for considerable research into the role of both corporate and subsidiary HR functions in the management of alternative international assignments.

For instance, in the case of selection, flexpatriate assignments are by nature briefer than traditional expatriate assignments, which means that there is a more limited time period to adjust to the different culture and working with people from that country. An interesting question that logically follows is based on the selection criteria for different types of global mobility: Does having cross-cultural competence become more important in shorter assignments due to not having the time to develop such skills or is the opposite true, cross-cultural agility is less important because the duration is short? And, are all measures of cross-cultural suitability useful and valid for each type of international working? There has been considerable attention placed on shortages of global talent, leading to discussion around the development of international managers, but what this actually means and how international assignments assist has not received much attention (Selmer, 1998). Relatedly, we know very little about how different types of international assignments fit in with approaches to career development within MNEs, which is something that should be redressed.

On an individual level, we call on researchers to investigate the individual motivations underscoring people undertaking international assignments and if there are differences in these according to the different mobility forms. There is an acute need to better appreciate the non-work issues and challenges faced by different international workers. For example, Collings et al. (2007) highlighted the high potential of international frequent fliers suffering from burnout. There is consequently a need for studies that investigate the strains and pressures on individuals and their partner/families involved in different mobility forms and how organizations can help ease these. Mayerhofer et al. (2004) found evidence of flexpatriates being active in gathering information from the Internet, and colleagues and friends to improve their experience and chances of succeeding on the assignment. Consequently, it would be useful to better understand how individuals manage the demands that are placed on their work and non-work life. The impact of undertaking an international assignment on one's career has started to gain a lot of attention (e.g. Suutari, 2003; Cappellen and Janssens, 2005). Much has been made on the learning experience garnered from an expatriate assignment leading to the development of three types of career capital (e.g. Jokinen et al., 2008): know-how (i.e. ability to see how things work differently in various situations); know-whom (i.e. the development of relationships); and, know-why (i.e. appreciating what is important to them). Research that investigates the career outcomes from different global mobility forms would make a very useful addition to existing knowledge on our understanding of the impact of international experience on one's career.

CONCLUSION

In this reading we have highlighted the changing topography of global mobility approaches in international organizations (see Table 1 for a summary). In particular we have highlighted that while the traditional corporate expatriate remains a mainstay in MNEs globally, there are a significant range of other types of global staffing assignments occurring which have received comparatively less attention by scholars. Practitioners also appear to have paid less attention to these global mobility forms, which might be based on the premise that they avoid many of the issues that are associated with long-term international assignments (Brewster et al., 2001). While this may be the case, it is not a truly accurate picture because it appears that alternative forms of global mobility bring new issues and challenges, as we have highlighted in this reading. An overarching issue in this is that there appears to be a lack of HR involvement in alternative forms of assignments. As a result, a key challenge is to enact a set of consistent and appropriate policies and practices for the different global mobility types.

Table 1. Summary of alternative global mobility types

Assignment	Assignment definition	Potential uses	Temporal issues	Challenges	HR issues
International business travel	Regular travel and communication between home and host location of an undefined duration.	Specialised irregular tasks e.g. production scheduling; budgeting; individual development; managerial control; development of networks.	Delineation of work and life roles, travel on personal time.	Burnout; stress; cost management; work–life balance.	Policy formation and implementation; recruitment; selection; training; reward; health and safety.
International commuter	Periodic travel between home and host location, frequently on a weekly, bi-weekly or monthly basis.	Project based tasks; network building; individual development; short term skills gap.	Tax issues; social security issues; compensation issues.	Costs; burnout; stress; cost management; work–life balance.	Work permit issues; policy formation and development; recruitment; selection; training; reward; health and safety.
Rotational assignment	Assignment of a pre-scribed period of time in host location followed by a break in home location before further relocation.	Managerial development; organisational functionality.	Tax and social security issues.	Work–life balance; strain on relationships.	Training and retention.
Short term assignment	Assignment of a duration longer than a business trip and shorter than one year.	Technical roles; organisational and individual development objectives; specific skill transfer.	Tax and social security issues.	Strain on personal relationships; health Issues; work–life balance; failure to build effective relationships.	Work permit issues; policy; recruitment; training; reward; health and safety.
Permanent transfer	One way transfer in which assignee works and resides in host location indefinitely.	Low margin industries, less strategic transfers.	Permanent break with home base.	Return on investment, identity, support.	Persuading individuals to accept permanent transfer.

NOTE

1.   Shaffer et al. (2012) prioritize assignments lasting several years in their definition. Given the incorporation of short-term assignments in the present discussion, we recognize the importance of such shorter-duration assignments.

REFERENCES

Arthur, M. B. and Rousseau, D. M. (1996). *The Boundaryless Career: A New Employment Principle for a New Organizational Era*. Boston, MA: Cambridge University Press.

Black, J. S., Gregersen, H. B. and Mendenhall, M. E. (1992). Toward a theoretical framework of repatriation adjustment. *Journal of International Business Studies*, 23: 737–760.

Black, J. S., Gregersen, H. B., Mendenhall, M. E. and Stroh, L. K. (1999). *Globalizing People through International Assignments*. New York: Addison-Wesley.

Bonache, J., Brewster, C. and Suutari, V. (2001). Expatriation: A developing research agenda. *Thunderbird International Business Review*, 43: 3–20.

Boyle, B. and McDonnell, A. (2013). Exploring the impact of institutional and organisational factors on the reaction of multinational companies to the global financial crisis. *Asia Pacific Business Review*, 19: 247–265.

Brewster, C. (1991). *The Management of Expatriates*. London: Kogan Page.

Brewster, C., Harris, H. and Petrovic, J. (2001). Globally mobile employees: Managing the mix. *Journal of Professional Human Resource Management*, 25: 11–15.

Briscoe, D. R. and Schuler, R. S. (2004). *International Human Resource Management* (2nd edn). New York: Routledge.

Brookfield GMAC (2013). *Global Relocation Trends: 2013 Survey Report*. Bun Ridge, IL: Brookfield.

Cappellen, T. and Janssens, M. (2005). Career paths of global managers: Towards future research. *Journal of World Business*, 40: 348–360.

Cartus (2012). *2012 Trends in Global Relocation*. Dandury, CT: Cartus.

Collings, D. G. (2014). Integrating global mobility and global talent management: Exploring the challenges and strategic opportunities. *Journal of World Business*, 49(2): 253–261.

Collings, D. G. and Scullion, H. (2012). Global staffing. In G. K. Stahl, I. Björkman and S. Morris (Eds), *Handbook of Research in International Human Resource Management* (2nd edn). (142–161) Cheltenham: Edward Elgar.

Collings, D. G. Scullion, H. and Morley, M. J. (2007). Changing patterns of global staffing in the multinational enterprise: Challenges to the conventional expatriate assignment and emerging alternatives. *Journal of World Business*, 42: 198–213.

Collings, D. G., Morley, M. J. and Gunnigle, P. (2008). Composing the top management team in the international subsidiary: Qualitative evidence on international staffing in US MNCs in the Republic of Ireland. *Journal of World Business*, 43(2): 197–212.

Collings, D. G., McDonnell, A., Gunnigle, A. and Lavelle, J. (2010). Swimming against the tide: Outward staffing flows from multinational subsidiaries. *Human Resource Management (US)*, 49(4): 575–598.

DeFrank, R. S., Konopaske, R. and Ivancevich, J. M. (2000). Executive travel stress: Perils of the road warrior. *The Academy of Management Executive*, 14(2): 58–71.

Demel, B. and Mayrhofer, W. (2010). Frequent business travelers across Europe: Career aspirations and implications. *Thunderbird International Business Review*, 52(4): 301–311.

Dickmann, M. and Debner, C. (2011). International mobility at work: Companies' structural remuneration, social security and risk considerations. In M. Dickmann and Y. Baruch (Eds), *Global Careers* (268–293). London: Routledge.

Dickmann, M. and Doherty, N. (2010). Exploring organizational and individual career goals, interactions and outcomes of developmental international assignments. *Thunderbird International Business Review*, 52: 313–324.

Doherty, N. (2013). Understanding the self-initiated expatriate: A review and directions for future research. *International Journal of Management Reviews*, 15(4): 447–469.

Doherty, N., Richardson, J. and Thorn, K. (2013). Self-initiated expatriation: Career experiences, processes and outcomes. *Career Development International*, 18(1): 6–11.

Dowling, P. J. and Welch, D. E. (2004). *International Human Resource Management: Managing People in an International Context*. London: Thomson/South-Western.

Dowling, P. J., Festing, M. and Engle, A. D. (2008). *International Human Resource Management* (5th edn). London: Thompson.

Edstrom, A. and Galbraith, J. R. (1977). Transfer of managers as a coordination and control strategy in multinational organizations. *Administrative Science Quarterly*, 22: 248–263.

Evans, P., Pucik, V. and Björkman, I. (2011). *The Global Challenge: International Human Resource Management*. New York: McGraw-Hill Irwin.

Feldman, D. C. and Thomas, D. C. (1992). Career management issues facing expatriates. *Journal of International Business Studies*, 23(2): 271–293.

Forster, N. (2000). The myth of the 'international manager'. *International Journal of Human Resource Management*, 11(1): 126–142.

Harvey, M., Speier, C. and Novicevic, M. M. (1999). The role of inpatriation in global staffing. *International Journal of Human Resource Management*, 10: 459–476.

Harvey, M. G., Novicevic, M. M. and Speier, C. (2000). Strategic global human resource management: The role of inpatriate managers. *Human Resource Management Review*, 10: 153–175.

Harvey, M., Speier, C. and Novicevic, M. M. (2001). A theory-based framework for strategic global human resource staffing policies and practices. *International Journal of Human Resource Management*, 12: 898–915.

Harzing, A. W. K. (1995). The persistent myth of high expatriate failure rates. *International Journal of Human Resource Management*, 6(2): 457–474.

Harzing, A. W. (2001). Of bears, bees and spiders: The role of expatriates in controlling foreign subsidiaries, *Journal of World Business*, 26: 366–379.

Harzing, A. W. (2002). Are our referencing errors undermining our scholarship and credibility? The case of expatriate failure rates. *Journal of Organizational Behavior*, 23(1): 127–148.

Jokinen, T., Brewster, C. and Suutari, V. (2008). Career capital during international work experiences: Contrasting self-initiated expatriate experiences and assigned expatriation. *The International Journal of Human Resource Management*, 19: 981–1000.

KPMG. (2013). *Global Assignment Policies and Practices Survey 2013*. Zurich: KPMG.

Kraimer, M. L., Shaffer, M. A. and Bolino, M. C. (2009). The influence of expatriate and repatriate experiences on career advancement and repatriate retention. *Human Resource Management*, 48: 27–47.

Lazarova, M. (2015). Taking stock of the repatriation research. In D.G. Collings, G. T. Wood and P.M. Caligiuri (Eds.), *Routledge Companion to International Human Resource Management*. (378–398) London: Routledge.

Lazarova, M. B. and Cerdin, J. L. (2007). Revisiting repatriation concerns: Organizational support versus career and contextual influences. *Journal of International Business Studies*, 38: 404–429.

Mayerhofer, H., Hartmann, L. C., Michelitsch-Riedl, G., and Kollinger, I. (2004). Flexpatriate assignments: A neglected issue in global staffing. *International Journal of Human Resource Management*, 15(8): 1371–1389.

Mayrhofer, W. and Brewster, C. (1997). Ethnocentric staffing policies in European multinationals. *International Executive*, 38: 749–778.

Mayrhofer, W. and Scullion, H. (2002). Female expatriates in international business: Empirical evidence from the German clothing industry. *International Journal of Human Resource Management*, 13: 815–836.

Mayrhofer, W., Sparrow, P. and Zimmerman, A. (2008). Modern forms of international working. In M. Dickmann, C. Brewster and P. Sparrow (Eds), *International Human Resource Management: A European Perspective*. (219–239) London: Routledge.

McDonnell, A., Russell, H., Sablok, G., Burgess, J., Stanton, P., Bartram, T., Boyle, B. and Manning, K. (2011). *A Profile of Human Resource Management in Multinational Enterprises Operating in Australia.* School of Management, Victoria University, Melbourne.

McNulty, Y., De Cieri, H. and Hutchings, K. (2009). Do global firms measure expatriate return on investment? An empirical examination of measures, barriers and variables influencing global staffing practices. *The International Journal of Human Resource Management,* 20: 1309–1326.

Meyskens, M., Von Glinow, M. A., Werther, W. B. Jr and Clarke, L. (2009). The paradox of international talent: Alternative forms of international assignments. *The International Journal of Human Resource Management,* 20: 1439–1450.

Moore, K. and Lewis, D. (1999). *Birth of the Multinational.* Copenhagen: Copenhagen Business Press.

Peltonen, T. (2001). *New Forms of International Work: An International Survey Study. Results of the Finnish Survey.* University of Oulu and Cranfield School of Management.

Pucik, V. (1992). Globalization and human resource management. In V. Pucik, N. M. Tichy and C. K. Barnett (Eds), *Globalizing Management: Creating and Leading the Competitive Organization* (61–84) New York: John Wiley & Sons.

PWC (2010). *Talent Mobility 2020: The Next Generation of International Assignments.* London: PWC.

Reiche, B. S. and Harzing, A. W. (2011). International assignments. In A. W. Harzing and A. Pinnington (Eds), *International Human Resource Management* (3rd edn) (185–226) London: Sage.

Salt, J. and Millar, J. (2006). International migration in interesting times: The case of the UK. *People and Place,* 14(2): 14–25.

Salt, J. and Wood, P. (2012). Recession and international corporate mobility. *Global Networks,* 12: 425–445.

Scullion, H. and Collings, D. G. (2006). *Global Staffing.* London: Routledge.

Selmer, J. (Ed.). (1995). *Expatriate Management: New Ideas for International Business.* Westport, CT: Greenwood Publishing Group.

Selmer, J. (1998). Expatriation: Corporate policy, personal intentions and international adjustment. *The International Journal of Human Resource Management,* 9: 996–1007.

Selmer, J. (1999). Career issues and international adjustment of business expatriates. *Career Development International,* 4(2): 77–87.

Shaffer, M. A., Kraimer, M. L., Chen, Y. P. and Bolino, M. C. (2012). Choices, challenges, and career consequences of global work experiences: A review and future agenda. *Journal of Management,* 38(4): 1282–1327.

Shay, J. P. and Baack, S. A. (2004). Expatriate assignment, adjustment and effectiveness: An empirical examination of the big picture. *Journal of International Business Studies,* 35: 216–232.

Sparrow, P., Brewster, C. and Harris, H. (2004). *Globalizing Human Resource Management.* London: Routledge.

Stahl, G. K. and Chua, C. H. (2006). Global assignments and boundaryless careers: What drives and frustrates international assignments? In M. J. Morley, N. Heraty and D. G. Collings (Eds), *International Human Resource Management and International Assignments.* (135–152) Basingstoke: Palgrave Macmillan.

Stahl, G. K., Miller, E. L. and Tung, R. L. (2002). Toward the boundaryless career: A closer look at the expatriate career concept and the perceived implications of an international assignment. *Journal of World Business,* 37: 216–227.

Stahl, G., Björkmann, I., Farndale, E., Morris, S., Paauwe, J., Stiles, P. and Wright, P. M. (2012). Leveraging your talent: Six principles of effective global talent management. *MIT Sloan Management Review,* 53: 25–42.

Starr, T. L. and Currie, G. (2009). 'Out of sight but still in the picture': Short-term international assignments and the influential role of family. *International Journal of Human Resource Management,* 20(6): 1417–1434.

Stroh, L. K., Gregersen, H. B. and Black, J. S. (2000). Triumphs and tragedies: Expectations and commitments upon repatriation. *International Journal of Human Resource Management*, 11(4): 681–697.

Stroh, L. K., Black, J. S., Mendenhall, M. E. and Gregersen, H. B. (2005). *International Assignments: An Integration of Strategy, Research, and Practice*. New York: Routledge.

Suutari, V. (2003). Global managers: Career orientation, career tracks, life-style implications and career commitment. *Journal of Managerial Psychology*, 18: 185–207.

Tahvanainen, M., Welch, D. and Worm, V. (2005). Implications of short-term international assignments. *European Management Journal*, 23: 663–673.

Tait, E., DeCieri, H. and McNulty, Y. (2014). The opportunity cost of saving money: An exploratory study of permanent transfers and localization of expatriates in Singapore. *International Studies of Management and Organization*, 44(3): 79–94.

Tornikoski, C., Suutari, V. and Festing, M. (2015). Compensation package of international assignees. In D.G. Collings, G. T. Wood and P.M. Caligiuri (Eds.), *Routledge Companion to International Human Resource Management*. (289–307) London: Routledge.

Tung, R. L. (1981). Selection and training of personnel for overseas assignments. *Columbia Journal of World Business*, 16(1): 68–78.

Tung, R. (1982). Selection and training procedures of US, European and Japanese multinationals. *California Management Review*, 25: 57–71.

Tung, R. L. (1988). Career issues in international assignments. *The Academy of Management Executive*, 2(3): 241–244.

Vaiman, V. and Hasleberger, A. (Eds). (2013). *Talent Management of Self-initiated Expatriates: A Neglected Source of Global Talent*. Basingstoke: Palgrave Macmillan.

Welch, D. E. (2003). Globalisation of staff movements: Beyond cultural adjustment. *MIR: Management International Review*, 43: 149–169.

Welch, D. E. and Worm, V. (2006). International business travellers: A challenge for IHRM. In G. Stahl and I. Bjorkman (Eds), *Handbook of Research in International Research Management*. (283–301) Edward Elgar: Cheltenham.

Gary R. Oddou and Mark E. Mendenhall

EXPATRIATE PERFORMANCE APPRAISAL: PROBLEMS AND SOLUTIONS

FOR MORE AND MORE COMPANIES, gaining a competitive edge increasingly means making decisions that reflect an acute understanding of the global marketplace – how other countries utilize and view marketing strategies, accounting and financial systems, labor laws, leadership, communication, negotiation and decision-making styles. Gaining a knowledge of these components is most directly accomplished by sending managers to work in an overseas subsidiary and utilizing them on re-entry.

Our research shows clearly that expatriates develop valuable managerial skills abroad that can be extremely useful to their development as effective senior managers. Based on current research on expatriates, including our own surveying and interviewing of more than 150 of them, probably the most significant skills expatriates develop as a result of their overseas assignments include the following:

- Being able to manage a workforce with cultural and subcultural differences.
- Being able to plan for, and conceptualize, the dynamics of a complex, multinational environment.
- Being more open-minded about alternative methods for solving problems.
- Being more flexible in dealing with people and systems.
- Understanding the interdependencies among the firm's domestic and foreign operations.

These skills are the natural outgrowth of the increased autonomy and potential impact expatriates experience in their international assignment. In fact, in our study, 67 percent reported having more independence, and they also indicated they had more potential impact on the operation's performance than in their domestic position. With increased decision-making responsibilities in a foreign environment, expatriates are subjected to a fairly intense working environment in which they must learn the ropes quickly.

The skills expatriate managers gain are obviously crucial to effectively managing any business operation, particularly at the international and multinational level. Nightmares abound in the business press of the inept decisions sometimes made by top management due to ignorance of cross-cultural differences in business practices. The ability to plan and conceptualize based on the complex interdependencies of a global market environment with significant cultural differences is required of top management in MNCs.

In short, expatriates can become a very valuable human resource for firms with international or multinational operations. However, one of the most serious stumbling blocks to expatriates' career paths is the lack of recognition of the value of expatriation and the informality with which firms accurately evaluate their expatriates' overseas performance. Although the attributes expatriates gain overseas can and do translate into concrete advantages for their firms, a quick glance at the skills previously listed indicates intangibles that are often difficult to measure and usually are not measured – or are measured inaccurately – by present performance evaluation methods. Hence, it is critical to more closely examine this potential stumbling block to expatriates' careers and to make specific recommendations to improve the process and accuracy of such reviews.

APPRAISING THE EXPATRIATE'S PERFORMANCE

Several problems are inherent to appraising an expatriate's performance. First, an examination of those who evaluate an expatriate's job performance is relevant. Those evaluators include the host national management and often the home office management.

Host National Management's Perceptions of Actual Job Performance

That local management evaluates the expatriate is probably necessary; however, such a process sometimes is problematic. Local management typically evaluates the expatriate's performance from its own cultural frame of reference and set of expectations. For example, one American expatriate manager we talked to used participative decision-making in India but was thought of by local workers as rather incompetent because of the Indian notion that managers, partly owing to their social class level, are seen as the experts. Therefore, a manager should not have to ask subordinates for ideas. Being seen as incompetent negatively affected local management's review of this expatriate's performance, and he was denied a promotion on return to the US. Local management's appraisal is not the only potential problem, however. In fact, based on our research with expatriates, local management's evaluation is usually perceived as being more accurate than that of the home office.

Home Office Management's Perceptions of Actual Job Performance

Because the home office management is geographically distanced from the expatriate, it is often not fully aware of what is happening overseas. As a result, for middle and upper management, home office management will often use a different set of variables than those used by local management. Typically, more visible performance criteria are used to measure the expatriate's success (for example, profits, market share, productivity levels). Such measures ignore other, less visible variables that in reality drastically affect the company's performance. Local events such as strikes, devaluation of the currency, political instability, and runaway inflation are examples of phenomena that are beyond the control of the expatriate and are sometimes "invisible" to the home office.

One expatriate executive told us that in Chile he had almost singlehandedly stopped a strike that would have shut down their factory completely for months and worsened relations between the Chileans and the parent company in the US. In a land where strikes are commonplace, such an accomplishment was quite a coup, especially for an American. The numerous meetings and talks with labor representatives, government officials, and local management required an acute understanding of their culture and a sensitivity beyond the ability of most people. However, because of exchange rate fluctuations with its primary trading partners in South America, the demand for their ore temporarily decreased by 30 percent during the expatriate's tenure. Rather than applauding the efforts this expatriate executive made to avert a strike and recognizing the superb negotiation skills he demonstrated, the home office saw the expatriate as being only somewhat better than a mediocre performer. In other words, because for home office management the most visible criterion of the expatriate's performance was somewhat negative (sales figures), it was assumed that he had not performed adequately. And though the expatriate's boss knew a strike had been averted, the bottom-line concern for sales dollars overshadowed any other significant accomplishments.

The expatriate manager must walk a tightrope. He must deal with a new cultural work group, learn the ins and outs of the new business environment, possibly determine how to work with a foreign boss, find out what foreign management expects of him, and so on. He must also understand the rules of the game on the home front. It is difficult, and sometimes impossible, to please both. Attempting to please both can result in a temporarily, or permanently, railroaded career. So it was with an individual who was considered a "high potential" in a semiconductor firm. He was sent to an overseas operation without the proper product knowledge preparation and barely kept his head above water because of the difficulties of cracking a nearly impossible market. On returning to the US, he was physically and mentally exhausted from the battle. He sought a much less challenging position and got it because top management then believed they had overestimated his potential. In fact, top management never did understand what the expatriate was up against in the foreign market.

In fact, expatriates frequently indicate that headquarters does not really understand their experience – neither the difficulty of it nor the value of it. One study found that one-third of the expatriates felt that corporate headquarters did not understand the expatriate's experience at all. In a 1981 Korn/Ferry survey, 69 percent of the managers reported they felt isolated from domestic operations and their US managers. It is clear from others' and our own research that most US senior management does not understand the value of an international assignment or try to utilize the expatriate's skills gained abroad when they return to the home office. The underlying problem seems to be top management's ethnocentricity.

Management Ethnocentricity

Two of the most significant aspects of management's inability to understand the expatriate's experience, value it, and thereby more accurately measure his or her performance are (1) the communication gap between the expatriate and the home office and (2) the lack of domestic management's international experience.

The Communication Gap

Being physically separated by thousands of miles and in different time zones poses distinct problems of communication. Not only does the expatriate have difficulty talking directly with his manager, but usually both the US manager and the expatriate executive have plenty of other responsibilities to attend to. Fixing the day-to-day problems tends to take precedence over other concerns, such as maintaining contact with one's boss (or subordinate) in order to be kept up to date on organizational changes or simply to inform him or her of what one is doing. Most of the expatriates in our research indicated they had very irregular contact with their home office and that often it was not with their immediate superior. Rarely did the boss initiate direct contact with the expatriate more than once or twice a year.

The Lack of International Experience

The old Indian expression "To walk a mile in another man's moccasins" has direct meaning here. How can one understand what another person's overseas managerial experience is like – its difficulties, challenges, stresses, and the like – without having lived and worked overseas oneself? According to one study, more than two-thirds of upper management in corporations today have never had an international assignment. If they have not lived or worked overseas, and if the expatriate and US manager are not communicating regularly about the assignment, the US manager cannot evaluate the expatriate's performance appropriately.

Of course, how the US manager and foreign manager perceive the expatriate's performance will depend partly on the expatriate's actual performance and partly on the managers' *perceptions* of the expatriate's performance. Up to now, we have discussed the managers' perceptions of the expatriate's performance. Let's now turn our attention to what usually composes the expatriate's *actual* performance to better understand why evaluating it is problematic.

Actual Job Performance

As repeatedly mentioned by the expatriates in our study and in other research, the primary factors relating to the expatriate's actual job performance include his or her technical job know-how, personal adjustment to the culture, and various environmental factors.

Technical Job Know-How

As with all jobs, one's success overseas partly depends on one's expertise in the technical area of the job. Our research indicates that approximately 95 percent of the expatriates believe that technical competency is crucial to successful job performance. Although common sense supports this notion, research shows that technical competence is not sufficient in itself for successful job performance. For example, an engineer who is an expert in his or her field and who tends to ignore cultural variables that are important to job performance will likely be ineffective. He or she might be less flexible with local personnel, policies, and practices because of his or her reliance on technical know-how or because of differences in cultural views. As a result, the host nationals might become alienated by the expatriate's style and become quite resistant to his or her objectives and strategies. A less experienced engineer, with less technical competence, might be more willing to defer to the host country's employees and their procedures and customs. A shade of humility is always more likely to breed flexibility, and in the long run, the less experienced engineer might develop the trust of the foreign employees and might well be more effective than the experienced engineer.

We have been given numerous examples by expatriates, in fact, where this has been the case. One expatriate who represented a large construction firm was sent to a worksite in India. The expatriate was an expert in his field and operated in the same fashion as he did in the US. He unintentionally ignored local work customs and became an object of hatred and distrust. The project was delayed for more than six months because of his behavior.

Adjustment to a New Culture

Just as important as the expatriate's technical expertise is his or her ability to adapt to the foreign environment, enabling him or her to deal with the indigenous people. Nearly every expatriate in our survey felt understanding the foreign culture, having an ability to communicate with the foreign nationals, and being able to reduce stress were as – if not more – important to successful job performance than was technical competence. Regardless of how much an expatriate knows, if he or she is unable to communicate with and understand the host nationals, the work will not get done.

An expatriate's adjustment overseas is also related to at least two personal variables: (1) one's marital and family status (that is, whether accompanied by a spouse and children) and (2) the executive's own personal and the family's pre-disposition to acculturation. Research clearly indicates that expatriates who have their family abroad are often less successful because of the stress on the family of being in a foreign environment. The stress on the spouse negatively affects the employee's concentration and job performance. With an increasing number of dual-career couples being affected by expatriation, the problems are even keener. A number of expatriates reported that their formerly career-positioned spouse suffered from depression most of the time they were overseas. Moving from experiencing the dynamics of a challenging career to having no business-world activity and being unable to communicate the most basic needs is a grueling transition for many career-oriented spouses.

Company variables affecting cultural and work adjustment also come into play. The thoroughness of the company's expatriate selection method and the type and degree of cross-cultural training will affect expatriate adjustment and performance. In other words, if the firm is not selective about the personality of the expatriate or does not appropriately prepare the employee and dependents, the firm may be building in failure before the manager ever leaves the US.

All these factors influence the expatriate's learning curve in a foreign business environment. More time is thus required to learn the ins and outs of the job than for the expatriate's domestic counterpart who might have just taken a comparable position stateside. In fact, most expatriates say it takes three to six months to even begin to perform at the same level as in the domestic operation. Hence, *performance evaluations at the company's normal time interval may be too early to accurately and fairly reflect the expatriate's performance.*

A SUMMARY OF FACTORS AFFECTING EXPATRIATION PERFORMANCE

In summary, an expatriate's performance is based on overseas adjustment, his or her technical know-how, and various relevant environmental factors. Actual performance, however, is evaluated in terms of perceived performance, which is based on a set of fairly complex variables usually below the evaluator's level of awareness. Much of the perceived performance concerns perceptions of the expatriate and his or her situation. Depending on whether the manager assessing the expatriate's performance has had personal overseas experience or is otherwise sensitive to problems associated with overseas work, the performance appraisal will be more or less valid. *The bottom line for the expatriate is that the performance appraisal will influence the promotion potential and type of position the expatriate receives on returning to the US.* Because expatriates generally return from their experience with valuable managerial skills, especially for firms pursuing an international or global market path, it behooves organizations to carefully review their process of appraising expatriates and the evaluation criteria themselves.

GUIDELINES ON HOW TO APPRAISE AN EXPATRIATE'S PERFORMANCE

Human Resource Personnel: Giving Guidelines for Performance Evaluation

Human resources departments can do a couple of things to help guide the evaluator's perspective on the evaluation.

A basic breakdown of the difficulty level of the assignment should be done to properly evaluate the expatriate's performance. For example, working in Japan is generally considered more difficult than working in England or English-speaking Canada. The learning curve in Japan will take longer because of the very different ways business is conducted, the language barrier that exists, and the isolation that most Americans feel within the Japanese culture. Major variables such as the following should be considered when determining the difficulty level of the assignment:

- Operational language used in the firm.
- Cultural "distance," based often on the region of the world (for example, Western Europe, Middle East, Asia).
- Stability of the factors affecting the expatriate's performance (for example, labor force, exchange rate).

Many foreigners speak English, but their proficiency does not always allow them to speak effectively or comfortably, so they rely on their native language when possible. In addition, they usually do not speak English among themselves because it is not natural. In Germany, for example, one expatriate said that while relying on English allowed a minimum level of work to be performed, the fact that he did not speak German limited his effectiveness. Secretaries, for example, had very limited English-speaking skills. German workers rarely spoke English together and therefore unknowingly excluded the expatriate from casual and often work-related conversations. And outside work he had to spend three to four times the amount of time to accomplish the same things that he did easily in the US. Most of the problem was because he could not speak good enough German, and many of the Germans could not speak good enough English.

Although sharing the same language facilitates effective communication, it is only the surface level of communication. More deep-rooted, cultural-based phenomena can more seriously affect an expatriate's performance.

Countries or regions where the company sends expatriates can be fairly easily divided into categories such as these: (1) somewhat more difficult than the US, (2) more difficult than the US, and (3) much more difficult than the US. Plenty of information is available to help evaluate the difficulty level of assignments. The US State Department and military branches have these types of ratings. In addition, feedback from a firm's own expatriates can help build the picture of the varying level of assignment difficulty.

Rather than having the manager try to subjectively build the difficulty level of the assignment into his or her performance appraisal, human resources could have a built-in, numerical difficulty factor that is multiplied times the quantity obtained by the normal evaluation process (for example, somewhat more difficult = × 1.2; more difficult = × 1.4; much more difficult = × 1.6).

Evaluator: Trying to Objectify the Evaluation

Several things can be done to try to make the evaluator's estimation more objective:

1. Most expatriates agree that it makes more sense to weight the evaluation based more on the on-site manager's appraisal than the home-site manager's notions of the employee's performance. This is the individual who has been actually working with the expatriate and who has more information to use in the evaluation.

Having the on-site manager evaluate the expatriate is especially valid when the on-site manager is of the same nationality as the expatriate. This helps avoid culturally biased interpretations of the expatriate's performance.

2. In reality, however, currently the home-site manager usually performs the actual written performance evaluation after the on-site manager has given some input. When this is the case, a former expatriate from the same location should be involved in the appraisal process. This should occur particularly with evaluation dimensions where the manager is trying to evaluate the individual against criteria with which he or she is unfamiliar relative to the overseas site. For example, in South America the dynamics of the workplace can be considerably different from those of the US. Where stability characterizes the US, instability often character- izes much of Latin America. Labor unrest, political upheavals, different labor laws, and other elements all serve to modify the actual effects a supervisor can have on the productivity of the labor force in a company in Latin America. A manager who has not personally experienced these frustrations will not be able to evaluate an expatriate's productivity accurately. In short, if production is down while the expatriate is the supervisor, the American boss tends to believe it is because the supervisor was not effective.

3. On the other hand, when it is a foreign on-site manager who is making the writ- ten, formal evaluation, expatriates agree that the home-site manager should be consulted before the on-site manager completes a formal terminal evaluation. This makes sense because consulting the home-site manager can balance an oth- erwise hostile evaluation caused by an intercultural misunderstanding.

One expatriate we interviewed related this experience. In France, women are legally allowed to take six months off for having a baby. They are paid during that time but are not supposed to do any work related to their job. This expatriate had two of the three secretaries take maternity leave. Because they were going to be coming back, they were not replaced with temporary help. The same amount of work, however, still existed. The American expatriate asked them to do some work at home, not really understanding the legalities of such a request. The French women could be fired from their jobs for doing work at home. One of the women agreed to do it because she felt sorry for him. When the American's French boss found out one of these two secretar- ies was helping, he became very angry and intolerant of the American's actions. As a result, the American felt he was given a lower performance evaluation than he deserved. When the American asked his former boss to intercede and help the French boss understand his reasoning, the French boss modified the performance evalution to something more reasonable to the American expatriate. The French manager had assumed the American should have been aware of French laws governing maternity leave.

Performance Criteria

Here again, special consideration needs to be given to the expatriate's experience. Expatriates are not only performing a specific function, as they would in their domestic operation, they are also broadening their understanding of their firm's total operations and the inherent interdependencies thereof. As a result, two recommendations are suggested:

1. Modify the normal performance criteria of the evaluation sheet for that particular position to fit the overseas position and site characteristics.

Using the Latin American example referred to before might serve to illustrate this point. In most US firms, maintaining positive management–labor relations is not a primary performance evaluation criterion. Stabilizing the workforce is not highly valued because the workforce is already usually a stable entity. Instead, productivity in terms of number of units produced is a highly valued outcome. As such, motivating the workforce to work faster and harder is important. In Chile, however, the workforce is not so stable as it is in the US. Stability is related to constant production – not necessarily to increasing production – and a stable production amount can be crucial to maintaining marketshare. In this case, if an expatriate is able to maintain positive management–labor relations such that the workforce goes on strike only two times instead of twenty-five times, the expatriate should be rewarded commensurately. In other words, while the expatriate's US counterpart might be rated primarily on increases in production, the expatriate in Chile should be rated on stability of production.

How can such modifications in the normal performance criteria be determined? Ideally, returned expatriates who worked at the same site or in the same country should be involved in developing the appropriate criteria or ranking of the performance criteria or both. Only they have first-hand experience of what the possibilities and constraints are like at that site. This developmental cycle should occur approximately every five years, depending on the stability of the site – its culture, personnel, and business cycles. Re-evaluating the criteria and their prioritization periodically will make sure the performance evaluation criteria remain current with the reality of the overseas situation. If expatriate availability is a problem, outside consultants who specialize in international human resource management issues can be hired to help create country-specific performance evaluation forms and criteria.

2. Include an expatriate's insights as part of the evaluation.

"Soft" criteria are difficult to measure and therefore legally difficult to support. Nevertheless, every attempt should be made to give the expatriate credit for relevant insights into the interdependencies of the domestic and foreign operations. For example, if an expatriate learns that the reason the firm's plant in India needs supplies by certain dates is to accommodate cultural norms – or even local laws – such information can be invaluable. Previously, no one at the domestic site understood why the plant in India always seemed to have such odd or erratic demands about delivery dates. And no one in India bothered to think that their US supplier didn't operate the same way. If delivering supplies by specific dates asked for by their Indian colleagues ensures smoother production or increased sales and profits for the Indian operation, and if the expatriate is a critical link in the communication gap between the US and India, the expatriate should be given credit for such insights. This should be reflected in his or her performance review.

To obtain this kind of information, either human resource or operational personnel should formally have a debriefing session with the expatriate on his or her return. It should be in an informal interview format so that specific and open-ended questions can be asked. Questions specific to the technical nature of the expatriate's work that relate to the firm's interdependencies should be asked. General questions concerning observations about the relationship between the two operations should also be included.

There is another, even more effective way this aspect of performance review can be handled. At regular intervals, say, every three to six months, the expatriate could be questioned by human resource or operational personnel in the domestic site about how the two operations might better work together. Doing it this way helps maximize the possibility of noting all relevant insights.

CONCLUSION

With the marketplace becoming increasingly global, the firms that carefully select and manage their internationally assigned personnel will reap the benefits. Today, there is about a 20 percent turnover rate for expatriates when they return. Such a turnover rate is mostly due to firms not managing their expatriates' careers well. Firms are not prepared to appropriately reassign expatriates on their re-entry. This obviously indicates that firms do not value the expatriate's experience. This further carries over into the lack of emphasis on appropriately evaluating an expatriate's performance. Appropriately evaluating an expatriate's performance is an issue of both fairness to the expatriate and competitive advantage to the firm. With the valuable experience and insights that expatriates gain, retaining them and effectively positioning them in a firm will mean the firm's business strategy will be increasingly guided by those who understand the companies' worldwide operations and markets.

Jaime Bonache and Luigi Stirpe

COMPENSATING GLOBAL EMPLOYEES

I T IS WIDELY RECOGNIZED that compensation and reward systems are key elements in attracting, retaining, and motivating a labor force. In order to achieve these objectives, the system of compensation should be welladjusted to key contingency factors of the firm (i.e. strategy, organizational culture, social and legal constraints, and regulations), as well as the expectations and characteristics of the labor force (Baron and Kreps, 1999).

Within multinational companies (MNCs), there are two distinct groups of the labor force with different expectations and characteristics. On the one hand, there are host country nationals (i.e. local employees who work in the various countries in which MNCs operate); on the other hand, there are global employees (i.e. expatriates either from the headquarters or from a third country). While admitting that international compensation is something more than expatriate compensation, the latter shall be the focus of this reading.

The academic research on the compensation of global employees is an underdeveloped area. In a review on historic developments in expatriates' management, Harvey and Moeller (2009) have shown that the literature on expatriation has focused on a wide number of issues, including the identification and selection of expatriate managers, adjustment and performance of international assignees, and repatriation planning and concerns. However, they point out the slight amount of theory and empirical research on compensation of expatriate employees. This is in sharp contrast to the abundant references that exist on compensation in the domestic human resources literature.

To find analyses of this issue, it is necessary to refer to magazines and work more oriented toward practitioners (e.g. Freeman and Kane, 1995; Krupp, 2008; McMorrow and Cummins, 2009; O'Neill, 2009; O'Reilly, 1996; Reynolds, 1997, 2000). This work reflects the concerns of professionals and there prevails a highly applied and descriptive orientation, focused on "how" MNCs compensate their expatriates rather than on the causes and effects of their compensation strategies. Two issues dominate this highly descriptive literature: the difficulties that are encountered when designing an expatriates' pay system, and the approaches and elements usually included in an international compensation package. We will begin by reviewing these two issues and then we will point out some areas that may guide further study.

CHALLENGES AND OBJECTIVES

Designing a pay system is always a challenging process, but doing so in MNCs is particularly complex and difficult (Harvey, 1993a, 1993b; Suutari and Tornikoski, 2001). A set of situational factors not normally encountered in a strictly domestic situation must be taken into account when designing the compensation package of an expatriate. For example, the nationality of the individual, their family situation (e.g. number and ages of their children, work situation of the spouse), floating exchange rates, differences in living costs, taxes, and inflation rates, the need to reconcile home and host country laws and regulations for compensation and benefits, and the geographically imposed problems of communication and control are all of great importance. These issues increase the complexity of the situation and the information needed as regards to the individual and his/her destination (Suutari and Tornikoski, 2001).

In addition to these situational factors, there are a number of objectives that must be incorporated into the design of expatriates' pay packages. According to Freeman and Kane (1995) and Suutari and Tornikoski (2001), an ideal expatriate compensation system should include five main objectives: (1) to attract personnel in the areas where the multinational has its greatest needs and opportunities; (2) to facilitate the transfer of international employees in the most cost-effective manner; (3) to be consistent and fair in the treatment of all its employees; (4) to facilitate re-entry into the home country at the end of the foreign assignment; and (5) to contribute to organizational strategy (that is, to support organizational goals, foster corporate culture, and help motivate employees to contribute their efforts to further organizational success). Taken individually, these objectives seem logical and achievable. However, the implementation of one may well contradict another. As an example, let us consider the first objective in relation to the others.

Attracting personnel to international service by offering generous compensation packages is a widespread practice in many MNCs (Toh and Denisi, 2003; Bonache, 2005). This initiative is designed to break the frequent barriers to international mobility. In addition to family and personal issues, such as the growing unwillingness to disrupt the education of children and the growing importance of quality of life considerations (Black et al., 1992; Shaffer et al., 1999), and the continued uncertainty regarding international terrorism and political and social unrest of certain destinations (Welch et al., 2008), it is well documented that the career implications of international assignments are often frustrating. A lack of respect for acquired skills, loss of status, and reverse culture shock upon return are recurring problems in many companies (Stahl et al., 2002). Because of these barriers, a logical way of encouraging individuals to accept a foreign assignment is to provide generous compensation packages to expatriates.

Yet this way of attracting individuals to the international service may conflict with other objectives of the system. First, it leads to costly assignments. This, in turn, puts an economic strain on the company and finally leads it to reduce the costs of assignments, in an attempt to save money. In doing so, the company might also reduce the pool of qualified candidates, thereby making the recruitment process all the more difficult (Hamil, 1989; Suutari and Tornikoski, 2001). Thus there is tension in the achievement of the first two objectives of the system. Second, it might also conflict with the repatriation objective. The incentives and allowances designed to encourage employees to take up a foreign assignment are not sustained when the expatriate returns home, leading to a substantial loss of income. In fact, such a loss of income is cited as one of the main difficulties upon return (Harvey, 1993b). In other words, a less attractive pay package facilitates re-entry, but reduces the ability of the company to attract employees for the international service. Finally, the generous incentives designed to help attract overseas employment have the side effect of creating large pay gaps between expatriates and local employees. The less fortunate position of the local employees relative to that of the expatriate may damage their perceptions of the company's procedural and distributive justice (Chen et al., 2002; Toh and Denisi, 2003), thus failing to achieve the objective of fairness.

That some empirical studies have pointed out the relative dissatisfaction with the expatriate compensation system (Harvey, 1993b) is perhaps the logical consequence of the difficulty of satisfying objectives that may work in opposite directions. As in many other areas of human resources, the compensation policy for multinational expatriates is bound to confront various dilemmas and conflicts. For example, the company faces the potential conflict of maintaining some form of internal equity while providing sufficient incentive to attract and motivate oversees assignees (Toh and Denisi, 2003). There is no magic formula that can solve these dilemmas, and so one should be wary of those who present this area of management as a science, to which one can limit oneself to applying technical solutions.

APPROACHES AND COMPONENTS

Bearing in mind the situational factors and objectives outlined above, the MNCs have a number of ways of dealing with the compensation of expatriates. Each way reflects the MNC's priorities when paying expatriates. Three main approaches, each with its strengths and weaknesses in achieving the five objectives (see Table 1), have been developed.

The first is the "host country approach." The main intention of this approach is to fit the expatriate into the assignment location salary structure. This approach is satisfactory when a number of eligible candidates for the particular position have a personal interest in living abroad, and so a local salary does not seem unattractive. In addition to reducing costs, this approach helps to create a sense of equity between expatriates and local employees, since nobody feels underprivileged. However, this method has only limited use in motivating international mobility because worldwide variations and the consequent inconsistencies may inhibit the transfer of expatriates. This approach is usually adopted when the expatriate has

Table 1. Compensation approaches and their impact on compensation objectives

Objectives of an international compensation system	Approach		
	Host-Country	Home-Country	Global
1. To attract personnel for the international service	−	+	+
2 To be cost-effective	+	−	−
3. To be fair			
With respect to local employees	+	−	−
With respect to other expatriates from a different nationality in the same location	+	−	+
With respect to other expatriates in another location	−	+	+
4. To facilitate re-entry	−	+	−
5. To support the company's international strategy	0	0	0

Note: "+" = Positive impact; "−" = Negative impact; "0" = Irrelevant.

become replaceable by a local hire but wants to remain abroad for personal reasons (O'Really, 1996).

The second is the "global approach." The intention is to pay on an international scale, with allowances derived from that base. An international basket of goods would be used across all expatriates regardless of country of origin (Freeman and Kane, 1995). This approach is most relevant in the case of expatriates who are expected to move to more than one foreign country, thereby losing direct connection with either their home country or host country grading and pay structure (O'Really, 1996). The high costs and difficulties of re-entry are often mentioned as the main shortfalls of this system (Dowling and Schuler, 1990).

The third is the "home country approach." The idea of this approach is to provide the expatriate with equivalent purchasing power abroad in order to maintain his/her standard of living in his/her home country. This is consistent with the so-called balance sheet approach. This system applies home country deductions and pays differential allowances (cost of living differential, housing allowance) to arrive at net disposable income which should maintain the expatriate's home country standard of living.

According to the 2008 Worldwide Survey of International Assignment Policies and Practices, conducted by the Organization Resources Counselors, Inc. (ORC Worldwide, 2008), most companies report that their intention is to provide expatriates with equivalent purchasing power abroad to help them maintain a home country lifestyle. This is the common practice among 67 percent of European, 62 percent of

Asian-Pacific, 76 percent of Japanese, and 72 percent of North American companies. The advantage of this approach is that, by keeping expatriates in line with conditions at home, they can readily fit back into their home country after their overseas posting. In addition, it enables a company to achieve worldwide consistency in its expatriate employment practices. However, it is not without drawbacks, which arise when different nationalities work together in similar jobs. Yet there exist solutions to this problem too. For example, Endesa, a Spanish electrical company, gets around this problem by giving all peer-group expatriates the same host country element, such as a housing or goods and services allowance.

Moreover, the home country approach is expensive, especially for some nationalities. For example, American expatriates are usually subject to higher income taxes abroad. The maximum marginal rate in the US is 31 percent, compared with 65 percent in Japan, 53 percent in Germany and 45 percent in Spain (Mercer HR Consulting, 2003). Maintaining the same level of net salary entails receiving a higher level of gross salary. The employers will have to carry that cost as part of the assignment terms. One should consider the possibility that these higher costs of expatriates of some nationalities influence recruitment policies. For example, according to the ORC Worldwide (2008) survey, American MNCs are less inclined to use expatriates than their European and Asian counterparts.

Although we know the prevalence of the above three approaches in MNCs, we do not know the reasons or determinants that lead companies to adopt them. Nor do we know the connection they may have with the international strategy of the MNC. Despite the claim that expatriate pay should be consistent with the overall strategy of the MNC (Freeman and Kane, 1995; Reynolds, 1997), the truth is that no indication is provided as to how the design of expatriate compensation packages can help to implement the company's international strategy (Bonache and Fernández, 1997). This omission regarding the connection between compensation and strategy was noted from the beginning of the literature on expatriation. Thus, Edström and Galbraith (1977: 253) justify the omission of the compensation system from the strategic dimensions involved in international transfers as follows: "Compensation packages ... do not differ with reasons for transfers; that is, all companies use compensation to maintain the expatriate's standard of living or slightly better it." Subsequent empirical research has been developed along the same lines. For example, Welch (1994), in her analysis of four Australian multinational firms, showed that, in spite of their differences in strategy, all four adopted a standardize focus on expatriate compensation (the balance sheet). More recently, another empirical study (O'Donnell, 1999) showed that few firms appear to be using compensation programs as a tool for implementing subsidiary strategy. Many companies limit themselves to using only standard compensation policies.

These "state of the art" compensation policies, mentioned by O'Donnell (1999), consist of including in the compensation package a series of key ingredients, such as cost of living and housing allowances, foreign service premiums (mobility premium, hardship pay),[1] income tax reimbursements, assistance programs (education, shipping and storage, travel and club membership), and performance incentives. (For a detailed description of how these elements are typically built and combined in a compensation package, see Suutari and Tornikoski, 2001.) The prevalence of these different elements in an international assignee compensation package is documented in the ORC Worldwide (2008) survey. We summarize this information in Table 2. We also distinguish between the prevalence of the different components for short- and long-term assignments (the differences between which two kinds of assignment will be addressed shortly).

The sum of all these elements allows us to understand the high costs incurred by employing expatriates. The data are quite compelling. The average compensation package of expatriates is two to five times as much as that received by their counterparts at home and certainly a great deal more than that received by the local nationals in the developing countries (O'Neill, 2009; Reynolds, 1997). Indeed, ORC Worldwide (2008) shows that expatriate program costs constitute a major concern for MNCs, and in many cases cost projections do influence assignment authorization.

Given such high costs, it is usual to debate the different ways or initiatives that companies can use to reduce the cost of expatriation, ways that will help to minimize or eliminate some of the items in Table 2. Among these initiatives, one should mention the following.

- Selection initiatives—To employ a greater number of local employees, expatriating only the most essential personnel (Dowling and Schuler, 1990). Organizations should establish a selection process which ensures that only employees who are interested in expatriate assignments are assigned to overseas positions (Wentland, 2003). The consequence of this would be that foreign service premiums, hardship premiums, and cost of living adjustments would be paid only to employees who accept assignments in undesirable or hazardous locations. Within Europe, where standards of living are converging, this initiative is relatively easy to implement, although there remain differences in tax systems, housing, and education standards. Another initiative is to fill international positions with third country nationals (TCNs) from subsidiaries located in countries with lower salaries and cost of living, when possible. By doing so instead of hiring higher paid parent country nationals (PCNs) a firm can reduce the magnitude of some of the elements in expatriates' compensation package mentioned above (Welch et al., 2008).
- Career planning initiatives—An alternative to selection initiatives is to require managers to have international experience as a criterion for promotion to higher level positions (Bonache and Fernández, 1997). This is fairly straightforward when dealing with a certain type of expatriate. Younger employees can be required to possess international experience if they want to move up the career ladder. They may then give up short-term earnings in exchange for long-term benefits. However, this initiative is not viable when dealing with more mature employees.
- Shorter assignments—As shown in Table 2, short term assignments are cheaper than their longer counterparts as they do not involve—or they do so in a lower level—many costly items included in the compensation package of the latter (e.g. education or spouse allowance).

Table 2. The use of different compensation components for global assignees (% of companies)

Elements	Short-term assignees Worldwide (N = 332)	Long-term assignees Worldwide (N = 930)
Cost of living and housing allowances		
Cost of living allowances (COLA)	29.3	93
Per-diem cost of living differential	63.8	–
Higher COLA/per-diem for accompanied assignees	18.9	86
Housing		
Free assignment housing	99.3	39
Hotel	29.0	–
Serviced apartment	57.7	–
Furnished accommodations	69.7	–
Unfurnished accommodations	2.9	–
Company owned apartment	11.4	–
Government housing	1.3	–
Other	7.8	–
Transportation		
Company car	35.7	71
Transportation allowance	34.8	–
Car and driver	19.7	27
Use of pool/fleet car	26.9	17
Public transportation allowance	19.0	–
Foreign service premiums		
Mobility premium	36.5	64
Hardship pay	45.6	73
Orientation and legal support		
Cross-cultural training	37.3	68
Work-permit support	93.9	99
Income tax reimbursement		
Tax equalization	75.7	80
Tax protection	6.3	5
Tax free	2.6	4
Other (e.g., laissez-faire)	15.5	12
Assistance programmes		
Spouse allowance	–	71
Education allowance		
Always	–	53
If no suitable education is available	–	42
Shipping and storage costs		
Baggage allowance	48.1	–
Shipping costs	12.5	97
Storage costs	41.0	83
First/business class air travel		
For senior management	–	46
Other expatriates	–	26

Table 2. *(continued)*

Elements	Short-term assignees	Long-term assignees
	Worldwide (N = 332)	Worldwide (N = 930)
Trips allowances provision		
For trips home	69.8	95
For visit from family	61.1	—
Remuneration approach		
Home-based balance sheet approach (BSA)	61.4	71
Headquarters-based BSA	5.3	8
Host-based approach	2.6	6
Other (for example, home plus approach)	30.7	14
Payroll handling		
Home-country payroll	88.5	—
Host-country payroll	2.3	—
International payroll	4.3	—
Other	4.9	—
Performance incentives	91.2	95

Source: Based on ORC Worldwide (2008; 2009).

FUTURE RESEARCH ISSUES

The components included in Table 2, as well as the different alternatives that exist in each one of them, are topics that attract the attention of professionals in this area. Often, the focus is on the relative advantages of, for example, tax equalization (the employee pays no more or no less than he/she would have paid in the home country) over the tax protection policy (employee pays no more than he/she have paid in the home country, but may pay less in certain situations), or on the advantages of offering free housing over other alternative housing policies (for example, the company may pay a housing differential).

Although these issues will continue to attract the attention of practitioners, there are a number of more strategic topics which should also attract academics' interest and guide future research in this area. Following the usual way of organizing HR topics, we will classify such topics around three big areas: (1) compensation and strategy; (2) compensation policy according to the type and form of global employees; and (3) compensation and HR outcomes (that is, satisfaction with pay packages, cost-efficiency, and justice). The following is a brief analysis of these themes as well as the theories that can support their investigation.

Compensation and its Link to Strategy

The fact that the majority of companies are simply using the "state of the art" compensation policy highlights an important issue. It is widely recognized that expatriates may perform different strategic roles and use different behaviors in different subsidiaries (Edström and Galbraith, 1977; Gupta and Govindarajan, 1991; Bonache and Fernandez, 1997). In some, for example, they are expected to transfer knowledge and procedures from the headquarters (HQs) while working independently with regards to other subsidiaries. Others, in contrast, are expected to develop their network of contacts with employees of other subsidiaries in order to personally import and export the knowledge within the integrated network of the multinational (see Gupta and Govindarajan, 1991). Given that compensation is an important mechanism to elicit different managerial roles and behaviors (Milkovich and Newman, 2008), how is it possible that multinationals limit themselves to the use of "state of the art" compensation policies instead of adapting the expatriate compensation system to the different roles of expatriates?

Although the strategic use of expatriate compensation (that is, compensation used to foster those behaviors required for the strategy of the company) has not been practically analyzed, we have some evidence that suggests its presence. For example, if we analyze the data in Table 2, we see that there are two types of incentive. One is classified under the category of premiums and allowances (that is, cost of living and housing allowances, foreign service premiums, hardship allowances, danger money, mobility premiums, and relocation allowances). These incentives are basically tools to encourage employees to take international assignments, and, as such, these have had a prominent place in the traditional international compensation arena. We also see that performance incentives are used by around 95 percent of MNCs. These are expected to be a mechanism to elicit the behaviors needed to implement the organization's strategy effectively. Little is known about these incentives although they are the ones that hold a greater theoretic and strategic interest.

A useful perspective to analyze the strategic use of performance incentives is agency theory (Gómez-Mejía, 1994). This theory is relevant to situations that have a principal–agent structure. The HQ–expatriate relationship responds to such a structure: HQ (the principal) delegates work and responsibilities to expatriates (the agent). In this type of relationship there is a risk that the "agency problem" may arise. This refers to the possibility that agents will pursue their own interests, which may diverge from the interests of the principal. This is a real possibility in the multinational arena. For example, in a subsidiary located in a culturally different environment, it is possible for an expatriate to enjoy excellent work conditions while making very little effort. His/her resulting poor performance can then be excused by attributing it to the lack of fit of the company's procedures to the local culture.

Incentive alignment is a traditional device used to address the agency problem. This is defined as the extent to which the reward structure is designed to induce managers to make decisions that are in the best interests of the principal (Gómez-Mejía, 1994). Properly designed, the reward structure promotes self-monitoring as it provides performance incentives that impel agents to minimize opportunism and promote their alignment with principal's interests. Through these performance incentives, expatriates, pursuing their own goals, will pursue the goal of the HQs.

From this theoretical perspective, one can analyze how different configurations of the expatriates' incentives (that is, the proportion of bonuses and long-term incentives versus salary and benefits, the short and long time horizon of incentives, the quantitative and qualitative criteria used to trigger rewards) respond to the intentions of the multinational to solve the agency problem and procure an appropriate alignment of interests between the company and expatriates. From Roth and O'Donnell's (1996) study on HQ–subsidiaries' relationships one may infer, for example, that when the potential for opportunism increases the percentage of expatriate incentive-based compensation rises accordingly and more weight is given to the performance of the host subsidiary in the expatriate compensation package. Although more work is clearly needed, such a study provides some support for the agency theory insight according to which particular compensation components are designed to reduce the agency problem by inducing expatriates to make decisions that are in the best interests of the HQs.

Not only is more research needed on the determinants of expatriate compensation systems but more research is also needed on the effects of these systems on firms' competitive advantages. In this regard, and contrary to the basic assumption underlying much of the research on traditional compensation literature, competitive advantage cannot be attained if companies simply implant a "state of the art" compensation package. As is well explained by the resource-based view of the firm, a competitive advantage must come from a resource that is valuable, rare, and difficult to imitate (Barney, 1991). Accordingly, instead of focusing on standard compensation packages, competitive advantage will come from crafting compensation and reward systems to create employment relationships that extract the value of firm-specific resources. We have no information about the way in which expatriate packages can be designed to create a shared mindset, extract tacit knowledge, encourage innovation, creativity, and responsiveness, and stimulate the development of important relationships among people. Investigation along these lines would undoubtedly be of great academic and professional interest.

Type and Form of Global Employees

While in the literature it is usual to refer to global employees as a homogenous group of employees, a closer look at the position they can occupy abroad allow us to make some distinctions that have important implications for international compensation strategies. Like other categories of employees, expatriates can perform different sorts of jobs. Specifically, we can discern between "star," "guardian," and "foot soldier" positions (Baron and Kreps, 1999). Such a distinction is based on the possible effects on total firm performance of the individual outcomes of those employees who occupy these positions.

Star jobs are those in which a bad performance is not too critical but a good performance is excellent for the company. At the international level, a global employee performing a star job would be a manager who runs a subsidiary that has very little dependence on its HQ (e.g. its products, brand image, or procedures) and where the essential thing is to develop new projects highly tailored to the local market. Guardian jobs are those in which an exemplary performance will be of little consequence for company's accomplishments but a bad performance will cause a disaster. A guardian job for an expatriate would be that of representing the firm to the key host country's external constituencies, where the reputation of the firm is a valuable asset. Subsidiary managers in the financial industry typically fall within this category. The last category of job that we can distinguish is the foot soldier. This includes positions in which neither a superlative nor a bad performance can determinedly impact the organization total performance. At the international level, "foot soldiers" would be young expatriates assigned abroad for learning and development purposes.

From expatriates occupying these different positions one would expect different behaviors and outcomes. Thus, for example, incentives for star global employees should be designed to induce risky behaviors. Positive performance should be proportionally rewarded, while small penalties (or no penalties at all) for failure should also be emphasized. Conversely, for guardian jobs an incentive system that contemplates severe penalties for any failure would possibly be more effective to foster the kind of conservative performance requested by global employees in this position. A different incentive system should be implemented for expatriates performing foot soldier jobs. While in the case of this kind of employees the firm does not significantly benefit by increasing a single worker's performance, it may do quite well by boosting the average performance of all employees in the same position through a meritocratic incentive system.

A fruitful avenue of future research would certainly be the analysis of the compensation plans that best support the specific kind of behavior requested in each type of position. Incentives constitute only an element of these plans. Other aspects such as base salary, benefits and so forth, are also worth researching.

Leaving aside the type of position that global employees can occupy abroad, another topic that deserves further research inquiry is that of new forms of international assignments, including "short-terms assignments," "commuters," "self-initiated expatriates," "virtual working," and "frequent flyers" (Bonache et al., 2010). While in the last few years efforts have been devoted to the exploration of the nature and functions of these assignments (e.g. Demel and Mayrhofer, 2010; Welch et al., 2008), much still remains to be understood about how compensation should be designed and implemented for employees on these assignments.

HR Outcomes

While compensation practices are relevant for a wide range of HR outcomes (Milkovich and Newman, 2008), three outcomes should be certainly addressed by future research on international assignees compensation. These are the satisfaction of global employees with their compensation package, the cost-efficient use of expatriates, and the impact of expatriate compensation on justice perceptions among host country nationals.

Satisfaction with Expatriate Compensation Packages

As has been mentioned before, MNCs often offer generous compensation policies to encourage international mobility. It would be reasonable to expect that this would lead to a high level of satisfaction among expatriates regarding their compensation. The evidence on this point is, however, contradictory. Suutari and Tornikoski (2001) studied the sources of salary satisfaction and dissatisfaction among Finnish expatriates and reported a high degree of satisfaction among expatriates with the principles and levels of their compensation packages. However, other studies on expatriates' attitudes have uncovered low levels of salary satisfaction among these employees. For example, Black et al. (1992) assert that 77 percent of expatriate employees are highly dissatisfied with their compensation systems. Similarly, Hamil (1989) suggests that salary dissatisfaction might be related with expatriate failure. The issue on salary satisfaction among expatriates clearly deserves more attention.

Salary satisfaction can be explained in terms of social comparison theory (Festinger, 1954; Adams, 1965). This theory asserts that satisfaction is a function of how "fairly" an individual is treated at work. Satisfaction results from one's perception that work outcomes, relative to inputs, compare favorably to another's outcomes/inputs. Dissimilar ratios lead to perceptions of inequity. This proposition implies that the same organizational circumstance may be perceived as fair or unfair depending on with which individual or group of individuals the worker chooses to compare himself/herself to. Accordingly, a main concern when analyzing someone's satisfaction with his/her salary is identifying the referent used in the individual's comparisons (Chen et al., 2002). The problem faced by expatriate workers is that there are multiple referents available to them when working abroad (Bonache et al., 2001; Bonache, 2005). They can compare themselves not only to other expatriates within the same company and host country but also with expatriates within the same company and other host countries, expatriates from other companies within their host country, local employees, and so on. With all these referents, lack of equity with respect to other employees is a very likely possibility. From this point of view, the low levels of salary satisfaction among expatriates that were reported by some studies can be easily explained.

In any case, a low level of salary satisfaction is a very common problem among all types of employees (Gómez-Mejía et al., 2006). This means that, even though expatriates might not feel satisfied with their pay, they might be relatively more satisfied than other groups of employees. However, the evidence to hand does not lead to this conclusion. Thus, in a study comparing job satisfaction among expatriates, repatriates, and domestic employees with international experience, conducted on a large sample of employees from a Spanish multinational, some significant differences in the satisfaction ratings on job characteristics, career prospects, and internal communication among these three groups of employees were found (Bonache, 2005). This study, however, did not find differences in the average level of satisfaction regarding salary. More research is clearly required on this issue.

The influence of nationality in the expatriates' attitudes toward their salaries is another important topic to examine. Some studies analyze the cross-cultural and motivational utility of various compensation strategies on managers and the larger workforce (Chiang & Birtch, 2006; Lowe et al., 2002). Their goal is to compare pay practices or preferences for pay practices across cultures. For example, when compared to individualist cultures, collectivist countries place more value on seniority. They see compensation according to needs as being fairer. Drawing on these studies, it would be illustrative to conduct in-depth academic cross-cultural research analyzing the motivational utility of various compensation strategies on expatriates from different nationalities. Such research would aim at providing some clues for companies as to which expatriate compensation strategy is most likely to mesh with a particular culture's values.

The Issue of Costs

Until now, the high costs of employing expatriates has been stressed. It is, therefore, surprising that MNCs continue to show a strong preference for expatriates to fill certain managerial positions. In fact, according to the ORC Worldwide (2008) survey, only 32 percent of companies from different countries declared a decreasing use of expatriates assigned in recent years. In other words, it is not clear why, in a business context under unremitting pressure to keep costs down, MNCs should continue to implement such a costly solution. To explain this apparent paradox would require more theoretical guidance than past work on expatriation has received.

On this point, the theory of transaction costs (Williamson, 1975) could be very useful because it considers a set of costs which are ignored in traditional expatriate compensation literature but which must be accounted for when an MNC is filling a management position in a subsidiary. Drawing on Jones and Wrights' (1992) classification of transaction costs in the employment relation, there are four main types of transaction costs that can be incurred when filling a management position in an MNC: (1) selection and recruitment costs, which are the costs of gathering information about the candidate as well as the costs associated with negotiation and final drawing up of the contract with the appointed candidate; (2) training and socialization costs, which are costs associated with the development of the skills and firm-specific abilities of the managers in the subsidiary; (3) monitoring and evaluating subsidiary's managers, which are the costs incurred in safeguarding the organization against moral hazard and these will include costs of managers from the HQs and managerial time spent on supervising the employees in the subsidiary, as well as costs associated with the implementation of appraisal and feedback systems; and finally (4) enforcement, which are the costs that the organization will have to take actions in the event of a breach of contract on the part of the subsidiary's manager. This will obviously produce new costs for the company.

The basic premise of transaction cost economics is that transactions will tend to take place in a form that minimizes the combined costs of the transaction. Accordingly, when deciding whether to recruit a local manager or an expatriate, relative salary levels are not the only economic items involved. Instead, the organization will have to consider the total costs associated with each alternative and opt for the most efficient one; that is, the one that minimizes salary and transaction costs. Without a doubt, determining when the transaction costs of using expatriates are lower than those of using local managers is of interest.

The first step in this direction was made by Bonache and Plá-Barber (2005). Building on the existence of the above-mentioned transaction costs, the authors argue that, in companies with a lower level of international expansion, that are less technologically innovative, with a global strategy, and with operations in very culturally distant environments, expatriates will have a lower level of associated transaction costs and, therefore, can be a cost-effective solution. They tested the viability of these arguments on a sample of 96 Spanish MNCs. Their data did not support the hypothesis concerning the diminished use of expatriates when companies operate in increasingly culturally distant environments. However, their empirical investigation supported their other three hypotheses, which illustrates the viability of this approach. Future research along these lines is clearly needed.

The Issue of Justice

In their review of HR literature, Ferris et al. (1999) insist upon the need to introduce the idea of justice into HR management. The topic of expatriate compensation provides an excellent opportunity to analyze the issue of justice. In fact, it has been stated that a compensation program should be fair in its treatment of all categories of employees (Milkovich and Newman, 2008). It is interesting to analyze this issue not only from the point of view of the expatriates, but also from that of the local employees.

Equity theory is the point of reference from which to evaluate the extent to which employees judge the fairness of their compensation. According to this theory, employees compare what they give to what they receive. This is based on their own evaluation of their value, a previous or later work, or what was promised to them. Such a comparison, as mentioned earlier, is made within a social setting by taking other employees as referents for comparison. On occasion, the referents are employees who are considered to be "similar," either in terms of age, seniority in the firm, or any other relevant variable. For example, the local employees may choose nationality as a variable and compare their level of compensation with that of other local employees, be it within the same MNC, other MNCs or in other local firms. Yet they also may choose "different" people to whom they compare themselves, as would happen if local employees were to compare themselves to expatriates. As seen in Table 2, the different allowances, additions and deductions included in a typical expatriate package, results in a pay package which is very different from that of other categories of employees. As compensation for their service abroad, it is logical that expatriates receive some of these elements (for example, overseas allowances, repatriation allowances), but other benefits (such as education allowances) are given to expatriates rather than to other groups (locals) with little justification.

Chen et al. (2002) analyzed the reactions of such comparisons of Chinese employees working in MNCs. These workers were at a salary disadvantage compared to the expatriates but at an advantage compared to other local employees. They found that local employees are more likely to feel a sense of injustice in compensation when comparing their salaries to expatriates' salaries than to locals'. This shows an egocentric bias: what they tend to see as fair is what benefits them the most.

The local's perception of salary inequity when comparing themselves to expatriates is unfortunate because local nationals are valuable socializing agents, sources of social support, assistance, and friendship to expatriates (Black et al., 1992; Toh and Denisi, 2003). The disparity in pay may lead local nationals to become uncooperative or antagonistic, which may lower the effectiveness of the expatriate on the job. Toh and Denisi (2003) theoretically analyzed the factors that determine this perception of inequity. They state that this perception occurs when a local employee does not perceive a salary advantage over locals in other companies, when they do not see logical reasons for the high expatriate compensation, and when expatriates do not have the appropriate interpersonal skills. Moreover, Toh and Denisi (2003) assert that such perceptions are greatly influenced by the national culture of the local employee. For example, we can expect that differences in salaries will be better accepted in cultures characterized by high power distance than by those of low power distance.

A number of empirical studies regarding the determinants and effects of salary inequity among local employees and expatriates have been published (e.g. Bonache et al., 2009; Leung et al., 2009; Paik et al., 2007). Paik et al. (2007) found that the host country workforce perceives significant gaps in their compensation relative to expatriates and that these gaps are inversely related to its affective organizational commitment. Bonache et al. (2009) identified diverse factors that may offset or attenuate the negative influence of pay differential on host country nationals' (HCNs') perceived pay unfairness, namely awareness of expatriate contributions and special needs, expatriate interpersonal sensitivity, HCN pay advantage over other locals, and HCN contact with expatriates. Similarly, Leung et al. (2009) found in foreign multinationals in China that perceived compensation and trustworthiness of expatriates are able to buffer the negative effects of distributive injustice on local employees.

Finally, while equity theory is the traditional reference used to analyze organizational justice, other approaches regarding justice are also possible. One possible and complementary alternative is Rawl's theory of justice (see Bonache, 2004, for an analysis of this theory as applied to HRM). According to this theory, different work arrangements for expatriates and local employees will be fair in cases where: (a) the groups have the same basic labor rights and opportunities, (b) greater rewards correspond to greater merits, and (c) the greater rewards of the expatriates group (the most-favored group) improve those of the less-favored local employees group. Theoretical and empirical research on the topic using this (or other) theoretical frameworks may be very instructive.

CONCLUSION

Traditionally, the literature on the compensation of expatriates has had a very descriptive and practitioner orientation. It basically describes the many difficulties encountered by MMCs in designing an "attractive" and "cost efficient" compensation approach that enables them to standardize salary decisions and apply the approach uniformly throughout the multinational network. Such an approach, however, is not easy to develop. As noted, there are conflicting objectives to be achieved, forcing MNCs to face a dilemma of achieving one objective at the expense of giving up another.

The difficulty involved in finding a satisfactory compensation system may explain why expatriate compensation literature has been dominated by interests of practitioners and has been characterized by an operative focus. Although these practical issues will continue to attract the attention of practitioners and academics, this reading has tried to show that this topic also brings to light many more theoretical issues, such as justice, satisfaction, costs, and strategy in expatriate compensation systems. The main challenge for academics is, from different theoretical perspectives, to shed light on these issues about which we still know very little.

NOTE

1.   ORC Worldwide's (2008) survey highlights that between 1998 and 2006 the percentage of companies no longer offering foreign service premiums have increased worldwide from 22 to 39 percent. In 2008 this percentage slightly reduced to 36 percent.

REFERENCES

Adams, J.S. (1965). Inequity in social exchange. In L. Berkowitz (Ed.), *Advances in Experimental Social Psychology*, vol. 2, (267–299). New York: Academic Press.

Barney, J. (1991). Firm resources and sustained competitive advantage. *Journal of Management*, 15: 175–190.

Baron, J. & Kreps, D. (1999). *Strategic Human Resources: Frameworks for General Managers*. New York: John Wiley & Sons, Inc.

Black, J.S., Gregersen, H.B. & Mendenhall, M.E. (1992). *Global Assignments*. San Francisco: Jossey-Bass.

Bonache, J. (2004). Towards a re-examination of work arrangements: an analysis from Rawls' Theory of Justice. *Human Resource Management Review*, 14(4): 395–408.

Bonache, J. (2005). Job satisfaction among expatriates, repatriates and domestic employees: the perceived impact of international assignments on work-related variables. *Personnel Review*, 34(1): 110–124

Bonache, J. & Fernández, Z. (1997). Expatriate compensation and its link to the subsidiary strategic role: a theoretical analysis. *International Journal of Human Resource Management*, 8(4): 457–475.

Bonache, J. & Plá-Barber, J. (2005). When are international managers a cost effective solution? The rationale of transaction costs economics applied to staffing decisions in MNCs. *Journal of Business Research*, 58(10): 1320–1329.

Bonache, J., Brewster, C., Suutari, V. & De Saá, P. (2010). Expatriation: traditional criticisms and international careers: introducing the special issue. *Thunderbird International Business Review*, 52(4): 263–274.

Bonache, J., Sánchez, J. & Zárraga, C. (2009). The interaction of expatriate pay differential and expatriate inputs on host country nationals' pay unfairness". *International Journal of Human Resource Management*, 20(10): 2135–2149.

Bonache, J., Suutari, V. & Brewster, C. (2001). A review and agenda for expatriate HRM. *Thunderbird International Management Review*, 42(1): 3–21.

Chen, C.C., Choi, J. & Chi, S.C. (2002). Making justice sense of local-expatriate compensation disparity: mitigation by local referents, ideological explanations, and interpersonal sensitivity in China-foreign joint ventures. *Academy of Management Journal*, 45(4): 807–826.

Chiang, F. & Birtch, T.A. (2006). An empirical examination of reward preferences within and across national settings. *Management International Review*, 46(5): 573–596.

Demel, B. & Mayrhofer, W. (2010). Frequent business travelers across Europe: career aspirations and implications. *Thunderbird International Business Review*, 52(4): 301–311.

Dowling, P.J. & Schuler, R.S. (1990). *International Dimensions of Human Resource Management*. Boston: PWS-Kent.

Edström, A. & Galbraith, J. (1977). Transfer of managers as a coordination and control strategy in multinational organizations. *Administrative Science Quarterly*, 22: 248–263.

Ferris, G., Hochwarter, W., Buckley, M.R., Harrell-Cook, G. & Frink, D. (1999). Human resource management: some new directions. *Journal of Management*, 25(3): 385–415.

Festinger, L. (1954). A theory of social comparison processes. *Human Relations*, 7: 117–140.

Freeman, K. & Kane, J. (1995). An alternative approach to expatriate allowances: an international citizen. *The International Executive*, 37(3): 245–259.

Gómez-Mejía, L.R. (1994). Executive compensation: a reassessment and a future research agenda. *Research in Personnel and Human Resources Management,* 12: 161–222.

Gómez-Mejía, L.R., Balkin, D. & Cardy, R. (2006). *Managing Human Resources* (5th edn). Upper Saddle River, NJ: Prentice Hall.

Gupta, A.K. & Govindarajan, V. (1991). Knowledge flows and the structure of control within multinational corporations. *Academy of Management Review,* 16: 768–792.

Hamil, J. (1989). Expatriate policies in British multinational. *Journal of General Management,* 14(4): 19–26.

Harvey, M.G. (1993a). Designing a global compensation system: the logic and a model. *Colombia Journal of World Business,* 28: 56–72.

——(1993b). Empirical evidence of recurring international compensation problems. *Journal of International Business Studies,* 24(4): 785–799.

Harvey, M. & Moeller, M. (2009). Expatriate managers: a historical review. *International Journal of Management Reviews,* 11(3): 275–296.

Jones, G. & Wright, P. (1992). An economic approach to conceptualizing the utility of Human Resource Management practices. *Research in Personnel and Human Resource Management,* 10: 271–299.

Krupp, N. (2008). International assignments: financing for retirement. *Benefits & Compensation International,* 37(7): 18–22.

Leung, K., Zhu, Y. & Ge, C. (2009). Compensation disparity between locals and expatriates: moderating the effects of perceived injustice in foreign multinationals in China. *Journal of World Business,* 44(1): 85–93.

Lowe, K.B., Milliman, J., De Cieri, H. & Dowling, P. (2002). International compensation practices: a ten-country comparative analysis. *Human Resource Management,* 41(1): 45–66.

McMorrow, V.G. & Cummins, S. (2009). Expatriate home leave policy in a volatile economy. *Benefits and Compensation International,* 38(8): 18–19.

Mercer HR Consulting (2003). *Estudio Mundial sobre diferencias salariales.* Mercer HR Consulting España.

Milkovich, G.T. & Newman, J.M. (2008). *Compensation* (9th edn). New York: McGraw-Hill/Irwin.

O'Donnell, S. (1999). Compensation design as a tool for implementing foreign sunsidiary strategy. *Management International Review,* 39(2): 149–165.

O'Neill, J. (2009). Relocating employees overseas: beyond cost projection and into the world of cost modeling. *Compensation and Benefit Review,* 41(3): 55–60.

O'Really, M. (1996). Expatriate pay: the state of the art. *Compensation and Benefits Review,* 12(1): 54–60.

ORC Worldwide. (2008). *2008 Worldwide Survey of International Assignment Policies and Practices.* Paris: ORC Worldwide.

ORC Worldwide. (2009). *2009 Survey of Short-Term and Commuter International Assignment Policies.* Paris: ORC Worldwide.

Paik, Y., Parboteeah, K.P. & Shim, W. (2007). The relationship between perceived compensation, organizational commitment and job satisfaction: the case of Mexican workers in the Korean Maquiladoras. *International Journal of Human Resource Management,* 18(10): 1768–1781.

Reynolds, C. (1997). Expatriate compensation in historical perspective. *Journal of World Business,* 32(2): 118–132.

——(2000). Global compensation and benefits in transition. *Compensation and Benefits Review,* 32(1): 28–39.

Roth, K. & O'Donnell, S. (1996). Foreign subsidiary compensation strategy: an agency theory perspective. *Academy of Management Journal,* 39: 678–703.

Shaffer, M.A., Harrison, D. & Gilley, M. (1999). Dimensions, determinants, and differences in the expatriate adjustment process. *Journal of International Business Studies,* 30(3): 557–581.

Stahl, G.K., Miller, E. & Tung, R. (2002). Toward the bounderyless career: a closer look at the expatriate career concept and the perceived implications of an international assignment. *Journal of World Business*, 37: 216–227.

Suutari, V. & Tornikoski, C. (2001). The challenge of expatriate compensation: the sources of satisfaction and dissatisfaction among expatriates. *The International Journal of Human Resource Management*, 12(3): 389–404.

Toh, S.M. & Denisi, A. (2003). Host country national reactions to expatriate pay policies: a model and implications. *Academy of Management Review*, 28(4): 606–621.

Welch, C.L., Welch, D. & Tahvanainen, M. (2008). Managing the HR dimension of international project operations. *International Journal of Human Resource Management*, 19(2): 205–222.

Welch, D. (1994). Determinants of international human resource management approaches and activities: a suggested framework. *Journal of Management Studies*, 31: 139–63.

Wentland, D. (2003). A new practical guide for determining expatriate compensation. *Compensation and Benefits Review*, 35(3): 45–52.

Williamson, O. (1975). *Markets and Hierarchies: analysis and Antitrust Implications*. New York: Free Press.

J. Stewart Black

FRED BAILEY: AN INNOCENT ABROAD

FRED GAZED OUT THE WINDOW of his 24th floor office at the tranquil beauty of the Imperial Palace amidst the hustle and bustle of downtown Tokyo. It had only been six months ago that Fred had arrived with his wife and two children for this three-year assignment as the director of Kline & Associates' Tokyo office. Kline & Associates was a multinational consulting firm with offices in nine countries worldwide. Fred was now trying to decide if he should simply pack up and tell the home office that he was coming home or whether he should try to somehow convince his wife and himself that they should stay and try to finish the assignment. Given how excited Fred thought they all were about the assignment to begin with, it was a mystery to him as to how things had gotten to this point. As he watched the swans glide across the water in the moat that surrounds the Imperial Palace, Fred reflected back on the past seven months.

Seven months ago, the managing partner, Dave Steiner, of the main office in Boston asked Fred to lunch to discuss "business." To Fred's surprise, the "business" was not the major project that he and his team had just successfully finished, but was instead a very big promotion and career move. Fred was offered the position of managing director of the firm's relatively new Tokyo office, which had a staff of 30, including seven Americans. Most of the Americans in the Tokyo office were either associate consultants or research analysts. Fred would be in charge of the whole office and would report to a senior partner (located in Boston) who was running the Asian region. It was implied to Fred that if this assignment went as well as his other assignments, then it would be the last step before becoming a partner in the firm.

How could Fred go back now? Certainly going back early would be the kiss of death for his career in Kline. But Jenny was not in a mood to discuss things. As far as she was concerned, there was nothing to discuss. She hated Japan. She felt that the company and Fred had oversold the country and how "well they would be looked after." Fred worked 80+ hours a week because of all the after-hours socializing that he had to do with the clients. He was never home and "had no idea what life was really like in Japan." Jenny had given Fred an ultimatum: either they left together or she would go home alone. That things had escalated this far just did not seem possible to Fred. What was he supposed to do? Sacrifice everything that he had worked for over the years? His Harvard MBA would no doubt get him another job, but he had a real future at Kline if he could just hit even a double in this assignment. But if he walked away from the plate now, his career was over. And yet he loved his wife and children and did not want to lose them. What had gone wrong?

FRED AND JENNY

Fred and Jenny met during their last year in college in a senior seminar class on business ethics. Fred was instantly attracted to Jenny's warm smile and flair for fashion. Jenny recognized in Fred ambition and a kind heart. The two started dating only a week after the class started.

Jenny came from a well-to-do family in Connecticut. Her father was a senior executive with a major firm headquartered in New York. She had majored in fashion merchandising as a way of combining her interest and talent for fashion and her father's advice about studying something practical.

Fred was the oldest of six children and was the first to go to college. His father was a construction worker and his mother a beautician. Fred had worked hard in high school and graduated second in his class. Even with a partial scholarship and loans, tuition help from his parents had placed a real financial burden on them. Fred was determined to take advantage of the opportunity he was being given and to make his parents proud.

Fred and Jenny were married on a warm June afternoon. Although skeptical at first, Jenny's parents gradually came to recognize in Fred what Jenny saw from the beginning. Fred was bright and determined but his humble background sparked in him a genuine interest in others that put them at ease whenever Fred was around.

Before and after getting married, Fred and Jenny talked at length about careers and family. Fred wanted to go back and get his MBA after a couple of years of work. He had landed a great job with American Express after graduation and hoped with two years experience in a name brand company, his stellar college grades, and good GMAT scores he could get into a top MBA program. Jenny wanted to be a buyer for a major store like Sacs Fifth Avenue and later have her own shop. They both wanted children but thought they would wait until Fred finished his MBA before starting a family. At that point, Jenny would take a few years off and then start her own small clothing store once the children were in school. They both thought that owning her own shop would give Jenny the flexibility and time to spend with their children that she wanted.

Everything had gone according to plan up until the offer to go to Japan.

THE OFFER

Fred joined Kline right after graduating from Harvard. He had a couple of other offers, but including expected performance bonuses, the job at Kline paid 20% more than any of the others. Fred took it and was immediately put on the San Francisco team of one of the hardest charging young consultants at Kline.

Rick Savage was one year away from the magical "up or out" decision concerning partner. This decision typically happened about the seventh year of employment for MBA hires. Rick had been given a very high profile assignment with Kline's largest client. Success here would guarantee a partnership. Fred felt that his life must be charmed to have landed on Rick's team out of the gate.

During his first three years at Kline, that first project and nearly every other project that Fred had been part of were successes. In his fourth year, he was given a major assignment and led a team of seven consultants and associates. Fred had just completed this 10-month assignment when Dave asked him to lunch.

Fred was stunned by the Tokyo offer. The Tokyo office was opened in part to serve major US clients' operations in Japan. From the same base, Kline would begin to develop relationships with Japanese firms. Once the relationships were formed, Kline would be able to service the Japanese multinationals' American operations from their established offices in seven major cities in the United States. The strategic significance of the office and the offer did not escape Fred.

Fred's predecessor in Japan had opened the office a year ago. George Woodward was a partner with a mixed reputation. George had friends at the very top of Kline, but he also had made enemies all along the away. Fred was not sure why George had been suddenly transferred to the UK. Because the transfer to England was taking place "right away," Dave told Fred that he and his family had about three weeks to get prepared for the move.

When Fred told his wife about the unbelievable opportunity, he was shocked at her less than enthusiastic response. Jenny thought that it would be rather difficult to have the children live and go to school in a foreign country for three years, especially when Christine, the youngest, would be starting first grade next year. Besides, now that the kids were in school, Jenny wanted to open her own clothing store.

Fred explained that the career opportunity was just too good to pass up and that the company's overseas package would make living in Japan terrific. The company would pay all the expenses to move whatever the Bailey's wanted to take with them. The company had a very nice house in an expensive district of Tokyo that would be provided rent-free. Additionally, the company would rent their house in Boston during their absence. The firm would provide a car and driver, education expenses for the children to attend private schools, and a cost of living adjustment and overseas compensation that would nearly double Fred's gross annual salary. After two days of consideration and discussion, Fred told Mr. Steiner that he would accept the assignment.

PREPARING FOR THE MOVE

Between getting things at the office transferred to Bob Newcome, who was being promoted to Fred's position, and the logistic hassles of getting furniture and the like ready to be moved, neither Fred nor his family had much time to really find out much about Japan, other than what they had quickly read on Wikipedia.

Kline handled many of the logistical and relocation details internally. Unfortunately, a number of things went wrong. For example, when the packers came, they were totally unprepared for the fact that some of the Baileys' stuff was going into storage and some was being shipped to Japan. On a "look see visit" a week after Fred had accepted the assignment, Jenny saw the house in Japan where they were to live and instantly knew that not even a third of their belongs would fit. In fact, none of the antiques would fit through the door, let alone in the house.

FRED'S EARLY EXPERIENCES

When the Bailey's arrived in Japan, they were greeted at the airport by one of the young Japanese associate consultants and the senior American expatriate. Fred and his family were exhausted from the long trip and the 90-minute ride back to Tokyo was a rather quiet one. After a few days of just settling in, Fred spent his first full day at the office.

Fred's first order of business was to have a general meeting with all the employees of associate consultant rank and higher. Although Fred did not really notice it at the time, all the Japanese staff sat together and all the Americans sat together. After Fred introduced himself and his general ideas about the potential and future directions of the Tokyo office, he called on a few individuals to get their ideas about how the things for which they were responsible would likely fit into his overall plan.

From the Americans, Fred got a mixture of opinions with specific reasons about why certain things might or might not fit well. From the Japanese, he got very vague answers. When Fred pushed to get more specific information, he was surprised to find that a couple of Japanese simply made a sucking sound as they breathed and said that it was "difficult to say." Fred sensed that the meeting was not meeting his objectives, and so he thanked everyone for coming and said that he looked forward to their all working together to make the Tokyo office the fastest growing office in the company.

After they had been in Japan about a month, Fred's wife complained to him about the difficulty she had getting certain products like maple syrup, peanut butter, and quality beef. She said that when she could get it at one of the specialty stores, it cost three and four times what it would cost in the States. She also complained that the washer and dryer were much too small and so she had to spend extra money by sending things out to be cleaned. On top of all that, unless she went to the American Club in downtown Tokyo, she never had anyone to talk to. After all, Fred was gone between 10 and 16 hours a day. Unfortunately, at the time Fred was pre-occupied, thinking about his upcoming meeting between his firm and a significant prospective client—a top 100 Japanese multinational company.

The next day, along with the lead American consultant for the potential contract, Ralph Webster, and one of the Japanese associate consultants, Kenichi Kurokawa, who spoke perfect English, Fred met with a team from the Japanese firm. The Japanese team consisted of four members—the vice president of administration, the director of international personnel, and two staff specialists. After shaking hands and a few awkward bows, the Japanese offered to exchange business cards. Fred's staff had prepared his cards in advance with Japanese on one side and English on the other. Fred handed his cards to each member of the Japanese team with the English side up.

After the card exchange, Fred said that he knew the Japanese gentlemen were busy and he did not want to waste their time so he would get right to the point. Fred then had Ralph Webster lay out Kline's proposal for the project and what the project would cost. After the presentation, Fred asked the Japanese what their reaction to the proposal was. The Japanese did not respond immediately and so Fred launched into his summary version of the proposal thinking that the translation might have been insufficient. But again, the Japanese had only the vaguest of responses to his direct questions.

The recollection of the frustration of that meeting was enough to shake Fred back to reality. The reality was that in the five months since the first meeting little progress had been made and the contract between the firms was yet to be signed. "I can never seem to get a direct response from Japanese," he thought to himself. This feeling of frustration led him to remember a related incident that happened about a month after his first meeting with this client.

Fred had decided that the reason not much progress was being made with the client was that Fred and his group just did not know enough about the client to package the proposal in a way that was appealing to them. Consequently, he called in the senior American associated with the proposal, Ralph Webster, and asked him to develop a report on the client so that the proposal could be re-evaluated and changed where necessary. Jointly, they decided that one of the more promising Japanese research associates, Tashiro Watanabe, would be the best person to take the lead on this report.

To impress upon Tashiro the importance of this task and the great potential they saw in him, they decided to have the young Japanese associate meet with both Fred and Ralph. In the meeting Fred had Ralph lay out the nature and importance of the task. At which point Fred leaned forward in his chair and said:

> You can see that this is an important assignment and that we are placing a lot of confidence in you by giving you this assignment. We need the report this time next week so that we can revise and re-present our proposal. What do you think?

After a somewhat pregnant pause, the Japanese responded somewhat hesitantly, "I don't know what to say." At that point Fred smiled, got up from his chair and walked over to the young Japanese associate, extended his hand, and said, "Hey, there's no need to thank us. We're just giving you the opportunity you deserve."

The day before the report was due, Fred asked Ralph how the report was coming. Ralph said that since he had heard nothing from Tashiro that he assumed everything was under control but that he would double check. Ralph later ran into one of the American research associates, John Maynard. Ralph knew that John was hired because of his language ability in Japanese and that unlike any of the other Americans, John often went out after work with some of the Japanese research associates, including Tashiro. So, Ralph asked John if he knew how Tashiro was coming on the report. John then recounted that last night at the office Tashiro had asked if Americans sometimes fired employees for being late with reports. John had sensed that this was more than a hypothetical question and asked Tashiro why he wanted to know. Tashiro did not respond immediately and since it was 8:30 in the evening, John suggested they go out for a drink. At first Tashiro resisted, but then John assured him that they would grab a drink at a nearby bar and come right back.

At the bar John got Tashiro to open up. Tashiro explained the nature of the report that he had been requested to produce. Tashiro continued to explain that even though he had worked long into the night every night to complete the report that it was just impossible and that he had doubted from the beginning whether he could complete the report in a week.

At this point Ralph asked John, "Why the hell didn't Tashiro say something in the first place?" Ralph did not wait to hear whether John had an answer to his question or not. He headed straight to Tashiro's desk.

The incident just got worse from that point. Ralph chewed Tashiro out and then went to Fred explaining that the report would not be ready and that Tashiro had worried that it might not be from the start. "Then why didn't he say something?" Fred asked. No one had any answers and the whole thing left everyone more suspicious of and uncomfortable with each other than ever.

There were other incidents, big and small, that had made especially the last two months frustrating, but Fred was too tired to remember them all. To Fred it seemed that working with Japanese both inside and outside the firm was like working with people from another planet. Fred felt that he just could not communicate with them and that he could never figure out what they were thinking. It drove him crazy.

JENNY'S EARLY EXPERIENCES

Jenny's life in Japan was equally frustrating. Jenny was determined at first to make an adventure of living in Japan. During the first week, she went down to the local grocery store to buy some food and basic household supplies. However, not being able to read the labels she had mistakenly bought a bottle of bluish colored liquid that was in a bottle of the same shape as "Scope" mouthwash back home. She discovered that it was actually bathroom cleaning liquid after "swishing," "gargling," and nearly choking to death on the stuff.

After about a month, Jenny tried to take the Tokyo subway system from her house to the American Club. What was supposed to be a 15-minute ride turned into a 2-hour ordeal. Jenny missed her stop but did not discover her mistake for several more stops. Then when she did, she got off the train, only to discover she had no idea of how to get to the other side of the tracks and head back in the opposite direction. She exited the station and tried to ask how to get to the other side. Finally, in broken English someone pointed out some stairs that led to a tunnel that went under the tracks to the other side. However, arriving there, she found, that she had no idea how much a ticket would cost to the stop she wanted and even though the map had had the stops in both English and Japanese, there were so many subway lines and stops that it was just overwhelming.

At this point she was frustrated nearly to the point of tears. The tears came when she saw a small group of young grade school kids buy tickets and go through the turnstile. Although she did not want to, she called Fred on her mobile. She reached his assistant who said he was in a meeting. "I understand, but I need to speak with him," Jenny said firmly. When Fred came to the phone Jenny was crying. Fred tried to be understanding but his irritation at being called out of a meeting because she was lost on the subway seeped through.

After a brief discussion, Fred and Jenny reasoned that she should take the escalator up out of the subway and hail a taxi. Fortunately, the Japanese taxi driver understood "American Club please" and Jenny arrived just as the group she was supposed to meet was breaking up.

Two people in the group were more than sympathetic to Jenny's ordeal and could not say enough about the "stupid" things that they had encountered in "this most frustrating of all developed countries." As part of this cathartic complaint session, Jenny related her "mouthwash" incident. After they all had a good laugh, one of the women told Jenny about National Azabu, a small but American grocery store. "At least there you can get key things from back home," she said.

THE BOMBSHELL

For Jenny, these incidents were only the tip of the iceberg. She wanted to go home, and yesterday was not soon enough. Even though the kids seemed to be doing okay, she was tired of Japan—tired of being stared at, of people trying to touch her hair, of not understanding anybody or being understood, of not being able to find what she wanted at the store, of not being able to drive and read the road signs, of not having anything to watch on television, of not being involved in anything. She wanted to go home and she could not think of any reason why they should not. After all, she reasoned that they owed nothing to the company because the company had led them to believe that this was just another assignment, like the two years they had spent in San Francisco, and it was anything but that!

Fred tried to reason with her, but the more he countered, the more determined she became. Suddenly she dropped the bombshell on him: either they could go home together or he could stay here alone.

THE DECISION

Fred looked out the window once more, wishing that somehow everything could be fixed, or turned back or something. What had gone wrong? Why was Jenny being so unreasonable? Did he dare call Dave and explain the situation? Dave was very old fashioned and had once made a derogatory comment about a promising young consultant whose future looked dimmer and dimmer because he "could control his complaining spouse."

Looking down again, Fred could see traffic backed up down the street and around the corner. Although the traffic lights changed, the cars and trucks did not seem to be moving. Fortunately, in the ground below, one of the world's most advanced, efficient, and clean subway systems moved hundreds of thousands of people about the city and to their homes.

Paula Caligiuri and
Henry W. Lane

SELECTING A COUNTRY MANAGER FOR DELTA BEVERAGES INDIA

PART 1

YOU ARE THE REGIONAL PRESIDENT, Asia, for Delta Beverages, a large US-based firm headquartered in Boston. Delta is one of the world's leaders in the beverage industry (bottled water, carbonated beverages, teas, juice beverages and sports drinks). After having been with Delta for ten years, you are now responsible for all of the firms' operations in Asia, including the major markets of China, India, Korea, and Japan. Along with the rest of Delta's regional leadership team, you live in the Boston area and travel extensively to the subsidiaries that you lead. In the two years since accepting this position, you have logged many frequent-flier miles and, on most days, greatly enjoy the challenges of leading the company's fastest growing global region.

One of the greatest challenges that you have in your role is selecting your direct reports, the country managers leading each of the country-level markets within your unit. Delta's country managers are hands-on leaders who effectively direct all areas of the subsidiary's operations, including supply chain, logistics, inventory, quality control, government, and customer service. Country managers need to operate with cultural agility, having a deep understanding of the company's culture, values, and standards of quality, safety, and ethics. At the same time, country managers need to, at times, adapt to the client demands and unique challenges inherent in each of their local markets.

For large markets, such as India, Delta has traditionally promoted country managers from within—leaders who have experience in the Boston-based headquarters and who have experience running smaller and less challenging markets. Currently, most of your country managers are international assignees, with the exception of a few who are running smaller markets.

You understand, firsthand, what it takes to do this role well. Prior to this role, you had three international assignments, all as country manager. Your spouse, two children, and yourself lived for three years in the United Kingdom, two years in Bulgaria, and, most recently, two years in China. You recall both the joys and the challenges of living and working in each of your host countries. It takes a special person—and a special family—to thrive in this type of work environment.

Today you need to make a critical staffing decision. Shortly, you are scheduled for a distance communication meeting with the Vice President of Human Resources for International Operations, Al Uccello and other members of your leadership team who are traveling. The meeting aims to select someone for the position of Country Manager, India. The job will not be far from New Delhi in the state of Haryana. This position became available a few years ahead of schedule when immediate concerns about government relations and quality control forced you to assign your strongest country leader, Canadian Xiao Zhang, the current country manager for India, to China—effective immediately.

The meeting today is important. India is among the largest and most important markets in your unit. You know that selecting the best country manager for India is critical.

EXCERCISE 1

Before looking at the personnel files you have decided to review what you know about selecting managers for international assignments. Exhibit 1 is a list of 15 important characteristics that you think should be considered. You believe that this ranking may help you in reviewing candidate files. Working alone, rank these characteristics in importance from high to low. Assign "1" to the most important characteristic and "15" to the least important. Although all are important, you know that some may be more important than others in contributing to a successful assignment. After completing your individual ranking, go to **Part 2**.

EXHIBIT 1. Ranking of expatriate selection criteria

(1 = most important, 15 = least important)

Item	1 *Your Individual Rank*	2 *Your Team's Rank*	3 *Experts' Rank*	4 *Your Score (Difference between 1 & 3)*	5 *Team Score (Difference between 2 & 3)*
Language fluency					
Prior postings					
Technical/business skills					
Availability for preparation training					
Cultural and social interests					
Low sickness record					
Spouse support					
Need for autonomy					
Interpersonal sensitivity					
Few family ties					
Vacations abroad					
Communication skills					
No school-age children					
Extroversion					
Need for achievement					
TOTALS					

Final Team Calculations

1	Average Individual Score (Sum of individual scores, divided by number in group)	_____	1
2	Team Score (from column 5 above)	_____	2
3	Gain Score (Average Individual Score (#1), minus Team Score (#2))	_____	3
4	Best Individual Score (Lowest Individual Score in Team)	_____	4
5	Ratio (Number of individuals in group who scored lower than Team Score (#2), divided by Number of individuals in the group)	_____	5
6	Relative Improvement (Gain score (#3), divided by Average Individual Score (#1))	_____	6

PART 2

FIVE CANDIDATES' NOTES FROM THE SUCCESSION PLANNING MEETING

To prepare for today's meeting, you have reviewed the materials from last year's performance review and succession planning meetings. This activity has surfaced five possible candidates for the role of Country Manager, India. Your notes on these candidates are as follows.

1. Anika "Ani" Navithar

    Ani has been with Delta for the past 15 years. She joined Delta immediately after completing her MBA at Northeastern University, joining us in the supply chain functional area. She has moved up ranks quickly to director-level positions in both supply chain and customer service. While based in Boston, Ani has successfully completed several short-term projects internationally, and in the Indian subsidiary specifically. Ani has never been a country manager. She speaks English, Hindi, and Telugu. Part of Ani's leadership development plan is an international assignment. Ani is American.

2. Carlos Delgado

    Between his experience at Delta and his previous employer (Delta's major competitor), Carlos has had three international assignments over the past 18 years. Carlos began his career with Delta at the Boston headquarters and is currently reporting sto you as the country manager in South Korea. He is highly regarded as a global leader and, as the succession plan indicates, he was on the slate of candidates for your current role. Prior to becoming the country manager in Korea, Carlos was the Argentinean country manager for Delta and he worked in a supply chain role in Poland with his previous employer. Carlos speaks Spanish and English. He is a Mexican national.

3. Haziq Tengku

    Haziq reports directly to you and he is currently the country manager for Malaysia, where he has been extremely successful. He has been serving in that role for the past six years and is ready for a promotion, according to the succession plan. With the exception of one three-month orientation at the Boston headquarters when he first joined Delta ten years ago, he has spent his tenure at Delta within the Malaysian subsidiary. Prior to joining Delta, Haziq worked for the Malaysian subsidiary of a US-based fast-food chain. Part of Haziq's leadership development plan is to be a country manager for a larger market. He speaks Malay and English and has a degree in business from the University of Malaya. Haziq is a Malaysian national.

4. Lucas Hansson

    Lucas was appointed as the vice president for Delta's Europe, Middle East, and Africa (EMEA) region one year ago. In this current role, he is living and working in Delta's EMEA headquarters at Basel, Switzerland. Prior to his current role he was country manager in Germany (four years) and he has had a variety of functional positions in the international division from the headquarters in Boston, including a two-year global quality initiative. Lucas speaks Swedish, English, French, and German. He is a Swedish national.

5. **Pranav Subramanium**

Pranav is the vice president of the Indian subsidiary, reporting to Xiao Zhang, the recently re-assigned country manager of India. Pranav joined Delta three years ago after spending five years in a consulting firm in Delhi. The succession plan states that his performance has been exemplary and he is considered in the top rank of the regional talent pool. Pranav has an MBA from the Institute of Advanced Management and Research in Ghaziabad. Part of Pranav's leadership development plan is a short-term assignment in the Boston headquarters. Pranav speaks English, Hindi, and Urdu. He is an Indian national.

YOUR PERSONAL REFLECTIONS

You know all of these candidates personally, some better than others. Here are the mental notes that you recall about each.

1. **Anika "Ani" Navithar**

You know Ani well and have been extremely impressed with her. She is intelligent and authentic, rising to every leadership role in which she has been placed across multiple functional areas. Last summer at the Delta Company picnic, you enjoyed meeting her family, her husband (who is a university professor in Boston) and their 9-year-old twin girls. Also, when Ani did her short-term project in India, Xiao Zhang said that she was very effective. Ani's husband used their short-term experience in India to conduct some research and work with colleagues at Delhi University. You learned at the picnic that he now has a joint appointment at Delhi University.

2. **Carlos Delgado**

If you were hit by a bus tomorrow, Carlos would probably be asked to step into your role. He has really proven himself at Delta, with a trajectory of success. He and his family have been willing to relocate to Korea, although the demands that they made regarding housing for their family, a cost of living allowance, and education for their teenage children seemed a bit excessive in your opinion. He would probably enjoy the expatriate community in Delhi but you wish that he was willing to integrate and acculturate more and, at least, attempt to learn the host national languages.

3. **Haziq Tengku**

Haziq is clearly proven himself in Malaysia and is probably ready for the next step in the Asia region. Six months ago when you were in Malaysia, Haziq was on a short leave of absence to support his wife and care for their two small children while she was going through cancer treatments. Last month you heard that Haziq's wife is doing well.

4. **Lucas Hansson**

Lucas and his family seem to "bloom wherever they are planted," becoming part of the local community in every host country where they have lived. At the last leadership offsite, you and Lucas were speaking about whether he would be interested in accepting the President of EMEA position in the future, becoming your counterpart in EMEA. He noted that he is always looking for the next exciting opportunity—but feels as though he needs more experience running a country in emerging markets. You thought that he was being exceptionally humble but appreciated his self-awareness, which is probably what makes him such a great international assignee. At one of the social events, Lucas also shared with you that he and his wife had begun to discuss whether they should retire in a few years and move back to Sweden to live with their elderly parents.

5. **Pranav Subramanium**

    Pranav is a solid performer but he seems as though he needs a few more years as the second-in-command. However, this could be exactly the stretch challenge that Pranav needs to launches a global leadership career at Delta.

EXCERCISE 2

Still working alone, consider the strengths and weaknesses of each of these four leading candidates for the job to prepare for your meeting with the leadership team. Decide which candidate you think is best suited for the job.

Günter K. Stahl and Mark E. Mendenhall

ANDREAS WEBER'S REWARD FOR SUCCESS
IN AN INTERNATIONAL ASSIGNMENT: A
RETURN TO AN UNCERTAIN FUTURE*

A NDREAS WEBER'S MIND would not stop racing. Normally, an intense run in the evening had the effect of dissipating his worries, but tonight this did not work. The further he jogged along his standard route on the banks of the Hudson River, the more he could not get out of his mind the letter he knew he must write tomorrow. "How had it all come to this?" he wondered. This thought triggered his memory back seven years, to the initial event that had set in motion the process that led to his current trouble.

ANDREAS' DECISION TO PURSUE AN INTERNATIONAL CAREER

Andreas remembered the occasion clearly; Herr Görner, the managing director, had walked into his office at the Frankfurt headquarters of his bank, and offered him the chance to participate in a company-wide international leadership development program. Herr Görner explained that the program involved an international assignment with the intention of fostering the professional development of young, aspiring managers. After their overseas assignments, the trainees would constitute a pool of internationally experienced young managers with the potential for senior management positions at corporate headquarters. Andreas accepted the offer on the spot, with pride. He had worked very hard since joining the bank and felt that his efforts had finally paid off.

The program started with a one-week seminar at a leading business school in the US. The CEO had flown in from Frankfurt, demonstrating the commitment of top management to this program. In his speech to the participants, the CEO stressed that the major challenge and "number one" priority for the bank in the future was globalization. He made it clear that international experience was a key value and a prerequisite for promotion into the ranks of senior management. Andreas felt confident that he had made the right decision in accepting the offer and in pursuing an international career.

Shortly after the program started, an unexpected vacancy opened up in the bank's New York branch and Andreas was asked if he was interested. He discussed the prospect of a three-year assignment to New York with his wife, Lina. The offer looked very attractive from all angles, and they quickly agreed that Andreas should accept it. Two months later, he was transferred to New York.

ASSIGNMENT NEW YORK: THE FIRST YEAR

Andreas remembered the day of his arrival as if it were yesterday. He arrived at JFK Airport early in the afternoon. Since his only contact point about the job assignment was corporate HR in Frankfurt, he assumed that they had made all the necessary arrangements with the New York office for his arrival. However, no one came to the airport to pick him up. He took a taxi and went directly to the New York branch of the bank. When he arrived, he was not sure where he should go. He had not been informed about whom he should contact after his arrival, so he went straight to the office of the head of the corporate finance department where he was supposed to work. When he entered the office and told the secretary that he was the new manager from Germany, she looked at her notebook, shook her head, and told him that they were not expecting anybody. Confused, Andreas rushed to the HR department and soon found that several misunderstandings had occurred. First, it was not the corporate finance department but the credit department that had requested his transfer. Second, contrary to what he was told in Frankfurt, there was only a non-management position vacant. They were looking for a credit analyst, basically the same job that he had done in Germany.

Andreas shook his head in reaction to the memory: "There I stood, in what was supposed to be my new office, with three pieces of luggage on the desk, and wondering whether I should stay or take the next plane home!"

Why he decided to stay in New York, he could never quite figure out. In retrospect, it was probably just a split-second decision to make the best of the situation. The whirl of images of the next two months flashed across his memory: rushed days and nights trying to learn the ropes of a new office with new procedures, looking for a place to live, meeting new people, and exploring new places. Then a clear memory intervened the collage of memories of those first two months — Lina's arrival. Lina, his wife, and their three-year-old daughter, Anne-Marie, followed Andreas to New York two months after his arrival. They moved into a small house in the outskirts of New York. Lina knew New York pretty well, as she had worked there for a couple of months as an intern at a reinsurance company. She arrived excited to re-discover her favorite restaurants, art galleries, and museums.

Except for occasional attacks of homesickness, Lina was satisfied with her new life. The week after they had moved into their new house, they received a dinner invitation from a young married couple next door. To their surprise, their American neighbors quickly embraced the Webers. Since Lina was not able to get a work permit, she joined her new acquaintance in doing volunteer work at a local art museum. Anne-Marie spent every second afternoon at a local kindergarten, which gave Lina plenty of time to pursue her own interests. At the end of their first year in the US, a second daughter, Elena, was born. By then, the Webers had already made several more new friends, both Americans and other expatriates. When the Webers stepped off the plane at JFK after their first home leave to Germany, it felt more like they were coming home than returning to a temporary assignment.

ANDREAS' FAST-TRACK CAREER AS AN EXPATRIATE

Professionally, things had gone extremely well during this time period. The New York branch of the bank had been right at the start of a boom-phase that lasted for several years. Throughout the boom, the bank's staff increased significantly. After eight months of working in the back office, Andreas was promoted to supervisor of a group of credit analysts. Then, one year after his first promotion, a position opened up at the senior management level. The deputy head of the rapidly expanding corporate finance department — a German expatriate — had unexpectedly left for a job at one of their American competitors, and the bank had to fill his position with a manager who spoke fluent German, was familiar with the finance departments of a number of German and other European companies, and was instantly available. Andreas was asked if he was willing to extend his foreign service contract for another three years and accept the position as deputy head of the corporate finance department. After discussing it with Lina, Andreas accepted.

In the fifth year of his assignment, Andreas made another step upward in his career. His boss retired, and Andreas was promoted to head of the corporate finance department. He was now one of five managing directors in the branch. When Andreas signed his new contract, it was agreed that he would stay with the New York branch of the bank for another three years and would then return to the bank's German headquarters.

These were warm memories, memories that somewhat buffered the intensity of Andreas' frustration and anger over his current situation. But as he continued running, the warmth of the past dissipated into the turmoil of the present.

"It all started with that promotion," he muttered to himself. As head of the corporate finance department, Andreas' professional and private lives had unexpectedly changed. He was now responsible for a huge area — his business activities no longer concentrated on North American subsidiaries of foreign-based companies, but included their headquarters in Europe and East Asia. In the first six months of his new job, Andreas had traveled almost 100,000 miles, mainly on business flights to Europe. His extensive traveling was hard on Lina. She felt alone, and was concerned about their children's education. Their eldest daughter, Anne-Marie, was now nine years old and had spent most of her life outside of Germany. Lina was also concerned about her missing out on a German high school education. Anne-Marie's German language skills had gradually deteriorated over the last two years, and that troubled Lina as well. Their second daughter, Elena, was attending kindergarten, and except for the yearly home leave, she had no contact with other German children. Elena's

German was quite poor. In fact, both Anne-Marie and Elena considered themselves Americans.

Lina also started to be more and more discontented with her life as a housewife. Obtaining a work permit in the US remained impossible, and it was not easy for her to find new volunteer activities to quench her interests. To make things worse, Lina's father fell ill and died in that same year, leaving her mother alone. Andreas remembered the long conversations he had had with Lina during this period of time, many of which were by telephone from hotel rooms in far away places. When he was home, they spoke often in the quiet of their living room, and on long walks — Andreas lost count of the multitude of times they had talked as they walked through the same park he was now running through.

ANDREAS' DILEMMA: STAYING IN NEW YORK OR RETURNING HOME TO AN UNCERTAIN FUTURE

"It was an extremely difficult situation," Andreas remembered, "not so much for the children, but for Lina and I . . . From a professional standpoint, my assignment to New York was the best thing that could ever happen to me: I worked in the financial center of the world; I loved my job, the freedom of being away from the bureaucracy at corporate headquarters, the opportunities to travel; I became a member of the senior management team at a very young age — impossible if I stayed in Germany. Personally, we were also happy: our children felt at home in New York; we were quickly embraced by our neighbors and the expatriate community; we had many friends . . . The question we continually wrestled with was: 'Does it make sense to give all these up for a return to an uncertain future in Germany?' In principle, the answer would clearly have been: 'No.' But on a long-term basis, moving back to Germany appeared to be the best solution for our children. After all, we felt responsible for their future."

After several weeks of consideration and discussion, Lina and Andreas decided to move back to Germany. This was about a year ago. Immediately after the decision was made, Andreas contacted the bank's corporate headquarters and informed the human resource executive in charge of international assignments about his decision. Three weeks later, Andreas received a short letter from him, stating that there were currently no positions available in Germany at his level. Part of the problem, Andreas was told, was due to the current economic downturn in Europe, but since several new branches were due to be opened in the eastern part of Germany over the course of the next year, he was told that chances were good that the company would be able to find him a suitable return assignment within the next six months. Since then, Andreas had several meetings with executives at corporate headquarters, as well as with managers of domestic branches of the bank, but he still had not been offered any re-entry position.

Lina gradually became discouraged. She had told her mother that they were coming home immediately after they made their decision to return to Germany, but eight months had passed, and her mother kept asking when they were coming. Andreas' parents were persistent in their queries as well. Finally, last week, Andreas received a telephone call from the corporate HR department, in which he was informed that they had found what they called a "challenging" return assignment. They offered him the position of deputy head of a medium-sized branch of the bank in the Eastern part of Germany. Andreas was told that a letter explaining the details of the position offer had already been sent.

THE OFFER

The memory of opening that letter and reading it, and the resulting emotions of anger, betrayal, disbelief, and frustration all came back to him. He stopped running, and sat down on a park bench alongside the jogging trail. "Not only will I earn little more than half the salary that I currently make in New York, I will not be able to use the skills and experiences that I gained during my overseas assignment, I will be out of touch with all the important decisions being made at headquarters, and on top of that, I will be posted to this God-forsaken place!" he thought, bitterly.

With all the frustrations and anger welling up in his chest, Andreas thought, cynically, "The bank's promotion policy — if there ever was any rational policy — is to punish those who are really committed to the organization. They assign you to one of those programs for high-fliers and send you abroad, but there is no career planning whatsoever. If there just happens to be a job vacant when you return, you are lucky. If not, they let you wait and wait and wait, until you finally accept the most ridiculous job offer ... Their slogan that international experience is a key value and a prerequisite for promotion into the ranks of senior management is garbage! If you look at the actual promotion and career development practices in this organization, it becomes clear it's only lip service ... and lies! ... In this bank, the better you perform overseas, the more you get screwed when you come back."

He began to wonder if he should accept the offer. Perhaps they should just stay in New York and make their home here. But then, images of Lina, Lina's mother, Anne-Marie, Elena, and his parents, and all of their combined needs enveloped him.

Leaning back on the park bench, he blankly stared down the path that would lead out of the park and into the street, and then home.

NOTE

* This case was prepared by Günter K. Stahl, Assistant Professor of Asian Business at INSEAD and Mark E. Mendenhall, J. Burton Frierson Professor of Leadership at the University of Tennessee. It is intended to be used as a basis for class discussion rather than to illustrate either effective or ineffective handling of an administrative situation. Financial support for the project "Expatriate Careers" (INSEAD research grant # 2010-502 R) is gratefully acknowledged.

PART IV

People Issues in Global Teams, Alliances, Mergers, and Acquisitions

Readings

- Tsedal Neeley
  GLOBAL TEAMS THAT WORK: A FRAMEWORK FOR BRIDGING SOCIAL DISTANCE

- Vladimir Pucik, Paul Evans, and Ingmar Björkman
  MANAGING ALLIANCES AND JOINT VENTURES

- Satu Teerikangas, Günter K. Stahl, Ingmar Björkman, and Mark E. Mendenhall
  IHRM ISSUES IN MERGERS AND ACQUISITIONS

Cases

- Carlos Sánchez-Runde, Yih-teen Lee, and B. Sebastian Reiche
  HAILING A NEW ERA: HAIER IN JAPAN

- Kathrin Köster and Günter K. Stahl
  LENOVO-IBM: BRIDGING CULTURES, LANGUAGES, AND TIME ZONES

- Ingmar Björkman and Ming Zeng
  GUANGDONG ELECTRONICS

Tsedal Neeley

GLOBAL TEAMS THAT WORK: A FRAMEWORK FOR BRIDGING SOCIAL DISTANCE

TO SUCCEED IN THE GLOBAL ECONOMY today, more and more companies are relying on a geographically dispersed workforce. They build teams that offer the best functional expertise from around the world, combined with deep, local knowledge of the most promising markets. They draw on the benefits of international diversity, bringing together people from many cultures with varied work experiences and different perspectives on strategic and organizational challenges. All this helps multinational companies compete in the current business environment.

But managers who actually lead global teams are up against stiff challenges. Creating successful work groups is hard enough when everyone is local and people share the same office space. But when team members come from different countries and functional backgrounds and are working in different locations, communication can rapidly deteriorate, misunderstanding can ensue, and cooperation can degenerate into distrust.

Preventing this vicious dynamic from taking place has been a focus of my research, teaching, and consulting for more than 15 years. I have conducted dozens of studies and heard from countless executives and managers about misunderstandings within the global teams they have joined or led, sometimes with costly consequences. But I have also encountered teams that have produced remarkable innovations, creating millions of dollars in value for their customers and shareholders.

One basic difference between global teams that work and those that do not lies in the level of social distance—the degree of emotional connection among team members. When people on a team all work in the same place, the level of social distance is usually low. Even if they come from different backgrounds, people can interact formally and informally, align, and build trust. They arrive at a common understanding of what certain behaviors mean, and they feel close and congenial, which fosters good teamwork. Coworkers who are geographically separated, however, cannot easily connect and align, so they experience high levels of social distance and struggle to develop effective interactions. Mitigating social distance, therefore, becomes the primary management challenge for the global team leader.

To help in this task, I have developed and tested a framework for identifying and successfully managing social distance. It is called the SPLIT framework, reflecting its five components: structure, process, language, identity, and technology—each of which can be a source of social distance. In the following pages I explain how each can lead to team dysfunction and describe how smart leaders can fix problems that occur—or prevent them from happening in the first place.

STRUCTURE AND THE PERCEPTION OF POWER

In the context of global teams, the structural factors determining social distance are the location and number of sites where team members are based and the number of employees who work at each site.

The fundamental issue here is the perception of power. If most team members are located in Germany, for instance, with two or three in the United States and in South Africa, then there may be a sense that the German members have more power. This imbalance sets up a negative dynamic. People in the larger (majority) group may feel resentment toward the minority group, believing that the latter will try to get away with contributing less than its fair share. Meanwhile, those in the minority group may believe that the majority is usurping what little power and voice they have.

The situation is exacerbated when the leader is at the site with the most people or the one closest to company headquarters: team members at that site tend to ignore the needs and contributions of their colleagues at other locations. This dynamic can occur even when everyone is in the same country: the five people working in, say, Beijing may have a strong allegiance to one another and a habit of shutting out their two colleagues in Shanghai.

When geographically dispersed team members perceive a power imbalance, they often come to feel that there are in-groups and out-groups. Consider the case of a global marketing team for a US-based multinational pharmaceutical company. The leader and the core strategy group for the Americas worked in the company's Boston-area headquarters. A smaller group in London and a single individual in Moscow focused on the markets in Europe. Three other team members, who split their time between Singapore and Tokyo, were responsible for strategy in Asia. The way that each group perceived its situation is illustrated in Figure 1.

To correct the perceived power imbalances between different groups, a leader needs to get three key messages across, as follows.

Who We Are

The team is a single entity, even though individual members may be very different from one another. The leader should encourage sensitivity to differences but look for ways to bridge them and build unity. Tariq, a 33-year-old rising star in a global firm, was assigned to lead a 68-person division whose members hailed from 27 countries,

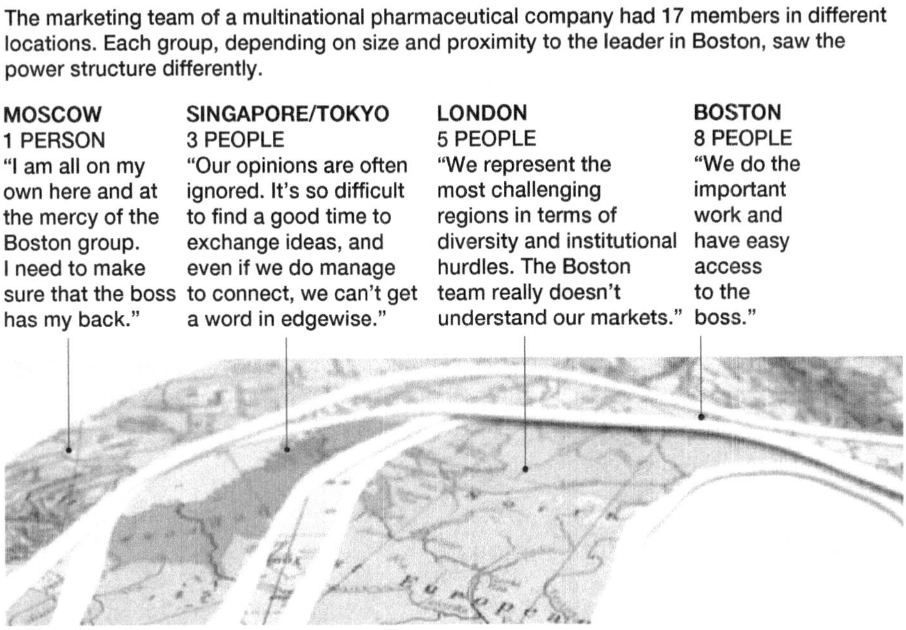

The marketing team of a multinational pharmaceutical company had 17 members in different locations. Each group, depending on size and proximity to the leader in Boston, saw the power structure differently.

MOSCOW	SINGAPORE/TOKYO	LONDON	BOSTON
1 PERSON	3 PEOPLE	5 PEOPLE	8 PEOPLE
"I am all on my own here and at the mercy of the Boston group. I need to make sure that the boss has my back."	"Our opinions are often ignored. It's so difficult to find a good time to exchange ideas, and even if we do manage to connect, we can't get a word in edgewise."	"We represent the most challenging regions in terms of diversity and institutional hurdles. The Boston team really doesn't understand our markets."	"We do the important work and have easy access to the boss."

Figure 1 Views from a dispersed team

spoke 18 languages, and ranged in age from 22 to 61. During the two years before he took charge, the group's performance had been in a precipitous decline and employee satisfaction had plunged. Tariq saw that the team had fractured into subgroups according to location and language. To bring people back together, he introduced a team motto ("We are different yet one"), created opportunities for employees to talk about their cultures, and instituted a zero-tolerance policy for displays of cultural insensitivity.

What We Do

It is important to remind team members that they share a common purpose and to direct their energy toward business-unit or corporate goals. The leader should periodically highlight how everyone's work fits into the company's overall strategy and advances its position in the market. For instance, during a weekly conference call, a global team leader might review the group's performance relative to the company's objectives. She might also discuss the level of collective focus and sharpness the team needs in order to fend off competitors.

I Am There for You

Team members located far from the leader require frequent contact with him or her. A brief phone call or email can make all the difference in conveying that their contributions matter. For instance, one manager in Dallas, Texas, inherited a large group in India as part of an acquisition. He made it a point to involve those employees in important decisions, contact them frequently to discuss ongoing projects, and thank them for good work. He even called team members personally to give them their birthdays off. His team appreciated his attention and became more cohesive as a result.

PROCESS AND THE IMPORTANCE OF EMPATHY

It almost goes without saying that empathy helps reduce social distance. If colleagues can talk informally around a water cooler—whether about work or about personal matters—then they are more likely to develop an empathy that helps them interact productively in more formal contexts. Because geographically dispersed team members lack regular face time, they are less likely to have a sense of mutual understanding. To foster this, global team leaders need to make sure they build the following "deliberate moments" into the process for meeting virtually.

Feedback on Routine Interactions

Members of global teams may unwittingly send the wrong signals with their everyday behavior. Julie, a French chemical engineer, and her teammates in Marseille checked and responded to emails only first thing in the morning, to ensure an uninterrupted workday.

They had no idea that this practice was routinely adding an overnight delay to correspondence with their American colleagues and contributing to mistrust. It was not until Julie visited the team's offices in California that the French group realized there was a problem. Of course, face-to-face visits are not the only way to acquire such learning. Remote team members can also use the phone, email, or even video-conferencing to check in with one another and ask how the collaboration is going. The point is that leaders and members of global teams must actively elicit this kind of "reflected knowledge," or awareness of how others see them.

Unstructured Time

Think back to your last face-to-face meeting. During the first few minutes before the official discussion began, what was the atmosphere like? Were people comparing notes on the weather, their kids, that new restaurant in town? Unstructured communication like this is positive because it allows for the organic unfolding of processes that must occur in all business dealings—sharing knowledge, coordinating and monitoring interactions, and building relationships. Even when people are spread all over the world, small talk is still a powerful way to promote trust. So when planning your team's call-in meetings, factor in 5 minutes for light conversation before business gets under way. Especially during the first meetings, take the lead in initiating informal discussions about work and non-work matters that allow team members to get to know their distant counterparts. In particular, encourage people to be open about constraints they face outside the project, even if those are not directly linked to the matter at hand.

Time to Disagree

Leaders should encourage disagreement both about the team's tasks and about the process by which the tasks get done. The challenge, of course, is to take the heat out of the debate. Framing meetings as brainstorming opportunities lowers the risk that people will feel pressed to choose between sides. Instead, they will see an invitation to evaluate agenda items and contribute their ideas. As the leader, model the act of questioning to get to the heart of things. Solicit each team member's views on each topic you discuss, starting with those who have the least status or experience with the group so that they do not feel intimidated by others' comments. This may initially seem like a waste of time, but if you seek opinions up front, you may make better decisions and get buy-in from more people.

A software developer in Istanbul kept silent in a team meeting in order to avoid conflict, even though he questioned his colleagues' design of a particular feature. He had good reasons to oppose their decision, but his team leader did not brook disagreement, and the developer did not want to damage his own position. However, four weeks into the project, the team ran into the very problems that the developer had seen coming.

LANGUAGE AND THE FLUENCY GAP

Good communication among coworkers drives effective knowledge sharing, decision making, coordination, and, ultimately, performance results (see also Tsedal Neeley and Robert Steven Kaplan, (2014). What's Your Language Strategy? *Harvard Business Review*, 92(9): 70–76). But in global teams, varying levels of fluency with the chosen common language are inevitable—and are likely to heighten social distance. The team members who can communicate best in the organization's lingua franca (usually English) often exert the most influence, while those who are less fluent often become inhibited and withdraw. Mitigating these effects typically involves insisting that all team members respect three rules for communicating in meetings.

Dial down Dominance

Strong speakers must agree to slow down their speaking pace and use fewer idioms, slang terms, and esoteric cultural references when addressing the group. They should limit the number of comments they make within a set time frame, depending on the pace of the meeting and the subject matter. They should actively seek confirmation that they have been understood, and they should practice active listening by rephrasing others' statements for clarification or emphasis.

Dial up Engagement

Less fluent speakers should monitor the frequency of their responses in meetings to ensure that they are contributing. In some cases, it is even worth asking them to set goals for the number of comments they make within a given period. Do not let them use their own language and have a teammate translate, because that can alienate others. As with fluent speakers, team members who are less proficient in the language must always confirm that they have been understood. Encourage them to routinely ask if others are following them. Similarly, when listening, they should be empowered to say they have not understood something. It can be tough for non-native speakers to make this leap, yet doing so keeps them from being marginalized.

Balance Participation to Ensure Inclusion

Getting commitments to good speaking behavior is the easy part; making the behavior happen will require active management. Global team leaders must keep track of who is and is not contributing and deliberately solicit participation from less fluent speakers. Sometimes it may also be necessary to get dominant-language speakers to dial down to ensure that the proposals and perspectives of less fluent speakers are heard.

The leader of a global team based in Dubai required all his reports to post the three communication rules in their cubicles. He soon noted that one heavily accented European team member began contributing to discussions for the first time since joining the group 17 months earlier. The rules had given this person the license, opportunity, and responsibility to speak up. As a leader, you could try the same tactics with your own team by distributing copies of Figure 2.

IDENTITY AND THE MISMATCH OF PERCEPTIONS

Global teams work most smoothly when members "get" where their colleagues are coming from. However, deciphering someone's identity and finding ways to relate is far from simple. People define themselves in terms of a multitude of variables—age, gender, nationality, ethnicity, religion, occupation, political ties, and so forth. And although behavior can be revealing, particular behaviors may signify different things depending on the individual's identity. For example, someone in North America who looks you squarely in the eye may project confidence and honesty, but in other parts of the world direct eye contact might be perceived as rude or threatening. Misunderstandings such

All team members should be guided by these three rules to ensure that influence on decisions is not dictated by fluency in the company's lingua franca.

FLUENT SPEAKERS DIAL DOWN DOMINANCE	LESS FLUENT SPEAKERS DIAL UP ENGAGEMENT	TEAM LEADERS BALANCE FOR INCLUSION
• Slow down the pace and use familiar language (e.g., fewer idioms).	• Resist withdrawal or other avoidance behaviors.	• Monitor participants and strive to balance their speaking and listening.
• Refrain from dominating the conversation.	• Refrain from reverting to your native language.	• Actively draw contributions from all team members.
• Ask: "Do you understand what I am saying?"	• Ask: "Do you understand what I am saying?"	• Solicit participation from less fluent speakers in particular.
• Listen actively.	• If you don't understand others, ask them to repeat or explain.	• Be prepared to define and interpret content.

Figure 2 Rules of engagement for team meetings

as this are a major source of social distance and distrust, and global team leaders have to raise everyone's awareness of them. This involves mutual learning and teaching.

Learning from One Another

When adapting to a new cultural environment, a savvy leader will avoid making assumptions about what behaviors mean. Take a step back, watch, and listen. In America, when someone says, "Yes, I can do this," it likely means that she is willing and able to do what you asked. In India, however, the same statement may simply signal that she wants to try—not that she is confident of success. Before drawing conclusions, therefore, ask a lot of questions. In the example just described, you might probe to see if the team member anticipates any challenges or needs additional resources. Asking for this information may yield greater insight into how the person truly feels about accomplishing the task.

The give-and-take of asking questions and providing answers establishes two-way communication between the leader and team members. And if a leader regularly solicits input, acting as a student rather than an expert with hidden knowledge, he empowers others on the team, leading them to participate more willingly and effectively. A non-Mandarin-speaking manager in China relied heavily on his local staff during meetings with clients in order to better understand the clients' perceptions of the interactions and to gauge the appropriateness of his own behavior. His team members began to see themselves as essential to the development of client relationships and felt valued, which motivated them to perform at even higher levels.

In this model, everyone is a teacher and a learner, which enables people to step out of their traditional roles. Team members take on more responsibility for the development of the team as a whole. Leaders learn to see themselves as unfinished and are thus more likely to adjust their style to reflect the team's needs. They instruct but they also facilitate, helping team members to parse their observations and understand one another's true identities.

A Case in Point

Consider the experience of Daniel, the leader of a recently formed multinational team spread over four continents. During a conference call, he asked people to discuss a particular strategy for reaching a new market in a challenging location. This was the first time that he had raised a topic on which there was a range of opinion.

Daniel observed that Theo, a member of the Israeli team, regularly interrupted Angela, a member of the Buenos Aires team, and their ideas were at odds. Although tempted to jump in and play referee, Daniel held back. To his surprise, neither Theo nor Angela got frustrated. They went back and forth, bolstering their positions by referencing typical business practices and outcomes in their respective countries, but they stayed committed to reaching a group consensus.

At the end of the meeting, Daniel shared his observations with the team, addressing not only the content of the discussion, but also the manner in which it took place. "Theo and Angela," he said, "when you began to hash out your ideas, I was concerned that both of you might have felt you weren't being heard or weren't getting a chance to fully express your thoughts. But now you both seem satisfied that you were able to make your arguments, articulate cultural perspectives, and help us decide on our next steps. Is that true?"

Theo and Angela affirmed Daniel's observations and provided an additional contextual detail: six months earlier they had worked together on another project—an experience that allowed them to establish their own style of relating to each other. Their ability to acknowledge and navigate their cultural differences was beneficial to everyone on the team. Not only did it help move their work forward, but it showed that conflict does not have to create social distance. And Daniel gained more information about Theo and Angela, which would help him manage the team more effectively in the future.

TECHNOLOGY AND THE CONNECTION CHALLENGE

The modes of communication used by global teams must be carefully considered, because the technologies can both reduce and increase social distance. Video-conferencing, for instance, allows rich communication in which both context and emotion can be perceived. Email offers greater ease and efficiency but lacks contextual cues. In making decisions about which technology to use, a leader must ask the following.

Should Communication be Instant?

Teleconferencing and video-conferencing enable real-time (instant) conversations. Email and certain social media formats require users to wait for the other party to respond. Choosing between instant and delayed forms of communication can be especially challenging for global teams. For example, when a team spans multiple time zones, a telephone call may not be convenient for everyone. The Japanese team leader of a US-based multinational put it this way: "I have three or four days per week when I have a conference call with global executives. In most cases, it starts at 9:00 or 10:00 in the night. If we can take the conference call in the daytime, it is much easier for me. But we are in the Far East, and headquarters is in the United States, so we have to make the best of it."

Instant technologies are valuable when leaders need to persuade others to adopt their viewpoint. But if they simply want to share information, then delayed methods such as email are simpler, more efficient, and less disruptive to people's lives. Leaders must also consider the team's interpersonal dynamics. If the team has a history of conflict, technology choices that limit the opportunities for real-time emotional exchanges may yield the best results.

In general, the evidence suggests that most companies over-rely on delayed communication. A recent Forrester survey of nearly 10,000 information workers in 17 countries showed that 94% of employees reported using email, but only 33% ever participated in desktop video-conferencing (with apps such as Skype and Viber), and a mere 25% used room-based video-conferencing. These numbers will surely change over time, as the tools evolve and users become more comfortable with them, but leaders need to choose their format carefully: instant or delayed.

Do I Need to Reinforce the Message?

Savvy leaders will communicate through multiple platforms to ensure that messages are understood and remembered. For example, if a manager electronically assigns one of her team members a task by entering notes into a daily work log, then she may then follow up with a text or a face-to-face chat to ensure that the team member saw the request and recognized its urgency.

Redundant communication is also effective for leaders who are concerned about convincing others that their message is important. Greg, for instance, a project manager in a medical devices organization, found that his team was falling behind on the development of a product. He called an emergency meeting to discuss the issues and explain new corporate protocols for releasing new products, which he felt would bring the project back on track.

During this initial meeting, Greg listened to people's concerns and addressed their questions in real time. Although he felt that he had communicated his position clearly and obtained the necessary verbal buy-in, he followed up the meeting by sending a carefully drafted email to all the attendees, reiterating the agreed-upon changes and asking for everyone's electronic sign-off. This redundant communication helped reinforce acceptance of his ideas and increased the likelihood that his colleagues would actually implement the new protocols.

Am I Leading by Example?

Team members very quickly pick up on the leader's personal preferences regarding communication technology. A leader who wants to encourage people to video-conference should communicate this way herself. If she wants employees to pick up the phone and speak to one another, she had better be a frequent user of the phone. And if she wants team members to respond quickly to emails, she needs to set the example.

Flexibility and appreciation for diversity are at the heart of managing a global team. Leaders must expect problems and patterns to change or repeat themselves as teams shift, disband, and regroup. But there is at least one constant: to manage social distance effectively and maximize the talents and engagement of team members, leaders must stay attentive to all five of the SPLIT dimensions. Decisions about "structure" create opportunities for good process, which can mitigate difficulties caused by "language" differences and "identity" issues. If leaders act on these fronts, while marshaling "technology" to improve communication among geographically dispersed colleagues, then social distance is sure to shrink, not expand. When that happens, teams can become truly representative of the "global village"—not just because of their international makeup but also because their members feel mutual trust and a sense of kinship. They can then embrace and practice the kind of innovative, respectful, and groundbreaking interactions that drive the best ideas forward.

Vladimir Pucik, Paul Evans, and Ingmar Björkman

MANAGING ALLIANCES AND JOINT VENTURES

I N THE LATE 1960S, the US-based chemical company Chemco (name disguised) decided to enter the booming Japanese market. However, Japan's investment policies at the time precluded direct entry. Facing the choice between licensing and a minority joint venture (JV), the company decided to establish a 49:51 percent partnership with a well-known Japanese firm to build a local plant and set up distribution. Chemco would contribute technology in exchange for help in market access. Soon after its launch, the JV, led entirely by local managers, became the leader in its industry segment.

Later, the US parent decided to take advantage of the liberalization of the Japanese economy to obtain a majority position in the JV. In their opinion, the JV was becoming "too independent," and they wanted more influence on its future direction. Besides, drawing upon the support functions of the head office could lower costs. After protracted negotiations, the Japanese partner agreed to sell 2 percent of equity to the Americans to give them control, and the board composition was changed accordingly. The JV management was instructed to streamline the product portfolio and to cut costs by integrating several support functions into the global organization. While the local managers never questioned the need for more efficiency, most of the integration projects never really got off the ground. This was officially justified by referring to pressing local customer needs that took up all available resources.

Frustrated by the difficulties in "integrating Japan," the US management decided that additional equity would give it the necessary influence to push through integration plans. After another round of long negotiations, the US parent gained control of 65 percent of the shares. The company was renamed, putting its US partner's name first. A senior vice president of finance (who did not speak Japanese) was dispatched to join the local management team. In spite of these changes, the venture continued to be run pretty much as before. While it was profitable, with nearly US$1 billion of sales, margins were well below corporate expectations. As Japanese customers began to migrate to lower cost sites in other areas of Asia, poor coordination with other affiliates became a serious business problem.

A third generation of US top management decided to address the problem head-on. They retained a consultant to advise them on what to do next. Should they buy even more equity? Send in more expatriates? Or even sell the existing business and start again?

It turned out that the company could not sell the plant in the open market because the surrounding infrastructure belonged to the Japanese parent. In addition, the Japanese partner (located right next door) was the legal employer of the vast majority of employees, including virtually all top managers. Even those recruited well after the JV was established were not employees of the joint venture. Their salaries were determined by their position in the Japanese parent company hierarchy and they were simply dispatched to the JV at the discretion of the Japanese partner. All the training, starting with new employee induction, was conducted jointly with employees of the Japanese parent—and they all belonged to the same company union.

All of this was seen as a "good deal" when the JV was originally set up in the 1960s—it meant that there was no need to invest heavily in staff or to worry about HRM issues in an unknown market. But ever since the original agreement was signed several decades ago, each step in the evolution of the relationship had focused only on the financial aspects of control. It was only when the consultant was brought in that HRM and organizational issues were analyzed thoroughly for the first time. So the questions had to be rephrased: would more equity buy more "respect"? Would more expatriates help the integration? What could be done to change the direction of the JV?

OVERVIEW

Alliances are a useful tool for internationalization, but they are also difficult to implement. The example of Chemco illustrates the complexity of alliances and the dangers of ignoring the management and people dimensions of such a strategy. So first, we review the many motives for entering an international alliance and the different organizational forms alliances can take, presenting several perspectives on what constitutes alliance success.

An important dimension of alliances is that they are inherently unstable. We next introduce a framework that helps us to think strategically about alliances and how they may evolve over time. Based on competitive context and knowledge creation requirements, we identify four types of alliances, each with a different set of management and HRM challenges. We illustrate how HR practices and tools can contribute to the long-term success of an alliance strategy.

We then focus on planning and negotiating alliances, paying particular attention to the human resource factors that must be taken into account. Key management roles in the alliance building process are presented, along with the implications for how managers for these positions are selected and developed.

Once an agreement has been negotiated, it must be implemented, so we next review the people and organizational factors involved, highlighting the HRM agenda in international JV management.

The final part of the reading explores the concept of alliance learning. We first analyze the key obstacles to alliance learning to show the importance of linking HRM to alliance learning objectives. We then describe the human resource processes that can contribute to successful alliance learning, contrasting examples of successful and unsuccessful learning. To conclude, we review the evolutionary perspective on alliances and raise the next-generation challenges facing HRM, as alliances become an organic part of the international operations of many multinationals.

THE WHYS AND WHATS OF ALLIANCES

JVs and other forms of cross-border alliance are important and commonly used tools for international growth. Companies engage in alliances for many reasons.[1] Some are created to cut the cost of entry, others to cut the cost of exit. Some are set up with the objective of leveraging opportunities, others with the aim of acquiring knowledge. Some alliances are focused on economies of scale, other on economies of scope. Understanding *why* a company participates in an international alliance is the first step towards deciding the approach to alliance human resource management.

Alliance Business Drivers

International alliances, usually in the form of JVs, began to multiply during the 1960s and 1970s.[2] Their primary objective was to enable firms expanding internationally to secure access to markets where direct presence was not permitted, or where market entry was deemed too costly, too risky, or both. For example, foreign companies targeting the Japanese market, like Chemco, were not allowed to invest independently in Japan until its foreign investment regime was deregulated in the mid-1970s. The only way to enter the booming market early was either to license technology to a local partner or to establish a JV. The early flow of foreign direct investment into China in the 1980s and 1990s followed a similar pattern.

Entering a protected market is only one reason why alliances are formed. Even when a wholly owned subsidiary may be feasible, there are many arguments in favor of market entry through partnership with a local firm. Such a partnership can provide knowledge of local business conditions, a desirable location and infrastructure, access to the distribution system, contacts with government, and a supply of experienced labor and management. The need to enter emerging markets rapidly while minimizing risk is another reason. After the collapse of the Berlin Wall, alliances minimized the risk of entry into uncharted territories in Eastern and Central Europe.[3] As anticipated in the initial agreements, many local partners have since been bought out. Many foreign investors in China and India are following a similar strategy.[4]

Alliances may support internationalization strategies. For example, while global competition often requires "insider" presence in a number of countries, it is difficult for all but the largest firms to achieve such universal market coverage. In car manufacturing, parts suppliers are expected to follow major car companies as they expand around the world, though it may not be viable to set up independent operations everywhere. "Sharing" the customer with a local partner may be a better idea. Many firms are left with only two choices: either to be acquired or to negotiate alliances with others in a similar position.

Some alliances can remain non-equity contractual agreements for long periods of time. The Airbus consortium was established in 1970 by leading European aerospace firms to compete against the then dominant US commercial aircraft manufacturers. Risk reduction, economies of scale and scope in research and development (R&D) and production were the primary drivers behind the push for collaboration.[5] But because the vast majority of Airbus employees were on the payrolls of the partner firms, the organization of the consortium presented major challenges, particularly with respect to managing mobility and coordinating cross-border projects. It was only in 2001 that a separate joint stock company was set up.[6]

In high-technology industries today, international alliances are the norm and not the exception. Most high-tech firms are engaged in scores of technological, manufacturing, and marketing alliances. Their objective is to leverage their current know-how quickly over the broadest possible number of markets and to foster the creation of tomorrow's know-how. The early success of IBM and Toshiba in the emerging laptop computer market was partly a result of their long-term collaboration in designing and manufacturing state-of the-art flat screens. While the two companies never ceased to compete for the final customer, the upstream collaborative efforts allowed them to maximize return on R&D investment, and to gain valuable economies of scale in manufacturing. The challenge for both firms was to ensure that competences created inside the alliance could be quickly transferred to the parents while maintaining learning parity. This was accomplished by a carefully balanced flow of personnel between the alliance and the two partners.

In short, there are many good reasons for companies to engage in international alliances. Some firms are heavily involved with alliances; others find them tangential to their global strategy. However, most companies will engage in some form of international alliance as they expand abroad. Consequently, it is important to understand the strategic and management issues relating to international alliances and the role of human resources management in alliance success. Indeed the question of what is a successful alliance is often not easy to answer, as we can see in the box "Defining alliance success."

DEFINING ALLIANCE SUCCESS

The Chemco case raises the question of what is a successful alliance. This may seem like an obvious question, but it does not have an obvious answer. Does the mere survival of an international alliance indicate success? Is success measured by the return on the funds originally invested? By current profitability and cash/dividend flow? By market share? By transfer of knowledge or creation of new knowledge? Obviously, the choice depends on the specific objective of the alliance, but objectives typically change as the alliance evolves. From this perspective, the only relevant measure of alliance success is the degree to which an international alliance helps the firm to improve its ability to compete.

Contrary to a popular metaphor, an alliance is *not* like a marriage—longer alliances are not necessarily better. Problematic alliances are a drain on management energy and resources, but they often limp on since shutting them down would imply "failure."

For an alliance to be sustainable, it must benefit all partners: respect for the partner's needs and mutual value creation is a prerequisite for a successful relationship. But this does not imply that value creation must be equal or that all alliances should be sustainable for an indefinite period. Most are transitory in nature, reflecting a particular competitive situation at a particular point in time. When the situation changes, so does the need for the alliance. A "win–win" strategy is only a tool to create a healthy alliance; it should not be seen as the goal in itself. The definition of a "win" may change as the company strategy evolves, as will the role that the alliance is expected to perform.

From this perspective, Chemco's alliance in Japan, although growing and profitable, was not as successful as it could have been. This does not mean that the original entry decision was wrong. In fact, in terms of return on investment, the deal was the best that the company had ever made. But as the company's internationalization strategy evolved, the alliance in Japan did not follow, largely because of inattention to the management and human resource issues involved.

There is ample data showing that many alliances fail to meet expectations and that the cause of the failure is, in many cases, poor implementation.[7] It has been estimated that fewer than 50 percent of early JVs in Japan met the foreign partner's business objectives,[8] and observations on more recent experiences with JVs in China suggest a similar pattern.[9] The complexity of managing a business with international partners is a challenge that few firms seem equipped to handle. When alliances break up, HRM issues are often cited as one of the key factors contributing to "irreconcilable differences."[10]

Understanding Alliances

Choosing the right type of alliance for a given strategy is difficult if the strategy is not clear. What is the business objective of the proposed alliance? What is the value-added of engaging in a business relationship that will inevitably consume significant resources before yielding results? What form of alliance should a company choose given its objectives? And, what are the human resource implications of such a choice?

There are a number of different ways to classify alliances. It is possible to take a functional orientation so as to identify R&D alliances, manufacturing alliances, marketing and distribution alliances, and so forth. Another way to classify alliances is to look at the number of partners involved, from a two-partner agreement to multiple partner consortia. However, the most common distinction is whether the contractual agreement covering the alliance creates a new jointly owned business unit—usually described as a JV—or whether the collaboration is essentially non-equity based, such as a licensing agreement.

Yoshino and Rangan (1995) present a comprehensive classification of alliances (see Figure 1) based on the fundamental nature of the contractual relationships between the partners.[11] There are many other classifications, some focusing specifically on HR issues.[12]

There is a general agreement that, as one moves through the spectrum of alliances from a "simple" marketing agreement with a foreign distributor or original equipment manufacturing (OEM) agreements to stand-alone JVs, the management challenges increase, as does the importance of paying attention to human resource management. Much of the discussion in this reading will, therefore, focus on the role of HR factors in the most complex of international alliances—JVs between firms based in different countries. However, even among JVs, the differences in strategic logic behind their formation may require different HRM strategies and HR tools to be applied.

An Alliance Strategy Framework

As the Chemco case illustrates, an alliance is typically a dynamic phenomenon. The nature of the alliance may change over time, and shifts in the relative bargaining power of the partners and in their expectations about the objectives of the alliance will have corresponding HRM implications.

There are two dimensions of alliances that require careful consideration from an HRM perspective: the strategic intent of the partners, and the expected contribution of the venture to the creation of new organizational capabilities and knowledge. With respect to strategic intent, alliances among firms with competitive strategic interests may require different approaches to HRM from those in which interests are

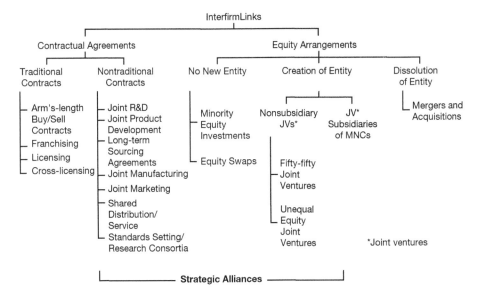

Figure 1. Classification of strategic alliances

Source: Yoshino and Rangan (1995)

complementary. With respect to capability and knowledge creation, while all alliances involve learning, some are actually formed with the main purpose of capability or knowledge creation. The learning aspect of alliances has major implications for the organizational arrangements, and thus for HR challenges and roles.

Figure 2 shows the four archetypes of alliance strategies based on their strategic and knowledge/capability-creation contexts: complementary, learning, resource, and competitive alliances.

A "complementary" alliance is formed when two (or more) partners with complementary strategic aims join forces to exploit their existing resources or competences—say, by linking different elements of the value chain—and where knowledge creation is not a prime objective. A typical complementary alliance is the traditional JV where one partner contributes technology and the other facilitates entry into a difficult market. Another example may be seen when two partners contribute complementary technologies that may lead to a new product stream. In non-equity alliances, this may take the form of a long-term contract, such as between TI and Nokia in the mobile phone chip manufacturing process.

Competitive	**RESOURCE ALLIANCE**	**COMPETITIVE ALLIANCE**
Long-term strategic context		
Complementary	**COMPLEMENTARY ALLIANCE**	**LEARNING ALLIANCE**

Low   **Opportunities for**   High
capability/knowledge creation

Figure 2. A strategic framework for understanding international alliances

Notes: Alliances can be evaluated on two dimensions. The first reflects the competitive context of the alliance. The second dimension reflects the need and opportunities for knowledge creation.

Strategic context: competition versus collaboration
The dimension of strategic context positions the alliance with respect to complementarity of interests between the alliance partners. Is the alliance a link with a partner whose long-term strategic interests are in principle complementary (e.g. Airbus), or are they more likely fundamentally competitive?[A]

Capability/knowledge-creation context: low versus high capability/knowledge creation opportunities
Some alliances rely exclusively on exploiting existing resources and competencies (partners contribute money, patents, production capacity, distribution networks); others are designed explicitly to generate new capabilities or knowledge by combining or extending the resources and capabilities of the partners.[B]

[A] It is important to bear in mind that the strategic interests can change over time, and that what was once a collaborative relationship may turn into a fierce competition or conflict. A common experience of many Western firms with their joint ventures in Japan and two decades later in China are often-cited examples in this regard (Reich and Mankin, 1986; Hamel et al., 1989; McGregor, 2005; Hamilton and Zhang, 2008).
[B] In principle, all alliances have the potential to generate new knowledge—at least partners can learn about each other, and how to work together—the difference is in the intensity of the knowledge-creation process.

A complementary alliance may evolve into a *learning alliance* if both partners share an interest in enhancing their individual capabilities. This can happen through the exchange of existing knowledge between the partners, or through the development of new knowledge where the partners jointly participate in the same value chain activities. An example of a learning alliance is the Fuji–Xerox JV in Japan, which will be discussed later in this reading.[13] Originally set up to facilitate Xerox's penetration of the Japanese market, it then shifted its focus to Asia Pacific and today serves as a critical source of competency development for the Xerox Corporation worldwide. Other alliances may be designed with learning in mind from the outset.[14] Compared to complementary alliances, learning alliances require much more interaction, including shared work and interface management, which creates demand for HR systems and processes that can facilitate effective knowledge creation.

Competitive pressures such as resource constraints, political and business risks, or economies of scale may lead competitors to join forces in a "resource alliance." Exploration consortia set up to develop and operate oil and gas fields are increasingly common in the energy industry. One company takes the lead but the others share the risk by contributing resources and often staff. For example, BP explored oil deposits off the coast of Vietnam together with Statoil from Norway and the Vietnamese state-owned oil company. Another example would be the sharing of manufacturing facilities in Australia by Nissan and Ford when the Australian government restricted the number of manufacturing sites in the country. Compared to complementary alliances, resource alliances place a greater requirement on HR practices that reduce the frictions that might hamper collaboration.

Finally, there are also learning alliances between partners who are competitors in global markets. One of the best-known examples is NUMMI—a 50:50 JV between General Motors and Toyota.[15] This venture was nominally designed for the joint production of small cars for the North American market but at the same time it was intended to serve as a "learning laboratory" for the two competitors. GM gained insights into Toyota's manufacturing system, and Toyota learned how to operate a US-based manufacturing facility. Such partnerships can be described as a *competitive* alliance. Another example is Boeing's long-term collaboration with a consortium of Japanese firms that built segments of Boeing airplanes, while at the same time pursuing a strategy of becoming aircraft designers themselves.[16] This type of alliance, with its emphasis on knowledge creation in a competitive context, is the most complex to manage and requires the highest level of attention to HRM.

None of these types of alliance is "better" than another. Alliances in all four quadrants can enhance a firm's competitive advantage. However, the management challenges associated with each alliance scenario are fundamentally different, and the HRM strategies, processes, and tools should reflect those differences. Problems occur when the company does not know what kind of alliance it has entered or, as in the case of Chemco, when it does not read and respond appropriately to early signals that the nature of the alliance is changing. For example, in a complementary alliance, it might be possible to rely on the local partner to recruit and train the alliance workforce since the loyalty factor may not be an issue—at least in the short term. However, such an approach in a competitive alliance could prove costly in the event of any subsequent conflict between the partners.[17]

In a complementary alliance, it may make sense to set up the venture as a stand-alone entity to promote internal entrepreneurship. In a resource partnership, there are also benefits in creating an entity with clear boundaries so that the competitive strategic context does not inhibit the performance of the alliance—good fences make good neighbors. However, learning alliances should not be constrained by too many fences, as opportunities for knowledge sharing will be greater when the boundaries between the venture and the parent are thin. HR practices in a learning alliance will, therefore, focus on facilitating the interface between the parent and the venture to increase the speed and quality of information exchange.

In contrast, it is not just fast learning that matters in a competitive alliance but also speed and effectiveness relative to the partner—maintaining learning parity is the key to sustaining such a relationship.[18] The HR approach has to reflect this, for example by integrating measures of the learning outcomes into the performance management process. At the same time, given the competitive context of the alliance, the flow of knowledge has to be monitored, if not restricted—an approach opposite to what is best for a learning alliance.

In all cases, it is important to remember that alliances do not always fit neatly into conceptual boxes. Some partnerships are complementary in some parts of the value chain but competitive in others and a nuanced approach to HRM may be needed. The critical issue is that the character of most alliances changes over time. Successful complementary alliances will become learning alliances, and learning alliances may turn into competitive alliances as the strategic intent of partners change over time.[19]

Precisely when a complementary alliance becomes a learning or a competitive alliance is a matter of interpretation. Alliances are typically defined as complementary in the opening public relations statements, but a shift in partnership orientation has to be expected. The anticipation of such shifts needs to be taken into account in formulating the HR strategy so that the appropriate tools can be used proactively to facilitate such a change. In the Chemco case, the alliance started as complementary, combining the technology of the US partner with the market access capability of the Japanese partner. However, the US partner failed to commit the necessary resources at an early stage to ensure the future integration of the JV into its global network (training, exchange of staff, and so forth). There were no incentives for the Japanese staff to pay attention to global strategy. They were rewarded solely on local results, and they saw no future for themselves in Chemco's global organization.

One of the few redeeming factors in the Chemco JV was that the alliance never migrated into the "competitive" domain, simply because the Japanese partner had no wish to enter this particular business segment. Had it chosen to do so, there was not much the US partner could have done to protect its market position because it had little influence over the employees or management in Japan. However, because the partner's position was essentially cooperative, Chemco's top executives and the HR managers did get another opportunity to consider long-term actions to remedy the unsatisfactory situation. We will review later what they did.

Alliance is a Process, not a Deal

An alliance is not just a deal between two or more partners; it is a complex process that is full of ambiguities and contradictions. Indeed, companies often learn to manage the contradictions of transnational organization through their alliance experiences. Most alliances either die early or evolve, just as any other business venture. Alliance stability is a contradiction in terms.

There is no best way to structure an alliance. Winning and losing alliances cannot be differentiated by specific configurations of organizing patterns, equity ratios, or reporting relationships.[20] In the case of JVs, some argue that 50:50 arrangements work best, since the partners are forced to anticipate each other's interest.[21] Others assert that such arrangements lead to paralysis, for example with respect to staffing and compensation issues, and that it is better when one partner has the power to make a decision when there is deadlock.[22] In fact, both types of venture appear to generate significant but distinct HRM challenges.[23]

It is not the structure of the deal, but the quality of the management process—in planning, negotiating, and implementing an international business partnership—that makes a difference. However, even here there are variations. In HP and Intel, two high-tech firms with extensive histories of successful alliances, the alliance management process is well defined, highly structured, and institutionalized. On the other hand, Corning, which derives most of its income from alliances, favors a more intuitive and informal approach that reflects the company's culture and mode of decision making. Others use a mix of the two extremes. Whether the approach is formalized or embedded in the company culture, successful alliance players have in common a rigorous and disciplined approach to alliances that includes an appreciation of the HRM contribution.

PLANNING AND NEGOTIATING ALLIANCES

The HR function should be involved early in exploring, planning, and negotiating alliances because a number of key issues relating to control and influence are closely tied to expertise, policies, and practices in human resource management. Unfortunately, HR is often left out at this stage.

Another reason why HR should be involved early is the fact that creating value through superior human resource management can be a source of competitive advantage for the partnership. For example, a partner with proven competence in implementing high-performing work systems, in staffing and recruitment, or in managing innovation through people, has additional negotiating leverage. This competence should contribute to the success of the venture—provided that it can be appropriately adapted to the different cultural and institutional circumstances, and strategic aims.

Outstanding HR strengthens bargaining power in the negotiations. A reputation for good HR systems and practices is part of the corporate "brand equity."[24]

Well-managed partners are more in demand than poorly managed ones. A company with poor foundations in its own approach to HRM and without proven know-how in aligning HRM with competitive strategy will find itself disadvantaged when it comes to negotiating and implementing alliances.

HRM Issues in Developing an Alliance Strategy

Successful alliances start with a strategy, not with a partner. This may seem an obvious statement, but it is not always followed in practice. Companies, or more precisely their chief executives, sometimes "fall in love." Notwithstanding the importance of personal relationships at the top, it is dangerous to select the partner before the strategic purpose is clarified.

As discussed in the previous section, it is difficult to identify what kind of relationship and what kind of a partner may be appropriate without fully understanding the long-term objectives. Japanese car component manufacturers entered the United States in the late 1980s because they were following their Japanese customers, for instance Toyota and Honda, into the United States. These customers expected just-in-time support for their newly transplanted assembly plants, but the component manufacturers knew that they did not have the competence themselves to operate in an alien environment. Given the urgency, the alliance route seemed the most feasible entry strategy, though in the long run they intended to establish an independent presence.

Consequently, human resource considerations played a major role in partner selection.[25] The Japanese firms searched for local partners situated in rural environments, perceived as having harmonious labor environments conducive to Japanese manufacturing methods. They also preferred partners who were family-owned but with no clear succession. This would give them the opportunity to acquire full control with a friendly bid once the US partner decided to retire.

While the HR issues in an alliance are always framed by the specific strategic and business context, these considerations are sometimes contradictory, requiring careful analysis. For example, when a firm decides to enter an unfamiliar foreign market, the choice of an experienced local partner may seem to be a smart move that overcomes the existing "market competence" handicap. Yet, with a strong local partner, there may be less urgency to develop internal market know-how, and investments in knowledge creation may not be a priority. In a complementary alliance, this may not matter. However, if the alliance ever becomes competitive, this may put the foreign partner at a serious disadvantage.

A well-defined alliance management process provides an arena for a full consideration of human resource issues.[26] Early involvement in strategy discussions allows the HR function to understand the business logic of the alliance, highlighting early the issues that may handicap implementation. In addition, important human resource decisions regarding the alliance may need to be taken early on in the implementation process (such as decisions on negotiation training or selection of an alliance manager).

HR's involvement in alliance strategy is often guided by a plan that is fleshed out as implementation proceeds. A sketch of the issues to be considered is shown in Table 1. Given the typical uncertainty surrounding alliance creation, such a plan is only a rough guide. It will become more specific when a partner is selected, paving the way for rigorous implementation when the alliance is launched.

Partner Selection

There are two main HR issues to consider in selecting a partner: the expected contribution of the partner, and how much the HR systems of the partners will interface within the alliance.

The first issue refers to the degree to which the partner's competences in human resource management are expected to contribute to the alliance. Will the partner be responsible for staffing the alliance? Or, will it be responsible for some of its critical

---

Table 1. The HR alliance strategy plan

HR issues that may influence partner selection:
- Desired competences that a partner should possess.
- Need for venture HR support from the partner.
- Assessment of HR skills and reputation of potential partners.
- Assessment of the organizational culture of potential partners.
- Exit options.

Venture HR issues that need to be resolved in negotiations:
- Desired negotiation outcomes and possible bargaining trade-offs
- Management philosophy, notably concerning HRM.
- Staffing: sourcing and criteria.
- Compensation and performance management.
- Who will provide what HR service support?

Specific HRM activities that must be implemented early and resources required:
- Negotiation stage:
  - Negotiation team selection.
  - Negotiation training.
- Start-up stage:
  - Staffing decisions.
  - Alliance management training.

Allocation of responsibility:
- Corporate responsibility.
- Local management team responsibility.
- Partner responsibility.

Measurements to evaluate the quality of HR support:
- Recruitment target.
- Training delivered.
- Skill/knowledge transferred.

---

functions? Is the partner expected to provide HR services to the alliance? Does the partner's HR reputation matter? As we will discuss later in this reading, getting the staffing right is the "make or break" issue for many alliances, and the probability of success can be enhanced by making these questions a part of the selection screen.

The second issue addresses the degree to which the organizational and people processes of the partners will be linked in the course of the alliance, which is likely if one of the strategic aims is learning. Will the alliance be clearly separated from the parents? Or, will the boundaries be ambiguous? Will there be a lot of mobility between the venture units and the parent companies? Who will evaluate the performance of the venture management? And, on what criteria?

When the partner is expected to contribute significantly to HRM, or when the venture is unlikely to be autonomous because of interfaces with the parents, it is vital to include the partner's HR philosophy, policies, practices, and culture as a factor in partner selection (see box "Assessing the culture and HR practices of the potential partner"). The issue here is not to find a perfect match—a partner who shares the same view on management selection criteria or the role of incentive compensation in the reward package; rather, the purpose is to identify potential differences and then to determine how these differences might influence the execution of the alliance strategy, whether any differences can be reconciled, and whether there are business risks if the gaps cannot be bridged.

ASSESSING THE CULTURE AND HR PRACTICES OF THE POTENTIAL PARTNER

HR policies and practices have a major impact on the culture of the organization, and research has shown that differences in organizational culture may influence alliance success.[27] A cultural audit is, therefore, an essential part of "due diligence," the audit of a potential partner. A number of factors may impact the cultural compatibility between partners and these should be included in the audit:

- Communication style (degree of formality),
- Hierarchical boundaries (rigid vs. flexible),
- Control mechanism (tight vs. loose),
- Mode of conflict resolution (explicit vs. implicit),
- Compensation philosophy (market position, degree of salary compression),
- Performance management (open vs. hidden), and
- Career stratification (gender, race, age, religion, qualifications).

Various maps exist to understand differences in culture. One simple but useful map has been developed by Goffee and Jones (1998), using two dimensions that are well established in sociological and management theory: *sociability* (friendships, emphasis on relationship, networking) and *solidarity* (collective task and goal orientation).[28] They map out four types of cultures: networked (strong on sociability), mercenary (strong on solidarity), fragmented (low on both), and communal (high on both). Each is reflected in different approaches to management and HRM, and each exists in a positive and negative form (for example, the danger for communal cultures is that they become arrogant and inward looking, while mercenary cultures can become ruthless).

It is particularly important is to clarify key operating HR policies and the actual practices:

- How do employees enter the company and what are the selection criteria?
- What are the promotion requirements and timetables?
- Which behaviors are encouraged and which are scorned?
- What are the performance criteria? And, how much do they matter?
- What are the determinants of salary? And, how large are the differentials?
- How open is the communication about individual performance?
- How open and transparent is the whole HR system?

This material may not be easily available, but it can be obtained through consultants, a thorough review of press coverage, and local intelligence—and not just leafing through annual reports. Doing the homework eliminates subsequent surprises.

A UK company decided to set up a JV in Malaysia to assemble its product for the local market. Soon after the results for the first year were in, the UK managing director proposed performance bonuses that differentiated by nearly 40 percent between managers at the same level of responsibility. A row erupted at the JV board meeting— the local partner objected because the bonus plan would violate the standards of internal equity among managers and hurt morale. The foreign managing director was puzzled: "You told us that bonuses in your company could be up to 40 percent of the total compensation. That is what I believe our best performers deserve." "Yes," came the answer, "but in our company the bonus percentage is the same for everyone."

Differences in management style and HR practices can, however, sometimes be a powerful argument in favor of an alliance. One of the factors that motivated Toshiba to join forces with General Electric in a Japan-based JV was to get an "insider" view on GE's renowned management system. Toshiba's top management actually encouraged GE to introduce many of its systems and practices into the JV to see how such practices might be adapted in Japan, and what learning the Japanese parent might gain from the experience.

Selecting Alliance Managers

An alliance manager is typically appointed at corporate level, responsible for planning, negotiating, and implementing alliances. Ideally, this role should be kept separate from the role of venture manager,[29] who is responsible for managing a specific project, business unit, or JV within the alliance (see Table 2), though obviously not all firms have the resources to do so.

Table 2. Alliance manager versus venture manager: roles and responsibilities[1]

Alliance Manager Roles and Responsibilities
- Building trust/setting the tone — unless there is trust and the right chemistry among managers involved in the alliance, it will not go anywhere.
- Monitoring partner contributions — how well a firm meets its obligations to an alliance is the most tangible evidence of its commitment.
- Managing information flow — drawing the line between information flow that ensures the vitality of the alliance, and unbridled information exchange that could jeopardize competitiveness.
- Assessing strategic viability/evaluating synergy — as strategic needs of the firm change over time, what are the implications for the alliance and overall relationship with the partner?
- Aligning internal relationships — since an alliance involves many people inside the firm, the alliance manager should mobilize the necessary support across the organization.

Venture Manager Roles and Responsibilities
- Managing the business — the venture manager assumes operational responsibility for the success of the venture.
- Representing venture interest — the venture manager has to represent without bias the interest of the venture as a business vis-à-vis its parents.
- Aligning outside resources — many resources are located outside the venture boundaries in the parent organizations; tapping effectively into those resources is a venture manager's responsibility.
- Building collaborative culture — irrespective of the competitive context of the alliance, trust inside the venture is an essential ingredient for success.
- Developing venture strategy — successful alliances evolve as any other ongoing business, and this evolution should be guided by solid strategy.

[1] Yoshino and Rangan (1995).

The alliance manager may monitor several existing alliances, supporting business units in identifying opportunities where a partnership could create value. When such opportunities are identified, the alliance manager will take the lead in developing the negotiating strategy and framing the partnership contract. After negotiations are completed and a new alliance has been formed, they will oversee the evolution of the alliance and the relationship with the partner. This is like managing a portfolio where new ventures get negotiated, added, and monitored.

The alliance manager has a determining impact on the quality of the relationship between the partners and on the ability of a firm to execute its alliance strategy. When selecting alliance managers, it is important to recognize that their role will change from visioning/sponsoring to networking/mediating as the alliance evolves from initial planning through negotiations, start-up, maturity, and on to eventual decline and dissolution.[30]

Typically, the key requirement for the alliance manager's position is a high degree of personal and professional credibility. Mutual trust is the glue that cements alliance relationships, and without credibility, it is difficult to establish trust. When Motorola established a strategically key semiconductor alliance with Toshiba, it appointed as alliance manager a corporate vice president with a stellar business record. This indi-vidual played a central role in developing overall corporate strategy in the sector.[31] The focus of the alliance was to share Motorola's microprocessor know-how with Toshiba in exchange for access to Toshiba's memory technology. The alliance manager's personal credibility and reputation were critical in aligning Motorola's internal resources behind the alliance, and in convincing Toshiba that Motorola's management was determined to make the alliance work.

The job of an alliance manager also requires a high degree of flexibility and adaptability in coping with different national and organizational cultures, manage-ment styles, and individual behaviors. As discussed, alliances are by nature unstable and uncertain, so it is difficult to operate under precise rules or to expect that an intended strategy will be followed to the letter. Managers who are not comfortable in working under ambiguity will find it difficult to cope. As one experienced alliance manager put it, "high tolerance for frustration is a must."

We have indicated that alliance managers are an example of one of the key lateral coordination roles in a multinational firm—much of what alliance managers are required to do involve mobilizing resources across organizational boundaries. They manage laterally in much the same way as a global account manager or an interna-tional project leader, but without large budgets or staff, and without direct authority over resource allocation.[32] Instead, the manager has to rely on influencing networks of people inside and outside the firm. As one senior executive in a Fortune 500 company put it:

> A leader is one who gets people to do what he wants, but who at the same time makes them think that it was all their idea in the first place. An alliance manager also has to work along the same lines. He has no battalions of his own, yet he has to get the job done. He has to get people to buy into his vision of the alliance, make it part of their own job assignment, and actively work to make the alliance a success.[33]

Preparing for Negotiations

Firms need to address HRM issues long before the first encounter between the poten-tial partners. The initial focus is primarily on selecting the negotiating team and facil-itating training in handling negotiations.

Selecting the Negotiation Team

Once the long-term strategy of the alliance is in place, its objectives set, and the poten-tial partners established, it helps if the negotiation team is selected quickly. Different types of venture may require different mixes of entrepreneurial, analytical, and political competences in the team.[34] The context might also influence the choice of the alliance manager, who in most circumstances should be the core member of the team.

There are different opinions as to whether future venture managers should take part in the negotiations. When venture managers are involved in negotiations they have a vested interested in "getting it right" rather than just "getting the deal," since they will be responsible for implementation. However, when negotiations are pro-tracted (most last longer than anticipated) it is not easy to free up managers who have other responsibilities to participate in negotiations that may fail. An alternative is to assign the responsibility for the venture before the negotiation is completed, but to have another position available in case the negotiations fail.

Training for Negotiations

Alliance negotiations resemble other business negotiations, though they tend to be more complex due to the strategic and cross-cultural issues involved. For team members who lack experience in alliance negotiations, properly structured negotiation training could be a worthwhile investment.

An essential part of such preparation is to help the negotiators to become familiar with the business and cultural context of the partner's country. Given the stakes involved, a number of studies suggest that companies underestimate the need to pre-pare carefully.[35] Without preparation, it is all too easy to fall back on cultural stereo-types. It is also important to sort out the individual roles in a team, and to review and practice different negotiation scenarios. HR professionals often have strong process facilitation skills, and they may serve as internal consultants in the alliance negotia-tions. Especially in more complex negotiations, the presence of an experienced facili-tator may be beneficial, observing the flow of interactions, interpreting behaviors, and coaching the key actors.

Negotiation Challenges in Joint Venture Formation

When an alliance takes the form of a joint venture, negotiations regarding control and management of the JV should include HR. There are several negotiation challenges where strategy and HRM interact closely. These include issues of:

- equity control versus operational influence;
- board composition;
- senior management appointments; and
- HR policies for the alliance.

Equity Control versus Operational Influence

The issue of control is often difficult to resolve in JV negotiations. Generally, both parties seek to be the majority owner, as this is considered the best way to protect one's long-term interests, particularly in the context of a competitive alliance. How-ever, in the absence of other supporting mechanisms, equity control is no guarantee that the venture will evolve in line with the intended strategy.

Gaining a majority position may provide a tax or financial reporting advantage. However, it is a fallacy to assume that equity control equals management control, as the Chemco case illustrates. A minority equity position, coupled with effective representation on the JV management team and an influence over the flow of know-how, may have more real impact on how the venture operates than a nominal majority exercised from a distance. From an accounting perspective, 51 percent of the shares may entitle the owner to 51 percent of the dividends, but these are often the last piece of the cash pie to be distributed. Internal transfer pricing, purchasing decisions, the cost of services provided by a local partner, payroll determined by compensation levels, all have an impact on cash flow long before any dividends are declared.

Not surprisingly, "the last 2 percent" (going from a 49 percent share to 51 percent) is the most expensive piece of equity. While intangible contributions (the infusion of technical or market know-how, transfer of depreciated assets, brand equity) may substitute for capital in a minority position, a majority position usually requires cash. The important point is that a careful human resource strategy that secures influence can be less costly and more effective than a strategy that focuses on securing equity control.

Acquiring such influence typically starts with the key appointments—the composition of the board and senior management appointments.

Board Composition

Companies often strive for a majority equity position simply to achieve a majority on the board of directors, thus protecting their voting interests in the event of a dispute between partners. In reality, JV boards seldom, if ever, vote. Pushing through a majority vote often constitutes the first step in dissolving an alliance. If the partners have a common interest in maintaining the relationship, then disputes are resolved in private and boards act only to approve such agreements. In addition, the protection of strategic interest can be achieved by other means, such as specific clauses in the agreement or articles of incorporation that stipulate what actions require unanimous or qualified majority consent of the shareholders.

There are side advantages to using the board primarily to oversee rather than to control. Positions on the board can be used for a variety of other purposes. An appointment to the board can be used to recognize the outstanding contribution of an alliance executive. In many countries, "company director" status is considered the pinnacle of a business career, and such opportunities may serve to increase the morale and retention of senior management. Board appointments can be used to expand linkages to outside business circles and the wider community in the local country, broadening learning and business opportunities. A position on the board can also be reserved for an individual who may mediate potential conflicts between the partners.

When setting up the board, there is a natural tendency to appoint alliance champions—people who favored the deal from the outset, who were involved in the negotiations, and who know the partner best. However, it is also useful to appoint at least one "bad cop," who will keep the champions from forgetting that the venture is a business rather than just a relationship—someone a little more skeptical, who sees the potential downfall of various alliance initiatives.[36]

Appointing Senior Management

In most JVs, senior managers wield far more strategic and operational control and influence than members of the board.[37] Tasks that determine the venture's success—setting business objectives, interfacing with key customers, monitoring the transfer of knowledge, developing the organization's culture—are all operational responsibilities of the senior managers inside the venture. Moreover, it is always preferable to resolve the inevitable conflicts and differences of opinion at the operational level rather than referring disputes to higher levels of alliance governance.

However, there is a paradox here. The shortage of international managers who can implement a market entry strategy in an unfamiliar environment is often a motive for choosing a JV over a wholly owned subsidiary; yet without a pool of suitable candidates, bargaining about positions is a meaningless exercise. Having such a pool ready requires attention to HR from the very early stage of alliance planning, since it takes time to select and groom potential candidates. It may be preferable to recruit in the local market and then provide them with opportunities to learn the organizational ropes before dispatching them to the JV—again, a time-consuming effort. If these HR issues are raised only after the agreement is signed, it may be difficult to find the right candidates in time for the launch. The cost of fixing the problems later grows exponentially with time since misaligned cultures, attitudes and behaviors are difficult to uproot once embedded.

Note, however, that executive role expectations may vary from one culture to another. In a 50:50 French–Swedish JV located in France, the Swedish company agreed to the appointment of a senior French executive as chairman in exchange for *de facto* control of the operations. But in the French organization, the chairman was not the honorary figure that the Swedes expected. He was seen as the ultimate decision-maker in the venture, while the opinions of the Swedish managers were ignored. Although the venture continued to make strategic sense, the operational frictions generated so much ill will on both sides that it had to be dissolved a few years later.

The leadership and behavioral demands on JV managers are greater than in wholly owned units, and finding suitable managers is not a simple task. Political skills are indispensable because top JV managers need to use influence to balance partner priorities and overcome conflicts. Cross-cultural sensitivity and flexibility are particularly important when partners come from different cultures and where JV staff represent two or more nationalities. Having a cooperative disposition, a high tolerance for ambiguity, and an internal locus of control are additional personal traits that help international alliance managers to perform well.[38]

In particular, the nomination of the venture general manager can generate intense debate. Who should "own" the JV manager? One can argue that the venture manager must have the goodwill of both parents in order to operate effectively.[39] Installing somebody as venture general manager who only represents the interest of one partner may be counterproductive. And special care is needed when the joint entity is essentially independent of the parents' operations, as in the case of many complementary or resource alliances.

However, if the venture activities need to be integrated with those of the parent, then an arms-length relationship may not be appropriate. There is a fine line between representing the best interests of the venture and that of the parent company. If an insider from one firm seems the logical choice as venture manager—because of his/her knowledge of the business or geographical area—it is important to minimize incentives that show favoritism. It should be clear that the manager's future career depends on the success of the venture. It also helps if alliance managers are seen as its champions—those, who believe in the purpose and who work hard to make it succeed—see the box "The role of venture champions."

THE ROLE OF VENTURE CHAMPIONS

An alliance succeeds because managers and employees believe in the promise of the concept and are willing to invest personal effort to make it happen. Alliances without champions do not survive for long because the ambiguity and uncertainty of the relationship impair participants' capacity to deal with the complex issues embedded in most partnerships.

When Whirlpool Corporation established a manufacturing JV with Tatramat, the Slovak washing machine maker, Tatramat's former top executive, Martin Ciran, became managing director of the JV.[40] The new company later ran into serious financial difficulties that enabled Whirlpool to gain majority control. Yet Ciran retained his position because he was recognized as the key champion of the alliance. His leadership was deemed essential to making the venture a success.

With access to Whirpool know-how, but under Ciran's leadership, the company was turned around. Today, Whirpool's Slovak factory—now fully owned— still ranks among its top performing European subsidiaries.

Identifying alliance champions and recognizing their contribution towards implementing the alliance strategy is a critical driver of its success. Not surprisingly, alliance champions, like alliance skeptics, can be found on both sides of the partnership. Knowing the venture champions on the "other side"—especially those who have sufficient internal credibility to mobilize resources for the benefit of the alliance—is of great value in the negotiations over managerial appointments.

Human Resource Policies within the Alliance Venture

The need to influence alliance strategy is only one of the arguments for addressing HRM issues early in the alliance formation process. When the success of the alliance depends heavily on people issues, such as competence transfer or reaching new standards in quality and productivity, leaving HR until later in order to simplify alliance negotiations may handicap the future chances of success.

It is particularly important to pay early attention to HR policies and practices when there are likely to be many complex interfaces between the venture and the alliance parents.[41] In contrast to licensing or supplier–buyer agreements, up-front agreement on HR philosophy and policies may be vital to success in manufacturing JVs or shared projects in new product development.

Some researchers advocate a detailed contract clarifying HR policies inside the alliance in order to reduce the uncertainty and conflict over matters of staffing, transfers, promotion, and compensation.[42] However, detailed contracts do not guarantee compliance. Venture synergy comes from shared business interests, not from legal formulations. A clear statement regarding HR principles is in most cases sufficient, without limiting contractually what can or cannot be done.

Sometimes companies take the position "when in Rome, do as the Romans" and delegate all responsibility for HR matters to the local partner. This makes sense provided that the "Roman" organization is a paragon of effectiveness, quality, and customer service. If it does not have solid HR foundations in place, then this attempt to show cultural sensitivity will only result in replicating the dysfunctional aspects of local practice. It is said of many foreign JVs in Japan that they represent "museums of Japanese management"—that is, they are repositories of obsolete practices that their Japanese parents ditched a long time ago, but which are still presented to the foreign parent as the "Japanese" way of managing people.

IMPLEMENTING ALLIANCES

Once the contract is signed and the partnership becomes operational, a new set of people related issues appear. How to manage the evolution of the partnership? How to ensure that the knowledge developed inside the alliance is properly shared among the partners? And, how to keep the partnership objectives aligned with those of the parent?

These issues have two major HR implications. The first is managing the interface with the parent, which involves influencing the attitudes and behaviors of staff at home who are in contact with the alliance. The second relates to the management of people inside the venture itself.

Managing the Interfaces with the Parent

An important challenge is to manage the interface between the parent organization and the partnership. The objective is to align the internal processes back home so that they support rather than hinder external collaboration. Often the organizational units that provide resources to the alliance are not those receiving its outputs. The asymmetry in the perceived costs and benefits of collaboration with the venture may cause internal tensions that undermine willingness to support the partnership. The value of collaboration is sometimes not visible in the hustle and bustle of daily operations, so explicit reinforcements of the message may be required. Ford learned from Motorola's experience, cited earlier, when it entered into broad cooperative agreements in Japan. The question "What have you done to support Ford's alliance strategy?" featured in the performance evaluations for a large part of the organization.

A rapidly growing US securities firm with global ambitions set up an alliance with a European brokerage to offer their European customers "preferential" access to US financial markets. However, even after the alliance was launched to great fanfare, the operational practices at the New York trading desk did not change. The relatively small orders from Europe did not get the same attention as those from large US institutional clients, reducing profit opportunities for the European partner. The new partner received a similar second-class treatment from other units of the US firm.

Why was this happening? The rigid "meet-the-numbers" reward system in the United States was incompatible with a strategy that did not yield immediate earnings, like the European partnership. No amount of presentations on the benefits of international expansion could make much difference. In Europe, the initial irritation quickly turned to anger and then to suspicions about the true motives of the American partner. Less than two years later the alliance was dissolved. As noted by one of the American HR managers involved: "If this alliance was important for our future, then perhaps it should have been partly my job to create an environment where phone calls from our partners would be returned without delay."

Top Management Role

The company's execution of its alliance strategy places particular demands on top management, who must "walk their talk." The box "The anniversary speech" illustrates what happens when top management is not involved.

THE ANNIVERSARY SPEECH

A 50:50 JV between a Japanese and a US firm celebrated its 25th anniversary. Over time, the JV had evolved from a small marketing start-up to a fully integrated firm with an independent R&D and manufacturing capability that enjoyed a very profitable leadership position in the Japanese market. Given its commercial success, the friction between the two partners in the early days regarding the future direction of the business was replaced by a grudging willingness to continue working together. However, on the American side, executives often voiced concerns that the JV operated as if it were a wholly owned affiliate of the Japanese parent, while their influence was being eroded. The loyalty of the workforce was seen as tilted in favor of the local partner.

On the anniversary date, the employees assembled in one of Tokyo's exhibition halls for an afternoon of celebration. The company's glee club warmed up with some speeches and songs. Then, the 96-year-old former chairman of the Japanese parent, who signed the original deal, was helped onto the stage in his wheelchair to deliver a message of thanks to all employees for bringing his dream to life. His speech was short, owing to his failing health, but it was emotional and made a big impact on the audience. His speech was followed by with a pre-recorded video message from the current American CEO who, in three years of tenure, had visited the venture once. He said nothing wrong, but the impersonality of the presentation defeated its purpose. Another skirmish in the loyalty battle was lost.

Capturing the loyalty of the alliance workforce is only one of the human resource tasks that require the support of top management. Internal communication is another; top management plays an indispensable role in ensuring that the reasons for the partnership are well understood inside the firm, especially when it comes to balancing the competitive and collaborative aspects of the alliance. Top management must also work closely with HR on the selection of alliance managers, on resource allocation for learning activities, and on ensuring that reward systems are well aligned with the partnership strategy.

Human Resource Management Issues in Managing the Alliance

Many of the international HRM issues discussed previously in this book are also relevant to international alliances. Here we will examine those that may have the biggest impact on the success of an alliance strategy:

- staffing of the alliance;
- mobility between the parent(s) and the venture;
- competence and capability development;
- performance management;
- rewards and recognition;
- building influence inside the alliance; and
- aligning the social architecture.

However, just as there are no generic alliance strategies, so too there are few generic blueprints for effective HR policies and practices. Attention to HRM in the alliance depends on the strategic objectives and the position of the alliance in the value chain. The more critical the role of the partnership in creating value, the larger is the need to commit HR resources and support.

Staffing Alliances

Staffing matters! Inappropriate staffing is of one the major causes of alliance failures, and this is typically the most important aspect of HRM in the venture. Perhaps the most important qualification for a potential alliance partner is having sound HR foundations at home. Without that credibility, it may be impossible to establish respect abroad.

Every strategic plan for an alliance should include a review of staffing requirements. Other HR matters, such as training and compensation, have an important impact, but problems in those areas can be addressed—with proper determination—in a relatively short time. Difficulties created by poor staffing, such as correcting the consequences of bad decisions made by people who are not qualified to meet the challenges of managing an alliance, may take years to fix. While the staffing issues will vary from one alliance to another, there are some generic matters to consider:

- What is the number and skill mix of employees required?
- Who is responsible for forecasting manpower demands?
- Who will do the recruiting? Each partner individually? Or will they work jointly?

- Which positions are to be filled by each parent?
- Which positions are to be filled by expatriates?
- In JVs, for whom do the new employees work—for one of the partners, or for the new entity?
- Who decides on new hires? Must there be an agreement among partners?
- How will staffing conflicts be resolved?

In virtually all JVs there will be staff from both partners. The box "'Managing' your partner's staffing" addresses the tricky question of how to influence the other company's staffing decisions.

"MANAGING" YOUR PARTNER'S STAFFING

Asymmetry in the quality of the assignees is often an early signal that the venture is heading for trouble, since it raises questions about the managerial competence or sincerity of the deficient partner. If the partner organization is to provide key operational staff, it is important to find ways of ensuring that they possess the required competences and skills. This means developing some way to identify the talented people in the partner organization, and understanding the basis by which the partner differentiates between high potentials, solid performers, and low performers.

Inappropriate staffing decisions are common. The partner's management may not understand the skill level required for jobs in the partnership venture, they may overestimate the capability of their internal candidates, or they may simply not have the necessary basic HR capabilities. It is essential to intervene before any decisions are taken. Forcing a change once an appointment has been made may be difficult.

The right to be consulted on key appointments is a useful stipulation in a partnership agreement. However, exercising this right requires familiarity with the "rules of the game" in the partner's organization, understanding the internal score cards, and knowing how careers evolve there, as well as gaining access to the levers of influence. Much of this is tacit knowledge, acquired through extensive informal interaction and built on trust and personal credibility.

Given the importance of staffing, there is a case for formally addressing these issues in the alliance contract, though, as noted earlier, views are divided since contractual arrangements may be too rigid for evolving staffing needs—mutual agreement on policies may suffice.

One Way versus Temporary Transfer

When partnerships are formed to create a new business, it is important to consider the costs and benefits of two alternative staffing strategies. One approach is to assign personnel to the JV on a temporary transfer from the partner firm. The other is to staff the JV positions on a "permanent" basis. While it is not unusual to combine the two methods, it is important to consider the conflicting priorities and career aspirations of the two groups of employees. Every position filled—usually at higher cost—by a temporary transferee is an opportunity lost for the permanent staff. If the value-for-money of the transferee is not readily apparent, then resentment and conflict are not far behind.

There is some evidence that it is better to staff JVs with dedicated management teams.[43] If employees are transferred from the parent, then they should expect to remain in the venture without a guaranteed ticket back to the parent, so that their future career opportunities are linked entirely to the growth of the new business. In Japan, a country where few JVs survive, several successful joint ventures have at their helm executives who have spent all or most of their careers in the venture. Fuji–Xerox, headed for many years by Yotaro Kobayashi, is probably the most notable example of what strong and stable leadership can do for JV performance.

On the other hand, temporary transfers do have merits. They are useful when a venture is evolving rapidly and the required management skills change, when skill gaps cannot be covered internally, or as a tool for organizational learning. Transferees are more likely to remember that their task is not to preserve the alliance at all costs. Indeed, temporary transfers are generally the only way in which the foreign partner can insert its employees into the venture. However, any assignments should be of a reasonable duration since new managers will pass through a learning stage before they can contribute fully to the venture. Frequent churn of key venture managers makes it difficult to establish a shared culture.

The foreign partner may experience greater difficulties than the local partner in convincing first-class employees from the parent firm to transfer to the JV.[44] In such cases, the personal involvement of top management can make a difference. When Procter & Gamble first entered the Chinese market in the 1980s, joint venturing with local partners was the only option. In order to encourage its best candidates to accept these challenging assignments, P&G's top management, including the CEO, took a visible role in candidate selection, acting as a mentor during the assignment and in repatriation. Such leadership commitment to staffing ensured a ready supply of good managers willing to work in China.

A shortage of qualified candidates or cost considerations may persuade foreign partners to limit their representation to a single executive. One person is expected to play the role of corporate ambassador, shadow CEO, chief learning officer, and business developer—quite a challenge! Notably in competitive alliances, this may not be in the best interest of the business.

In most cases, the best strategy is to recruit and develop local talent. When JVs are an important part of a company's strategy in a particular market, it may be worthwhile establishing a corporate unit that can serve as a holding company for all operations in the country. Local managers can then be hired by the holding company, and trained and dispatched to JVs to represent the interests of the foreign partner, thus lessening the reliance on expensive expatriates with limited local know-how. Many foreign firms investing in JVs in China; for example, ABB and GE have chosen this route to develop their local management teams.[45]

Developing Capabilities

The strategic objectives of an alliance often require developing new knowledge, skills, and competences, as in the case of learning and competitive alliances. This in turn requires actions to create a learning environment, including:

- building understanding among people in the parent company who will be involved directly or indirectly in the partnership;
- training employees and managers dispatched to the alliance;
- enhancing collaboration inside the partnership; and
- facilitating integration with the parent firm.

In companies where alliances are critical to the business strategy, alliance training is often used as an integral part of the implementation process. For example, Hewlett Packard, which is engaged in scores of international partnerships, organizes workshops on a massive scale for managers involved in alliances. The HP alliance management framework, an elaborate knowledge management system focused on alliances, is disseminated using case histories, toolkits and checklists, as well as comparisons of best practice from other firms.[46]

One of the dilemmas in preparing executives for alliance assignments is that companies may be reluctant to devote resources to alliance management training, or even to select potential venture staff, until the partnership has been agreed. This is a double bind since there is seldom time for extensive training once an agreement has been reached. Estimates suggest that only a third of firms involved in alliances offer alliance training.[47] One of the authors has directed alliance management seminars for over 25 years. It is not unusual to see participants subscribing for the course at the last minute, departing for a foreign location virtually as soon as the course ends.[48]

One of the focal areas for management development within the alliance venture itself is in helping the members of venture team to interact and work effectively with each other and with the parents. This process ideally starts when the alliance is launched, helping employees to get to know each other, and learning about each other's company culture and mode of operations. When Corning creates new alliances, venture staff are briefed on the respective organizational cultures and traditions, corporate values, and venture organization in order to minimize confusion and misunderstanding.[49] Other companies organize team-building workshops, ranging from traditional organizational development interventions to outdoor experiential learning.[50] It also pays to follow up the "honeymoon training" with periodic workshops, working jointly through specific business and cultural challenges facing the partnership.

In the Chemco case, the US partner realized that it had to modify the structure of functional training workshops it held to improve coordination in Asia Pacific. Previously, these had been limited to wholly owned subsidiaries. Although participants complained about the lack of support from the Japanese, no action could be taken since the Japanese, as part of a JV rather than a wholly owned subsidiary, did not attend. In the new format, Japanese JV employees were invited to take part, and the program was redesigned to take language problems into account and to facilitate dialogue.

Participants were now able to identify jointly the obstacles to collaboration, suggest actions to remedy the problems, and commit to new joint business initiatives. The bottom line? Profits from joint projects generated by the first three workshops equaled the annual training budget for the whole region.

A good and relatively inexpensive way to foster the alliance integration process is to open up in-house training to the staff in the alliance unit, and when appropriate to those from the partner. Aside from skill development, this may lead to the creation of personal networks across the alliance boundaries. Real trust cannot be built through contracts, only through human relationships.

Defining Performance

During the planning stage, it is generally not difficult for alliance partners to agree that "performance matters." However, for the operating managers dispatched to the actual JV, it can be much more difficult to agree on what constitutes "performance," how to measure it, and what the consequences of high or low performance should be.

Most fundamentally, the partners may have different objectives for the JV and, therefore, use different criteria to assess performance. A study of Chinese–German JVs revealed that the Chinese parent organization put much higher value on the acquisition of technology and knowledge, while growth and market share were more important for the German parents.[51] However, disagreements about how to appraise performance are often less obvious.

In an oil exploration JV created by British, Norwegian (state-owned), and Vietnamese (government) partners, the parties did not hold the same views about performance management. Yet the split did not cut along East–West cultural lines. British expatriates and locally recruited young Vietnamese managers were in favor of individually focused, achievement-oriented performance criteria with substantial financial benefits for top performers. The Norwegians and the senior representatives of the Vietnamese partner, concerned with equity and harmonious work relations, preferred to give more emphasis to team goals and process implementation, with much less internal differentiation. Although the business principles in the agreement contained a commitment to create a performance-oriented culture, the specifics were never spelled out. The net result was confusion, frustration, conflict, and high turnover—the opposite of what a performance management system is supposed to achieve. It was not that one partner was "right" and the other "wrong," the real issue was the lack of a common perspective.

Many of the dualities involved in performance management can lead to disagreement—short-term versus long-term time horizon, focus on output versus behavior, individual versus group scope, objective versus subjective evaluation, direct versus indirect feedback, and in addition parent versus venture orientation. This last issue—whether managers are evaluated on the performance of the venture or the parent—can become particularly contentious. But an even bigger problem is to align strategic aims. In Chemco's case, as long as the objective of the local management team was only to grow profitably in Japan, the wider strategic aims of the US firm to grow in the region remained neglected.

Many of the tensions around performance management come from three sources: (1) applying homegrown principles inappropriately in a different context; (2) using different standards for parent company and alliance employees; and, (3) attempting to combine incompatible approaches.

In a Japanese-controlled JV in the United States, merit increases were linked to performance evaluations, according to local practice. However, the performance feedback process was decidedly "Japanese," indirect and informal. Japanese bosses spent most time with the laggards, hoping that with some encouragement their performance would improve. On the other hand, they loaded more responsibility on those considered outstanding so as to signal that they were trusted and were on the way to a bright future in the firm. While these signals might have been correctly interpreted in Japan, several of the top American performers quit, complaining that the merit increases did not reflect the additional responsibilities, that the bosses did not care, and that they did not know where they stood. Others complained that the Japanese were not honest, since the encouraging words were not matched by what they saw on their paychecks.

Strategy matters—in a complementary alliance, a hands-off approach to setting the performance objectives may be appropriate, whereas in a competitive alliance this may be a recipe for disaster. Not surprisingly, resistance to "foreign" ways of managing performance is most pronounced in competitive alliances. This happens because managing performance is one of the keys to having an influence inside the venture. The way that performance is managed indicates to the alliance staff who is in charge, whose interests have to be taken seriously. Without influence over the performance management process, a partner (especially a distant partner) can expect only nominal control over the direction of the venture. Therefore, performance management issues often become a lightning rod in the latent struggle for influence.

The proper measure of influence is not how much the performance management of the alliance resembles that of the parent but how it furthers the parent company's strategy. First, this means making sure that the parent's strategic objectives are reflected in the performance targets for the alliance. Second, achieving these targets has to be measured. Third, meeting or failing to meet targets should have consequences.

In Chemco's case, the first and second requirements for effective performance management processes were met once the US partner attained formal majority control and regional targets were included in the annual objectives set for the local management team. However, target setting was merely a ritual since the results had no consequences, positive or negative—and this would remain the case as long as Chemco had no influence over salaries, bonuses, or promotions. This leads us to the reward aspects of performance management.

Aligning Rewards

One of the first actions that Chemco took to increase its influence was to negotiate a gradual transfer of all employees in Japan from the payroll of the Japanese parent to JV employee status. The work conditions offered were more favorable but did not increase the cost as the compensation and benefit system was tailored to the

JV workforce. The union and nearly all employees accepted these conditions. As a next step, the management bonus was linked to the achievement of two sets of targets, regional and local, with regional targets being the key objective for senior management. In addition, the variable part of total compensation was increased dramatically, and the company began discussing a stock option scheme. Today, the Japanese partner considers its JV as a "human laboratory" where new HR—novel to the Japanese market—can be tested before being introduced into the parent company.

Of all compensation issues, those relating to variable pay require the most sensitivity and flexibility. Compensation can have a strong impact on strategy implementation because people tend to do what they believe they get rewarded for.[52] But beyond that, people in different countries have very different attitudes to variable pay. This is partly the result of wide differences in accounting standards and tax regimes, for example regarding stock options.[53] There are also different cultural attitudes to issues like uncertainty avoidance and salary differentials. Again, the primary consideration is to align rewards with the alliance strategy rather than blindly import HR practices because they are successful in the parent firm.[54]

No compensation formula or measurement matrix can overcome a disagreement about strategy. If one partner wants to build market share and the other is interested in cash flow, then developing common performance targets is going to be difficult unless the two partners first agree on priorities. In more complex alliances, building a clear linkage between strategic aims and rewards may not be possible, which is an additional argument for keeping alliances simple and focused.

Another important compensation issue to consider is the tension between external equity with the parent for expatriates and internal equity for venture staff, frequently leading to asymmetry in earnings among different groups of employees within the alliance. For example, expatriate managers often earn many times more than the income of a typical local JV employee (whose pay in turn may be considerably higher than that of a counterpart in a local firm). The differences in compensation levels may also impact the balance of influence in the alliance since loyalties, not surprisingly, tend to shift towards the higher paying partner.[55]

These differences, while unavoidable in ventures involving companies from countries with widely different standards of living, may lead to motivational problems and conflict unless the added value of staff who receives superior compensation is visible and appreciated. Disparity in compensation sometimes makes it difficult to persuade the local partner to accept expatriates, even when this could be in the best interest of the venture.[56] Local partners may also try to use the disparity to their own advantage. For example, compensation "equality" between foreign expatriates and local managers was often one of the conditions for JV approval by local authorities in China. In reality, the Chinese managers were paid only a fraction of what was stipulated in the contract, while their state-owned employer retained the rest. Foreign partners in Chinese JVs had to bear the expatriation costs of foreign managers while the Chinese partner earned a corresponding profit.

Internal equity issues within the parent firm must also be balanced against the supply and demand for high quality venture managers. Alliances, in comparison with wholly owned subsidiaries, are difficult to manage. They may be seen as risky since the venture is removed from the politics of getting ahead in the parent company. High performers, who tend to have options, may elect to stay clear of such assignments unless they are sufficiently compensated. On the other hand, corporate cohesion is better facilitated by a degree of consistency in compensation strategy across all affiliates, irrespective of the organizational form.

This paradox cannot be solved simply by re-calibrating compensation. To achieve the necessary balance, other components of the HR system have to be aligned as well. The deliberate positioning of alliance assignments as a key element of long-term career progression is a powerful tool for ensuring a supply of requisite talent, as we saw in the case of P&G's staffing strategy for entering China. Influencing and shaping careers provides stronger leverage over expatriate staffing than short-term financial incentives.[57]

Building and Maintaining Influence

One of the best ways to gain allegiance among JV employees is to show commitment to their career development. Shortly after transferring Japanese employees to the JV payroll, Chemco offered some younger staff the possibility of moving to their subsidiaries in South East Asia with the assignment of coordinating sales with Japanese customers in the region. The conditions offered were the same as for any other Chemco expatriate. One benefit for Chemco was improved customer service and sales. The other was a dramatic change in how the Japanese staff perceived regional integration. The earlier view that integration was a power game—us versus them—quickly faded. Expatriate perks such as housing were attractive for the young Japanese since they could not afford this at home. But what made the difference was the feeling that career opportunities were now visibly open to all.

Such career development can promote organizational cohesion, though as with any HRM practice, the execution depends on the alliance's strategic context. In competitive alliances, this needs to be carefully considered. The worst outcome is to accept a transferee for the sake of the relationship, and then to cut him/her off from information and influence because he/she is perceived as untrustworthy. Some transferees will view this as another example of the partner's duplicity and bad intentions.

The form of the alliance also has implications for career development, and again JVs pose most of the challenges.[58] Employees transferred from the parent to a JV can feel left behind, especially if the number of expatriates inside the venture is small. The temporary nature of the assignment only reinforces anxiety about career prospects. Assurances from corporate HR—"Don't worry, we'll take care of you when you come back"—lack credibility in an era of continuous restructuring. The difficulty of managing dual allegiance is one of the arguments in favor of "one-way-transfer" staffing strategies. However, this is often not practical from a staffing perceptive, as we will discuss in the next section, or desirable because of a need to foster knowledge exchange between the venture and the parent.

Visible involvement in career development decisions is one of the most effective ways to build influence. Being an "absentee" parent may be a cost-efficient strategy in the short term, but it can be costly in the long term. In a stand-alone JV, when the initial growth levels off, career development prospects may diminish and the best and the brightest may leave unless they see the same opportunity to move to increased responsibilities, as they would have in a wholly owned subsidiary. If only one of the parents seems to care, then it is likely that commitment and loyalty will shift accordingly.

Developing Shared Culture

In contrast to acquisitions, one has to live with conflicting loyalties in alliances. Whether or not this becomes dysfunctional depends on the type of alliance and the ability of the partners to deal with the contradictions in the alliance relationship. One way to cope is to foster a distinct and shared culture inside the alliance that eases tensions between partners, another is to build strong personal relationships. However, as always, this depends on the business strategies underlying the venture. Alliance independence is not a goal in itself—the purpose of an alliance is to create value for the partners. Instructions to general managers, such as "run this like your own business" when the venture does not have decision-making autonomy can only create mistrust and cynicism.

The key outcome of a shared culture is trust.[59] Creating a shared culture inside an alliance does not mean ignoring differences between the partners' strategic priorities. However, even in a competitive alliance, the partnership will not succeed without trust on an operating level. The best way to build trust is to get to know each other. This can be supported by promoting personnel exchanges and by providing visible examples of commitment to common goals.

Another source of cohesion may be a common enemy, as illustrated by the experience of three middle-sized manufacturers of electronic components. American, German, and Japanese respectively, they established a global alliance aimed at combining R&D resources in a market dominated by two giant competitors. Management teams met regularly around the world to coordinate development activities. However, traditional rivalry, parochial departmental interests, and cultural insensitivity slowed down decision making, causing the alliance to miss several critical deadlines and to jeopardize relationships with key customers. On the initiative of one of the HR managers, signs bearing the logos of the two competitors were installed on the walls in the conference rooms. The signs could be made to light up by pushing a button hidden under the conference desk, reminded everyone that the competition did not go away while they wasted time in unproductive arguments. After only a few meetings, it became embarrassing for anyone to get flashed for allowing a parochial agenda to get in the way of common interest. The speed, decision making, and quality of implementation improved dramatically.

SUPPORTING ALLIANCE LEARNING

All alliances include some learning aspects, the least of which is how to work effectively with partners.[60] However, some alliances are created with capability development, knowledge creation, and learning as the focal objectives.

In both learning and competitive alliances, effective alliance learning is important not only to prevent the erosion of a firm's market position but also as a building block for future competitive advantage. In the case of Fuji–Xerox, the venture was started to facilitate Xerox's entry into the Japanese market. In the late-1980s, other Japanese companies such as Canon and Ricoh aggressively attacked Xerox in its home US market with innovative products, competing on price and quality. Initially, Xerox was not able to respond and lost significant market share. However, recognizing that Fuji–Xerox competed successfully against the same players in Japan, the company launched a massive "learning from Japan" campaign aimed at transferring Fuji–Xerox's capabilities back to the US mother firm.[61] Because of this "reverse technology transfer," Xerox was able to stem the market erosion and began to recapture lost share.

The long-term success of Fuji–Xerox illustrates the fact that many strong strategic alliances focus on mutual learning. Indeed, selecting partners who are known to be poor learners so as to guard against capability leaks is short-sighted. Weak learning capability is a sign of poor management, and poorly managed firms make poor partners. Trust between the partners allows them to concentrate on managing the business rather than on monitoring and control, and their mutual learning strengthens their position in markets worldwide.

An organization has many tools to manage the process of learning, but in principle, the learning ability of an organization depends on its ability to transfer and integrate tacit knowledge that is difficult to copy, thereby building organizational capabilities. Since the capabilities are typically embedded in people, HRM is critical to organization learning. This is especially true in international alliances where the learning occurs in a complex context of competition and cultural differences. Many of the difficulties in implementing long-term alliance strategies can be traced to the quality of the learning process and the underlying human resource policies and practices. The ability to learn is even more important in competitive alliances, where asymmetry in learning can result in an uneven distribution of benefits.[62]

One objective of human resource management in international alliances is, therefore, to complement business strategy by providing a climate that encourages organizational learning, and by installing appropriate tools and processes to guide the process of knowledge creation.[63] We have already discussed many of these, but alliances, particularly competitive alliances, bring particular challenges for HRM.

Obstacles to Alliance Learning

The rapid development of competitive capabilities among leading Japanese firms in the second half of the twentieth century is often attributed to successful alliance learning. Alliances were used as the main vehicle for inward technology transfer and capability improvement. More recently, many other companies in developing countries in Asia and Latin America have pursued the same strategy with success. By contrast, many of the traditional US and European firms have struggled to kick start the learning process and examples of alliance learning like that of Fuji–Xerox are relatively rare. So what are the obstacles? Some stem from ill-conceived strategies; others, from poor HRM practices; yet others, from a combination of both (see Table 3).

Table 3. Obstacles to organizational learning in international strategic alliances

HR Activities	HR Practices
Planning	• Strategic intent not communicated.
	• Short-term and static planning horizon.
	• Low priority for learning activities.
	• Lack of involvement by the HR department.
Staffing	• Insufficient lead-time for staffing decisions.
	• Resource-poor staffing strategy.
	• Low quality of staff assigned to the JV.
	• Staffing dependence on the partner.
Training and development	• Lack of cross-cultural competence.
	• Uni-directional training programs.
	• Career structure not conducive to learning.
	• Poor culture for transfer of learning.
Appraisal and rewards	• Appraisal focused on short-term goals.
	• No encouragement to learn.
	• Limited incentives for transfer of know-how.
	• Rewards not tied to global strategy.
Organizational design and control	• Responsibility for learning not clear.
	• Fragmentation of the learning process.
	• Control over the HR function given away.
	• No insight into partner's HR strategy.

Source: Adapted from Pucik (1988b).

Defensive Strategic Intent

One obstacle to alliance learning may arise because many alliances are driven by a defensive strategic intent. Firms perceive partnerships primarily as a way of reducing risk and conserving valuable resources.[64] This built-in defensive posture may make managers reluctant to make the necessary investments in learning, especially if one of the alliance objectives is to minimize the cost of developing new competences. Failing to invest in learning will invariably result in the deterioration of a firm's competitive position, leading to an asymmetry in the relationship and eventually to a conflict with the partner. Dissolution of the relationship is then the logical next step. Successful learning alliances are most often driven by a "top-line" orientation where investment in the development of new competences is recovered through the growth of business.

A corollary to defensive intent is the belief that preventing the partner from learning (and thus avoiding asymmetry) may be easier and cheaper than investing in one's own learning. A partner committed to learning will always learn, even if this is made difficult by obstacles put in the way. Meanwhile, the customer feels the obstacles. Secrecy and internal walls lead to sub-optimal solutions, excessive costs, and delays. In highly competitive markets, companies that hope to build defensive walls around themselves to prevent knowledge "seeping" to the partner often end up losing the customer.

Low Priority for Learning Activities

Decisions on alliance learning strategy are often based on the assumption that the existing balance of contributions to the venture will not change over time. Consider the case of a partnership where one party provides technology and the other secures market access. The executives of the technology firm may believe that the partner will have to rely on their technological leadership for the foreseeable future, so they see few incentives to invest in learning about the market. However, if the other partner gradually closes the technological gap—after all, technology transfer is often a part of the deal—the basis for the alliance becomes problematic. One partner now has both technology and market access, so why share the benefits?

One problem here is that many firms do not recognize the importance of developing soft or invisible competences. Learning often has to be focused on mastering tacit processes underlying product quality, speed of product development, or linkage to key customers. Firms frequently fail to benefit from alliance learning because they do not recognize the benefits of acquiring the ''soft'' skills.[65]

Learning through alliances may be faster than learning alone but it still requires investment. The learning strategy may be compromised by a reluctance to commit the necessary financial resources. In many companies, the traditional focus of the business planning process is return on financial assets, while the accumulation of invisible assets is not evaluated directly since a financial value is hard to assign to these outcomes. Activities that cannot be evaluated in financial terms may be seen as less critical, so learning efforts are given only token support.

Inappropriate Staffing

Expatriate staffing is costly, and firms are tempted to reduce alliance costs by limiting the number of expatriate personnel assigned to the foreign venture. As a result, the few expatriates (sometimes only one) are often overwhelmed with routine work, struggling just to get by in an unfamiliar culture. The opportunities for active involvement in new knowledge acquisition—for example through relationships with local customers or interactions with the partner—are minimal. However keen the expatriate may be to learn, operational matters prevent him/her from doing so.

In Chemco's case, company policy for nearly 20 years was to dispatch only one senior-level executive to Japan, occasionally augmented with an experienced engineer bringing knowledge into Japan. In most cases, the expatriates retired after their assignment in Japan so there was no organizational transfer of learning. When the company decided to refocus its Japan strategy, the total accumulated experience in the Japanese market among the top management team (Japan was at that time the largest overseas market for Chemco), including business trips longer than one week, was less than six months.[66]

The staffing agenda, however, is not just about how many and where but also about who. If the managers assigned to oversee or manage an alliance are not credible within their own organization and with the partner, learning will be difficult to achieve. Because these are relatively long-term assignments, they clash with the expectations of fast upward mobility and may not be attractive to high-potential managers. The managers who land in this role may not have the influence to cope with the complex give-and-take of a learning relationship. Long-term career planning is often lacking, as is effective repatriation (as in Chemco's case), which may hinder effective exploitation and dissemination of the acquired know-how.

Poor Climate for Knowledge Exchange

A characteristic of alliance learning is that partner interactions often take place in a context of competitive collaboration.[67] Not surprisingly, competition and learning commonly go hand in hand in high-tech industries in which fast learning is an imperative of the business model.

In a competitive alliance, transfer of knowledge to a competitor will often generate legitimate concern among staff over what will happen to job and work groups when their unique knowledge is disseminated to others. Principles of equitable exchange agreed at the venture board meeting do not necessarily translate into perceptions of equity at the operational level. Initial obstacles such as lack of focus and unclear priorities can quickly mushroom into widespread resistance to knowledge exchange. When one partner ignores requests for learning support, it may awaken suspicions of duplicity, inviting retaliation. Very soon, the whole atmosphere of partnership is poisoned.

Internal barriers to the acquisition of learning are often just as serious as unfriendly actions by the partner. The learning from the outside threatens the status quo. The typical attitude is defensive: "It's a good idea, but it will never work here." Contrast this with the attitude guiding GE's approach to alliances: "Stealing with pride" is a message that made it into the company's annual report.

No Accountability or Rewards for Learning

Some years ago, one of the authors conducted a survey among foreign JVs in Japan. One of the questions put to the HR managers was "Who in the parent firm organization is responsible for learning from Japan?" Less then 10 percent identified a person or a function (usually the top representative in Japan), about a third mentioned "nobody" and over half considered the question "not applicable." Since learning is taken more seriously today, the answers might be more positive, but the lack of clear responsibility remains a major obstacle to alliance learning.

Learning targets are unlikely to be taken seriously if there is no accountability for meeting them. In complex organizations, perceptions of the potential value of learning from an alliance may vary according to the business unit, function and territory, and the commitment to provide the necessary support will vary accordingly. This can lead to asymmetry, where one unit supplies the people while another unit expects the learning. During the dot.com boom, a European high-tech company entered a number of partnerships with companies in Silicon Valley, with the aim of exploring ways of leveraging its technology in the Internet world. Several young engineers were dispatched to California to work on specific projects as well as to provide feedback to the technology managers in the mother company. Within a few months, the word came back: "If you want to learn about exploiting the Internet, do it yourself. We don't have the time to teach you."

Traditional market-driven reward systems may implicitly encourage the hoarding of critical information, rather than the diffusion of learning. People who have valued knowledge can command higher salaries on the market, so diffusing their knowledge to others (for example by sharing critical alliance contacts) may diminish their market value. Being indispensable is the ultimate in "employability."

HRM Foundations for Effective Alliance Learning

A major role for HR is to help create an organizational context in which alliance learning can flourish (see Table 4). Importantly, alliance learning is not about collecting binders of data in the alliance "war room." Rather, effective alliance learning is focused on absorbing know-how and developing or broadening capabilities.

In the context of learning and competitive alliances, the need to focus on HRM from an early stage is especially critical. Acquisition of new knowledge and competences happens only through people, and if the people strategy is not aligned with the learning objectives, then the chances of this happening are greatly diminished.

Setting the Learning Strategy

One of the first questions to address in developing an alliance learning strategy is the extent to which this issue should be considered in the alliance agreement.

When the alliance is set up as a separate organization, for example as a JV, the partnership agreement or operating principles should provide for at least broad guidelines on key HR policies and practices that influence learning effectiveness. These may involve issues such as freedom to move people across alliance boundaries as necessary, and determination of their learning roles and responsibilities. Clarifying HR issues that influence learning is especially important if the alliance operates abroad

Table 4. Core principles for alliance learning

1. Build learning into the alliance agreement.
2. Communicate the learning intent inside the parent.
3. Assign responsibility for alliance learning.
4. Secure early HR involvement.
5. Maintain HR influence inside the alliance.
6. Staff to learn.
7. Support learning-driven careers, including repatriation.
8. Stimulate learning through training.
9. Reward learning activities.
10. Monitor your partner's learning.

Source: Adapted from Pucik (1988b).

since it is often difficult—and costly—to renegotiate HR policies for the benefit of one of the partners after the venture is launched.

In a learning alliance, the benefits of being clear about learning expectations among partners are self-evident. But what if the learning is to take place in the context of a competitive alliance? Does it make sense to be open about one's learning strategy, or should this remain a closely guarded secret?

The best, but probably hardest, way to deal with the competitive collaboration is to accept and be open about the "race to learn." Hiding the learning agenda increases mistrust and encourages opportunistic behavior. Both parties should be explicit about their learning objectives, put forward strategies to accomplish such learning together with their HRM implications, monitor mutual progress, and discuss with each other any important reservations. If the learning objectives cannot be openly discussed, then the merits of the whole alliance may become questionable.[68]

Once the strategy is set, it has to be clearly and consistently communicated across the organization. What is the purpose of the alliance? What are its boundaries? What needs to be learned? What is the partner expected to gain? Sometimes, companies are reluctant to communicate clearly that the alliance is actually competitive in nature because of the fear that such communication may set a bad tone for the relationship. In fact, the lack of communication does not change the reality; competition does not disappear because it is not talked about. The result is confusion and disbelief among the employees. Clear and unequivocal rules of engagement are essential.

While aligning HR processes to the learning strategy is vital, the responsibility for managing learning belongs to the line, not to HR or any other staff function. Who is responsible for learning sends a signal about how important this is. In a product development alliance between an American and Japanese high-tech firm, the HR function put itself forward as the champion of alliance learning, one of the explicit objectives for the alliance. [69] Many of the engineers who were expected to participate dismissed the whole activity as another "HR program." As for the Japanese, the role of the American HR "learning manager" remained a mystery throughout.

There are four basic HR areas where line management and the HR function can leverage alliance learning:

1. Selection and staffing
2. Training and development
3. Career planning
4. Performance management.

Staffing to Learn

The focus on learning starts with appropriate staffing, since the quantity and quality of people involved in the learning effort is fundamental to its credibility and success.[70] There is no such thing as free alliance learning. Strategic intent is no substitute for resource commitment.[71] Obviously, justifying the necessary staffing investments requires fixing clear and measurable learning outcomes. And when some of the desired knowledge resides with partner's employees, as is usually the case, then the partner's commitment to support the alliance with competent staff is also essential.

The most powerful learning often happens in joint alliance teams where employees from both partners work together on solving business issues. Here it is important to consider the difference between traditional in-company teams and alliance teams. A common company culture and above all shared long-term goals facilitate the team process when working in the company. In alliance teams, none of these "glue" factors exist, which introduces additional ambiguity and uncertainty into the learning environment. Selection criteria for alliance learning teams need to take into account the ability of employees to cope with this complexity.

Several years ago, a European consumer products company assigned a group of its fast-track employees to work on a team with its Chinese partner in developing strategies for expansion in China. All assignees had a record of successful postings to wholly owned subsidiaries in the region. However, the added difficulties of working with a partner organization required an adjustment in behavior, communication, and leadership style that several of them could not handle. The project team had to be restructured several times, causing delays and disruptions to the new product launch schedule.

Another critical staffing issue concerns the tradeoff between staffing for learning and staffing for effective execution. Consider the case of a joint development project between a US and a European telecommunication company. The main idea behind the collaboration is to pool the complementary technical capabilities of the two firms in order to deliver a novel solution to global customers. A second objective is to learn from each other so that both companies could improve their competitive offerings at home. The execution perspective suggests that each partner should field a team in its areas of special expertise, which will foster speed and efficiency in executing the business plan. However, if the partners only focus on what they are good at, then how will they acquire new skills? In order to learn, additional staff will have to be assigned to join the team, which might hinder progress in getting the job done, not to mention the additional cost that the project would have to bear. Getting this balance right requires a very clear understanding of the strategic objectives behind the alliance.

Learning to Learn

Different types of training and development activities can stimulate a climate conducive to effective alliance learning. Some training is best conducted internally, with attendance limited to the parent firm so that sensitive issues can be openly discussed. Internal training can help employees to understand the importance of the learning aims of the alliance, as well as how to learn through collaboration, and this type of training should take place early on in the alliance lifecycle. This is especially important if the alliance is or is likely to become competitive in nature.

When a US high-tech manufacturer decided to set up a joint new product development project with a Japanese partner, one of its first actions was to conduct a series of alliance management workshops for all key employees who would be directly or indirectly involved. The strategic logic of the project, its scope and boundaries, the learning objectives and opportunities as well as ideas on specific learning processes were presented and discussed in detail. As a result of these discussions, top management decided to redesign the alliance manager role in order to foster clearer accountability for learning and to adjust the resources allocated to specific learning activities.

Since alliance learning is based on relationships with the partner, joint training activities can enhance collaboration by raising both competence and trust. Team building and joint cross-cultural communication training are especially useful to speed up the getting-acquainted process. These can include intensive discussion on organizational values, structures, decision-making patterns, and the like, so that employees understand the context in which they are expected to work together. Communication problems may otherwise be attributed to "cultural differences"— people learn through such workshops that the real problems are often more tangible matters, such as different interpretations of performance expectations and rewards.

Manager Career Paths to Facilitate Learning

The rotation of employees through alliance positions and back to the parent firm facilitates the transfer of knowledge between the venture and the parent.[72] This requires addressing such issues as the harmonization of salaries/benefits to facilitate moving people back and forth. While these issues do not have to be addressed in the text of the partnership agreement, the transfers need to be planned carefully, especially with respect to future career expectations. [73] If the individual knows that the knowledge acquired in the venture will be put to good use on return, this increases his/her motivation to learn during the assignment.[74]

The need for an explicit strategy to transfer and implement acquired knowledge is well illustrated by the case of NUMMI. Only a handful of selected General Motors managers were assigned to the venture in the early years—apparently in order not to "contaminate" its new culture with old GM practices.[75] After two to three years of working with the Japanese, these managers were converted to the virtues of Toyota's lean manufacturing system, with a good grasp of its workings. They moved back to different GM locations with the mission of implementing the learning from NUMMI within the GM organization. All these efforts ended in failure—not because of inadequate personal learning but because there was never a critical mass of ex-NUMMI staff to make a difference.

Asymmetry in personnel transfers is usually a good indication of asymmetry in learning. While GM shuffled isolated individuals, Toyota trained more than 100 of its personnel on how to collaborate with NUMMI's American workforce. They were then assigned to Toyota's new wholly owned plant in Kentucky to replicate the NUMMI experience. In contrast, it took over a decade for General Motors to properly leverage its own acquired knowledge. An alumni team from the ventures at NUMMI and CAMI (GM's JV with Suzuki Motors) took charge of a decrepit East German car plant in Eisenach, and within three years they had turned it into the most advanced car manufacturing facility in Europe.[76] The knowledge that specific individuals had gained about Toyota's manufacturing system resulted in action only when there was a coherent organizational strategy for applying that learning.

Reinforcing Learning through Performance Management

While successful learning from alliances requires champions of knowledge creation — people who believe in the value of learning and who support the necessary investments — this may not be enough. Thus, alliance learning objectives should be translated into specific measures wherever possible, such as quality or productivity improvement, speed of new product development, or customer expansion.

In Motorola's 12-year alliance with Toshiba to design and manufacture advanced semiconductors (a typical competitive alliance), both companies used explicit learning targets. In Motorola's case, these were translated into individual-level objectives linked to rewards. The explicit measurements allowed both firms to mobilize their internal resources to support learning efforts. Externally, the tangible learning outcomes provided a valuable benchmark for assuring learning symmetry during the life of the alliance. It should be noted that the two executive positions considered most important in this alliance were split between the partners, but rotated every couple of years. One was the role of venture chief executive, the other that of human resource manager.

The climate for learning is best when alliance performance is satisfactory. When the alliance does not meet its expected targets, it may be more difficult to focus attention on the learning agenda, and necessary investments may be cut.[77] But even a failed alliance can be a source of valuable lessons. During its ambitious drive to internationalize in the early 1990s, GE organized a workshop in which executives who had been involved in failed alliances presented their experiences at a company forum. No amount of lectures on alliance strategy can match the impact of a high-level manager explaining how his assumptions about the foreign partner's business culture were wrong, resulting in a loss to GE of US$50 million. Why were these managers willing to share their painful experiences? Because sharing experience with others, positive or negative, was part of their performance objectives.

There are also alliances designed solely for the purpose of learning, where the business results are secondary, at least in the short term. However, problems quickly surface if the partners have different priorities in terms of business results versus learning, especially if this issue was not addressed during the formation of the partnership. In the words of a German manager in a Chinese JV: "We pay the tuition and they go to school." Conflicting priorities usually translate into ambiguous performance indicators for managers assigned to the venture, generating tension and disagreements among the executive team.

Successful learning alliances exhibit a bias for action. The best way of learning, sometimes the only way, is to do things together. "Don't just talk about learning and collaboration. Do it!" Such was the advice of a Japanese executive in charge of a highly successful learning alliance in the electronics industry. In this alliance, the approach to stimulating mutual learning was straightforward: focused joint development teams were assigned to specific tasks and then held responsible for achieving results, with the co-leaders being directly accountable to their parents. Those who were unwilling to share their know-how were quickly moved aside, those who were not keen to apply what they had learned did not last much longer. The race to learn lasted three years. With the learning mission accomplished, the alliance was dissolved, and the companies renewed their competition, both of them stronger than they would have been if they had operated alone.

THE EVOLVING ROLE OF ALLIANCES

Just as alliances themselves evolve, so the role of alliances as part of corporate strategy is evolving. One increasingly frequent pattern of alliance development is the emergence of alliance networks, whereby firms engage in multiple linkages and relationships, often across the whole spectrum of the value chain from R&D and manufacturing all the way to distribution and after-sales service.[78] Originally limited to the high-tech sector, in which multiple alliances were used as a protective device against obsolescence and other technology risks, today they can be found in a number of sectors, from airlines to fashion to pharmaceuticals. Such networks pose new challenges for HRM.

Managing Network Boundaries

Alliances among carriers in the airline industry are spreading. Such alliances promise the customer a seamless package of air services around the world. Code sharing (where a particular flight is shared by several airlines) is the most visible example. For example, traveling around the world with Star Alliance[79] may involve purchasing a ticket in Asia from Singapore Airlines, flying to Europe via Cape Town with South African Airlines, then on a Lufthansa plane serviced by United to the United States, and completing the final leg of the trip with a Japan-based air carrier. If a service complaint on such a journey were met with the response "sorry, but those people were not our employees," then customer loyalty would clearly be compromised. So this raises the question of who the employees work for—their own airline, or also for the Star Alliance?

From the time of reservation until the delivery of luggage at the end of the trip, airlines are a people-intensive business. Some argue that people and the service experience that they provide is the only differentiator among carriers.[80] Is it possible to deliver a seamless experience without coordinating or perhaps ultimately integrating HR strategies, ranging from the profile of who will be hired, to the kind of training they receive, and how they will get paid? How can the airlines share best practices? If at least some amount of coordination of airline HR standards is essential, then what kind of process is needed to make it happen? Who should lead it? And, where is the accountability?

These are new challenges for HRM, particularly since historically the approach for airlines has been strongly domestic in orientation. A typical airline today is international only because it flies to foreign locations. Most major airlines outside the United States are national flag carriers, with close relationships to their home government and strong national unions. Even if the respective management teams in an alliance agree on what behaviors are expected from the employees, the implementation of HR policies influencing these behaviors may be restricted by historic, institutional, and cultural factors.

In the case of Star Alliance, the Lufthansa Business School took a lead, perhaps because it had played an important role in transforming a bankrupt national carrier with a civil service mentality into one of the most profitable global leaders in the industry in the 1990s. Participation on its project-oriented programs was broadened to include partner members, with the aim of not only facilitating coordination, but also speeding up the internal transfer of learning from one partner to another. Most of the partners bring particular distinctive strengths — Singapore Airlines in customer bonding, United in logistics, Lufthansa itself in maintenance and managing learning. The HRM vision is that the alliance can be used for mutual learning, to convert weaknesses on the part of individual partners into collective strengths.

The HR challenge in airline alliances is an indicator of things to come. As one senior HR executive in a European airline put it: "Anybody who delivers value to my customer is my employee." This is a bold statement, not yet backed up by practice, but with broad implications that go well beyond the airline industry. The density of international alliances is increasing in all sectors as companies engage in a broader variety of relationships across the supply and value chains to the customer. This raises the question of where the boundary of HR's responsibility lies.

Alliances as a Journey towards Transnationalism

The ambiguity of boundaries in an alliance and the need to anticipate future shifts is only one of the tensions in this domain. Alliances are full of tensions between competition and collaboration, between global and local interests, between the venture and its parents, between leveraging and developing competences. Ambiguity and complexity are the norm. Bearing in mind that the principal challenge in the internationalization process is learning to manage tension, dilemma and duality, mastering alliance dilemmas and contradictions help firms to learn to manage transnational pressures.

In conclusion, let us therefore summarize some of the paradoxes and dualities that the multinational firm learns to confront through its experience in managing alliances.

- Learning how to manage differentiation. There is no such thing as "an alliance" — each alliance has different aims and strategic objectives, implying different courses of management and HR action. The parallel for the transnational is that it has to differentiate the roles of its units and subsidiaries, managing them in different ways.
- Learning to balance the fundamental tension between short-term performance and the long-term learning or knowledge creation that comes through collaboration (the exploitation versus exploration duality). As in the Chemco example, being a hands-off parent can be advantageous in the short term but it can carry a corresponding long-term cost.

- Learning to recognize and deal with trade-offs where a pathology can be created if one extreme is pushed too far. We see many examples in alliances—if either the interests of the venture itself or the interests of the parent are pushed too far, this can make it impossible to achieve the alliance aims. Similarly, the deal itself is critical, though excessive attention to detail can create rigidities (the first Star Alliance document was only one page long).
- Learning that a delicate balance is needed between external equity for expatriates and internal equity for long-term venture staff.
- Learning to take important but "soft" aims such as learning and convert them into "hard" objectives through measurement and accountability.
- Learning "to manage the future in the present"—the strategic aims of tomorrow may be quite different from those of today. Success of the venture must not be confused with the wider strategic aims of the parent.

Individuals involved in alliances face many challenges. They must learn how to manage boundaries, how to deal with ambiguity and conflicting interests, how to mold a culture that balances competing interests, and how to manage the tensions between exploitation (operating results, cash flow, and profit) and exploration (learning). One of the best breeding grounds for transnational managers may be alliance management.

TAKEAWAYS

1. Initially considered only as a means of securing market access, alliances today are an integral part of global strategies in all aspects of the value chain. Using alliances to generate new knowledge is increasingly important.
2. Alliances are mostly transitional entities; therefore, longevity is a poor measure of success. The aim is not to preserve the alliance at all costs but to contribute to the parents' competitive position.
3. There are four types of alliances: complementary, learning, resource, and competitive. Alliances are dynamic, migrating from one strategic orientation to another. Very few alliances remain complementary for long. Alliances among competitors are increasingly frequent, but they are also the most complex.
4. The approach to HRM is largely driven by the strategic objectives of the partnership. This requires a focus on both managing the interfaces with the parent companies as well as managing people inside the alliance itself.
5. The firm's HRM skills and reputation are assets when exploring and negotiating alliances. Do not enter a complex alliance unless both sides of the partnership have a good grasp of HRM basics. The greater the expected value from the alliance, the more HR support is required.
6. The failings of an alliance are too easily attributed to cultural differences when the real culprit may be the lack of attention to HRM issues, such as appropriate staffing, performance measures, compensation equity, and career management.
7. Equity control is a costly and relatively ineffective form of alliance control when compared to investing in a carefully designed and implemented HRM strategy.

8. Conflicting loyalties, complex relationships, and boundary management issues, coupled with uncertainty and instability, are characteristic of most alliances. Managers assigned to the alliance need high tolerance for ambiguity.

9. Alliance learning is neither automatic nor free—there must be clear learning targets, sufficient investment in people, and a tight alignment of HRM practices with learning objectives.

10. Alliances are full of tensions between competition and collaboration, between global and local interests, between leveraging and developing competences. Mastering alliances helps firms to learn to manage transnational pressures.

NOTES

1. Contractor and Lorange (1988: 9) identify seven overlapping objectives for the formation of various types of alliances: (1) risk reduction; (2) achievement of economies of scale and/or rationalization; (3) technology exchanges; (4) co-opting or blocking competition; (5) overcoming government-mandated trade or investment barriers; (6) facilitating initial international expansion; and, (7) linking the complementary contributions of the partners in a "value chain." See also Kogut (1988).

2. Hergert and Morris (1988); Gomes-Casseres (1988).

3. Cyr and Schneider (1996).

4. Kale and Anand (2006); Luo (2001).

5. Rossant (2000).

6. BAE sold its share in Airbus to EADS in 2006, transforming Airbus into a wholly owned subsidiary.

7. Kanter (1994); Morosini (1998).

8. Pucik (1988a).

9. Luo (2000).

10. Pucik (1988a); Cascio and Serapio (1991).

11. Yoshino and Rangan (1995) describe alliances as linkages based on non-traditional contracts that reflect the long-term and unique nature of the relationship between the partners, such as long-term product development collaboration, not just routine buy–sell agreements. They point out that not all relationships between businesses should be considered alliances—although the word "alliance" has become quite fashionable. They also note that not all equity-based alliances need to be joint ventures; partners may simply decide to invest in each other in order to cement the relationship, or one partner may make a unilateral investment in the other partner. Joint ventures can be further classified based on dominant (majority) or non-dominant (50:50) partnerships and where they fit in the organizational structure of the firm (integrated or stand-alone).

12. One of these classifications compares different forms of alliances, from licensing arrangements to manufacturing joint ventures, based on the degree of *interaction* between partners and alliance entity employees. This scale is determined by the level and frequency of interaction, and the number of people interacting (Cascio and Serapio, 1991). The intensity of focus on human resource factors and the involvement of the HR function are expected to mirror the intensity of people interaction.

    Another framework links the HR role with two dimensions of business strategy: the strategic importance of the cooperative venture for the parent organization and the degree of control over own resources by each partner (Lorange, 1996). Alliances fall into four groups: project-based cooperative networks, strings of renegotiated cooperative agreements, ventures with permanently complementary roles, and jointly owned business ventures. Each alliance type requires a different approach to staffing, personnel control, and evaluation.

Salk and Simonin (2003) offer a multidimensional map of alliances, encompassing their form, mode, cycle, organization, number of partners, and scope.

13. Fuji-Xerox was established in 1962 as a 50:50 partnership of Fuji Photo with Rank Xerox. Rank Xerox was absorbed into Xerox Corporation in 1997. Xerox Corporation transferred its China/Hong Kong Operations to Fuji Xerox in 2000 and Fuji Photo Film Co. raised its stake in the venture to 75 percent in 2001.

14. Inkpen (2005).

15. O'Reilly (1998).

16. Moxon, Roehl, and Truitt (1988).

17. When the Danone and Wahaha alliance in China collapsed, the workforce and managers in the joint ventures overwhelmingly supported the local partner. Danone discovered too late in the game that it had no management capability on the ground to protect its interests (Liu and Liu, 2007).

18. Hamel, Doz, and Prahalad (1989).

19. When business is profitable and provides advantages for both partners in the market as well as contributing to the creation of new knowledge, an alliance may continue even after the original learning objectives of the partners have been fulfilled. NUMMI is a good example.

20. Janger (1980).

21. Beamish (1985).

22. Killing (1982).

23. Zeira and Shenkar (1990).

24. Ulrich (1997).

25. Cole and Deskins (1988); Kenney and Florida (1993).

26. Pucik (1988b); Schuler (2000).

27. Parkhe (1991).

28. Goffee and Jones (1998).

29. Yoshino and Rangan (1995).

30. Spekman et al. (1998).

31. Yoshino and Rangan (1995).

32. Yoshino and Rangan (1995).

33. Cited by Yoshino and Rangan (1995: 146).

34. Lorange and Roos (1990).

35. Weiss (1994).

36. Killing (1997).

37. For a review of strategic control and staffing issues in international joint ventures, see Petrovic and Kakabadse (2003).

38. Adobor (2004).

39. Killing (1997).

40. Ferencikova and Pucik (1999).

41. Cascio and Serapio (1991).

42. Shenkar and Zeira (1990).

43. Killing (1982).

44. Tung (1988).

45. Lasserre (2008).

46. In the H P framework, workshop materials are organized in a 400-page proprietary manual, supported by an electronic library devoted to alliances. This serves as a repository for the know-how accumulated by H P over time. Internal knowledge management is important for learning from alliance experience and disseminating that know-how, complemented by internal training if the company has the resources to develop this.

47. Findings from Booz Allen's 1997 survey, as cited in Conference Board (1997).

48. This is one of the management development areas where Web-based distance learning may create opportunities for greater flexibility—providing access to just-in-time relevant information anywhere, including links to the in-company alliance knowledge base.

49. Conference Board (1997).

50. The context of the relationship will determine the most beneficial development applica-tions. However, off-the-shelf cultural training using the traditional "Doing Business with..." approach is probably of limited value—perhaps even dangerous in building stereotypes.

51. Mohr (2006).

52. Kerr (1995).

53. A common incentive plan (e.g. stock options) could be a logical tool to support synergy among alliance staff. However, among various tax issues that hinder harmonization of compensation across boundaries, incentive plans are probably the area where the differences are the widest. In some countries, such as France, even the initial exercise of stock option rights is a taxable event, which makes awarding options risky and expensive. In addition, even when tax benefits are available, there are differences—for example, which kind of stock option qualifies for tax benefits in the United States and in Germany.

54. Geringer and Frayne (1990).

55. Shenkar and Zeira (1990).

56. Sometimes, expatriate cost alone makes a difference between profit and loss. In a dispute between P&G and its Vietnamese partner, the local company alleged that the high cost of expatriates, brought in to deal with unanticipated product launch difficulties, caused the JV to incur major losses. The local partner was ultimately faced with the choice of accept-ing the JV bankruptcy or allowing P&G to gain equity control through a recapitalization that the local partner could not match.

57. Lorange (1996).

58. Non-equity alliances are generally temporary, and from a legal perspective, have no "direct" employees. Even those who are assigned to the alliance on a full time basis are typically paid by and report to their own parent. They expect to return to the parent organization, so that there is no confusion about the focus of their careers. Even if a foreign assignment is involved, a disciplined career development process, which ensures mentoring and a periodic dialogue with the employee, is generally sufficient to avoid a sense of isolation.

59. Child and Faulkner (1998); Parkhe (1993).

60. Barkema et al. (1997); Westney (1988).

61. Gomes-Casseres and McQuade (1992); Kennedy (1989).

62. Hamel (1991).

63. Pucik (1988b).

64. For example, when both partners perceive the partnership as a complementary or resource alliance, the collaboration can be mutually beneficial for a long period of time without much need for new knowledge creation. However, as we discussed earlier in the reading, the focus of the alliance often shifts as the partnership evolves.

65. Doz and Hamel (1998); Tsang (2002).

66. One of Europe's largest banks formed a learning alliance with a major Japanese bank about 20 years ago. The Japanese used this as an opportunity to send hundreds of managers over on two- to six-month learning assignments to Europe, during which time the Europeans only got around to sending two people to learn from the Japanese. By the time the financial services industry started to globalize seriously in the early 1990s and the Europeans awak-ened to the benefits of the deal, the Japanese had reached their learning objectives and lost interest in maintaining the alliance.

67. Hamel (1991).

68. Open discussion about learning needs may result in explicit limitations on knowledge exchange. A clear definition of what is in and what is out is preferable to fuzzy learning boundaries, which only encourage illicit behavior detrimental to trust between the partners.

69. Pucik and Van Weering (2000).

70.   Westney (1988); Schuler (2000); Cyr (1995); Cyr and Schneider (1996).
71.   Simonin (1999).
72.   Harrigan (1988); Pucik (1988b).
73.   Lei, Slocum, and Pitts (1997).
74.   Conversely, if there is a perceived imbalance in career opportunities, employees may either be willing to move to the alliance venture but less willing to return to the parent, or not want to move to the venture in the first place (Inkpen, 1997).
75.   Inkpen (2005); O'Reilly (1998).
76.   Haasen (1996).
77.   As argued by Inkpen (1998), unexploited learning opportunities may in turn lead to perceptions that the performance of the alliance is not satisfactory.
78.   Doz and Hamel (1998).
79.   Star Alliance links the operations of 13 major international airlines, such as United, Lufthansa, and Singapore. The member airlines coordinate schedules, share codes, match frequent flier programs, and coordinate activities to benefit from lower costs in areas such as plane maintenance, ground service, and purchasing.
80.   Pfeffer (1998).

REFERENCES

Adobor, H. (2004). Selecting management talent for joint ventures: A suggested framework. *Human Resource Management Review* 14(2): 161–178.

Barkema, H.G., O. Shenkar, F. Vermeulen, and J.H.J. Bell (1997). Working abroad, working with others: How firms learn to operate international joint ventures. *Academy of Management Journal* 40(2): 426–442.

Beamish, P.W. (1985). The characteristics of joint ventures in developed and developing countries. *Journal of World Business* 20(3): 13–19.

Cascio, W.F., and M.G. Serapio, Jr. (1991). Human resources systems in an international alliance: The undoing of a done deal? *Organizational Dynamics* 19(3): 63–74.

Child, J., and D. Faulkner (1998). *Strategies of cooperation: Managing alliances, networks, and joint ventures.* New York: Oxford University Press.

Cole, R.E., and D.R. Deskins, Jr. (1988). Racial factors in site location and employment patterns of Japanese auto firms in America. *California Management Review* 31(1): 9–22.

Conference Board (1997). HR challenges in mergers and acquisitions, *HR Executive Review* 5(2).

Contractor, F.J., and P. Lorange (1988). Why should firms cooperate? The strategy and economics basis for cooperative ventures. In *Cooperative strategies in international business*, eds. F.J. Contractor, and P. Lorange. (3–30) Lexington, MA: Lexington Books.

Cyr, D.J. (1995). *The human resource challenge of international joint ventures.* Westport, CT: Quorum Books.

Cyr, D.J., and S.C. Schneider (1996). Implications for learning: Human resource management in East-West joint ventures. *Organization Studies* 17(2): 207–226.

Doz, Y., and G. Hamel (1998). *Alliance advantage: The art of creating value through partnering.* Boston, MA: Harvard Business School Press.

Ferencikova, S., and V. Pucik (1999). Whirlpool Corporation: Entering Slovakia. Case study no. IMD-3-0796. IMD, Lausanne.

Geringer, M. J., and C.A. Frayne (1990). Human resource management and international joint venture control: A parent company perspective. *Management International Review* 30 (Special Issue): 103–120.

Goffee, R., and G. Jones (1998). *The character of a corporation: How your company's culture can make or break your business.* New York: Harper Business.

Gomes-Casseres, B. (1988). Joint venture cycles: The evolution of ownership strategies of US MNEs, 1945–75. In *Cooperative strategies in international business*, eds. F.J. Contractor, and P. Lorange. (111–128) Lexington, MA: Lexington Books.

Gomes-Casseres, B., and K. McQuade (1992). Xerox and Fuji Xerox. Case study no. 391156. Harvard Business School, Boston, MA.

Haasen, A. (1996). Opel Eisenach GmbH: Creating a high-productivity workplace. *Organizational Dynamics* 24(4): 80–85.

Hamel, G. (1991). Competition for competence and inter-partner learning within international strategic alliances. *Strategic Management Journal* (Summer Special Issue) 12: 83–103.

Hamel, G., Y. Doz, and C.K. Prahalad (1989). Collaborate with your competitors—and win. *Harvard Business Review* (January-February): 133–139.

Hamilton, S., and J. Zhang (2008). Danone & Wahaha: A bitter-sweet partnership. Case study no. IMD-3-1949. IMD, Lausanne.

Harrigan, K. (1988). Strategic alliances and partner asymmetries. *Management International Review* (Special Issue) 28: 53–72.

Hergert, M., and D. Morris (1988). Trends in international collaborative agreements. In *Cooperative strategies in international business*, eds. F.J. Contractor, and P. Lorange. (99–109) Lexington, MA: Lexington Books.

Inkpen, A.C. (1997). An examination of knowledge management in international joint venture. In *Cooperative strategies: North American perspectives*, eds. P.W. Beamish and J.P. Killing. San Francisco, CA: New Lexington Press.

Inkpen, A.C. (1998). Learning and knowledge acquisition through international strategic alliances. *Academy of Management Executive* 12(4): 69–80.

Inkpen, A.C., and E.W.K. Tsang (2005). Social capital, networks, and knowledge transfer. *The Academy of Management Review* 30(1): 146–165.

Janger, A.H. (1980). *Organization of international joint ventures*. New York: Conference Board.

Kale, P., and J. Anand. (2006). The decline of emerging economy joint ventures: The case of India. *California Management Review* 48(3): 62–76.

Kanter, R.M. (1994). Collaborative advantage: The art of alliances. *Harvard Business Review* (July-August): 96–108.

Kennedy, C. (1989). Xerox charts a new strategic direction. *Long Range Planning* 22(1): 10–17.

Kenney, M., and R. Florida (1993). *Beyond mass production: The Japanese system and its transfer to the US*. New York: Oxford University Press.

Kerr, S. (1995). An academic classic: On the folly of rewarding A, while hoping for B. *Academy of Management Executive* 9(1): 7–14.

Killing, J.P. (1982). How to make a global joint venture work. *Harvard Business Review* (May-June): 120–127.

Killing, J.P. (1997). International joint ventures: Managing after the deal is signed. *Perspectives for Managers*, no. 1. Lausanne: IMD.

Kogut, B. (1988). Joint ventures: Theoretical and empirical perspectives. *Strategic Management Journal* 9(4): 319–332.

Lasserre, P. (2008). *Global strategic management*. London: Palgrave Macmillan.

Lei, D., J.W. Slocum, Jr., and R. Pitts (1997). Building cooperative advantage: Managing strategic alliances to promote organizational learning. *Journal of World Business* 32(3): 203–223.

Liu, G., and D. Liu (2007). Danone and Wahaha: China-style divorce (A) and (B). Case study nos. 207-021-1 & 207-022-1. China Europe International Business School (CEIBS), Shanghai.

Lorange, P. (1996). A strategic human resource perspective applied to multinational cooperative ventures. *International Studies of Management and Organization* 26(1): 87–103.

Lorange, P., and J. Roos (1990). Formation of cooperative ventures: Competence mix of the management teams. *Management International Review* (Special Issue) 30: 69–86.

Luo, Y. (2000). *Partnering with Chinese firms: Lessons for international managers*. Aldershot: Ashgate.

Luo, Y. (2001). *Strategy, structure, and performance of MNCs in China*. Westport, CT: Greenwood Publishing Group.

McGregor, J. (2005). *One billion customers: Lessons from the front lines of doing business in China*. London: Nicholas Brealey.

Mohr, A.T. (2006). A multiple constituency approach to IJM performance management. *Journal of World Business* 41(3): 247–260.

Morosini, P. (1998). *Managing cultural differences: Effective strategy and execution across cultures in global corporate alliances*. Oxford and New York: Pergamon.

Moxon, R.W., T.W. Roehl, and J. Truitt (1988). International cooperative ventures in the commercial aircraft industry: Gains, sure, but what's my share? In *Cooperative strategies in international business*, eds. F.J. Contractor, and P. Lorange. (255–277) Lexington, MA: Lexington Books.

O'Reilly, C.A. (1998). New united motors manufacturing, Inc. (NUMMI). Case study. Stanford Graduate School of Business, Stanford.

Parkhe, A. (1991). Interfirm diversity, organizational learning, and longevity in global strategic alliances. *Journal of International Business Studies* 22(4): 579–601.

Parkhe, A. (1993). Partner nationality and the structure-performance relationship in strategic alliances. *Organization Science* 4(2): 301–324.

Petrovic, J., and N.K. Kakabadse (2003). Strategic staffing of international joint ventures: An integrative perspective for future research. *Management Decisions* 41(4): 394–406.

Pfeffer, J. (1998). *The human equation: Building profits by putting people first*. Boston, MA: Harvard Business School Press.

Pucik, V. (1988a). Strategic alliances with the Japanese: Implications for human resource management. In *Cooperative strategies in international business*, eds. F.J. Contractor, and P. Lorange. (487–498) Lexington, MA: Lexington Books.

Pucik, V. (1988b). Strategic alliances, organizational learning, and competitive advantage: The HRM agenda. *Human Resource Management* 27(1): 77–93.

Pucik, V., S. Fiorella, and E. van Weering (2000). American Diagnostic Systems. Case study no. IMD-3-0870. IMD, Lausanne.

Reich, R.B., and E.D. Mankin (1986). Joint ventures with Japan give away our future. *Harvard Business Review*, 64(2): 78–86.

Rossant, J. (2000). Airbus: Birth of a giant. *Business Week*.

Salk, J.E., and B.L. Simonin (2003). Beyond alliances: Towards a meta-theory of collaborative learning. In *The Blackwell handbook of organizational learning and knowledge management*, eds. M. Easterby-Smith, and M.A. Lyles. (253–277) Malden, MA: Blackwell.

Schuler, R.S. (2000). HR issues in international joint ventures and alliances. In *Human resource management: A critical text*, ed. J. Storey. (314–316) London: International Thomson.

Shenkar, O., and Y. Zeira (1990). International joint ventures: A tough test for HR. *Personnel* 67(1): 26–31.

Simonin, B.L. (1999). Ambiguity and process of knowledge transfer in strategic alliances. *Strategic Management Journal* 20(7): 596–623.

Spekman, R.E., L. Isabella, T. MacAvoy, and T.M. Forbes III (1998). Alliance management: A view from the past and a look to the future. *Journal of Management Studies* 35(6): 747–772.

Tsang, E.W.K. (2002). Acquiring knowledge by foreign partners from international joint ventures in a transition economy: Learning-by-doing and learning myopia. *Strategic Management Journal* 23(9): 835–854.

Tung, R.L. (1988). Career issues in international assignments. *Academy of Management Executive* 2(3): 241–244.

Ulrich, D. (1997). *Human resource champions: The next agenda for adding value and delivering results*. Boston, MA: Harvard Business School Press.

Weiss, S.E. (1994). Negotiating with 'Romans'—Part 1. *Sloan Management Review* 35(2): 51–61.

Westney, D.E. (1988). Domestic foreign learning curves in managing international cooperative strategies. In *Cooperative strategies in international business,* eds. F.J. Contractor, and P. Lorange. (332–337) Lexington, MA: Lexington Books.

Yoshino, M., and U.S. Rangan (1995). *Strategic alliances: An entrepreneurial approach to globalization.* Cambridge, MA: Harvard Business School Press.

Zeira, Y., and O. Shenkar (1990). Interactive and specific parent characteristics: Implications for management and human resources in international joint ventures. *Management International Review* (Special Issue) 30: 7–22.

Satu Teerikangas, Günter K. Stahl, Ingmar Björkman, and Mark E. Mendenhall

IHRM ISSUES IN MERGERS AND ACQUISITIONS

INTRODUCTION

THIS CHAPTER ADDRESSES THE KEY international human resource management concerns when undertaking mergers and acquisitions (M&As) across borders. M&As are a form of an inter-organizational encounter; thus they share, in part, features with other forms of inter-organizational encounters, including joint ventures, alliances or outsourcing arrangements (Borys & Jemison, 1989; Parmigiani & Rivera-Santos, 2011). The distinguishing feature of M&A transactions is that beyond mere strategic change they result in a change in ownership. It is this change of ownership that lies at the heart of many of the human resource-related concerns experienced in many M&As. Indeed, for the employee, a change of ownership represents not only a change in employer, but a change in the psychological contract with one's employer as well.

The study of M&As had an early focus on the management of the M&A process, starting with the works of Mace and Montgomery (1962), and Howell (1970). A financial and strategic focus arose in the 1970s, followed by an interest in the people and cultural sides of M&A activity in the 1980s. The 1990s saw an increase in work on the cross-border dimensions of M&As, including their cultural and language implications for managers (Cartwright, 1998; Cartwright & Schoenberg, 2006). The early twenty-first century has seen identity and power considerations emerge, and samples have been broadened from US and European acquirers to also include acquiring firms from emerging markets, including China and India (Teerikangas et al., 2012). Although studied through many lenses, including finance and strategy

(Haleblian et al., 2009; Faulkner et al., 2012), the analysis in this chapter focuses on extant theoretical and empirical studies on the sociocultural dimensions underlying M&A activity.

The first section of this chapter serves as an extended introduction to the M&A phenomenon and its human dimensions. Trust, M&A process management, and cultural dynamics are addressed in subsequent sections, and the chapter concludes with implications for HR practice and future research.

WHAT ARE M&AS?

The collective term, "mergers and acquisitions," is somewhat misleading given that in terms of transaction numbers 98 percent of all M&A transactions are acquisitions (Buckley & Ghauri, 2002). In acquisitions, the "acquiring" firm purchases the "target" or "acquired" firm either using cash or stock, whereas in mergers two or more organizations are combined into one new entity. From a managerial perspective, this means that acquisitions often incur a "takeover" approach by the acquiring firm, which seemingly has the upper hand in the transaction. The post-acquisition era can also be termed a "merger" even though the transaction has been an acquisition. Thus, the term "merger" can be used metaphorically to portray an image of a "collective, shared" future, and thus alleviate acquired firm employee concerns (Faulkner et al., 2012).

Taking a historical lens, throughout the twentieth century, fueled by the internationalization of firms, the globalization of the business world, and the liberalization of trade, M&A activity has increased rapidly, becoming by the dawn of the twenty-first century a worldwide phenomenon spanning most sectors and industries (Kolev et al., 2012), and driving industry consolidation. Firms have engaged in M&A activity for various reasons. Strategic rationales include product or market expansion, internationalization, access to resources including technology, research and development, people, and elimination of excess capacity on the market. M&A are at times also defensive moves to purchase a competitor or protect against a takeover. In addition to these overt motives, unstated psychological motives have also been reported, including empire-building, managerial hubris, and overconfidence, CEO narcissism, the thrill of making deals, and the systemic effect of herd-like behavior (Sudarsanam, 2012). In essence, a view of M&A activity emerges that combines not only its strategic and financial dimensions but also its less overtly visible psychological and human dimensions as well.

The apparent corporate obsession with M&A activity that is suggested by the rising numbers of M&A deals over the past three decades is not matched by the performance of M&As. Although the vending side has been found to gain financial profit from such transactions, the acquiring firms' financial performance, whether measured in months or years, portrays a more challenging image (King et al., 2004; Haleblian et al., 2009). It appears that many acquiring firms never gain financially from their M&A activity, and when they do, the positive impact is visible three to twelve years after the transaction (Biggadike, 1979; Birkinshaw et al., 2000; Quah & Young, 2005).

THE CENTRALITY OF THE HUMAN FACTOR IN M&A ACTIVITY

In seeking reasons for the difficulty in making M&As succeed, a number of causal factors have been brought forward by scholars. The difficulty of post-deal integration and implementation management is typically seen as "the" challenge in making M&As succeed (Haspeslagh & Jemison, 1991; Larsson & Finkelstein, 1999). The question is not only one of change management or strategy implementation, both of which are difficult endeavors in their own right, but further one of combining two hitherto separate organizations into one. This combination of organizations introduces cultural clashes, be it at the level of team, organizational, or national cultures (Teerikangas & Véry, 2006; Stahl & Voigt, 2008). The change of ownership further represents a violation to the employees' psychological contract; this enforced, and often sudden ownership change tends to be a cause of great concern for employees that in turn causes high levels of uncertainty, stress, and turnover rates in M&As (Napier, 1989; Cartwright and Cooper, 1990). Issues of identity also arise, as do power conflicts between the two sides as they struggle for authority in the new regime (Giessner et al., 2012; Stahl et al., 2013; Tienari & Vaara, 2012).

Beyond these challenges in the post-deal implementation phase, the pre-deal phase is also mired by human resource challenges (Sudarsanam, 2012). How should the target firm be valued? How should the target firm's intangible assets be valued? What psychological biases will intervene in the decision-making processes leading to the acquisition? Is there sufficient time to assess the target firm (Harding & Rouse, 2007)? Is the information for the valuations reliable?

If well managed, the human side in M&A has been found to have a long-lasting impact on the performance of the acquisition and the buying firm. These consequences have been quantified by Larsson & Finkelstein (1999), who found that employee motivation enables the realization of synergies potentially available through an acquisition. Birkinshaw et al. (2000) conclude that a well managed human integration has an enabling effect on the progress of integration. In contrast, stress, uncertainty, and rumoring in the post-merger integration time period have been found to negatively impact the financial performance of the parent firm (Buono & Bowditch, 1989; Davy et al., 1998; Marks & Mirvis, 1985) amounting even to "the loss of two hours of productive work per employee per day" (Wishard, 1985 quoted by Napier, 1989: 275). High levels of uncertainty have, moreover, been evidenced to lead to rumoring (Ivancevich et al., 1987) that runs counter to effective work. M&As, if badly managed, also lead to labor and managerial turnover (Hambrick & Cannella, 1993; Hayes, 1979; Krug & Nigh, 2001; Véry et al., 1997) and higher degrees of absenteeism (Davy et al., 1998), both of which have a potentially detrimental effect on firm effectiveness. The significance of the people dimension in M&As gains more weight if considered in terms of the long-term nature of these reactions—they persist and tend even to become emphasized over time (Schweiger & Denisi, 1991). In the following section, as we proceed to an overview of the human and managerial considerations in M&As, our aim is to give voice to some of the prominent themes that this broad body of work and experience has led us to identify.

DEALING WITH EMPLOYEE UNCERTAINTIES IN M&AS

How do Employees React to M&As?

Prior research has emphasized the negative impact of M&As on employees in the acquired firm. This has been termed the "merger syndrome" (Buono & Bowditch, 1989; Marks & Mirvis, 1985), referring to the psychological challenge caused by the change that an M&A represents to employees. Moreover, negative reactions, such as increased levels of employee uncertainty (Buono & Bowditch, 1989; Marks, 1982; Risberg, 2001), rising levels of stress (Cartwright & Cooper, 1992), lower morale (Sinetar, 1981), and rumoring (Ivancevich et al., 1987) have been shown to occur. Feelings of loss and deprived identity abound (Cartwright & Cooper, 1990), as do worries about job security (Mace & Montgomery, 1962). Acquisitions have even been described in terms of "organizational death" (Marks & Vansteenskiste, 2008). These studies tend to paint a bleak and negative image of the human toll resulting from M&As.

Although they do exist, the positive effects of M&As on the employees concerned have received less attention than the negative effects (Teerikangas, 2012). In particular, findings from recent studies lend evidence to the presence of positive employee reactions. In a comparative study of hostile versus friendly mergers, Fairfield-Sonn et al. (2002) found that whilst hostile mergers result in long-term negative employee reactions, friendly mergers result in long-term positive reactions. Further, certain kinds of post-acquisition changes (e.g. in human resource management practices and organizational culture), have been shown to have a positive effect on employee attitudes, as recently exemplified by Froese et al. (2007) in a study of cross-border acquisitions in Korea. Teerikangas (2012) found that target firm employees react positively to forthcoming transactions. This occurs especially when the transaction is viewed as an opportunity. In such cases, acquired firm managers become proactive agents leading the transformation, and in so doing engage the organization in the change process.

Other factors come into play to provide a nuanced view of employee reactions to M&As. In phase-based studies of human reactions during M&A (e.g. Ashkanasy & Holmes, 1995; Buono & Bowditch, 1989; Graves, 1981; Ivancevich et al., 1987; Schweiger et al., 1987), employee reactions have been shown to lean toward the negative in the pre-deal phase, and gradually, depending on the quality of integration management and the way in which the acquisition is experienced, turn to the positive in the post-acquisition era. In summary, it would seem that M&As are greeted with a mix of positive and negative reactions by employees; however, the media and many management scholars have tended to emphasize negative reactions of employees to M&A activity.

What Explains Employee Reactions to M&A?

Previous research has suggested that the extent of culture shock (Buono et al., 1985; Buono & Bowditch, 1989) and the direction of post-deal changes implemented (Cartwright & Cooper, 1992; Froese et al., 2007) influence acquired firm employee reactions. However, the issue of whether domestic or cross-border deals result in higher levels of stress has produced conflicting evidence (Larsson & Risberg, 1998; Véry et al., 1996; Weber, 1996). Nahavandi and Malekzadeh (1988) see that the match between the preferred acculturation modes of involved firms dictates the likely degree of "acculturative stress" following acquisitions. In their paper, the acquired reactions to the buying firm are conceptualized as stemming from the degree of partner attractiveness and the extent to which the acquired firm wishes to preserve its own culture. Expectations of the future have also been found to predict employee reactions (Dackert et al., 2003). In summary, the greater the cultural discrepancy between the organizations involved and the less attractive the partner and the vision of a future with the partner, the more likely it is that employees will react negatively to an acquisition.

It has been established that the manner in which the change process is managed has a significant effect on the outcome of a merger or acquisition (Kavanagh & Ashkanasy, 2006). For example, leadership has been found to affect the extent to which post-deal cultural change is accepted (Kavanagh & Ashkanasy, 2006). Where the effect of leadership style on post-merger satisfaction has been studied (Covin et al., 1997), the characteristics of transformational leadership (i.e. a leadership style involving charisma, inspiration, and transcendental goals) have been found to be the strongest predictors of merger satisfaction. Yet, the ability and competence of managers to effectively deal with a process as complex as a merger or acquisition has been questioned (Covin et al., 1997; Kavanagh & Ashkanasy, 2006).

The significance of timely and honest communication throughout the M&A process has been emphasized (Bastien, 1987; Ivancevich et al., 1987; Schweiger & Denisi, 1991). A host of practical tips (e.g. with regard to the use of courses, workshops, and psychological counseling) have also been suggested as a means of dealing with the human challenge in M&As (Buono & Bowditch, 1989; Marks & Mirvis, 2001). The buying firm's cooperative pre-deal attitudes have been found to help steer employee reactions toward the positive (Marks, 1991; Schweiger et al., 1987). The way that employees are treated matters, and thus respect has been emphasized as a critical variable to M&A success (Krug & Nigh, 2001). The significance of retaining key target firm talent, for example, through their early involvement (Krug & Nigh, 2001; Schuler et al., 2004) and mutual relationship building (Marks & Mirvis, 2001) has also been highlighted in the literature, and the role of the human resource function pre and post-deal has been emphasized by some scholars as being critical (Antila, 2006; Lorange, 1996; Schuler et al., 2004).

BUILDING AND MAINTAINING TRUST IN M&A

Recently, the role of trust has been discussed as a critical success factor in M&A processes. Whilst few attempts have been made to systematically examine trust dynamics in M&As, indirect evidence about the critical role of trust in the M&A process can be drawn from a large body of research that suggests that the development of trust is critical to the successful formation and implementation of cooperative alliances between firms, such as joint ventures, R&D collaborations, and marketing partnerships (Child, 2001; Inkpen & Currall, 2004; Krishnan et al., 2006; Zaheer et al., 1998). For example, in joint ventures factors such as open communication and information exchange, task coordination, informal agreements, and levels of surveillance are all manifestations of trust between joint venture partners (Currall & Inkpen, 2002; Krishnan et al., 2006).

In the context of M&As, case studies (e.g. Chua et al., 2005; Olie, 1994) as well as interviews with managers and employees affected by M&As (e.g. Krug & Nigh, 2001) suggest that trust is critical to post-merger integration process dynamics and outcomes because it helps management to overcome resistance, gain commitment from the employees, and develop a sense of shared identity. It has been observed that the turbulence following the announcement of a merger or an acquisition creates a breeding ground for distrust because the situation is unpredictable, easy to misinterpret, and people tend to feel vulnerable (Hurley, 2006; Krug & Nigh, 2001; Marks & Mirvis, 2001). Social networks and mutual understanding established through years of working together are sometimes destroyed in an instant. With a new organization, a new top management team, and a new superior, there is little trust initially and employees are left wondering what the next wave of changes will bring. Employees may perceive a merger as a psychological contract violation or a breach of trust, requiring renegotiation of the broken psychological contract (Buono & Bowditch, 1989; Cartwright & Cooper, 1992). The period following the announcement of a merger or takeover is thus one of vulnerability and intense risk assessment in which employees have to judge whether the acquiring firm's management (and their own management) can be trusted.

The following quote from Daniel Vasella, CEO of Novartis, concerning the merger that created the Swiss pharmaceutical giant highlights both the importance and fragility of trust in M&As:

> Only in a climate of trust are people willing to strive for the slightly impossible, to make decisions on their own, to take initiative, to feel accountable; trust is a prerequisite for working together effectively; trust is also an ally to fight bureaucracy. . . . We must fill this vacuum as fast as we can, we must restore confidence [after the merger]. We must earn it by "walking the talk," with candour, integrity, openness, fairness . . . We need to create a culture based on trust.
>
> (Chua et al., 2005: 391–392)

Despite the large body of anecdotal evidence supporting the critical role of trust in M&As, surprisingly little is known about the factors that facilitate or hinder the development of trust in acquired or merging organizations. Stahl and Sitkin (2010) propose that factors related to the firms' relationship history and inter-firm distance, as well as process variables related to the acquirer's integration approach affect target firm member trust in the acquiring firms' management (see Figure 1).

Relationship History

The extent to which the members of a target firm perceive the acquirer to be trustworthy is a function of prior "inter-firm contact" or, in the absence of a history of

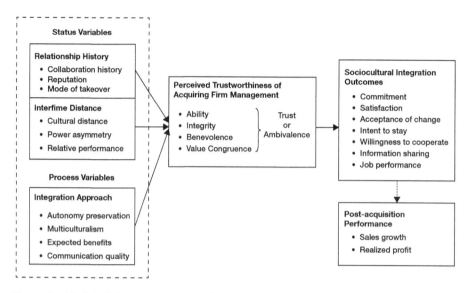

Figure 1. Model of the antecedents and consequences of trust in M&As

collaboration, the "reputation" of the acquirer. A large body of research on the role of trust in work groups, strategic alliances, and socially embedded partnerships suggests that trust evolves over time through repeated interactions (Inkpen & Currall, 2004; Ring & Van de Ven, 1992; Zaheer et al., 1998). If members of the combining firms had a conflict-rich, inequitable, or otherwise problematic exchange prior to the acquisition (e.g. a failed joint venture), this is likely to limit the potential for trust to emerge. Another important factor in determining target firm members' trust is the "mode of takeover" or tone of the negotiations (whether it is friendly or hostile). It has been argued that hostile takeover tactics can result in sharp inter-organizational conflict and difficulties integrating acquired firms (Buono & Bowditch, 1989; Hitt et al., 2001). Hambrick and Cannella (1993) have observed that the atmosphere surrounding a hostile takeover is often characterized by bitterness and acrimony, making smooth social integration after the deal less likely. This is supported by research showing that hostile takeover attempts lead to resistance and increased "in-group out-group" bias (Elsass & Veiga, 1994; Krug & Nigh, 2001).

Inter-firm Distance

Cultural distance, power asymmetry, and relative performance may affect trustworthiness attributions through perceptions of inter-firm distance. Although studies that tested the impact of cultural distance on post-acquisition integration process dynamics and outcomes have yielded inconclusive results (see Cartwright & Schoenberg, 2006; Stahl & Voigt, 2008; Teerikangas & Véry, 2006; Weber & Drori, 2008 for reviews), trust research has clearly shown that shared norms and values facilitate the development of trust and the emergence of a shared identity (Lewicki et al., 1998; Sarkar et al., 1997). Conversely, trust can erode and the potential for conflict increase when a person or group is perceived as not sharing key values (Sitkin & Roth, 1993).

Social Identity Theory suggests that in a merger situation, the mere existence of two different cultures is enough to lead to in-group/out-group bias and conflict: organizational members, whilst emphasizing their own positive distinctiveness, tend to exaggerate the differences between their own and the other's culture (e.g. Hogg & Terry, 2000; Kleppestø, 2005; Vaara, 2003). In cross-border acquisitions, feelings of resentment, hostility, and mistrust may be further fueled by cultural stereotypes, prejudices and xenophobia (Vaara, 2003). In addition to cultural distance, "differences in power" between the acquiring and acquired firm is likely to affect trust dynamics. In the case of asymmetrical power relations, target firm members' needs are often overlooked or trivialized by the acquirer (Datta & Grant, 1990; Hambrick & Cannella, 1993; Marks & Mirvis, 2001). Acquiring executives tend to adopt an attitude of superiority and treat the members of the target firm as inferior, thus leading to status degradation and the voluntary departure of key employees (Hambrick & Cannella, 1993; Krug & Nigh, 2001).

"Poor target firm performance" in the past relative to the acquirer may have a similar effect, as it is likely to increase an acquirer's tendencies toward arrogance and domination. For instance, Hambrick and Cannella (1993) have observed that even if executives of a poorly performing firm are not fired outright after their acquisition, they may feel inferior or depart voluntarily because they are anticipating the dominating behaviors of their "conquerors." Lower-level employees are likely to experience anxiety from fears that they might lose their jobs or be unable to meet the acquirer's performance standards. Paradoxically, though, it has been observed that when a smaller or underperforming firm is acquired by a significantly larger or financially healthy buyer, the target firm members often welcome the takeover and are energized to become part of something larger or more successful than themselves (e.g. Chaudhuri, 2005; Evans et al., 2002). This is especially true when they see the acquiring company as being a savior or having a more enlightened culture, or when they see other positive outcomes in being associated with the acquirer (better pay, more prestige, etc.). Thus, there is not a general effect of power asymmetry and relative performance; rather, the effect on target firm members' trust will depend on the perceived personal risk and benefits resulting from the merger or takeover, as discussed below.

Integration Approach

In addition to the status variables discussed above, trust is influenced by a set of process variables relating to the acquirer's post-acquisition integration approach, most notably the removal of autonomy. Autonomy removal can be devastating from the perspective of the members of the target firm and lead to feelings of helplessness and open hostility (Hambrick & Cannella, 1993; Marks & Mirvis, 2001), as managers and employees vigorously defend their autonomy—a situation that Datta and Grant (1990) have termed the "conquering army syndrome." Research suggests that the degree to which an acquiring firm tends to impose its policies, norms, and expectations on the target firm partly depends on the acquirer's "multiculturalism" (Nahavandi & Malekzadeh, 1988; Pablo, 1994). The term multiculturalism refers to the degree to which an organization values cultural diversity and is willing to tolerate and encourage it (Nahavandi & Malekzadeh, 1988). A multicultural acquirer considers diversity an asset, and is therefore likely to allow an acquired firm to retain its own values and modus operandi. In contrast, a unicultural acquirer emphasizes conformity and adherence to a unique organizational ideology, and is therefore more likely to impose its culture on the target firm. Furthermore, there is evidence that the "expected benefits" of the organizational changes that result from the takeover, particularly the quality of the post-acquisition reward and job security changes, is a critical factor in determining employees' reactions to an acquisition (Cartwright & Cooper, 1992; Van Dick et al., 2006). For instance, Bartels et al. (2006) found that the expected utility of a merger (anticipated benefits such as salary increases or more job security) was the strongest predictor of employees' identification with the post-merger organization. Chaudhuri (2005), in an in-depth case study of one of Cisco's acquisitions, found that strong financial incentives and a vision of the merged entity that included an important role for the acquired employees helped to promote trust and encouraged acquired employees to stay.

Finally, the "quality of communication" is a key factor in determining the level of trust that target firm members have in the acquirer's management. M&As are associated with high degrees of stress and uncertainty for the individuals affected by them, especially those of the target firm. Providing acquired employees with credible and relevant information can reduce this uncertainty and mitigate feelings of mistrust and suspicion (Bastien, 1987; Schweiger & Denisi, 1991), as well as increase employees' identification with the post-merger organization (Ellis et al., 2009). A lack of credible and open communication, on the other hand, has been found to result in intense rumor activity, anxiety over job security, and feelings of suspicion and mistrust (Buono & Bowditch, 1989; Marks & Mirvis, 1998).

Preliminary evidence from several empirical studies (Stahl et al., 2006, 2012; Stahl et al., 2011) suggests that the degree to which target firm members trust the acquiring firm management affects a variety of behavioral and attitudinal outcomes, including employee commitment (e.g. Weber et al., 1996), resistance (e.g. Larsson & Finkelstein, 1999), turnover (e.g. Schoenberg, 2004), level of acculturation (e.g. Larsson & Lubatkin, 2001), and cooperation (e.g. Weber et al., 1996), and, ultimately, the post-acquisition performance. For example, the results of a case survey (Stahl et al., 2011) suggest that whilst aspects of the combining firms' relationship history and inter-firm distance, such as pre-acquisition performance differences, power asymmetry, and cultural distance, seem to be relatively poor predictors of trust, integration process variables such as the acquirer's tolerance for diversity, the adoption of a hands-off integration approach, the quality of communication, and the quality of the post-acquisition reward and job security changes are major factors influencing target firm member trust. This study further suggests that not only does trust have a powerful effect on target firm members' attitudes and behaviors but it may also contribute to the realization of synergies, as reflected in accounting-based performance improvements. This is consistent with research on post-merger integration that indicates that aspects of the sociocultural integration process, such as the acquirer's ability to build an atmosphere of mutual respect and trust, facilitate the transfer of capabilities, resource sharing and learning; and, conversely, sociocultural and human resources problems can undermine the realization of projected synergies (e.g. Birkinshaw et al., 2000; Larsson & Finkelstein, 1999; Stahl & Voigt, 2008).

MANAGING M&AS

Having acknowledged the challenge that M&As represent to employees and the need for the establishment of mutual trust, the focus in this section shifts to an appreciation for the variables associated with M&A process management. The role of the HR function is to support managers in the challenging task of M&A management; the better the HR professionals comprehend M&A process dynamics, the better they are able to support managers throughout its phases.

Overview of the M&A Process

Whilst insights to the managing of M&As can be found in early publications (e.g. Mace & Montgomery, 1962; Kitching, 1967; Howell, 1970), it was the seminal work of Jemison and Sitkin (1986) and Haspeslagh and Jemison (1991) that formally posited a "process" perspective to M&As. On the basis of a series of in-depth case studies of international acquisitions, Haspeslagh and Jemison (1991) articulated the tenet that what distinguishes successful acquisitions is an understanding of the processes through which acquisition decisions are made and through which acquisition integration is managed.

Prior to this perspective, many scholars claimed that acquisitions were viewed as individual deals, with a primary focus on price. Moreover, the decision-making process leading to acquisitions tended to be considered a sequential, linear process involving setting strategic objectives, search and screening, strategic evaluation, financial evaluation, negotiation, agreement, and integration. In contrast, the process view advocated by Haspeslagh and Jemison (1991) portrays acquisitions not as independent, one-off deals, but rather as belonging to a firm's long-term renewal strategy. What is more, they contend, whilst concluding a deal is significant, value is realized only if the target is rightly integrated—hence, "integration management" matters. Their key argument is that instead of viewing (pre-acquisition) decision-making and (post-acquisition) management as separate activities and phases, as they often are in M&A practice, M&A scholars and practicing managers should treat them as interdependent processes.

This leads to the view of the acquisition process as consisting of two interrelated phases: the phase preceding the deal (the pre-acquisition phase) and the phase following the deal (the post-acquisition phase). The aim of the pre-acquisition evaluation process is to decide whether to engage in an acquisition or not. The acquiring company has a strategic rationale for the purchase, including potential value creation, against which it assesses the attractiveness of the deal. The integration process can be defined as a guided process to implement organizational change affecting mainly the acquired unit (possibly the acquiring organization too, depending on the integration strategy), and ultimately the parties involved, with the aim of aligning the new unit with the sought strategic direction.

Not all M&As are alike, and this bears consequences on the human side of M&A dynamics. The more the transaction incurs integration and post-deal change, the more likely it is that "people needs" will require significant attention from management. Several typologies of M&A integration strategies have been proposed (see e.g. Kitching, 1967; Howell, 1970; Buono & Bowditch, 1989; Napier, 1989; Cartwright & Cooper, 1992; Bower, 2001). An often cited approach is the typology proposed by Haspeslagh and Jemison (1991), which identifies four integration strategies for the post-deal time period: "absorption," "symbiosis," "preservation," and "holding." These integration strategies differ with respect to the desired degree of target firm strategic interdependence, and target firm autonomy.

In "holding" acquisitions, the acquiring firm does not seek to integrate the target nor create value from the deal; rather, it might seek financial integration or managerial cooperation. This strategy is appropriate for the acquisition of unrelated entities, or acquisitions that are not inherently strategic in nature. In the "preservation" mode, the target firm retains autonomy, usually as a separate subsidiary or division of the acquiring firm. It is likely that little integration takes place, and as a result, the target is not likely to incur much change in the post-deal era. By contrast, in "absorption" acquisitions where the aim is explicitly to "absorb" the acquired firm into the acquiring firm's organization, a strong integration of the acquired firm into the acquiring firm is expected. Integration is likely to be a "one-way only" affair, where the acquiring firm's best practices and operational processes are imposed on the target with little interest in mutual learning or knowledge transfer.

In "symbiotic" acquisitions the aim is to ensure a balance between target firm autonomy on the one hand, and integration into the acquiring firm on the other hand. Central to the implementation of the symbiotic approach is the reciprocal exchange of knowledge, skills, and capabilities between the two firms. Given that the process is inherently bi-directional, the management of symbiotic acquisitions is deemed the most challenging of all integration types (Haspeslagh & Jemison, 1991).

The four-quadrant typology of integration strategies suggests that not all acquisitions are alike in terms of their integration processes, management challenges, and requirements. Using this typology, integration management seems to be the most critical and demanding in "absorption" or "symbiotic" acquisitions. One limitation of this typological scheme is that the integration strategies adopted by acquiring firms rarely fit neatly into existing typologies. In practice, acquiring firms tend to adopt integration strategies that combine various features of different integration approaches (Haspeslagh & Jemison, 1991). Another limitation is that the typology assumes that acquiring firms explicitly decide on post-acquisition integration strategies. This decision might not always be explicit, nor might it involve the entire firm. In practice, there are likely to be a myriad of different post-deal strategies implemented throughout the organizations. Ultimately, the number of different post-acquisition strategic regimes is reflected in the number of parallel integration processes at work (e.g. Teerikangas, 2006).

Best Practices in Integration Management

Planning

Planning has been referred to in the research literature as a critical factor in ensuring the success of M&A integration. As early as 1970, Howell's study of over 40 acquiring companies found many to be poorly prepared for acquisitions because of a lack of planning. In their survey of 751 cross-border acquisitions, Colombo et al. (2007) confirm that planning, through its positive impact on the post-acquisition climate and managerial appointments in the target firm, significantly impacts acquisition performance.

Speed and Timing

Timing is also critical to the success of acquisitions. There is an ongoing debate about the significance of the speed of integration to M&A success. There are diverging views as to whether a quick or slow start is best to accomplish the acquisition (Schweiger et al., 1993; Schweiger & Goulet, 2000; Ranft & Lord, 2002; Stahl et al., 2013). Whilst practitioner cases point to the need for "swift" action (De Noble et al., 1988; Epstein, 2004), academic findings have maintained a more nuanced stance. Among proponents of swift post-deal action, the immediate post-deal period has been referred to as the "window of opportunity" (Ranft & Lord, 2002). In the weeks and months following the acquisition, the target organization expects and awaits change to take place. Implementing change has been found to be easier in this period because change is expected.

A link to performance has also been identified. In their large-scale survey of acquisitions related to Italian firms, Colombo et al. (2007) found a negative correlation between a temporal lag (i.e. time between deal closure and start of integration) and performance and climate. It is in this respect that the concept and argued importance of the "first 100 days" (e.g. Angwin, 2004) is well-known in M&A practice. In a study of General Electric (GE) Capital's acquisitions, Ashkenas et al. (1998) reported that the first 100 days are typically spent creating an integration plan, whilst some argue that the first 100 days constitute the timeframe during which all critical actions should be launched. Yet, in a study of whether and how the first 100 days impact the performance of acquisitions, Angwin (2004) found little evidence of such an impact, thus suggesting that this timeframe might be "more of convenience than substance" (2004: 428). On the other hand, Angwin (2004) found a correlation between the volume of changes implemented in the first 100 days and perceptions of success three-four years post-deal.

By contrast, in the context of cross-border acquisitions, recent research evidence suggests that changes should not be made immediately after the deal. Rather, post-deal changes should be made over time, as the acquiring firm will be better able to target the changes required, once its knowledge of the acquired organization increases (Quah & Young, 2005). It is possible that both slow and rapid integration speeds may be necessary at different intervals. Teerikangas (2006) found that rapid action is needed at the early start of the integration phase with regard to communications and changes that are implemented soon after the deal in order to ensure that acquired firm staff understands what is taking place. Thereafter, a gradual integration pace created space for making longer-term decisions on more significant, larger-scale changes required in the acquired firm. These findings suggest that both kinds of integration actions are needed and that the choice between quick versus slow pace is not an "either/or" proposition. Timing and speed are critical, yet they depend on the deal type, context, relatedness of firms, and the nature of the acquisition/integration strategy.

Socialization and Interactions

M&As are at heart social encounters—encounters of people who differ from each other. In this respect, it is not surprising that socialization and interactions have been found to be critical to successful post-deal integration. Calori et al. (1994) discussed the importance of "informal control mechanisms" (Ouchi, 1981; Bartlett and Ghoshal, 1989) in M&A integration. Larsson and Lubatkin (2001) emphasized the importance of "social controls" in fostering acculturation following M&As. The role of mutual interaction to the success of M&A integration has been addressed by Buono and Bowditch (1989), Olie (1990), Cartwright and Cooper (1992), and Larsson and Finkelstein (1999). These studies call for recognition of the importance of exchange and interaction in promoting learning, sharing knowledge, and ensuring successful post-deal integration (Schweiger & Goulet, 2000; Larsson & Lubatkin, 2001). Given the significance of knowledge transfer in the context of R&D acquisitions, work on the integration of acquired R&D units Håkanson (1995) also emphasizes the importance of informal means of communication. Larsson and Finkelstein (1999) regard the degree of organizational integration and the ensuing degree of inter-firm interaction as significant for the success of M&As.

Communications

The centrality of integration-related communications has been found to be a critical factor to M&A success (Bastien, 1987; Ivancevich et al., 1987; Schweiger & Denisi, 1991). Haspeslagh and Jemison (1991) posit that inter-firm interactions are "at the heart of integration" (1991: 117). In their study of technology acquisitions, Ranft and Lord (2002) found that frequent and open communications facilitate post-deal integration. In particular, they found the richness of exchanges to be determinative of the effectiveness of communication (i.e. face-to-face contact has more effect than virtual contact). They concluded that rich communications in turn support knowledge transfer and the establishment of a climate favorable to change. Similarly, Ellis et al. (2009) found that the degree of open communications is positively related to value creation during and after integration. Involving target firm managers in decision-making was found to have positive performance effects only if previously supported by open communications. Intriguingly, communications and involvement impact acquisition performance in different ways: whilst open communications have a positive effect on financial returns, involvement has a positive effect on gains in market position. This would mean that managers involved in acquisitions should revert to different managerial approaches, depending on the desired objectives in the deal (Ellis et al., 2009).

The role of HR is critical with respect to post-deal communication effectiveness. Notwithstanding, this role will bear different consequences depending on the size of the acquiring firm. In larger organizations the communications department coordinates external communications, whilst HR typically is in charge of within-firm communications and coaching management teams with respect to the right tone of communicating information. In the Nokia Siemens Networks merger in 2007, HR coordinated a series of town-hall meetings for staff in certain countries at the start of the merger, where the merger's strategic aims and typical psychological issues that surface in M&As were presented and discussed. In contrast, in smaller-sized firms that potentially lack a proper HR function per se, communication protocols remain the remit of the founding owner or entrepreneur, with all the risks and opportunities that such a state of affairs involves.

Attitudes

Attitudes have been found to derive both value enhancing and value destructive effects on the progress and outcomes of M&As. The M&A literature shows the importance of the buying firm's attitudes in enhancing mutual cooperation in the post-deal phase (Olie, 1994; Deiser, 1994), the need to create an atmosphere supportive of capability transfer (Haspeslagh & Jemison, 1991), the role of "assertive tolerance" in managing the post-deal integration phase (Napier et al., 1993), and the importance of fairness during post-acquisition integration (Hambrick & Cannella, 1993). The importance of "respect" in the way acquired firm management and employees are treated was noted by Krug and Nigh (2001) in their study of acquired firm executive departures.

Recent findings support this view. A study of European and American firms' acquisitions in Eastern Germany (Thomson & McNamara, 2001) cites the role of "corporate entrepreneurship" in enabling integration, thereby affecting acquisition success.[1] In her study of acquisitions by worldwide industry leaders, Kanter (2009) found that successful buyers have been able to integrate and motivate new staff members. Such "winners" can be distinguished from other firms on the basis of their attitudes: they do not act like conquerors. Rather, they act as "welcoming hosts," "eager learners," and "fixers vs. destroyers." Teerikangas (2012) found that attitudes of cooperation and mutuality need to be balanced with attitudes associated with enabling change in order for post-merger success to occur.

Whilst fairness and equality are often raised as cornerstones of successful mergers, cases of failed mergers point to the potential ambiguities therein. In a study of the failed Telia and Telenor merger, Meyer and Altenborg (2007) contend that the notion of equality is in practice not an objective concept but subject to a myriad of local interpretations. Moreover, they point out that in the context of a merger the principles of equality in roles and responsibilities might lead to "structural paralysis" because decisions cannot be taken, and national interests cannot be bridged.

Scholars have also cautioned against the presence of potentially negative attitudes in the aftermath of M&As. Deiser (1994) alludes to the impact of the buying firm's attitude in the post-acquisition process and advises against the buying firm blindly imposing its ideas upon the acquired firm. The presence of a "not-invented-here" syndrome has been referred to by Blake and Mouton (1984), and Buono and Bowditch (1989). They note that interpersonal relations can be tense in times of M&As, even moving toward hostility owing to group dynamics. They caution that employees are likely to resent ideas not coming from their group. Inter-organizational problems in times of M&As typically relate to "competing claims," "secrecy vs. deception" (Buono & Bowditch, 1989), "we vs. they," "superior vs. inferior," "attack and defend," and "win vs. lose" behaviors (Marks, 1991). These findings touch on the debate on inter-group relations in social psychology, where it is argued that social conditions should be positive in order for inter-group encounters to succeed. Otherwise, the groups will revert to dysfunctional behavior, through which each will favor their in-group members at the expense of the out-group members (Sherif, 1962; Tajfel, 1978).

Among potentially destructive attitudes, Haspeslagh and Jemison (1991) identify "determinism" as a problem in acquisitions. By determinism, they mean situations, where managers cling to their initial goals for the deal regardless of mounting evidence of the need to change these objectives. The source of determinism can be traced to how and when the acquisition decision was justified in the pre-deal phase. Indeed, in retrospect, the initial justification for the acquisition might be flawed, based on limited information, or might have been purposefully communicated in simplistic terms in order to be understood. Also, unexpected events such as industry or contextual changes might have prompted changes to the initial strategy.

To summarize, attitudes can bear positively or negatively on M&As. Whilst attitudes of fairness, experimentation, learning, ambition, and humility underlie experiences of successful integration, one must beware of the potential for destructive reactions in the post-acquisition encounter of any two organizations.

Who is in Charge of Integration?

Extant research has found the following roles as significantly impacting M&A success: top management teams, change agents, acquired firm managers, and key target firm talent. These roles will be reviewed in this section.

Top Management Attention

In addition to demanding the attention of business or integration managers, acquisitions require the attention of senior managers (Haspeslagh & Jemison, 1991). Without such attention a "leadership vacuum" might occur in the post-acquisition phase. At worst, top managers forget the acquisition soon after the deal. Yet this omission masks the targets' need for top management attention and steering. At worst, such inattention can result in the failure to make, implement, or effectively communicate decisions throughout the organization. The role of top management is to set the right atmosphere or tone for integration, so that both sides are interested in sharing ideas and are willing to collaborate in a mutually respectful manner. Haspeslagh and Jemison (1991) term this "institutional leadership."

Integration Teams and Boundary-spanning Change Roles

Who is responsible for integration? In their study of GE's acquisition process across a number of deals, Ashkenas et al. (1998) identified the integration manager as key to the success of the company's acquisitions. The authors note that it was after significant acquisition experience that GE realized the appointment of a manager in charge of the integration process to be critical to acquisition success. Regarding GE Capital's acquisitions, Ashkenas et al. (1998) identified the integration manager's role as (1) facilitating and managing integration activities, (2) helping the acquired business to understand GE Capital, (3) helping GE Capital to understand the target business, and (4) building a connective tissue between the organizations. In a follow-up study of companies across industries, Ashkenas and Francis (2000) clarified the role of the integration manager; they observed that so-called "enlightened" companies typically appoint an executive, "guide" or "shepherd," to coordinate post-acquisition phase activities.

In a similar vein, Haspeslagh and Farquhar (1994) found interface management or "gatekeeping" between the buying and acquired firms to be a critical variable that impacts the progress of post-acquisition integration. Effectively this task is incidental to the role of the "integration manager." In acquisitions where exchange and integration between the combined firms is to be expected, "interface management" becomes important to the extent that "the quality of interface management becomes a key to unlocking acquisition value" (Haspeslagh & Jemison, 1991: 156). The role of interface management is to control the pace, nature, and timing of inter-firm interactions. Depending on the integration approach, interface management serves a gatekeeping function to: (1) provide transitional management in a full integration "absorption" acquisition, (2) support mutual knowledge transfer in a "symbiotic acquisition," or (3) protect target firm boundaries in a "preservation" strategy where granting target firm autonomy is high priority.

In a recent study of Nordic multinational firms' cross-border acquisitions (Teerikangas et al., 2011), the presence and proactivity of integration managers was found to have a performance enhancing versus a destructive impact. In the pre-acquisition phase, integration managers support the capturing of value by relationship building. Negative media coverage or internal rumoring about a forthcoming transaction can result in unnecessary staff turnover. If change is sought post-deal, then the presence of an integration manager (team) is critical with respect to pursuing the set targets, implementing change, and supporting the processes of knowledge transfer and cultural change. Also, the target firm's knowledge base needs to be nurtured and respected, lest its value come to be under-utilized.

What capabilities are required of such individuals? Excellent integration managers combine professional expertise with human touch and linguistic and cultural intelligence (Teerikangas, 2006). In a study of individuals engaged in boundary-spanning activities in times of organizational change including mergers, Balogun et al. (2005) found that these individuals typically align agendas and sell the initiative, manipulate situations to ensure that the message is effectively delivered, gather intelligence, and lobby for help from senior managers. A key factor characterizing these individuals is that they work within social networks and strongly rely on their networks to achieve results. By implication, the work of these individuals is highly network-dependent.

Use Insiders or Outsiders in Management?

A major discussion in the M&A field centers on the destiny of top managers in the post-deal regime: Should top managers stay or go? Angwin and Meadows (2009) suggest that the choice of whether to use target or outsider managers depends on the integration strategy. Where there is low interdependency between the firms or the target is given considerable autonomy following the deal (i.e. "preservation" acquisitions), the tendency to use insiders (i.e. target firm managers) is predominant. Insiders also appear to be favored when the target is granted little autonomy and is in financial difficulty (it is assumed that an insider is best positioned to deal with the dire situation). In contrast, where there is high interdependency between the firms (i.e. "absorption" acquisitions), and change and new perspectives are required, the tendency to opt for outsiders in top managerial positions prevails. In "symbiotic" acquisitions, firms typically start with an insider manager, only to replace him or her later by an outsider. In "holding" acquisitions, although insiders are predominant, outsiders, when used, tend to achieve better results. In sum, the integration strategy and the acquisition context dictate the choice of management.

The Selling Side and Involving Acquired Firm Management

Evidence advises involving the acquired organization (Haspeslagh & Farquhar, 1994; Angwin, 2004; Graebner, 2004) as a means of fostering integration and mutual learning. Véry and Schweiger (2001) stressed the importance of such involvement, especially where the acquisition occurred in a country in which the acquiring firm had no prior experience. Graebner's (2004) study of technology acquisitions suggested that target firm managers have a distinct and crucial role in ensuring the successful integration of their entity into the new parent firm. These managers usually enable realizing expected and serendipitous value creation in acquisitions. In order to realize expected values, acquired firm managers typically engage in "mobilizing actions" that help maintain the momentum of change, be it by setting goals and clear tasks for target firm employees or coordinating with acquiring firm management for support. Moreover, in successful acquisitions, acquired firm leaders also engage in "mitigating actions" that address personnel issues and uncertainties in times of the change. Graebner (2004) further found that serendipitous value was created when acquired firm engineers and managers were provided with cross-organizational responsibilities. Teerikangas (2006) claims that when target firm managers are pro-acquisition, talent retention bears beneficial consequences—it is appreciated as a sign of trust.

Acting locally, they can drive the target's "self"-integration. However, this choice bears negative consequences if target firm managers resist the new regime.

The majority of M&A research has focused on the perspective of the buying firm. However, the work of Graebner and Eisenhardt (2004) takes the seller's view in their research on M&As. They find that sellers are triggered to be positive toward their firm being acquired if they are facing strategic hurdles or have a personal motivation to sell the firm due to fear of failure, stress, financial gain, or dilution risk. Moreover, target company leaders were found to be ready to sell their firm when they identified combination potential between the acquiring and target firms, or when organizational rapport (e.g. cultural fit, personal fit, trust, and respect) existed between the two firms. Graebner and Eisenhardt (2004) provide not only a seller-focused but also a relationship-focused perspective on acquisitions, in contrast to a buyer-focused, and agency-theory focus that is common in the existing literature. In light of this result, Graebner and Eisenhardt (2004) posit the acquisition process not as a takeover, but rather at best as a courtship.

Key Talent

In terms of ensuring future performance, retaining key employees is critical. This applies especially to sectors that are highly reliant on human capital. In biotechnology acquisitions, retaining engineers is perhaps more critical than retaining senior managers, owing primarily to the unique expertise of the former. In their study of targets acquired by pharmaceutical companies, Paruchuri et al. (2006) found that negative effects of acquisitions are not homogenous across employee types; rather, acquisitions affect the productivity of some employees more than others, depending on their particular skill sets. They also found that acquisition integration has an overall negative effect on the productivity of inventors following acquisitions, and that inventors whose work is far from the acquiring firm's core tend to suffer more than others. Moreover, engineers who boasted a strong pre-acquisition network are likely to suffer most in the aftermath of a takeover because the acquisition and resulting integration tend to redefine the structure of social networks. Whilst these changes are constructive from an integration perspective, they are destructive from an innovation perspective because inventors tend to rely on strong social networks to collaborate. It generally takes some time after the acquisition for these networks to become functional again.

Synthesis

The task of achieving M&A integration rests on a number of shoulders. It falls primarily on acquiring firm top management, who should be fully committed to integration, and should visibly express this commitment to the members of the target firm. Second, successful integration rests on the work of transition teams and integration managers who are appointed for an interim period to coordinate change efforts. At best, such teams should involve members of both organizations. In particular, involving an acquired firm's managers has been found to have beneficial effects. The question of whether acquired firm managers should stay or go depends on the acquisition and integration type.

CULTURAL CLASHES AND CULTURAL CHANGE IN M&AS

Beyond employee concerns and the challenge of post-deal integration, a central question concerns the nature and dynamics of cultural encounters during M&A activities. This question has been studied through the lenses of performance consequences, change dynamics, cultural change, and the intercultural dimensions inherent in M&As.

Culture and M&A Performance

Many M&A scholars who studied the impact of organizational culture differences on the performance of domestic transactions found contradictory evidence. Whilst Datta (1991), Chatterjee et al. (1992), and Weber and Camerer (2003) find that cultural differences have a negative impact on performance, Krishnan et al. (1997) found that differences in the functional backgrounds of the top management team have a positive impact. However, Weber (1996) did not find a direct relationship between cultural differences and M&A financial performance but he did find that corporate culture differences have a negative impact on both integration progress as well as commitment. These relationships are likely to be stronger for service than for manufacturing firms, and the impact of cultural differences is also likely to be stronger, when high degrees of integration and autonomy removal are sought (Weber, 1996). Interestingly, Datta's (1991) findings were robust regardless of the degree of integration; thus, even the question of "depth of integration" needs to be treated with caution.

In parallel to the above studies, another group of scholars explored the impact of national culture differences on the performance of international M&As. Here, two types of findings are identified. On the one hand, national culture differences are found to bear positive outcomes (Morosini et al., 1998; Chakrabarti et al., 2009; Gubbi et al., 2010). On the other hand, researchers argue for a more nuanced picture of the impact of national culture on post-deal performance. Slangen (2006) found that the effect of national culture depends on the degree of integration (i.e. it is not static from one deal to another). Brock (2005) and Reus and Lamont (2009) argue that national cultures have an indirect effect on acquisition performance through their effect on "interim" metrics, such as resource sharing and integration (Brock, 2005), communication, retention, and understanding. Also, differing dimensions of cultures were found to have differing performance effects (Brock, 2005), and buyers from economically more developed countries fared better as well (Chakrabarti et al., 2009; Gubbi et al., 2010). The performance effect becomes more positive the greater the distance between the participating firms' home countries (Morosini et al., 1998; Chakrabarti et al., 2009). Finally, Reus and Lamont (2009) noted a simultaneous negative and positive impact of national cultures.

Research on the dual impact of organizational and national culture on M&A performance points to an increasingly nuanced, yet mixed picture. Whilst organizational culture is found to positively affect attitudes, stress, and behaviors (Weber et al.,1996), it is in parallel found to increase post-acquisition conflict (Sarala, 2010), and not affect knowledge transfer (Sarala and Vaara, 2010). National culture is found to negatively impact attitudes, stress and behaviors (Weber et al., 1996), positively impact acculturative stress (Véry et al., 1996), have no impact on post-acquisition conflict (Sarala, 2010), and provide opportunities for knowledge transfer (Sarala & Vaara, 2010). Further, buyers from some countries would tend to outperform others (Véry et al., 1997). In general, related deals perform better the longer the timeframe of the measurement (Véry et al., 1997).

In synthesis, the issue of whether and how cultural differences impact merger and acquisition performance continues to be open to debate (Stahl & Voigt, 2008; Teerikangas & Véry, 2006). The field has moved from an initial focus on US deals, to a focus also on European, Asian, and worldwide transactions. Whilst the work was initially dominated by a focus on organizational culture, this early shift was rapidly replaced by studies on national culture, and studies combining the effects of national and organizational cultures on performance. It is worth noting that studies rely on existing models of national cultural differences, especially Hofstede's (2004) or more recently House et al.'s (2004) dimensions. Likewise, organizational culture is largely proxied using differences at the level of management teams. In terms of performance measurement, the study of organizational or national cultures on M&A performance has largely relied on financial metrics, whilst the study of national and organizational cultures has operationalized performance using non-financial measures (Teerikangas, 2012).

The Cultural Clash in M&As

If interest in the domestic dimensions of culture clash following M&As has been relatively scant since the 1980s, this seeming disinterest has been replaced by an emerging interest in the cultural dynamics at stake in cross-border M&As.

Cultures Clashing in Domestic M&As

Among the early studies was that of Marks (1982), who found that cultural clashes occur in the merging of domestic firms. Buono et al. (1985) introduced the concept of "culture shock" occurring when two organizational cultures merge. As culture provides a frame of life for its members, cultural changes are among the most difficult for people to cope with. Buono et al. (1985) found that a culture shock follows an organizational merger and affects the members by contributing to changing feelings and discomfort. Despite the employees' rational understanding of the need to merge, culture shock impacts their willingness to view the deal in a positive light. These findings were among the first in the study of M&As to point to the fact that the cultural side of mergers warrants attention (Buono et al., 1985; Buono & Bowditch, 1989).

The introduction of the concept of acculturation by Nahavandi and Malekzadeh (1988) was the next conceptual milestone in this stream of research. The concept of acculturation, borrowed from cross-cultural psychology (Berry, 1983), represents the cultural adaptation process and alternative scenarios in the merging of two organizational cultures. The choice of the acculturative mode depends on both the acquirer and the acquired company. When an acculturative mode accepted by both companies is chosen, less acculturative stress is expected to occur. The contribution is significant in that it recognizes different approaches and choices for cultural integration. The concept of acculturative stress is useful in highlighting the emotional distress incurred by the acquired company's members. It is also noted that different sub-units within the company can experience different levels of acculturative stress, and unrelated acquisitions can be made to succeed if the correct acculturative mode is chosen. A year later, Buono et al. (1985) defined four modes of integrating cultures in M&As: cultural pluralism, cultural blending, cultural takeover, and cultural resistance. These modes mirror the acculturative modes presented by Nahavandi and Malekzadeh (1988).

These early initiatives based on either US domestic mergers or conceptual work have thereafter maintained an almost "unrivalled" position in the literature on M&As given that few scholars have thereafter sought to study the cultural dynamics of domestic deals. A notable step in this direction was the introduction of the stepfamily metaphor (Allred et al., 2005) as a means of understanding the challenge of managing M&As. The two phenomena are argued to share similar characteristics (e.g. culture shock, high levels of stress, role ambiguity), tasks (e.g. establishing new relationships), and issues (e.g. high failure rates, power issues). Based on the stepfamily literature, they posit that challenges experienced in times of M&As could be extrapolated from those experienced by stepfamilies. Drawing a parallel, this would mean that M&As would suffer from biological discrimination (i.e. buying firm discrimination), incomplete institutionalization (i.e. leading to misunderstandings), and deficit-comparison (i.e. acquired firms ending in a disadvantageous position as compared to the buying firm and competitors). In order to sustain high success rates in M&As, Allred et al. (2005) suggest that firms: (a) acquire similar targets, (b) properly evaluate the target prior to the deal, and (c) ensure the buying firm's full commitment to the venture.

Cultural Clashes in Cross-border M&As

The first papers to address cultural encounters in cross-border mergers were by Olie (1990, 1994), who focused on cross-border merger integration. He argued that both organizational and national cultures meet in cross-border mergers, with the latter influencing the former. Olie (1990) found obstacles in international M&As as being related to the way people react as culture-bearers. First, there is resistance to changing working methods and opposition against any alienation from the national character of the environment. Second, there is a perceived threat to one's own position in the company. A third issue concerns nationalism existing in the countries owing to their historical backgrounds. He argued that integration success of cross-border mergers depends on the degree of interaction between the two firms, the degree of integration, and the extent to which the firms value their original cultures. In a later study, Olie (1994) looked at the nation and firm-specific factors influencing cross-border mergers. He found that the degree of compatibility of administrative practices, management styles, organizational structures and cultures, kind and degree of post-merger consolidation, the extent to which parties value and want to retain their organizational integrity, and the nature of the relationship between the two organizations together contribute to explain the difficulties encountered in the post-merger integration process in a cross-border merger setting.

Building on the work of Nahavandi and Malekzadeh (1988) in a cross-border setting, Larsson (1993) found that national cultures create additional barriers to the development of joint corporate cultures in the post-acquisition phase. In a similar vein, Malekzadeh and Nahavandi (1998) discuss acculturation in the context of cross-border M&As, wherein double-layered acculturation (Barkema & Bell, 1996), that is, changes in both national and corporate cultures, occurs. Despite these advances, there is a relative scarcity of research on the dual impact of national and organizational cultures on cross-border M&As.

The Management of Cultural Change Following M&As

Another stream of research in the literature has focused on cultural change following M&As (Buono & Bowditch, 1989; Olie, 1990; Cartwright & Cooper, 1992, 1993; Schweiger et al., 1993; David & Singh, 1994; Forstmann, 1998). The direction of cultural change has been found to dictate the ease of change, especially if the change is paralleled with increased levels of openness in the organizational culture (Cartwright & Cooper, 1992, 1993). Where beliefs are widely shared and strongly held, cultural change is likely to be challenging (Buono & Bowditch, 1989). Cartwright and Cooper (1992) identify four approaches to culture change: aggressive, conciliative, corrosive, and indoctrinative. They found that a combinative use of these approaches is fruitful, and argue that culture change should begin with an understanding of both participating cultures followed by an "unfreezing" of these cultures. Next, a positive and realistic view of the future should be presented to people in both organizations—this ensures that organizational members are involved on a wide-scale and creates a realistic timescale for the integration process. Finally, it is necessary to monitor the change process and take corrective action where necessary.

Sales and Mirvis (1984) argue that managing a culture in transition requires understanding not only the factors influencing acculturation, but also the processes underlying them. They contend that the new culture must first perceive a threat to its culture. This phase can best be managed by preparing strategically and emotionally for the change, rehearsing the possible implications, and developing ground rules for cross-cultural contact. Second, there should be cross-cultural contact between the two firms. The management of this phase entails managing the processes of polarization, evaluation and ethnocentrism as well as the conflicts resulting from cultural differences. Third, acculturation begins. This phase should be accompanied by a conscious scanning of culture and its re-examination.

Buono et al. (1985) unfold the process of culture change and identify the following factors as meaningful ways of influencing integration in M&As: changing the behavior of organizational members, justifying this change, using cultural communication to facilitate the change, hiring and socializing new recruits to speed up the change, and removing deviants. The extent to which cultural change can be achieved has also been questioned (Buono & Bowditch, 1989), and the importance of attitudes (Napier et al., 1993; Deiser, 1994; Morosini, 1998) when implementing cultural change has been viewed as critical. In a review of existing literature, Schraeder and Self (2003) found that training, support, and socialization are important means of fostering acculturation in the post-acquisition period.

In her study of organizational culture change following M&As, Bijlsma-Frankema (2001) identified factors that promote the progress of cultural integration following M&A. The identified factors include the degree of mutual trust between the parties, which is then strengthened by shared norms, and further enabled by dialogue—even in instances of deviance or conflict resolution. Whilst Bijlsma-Frankema (2001) notes that the factors have been already identified in the literature, the same factors were present in all of the successful M&A cases in her study, and likewise absent in the unsuccessful cases.

More recent findings focus on the human reactions to cultural change as well as the practice of cultural changes in cross-border M&As. Styhre et al. (2006) point to "cultural anxieties" that are raised in employees' minds in times of cross-border mergers. In other words, cultural changes following cross-border mergers represent an emotionally painful process for organizational members who have to gradually let go of their previous culture whilst developing an allegiance toward the new one.

In a study of cultural change following a cross-border acquisition in the retail sector in the UK, Pioch (2007) found that whilst top management sees post-acquisition cultural change from a company-wide integration perspective, the larger part of employees experience a daily differentiation of cultures at the shop floor. The former have internalized the new organizational culture at Schein's (1985) level of assumptions, whereas for the majority of employees only surface-level cultural changes are experienced. Moreover, Pioch points to the presence and impact of industrial cultures and notes that in industries that increasingly share global practices, such as the retail sector, an acquisition does not necessarily entail as much change as one might assume, given that industry-wide, the sector has been globally moving toward a similar direction for some time.

A study of research and development unit acquisitions found that post-acquisition structural and cultural integration processes are intertwined (Teerikangas & Laamanen, 2013). Thus, cultural integration begins only once structural integration is in progress. All the while, national and organizational cultures impede structural integration if structural integration is not adjusted to the target's cultural regime. Once structural integration begins, cultural change is then facilitated in an iterative manner over time by the emerging, new structure. These findings demonstrate the mutually reinforcing effects of structural and cultural integration in cross-border acquisitions.

Calling for recognition of the parallel presence of espoused versus practiced cultures in organizations, Teerikangas and Irrmann (2014) present post-acquisition cultural change as a dyadic, bipolar process, whereby targets cohabit the space between espoused and practiced values. Depending on the acquirer's cultural maturity, targets align with either the espoused or the practiced culture. Further, whereas previous research parallels cultural change with explicit "initiatives," it is argued that cultural change results also from all post-acquisition integration activity, that is, integration and interactions drive cultural change. This emergent nature of cultural change reflects Brannen and Salk's (2000) work on negotiated cultures in joint ventures, where organizational cultures emerge dynamically. Whereas much of the research on culture in M&As assumes that firms not only "have" cultures but, further, "know" their cultures and cultural integration strategies, the studied acquisitions pointed to greater naiveté and lacking cultural awareness than is suggested (Teerikangas & Irrmann, 2014).

In conclusion, existing research has highlighted that there are alternative approaches to cultural change and that cultural change occurs in phases. Best practices with regard to enabling cultural change revolve around attitudes conveying trust and safety, communications, dialogue, clarity of goals, and employee rotation. However, there are complexities surrounding cultural change; for example, the links between cultural change and the overall progress of integration need to be considered, and cultural change relates to change toward both espoused and practiced acquiring firm cultures.

Cross-cultural Interactions and Dynamics

How do national cultural differences bear upon the progress of cross-border acquisitions? A series of studies on acquirer behavior across national boundaries confirm that acquirers from different countries differ in their approach toward due diligence (Angwin, 2000) and integration management (Dunning, 1958; Jaeger, 1983; Calori et al., 1994; Lubatkin et al., 1998; Child et al., 2001; Larsson & Lubatkin, 2001; Pitkethly et al., 2003; Teerikangas, 2006). These differences can be reflected back onto the national culture of the involved firms. All the whilst, some constants across acquirers have been found, just as some acquiring nations would not seem to conform to their cultural stereotype when engaged in acquiring activities (Child et al., 2001). In this respect, based on a recent study of international firms' acquisitions in Japan, Olcott (2008) points to there not being one approach that characterizes international firms' integration styles in Japan.

Also, target firms from different countries have been found to prefer different kinds of integration approaches, in line with their home countries' national cultures (Morosini, 1998; Cartwright & Price, 2003). Particular emphasis has been placed on the dimensions of uncertainty avoidance (Morosini, 1998; Schoenberg, 2000), risk orientation (Schoenberg, 2000), and individualism versus collectivism (Morosini, 1998). Despite these preferences, it seems that acquisitions in which the target firm has been involved in the integration through informal activities meet greater success than others (Calori et al., 1994; Child et al., 2001; Larsson & Lubatkin, 2001). This would seem to suggest that the involvement of acquired firms is a critical success factor in M&A activity.

Surprisingly, less effort has been placed at studying the reality of national cultures interacting in times of M&A. In this respect, the findings of Barmeyer and Mayrhofer (2007) in a study on the European EADS tri-party merger are of interest.

They found that intercultural team-working was negatively affected by the French, German, and Spanish parties' differing perceptions and interpretations of what team-work and cooperation mean. This resulted in misunderstanding as regards to how one ought to behave in teams. What is more, Barmeyer and Mayrhofer (2007) identified differences in perceptions and interpretations of leadership, especially around the notion of "authority" and what it means across country contexts. The authors conclude that these differences are likely to complicate the process of integration, as members involved in the merger adopt different behavioral strategies to reach their goals. Whilst the strategies are aligned with their respective national cultural backgrounds, their everyday presence makes intercultural work prone to misunderstanding.

Teerikangas (2012) found that the effectiveness of integration progress in cross-border M&As depends on the extent to which differences in institutions, national cultures, and language are recognized. Inattention to the behavioral, managerial, and communication-related dimensions of national cultures (Hall, 1967; Hofstede, 2001) leads to different expectations with regard to appropriate organizational behavior and results in misunderstandings. Longer-term, this can lead to reducing the effectiveness of cross-border interactions. The national cultural roots of both parties' behaviors help to explain the challenge that acquired firm's managers' experience in adapting to a new parent firm's managerial environment (Morosini, 1998; Teerikangas, 2006). Indeed, the prevailing management style in the buying firm is influenced by its respective home country's national culture (Calori et al., 1994; Lubatkin et al., 1998; Child et al., 2001). Unless this influence is recognized, however, "mistakes" made by acquired firm managers tend to be termed as "deviant" or "wrong" behavior. In other words, for successful intercultural cooperation to occur, both parties need to recognize the influence of their respective cultural heritage on their interactions. Until this occurs, both sides will continue to complain about the other's seemingly "deviant" or "wrong" behavior.

In cross-border contexts, the effectiveness of inter-organizational interfaces is further impacted by language (Marschan et al., 1997; Feely & Harzing, 2003). The lack of a joint native language slows down cooperation, causes misunderstandings, and makes it more difficult and time-consuming to develop a relationship based on trust (Teerikangas & Irrmann, 2013). Moreover, acquired firm managers fear that longer-term, the lack of a joint language has consequences for their potential to climb the parent firm's corporate career ladder (Marschan et al., 1997; Piekkari et al., 2005; Vaara et al., 2005).

Working across National Cultures in M&As

Some studies have taken a step further to understanding how national cultures should be accounted for throughout the international M&A process, and they contend that cultural differences should be managed throughout the entire process. In a study on the impact of organizational fit on post-acquisition performance, Datta (1991) found that organizational fit should be evaluated together with the financial evaluation of the deal. Datta defined organizational fit as the differing management styles, reward, and evaluation systems between the acquired and acquiring firms. He found that management styles were especially prone to causing difficulties in all types of acqui-sitions. Cartwright and Cooper (1993) noted that effective evaluation of cultural differences and similarities of the partners prior to entering the deal and starting integration is an early means of assessing the success potential in the merger.

Schweiger et al. (1993) argue that strategy is critical in guiding the change. Morosini and Singh (1994) studied the management of cultural differences in post-acquisition integration and suggested acquirers to adopt a culture-related post-acquisition strategy, coherent with the target country's national culture. They termed this the "national culture compatible strategy." This was deemed especially relevant in cross-border acquisitions, as characteristics influenced by national culture are especially difficult to change. This kind of strategy was seen as a way of ensuring that the aspects of national culture most likely to cause challenges would be ade-quately managed.

In their study of the creation of the European Aeronautic Defence and Space Company, a tri-party merger between the French Aerospatiale Matra, the German DASA, and the Spanish CASA, Barmeyer and Mayrhofer (2007) describe how shared organization structures, the development of an organizational culture geared toward an "EADS spirit," as well as specific human resource management practices geared toward enhancing team-working and cooperation between members of the formerly separate organizations, as well as leadership and career development, were used to further the ties between the formerly disparate organizations.

Tolerance has been found key in intercultural management. Napier et al. (1993) looked at how organizational diversity is managed in cross-border mergers from a human resource management perspective. They found that assertive tolerance is a powerful integration tool. Chatterjee et al. (1992) found a tolerant attitude as a posi-tive factor toward ensuring acquisition success; an over-controlled approach should thus be avoided.

Intercultural training has been established as a means of enhancing awareness of cultural differences (Black & Mendenhall, 1990; Thomas & Inkson, 2005), the assumption being that cultural differences can be learnt about, and in so doing, man-aged or even manipulated (David & Singh, 1993). Schweiger and Goulet (2005) tested the effect of deep versus surface-level cultural learning interventions on acquired firm employees' experiences of being acquired. They argue that the positive experience of an acquisition is not a matter of merging similar cultures, but rather a matter of cultural learning. Consistent with their hypotheses, they find that deep-level cultural learning interventions resulted in enhanced intercultural awareness, understanding, and communication, as well as geared attitudes toward cooperation and integration, in contrast to units that received no learning interventions, where as a result, cultural misunderstandings flourished. Despite these positive findings, surface-level cultural interventions did not result in the partner being better accepted. Interestingly, surface-level learning interventions were found to have limited effect, possibly even furthering existing stereotypes.

In a recent study of EADS, Barmeyer and Mayrhofer (2007) identified distinct intercultural training practices geared to improving the organizational members' intercultural skills. This was particularly salient in the context of this merger, which was formed on the basis of a simultaneous merger of three formerly separate European national organizations (French, German, and Spanish respectively) in the aerospace industry. The intercultural training sessions were part of EADS's management's goal of creating the "Corporate Business Academy" that trained the organization's managers in leadership, change management, business excellence skills in addition to intercultural management.

Morosini (1998) looked at how cultural differences can be managed in cross-border M&As. He argues that pragmatic cross-cultural skills are required to successfully manage in the international arena. National cultural differences also provide a competitive advantage to the firm, as each national culture introduces new organizational routines into the organization.

In summary, we conclude that the behaviors of both the buying and acquired parties are dependent on their national culture heritage. Differences in the merging partners' national cultures should be included in the management of the acquisition process, starting from evaluation, through strategy, and the building of cross-cultural skills in integration work. The impact of national cultural distance on post-merger integration is likely to be negative if these measures are not undertaken.

Implications for HR Processes in M&As

Having completed our overview of the human and managerial dimensions of M&A activity, we now turn to addressing the direct HR implications of M&A activity. It needs to be recognized that a plethora of acquirer profiles exist. In addition to experienced serial acquirers with M&A program management offices that include professional HR expertise (Laamanen & Keil, 2008), there is a spectrum of acquirers who range from zero to high in terms of their past acquisition experience. This experience tends to parallel the firms' maturity in terms of HR expertise. Whilst the larger-sized multinationals with active acquisition programs tend to boast upper-end HR capability, a large portion of acquisitions are made by small to medium-sized firms with little HR expertise.

Four acquirer scenarios with respect to the degree of the firm's HR expertise and its degree of HR awareness in times of M&A can be identified (see Figure 2). Depending on the acquirer's profile, the human resource challenge in an M&A will be tackled more or less professionally from a human resource standpoint. Whilst the active acquirers aware of human factors in M&A would naturally acknowledge HR as a strategic M&A partner (as in the upper right hand quadrant of Figure 2), in other cases a formal HR department may not exist (this is the case in both of the left-hand quadrants of Figure 2). If an HR function exists, but its significance in the M&A process has not been recognized by top management, then the local HR staff will need to sell themselves to management in order to be able to join the negotiating table (this is the case in the lower right hand quadrant).

HR Roadmap in Times of M&A

The challenge that the HR function faces is not only one of supporting line and top management in dealing with the human dimensions of this change, but further, in

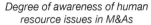

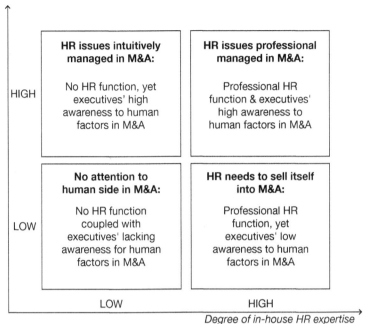

Figure 2. HR's involvement in M&As—four scenarios

enabling simultaneously the change amidst its own organization, that is, the HR function (Galpin & Herndon, 2000; Antila, 2006), see Figure 3. Thus, HR bears two roles.

HR professionals need to secure the integration of the HR function in M&A transactions; we term this, "transactional" HR activity. As administrative experts (Antila, 2006), HR professionals are engaged in conducting pre-acquisition HR due diligence (Harding & Rouse, 2007), including compensation and benefits audits, which feed directly onto the financial deal valuation schemes driving decision-making about whether to go/not go for the deal. Once a deal has been decided upon, HR needs to secure that basic HR activities function regardless of the change in ownership. Rewards, pay, benefits, and pensions become strategic factors that need to be in place before a transaction goes live—who wants to work let alone engage if one's pay is not secured? The task of coordinating reward and pay packages in major mergers is a strategic task requiring enormous amounts of work and politics. Finally, HR professionals need to plan and coordinate the integration of HR policies and practices across the merging organizations. Whose sickness absence policy is adhered to? What are the consequences on the party that seemingly loses many of its benefits?

In parallel, HR professionals are ideally called in to support the decision-making, planning, and implementation of the organizational transformation that a merger or acquisition represents. We term this "transformational" HR activity following an M&A. We use the term "ideally," as industry experience posits differences between acquirers in this respect. Here, the acquirer types previously identified come into play, see Figure 2.

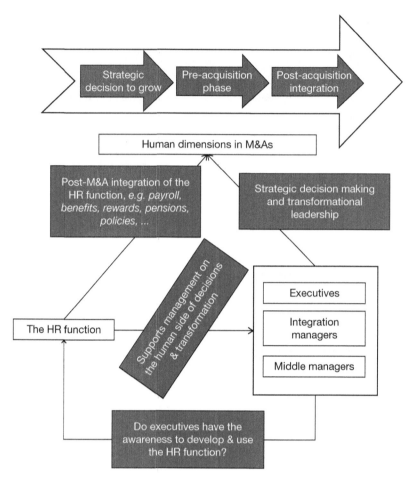

Figure 3. Situating HR's and management's roles in dealing with human dimensions of M&A activity

In order for HR professionals to be able to perform this role, however, they need to step out of an administrative HR role toward a strategic HR role. Using Ullrich's typology of HR roles, in her study of HR roles in M&As, Antila (2006) terms this the strategic partner role. This requires not only courage to act, but beyond this, an appreciation of the M&A process, its strategic, financial, and sociocultural implications. This was the purpose of the front-end and middle sections of this chapter: provide HR professionals a bird's eye understanding of M&As, the M&A process, and management dynamics therein. It is critical to note that despite frameworks and process maps, the contingency variables shaping M&A activity are numerous (Teerikangas et al., 2012): deals differ depending on type of purchase, payment method, countries involved, and so on. Thus, whilst an appreciation of M&A process dynamics is critical, it is also important to appreciate how HR approaches might need to be adjusted from one deal and transformation project to the next. In particular, the role of HR will depend on the degree of integration sought in the transaction;

when medium to high degrees of integration are sought, the role of HR in transformation support increases. In this role, HR ideally supports executives and middle managers in strategic decision-making and M&A process management both pre-and post-deal. The strategic support roles that HR professionals engage in support of management thus include:

- Identifying the strategic and sociocultural success factors behind M&As, and ensuring that key decision-makers and change agents are made aware of them;
- Engagement from the pre-deal phase onward in identifying the strategic rationale for the transaction, partner search and selection, and M&A process planning and management;
- Gaining early entry into the pre-acquisition phase to provide strategic decision-making support on sociocultural dimensions, including the conduct of management and cultural audits;
- Being involved in the selection of change agents for the transformation phase; that is, the acquiring firm integration manager(s) and target firm managers in charge of integration;
- Making a change management game plan for the transformation phase;
- Ensuring that a communications plan toward internal and external stakeholders exists;
- Appreciating the challenge that a change of ownership incurs on employees throughout the organizational hierarchy, and providing adequate support;
- Emphasizing the significance of motivating and engaging employees in times of major change, such as acquisitions and mergers;
- Securing the retention of key talent through talent planning exercises; managing the layoff process, if relevant, and liaising with local staff/trade unions;
- Facilitating the cultural clashes and opportunities involved, as well as the sought processes of cultural change; and,
- Coaching management on the above-mentioned sociocultural dimensions of M&A activity to ensure that in their decision-making and daily behaviors, executives and line managers begin to walk the right talk.

FUTURE RESEARCH DIRECTIONS

Looking forward, the domain of M&A management and its human implications offer exciting and important avenues for future research. Despite the corporate significance of M&As, ample research opportunities in its study remain. In the broader realm, calls have been made to further our appreciation of the dynamics underlying and predicting M&A performance (King et al., 2004; Haleblian et al., 2009). Despite the acknowledged significance of the human factor to M&A success, this raises the question—how does HR enable the creation of value in M&As? Further, which HR related factors impact M&A performance? And, what is the process through which this implication occurs? What is the array of human dimensions that needs to be accounted for? And, how do they account for M&A performance? In parallel, calls for greater methodological and philosophical pluralism in the study of M&As have been made (Meglio & Risberg, 2010; Cartwright et al., 2012) in order to secure enhanced appreciations of its dynamics.

A number of specific HR related research directions can be identified. For one, we noted how extant theorizing has preferred seeming negative takes on the employee outcries in the portrayal of M&As. This begs the question—under which conditions employee reactions veer toward the positive (Teerikangas, 2012)? Further, what explains employee engagement and talent retention in M&As? Where are examples of corporations that have successfully maneuvered the human mires following M&As? There would thus appear to be a need to parallel the rise of positive organizational scholarship (Cameron et al., 2003) in the study of M&A processes.

Furthermore, what are the HR and human implications in mega-mergers vs. (smaller scale) acquisitions? Clearly, human and HR dynamics as well as HR roles differ per transaction type. Yet, extant theorizing appears to have paid lip-service to this distinction (Faulkner et al., 2012). There is a need to further refine our appreciation of M&A transactions across contexts. Here, beyond transaction types, country contexts come into play. Whilst emerging market acquirers seem to perform better than acquirers from traditional markets (Gubbi et al., 2010), what are the underlying HR antecedents explaining these results? For example, Indian acquirers are witnessed to bear a more "human" touch than UK or US acquirers (Kale & Singh, 2012).

Third, whilst the culture-performance debate has intrigued scholars, several important questions remain unanswered. In particular, processual research detailing the complex cultural dynamics at play during mergers versus acquisitions is in need (Teerikangas & Véry, 2006; Stahl & Voigt, 2008). Here, recent insights from international business research on the complexity of the modern cultural encounter will be useful.

Fourth, in the realm of M&A integration management, only a handful of papers have addressed individual actors and roles in M&As. Paralleling the increasing interest in strategy as practice (Johnson et al., 2003; Whittington, 2006) and the role of middle managerial agency (Huy, 2002; Buchanan, 2003; Mantere, 2008), HR scholars could further our appreciation of HR roles in mergers versus acquisitions. Under which conditions do acquirers have a mature HR function that is ready to act, when an opportunity to purchase emerges? Who has responsibility for the human agenda in M&As? Whilst prior research has seemingly signed this responsibility onto HR, the reality is more complex. What is the process whereby line managers/executives on the one hand, and HR professionals on the other, come to jointly create a positive HR agenda in M&As? Are there elements of positive emotional contagion in this process (Barsade, 2002; Losada & Heaphy, 2004)? Finally, whilst M&A integration has created much buzz in the 1990s in the scholarly literature, less is known about integration within the HR function prior to and following M&A transactions. Looking ahead, there are many opportunities to take these important lines of inquiry forward. Beyond scholarly impact, there is a need for an appreciation of the practiced reality of M&As.

NOTES

1.   Corporate entrepreneurship refers to post-acquisition behaviors characterized by a learning capability, a team orientation, a culture of experimentation, and ambition in terms of high aspirations.

REFERENCES

Allred, B. B., Boal, K. B., & Holstein, W. K. (2005). Corporations as stepfamilies: A new metaphor for explaining the fate of merged and acquired companies. *Academy of Management Executive*, 19(3): 23–37.

Angwin, D. (2000). Mergers and Acquisitions across European Borders: National Perspectives on Pre-acquisition Due Diligence and the Use of Professional Advisers. *Journal of World Business*, 36(1): 32–57.

Angwin, D. (2004). Speed in M&A integration: The first 100 days. *European Management Journal*, 22(4): 418–430.

Angwin, D., & Meadows, M. (2009). The choice of insider or outsider top executives in acquired companies. *Long-Range Planning*, 42: 359–389.

Antila, E. (2006). The role of HR managers in international mergers and acquisitions: A multiple case study. *International Journal of Human Resource Management*, 17: 999–1020.

Ashkanasy, N. M., & Holmes, S. (1995). Perceptions of organizational ideology following merger: A longitudinal study of merging accounting firms. *Accounting, Organizations and Society*, 20: 19–34.

Ashkenas, R. N., & Francis, S. C. (2000). Integration managers: Special leaders for special times. *Harvard Business Review*, 78(6): 108–116.

Ashkenas, R. N., DeMonaco, L. J., & Francis, S. C. (1998). Making the deal real: How GE Capital integrates acquisitions. *Harvard Business Review*, 76(1): 165–178.

Balogun, J., Gleadle, P., Hope Hailey, V., & Willmott, H. (2005). Managing change across boundaries: Boundary-shaking practices. *British Journal of Management*, 16: 261–278.

Barkema, H. G., & Bell, H. J. (1996). Foreign entry, cultural barriers, and learning. *Strategic Management Journal*, 17: 151–166.

Barmeyer, C., & Mayrhofer, U. (2008). The contribution of intercultural management to the success of international mergers and acquisitions: An analysis of the EADS Group. *International Business Review*, 17(1): 28–38.

Barsade, S. G. (2002). The ripple effect: Emotional contagion and its influence on group behavior. *Administrative Science Quarterly*, 47: 644–675.

Bartels, J., Douwes, R., De Jong, M., & Pruyn, A. (2006). Organizational identification during a merger: Determinants of employees expected identification with the new organization. *British Journal of Management*, 17: 49–67.

Bartlett, C. A., & Ghoshal, S. (1989). *Managing Across Borders: The Transnational Solution*. London: Random House Business Books.

Bastien, D. T. (1987). Common patterns of behaviour and communication in corporate mergers and acquisitions. *Human Resource Management*, 26: 17–33.

Berry, J. W. (1983). Acculturation: A comparative analysis of alternative forms. In R. Samuda and S. Woods (Eds.), *Perspectives in Immigrant and Minority Education*. (65–78) New York: University Press of America.

Biggadike, R. (1979). The risky business of diversification. *Harvard Business Review*, 57(3): 103–111.

Bijlsma-Frankema, K. (2001). On managing cultural integration and cultural change processes in mergers and acquisitions. *Journal of European Industrial Training*, 25: 192–207.

Birkinshaw, J., Bresman, H., & Håkanson, L. (2000). Managing the post-acquisition integration process: How the human integration and task integration processes interact to foster value creation. *Journal of Management Studies*, 37(3): 395–425.

Black, J. S., & Mendenhall, M. (1990). Cross-cultural training effectiveness: A review and a theoretical framework for future research. *Academy of Management Review*, 15(1): 113–136.

Blake, R. B., & Mouton, J. S. (1984). How to achieve integration on the human side of the merger. In R. B. Black and J. S. Mouton (Eds.), *Solving Costly Organisational Conflicts: Achieving Intergroup Trust, Cooperation and Teamwork*. (41–56) San Francisco: Jossey-Bass.

Borys, B., & Jemison, D. B. (1989). Hybrid arrangements as strategic alliances: Theoretical issues in organizational combinations. *Academy of Management Review*, 14(2): 234–249.

Bower, J. L. (2001). Not all M&As are alike—and that matters. *Harvard Business Review,* 79(3): 93–101.

Brannen, M. Y., & Salk, J. E. (2000). Partnering across borders: Negotiating organizational culture in a German-Japanese joint venture. *Human Relations,* 53(4): 451–487.

Brock, D. (2005). Multinational acquisition integration: The role of national culture in creating synergies. *International Business Review,* 14(3): 269–288.

Buchanan, D. (2003). Demand, instabilities, manipulations, careers: The lived experience of driving change. *Human Relations,* 56(6): 663–684.

Buckley, P. J., and Ghauri, P. N. (2002). *International Mergers and Acquisitions: A Reader.* London: Thomson.

Buono, A. F., & Bowditch, J. L. (1989). *The Human Side of Mergers and Acquisitions: Managing Collisions between People, Cultures and Organizations.* London: Jossey-Bass.

Buono, A. F., Bowditch, J. L., & Lewis, J. W. (1985). When cultures collide: The anatomy of a merger. *Human Relations,* 38(5): 477–500.

Calori, R., Lubatkin, M., & Véry, P. (1994). Control mechanisms in cross-border acquisitions: An international comparison. *Organization Studies,* 15(3): 361–379.

Cameron, K. S., Dutton, J. E., & Quinn, R. E. (2003). *Positive Organizational Scholarship.* San Francisco: Berrett-Koehler.

Cartwright, S. (1998). International mergers and acquisitions: The issues and challenges. In M. Gertsen, A.-M. Søderberg and J. E. Torp (Eds.), *Cultural Dimensions of International Mergers and Acquisitions.* (5–16) Berlin: De Gruyter.

Cartwright, S., & Cooper, C. L. (1990). The impact of mergers and acquisitions on people at work: Existing research and issues. *British Journal of Management,* 1: 65–76.

Cartwright, S., & Cooper, C. L. (1992). *Managing Mergers, Acquisitions and Strategic Alliances: Integrating People and Cultures.* Oxford: Butterworth-Heinemann.

Cartwright, S., & Cooper, C. L. (1993). The role of culture compatibility in successful organizational Marriage. *Academy of Management Executive,* 7(2): 57–70.

Cartwright, S., & Price, F. (2003). Managerial preferences in international merger and acquisition partners revisited: How much are they influenced? In C. Cooper and A. Gregory (Eds.), *Advances in Mergers and Acquisitions.* (1, 81–95) Amsterdam: JAI Press.

Cartwright, S., & Schoenberg, R. (2006). Thirty years of mergers and acquisitions research: Recent advances and future opportunities. *British Journal of Management,* 17(1): 1–5.

Cartwright, S., Teerikangas, S., Rouzies, A., & Wilson-Evered, E. (2012). Methods in M&A: A look at the past, and the future, to forge a path forward. *Scandinavian Journal of Management,* 28(2): 95–106.

Chakrabarti, R., Gupta-Mukherjee, S., & Jayaraman, N. (2009). Mars-Venus marriages: culture and cross-border M&A. *Journal of International Business Studies,* 40: 216–236.

Chatterjee, S., Lubatkin, M. H., Schweiger, D. M., & Weber, Y. (1992). Cultural differences and shareholder value in related mergers: Linking equity and human capital. *Strategic Management Journal,* 13: 319–334.

Chaudhuri, S. (2005). Managing human resources to capture capabilities: Case studies in high-technology acquisitions. In G. K. Stahl & M. E. Mendenhall (Eds.), *Mergers and Acquisitions: Managing Culture and Human Resources.* (277–301) Stanford: Stanford Business Press.

Child, J. (2001). Trust—The fundamental bond in global collaboration. *Organizational Dynamics,* 29(4): 274–288.

Child, J., Faulkner, D., & Pitkethly, R. (2001). *The Management of International Acquisitions.* Oxford: Oxford University Press.

Chua, C. H., Engeli, H.-P., & Stahl, G. (2005). Creating a new identity and high-performance culture at Novartis: The role of leadership and human resource management. In G. K. Stahl & M. Mendenhall (Eds.), *Mergers and Acquisitions: Managing Culture and Human Resources.* (379–400) Stanford: Stanford University Press.

Colombo, G., Conca, V., Buongiorno, M., & Ghan, L. (2007). Integrating cross-border acquisitions: A process-oriented approach. *Long-Range Planning*, 40: 202–222.

Covin, T. J., Kolenko, T. A., Sightler, K. W., & Tudor, R. K. (1997). Leadership style and post-merger satisfaction. *Journal of Management Development*, 16: 22–33.

Currall, S. C., & Inkpen, A. (2002). A multilevel approach to trust in joint ventures. *Journal of International Business Studies*, 33: 479–495.

Dackert, I., Jackson, P., Brenner, S-O., & Johansson, C. R. (2003). Eliciting and analysing employees' expectations of a merger. *Human Relations*, 56: 705–725.

Datta, D. K. (1991). Organizational fit and acquisition performance: Effects of post-acquisition integration. *Strategic Management Journal*, 12: 281–297.

Datta, D. K., & Grant, J. H. (1990). Relationships between type of acquisition, the autonomy given to the acquired firm, and acquisition success: An empirical analysis. *Journal of Management*, 16: 29–44.

David, K., & Singh, H. (1993). Acquisition regimes: Managing cultural risk and relative deprivation in corporate acquisitions. In D. E. Hussey (Ed.), *International Review of Strategic Management*. (4, 227–276) New York: Wiley.

David, K., & Singh, H. (1994). Sources of acquisition cultural Risk. In G. von Krogh, A. Siknatra, H. Singh (Eds.), *The Management of Corporate Acquisitions*. (251–292) London: Macmillan.

Davy, J. A., Kinicki, A., Kilroy, J., & Scheck, C. (1998). After the merger: dealing with people's uncertainty. *Training and Development Journal*, November: 57–61.

Deiser, R. (1994). Post-acquisition management: A process of strategic and organisational learning. In G. von Krogh, A. Siknatra & H. Singh (Eds.), *The Management of Corporate Acquisitions*. (359–390) London: Macmillan.

De Noble, A. F., Gustafson, L. T., & Hergert, M. (1988). Planning for post-merger integration–Eight lessons for merger success. *Long-Range Planning*, 21(4): 82–85.

Dunning, J. H. (1958). *American Investment in British Manufacturing Industry*. London: Allen and Unwin.

Ellis, K. M., Reus, T. H., Lamont, B. T. (2009). The effects of procedural and informational justice in the integration of related firms. *Strategic Management Journal*, 30: 137–161.

Elsass, P. M., & Veiga, J. F. (1994) Acculturation in acquired organizations: A force-field perspective. *Human Relations*, 47: 431–453.

Epstein, M. J. (2004). The drivers of success in post-merger integration. *Organisational Dynamics*, 33(2): 174–189.

Evans, P., Pucik, V., & Barsoux, J.-L. (2002). *The Global Challenge: Frameworks for International Human Resource Management*. Boston, MA: McGraw-Hill.

Fairfield-Sonn, J. W., Ogilvie, J. R., & DelVecchio, G. A. (2002). Mergers, acquisitions and long-term employee attitudes. *Journal of Business & Economic Studies*, 8: 1–16.

Faulkner, D., Teerikangas, S., & Joseph, R. (2012). *The Handbook of Mergers and Acquisitions*. Oxford: Oxford University Press.

Feely, A. J., & Harzing, A.-W. (2003). Language management in multinational companies. *Cross-Cultural Management: An International Journal*, 10(2): 37–52.

Forstmann, S. (1998). Managing cultural differences in cross-cultural mergers and acquisitions. In M. Gertsen, A.-M. Søderberg, & J. E. Torp (Eds.), *Cultural Dimensions of International Mergers and Acquisitions*. (57–84) Berlin: De Gruyter.

Froese, F. J., Pak, Y. S., & Chong, L. C. (2007). Managing the human side of cross-border acquisitions in South Korea. *Journal of World Business*, 43: 97–108.

Galpin, T. J., & Herndon, M. (2000). *The Complete Guide to Mergers and Acquisitions: Process Tools to Support M&A Integration at Every Level*. San Fransisco. CA: Jossey-Bass.

Giessner, S. R., Ullrich, J., & Van Dick, R. (2012). A social identity analysis of mergers and acquisitions. In D. Faulkner, S. Teerikangas, & R. Joseph (Eds.), *Handbook of Mergers & Acquisitions*. (474–494) Oxford: Oxford University Press.

Graebner, M. E. (2004). Momentum and serendipity: How acquired firm leaders create value in the integration of technology firms. *Strategic Management Journal*, 25: 751–777.

Graebner, M. E., & Eisenhardt, K. M. (2004). The seller's side of the story: Acquisition as courtship and governance as syndicate in entrepreneurial Firms. *Administrative Science Quarterly*, 49: 366–403.

Graves, D. (1981). Individual reactions to a merger of two small firms of brokers in the re-insurance industry: A total population Survey. *Journal of Management Studies*, 18: 89–114.

Gubbi, S. R., Aulakh, P. S., Ray, S., Sarkar, M. B., & Chittoor, R. (2010). Do international acquisitions by emerging-economy firms create shareholder value? The case of Indian firms. *Journal of International Business Studies*, 41: 397–418.

Håkanson, L. (1995). Learning through acquisitions: Management and integration of foreign R&D laboratories. *International Studies of Management and Organization*, 25(1–2): 121–157.

Haleblian, J., Devers, C. E., McNamara, G., Carpenter, M. A., & Davison, R. B. (2009). Taking stock of what we know about mergers and acquisitions: A review and research agenda. *Journal of Management*, 35: 469–502.

Hall, E. T. (1967). *Beyond Culture*. New York: Doubleday.

Hambrick, D. C., & Cannella, A. A. (1993). Relative standing: A framework for understanding departures of acquired executives. *Academy of Management Journal*, 36: 733–762.

Harding, D., & Rouse, T. (2007). Human due diligence. *Harvard Business Review*, 85/(4): 124–131.

Haspeslagh, P. C., and Jemison, D. B. (1991). *Managing Acquisitions: Creating Value Through Corporate Renewal*. New York: The Free Press.

Haspeslagh, P., & Farquhar, A. B. (1994). The acquisition integration process: A contingent framework. In G. von Krogh, A. Siknatra & H. Singh (Eds.), *The Management of Corporate Acquisitions*. (414–447) London: Macmillan.

Hayes, R. H. (1979). The human side of acquisitions. *Management Review*, 68: 41–46.

Hitt, M. A., Harrison, J. S., & Duane Ireland, R. (2001). *Mergers and Acquisitions: A Guide to Creating Value for Stakeholders*. New York: Oxford University Press.

Hofstede, G. (2001). *Culture's Consequences. Comparing Values, Behaviours, Institutions and Organisations Across Nations*. Thousand Oaks: Sage.

Hogg, M. A., & Terry, D. J. (2000). Social identity and self-categorization processes in organizational contexts. *Academy of Management Review*, 25: 121–140.

House, R. J., Hanges, P. J., Javidan, M., Dorfman, P. W., & Gupta, V. (2004). *Culture, Leadership, and Organizations: The GLOBE Study of 62 Societies*. Thousand Oaks, CA: Sage.

Howell, R. A. (1970). Plan to integrate your Aacquisitions. *Harvard Business Review*, November–December: 66–76.

Hurley, R. F. (2006). The decision to trust. *Harvard Business Review*, September: 55–62.

Huy, Q. N. (2002). Emotional balancing of organizational continuity and radical change: The contribution of middle managers. *Administrative Science Quarterly*, 47: 31–69.

Inkpen, A. C., & Currall, S. C. (2004). The coevolution of trust, control, and learning in joint ventures. *Organization Science*, 15(5): 586–599.

Ivancevich, J. M., Schweiger, D. M., & Power, F. R. (1987). Strategies for managing human resources during mergers and acquisitions. *Human Resource Planning*, 10: 19–35.

Jaeger, A. M. (1983). The transfer of organisational culture overseas: An approach to control in the multinational corporation. *Journal of International Business Studies*, Fall: 91–104.

Jemison, D. B., & Sitkin, S. B. (1986). Corporate acquisitions: A process perspective. *Academy of Management Review*, 11(1): 145–163.

Johnson, G., Melin, J., & Whittington, R. (2003). Guest editors' introduction — Micro strategy and strategizing: Towards an activity-based view. *Journal of Management Studies*, 40(1): 3–22.

Kale, P., & Singh, H. (2012). Characteristics of emerging market mergers and acquisitions. In D. Faulkner, S. Teerikangas, & R. Joseph (Eds.), *Handbook of Mergers & Acquisitions*. (545–565) Oxford: Oxford University Press.

Kanter, R. M. (2009). Mergers that stick. *Harvard Business Review*, October: 121–125.

Kavanagh, M. H., & Ashkanasy, N. M. (2006). The impact of leadership and change management strategy on organizational culture and individual acceptance of change during a merger. *British Journal of Management*, 17: S81–S103.

King, D. R., Dalton, D. R., Daily, C. M., & Covin, J. G. (2004). Meta-analyses of post-acquisition performance: Indications of unidentified moderators. *Strategic Management Journal*, 25(2): 187–200.

Kitching, J. (1967). Why do mergers miscarry? *Harvard Business Review*, November–December: 84–100.

Kleppestø, S. (2005). The construction of social identities in mergers and acquisitions. In G. K. Stahl & M. Mendenhall (Eds.), *Mergers and Acquisitions: Managing Culture and Human Resources*. (130–151) Stanford: Stanford Business Press.

Kolev, K., Haleblian, J., & McNamara, G. (2012). A review of the merger and acquisition wave literature: History, antecedents, consequences and future directions. In D. Faulkner, S. Teerikangas, & R. Joseph (Eds.), *Handbook of Mergers and Acquisitions*. (19–39) Oxford: Oxford University Press.

Krishnan, H. A., Miller, A., & Judge, W. Q. (1997). Diversification and top management team complementarity: Is performance improved by merging similar or dissimilar teams? *Strategic Management Journal*, 18(5): 361–374.

Krishnan, R., Martin, X., & Noorderhaven, N. G. (2006). When does trust matter to alliance Performance? *Academy of Management Journal*, 49/5: 894–917.

Krug, J. A., & Nigh, D. (2001). Executive perceptions in foreign and domestic acquisitions: An analysis of foreign ownership and its effect on executive fate. *Journal of World Business*, 36: 85–98.

Laamanen, T. & Keil, T. (2008). Performance of serial acquirers: Toward an acquisition program perspective. *Strategic Management Journal*, 29(6): 663–672.

Larsson, R. (1993). Barriers to acculturation in mergers and acquisitions: Strategic human resource implications. *Journal of European Business Education*, 2(2): 1–18.

Larsson, R., & Risberg, A. (1998). Cultural awareness and national versus corporate barriers to acculturation. In M. Gertsen, A.-M. Søderberg and J. E. Torp (Eds.), *Cultural Dimensions of International Mergers and Acquisitions*. (39–56) Berlin: De Gruyter.

Larsson, R., & Finkelstein, S. (1999). Integrating strategic, organizational, and human resource perspectives on mergers and acquisitions: A case survey of synergy realization. *Organization Science*, 10(1): 1–26.

Larsson, R., & Lubatkin, M. (2001). Achieving acculturation in mergers and acquisitions: An international case study. *Human Relations*, 54(12): 1573–1607.

Lewicki, R. J., McAllister, D. J., & Bies, R. J. (1998). Trust and distrust: New relationships and realities. *Academy of Management Review*, 23: 438–458.

Lorange, P. (1996). A strategic human resource perspective to multinational cooperative ventures. *International Studies of Management and Organization*, 26: 87–103.

Losada, M. & Heaphy, E. (2004). The role of positivity and connectivity in the performance of business teams. *American Behavioral Scientist*, 47(6): 740–765.

Lubatkin, M., Calori, R., Véry, P., & Veiga, J. (1998). Managing mergers across borders: A two-nation exploration of a nationally bound administrative heritage. *Organisation Science*, 9(6): 670–684.

Mace, M. L, & Montgomery, G. (1962). *Management Problems of Corporate Acquisitions*. Cambridge, MA: Harvard University Press.

Malekzadeh, A. R., & Nahavandi, A. (1998). Leadership and culture in transnational strategic alliances. In M. C. Gertsen, A.-M. Søderberg, and J. E. Torp (Eds.), *Cultural Dimensions of International Mergers and Acquisitions*. (111–128) Berlin: De Gruyter.

Mantere, S. (2008). Role expectations and middle manager strategic agency. *Journal of Management Studies*, 45(2): 294–316.

Marks, M. L. (1982). Merging human resources: A review of the literature. *Mergers and Acquisitions*, Summer: 38–44.

Marks, M. L. (1991). Combating merger shock before the deal is closed. *Mergers and Acquisitions*, January/February: 43–48.

Marks, M. L., & Mirvis, P. (1985). Merger syndrome: Stress and uncertainty. *Mergers and Acquisitions*, Summer: 50–55.

Marks, M. L., & Mirvis, P. H. (1998). *Joining Forces: Making One Plus One Equal Three in Mergers, Acquisitions, and Alliances*. San Francisco: Jossey-Bass.

Marks, M. L., & Mirvis, P. (2001). Making mergers and acquisitions Work: Strategic and psychological preparation. *Academy of Management Executive*, 15: 80–94.

Marks, M. L., & Vansteenkiste, R. (2008). Preparing for organizational death: Proactive hr engagement in an organizational transition. *Human Resource Management*, 47: 809–827.

Marschan, R., Welch, D., & Welch, L. (1997). Language: The forgotten factor in multinational management. *European Management Journal*, 15(5): 591.

Meglio, O., & Risberg, A. (2010). Mergers and acquisitions: Time for a methodological rejuvenation of the field? *Scandinavian Journal of Management*, 26(1): 87–95.

Meyer, C. B., & Altenborg, E. (2007). The disintegrating effects of equality: A study of a failed international merger. *British Journal of Management*, 18: 257–271.

Morosini, P. (1998). *Managing Cultural Differences: Effective Strategy and Execution Across Cultures in Global Corporate Alliances*. Oxford: Pergamon.

Morosini, P., & Singh, H. (1994). Post-cross-border acquisitions: Implementing national culture-compatible strategies to improve performance. *European Management Journal*, 4: 390–400.

Morosini, P., Shane, S., & Singh, H. (1998). National cultural distance and cross-border acquisition performance. *Journal of International Business Studies*, 19(1): 137–158.

Nahavandi, A., Malekzadeh, A. R. (1988). Acculturation in mergers and acquisitions. *Academy of Management Review*, 13(1): 79–90.

Napier, N. K. (1989). Mergers and acquisitions, human resource issues and outcomes: A review and suggested typology. *Journal of Management Studies*, 26(3): 271–289.

Napier, N. K., Schweiger, D. M., & Kosglow, J. J. (1993). Managing organizational diversity: Observations from cross-border acquisitions. *Human Resource Management*, 32(4): 505–523.

Olcott, G. (2008). Politics of institutionalization: The impact of foreign ownership and control on japanese organizations. *International Journal of Human Resource Management*, 19: 1569–1587.

Olie, R. (1990). Culture and integration problems in international mergers and acquisitions. *European Management Journal*, 8(2): 206–215.

Olie, R. (1994). Shades of culture and institutions in international mergers. *Organization Studies*, 15(3): 381–405.

Ouchi, W. G. (1981). *Theory Z: How American Business Can Meet the Japanese Challenge*. Reading, MA: Addison-Wesley.

Pablo, A. L. (1994). Determinants of acquisition integration level: A decision making perspective. *Academy of Management Journal*, 37: 803–836.

Parmigiani, A., & Rivera-Santos, M. (2011). Clearing a path through the forest: A meta-review of interorganizational relationships. *Journal of Management*, 37(4): 1108–1136.

Paruchuri, S., Nerkar, A., & Hambrick, D. C. (2006). Acquisition integration and productivity losses in the technical core: Disruption of inventors in acquired companies. *Organization Science*, 17(5): 545–562.

Piekkari, R., Vaara, E., Tienari, J., & Säntti, R. (2005). Integration or disintegration? Human resource implications of a common corporate language decision in a cross-border merger. *International Journal of Human Resource Management*, 16: 330–344.

Pioch, E. (2007). 'Business as usual?' Retail employee perceptions of organizational life following cross-border acquisition. *International Journal of Human Resource Management*, 18(2): 209–231.

Pitkethly, R., Faulkner, D., & Child, J. (2003). Integrating acquisitions. In C. Cooper and A. Gregory (Eds.), *Advances in Mergers and Acquisitions*. (1, 27–58) Amsterdam: JAI Press.

Quah, P., & Young, S. (2005). Post-acquisition management: A phases approach for cross-border M&A. *European Management Journal*, 23(1): 65–75.

Ranft, A. L., & Lord, M. D. (2002). Acquiring new technologies and capabilities: a grounded model of acquisition implementation. *Organization Science*, 13: 420–441.

Reus, T. H., & Lamont, B. T. (2009). The double-edged sword of cultural distance in international acquisitions. *Journal of International Business Studies*, 40: 1298–1316.

Ring, P. S., & Van de Ven, A. H. (1992). Structuring cooperative relationships between organizations. *Strategic Management Journal*, 13: 483–498.

Risberg, A. (2001). Employee experiences of acquisition processes. *Journal of World Business*, 36: 58–84.

Sales, A. L., & Mirvis, P. H. (1984). When cultures collide: Issues in acquisitions. In J. Kimberley and R. E. Quinn (Eds.), *New Futures: The Challenges of Managing Corporate Transitions*. (107–133) Homewood: Dow Jones-Irvin.

Sarala, R. (2010). The impact of cultural differences and acculturation factors on post-acquisition conflict. *Scandinavian Journal of Management*, 26(1): 38–56.

Sarala, R., & Vaara, E. (2010). Cultural differences, convergence, and crossvergence as explanations of knowledge transfer in international acquisitions. *Journal of International Business Studies*, 41: 1365–1390.

Sarkar, M., Cavusgil, T., & Evirgen, C. (1997). A commitment-trust mediated framework of international collaborative venture performance. In P. W. Beamish & J. P. Killing (Eds.), *Cooperative Strategies: North American Perspectives*. (255–285) San Francisco, CA: New Lexington.

Schein, E. (1985). *Organisational Culture and Leadership: A Dynamic View*. London: Jossey-Bass.

Schoenberg, R. (2000). The influence of cultural compatibility within cross-border acquisitions. In C. Cooper & A. Gregory (Eds.), *Advances in Mergers and Acquisitions*. (1, 43–60) Amsterdam: JAI Press.

Schoenberg, R. (2004). Dimensions of management style compatibility and cross-border acquisition outcome. *Advances in Mergers and Acquisitions*, 3: 149–175.

Schraeder, M., & Self, D. R. (2003). Enhancing the success of mergers and acquisitions: An organizational culture perspective. *Management Decision*, 41(5): 511–522.

Schuler, R. S., Jackson, S. E., & Luo, Y. (2004). *Managing Human Resources in Cross-Border Alliances*. London: Routledge.

Schweiger, D. M., & Denisi, A. S. (1991). Communication with employees following a merger: A longitudinal field experiment. *Academy of Management Journal*, 34: 110–135.

Schweiger, D. M., & Goulet, P. K. (2000). Integrating mergers and acquisitions: an international research review. In C. Cooper and A. Gregory (Eds.), *Advances in Mergers and Acquisitions*. (1, 61–91) Amsterdam: JAI Press.

Schweiger, D. M., & Goulet, P. K. (2005). Facilitating acquisition integration through deep-level cultural learning interventions: A longitudinal field experiment. *Organization Studies*, 26(10): 1477–1499.

Schweiger, D. M., Ivancevich, J. M., & Power, F. R. (1987). Executive actions for managing human resources before and after acquisition. *Academy of Management Executive*, 1: 127–138.

Schweiger, D. M., Csiszar, E. N., Napier, N. K. (1993). Implementing international mergers and acquisitions. *Human Resource Planning*, 16(1): 53–70.

Sherif, M. (1962). *Intergroup Relations and Leadership*. New York: Wiley.

Sinetar, M. (1981). Mergers, morale and productivity. *Personnel Journal*, 60: 863–867.

Sitkin, S. B. & Roth, N. L. (1993). Explaining the limited effectiveness of legalistic 'remedies' for trust/distrust. *Organization Science*, 4: 367–392.

Slangen, A. (2006). National cultural distance and initial foreign acquisition performance: The moderating effect of integration. *Journal of World Business*, 41: 161–170.

Stahl, G. K., & Voigt, A. (2008). Do cultural differences matter in mergers and acquisitions? A tentative model and examination. *Organization Science*, 19(1): 160–176.

Stahl, G. K., & Sitkin, S. (2010). Trust dynamics in acquisitions: The role of relationship history, interfirm distance, and acquirer's integration approach. *Advances in Mergers and Acquisitions*, 9: 51–82.

Stahl, G. K., Chua, C. H., & Pablo, A. (2006). Antecedents of target firm members' trust in the acquiring firm's management: A decision-making simulation. *Advances in Mergers and Acquisitions*, 5: 69–89.

Stahl, G. K., Larsson, R., Kremershof, I., & Sitkin, S. (2011). Trust dynamics in acquisitions: A case survey. *Human Resource Management*, 50: 575–603.

Stahl, G. K., Chua, C. H. & Pablo, A. (2012). Does national context affect target firm employees' trust in acquisitions? A policy-capturing study. *Management International Review*, 52(3): 395–423.

Stahl, G.K., Angwin, D. N., Very, P., Gomes, E., Weber, Y., Tarba, S. Y., Noorderhaven, N., Benyamini, H., Bouckenooghe, D., Chreim, S. & Durand, M., (2013). Sociocultural integration in mergers and acquisitions: Unresolved Paradoxes and Directions for Future Research. *Thunderbird International Business Review*, 55: 333–356.

Styhre, A., Börjesson, S., & Wickenberg, J. (2006). Managed by the Other: Cultural anxieties in two Anglo-Americanized Swedish firms. *International Journal of Human Resource Management*, 17(7): 1293–1306.

Sudarsanam, S. (2012). Value creation and value appropriation in M&A Deals. In D. Faulkner, S. Teerikangas, & R. Joseph (Eds.), *Handbook of Mergers & Acquisitions*. (195–253) Oxford: Oxford University Press.

Tajfel, H. (1978). Interindividual behaviour and intergroup behaviour. In H. Tajfel (Ed.), *Differentiation between Social Groups: Studies in the Social Psychology of Intergroup Relations. European Monographs in Social Psychology*, 14. (27–60) London: Academic Press.

Teerikangas, S. (2006). Silent forces in cross-border acquisitions—An integrative perspective on post-acquisition integration. Espoo: Helsinki University of Technology, Department of Industrial Engineering and Management, Institute of Strategy. Doctoral Dissertation Series 1/2006. Available online at lib.tkk.fi/Diss/2006/isbn9512280930/isbn9512280930.pdf [accessed June 1, 2016].

Teerikangas, S. (2012). Dynamics of acquired firm pre-acquisition employee reactions. *Journal of Management*, 38(2): 599–639.

Teerikangas, S., & Véry, P. (2006). The culture-performance relationship in M&A: From yes/no to how. *British Journal of Management*, 17(S1): 31–48.

Teerikangas, S., & Irrmann, O. (2013). Unbundling the linguistic dynamics in cross-border acquisitions. Paper presented at the Annual Meeting of the Academy of Management, Orlando, August 2013.

Teerikangas, S., & Irrmann, O. (2014). Post-acquisition cultural change: cohabiting the tension between practiced and espoused values. *Management International Review*, forthcoming.

Teerikangas, S., & Laamanen, T. (2013). Structure first! Temporal dynamics of structural & cultural integration in cross-border acquisitions. In C. Cooper, & S. Finkelstein (Eds.), *Advances in Mergers and Acquisitions*, Vol. 12. (109–152) Amsterdam: JAI Press.

Teerikangas, S., Véry, P., & Pisano, V. (2011). Integration manager's value-capturing roles and acquisition performance. *Human Resource Management*, 50(5): 651–683.

Teerikangas, S., Joseph, R., & Faulkner, D. (2012). Mergers & acquisitions: A synthesis. In D. Faulkner, S. Teerikangas, & R. Joseph (Eds.), *Handbook of Mergers & Acquisitions*. (661–685) Oxford: Oxford University Press.

Thomas, D. C., & Inkson, K. (2005). Cultivating your cultural intelligence. *Security Management*, 48(8): 30–32.

Thomson, N., & McNamara, P. (2001). Achieving post-acquisition success: The role of corporate entrepreneurship. *Long-Range Planning*, 34: 669–697.

Tienari, J., & Vaara, E. (2012). Power and politics in mergers and acquisitions. In D. Faulkner, S. Teerikangas, & R. Joseph (Eds.), *Handbook of Mergers & Acquisitions*. (495–516) Oxford: Oxford University Press.

Ulrich, D. (1997). *Human Resource Champions: The New Agenda for Adding Value and Delivering Results*. Boston, MA: Harvard Business School Press.

Vaara, E. (2003). Post-acquisition integration as sensemaking: Glimpses of ambiguity, confusion, hypocrisy, and politicization. *Journal of Management Studies*, 40: 859–894.

Vaara, E., Tienari, J., Piekkari, R., & Säntti, R. (2005). Language and the circuits of power in a merging multinational corporation. *Journal of Management Studies*, 42(3): 595–623.

Van Dick, R., Ullrich, J., & Tissington, P. A. (2006). Working under a black cloud: How to sustain organizational identification after a merger. *British Journal of Management*, 17: 69–79.

Véry, P., & Schweiger, D. (2001). The acquisition process as a learning process: Evidence from a study of critical problems and solutions in domestic and cross-border deals. *Journal of World Business*, 36(1): 11–31.

Véry, P., Lubatkin, M., & Calori, R. (1996). A cross-national assessment of acculturative stress in recent European mergers. *International Studies of Management and Organization*, 26(1): 59–86.

Véry, P., Lubatkin, M., Calori, R., & Veiga, J. (1997). Relative standing and the performance of recently acquired European firms. *Strategic Management Journal*, 18(8): 593–614.

Weber, R. A., Camerer, C. F. (2003). Cultural conflict and merger failure: an experimental approach. *Management Science*, 49(4): 400–415.

Weber, Y. (1996). Corporate cultural fit and performance in mergers and acquisitions. *Human Relations*, 49(9): 1181–1202.

Weber, Y., Shenkar, O., & Raveh, A. (1996). National and corporate cultural fit in mergers/acquisitions: An exploratory study. *Management Science*, 42(8): 1215–1227.

Weber, Y., & Drori, I. (2008). The linkages between cultural differences, psychological states, and performance in international mergers and acquisitions. *Advances in Mergers and Acquisitions*, 7: 119–142.

Whittington, R. (2006). Completing the practice turn in strategy research. *Organization Studies*, 27(5): 613–634.

Zaheer, A., McEvily, B., & Perrone, V. (1998). Does trust matter? Exploring the effects of inter-organizational and interpersonal trust on performance. *Organization Science*, 9: 141–159.

Carlos Sánchez-Runde, Yih-teen Lee, and B. Sebastian Reiche

HAILING A NEW ERA: HAIER IN JAPAN

A S ONE OF THE MOST valuable brands in China, Haier designs, manufactures, and sells various home appliances, including refrigerators, air conditioners, and washing machines in over 100 countries. Under the leadership of its well-respected and visionary founder and CEO, Zhang Ruimin, Haier Group has rapidly grown from a small refrigerator plant in Qingdao, Shandon Province, China, to a global leader in home appliances. Haier's 2011 annual sales reached RMB151 billion. As part of its internationalization strategy, Haier entered the Japanese market in 2002 and formed a joint venture with Sanyo in 2007 to produce and sell refrigerators and washing machines in Japan.

In 2012, after five years of collaboration with Sanyo, Haier acquired Sanyo's white goods business in Japan and the related operations in six other Southeast Asian countries. Du Jingguo, president of Haier Asia International, moved from China to live in Japan in 1998 and learned the specificities of the Japanese culture well. Knowing his role in realizing Haier's globalization strategy that aims to turn each localized brand into a mainstream product in its respective market, Du is pondering how he can more effectively lead the team based in Japan. In particular, he needs to instill Haier's culture and innovative management system into its Japanese operation.

COMPANY BACKGROUND AND ITS INTERNATIONAL EXPANSION

Established in 1984, Haier has experienced four stages of expansion over the past 28 years, each representing the formulation and execution of different strategies: brand building (1984–1991), diversification (1991–1998), internationalization (1998–2005) and developing a global brand (2006–now).

Brand Building Period (1984–1991)

When Zhang took control of Haier in 1984 at the age of 35, the company was in financial distress and it lacked basic standards and procedures. It was not uncommon for workers to steal materials from company premises or simply not show up to work. Zhang inherited a workforce that, due to the Cultural Revolution, was largely under-educated. To foster discipline and proper work processes, Zhang began by defining a list of simple rules of conduct (see Exhibit 1) that would later evolve into sophisticated policies. This was particularly important because Haier faced fierce competition from over 300 local refrigerator plants. At that time, demand in home appliance products in China was growing and customers were willing to pay for second-rate products. Quality was a rare concept. Zhang, however, believed that customers would be willing to pay more for higher quality products and services. Hence, whereas its competitors strived to pursue economies of scale to meet increasing demand and ignored quality control, Haier focused on the manufacture of refrigerators and strictly emphasized product quality. To demonstrate his commitment to high quality, Zhang once personally pulled 76 refrigerators with minor defects from the production line and smashed them in public. This event marked an inflexion point in Haier's culture and is still the object of commentaries by current employees today, some 30 years later.

By 1990, Haier had become the leading refrigerator maker in China along with an average 9.5% growth rate over the preceding decade. At this early stage, Haier had also already started its international collaborations. In 1984, Haier signed a technology licensing agreement with Liebherr, a German refrigerator maker. Later, Haier imported freezer and air conditioner production lines from Derby (Denmark) and Sanyo (Japan). Joint ventures with Mitsubishi (Japan) and Merloni (Italy) further introduced advanced technology and innovation into Haier's operations and culture.

Diversification Period (1991–1998)

In its second phase, Haier adopted a "stunned fish" tactic to diversify its product lines. "Stunned fish" referred to those companies that performed poorly due to weak management and yet owned advanced technology and equipment. Haier actively identified and acquired 20 of these companies and turned them around.

Haier also started to demonstrate its capability in management innovation by introducing the OEC (Overall, Every, Control and Clearance) approach, referring to Haier's practice of planning, executing, and clearing every task and performance dimension on a daily basis. This practice proved to be instrumental to Haier's success in changing the mentality of its workers to the pursuit of high quality. Later, Zhang introduced the concept of Miniature Companies within Haier, whereby each employee's tasks and responsibilities would be understood in terms of income and expenses to be recorded in a personal bankbook that served as an individual profit-and-loss statement and determined a person's salary.

While the various acquisitions provided access to advanced technology and sources of diversification, they also added a substantial number of workers with

EXHIBIT 1. The rules introduced by Zhang in 1984

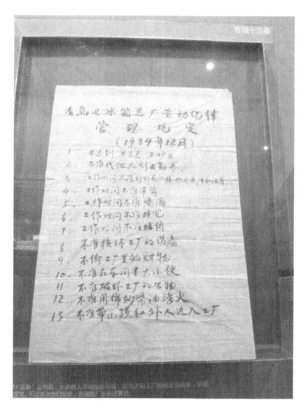

Note: The rules in English:

1. No late arrivals, no leaving early, no absenteeism.
2. No signing in for others at work.
3. No playing poker or chess or knitting sweaters during work hours.
4. No visiting friends for personal reasons during work hours.
5. No drinking alcohol during work hours.
6. No sleeping during work hours.
7. No gambling during work hours.
8. No damaging the production facilities of the factory.
9. No stealing equipment from the factory.
10. No defecating and urinating on the work floor.
11. No damaging public goods in the factory.
12. No using cotton yarn and diesel fuel to make fires in the factory.
13. No bringing children or unrelated persons into the factory.

Source: Picture taken by the case authors at the Haier Museum in Qingdao, May 2012.

different profiles and who used different forms of work organization. Haier then had to align the acquired companies with its increasingly sophisticated management systems. The formalization of Haier's systems helped provide a guiding framework, but it was insufficient by itself to unify the entire workforce. In fact, the pressure to quickly turn around the acquired companies meant that Haier had to socialize the new work-force into Haier's corporate culture and operating systems, often within short periods of time. Haier started to provide formal training, which later led to the creation of Haier University. The company also deployed staff from its Corporate Culture Center to the newly acquired companies to help with the integration.

Internationalization Period (1998–2005)

After Haier's refrigerators outperformed Liebherr's in a blind quality test held by a German magazine, Haier decided to develop its own brand globally. Influenced by suc-cessful Japanese and Korean companies such as Sony and Samsung, Haier also decided to bear the cost of building up the firm as an independent brand overseas. Haier adopted a strategy to enter more difficult, mature markets first and leave the easier ones for later. Initially, Haier focused on the European and US markets, which contributed to over 3% of group sales. In the late 1990s, China joined the World Trade Organization and the government called on enterprises to follow its national policy of expanding operations overseas. In 1999, Haier established the Overseas Promotion Division, and aggressively pursued exports and overseas production in Asia (Indonesia, Philippines, Pakistan, India, and Japan), the Americas (South Carolina), Europe (Italy and Germany), and the Middle East (Dubai, Saudi Arabia, Iran, Algeria, Syria, and Jordan).

The internationalization period tested Haier's ability to effectively manage its workforce across an increasingly wide network of foreign operations. While Haier had successfully integrated a host of different product divisions into its domestic organi-zation and created an overarching management system, moving across borders meant that Haier now faced the challenge of expanding its systems abroad and managing across growing geographic and cultural distances. In contrast to many multinationals that staffed their foreign operations with managers from headquarters, Haier selected experienced local staff to manage its foreign operations from the beginning. Haier was convinced that, to ensure proximity to local customers, the company needed local people to develop the sales and distribution channels and better understand local customer needs. Although many aspects of Haier's systems were successfully trans-ferred to other countries, Haier also adapted specific practices to the local context. For example, after the practice of having low performers publically share their mistakes in front of their peers was deemed a violation of human rights in the United States, it was replaced by having top performers share best practices. The European context required further adaptations of Haier's management practices.

Global Brand Period (2006–Present)

Since 2006, Haier has continued to evolve its business models and extend its global reach. During the latest phase, Haier developed a global brand strategy. Unlike its previous internationalization strategy, which saw Haier expand to international markets while maintaining a focus on its home market, the new strategy aims to make each localized brand of Haier a mainstream product in the respective local market with the ultimate goal of leading local market trends.

As the company grew larger throughout the years, Zhang noticed that it was becoming harder for Haier to respond to the market in a speedy and timely fashion. Recognizing the need to adapt to the Internet era with a high level of speed and responsiveness to customers, Zhang introduced a new business strategy called a "Win–Win Mode of Individual–Goal Combination" to (1) link each employee more closely to the clients that he or she serves, and (2) satisfy the clients' specific needs by consolidating R&D, manufacturing, and marketing resources via the Internet. To implement this strategy, Zhang proposed a restructuring that would organize employees into self-managed units (called ZZJYTs (from *zizhu jingyin ti*—自主经营体 in Chinese) with an inverted triangular structure. Haier also made a conscious effort to develop the corresponding corporate culture (the system will be discussed in more detail later). Haier has been experimenting with this model in China and aims to gradually implement it overseas.

It is in this context that Du was asked to acquire Sanyo's white appliances operations in Japan and Southeast Asia, and turn them into an integral part of the Haier Group in building its global brand.

HAIER'S INNOVATIVE ORGANIZATIONAL STRUCTURE AND CULTURE

Since 1984, Zhang has continuously proposed new strategies, most of which combined Western management concepts and Chinese philosophical thought. While unable to receive a systematic, formal education due to the Cultural Revolution, Zhang is a diligent autodidact and has educated himself in different ways. He reads extensively, especially on topics related to traditional Chinese philosophy and literature, and Western management theories, from which he created the unique Haier management models. In many public interviews, Zhang has consistently maintained that it is the ancient Chinese teachings, such as Confucius' *Analects*, Lao Tzu's *Tao-De Ching* and Sun Tzu's *The Art of War*, that helped him face Haier's various challenges and form its management philosophy and corporate culture.

As a result, Haier adopted Western management theories, infused them with Chinese ancient philosophy, and then executed them according to local practice. These concepts emerged gradually and were developed by trial and error over time. The ZZJYT is a vivid example. "ZZJYT" refers to a self-operating, self-managing entity that determines goals, recruits members, and formulates rules. The concept was already mentioned by Zhang in 2002, when he witnessed how the Internet changed traditional business models in various industries. To address the essential transformation from manufacturing to services and customer-centric models of operation, Zhang proposed an inverted triangular corporate structure to serve customers in the future. With the aim of leading the company into the Internet era, Haier formally adopted ZZJYTs in 2007.

ZZJYT (Self-Managed Unit) and the Inverted Triangle

Traditional management theory tends to see a company as a triangle that locates senior executives at the top, followed by middle managers in charge of different functional areas, and employees facing the markets and other external stakeholders at the bottom. In such a structure, top executives assume traditional roles as decision makers. Employees then follow managers' instructions and guidance in their daily operations. By contrast, the ZZJYT concept subverts this organizational structure by adopting an inverse triangle. At the company level, Haier differentiates between three vertical levels. Each level consists of specialized ZZJYTs (see Exhibit 2).

The first vertical level consists of ZZJYTs of manufacturing, marketing, and R&D functions that directly face customers. Employees of this level will directly contact customers, assess demand, and formulate and execute projects to efficiently satisfy customer needs. For instance, with the support of marketing and sales colleagues, R&D staff will communicate with customers and identify customers' needs on-site. As a manager of Haier explained: "Employees don't get orders from executives, but rather actively listen to the market. They are their own CEOs." In Zhang's view, the most unique characteristic of ZZJYTs was their ability to shorten the gap between internal and external users. It would be the employees who would closely coordinate with each other to directly create value for their internal and external customers, achieving "zero" distance between Haier and its end users.

The second level of ZZJYTs comprises a number of platforms that provide support to first-level ZZJYTs, including specific R&D, human resources, and finance support. The third level, the same as the executive level in a traditional triangular organization, is responsible for identifying and formulating strategic opportunities. It is expected to support the second-level platforms and facilitate resource allocation to the first-level ZZJYTs. In other words, the second-level and third-level ZZJYTs, serving as a resource

EXHIBIT 2. ZZJYT and the inverted-triangular organizational structure

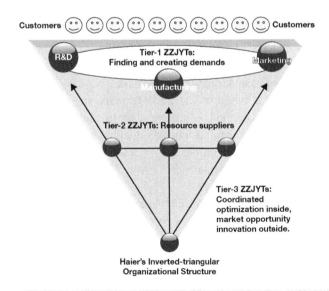

Source: Haier (2012).

platform and resource allocators, stand behind the first-level ZZJYTs to integrate ZZJYTs and employees and achieve another "zero" gap in Haier internally. This also translates into a "zero inventory" policy that requires specific planning of user resources to avoid any inventory. Manufacturing only produces according to the specific orders that sales units provide—and that is agreed upon in an internal order contract.

According to Zhang, ZZJYTs transform the company from a static organization into a network of units that can offer customized solutions to satisfy the unique, fragmented users of the Internet era. In Haier's jargon, users and hence markets not only represent external customers and stakeholders but also internal "customers;" that is, other ZZJYTs. The adoption of the ZZJYT concept goes as far as replicating the three-level inverted triangular structure within each ZZJYT. By 2012, Haier had established more than 2,000 ZZJYTs among its 80,000 employees. The ZZJYTs usually comprised between 9 and 30 members. While the majority operates in China, Haier aims to transfer the concept to its foreign operations, notably to the newly acquired operations in Japan and the rest of Southeast Asia.

As independent and self-governed organizational units, ZZJYTs function in an open-system fashion to motivate employees to reinforce this self-driven mechanism in their respective ZZJYT. Specifically, Haier implements this open system in the following aspects. The degree of autonomy is such that it is basically for tax purposes that each unit does not become a fully independent company by itself.

Win–Win Mode of Individual–Goal Combination (人单合一双赢)

This is the founding philosophy of ZZJYTs. Here *individual* refers to employees; *goal* refers to customer orders in general but further implies the needs and value of resources of both internal and external users. Thus, the *Individual-Goal Combination* focuses on the integration of employees' capabilities with the value that they create for users and the user resources. Unlike traditional management theory that defines an enterprise in terms of the contract relationships between the company and its employees, Haier uses this new concept to redefine its organization as a network between users and employees. Thus, Haier becomes a dynamic and evolving organization that can meet the end users' changing and fragmented needs. The win-win principle is shown in the incentive system that is based on the ZZJYTs managing their own profit-and-loss statement, in close collaboration with other units (including internal and external clients), to create profit. As a result, each individual has to achieve key performance indicators that, in turn, determine his/her salary. Ji Guangqiang, general director of Haier's Corporate Culture Center, explained:

> Haier doesn't provide a job for you—you are working in an open market. As an employee you need to find your own job and resources to meet your ever-changing goals. Of course, you can't always grow, but your targets may continuously change and it is your responsibility to account for these changes. Maybe your customer doesn't want a three-door fridge anymore, but rather prefers four or five doors. It is the customer that demands and you will need to follow suit to succeed.

Catfish Mechanism

The team leader is elected through a voting process with each ZZJYT member exercising voting rights. The voting process can be initiated at any time. This results in a dynamic optimization of operations and equal opportunities for all employees. It also actively encourages internal competition for positions. If a ZZJYT member showed higher performance levels than the current leader, he or she could then assume the leadership of the unit. In addition to the actual team leader, ZZJYTs also comprise a leader in waiting—a role that Haier, drawing from a Norwegian tale, referred to as the "catfish." The team leader is responsible for taking care of and developing the catfish so that the latter may be able to step in and substitute for the leader in the future.

Negative Entropy and Positive Feedback Loops

Negative entropy refers to the constant influx of first-class talent into Haier. For example, ZZJYTs are temporary organizational units in the sense that if they do not perform they are quickly disbanded. The positive feedback loop emphasizes the positive correlation between Haier employees' capabilities and market objectives. Based on new talent and a positive loop between talents and their market goals, Haier aims to form a self-managed virtuous cycle in its ZZJYT structure (see Exhibit 3).

ZZJYT in Practice

The ZZJYT and inverted triangle system is continuously evolving. Sometimes even the managers at Haier's Qingdao headquarters find it difficult to define how the system works because it is constantly revised. Operationally, Haier uses three forms to assess the performance of a ZZJYT: a Strategic Income Statement, a Clearance Form, and a People-Goal Incentive Form. In contrast from the traditional balance sheet, income statement, and cash flow statement, Haier designed its *Strategic Income Statement* to track the performance of each ZZJYT and each individual employee. Based on managerial accounting theory, the Strategic Income Statement emphasizes pre-budget and execution. It contains four quadrants: user value created, human resources, process (forecasting and accounting), and gap-closing optimization. The performance of each individual employee is thus determined by the user value created rather than the completion of tasks or seniority in the organization. The *Clearance Form* comes from the OEC (Overall, Every, Control and Clearance) approach that was implemented by Haier several years before and referred to Haier's practice of planning, executing and clearing every task and performance dimension on a daily basis. This form, in support of the Strategic Income Statement, tracks the progress of pre-budget plans and pursues zero discrepancy between plan estimation and actual result. Finally, the *People-Goal Incentive Form* sets goals for each employee in relation to market factors (rather than internally determined targets). Employees' salaries are calculated based on customer value recorded in this form.

EXHIBIT 3. Negative entropy and positive feedback loops

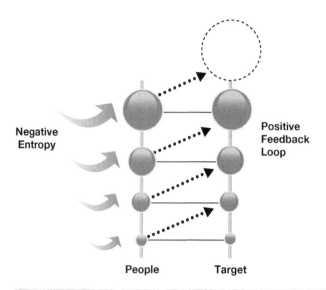

Source: Haier (2012).

Ultimately, this means that the salary is paid by the market, not Haier. As Zhang explained:

> The ZZJYT concept completely changes traditional incentive systems. Before, you were paid a salary from the company. Now, however, you are paid by the market, not Haier. There is no glass ceiling for what you can earn. If you want to get paid more, you need to develop your capability to meet more customer needs. People who leave the company often complain about the low salary they received from Haier, but the main problem is that they don't feel comfortable with being their own boss.

Naturally, income can also go down because of underperformance. For instance, in 2012, a new 24-hour delivery for all home appliances was established by Haier in China. If the goods are not delivered within 24 hours, then the customer receives them free of charge and the responsible employee is made to personally pay for them. During the year, this actually happened just four times, which is still considered a success. Similarly, if a given unit does not perform adequately, then the unit is disbanded and its members are left on their own to find a place in another unit that is willing to hire them, or they can leave the company. This is no different from actually starting a new firm and failing. Nobody will give you any guarantees in case of failing in your new venture.

Although the pressure to perform is relentless, Haier recognizes employee loyalty. Employees who have served the company for a long time are often given less demanding jobs that allow them to still keep pace with the Haier rhythm. A Haier manager explained that "it is a bit like a chair. You don't need four legs to sit on and yet you won't cut off the fourth leg."

In the end, the CEO likes to stress that the key to success is not in doing or not doing something specific, but in being aligned with the major tendencies of the times. In that sense, Haier does not aim at being successful (such success comes and goes too easily) but at being a "company of the times," thus moving in the flow of the overall context, worldwide.

HAIER IN JAPAN

Due to a traditional preference for local brands and strong competition among Japanese home appliances makers, Japan is one of the most difficult markets in the world for foreign brands to step into. Haier officially entered Japan in 2002 when it established an alliance with Sanyo Electric Co. In 2007, this alliance was formalized through a joint venture between the two partners, in which Haier owned 60%. Under this alliance, Sanyo products were sold under both the "Sanyo" and "Haier" brand names in China through Haier's sales-and-service network. The joint venture in Japan was responsible for sales of Haier products in Japan through Sanyo's distribution and service outlet. This was the first time that a major Japanese company had ever promoted Chinese products. Such an alliance, however, was a smart move for both sides because they were able to take advantage of each other's resources. It helped Haier break into the Japanese market and gradually establish its brand name through unique design and competitive prices.

On July 28, 2011, Haier and Sanyo Electric signed a merger and acquisition (M&A) memorandum of understanding. In October 2011, both sides agreed for Haier to acquire Sanyo's white goods business in Japan, Vietnam, Indonesia, the Philippines and Malaysia. The first delivery was made in January and the whole process was completed in March 2012. All remaining parts of Sanyo were acquired by Panasonic. During integration, Haier implemented a system-wide M&A approach to maximize synergy among the various functional teams in the different countries and sustain its global brand strategy. Specifically, it rearranged resources in technology, manufacturing, marketing and sales, and the service network. Ultimately, Haier came to comprise two R&D centers, four manufacturing bases (in Kyoto and Tokyo), four manufacturing bases in Hunan Motor (Japan), Vietnam, Thailand and Indonesia, and six marketing frameworks for six Asia-Pacific regions. The company adopted a dual brand strategy, with Haier and Aqua brands focusing on different market segments.

The Leader in Japan – Du Jingguo

Du Jingguo, the current president of Haier Asia International (HAI), has served at Haier since 1985. With an engineering background, Du started his career as an engineer on the production line before being promoted to manager and product developer. He was then assigned to introduce the technology transfer from Germany and became involved in operations management in the refrigerator plant. Later, he was in charge of business management, including sales service and advertisements, and was named president of the Haier Sales Company. In 1998, Du left Haier and moved to Japan for three years due to family reasons. During this period, he learned the language, customs and business practices of Japan. In 2002, at the age of 36, Du rejoined Haier and was responsible for the overall management of Haier's operations in Japan, including sales and R&D. He has also been the key person leading the Haier–Sanyo joint venture since 2007. In 2011, Du executed the acquisition of Sanyo's white goods business and established HAI.

As the presence of Haier in Japan gradually evolved from a simple import center to a joint venture, and finally to acquiring Sanyo to enter the mainstream market, Du realized that he had to instill the Haier system and culture in its Japanese operation, yet at the same time adapt to the local cultural values and traditions. Although for Western outsiders the Japanese culture may seem close to the Chinese, the invisible divides can be huge. What is more, Haier is implementing an unconventional organizational structure and management system in an attempt to be an "enterprise of its time that can adapt well to the trend," in the words of Zhang. Du needs to introduce this system in the units that he leads in Japan and the operations in other Southeast Asian countries.

CHALLENGES IN LEADING THE NEW HAIER IN JAPAN

Du adopted the following guiding principles in leading Haier Japan: respecting Japanese culture, integrating Haier culture, and, finally, shaping a unique local culture of Haier Japan. CEO Zhang commented: "It is very easy to merge and purchase any enterprise with capital, but success can only be achieved with culture and strategy, and culture integration is the most decisive factor." As a keen follower of Zhang's management philosophy, Du paid special attention to cultural differences and made extra efforts to communicate with workers at different levels so as to ensure a better mutual understanding and a smooth introduction of Haier's system.

In total, Du leads 350 employees in Japan and 6,700 workers in other Southeast Asian countries. In implementing the ZZJYT and inverted triangular system in Japan, Du faces huge challenges, which are intensified by the many cultural differences. How can he lead a Chinese brand to break into a market that has been traditionally dominated by well-known Japanese brands such as Hitachi, Panasonic, Sharp, and Mitsubishi? Also, customers in China and Japan, much like the employees in Haier and Sanyo, hold a different understanding of quality. Although generally Haier enjoys a reputation for its product quality, the quality standard in Japan tends to be higher and customers are much more demanding, not tolerating, for instance, a slight scratch on the packaging materials of an otherwise perfect product.

Internally, a strong collectivistic culture in Japan prevents companies from adopting a more individual-based compensation system, which is the core of the Individual-Goal Combination mechanism in Haier. While leading the joint venture, Du once wanted to distribute individualized incentives and encountered strong objections from Sanyo managers, who insisted on the importance of team spirit and equality.

Moreover, traditional lifelong employment and seniority-based reward and promotion systems, though gradually abandoned by some Japanese companies, still exist in big Japanese firms. This makes merit-based promotions extremely difficult to implement.

Finally, Du also faced the ultimate question of whether Sanyo workers would be willing to join Haier, since they had the choice to stay with Sanyo, now part of the Panasonic Group. When Du first started running the Haier–Sanyo joint venture, a Japanese director came to him with a provoking comment: "Each Chinese individual alone is smart and competent, but when you put two Chinese workers together, they will not be able to perform. The Japanese are different—we play collective games."

Aiming High

One day, Du was reviewing the first post-acquisition annual sales target prepared by the sales team. "JPY7 billion seems a bit low," Du thought. But he did not want to impose a sales target on the team.

Du had always kept in mind the vision of CEO Zhang of making Haier the number one brand in home appliances in the world, and he decided to move quickly toward this goal. He was determined to revise the first sales target of JPY7 billion and push it higher. As Du remarked:

> The goal is to one day be number one. Although we cannot reach it overnight, we need to start with number five, then number three, then eventually reach the place of number one. I did a calculation based on the idea of being number five in the market as a baseline for the discussion, but I did not reveal it to the sales team.

He then called a series of meetings with the sales team and asked them to explain how they derived the JPY7 billion figure. The team pointed to the specific constraints they faced for a higher target. For example, the team emphasized that several negotiations would still be ongoing, leaving uncertainty as to the overall project. It would take three months after the January delivery date to withdraw all of the old products from the market. Furthermore, more time would be required to prepare the new product launch. Communication and coordination with the marketing team would also take time. In total, it would take another six months to improve the products and develop new designs.

Du then went through the list of constraints and asked the team for alternatives in overcoming them. Du explained:

> I wanted them to operate as an inverted triangle. They would make decisions and I would offer support and resources.

The R&D team originally planned to start developing new products for Haier Japan after the initial delivery of the M&A, with a possible launch date around March/April 2012. However, Du came up with a bold strategy—he decided to launch all new products right after the M&A delivery. To achieve this, he would need the R&D team to start working on completely newly designed products even before the Haier R&D office and facility were ready and the employees had been officially transferred from Sanyo to Haier. Du rented an empty building near Kyoto that would be the future

R&D Center of Haier washing machines and asked the R&D staff to start designing new products with the objective of launching new products on January 6. For some weeks, the building had no windows, yet the team was already working inside. It was winter and extremely cold. "The team needed to wear heavy coats and worked very long hours in the building without the protection of windows in the cold winter to meet the deadline," Du commented.

Finally, they accomplished the challenging goal and launched 33 new products designed for Japanese customers on January 6, and had them distributed all over Japan within two weeks. This "instant launch" was something never seen before and it surprised the Japanese competitors.

When Du met with the sales team and they together found solutions to overcome the obstacles one by one, they were able to move the target of JPY7 billion first to JPY27 billion, then to JPY32 billion, and, finally, to JPY35 billion. All members of the sales team expressed their commitment to reaching the target of JPY35 billion in their own way, displayed as an inverted triangle in the office of the sales team in Osaka (Exhibit 4). In July 2012, this target was 100% on schedule, with the sale of Haier washing machine and refrigerator brands occupying third and fourth place, respectively, in the Japanese market. Du remarked:

> In fact, Japanese workers are very diligent and hardworking. It is only that they could not imagine that reaching such ambitious goal within such a short time was attainable. Once I broke these mental obstacles and set up clear goals for them, they became committed to the goals and did their best to make them happen. When they saw the first results, they knew that it was really possible and gained the confidence to achieve future challenging goals.

BRIDGING CULTURAL DIFFERENCES

Having lived in Japan for years and being married to a Japanese woman, Du had learned about Japanese culture and was able to clearly see the cultural differences. When Du first took charge of the Haier–Sanyo joint venture in 2007, Japanese workers would often not express their feelings openly to Du. To communicate better with the Japanese workers, he divided the 160 employees at that time into 16 teams of 10. Every few nights, he would go out drinking with a team. After two years of drinking, the Japanese workers finally felt comfortable talking and drinking with Du in a more open way. "However," Du said with a wry smile, "I got all kinds of gastric and duodenal ulcers after that." Little by little, in his way, Du gained acceptance from the Japanese workers.

Merit-Based Rewards and Promotions

One of the core concepts of the ZZJYT is to connect each worker's performance with the market and reward him or her accordingly (that is individual–goal combination

EXHIBIT 4. Commitment of the sales team to the JPY35 billion target

In the photo: Du Jingguo, president of Haier Japan.
Source: Picture taken by the case authors at the Haier Japanese headquarters in Osaka, July 2012.

and win–win). This means that workers do not receive equal amounts of incentive bonuses but rather receive rewards according to their contribution. For Japanese workers, this practice was hard to accept. While leading the joint venture, Du spent six months communicating with the Japanese team on this issue. Finally, he decided to withhold the part of the bonuses representing Sanyo's share because his Japanese counterpart did not agree with his approach but insisted on implementing the system in the Haier way and gave out 60% of the bonuses that represented Haier's share in the joint venture.

Similarly, Du at one point wanted to promote a 35-year-old worker to the position of director. However, it would go against the Japanese value of seniority if he got promoted sooner than an older colleague. Over the course of a year, Du publicized the performance of this young man in the company and indicated the problem of the current appraisal system that failed to reveal the outstanding performance of the young man. Two years later, Du promoted the young man to director, while at the same time assigning the more senior colleagues titles of "Responsible Director" with clear roles and responsibilities so that they would not feel ignored. Little by little, the merit-based system embedded in Haier's ZZJYT was accepted in Haier's Japanese operation.

After the acquisition, Du talked to former Sanyo sales people and tried to convince them to sign an Individual-Goal Combination contract, offering them higher incentives for higher performance (win–win). Some of them did not feel comfortable and refused to sign it in the beginning. Rather than pushing them, Du tried to help them understand the underlying logic of the contract.

Retaining Japanese Workers

When Haier was about to acquire Sanyo's home appliances operation, Du and his management team estimated that about 30% of employees might quit. Indeed, many workers had joined Sanyo with the idea of staying there until retirement. They were afraid of moving to a Chinese company. At that moment, Sanyo had very limited new product development and resource investment, but Du kept communicating with the employees about the plan, system, and prospects if they stayed with Haier.

CULTURAL INTEGRATION AS AN ONGOING PROCESS

Haier Japan seemed to be off to a successful start under the leadership of Du, who attributes his achievement to the well-devised strategy and management system defined by Zhang. "What I am doing is simply trying to understand the thinking and strategy of Mr. Zhang, trying to align my operation with it, and continuously adapting it to local realities," said Du.

Yet, cultural integration is an ongoing process—challenges may persist and require further effort to handle them. For example, some Japanese workers continue to feel confused about the structure. They see Haier Japan functioning as a star (that is the juxtaposition of a normal and the inverted triangular structures). Du and Haier Japan will need to continuously experiment with the ZZJYT system (which is still quite new and in a fine-tuning stage back in China) and instill the Haier values into the Japanese operation.

Conversations among Japanese Employees

The day after a regular visit of Du to the washing machine R&D center near Kyoto, three senior managers and two chief engineers of the center had lunch together.

"We knew Sanyo was not performing at the levels at which it used to perform some years ago," one manager said. "In fact, the company was putting itself in the same position that other companies faced in the final years of the last century, when Sanyo bought them. In the end, it all worked out for the best, for the former independent companies and for Sanyo. So we keep asking ourselves if this is not the same situation."

"Yes, the situation is similar, but there are some differences. Haier is a Chinese company, and when we talk with Mr. Du we feel confident about his capabilities and his intentions. But where will Mr. Du be in 20 years? With Sanyo we did not have to think about this because we were confident that Sanyo was going to be there for us always, forever. We used to say that we were Sanyo employees the same way I say

I belong to my family. Can we say the same now? Are we going to 'be' Haier employees, or should we say that we are 'now' Haier employees?" added another manager.

"There is little we can do about that," commented one chief engineer. "We will never see ourselves as Haier employees the same way we saw ourselves as Sanyo employees, but Haier provides us with important challenges in developing new technologies, and the market will respond to that. In fact, Haier is being very brave entering the Japanese market, competing head-to-head with the most advanced brands and products. It shows an amazing drive to succeed in the most difficult environment. And this is our environment. If we succeed here, we will succeed anywhere. There was a time when we felt exactly the same with Sanyo, but that was gone well before Haier acquired us. We just might have an interesting combination: a resourceful company, strong market prospects and the will to face all the technological challenges. What else do we need?"

The other chief engineer responded, "Well, we need to combine those aspects into a new way of organizing ourselves through the inverted triangle, and this does not seem easy. Mr. Du is telling us that we are an inverted triangle but he talks from his top position. I would like to see how that works in practice."

"Actually, Mr. Du says that he is the one who wants to see how it works—that he is here to see (not us) and we are here to act (not he)," explained one senior manager. "Also, I find that the idea of an inverted triangle is promising in helping us move beyond country issues. So far, it makes a difference for us to think in terms of whether our boss is Chinese or Japanese. But if the inverted triangle idea works out the way it should, there is nobody above of us, neither Chinese nor Japanese, just our customers. It is just us figuring out the best way to produce something. Haier probably has an advantage here in terms of how to deal with global and local tensions (as long as the idea really works, obviously)."

"Actually, Sanyo had tried some empowerment approaches in the past that somehow remind us of the inverted triangle, but they never really worked. They seemed to be very fashionable in the United States, but not here," echoed one chief engineer.

"Indeed, but we need to be careful. If possible, I would still prefer a Japanese boss," said one manager. "On the other hand, the Chinese seem to behave differently from the Japanese. We prefer someone who is Japanese because we think of how Japanese leaders behave. But these people are not Japanese; they will behave differently, so it may not be relevant at all whether they are Japanese or not. Mr. Du and most of the Chinese Haier employees in Japan actually speak very decent Japanese. They do not speak like us, but they are closer to fully mastering our language than anyone who has been around here in the past. It may actually be easier for them to adapt to us than the other way around. And yet, this idea of the inverted triangle can be very powerful; it may relativize these differences. We need to see how it really works."

"That is up to us," said a manager. "Remember, we are not here to see it happen, we are here to make it happen. It is for headquarters to see that we, not they, do it."

Yet, another chief engineer commented, "A few days ago I performed a little experiment at home with my two kids. They are 16 and 14 years old. I told them that we at Haier were going to begin to work under a different system, the inverted triangle. I asked them how that would work in their school. They could not understand at all what I was telling them. They were afraid their class would turn into total chaos if the teacher proposed something like that, and that students would not know what to do. My wife nearly suggested that I was a little bit crazy. The question is whether we are prepared for this: to become our own bosses and answer not only for our work and hours, but for our initiative and creativity as well. It is like we have been under a school system, with someone always monitoring our work, and now we have to become the teachers. This is not going to be easy, at least not for the older people, and they are our masters. Should we expect everybody, absolutely everybody, to be able to perform under this new system? I am afraid it may create a division between those who enjoy the system more, especially the younger people, and those who have worked too many years under the Sanyo system. How are Haier and Mr. Du going to deal with this?"

Kathrin Köster and Günter K. Stahl

LENOVO–IBM: BRIDGING CULTURES, LANGUAGES, AND TIME ZONES

(A) AN AUDACIOUS DEAL

...Cultural integration is still one of the biggest challenges.... We face the combined effect of different corporate cultures and the difference between the cultures of the East and the West.

—Orr & Xing, 2007[1]

ON TUESDAY, DECEMBER 20, 2005, the public learned of the departure of Steve Ward, the CEO of Lenovo. He had lasted just eight months in the position before he was replaced by William Amelio, a former Dell executive.[2] The move came as China's Lenovo seemed poised to become the world's leading PC maker, despite its difficult start.

Just 12 months prior, on December 8, 2004, Yang Yuanqing, who was then Lenovo's CEO, announced his intention to purchase IBM's PC division for US$1.75 billion—an unprecedented move for a company based in an emerging market (for a timeline of the deal, see Exhibit 1). The radical deal would transform Lenovo from a company that sold exclusively in China into a major global player. Furthermore, IBM's PC division accounted for three times the sales that Lenovo earned, so the announcement seemed less like a merger and more like David trying to swallow Goliath.

THE LONG MARCH FROM LEGEND TO LENOVO

Prior to 2004, Lenovo had been known as Legend, a company established by Liu Chuanzhi, a graduate of the Xi'an Military Communications Engineering College. In 1984, he and a few colleagues spun off Legend from the state-owned Chinese Academy of Sciences, which provided seed money of US$25,000 that the young

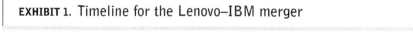

EXHIBIT 1. Timeline for the Lenovo–IBM merger

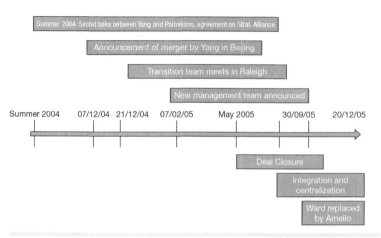

entrepreneurs used to set up shop in a ramshackle building in "Swindler's Alley," Beijing's electronics black market. Very quickly, Liu Chuanzhi realized that differentiation through innovation was the only way forward. The Legend brand thus developed an add-on card that allowed Chinese applications to run on English-language operating systems, which catapulted China into the PC age. For this innovation, Legend received one of China's highest honors, a National Science Technology Progress Award.

In contrast to its main competitor Great Wall, Legend was not well connected to or protected by government authorities. For example, the company was refused a license to manufacture in China. But with innovation as its watchword, Legend came up with the idea of entering into a joint venture in Hong Kong, in which capacity it would also build motherboards and PCs and thereby outmaneuver its better-connected Chinese rivals. However, it was not until 1990 that Liu Chuanzhi could realize his dream to build PCs in his home country.

In 1994, Legend went public to raise capital in Hong Kong and thus be able to compete with foreign computer manufacturers, whose products had been flooding the Chinese markets since the beginning of the 1990s. Legend introduced a Pentium PC in China before its competitors. This first-mover advantage contributed greatly to its status as the leading PC maker on the Chinese market.

Although Legend diversified into a few non-core businesses, such as IT services, the PC business remained the center of its operations. During the mid-1990s, a young manager, Yang Yuanqing, stood out for his work in this division. An unusually bright engineer with a strong desire for clarity and precision, Yang had been hired straight out of school and, like many of the company's high fliers, had been promoted at a very young age. A forceful personality and firm believer in discipline and centralized decision making, the young Yang Yuanqing prompted descriptions such as acutely intelligent, tough, and decisive,[3] as well as autocratic in his leadership and abrasive. As an observer noted:

> Yang's colleagues thought himself both strict with others and immodest about himself. For sure, he was honest and straightforward to the point of being blunt. Sometimes people were afraid to enter his office. Yang would eventually have to learn a more co-operative management style but for the moment there was no time.[4]

Yet Yang also proved a visionary, with a sharp eye for promising innovations and new business opportunities. In retrospect, his arrival at the company was a true turning point in Legend's history.

With Liu, Yang shared the conviction that to achieve ambitious goals, Legend needed to attract China's best and brightest and then imbue them with the Legend spirit. Newcomers had to "fit the mold," and the company went to great lengths to instill the right mindset, values, and work ethic.

Legend's vice president Du Jianhua described the desired corporate culture, as well as required changes in management practices and individual behavior, using the "1-2-3-4-5 formula.[5]"

1. Adopt one common culture and vision that all Legend employees and managers share.
2. Require dual attitudes from employees. That is, Legend employees were expected to treat customers with the utmost respect and care, in line with the motto, "the customer is the emperor," and go the extra mile to meet customers' needs. Legend's definition of "customers" included internal customers, suppliers, dealers, and distributors, so employees also were warned not to offend or exploit these members of the extended Legend family. The second employee characteristic that the company prioritized was frugality. Every employee needed to be aware that Legend was a profit-maximizing organization, with the motto "save money, save energy, save time."
3. Concentrate on three fundamental leadership tasks: build the management team, determine the strategy, and lead the troops. These tasks, reflecting the philosophy of Sunzi, constituted not only the capabilities that leaders needed to possess but also the recommended approach to managing people. Thus, management was to instill discipline and obedience in the rank-and-file staff, and ensure that the employees strictly adhered to company rules and policies. Only in the case of an emergency or crisis that might cause severe damage to the company could employees act according to their own judgment.
4. Adhere to four commandments: (1) do not abuse your position to line your own pockets; (2) do not accept bribes; (3) do not take any second job outside the company; and (4) do not discuss your salary with anybody in the company. These rules defined minimum requirements; employees also were expected to meet additional standards of conduct. In a management meeting in August 1997, Yang described the ideal Legend employee as follows: Accurate, careful, and meticulous

when it comes to details; able to analyze the root causes of problems and come up with practicable solutions; able to effectively communicate and cooperate with others; and marked by relentless self-discipline. At Legend, such military-like discipline was strictly enforced and backed by stiff penalties for misbehavior. Yang was convinced that only under pressure and with clear rules and accountabilities would employees perform and thrive. Employees had to clock in and out. If they came late to a meeting, they had to stand for 1 minute behind their chair. If they were seen outside the office building without a plausible explanation, they had to accept a pay deduction.

5. Consider five changes. As the twentieth century drew to a close, Legend's top management perceived a need to move away from hierarchical control toward a more participative style of leadership that encouraged people to take ownership and responsibility of their performance. Strict lines of authority and top-down control, Yang and Liu came to realize, would prevent Legend from responding to market needs and trends and achieving international significance. Thus, the company faced the significant challenge of delegating responsibility broadly and promoting an entrepreneurial spirit, as well as leadership at all levels. Five changes in behavior and skills would be needed to implement Legend's new management model, which Yang introduced in 1998. Specifically, managers were expected to:

    5.1. Work toward meeting goals and objectives rather than blindly following a supervisor's instructions;
    5.2. Develop from a people-oriented into a task-oriented manager;
    5.3. Do what needs to be done to respond to the needs of the customer;
    5.4. Think in terms of numbers and specify concrete, quantifiable objectives to be achieved; and
    5.5. Become more inquisitive and open-minded.

These management principles and rules aimed to impart a greater performance orientation and to cultivate a culture of accountability throughout the company. They were also designed to reflect the company's core values: customer service, innovative and entrepreneurial spirit, accuracy and truth-seeking, trustworthiness, and integrity.

To instill these values, Legend's top managers decided to adopt Western-style performance management and human resource (HR) practices. It was among the first Chinese companies to introduce a stock option program for managers. It also implemented a forced ranking, or "rank and yank," system that required managers to identify the top and bottom 10 percent of performers, similar to the appraisal system introduced by Jack Welch at General Electric. This prompted some observers to conclude that Legend was not a "typical" Asian company.[6]

In 2001, when Yang was appointed CEO and Liu took on the chairman role, Legend also began globalizing. Yang and Liu had become convinced that growth opportunities in China were limited by the increasingly fierce competition in the Chinese market. To pursue opportunities outside China, they established a new vision for Legend, namely, to join the Fortune 500 and become the first global Chinese player. But the name Legend was already copyright-protected outside of China, so the company renamed itself Lenovo—"Le" from Legend and "Novo" to indicate a new start. Also in 2004, Lenovo announced its decision to become the worldwide partner of the International Olympic Committee, as the computer equipment provider for the 2006 Winter Olympics in Turin, Italy, and the 2008 Beijing Olympic Games.

THE IBM OPPORTUNITY: ACQUIRING AN AMERICAN ICON

IBM, an icon of corporate America, was founded in 1911 as The Computer-Tabulating-Recording Company. After its geographical expansion into Europe, South America, Asia, and Australia, the company took the new name International Business Machines, or IBM, under the leadership of Sir Thomas J. Watson Sr., the head of the organization from 1915 to 1956. A self-made man with no higher-level education, he reportedly stated: "The trouble with every one of us is that we don't think enough. We don't get paid for working with our feet; we get paid for working with our heads" (Forbes, 1948).[7] The slogan "THINK" was thus a mantra for IBM; it was also the motto above the door of the IBM schoolhouse where all new hires, usually fresh from college, had to undergo 12 weeks of education and orientation.[8]

The beliefs of Sir Watson not only prompted the company's innovativeness but also had long-term impacts on the attitudes and behaviors of its workforce. Watson emphasized impeccable customer service and insisted on dark-suited, white-shirted, alcohol-abstinent salesmen. With fervor, he instilled company pride and loyalty through job security for every worker, company sports teams, family outings, and a company band. Employees received comprehensive benefits and were convinced of their own superior knowledge and skills.[9]

IBM also prided itself on shaping the entire computer industry. With the advent of high-performing integrated circuits, "Big Blue"—a corporate nickname that recognized IBM's army of blue-suited salesmen and blue logo—could launch the System/360 processors that enabled it to lead the market with high profit margins and few competitive threats for decades. This position changed with the rise of UNIX and the age of personal computing. In 1986, IBM developed the first laptop, which weighed 12 lbs; by 1992, it was promoting the ThinkPad, the first notebook computer with a 10.4" color display that used Thin Film transistor technology.

Despite its pioneering entries into the PC market, IBM did not make its PC business a top priority and it surrendered control of its highest-value components, namely, the operating system and the microprocessor, to Microsoft and Intel, respectively. Critics widely attributed IBM's decline in the late-1980s and early-1990s to its failure to protect its technological lead; it became a follower rather than an innovator.[10] The once-dominant giant came close to collapse when its mainframe computer business, the primary growth engine of the 1970s and 1980s, ground to a halt.

But the CEO in what were arguably IBM's darkest hours brought the company back from the brink. When he took over in 1993, Louis Gerstner recognized that IBM's cherished values—customer service, excellence, and respect—had become a sort of rigor mortis, which turned them from strengths into liabilities. "Superior customer service" had come to mean servicing machines on the customers' premises;

"excellence" had mutated into an obsession with perfectionism. The numerous required checks, approvals, and validations nearly paralyzed the decision-making process. Even the belief in respect for the individual had turned into an entitlement, such that employees could reap rich benefits without earning them.[11]

Under Gerstner's leadership, the company was recentralized and structured around processes. He introduced global customer relationship management, a complex web of processes, roles, and IT tools that affected tens of thousands of employees. It took IBM nearly a decade to remake itself into a comprehensive software, hardware, and services provider, but Big Blue's successful strategic repositioning increased the "we feeling" and strengthened what has been described as an almost cult-like culture.[12]

Thus, when Sam Palmisano took over as CEO in 2002, his challenge was to come up with a mandate for the next stage in the company's transformation. His primary aim was to get different parts of the company to work together so IBM could offer a bundle of "integrated solutions"—hardware, software, services, financing—at a single price. A set of shared values supported the change in strategy and ensured consistency across the globe:

1. Dedication to every client's success.
2. Innovation that matters—for our company and for the world.
3. Trust and personal responsibility in all relationships.[13]

These core values provided the basis for IBM's management system and a crucial orientation frame for its diverse workforce, which serves clients in more than 170 countries.

Along with these changes to the company's orientations and values, in 2004 it made another sharp break with its history: IBM would sell off its PC business. The move would affect 10,000 IBMers working in the PC business, which was part of the company's Personal Systems Group. Although this division contributed 13% of the company's overall turnover of US$96.3 billion in 2004, it also incurred losses from the PC business.[14]

THE GREAT LEAP FORWARD

When IBM announced its interest in selling its PC division, Lenovo jumped at the chance; for Lenovo, the IBM deal was a giant leap forward. It gave Lenovo access to the computer giant's technology and expertise, a foothold into the lucrative US and European markets, and worldwide brand recognition.

As a well-established brand worth an estimated US$53 billion,[15] IBM was globally present and enjoyed a reputation for high quality, innovation, and reliability. As part of the deal, Lenovo obtained the right to use the IBM brand name for five years. This agreement would help maintain customer loyalty and avoid the risk that customers would notice any major changes. IBM also committed to continuing to provide service for its PCs and laptops, a move aimed to dispel customers' service concerns. Moreover, Lenovo hoped to benefit from IBM's long experience in global marketing and sales. Lenovo's own sales channels were limited to China, where it maintained excellent relations with major distributors, mainly due to the organization's transparent rules and procedures. But IBM had sales, support, and delivery operations all around the world.

In addition, IBM's huge sales volume would help lower the company's component costs. In the PC industry, 70–80% of total revenues go to components, so economies of scale are key contributors to keeping costs low. Lenovo expected to realize annual savings of US$200 million just through larger purchasing volumes. The "new Lenovo" thus could tackle price-sensitive markets, such as India, and appeal more to small and medium-sized enterprises around the world. Lenovo estimated that these markets offered growth opportunities of about US$1 billion.[16] Finally, Lenovo extended its product portfolio overnight, immediately offering a broad range of products and services to diverse customers.

The deal also seemed to make sense for IBM. Since its reinvention in the 1990s, IBM had been moving constantly toward becoming a software and integrated services provider. In 1993, revenues from the hardware business represented more than half of IBM's total revenues; by 2004, they were less than a third.[17] With this strategic reorientation, the low-margin hardware business lost importance. In addition, IBM's PC division continued to be a source of ongoing profit drains. From 2001 to mid-2004, the unit accumulated losses of US$965 million, which imposed a major burden on the overall organization.[18] The Lenovo deal promised to stop this profit drain and pave the way into the lucrative Chinese market. Lenovo's well-developed distribution network provided inroads into China, especially those leading to new corporate customers of IBM's software and service solutions. Lenovo's existing relationships with regulatory bodies and potential corporate customers, as well as its well-established brand name, could help IBM gain footing and expand quickly in mainland China.

Thus, Lenovo–IBM would obtain a competitive advantage that its closest competitors, Hewlett-Packard and Dell, could not match. As one Lenovo executive recalled: "On paper this was pretty much a match made in heaven."[19] The challenge was to make it work in practice.

NOTES

All interview excerpts were taken from Baumeister, B. (2009). Lenovo's acquisition of IBM's PC division: A success story of cultural post-combination integration? Unpublished master thesis, WU Vienna, unless referenced otherwise.

1. Orr, G. and Xing, J. (2007). When Chinese companies go global: An interview with Lenovo's Mary Ma. *McKinsey on Finance,* 23: 18–22. Available from http://corporatefinance. mckinsey.com/knowledge/knowledgemanagement/mof.htm [accessed May 16, 2013].
2. Einhorn, B. (2005). Lenovo's new boss–from Dell. *Business Week,* December 21, 2005. Available from http://www.businessweek.com/technology/content/dec2005/tc20051221_376268. htm [accessed May 16, 2013].
3. Ling, Z. (2006). *The Lenovo Affair–The Growth of China's Computer Giant and Its Takeover of IBM-PC.* Singapore: Wiley & Sons.
4. Feng, S. and Elfring, J. (2006). *The Legend behind Lenovo: The Chinese IT Company that Dares to Succeed.* Hong Kong: Asia 2000.

5. N.N. (2009). Lianxiang qiye wenhua yu guanli sixiang 12345, June 16. Available from http://oxford.icxo.com/htmlnews/2009/06/16/1389015.htm [accessed May 16, 2013].

6. London, S. (2005). The making of a multinational part II: Your rules and my processes. *Financial Times,* November 10, 13.

7. Bell, L. (1948). Thomas J. Watson. In Forbes, B. (ed.), *America's Fifty Foremost Business Leaders*. New York: Forbes and Son 427.

8. Weeks, J. (2004). Culture and leadership at IBM. INSEAD case no. 10/2004-5239.

9. Collins, J. and Porras, J (2002). *Built to Last, Successful Habits of Visionary Companies*. New York: HarperCollins Publishers.

10. Mills, D. and Friesen, G. (1996). *Broken Promises—An Unconventional View of What Went Wrong at IBM*. Cambridge, MA: Harvard Business Press.

11. Gerstner, L. V. Jr. (2002). Who Says Elephants Can't Dance? Inside IBM's Historic Turn-around. London: Harper Collins.

12. Ibid.

13. Palmisano, S. (2004). IBM Annual Meeting of Stockholders, Providence, Rhode Island, April 27, 2004. Available from: www.ibm.com/ibm/sjp/04-27-2004.html [accessed May 16, 2013].

14. IBM (2004). *IBM Annual Report 2004*. Available from: ftp://ftp.software.ibm.com/annualreport/2004/ [accessed May 16, 2013].

15. Wolf, D. (2009). Lenovo: Amelio's exit a sign that IBM integration hitting the rocks? *Seeking Alpha*, February 5. Available from: http://seekingalpha.com/article/118829-lenovo-amelio-s-exit-a-sign-that-ibm-intetration-hitting-the-rocks [accessed May 16, 2013].

16. Ibid.

17. IBM (2004). IBM and Lenovo: New leadership in global PCs. Available from: http://i.i.com.com/cnwk.1d/html/news/all_hands_presentation_final.ppt [accessed May 16, 2013].

18. Pilzweger, M. (2006). IBM: PC-Sparte seit Jahren im Minus, *PC-Welt*, January 19. Available from: www.pcwelt.de/news/IBM-PC-Sparte-seit-Jahren-im-Minus-18253.html [accessed May 16, 2013].

19. Quelch, J. and Knoop, C.-I. (2006). Lenovo: Building a global brand. Case no. 9-507-014. Harvard Business School, Cambridge, MA.

(B) INTEGRATION CHALLENGES

POST-MERGER INTEGRATION

While the synergies between Lenovo and IBM looked great on paper, the roadblocks to making Lenovo–IBM the PC industry's world leader remained formidable. Not only would the process need to merge two companies with vastly different business models and cultures across 12 times zones, but also the combined company needed to stay constantly competitive in the fast-paced PC industry. Michael Dell, chairman of Lenovo's main rival, asserted: "It won't work."[1] Most observers agreed.

But Lenovo's top executives vowed to prove these skeptics wrong. Their vision for the new Lenovo was to create a computer powerhouse that would combine the best of both worlds and thereby reinvent the entire global PC industry. As Lenovo executives stated:

> What Lenovo brings to the table is the best from East and West. From the original Lenovo we have the understanding of emerging markets, excellent efficiency, and a focus on long-term strategy. From IBM we have deep insights into worldwide markets and best practices from western companies.[2]

This best-of-both-worlds integration approach could work if the combination represented a partnership rather than a takeover. Lenovo's CEO Yang repeatedly stressed his perception of the IBM deal as a "marriage of equals," based on trust, respect, and compromise. Yang demonstrated his willingness to compromise right from the start: he stepped down as CEO to make way for IBM's Steve Ward, while he became chairman. Yang also accepted Ward's proposal to locate the new headquarters in New York, rather than establishing dual headquarters in the United States and China. Lenovo's new global headquarters took up the top floor of a non-descript office building outside the city; the staff of the IBM PC division mainly continued to work out of their existing site in Raleigh, North Carolina.

Despite the seeming friendliness of the deal, cross-border problems soon emerged. Simple geographical distance was a major barrier: the flight from Beijing to New York took 13 hours and crossed 12 time zones. Without any direct flights from Beijing to Raleigh, North Carolina, that trip took an additional few hours. Making the trip, in either direction, for a day of meetings or workshops was not possible, and any gathering or information exchange had to be planned weeks in advance to make the trip worthwhile. The thousands of miles separating the company's main locations made exchanging information about best practices incredibly difficult. The regular business hours of New York and Beijing overlap only for three to four hours each day; if the company needed to include European colleagues, the operation became nearly impossible—or required employees to arrive at the office at very odd hours.

Even as they racked up miles of travel and readjusted their alarm clocks, the management teams on both sides continued to view the deal as an opportunity to learn. They displayed a genuine and remarkable willingness to set aside their own egos and make decisions in the best interest of the combined company. As one former IBM executive recalled:

> Where the Chinese approach worked best, we borrowed it, and where the IBM approach worked best, we borrowed that. Or maybe an outside approach. The point was to do the right thing ... because the fundamental mission [was] to be seen as a global corporation, not a Western and not a Chinese company. And wherever we could get ideas or implement tools that advance that idea, we did.

This pragmatic and learning-oriented approach also featured what appeared to be an honest enthusiasm for creating something new and better. Ravi Marwaha, the Indian-Australian in charge of running Lenovo's worldwide sales, admitted, "I spent 36 years in IBM. I could easily have retired. Why am I here? Because it is exciting."[3] Another senior Lenovo executive explained:

> We are the first of this kind in the world, and I think people are authentically and genuinely excited about being in a place that is very fresh, and young, and new. ... It is an experiment and something that has never been done before, and there is no company like us in the world.

Such enthusiasm might have been expected from Lenovo, given that it was Lenovo that had acquired IBM's PC business. But the general sense of excitement also seemed shared among the IBM PC executives, who had for years felt like the unpopular stepsister in their former company. IBM had considered hardware a peripheral business and thus made few investments in the PC division; with the merger, the PC division became a core business again, even if for Lenovo.

This positive attitude spanned various levels of the organization. In the first days of the new Lenovo, people took creative steps to bridge their geographical distance. IBM sent camera teams to Raleigh and Beijing, to enable video greetings to various counterparts around the globe. In the call center in Raleigh, employees filmed themselves throwing their IBM badges into the trash. Frances O'Sullivan, COO of Lenovo International, initiated a program called the "Trash Bin Project," which encouraged ex-IBMers to submit examples of what they had done in their previous work life but did not want to do in the new Lenovo.[4]

CREATING A STRUCTURE

The new Lenovo started with three separate business units: China PCs, China Cell Phones, and International Operations (the former IBM PC division). In this sense, business continued much as usual for the IBMers, except that project teams formed to support different functions, such as sales, finance, and order management. The project teams consisted of former Lenovo and IBM managers and they took the responsibility of preparing the further integration of the functions.

Yang Yuanqing announced a managerial restructuring on September 30, 2005. Top management jobs would be split approximately evenly between the Chinese and Western sides (Exhibit 2). A third of the board members would be from Hong Kong (where Lenovo is registered); another one-third would come from the United States and Europe; and the rest would be from China.[5] This restructuring aimed to provide a framework for further integration, but it also was designed in accordance with Lenovo's goal of joining the league of global technology powerhouses in that it provided a multinational management team spread across national boundaries and several time zones.

The new management structure then led to closer integration in functions such as supply chain management, planning and control, product development, and marketing. In support of its global supply chain, the company applied a unified IT system that enabled it to ship directly to 100 countries, usually with products configured to order.[6] In the wake of this integration, the corporate headquarters moved from New York to Raleigh.

But the integration also meant that there were some redundancies, especially in IBM's sales structure. Therefore, the layoffs announced in March 2006 affected approximately 1,000 of the company's 21,400 employees. The cuts spread across company offices in the Americas, Asia-Pacific, and EMEA regions.[7]

UBIQUITOUS DIFFERENCES

The functions integrated, headquarters moved, and managerial responsibility was shared. Yet without a common language and shared values, it would be impossible to form a unified, global management team.

A year before the acquisition, Lenovo had launched a major campaign to improve the English-language skills of its managers and employees. Most of the company's

---

EXHIBIT 2. "New" Lenovo's executive team

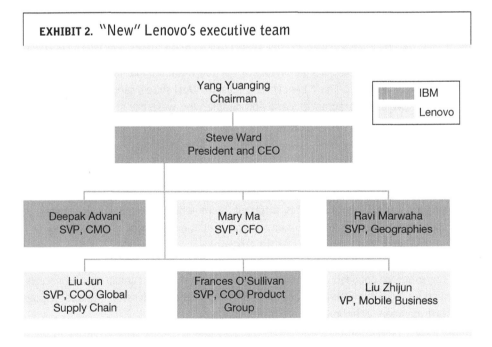

senior Chinese executives could speak some English, though not all were able to do so fluently or with sufficient ease to support effective working relationships. Few of the lower-level managers were fluent in English. Of the IBM managers, virtually no one had even rudimentary knowledge of Mandarin. These immense language barriers led to lengthy meetings and frequent misunderstandings. For example, one of the most senior executives did not speak English, so board meetings had to include a translator. Yet the company determined that English would be its corporate language.

The language barriers seemed obvious from the start; less apparent were the widely divergent preferences regarding communication styles. Especially tricky were conference calls, which offered no visuals to help the participants to interpret the true meanings and nuances of others' verbal comments. Bill Matson, the HR Director of Lenovo, observed:

> IBM leaders would do most of the talking and the Lenovo leaders would do most of the listening. The Chinese, and Asian cultures in general, are much more silent in a conversation. They first think about what they want to say before they say it. And if you think about what you want to say before you say it, and you also translate it from your native language into English ... you can understand that a 5 second or a 7 second gap in a conversation is not a long time. Yet, to a Western person, 5 seconds silence in a conversation seems like an eternity. So, often times what you would see in meetings is that the Western leaders would be filling in the gap in conversation, and therefore would dominate these discussions, and all too often would not spend as much time as they probably should have seeking out the perspectives and experiences of their Lenovo colleagues.

These differences in communication style were not just frustrating; they affected decision-making and problem-solving quality.

Therefore, the company established a culture integration committee[8] and instituted several programs, designed to overcome such barriers. The "East Meets West" program taught the company's global executives about the foundations of both Chinese and American cultures. The "Lenovo Expression Workshop" targeted the Chinese managers—typically, pragmatic, hands-on people who were not strong communicators, according to Western standards. One Chinese manager explained:

> When Chinese people talk, we start from the background, and then we ... talk about the present situation and the challenges that we are facing, and then we gather lots of supporting materials, so at the end we say 'ok, this is our proposal.' I guess this is different from what you call the Western approach: You have an executive summary at the very beginning, basically you tell what you want to tell on the first page.

The program coached Chinese executives in Western communication and presentation styles, with the ultimate goal of facilitating mutual understanding and helping the staff members collaborate more effectively.

Beyond these differences, the variance in cultural norms and values became something of an issue; the United States and China can be worlds apart, both literally and figuratively. In particular, their attitudes toward hierarchy and authority are widely divergent. As one former senior IBM executive observed:

> Lenovo was a more hierarchically driven company. . . . You didn't challenge authority quite as much, and the leadership was certainly revered. . . . In IBM, you are probably a bit more process oriented, a culture that is a bit more accepting of challenges and bottom-up kind of thinking.

Another former IBM manager was surprised to receive, during his first meeting with his Chinese counterpart, gifts of a cell phone and a portable music player. He also noted a significantly greater level of attention to detail by his new Chinese colleagues.[9]

For the American managers, these differences were notable; for the Chinese delegates, they often verged on offensive. For example, Yang and several other Lenovo executives arrived at John F. Kennedy International Airport in New York for their first planning meeting and found no representatives of IBM waiting to greet them. In China, any such high-ranking guests would have found not only counterparts at the airport to greet them but also a limousine to whisk them away to their hotels.

The potential for offense was mitigated somewhat by the commonalities in the corporate cultures—both sides shared strong beliefs in innovation, personal responsibility, and responsiveness to customer needs. Both sides also talked about the need for commitment. However, on this topic, the interpretations were rather different:

> In Lenovo, planning before you pledge, performing as you promise, delivering your commitment is really deeply ingrained in the culture. And when people sign up for a plan, they execute it. And that was probably not as effectively implemented in the old company [i.e., IBM's PC Division] that we bought.

These ubiquitous differences were not only limited to the relationships between the two companies but they also influenced customer relationships. The deal had been tailored to minimize disruptions and offer service as usual to customers, but some refused to work with the new entity. The US State Department, citing fears of spyware in Lenovo computers, altered its use of some 14,000 PCs that it had ordered from Lenovo.[10] The bias against the Chinese company also reared its head in some former IBM sites. In Japan, the former IBM staff fiercely resisted the idea of Chinese ownership. The Japanese design team in particular expressed deep concerns about any attempts to change the look or feel of Think-Pad notebooks—a design inspired by a Japanese lunch box that had remained unchanged since 1992.

EXHIBIT 3. Lenovo's market share, 2005

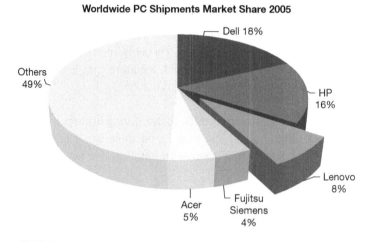

Worldwide PC Shipments Market Share 2005

Dell 18%
HP 16%
Lenovo 8%
Fujitsu Siemens 4%
Acer 5%
Others 49%

Source: Adapted from Quelch and Knoop (2007).

LEADERSHIP

A year into it, the "new" Lenovo could look back on some major achievements. It had launched its operations and brand in more than 65 countries, without any major disruptions to deliveries and support. No mass exodus of customers had occurred, as some had predicted. It managed to retain 98% of its employees. And it had gained global market share, including in BRIC countries, making it the world's third-largest PC manufacturer, behind Dell and HP (Exhibit 3).

Then, in December 2005, the skeptics felt a sense of vindication, because something had to be wrong: the American CEO Steve Ward resigned. Why did Ward last only eight months? Some guessed a personality clash with Yang Yuanqing—a man ten years his junior who embraced a completely different style. Others speculated that Ward had been too accustomed to the "IBM way" and could not adapt to the new culture. Perhaps his departure marked the end of a power struggle between the Lenovo and former IBM executives, won by Yang. No one outside the company's top management team knew the answer for sure, which kept observers buzzing. Whether the IBM deal would help Lenovo become the global market leader in the PC industry remained uncertain, but this incident certainly raised questions about Lenovo's ability to build a strong multinational management team and successfully run a global business.

NOTES

All interview excerpts were taken from Baumeister, B. (2009). Lenovo's acquisition of IBM's PC division: A success story of cultural post-combination integration? Unpublished Master's thesis, WU Vienna, unless referenced otherwise.

1. London, S. (2005). Lenovo: The making of a multinational, part I. A global power made in China. *Financial Times*, 09/11/2005.

2. Quelch, J. and Knoop C.I. (2007). Lenovo — Building a Global Brand, Harvard Business School Case Study 9-508-703, Boston, MA: Harvard Business School.

3. London, S. (2005). Lenovo: The making of a multinational, part I. A global power made in China. In: Financial Times, November 9, 2005.

4. Hamm, S. and Wildstrom, S. (2005). Turning two tech teams into one. *Information Technology Online Extra*, May 9. Available from: www.businessweek.com/print/magazine/content/05_19/b3932116_mz063.htm?chan=gl [accessed May 16, 2013].

5. Liu, C. (2007). Lenovo: An example of globalization of Chinese enterprises. *Journal of International Business Studies*, 38: 573–577.

6. Van Duijl, M. (2006). Lenovo: An example of Chinese globalization. Lenovo internal presentation delivered June 15, by EMEA and SVP president. Available from: www.oecd.org./dataoecd/60/43/36929454.pdf [accessed May 16, 2013].

7. Ames, B. (2006). Lenovo to lay off 1,000, move headquarters to N.C. *Computerworld*. March 16. Available from: www.computerworld.com/s/article/109604/Lenovo_to_lay_off_1_000_move_headquarters_to_N.C [accessed May 16, 2013].

8. Peng, S. (2008). Achieving successful cross-cultural and management integration: the experience of Lenovo and IBM. Available from: http://aut.researchgateway.ac.nz/bitstream/handle/10292/486/PengS.pdf;jsessionid=1C6170BE36AF1D8E75ECCAB62E8BCF1E?sequence=4 [accessed May 16, 2013].

9. Tang, Y. (2006). "We are trying everyday to make Lenovo a global brand" — Interview with Deepak Advani. Available from: http://english.peopledaily.com.cn/200606/19/eng20060619_275249.html [accessed May 16, 2013].

10. Peng, M. (2009). *Global Business Update 2009*. Mason, OH South-Western College.

Ingmar Björkman and Ming Zeng

GUANGDONG ELECTRONICS*

SITTING IN HIS OFFICE in a mid-sized city in Guangdong Province, China, Gunther Dane realized that he had inherited a difficult situation. It was late October 1998, and Dane was the new general manager of Guangdong Electronics Co. Ltd. (GE), a joint venture between Deutsche Elektro-Informatika (DEI), a huge German electronics company with a global presence, and Rural Red Star, a Chinese state-owned electronics company with 1,200 employees. Dane was a German expatriate.

Over the two months since his appointment as general manager in August 1998, Dane had learned that Guangdong Electronics was stumbling badly. The company was going to show a loss for 1998 and the latest forecasts indicated a 20 percent drop in sales when compared with the preceding year. The company had no formal sales planning and existing contracts received only haphazard follow up. Moreover, project management was virtually non-existent and was carried out with little, if any, documentation regarding resource planning, job responsibilities, and formal schedules. Now, as general manager, he had to decide what to do next. His first management group meeting was scheduled for November 5, 1998.

ESTABLISHING THE JOINT VENTURE

The agreement to establish GE was signed in 1991, and operations started the following year. It was DEI's first joint venture in the People's Republic of China. The company had operated for almost ten years in China with only a representative office in Beijing with a total of 25 employees. By 1991, it had carved out a relatively small niche market with modest sales. However, because the company viewed China as a potentially important market, corporate headquarters were encouraging an expansion of the operations in the country. Furthermore, several of its international competitors had already established local manufacturing units in China.

Operating in an industry that was tightly controlled by the Chinese government, the company viewed the establishment of a joint venture principally as a political move. The investment, its managers reasoned, would demonstrate to authorities that DEI was committed to China and was willing to transfer its technology to the country. If handled correctly, it was to be DEI's means to gain wider access to the Chinese market. Nonetheless, the managers had few concrete ideas about what products to manufacture in the joint venture.

In 1990, DEI started to search for a joint venture partner in the state-owned sector. Negotiations were undertaken in one of China's largest cities with the central ministry's support. However, the negotiations ended when the city government chose a Japanese company in DEI's place.

The Chinese authorities then suggested Rural Red Star as a suitable partner, even though it was not ideally located and its line of business was somewhat different from that of DEI. Nonetheless, as DEI was determined to establish a joint venture in China, Rural Red Star was accepted as the partner. DEI executives viewed the agreement as an important step towards enhancing their goodwill and relationships with the ministry in Beijing, and the Chinese vice minister agreed to attend the joint venture signing ceremony.

GE was established as a 50–50 joint venture. The chairman of the board was to come from the Chinese partner's organization—eventually, the president of Rural Red Star was appointed—while the deputy chairman was to come from the German firm. The contract also stated that the foreign partner was to appoint the GM, while the local partner held the right to appoint the deputy GM. The joint venture was going to start by importing products from DEI, but would soon start some kind of manufacturing. Hence, according to the plans that the partners had agreed upon, GE was to engage in sales, project implementation, customer service, customer training, and production. The venture was located on the premises of Rural Red Star, to which it paid rent.

THE EARLY DEVELOPMENT OF THE JOINT VENTURE

Two German managers arrived during the fall of 1992. Both had worked at DEI for several years. The general manager (GM) was a German in his 50s who had had a couple of years of international experience in the US. The other was a young engineer on his first overseas assignment. He was going to work with customer service and answer questions concerning future production. All local employees were transferred from the Chinese partner. Mr Chen, the deputy GM appointed by the Chinese partner, had been working in sales for Rural Red Star, which would be his principal function in GE. By the end of 1992, the company had 45 employees.

During 1994–96, DEI established several additional joint ventures in China. GE became a relatively small part of DEI's China business and received scant attention by top management, operating like "an unguided missile that people didn't pay attention to." The joint venture reported both to the product division in Germany and to DEI's China headquarters in Beijing; operating rather autonomously, the company was little integrated into DEI's China organization. Few corporate policies and practices that were implemented in the other DEI units were transplanted to GE, though its employees' technological knowledge of DEI product lines improved. The culture of the joint venture remained "Chinese" rather than "Western." In fact, DEI's other joint ventures shared more of DEI's corporate culture than did GE. Within the joint venture, Chinese employees felt that "they should manage by themselves" and should avoid dealing much with DEI.

During 1992–96, the joint venture grew steadily both in terms of sales and number of employees. By the end of 1996, GE had 105 employees and net sales of close to 140 million yuan, approximately US$16 million. While small-scale manufacturing had begun, it never achieved economic feasibility and was closed down in 1997. In financial terms, the company was not quite living up to the profitability expectations of the parent organizations. Nonetheless, DEI benefited from supplying components to the joint venture. For Rural Red Star, GE had become a crucially important source of revenues through dividends, service fees, and rent. As a floundering state-owned enterprise, Rural Red Star was clearly unable to participate in financing the growth of the joint venture.

Herbert Klein, the immediate predecessor of Gunther Dane, was appointed in the summer of 1996. Klein, who was GE's third general manager, had previously worked as quality and factory manager in Germany. Up until the end of 1996, the joint venture had only two German expatriates: the GM and a German engineer working with customer service. Mr Chen continued to serve as deputy GM. In November 1996, DEI informed GE employees that on January 1, 1997, the financial statement of the joint venture would be consolidated into DEI's total operations. To develop compatible accounting and reporting procedures, the joint venture required a DEI financial controller. (The organizational chart of GE at the beginning of 1997 is presented in Exhibit 1.)

DEVELOPMENTS IN 1997

In 1997, GE received a large number of orders and its employees were busy filling them. However, employee relations in the company had begun to deteriorate.

EXHIBIT 1. The Guangdong Electronics organization in early 1997

First, there was the new financial controller, a British citizen and the first non-German expatriate in GE. Looking over the joint venture's books, he quickly realized that most financial procedures and tools were poorly developed and there was an urgent need to develop the financial planning and control processes. Unfortunately, his effort was undermined by a series of new problems. His wife, a Chinese woman from Shanghai who had been offered a job at GE, antagonized local Guangdong employees from the beginning; she was asked to resign. Then his relationship with the GM soured, until finally Klein fired him. During the fall of 1997, the company hired an interim expatriate financial controller, who tried to address the firm's most pressing concerns.

Second, Klein, who at that time served as GM, was not much involved in the day-to-day operations of the company. He spent relatively little time in the joint venture, preferring instead to travel within China and abroad; increasingly, he communicated with his managers through letters. Moreover, his relationship with Mr Chen and the chairman of the board gradually deteriorated.

In April 1997, Bernd Fischer, a new expatriate, arrived from Germany. His background at DEI was in production and he had visited GE a few times to help the company in the early stages of its attempts at manufacturing. Apart from a couple weeks of training in Germany, he had no experience with customer service, the area that he was appointed to manage. With little guidance from the GM concerning his responsibilities, he started to familiarize himself with the company's internal operations. It soon became clear to him that a number of things in the company badly needed improvement. For example, nobody knew the exact number of products in stock. While inventories were high, the "right" products were often out of stock. There was nobody in the company responsible for logistics.

Upon hearing Fischer's observations, Klein agreed that they should do something about these matters. Once contacted, the logistics department of DEI's product division suggested that GE adopt a sophisticated materials flow management program (STAR), which had been developed for use in the manufacturing operations in Germany. In spite of the fact that GE was shutting down its manufacturing operations, the head of the logistics department was convinced that the STAR program would be suitable for handling logistics issues in China as well. During the fall of 1997, Klein decided to implement STAR.

Logistics was not the only problem that Fischer identified. His overall impression was that "there were no procedures for doing anything, and very little documentation. Everything seemed ad hoc. The company was totally sales driven. And there were no formal project management tools in use." Perhaps the company could function without detailed procedures when it was smaller, he reasoned, but now they needed to do something about it. Fischer was not the first German to notice these problems, but the previous observers apparently had failed to do anything about them.

Klein discussed the issue with Fischer, whom he asked to make a presentation to the board of directors in June 1997 based on his observations. For starters, the board decided that an expatriate quality manager should be hired. Klein also suggested to the board that, by 1999, GE should fulfill the requirements for ISO 9002; because several Chinese customers recently had mentioned that their suppliers should have this certification, Mr Chen also supported the idea. Regarding other aspects of the company's operations, Klein pointed out a gap in human resource development, including both technical and general management skills. So far, he argued the company had no human resource (HR) manager; the board decided to appoint a local employee as HR manager.

Klein also formulated some ideas that he did not present at the board meeting. The salary system, for example, should be "totally updated." The yearly bonus obtained by the employees was currently linked only to sales, not to other relevant performance measures such as company profitability. More Germans should be brought in to develop the competence level in the company. Finally, DEI should acquire majority ownership of GE, and "take over and have a leading role in [GE's] overall development," including its full integration with DEI's other activities. Because Klein's views were in line with those of DEI's top executives in China, negotiations were initiated during the fall of 1997 to increase DEI's share of ownership. Klein neither discussed nor communicated his plans with his management team in GE.

During the summer and early fall, Fischer became convinced that there was a need to examine all existing sales contracts, a task that came to occupy a significant part of his time. The company signed some 300 contracts per year, most of which were very small. Unfortunately, Fischer found that the contracts did not contain enough information for the customer service department to devise plans. Some contracts contained no information about deadlines and no system existed to ensure that delivery commitments would be honored. Many contracts were written in Chinese, which violated company policy that they should be written in English as well. Indeed, some contracts were entirely missing. Perhaps most alarmingly, Fischer learned, the GE contract template contained clauses that stipulated stiff penalties for late deliveries, including discounts of up to 1 percent per day delayed. When asked about this, Chinese employees advised him not to worry about the content of the contract "as they had good relationships with the buyers [who] therefore would not demand any compensation." Fischer was not reassured, however, especially since the company consistently failed to meet delivery deadlines. Looking back, his first six months had been very frustrating.

In October, a German expert from the quality department visited GE. The purpose of the visit was to audit Rural Red Star as a potential supplier of some simple components to GE, an initiative that Fischer had spearheaded earlier by obtaining design drawings for the products. Upon approval as a supplier, which made Mr Chen "very happy," Fischer asked the quality expert to examine other operations at GE. The German expert found serious quality management problems, which led him to recommend that his boss in Germany, quality manager Rudolf Steiner, visit GE himself.

Steiner arrived in November and made a number of alarming observations regarding quality management. In the discussion that followed, he bluntly asked Klein why they had not been rectified. The general manager replied: "this is China, everything is very difficult!" Despite their somewhat tense introduction, Klein agreed to take Steiner on as the quality manager of the company at the beginning of the next year. The idea was to use the ISO 9002 certificate as a spur to improve the entire operation of the company. Though Steiner had not personally implemented an

ISO 9002 project, he had worked as a quality manager in the parent organization; he estimated that it would take about two years to obtain the ISO 9002 certificate. The Chinese manager who had been in charge of production would serve as his assistant. German expatriates viewed the certificate as a good way to engage the Chinese partner and managers in a project that would lead to significant change.

FINANCE AND CONTROL

In 1998, Rudolf Steiner arrived with a new financial controller, Uli Beck. For both Germans, the beginning of their assignment brought unpleasant surprises.

Just before Beck arrived, Klein had told the expatriate interim controller that his services were no longer needed. This deprived Beck, who had left a position in an international accounting firm to take this job in China, of any introduction from his predecessor. When he examined his department in more detail, he was shocked at the number of errors he found. For instance, the 1997 accounts, which had boasted sound financial results, were revealed to be misleading: certain costs had simply been omitted.

Furthermore, though GE's lawyer had visited the company to instruct employees in contractual procedures, few changes had been made. Contracts tended to be incomplete, often still written exclusively in Chinese, which Klein had continued to sign in violation of company policy. In addition, oral commitments were often made to the buyers concerning delivery times. Even more seriously, one of the company's official stamps (the so-called "chop" routinely used in China to sign official company documents) was missing and it appeared that Rural Red Star had signed some of the deals in GE's name. It was only after strong pressure from Beck and Fischer that the stamp was returned to GE.

THE ISO 9002 PROJECT

When the new quality manager Rudolf Steiner arrived in China, he was informed that his assistant had left GE in order to return to the Rural Red Star organization. This reflected a lack of control in the joint venture's personnel issues about which Germans had long complained. In his place, a young Chinese-American, Patricia Gui, had been hired as his assistant. Ms Gui, whose husband worked in a US–Chinese joint venture in the same city, had graduated from a top US university with a degree in engineering, spoke fluent Mandarin, and appeared to be straightforward and direct in how she communicated with both the Germans and the Chinese. Nonetheless, she had very little practical experience. A local person was hired in March to provide further support in the quality department. Klein soon ordered Steiner to "speed up" the ISO 9002 certification process (Exhibit 2 summarizes some features concerning ISO certification).

To his astonishment, Steiner was asked immediately by the Chinese managers, "When will you give us the certificate?" The Chinese managers, he realized, understood neither the role he was going to play in the company nor the rigor that the ISO process would impose. In February, at his kick-off meeting with the managers, Steiner explained that their first tasks were to train the department heads in quality

---

EXHIBIT 2. The ISO 9000 series of quality standards

ISO 9000 was created by the International Organization for Standardization in 1987 to denote quality systems and standards. Although ISO certification began and initially grew mostly in Europe, by the late 1990s it was increasingly popular in both North America and Asia. In China, the government was encouraging companies to obtain ISO certification.

There are basically five standards associated with the ISO 9000 series:

1. ISO 9000
   Essentially a set of guidelines for the selection and use of the appropriate systems standards ISO 9001, 9002, and 9003
2. ISO 9001
   Model for quality assurance in design, development, production, installation, and servicing.
3. ISO 9002
   Model for quality assurance in production, installation, and servicing.
4. ISO 9003
   Model for quality assurance in final inspections and testing.
5. ISO 9004
   Guide for the application of various elements of a quality management system.

The ISO 9000 standards have 20 elements concerning how well the company's quality system operates (see, for example, R.B. Chase and N.J. Aquilano: *Production and Operations Management: Manufacturing and Services*. Irwin, Chicago, 1995). The company, not ISO, determines what quality standards to assure. Hence, the series are dealing with the management of quality systems rather than with the quality of the company's products and services.

The following activities are often parts of the process leading up the certification:

- assignment of responsibility;
- training of key people;
- assessment of existing practices and procedures;
- documentation of practices and procedures;
- implementation of procedures;
- internal audit and/or outside party pre-assessment;
- formal independent assessment; and
- certification and registration.

---

management and to document existing company practices. Nobody objected to this plan, which Patricia Gui was charged with implementing. As it turned out, the managers were unwilling to fully participate. Even those who showed up for meetings exhibited little interest, preferring to chat together or leaving frequently to take care of other tasks.

It was even more difficult to get the managers to document existing practices. Arguing that "the role of the quality manager is not to write them," Steiner refused to supply them himself. It fell to Ms Gui to meet with people in all the departments, but few cooperated. For example, Ms Gui provided a diagram of the overall marketing structure to the marketing manager and asked him to fill in the missing details; but somehow, he never got around to supplying them. The Germans in GE suggested various reasons why the local employees refused to cooperate in the documentation exercise, including:

- "They usually go against everything that the foreigners present."
- "They want to be free to do whatever they like."
- "They thought [Steiner] was brought here to do it."
- "They were not able to understand what this thing will do to their normal life."
- "They were not prepared for it."
- "He didn't know how to do it."
- "They were busy doing more important things and delegated it to their secretaries."

However, perhaps none of the Germans understood the real reason why local employees were reluctant to collaborate on this matter. As pointed out by customer service manager Fischer, "In the beginning it was often difficult to understand the concrete reasons why people didn't want to change. It's very important to know that they often had very concrete reasons, and it was not because people are lazy or unwilling to do new things!"

In May, Klein suddenly appointed Patricia Gui as the logistics manager, which Steiner learned after the fact. It was a serious blow for Steiner, who felt deeply disappointed to lose his assistant. Klein, he came to believe, was demonstrating how little he appreciated his work. From that moment on, the ISO 9002 project ran increasingly behind schedule. While employees had been promised a 100-yuan bonus upon the first successful internal audit, it was unclear whether this promise had provided any incentive for them to cooperate. The first task of Steiner's new assistant was to build a filing system for GE. He complained, however, that "[I] haven't come very far yet as people don't provide me with their files!"

THE STAR PROGRAM

A project team from Germany arrived in February 1998 to install the STAR program and train employees in the system. The objective was to create an integrated logistics system, in which the STAR program would monitor stock levels and transmit product orders to Germany. In addition, the program would be supported by the price quotation system, PREIS, which generated equipment lists with prices. For the experts arriving from Germany, it was an exciting pilot project—nowhere else had the two programs been integrated. To do so made lots of sense: data from the price quotation system could boost the efficiency with which the ordering process would be handled. Furthermore, the logistics department in Germany believed that the experience in GE would prove useful in a new manufacturing joint venture that DEI was planning to establish in China.

Unfortunately, the project did not proceed according to expectations. Because Patricia Gui was not yet serving as logistics manager, GE had no logistics department and thus nobody in the organization had responsibility for the project. An additional problem was that the programs' computer language had never been used in China— it was impossible to find anybody there who could work with the program itself.

Program documentation was also written in German, and the program would neither accept entries in, nor print, Chinese characters. Moreover, despite numerous attempts to train them, the sales staff found it "too complicated;" customers did as well. Finally, the program had been developed for production management, and thus was apparently unsuitable for a company devoted solely to sales and service. Eight months after the arrival of the project team, the STAR program could only be used to place orders in Germany. In retrospect, the German manager in charge commented that: "we tried to copy [the program] 100 percent in China—it wasn't a very good idea, and I'm not sure whether I think it's suitable there."

In order for the STAR system to work, the company's sales force had to use PREIS, a system that DEI used in a number of countries. To persuade them to do so became the task of Davi Mann, the fifth manager to arrive from Germany.

SALES AND MARKETING

Mann had previously worked as an international sales manager. When he signed his contract, Klein had told Mann that his main task was going to be to "help bring 'the DEI Way' to the company." His job title was "sales manager," with three sales team managers reporting directly to him. However, the local marketing manager was soon transferred to the training department, which added marketing management to his job title.

One of Mann's first challenges was to convince people to use the new sales contract templates. He began by telling the sales managers that they had to start using DEI templates in China, "as it's company procedure" and also because it included clauses that were regarded as necessary safeguards for the company. However, he made little progress with GE's sales people. While many were evasive in their answers, some told him directly that, because "customers refuse to read so many pages," the contract template was a useless handicap to their sales. Mann was not certain whether or not that was the main reason for their reluctance.

Mann later revised some of the clauses and tried a shorter version of the contract. This time, however, he began by discussing the matter with Chen. It's "the only way to get things done," he said. "They always check with him anyway before they do it." During the fall of 1998, sales people started to use the new template. However, it was still unclear whether the contracts included all necessary information, such as promises made to buyers during the negotiation process.

ISO 9002 added a few requirements to contracting procedures. Before contracts were signed, representatives of all the relevant departments should meet together to review them. For GE, this meant that sales and marketing, product competence center, customer service, and finance and control should meet. However, such a meeting had taken place only once, with the largest project signed by GE to date. In this meeting, managers noted that not only was the timetable too tight, but penalties for delivery delays were too severe. However, the sales people reassured everybody that the company would not need to pay: they had good relationships with buyers, whom, they said, they would keep happy. Because there was some pressure from DEI China to accept the project as well, eventually the contract was signed.

Another major challenge for Mann was to change the way in which project offers were made. The Controller Uli Beck also pushed him to work on this. So far, sales people included only the direct costs of the products in their calculations; other costs tended to be added at a later stage and thus were rarely included in their calculations. This also meant that GE signed contracts without knowing the real sales margins. What was needed, Mann thought, was a tool to calculate total project costs, which included after-sales services, agent commissions, finance charges according to pay-back conditions, kick-backs, and the like.

After six months into his job, Mann was beginning to have trouble handling all of the issues that came his way. The sales teams were still functioning on a rather ad hoc basis, without formal plans for their activities, that is, how to identify customers, how to qualify customers as well as gauge their prospects for winning a certain contract, how to make bids, and how to follow up on project implementation. They also seemed to spend too much time trying to win small contracts. As it turned out, the only sales team likely to meet its sales budget for 1998 was the group focusing on large projects.

Mann hoped to systematize the activities of the sales teams. But he knew that it would be a "very big change for the [sales people] from traveling and running around" to sitting in headquarters to "plan activities, write reports, etc. It's new terminology and a new way of thinking." Furthermore, communication across units was sporadic at best. It appeared that employees found it very difficult to think and work in terms of processes; their focus seemed to be entirely on the on-going activities of their own unit.

KLEIN LEAVES THE COMPANY

During the spring of 1998, morale in the company plummeted. Carrying out an old threat, Klein canceled the existing bonus scheme for the local employees, eliminating all the bonuses they had earned during the last six months. Enraged by this action, the sales people went on strike. When Klein refused to discuss the matter, it fell to Beck to negotiate with local employees. Although the issue was not entirely settled, the sales people did return to their jobs. Klein then decided to specify the size of the contracts that certain employees were allowed to sign. According to the new regulations, only he could sign major contracts, while the signatures of both deputy GM Chen and Mann would be required for medium-sized contracts. When he heard that he was not any more allowed to sign contracts by himself, Chen angrily refused to sign any contracts at all. Chen stopped working almost entirely, preferring to read business books during working hours instead. There were virtually no management meetings, which Chen would have refused to attend anyway. As contact dwindled between the German expatriates in GE and Rural Red Star, financial controllers became the only viable channel of communication. On the initiative of Rural Red Star, Beck regularly met his Chinese counterpart for informal discussions.

Klein, employees knew, had serious personal problems. He was consuming large quantities of alcohol. His relationship with the other Germans had become so bad that a fistfight broke out during a company outing that all employees witnessed. Gradually,

Beck became the informal leader of the company. As people in DEI's China headquarters received information about the situation in GE, Fischer was asked to write a report to DEI's Controller in the China headquarters on the situation.

While there were sporadic attempts to negotiate with the Chinese partner concerning a change in the equity distribution, they proceeded only slowly. A decision, enshrined in a new contract, was finally reached: DEI would become the majority shareholder. The contract contained other important changes, including a provision that mandated DEI to appoint the chief controller, while Rural Red Star was responsible for naming an assistant controller. Regardless of the profitability of the company, the local partner would be paid a specified dividend.

At a board meeting in May 1998, the new contract was formally approved. There was also an informal meeting between one of DEI's board members and Fischer. During this meeting, Fischer was promised that action would be taken within two weeks. In reality, three months of virtual paralysis ensued. Then finally, employees were informed that Klein was going to be replaced by Gunther Dane.

THE NEW GM ARRIVES

In late August 1998, a management meeting took place. Klein chaired the meeting, introducing Gunther Dane, the new GM, to the management group. Dane had been offered the job in July. The message that he received from DEI's top executives was that: "There are some problems [in GE], go there and fix it!" After some hesitation, he accepted the position. By October, Dane had finally managed to finish most of his ongoing tasks in Beijing and moved permanently to GE. However, he gave no indication how long he was willing to serve as the company's general manager.

Like all his predecessors, Dane was German. But he had already spent three years in China, based at the headquarters in Beijing. During this period he had visited GE a number of times, and had developed a good relationship with Mr Chen, now his deputy GM. The employees immediately noticed that Dane engaged in many more face-to-face interactions than his predecessor had done. Dane asked questions, listened, and discussed solutions with people in the company (See Exhibit 3 for the organizational structure of the company at the end of October 1998). His approach, to both German and local managers, was very personal.

LOOKING TO THE FUTURE

Now fully installed in his new office, Dane recognized a number of fundamental challenges. In addition to the managerial problems he had inherited, the company's products were not on the central government's list of "approved" and "suggested" products. There was also a new "buy local campaign." Already, local competitors had offered a number of good, yet cheaper products. In addition, the local Chinese firms had considerably more sales people at their disposal. Confirming the new GM's fears, the controller Uli Beck reported that sales lagged behind target and costs were rising. Finally, there was always the question of whether customers would start to demand

EXHIBIT 3. The Guangdong Electronics organization in November 1998

penalties for late deliveries. Mr Chen had told him that at least one customer was likely to do so. With several other projects running behind schedule, Dane wondered whether more would demand the penalty payments to which they were entitled under contract. With a new building about to be constructed, GE's financial situation appeared increasingly precarious.

Nonetheless, Dane knew that GE stood on solid ground. The company's sales force appeared to have built a reliable network of customer relationships, and, in spite of some delays in the deliveries, the company enjoyed a good reputation. Many of the employees were competent and skillful, and their English skills had improved. Moreover, DEI's majority ownership had simplified decision-making.

Perhaps the most pressing question was what to do about the internal management of GE. The bonus system remained a divisive question. GE also needed to develop the HR function from the ground up. With the ISO 9002 project apparently stalled, Rudolf Steiner, the quality manager, had announced that he would return to Germany in December. In addition, customer service manager Bernd Fischer, the German with the longest tenure, planned to leave the company around then. On the technical front, STAR continued to suffer from technical problems that the logistics department had worked very hard to solve, including the Chinese character issue; PREIS also functioned in a less than satisfactory manner.

Further food for thought came from a quality audit report that was written by a DEI expert group following their visit to GE in October. The purpose of their visit had been to monitor GE's progress in the pursuit of the ISO 9002 benchmark standards and to suggest areas for improvement. In their report, the quality experts observed:

> Visions and long range plans of [GE] were not available. There is no evidence available that quality planning in general is done; [there appear to be] no defined processes, few documented procedures, and no defined objectives and targets; no evidence [emerged] that management is reviewing customer satisfaction, achievement of objectives, audit results, etc. [GE's] quality manual is not yet available, and many procedures have not been documented.

The summary of the report is reproduced in Exhibit 4.

Dane knew that morale in the joint venture would have to improve. He believed that he could motivate Chen again, but what kind of role should he give Chen in the management of the company? Up to now, GE appeared to be split between two "camps" in the firm, with Chinese employees on one side and German expatriates on the other. Patricia Gui seemed to be an outsider in both groups. Did he need to try to change this situation, and if so, how?

Dane's first management meeting would take place next week. What should he do?

EXHIBIT 4. Summary of the report made by the quality audit group in October 1998

[GE] has no issued performance objectives. It seems that the organization is managed case by case, department by department.

Customer needs are not a self-evident goal. There are no defined processes [regarding how] to meet customer requirements.

The people in [GE] know their tasks and responsibilities; they have skills to do the tasks required by their departments.

There are many deficiencies to rectify before the third party certification to ISO 9002 can be achieved. The non-conformities recorded could have been divided into numerous detailed non-conformities. However, it is important to plan the objectives and business processes before the specific elements of quality management can be implemented.

The audit covered all elements of ISO 9002. For this reason the auditors recommend that the next audit covering the whole organization should be in 1999.

NOTE

* This case was written by Ingmar Bjorkman, Visiting Professor of International Management at INSEAD, France & Professor at the Hanken School of Economics, Finland, and Ming Zeng, Assistant Professor of Asian Business at INSEAD. It is intended to be used as a basis for class discussion rather than to illustrate effective or ineffective handling of a situation. The identity of the companies and persons involved has been disguised.

PART V

Responsible Leadership in a Global and Cross-Cultural Context

Readings

- **Thomas Donaldson**
  VALUES IN TENSION: ETHICS AWAY FROM HOME

- **Günter K. Stahl, Christof Miska, Laura J. Noval, and Verena J. Patock**
  THE CHALLENGE OF RESPONSIBLE GLOBAL LEADERSHIP

- **Ina Aust and Marie-Thérèse Claes**
  GLOBAL LEADERSHIP FOR SUSTAINABLE DEVELOPMENT

Cases

- **Charlotte Butler and Henri-Claude de Bettignies**
  CHANGMAI CORPORATION

- **Nicola Pless and Thomas Maak**
  LEVI STRAUSS & CO.: ADDRESSING CHILD LABOUR IN BANGLADESH

- **Barbara Coudenhove-Kalergi and Christian Seelos**
  EVN IN BULGARIA: ENGAGING THE ROMA COMMUNITY

Thomas Donaldson

VALUES IN TENSION: ETHICS AWAY FROM HOME

WHEN WE LEAVE HOME AND CROSS our nation's boundaries, moral clarity often blurs. Without a backdrop of shared attitudes, and without familiar laws and judicial procedures that define standards of ethical conduct, certainty is elusive. Should a company invest in a foreign country where civil and political rights are violated? Should a company go along with a host country's discriminatory employment practices? If companies in developed countries shift facilities to developing nations that lack strict environmental and health regulations, or if those companies choose to fill management and other top-level positions in a host nation with people from the home country, then whose standards should prevail?

Even the best-informed, best-intentioned executives must rethink their assumptions about business practice in foreign settings. What works in a company's home country can fail in a country with different standards of ethical conduct. Such difficulties are unavoidable for business people who live and work abroad.

But how can managers resolve these problems? What are the principles that can help them work through the maze of cultural differences and establish codes of conduct for globally ethical business practice? How can companies answer the toughest question in global business ethics: What happens when a host country's ethical standards seem lower than the home country's?

COMPETING ANSWERS

One answer is as old as philosophical discourse. According to cultural relativism, no culture's ethics are better than any other's; therefore, there are no international rights and wrongs. If the people of Indonesia tolerate the bribery of their public officials, so what? Their attitude is no better or worse than that of people in Denmark or Singapore who refuse to offer or accept bribes. Likewise, if Belgians fail to find insider trading morally repugnant, who cares? Not enforcing insider-trading laws is no more or less ethical than enforcing such laws.

The cultural relativist's creed — When in Rome, do as the Romans do — is tempting, especially when failing to do as the locals do means forfeiting business opportunities. The inadequacy of cultural relativism, however, becomes apparent when the practices in question are more damaging than petty bribery or insider trading.

In the late 1980s, some European tanneries and pharmaceutical companies were looking for cheap waste-dumping sites. They approached virtually every country on Africa's west coast from Morocco to the Congo. Nigeria agreed to take highly toxic polychlorinated biphenyls (PCBs). Unprotected local workers, wearing thongs and shorts, unloaded barrels of PCBs and placed them near a residential area. Neither the residents nor the workers knew that the barrels contained toxic waste.

We may denounce governments that permit such abuses, but many countries are unable to police transnational corporations adequately, even if they want to. And in many countries the combination of ineffective enforcement and inadequate regulations leads to behavior by unscrupulous companies that is clearly wrong. A few years ago, for example, a group of investors became interested in restoring the SS *United States*, once a luxurious ocean liner. Before the actual restoration could begin, the ship had to be stripped of its asbestos lining. A bid from a US company, based on US standards for asbestos removal, priced the job at more than US$100 million. A company in the Ukrainian city of Sevastopol offered to do the work for less than $2 million. In October 1993, the ship was towed to Sevastopol.

A cultural relativist would have no problem with that outcome, but I do. A country has the right to establish its own health and safety regulations, but in the case described above, the standards and the terms of the contract could not possibly have protected workers in Sevastopol from known health risks. Even if the contract met Ukrainian standards, ethical business people must object. Cultural relativism is morally blind. There are fundamental values that cross cultures, and companies must uphold them. (For an economic argument against cultural relativism, see Exhibit 1.)

At the other end of the spectrum from cultural relativism is ethical imperialism, which directs people to do everywhere exactly as they do at home. Again, an understandably appealing approach but one that is clearly inadequate. Consider the large US computer products company that in 1993 introduced a course on sexual harassment in its Saudi Arabian facility. Under the banner of global consistency, instructors used the same approach to train Saudi Arabian managers that they had used with US managers: the participants were asked to discuss a case in which a manager makes sexually explicit remarks to a new female employee over drinks in a bar. The instructors failed to consider how the exercise would work in a culture with strict conventions governing relationships between men and women. As a result, the training sessions were ludicrous. They baffled and offended the Saudi participants, and the message to avoid coercion and sexual discrimination was lost.

The theory behind ethical imperialism is absolutism, which is based on three problematic principles. Absolutists believe that there is a single list of truths, that

---

EXHIBIT 1. The culture and ethics of software piracy

Before jumping on the cultural relativism bandwagon, stop and consider the potential economic consequences of a when-in-Rome attitude toward business ethics. Take a look at the current statistics on software piracy: In the United States, pirated software is estimated to be 35% of the total software market, and industry losses are estimated at $2.3 billion per year. The piracy rate is 57% in Germany and 80% in Italy and Japan; the rates in most Asian countries are estimated to be nearly 100%.

There are similar laws against software piracy in those countries. What, then, accounts for the differences? Although a country's level of economic development plays a large part, culture, including ethical attitudes, may be a more crucial factor. The 1995 annual report of the Software Publishers Association connects software piracy directly to culture and attitude. It describes Italy and Hong Kong as having "'first world' per capita incomes, along with 'third world' rates of piracy." When asked whether one should use software without paying for it, most people, including people in Italy and Hong Kong, say no. But people in some countries regard the practice as *less* unethical than people in other countries do. Confucian culture, for example, stresses that individuals should share what they create with society. That may be, in part, what prompts the Chinese and other Asians to view the concept of intellectual property as a means for the West to monopolize its technological superiority.

What happens if ethical attitudes around the world permit large-scale software piracy? Software companies will not want to invest as much in developing new products because they cannot expect any return on their investment in certain parts of the world. When ethics fail to support technological creativity, there are consequences that go beyond statistics—jobs are lost and livelihoods jeopardized.

Companies must do more than lobby foreign governments for tougher enforcement of piracy laws. They must cooperate with other companies and with local organizations to help citizens understand the consequences of piracy and to encourage the evolution of a different ethic toward the practice.

---

they can be expressed only with one set of concepts, and that they call for exactly the same behavior around the world.

The first claim clashes with many people's belief that different cultural traditions must be respected. In some cultures, loyalty to a community—family, organization, or society—is the foundation of all ethical behavior. The Japanese, for example, define business ethics in terms of loyalty to their companies, their business networks, and their nation. Americans place a higher value on liberty than on loyalty; the US tradition of rights emphasizes equality, fairness, and individual freedom. It is hard to conclude that truth lies on one side or the other, but an absolutist would have us select just one.

The second problem with absolutism is the presumption that people must express moral truth using only one set of concepts. For instance, some absolutists insist that the language of basic rights provide the framework for any discussion of ethics. This means, though, that entire cultural traditions must be ignored. The notion of a right evolved with the rise of democracy in post-Renaissance Europe and the United States, but the term is not found in either Confucian or Buddhist traditions. We all learn ethics in the context of our particular cultures, and the power in the principles is deeply tied to the way in which they are expressed. Internationally accepted lists of moral principles, such as the United Nations' Universal Declaration of Human Rights, draw on many cultural and religious traditions. As philosopher Michael Walzer has noted, "There is no Esperanto of global ethics."

The third problem with absolutism is the belief in a global standard of ethical behavior. Context must shape ethical practice. Very low wages, for example, may be considered unethical in rich, advanced countries, but developing nations may be acting ethically if they encourage investment and improve living standards by accepting low wages. Likewise, when people are malnourished or starving, a government may be wise to use more fertilizer in order to improve crop yields, even though that means settling for relatively high levels of thermal water pollution.

When cultures have different standards of ethical behavior—and different ways of handling unethical behavior—a company that takes an absolutist approach may find itself making a disastrous mistake. When a manager at a large US specialty-products company in China caught an employee stealing, she followed the company's practice and turned the employee over to the provincial authorities, who executed him. Managers cannot operate in another culture without being aware of that culture's attitudes toward ethics.

If companies can neither adopt a host country's ethics nor extend the home country's standards, then what is the answer? Even the traditional litmus test—What would people think of your actions if they were written up on the front page of the newspaper?—is an unreliable guide, for there is no international consensus on standards of business conduct.

BALANCING THE EXTREMES: THREE GUIDING PRINCIPLES

Companies must help managers distinguish between practices that are merely different and those that are wrong. For relativists, nothing is sacred and nothing is wrong. For absolutists, many things that are different are wrong. Neither extreme illuminates the real world of business decision making. The answer lies somewhere in between.

When it comes to shaping ethical behavior, companies must be guided by three principles:

- Respect for core human values, which determine the absolute moral threshold for all business activities.
- Respect for local traditions.
- The belief that context matters when deciding what is right and what is wrong.

Consider those principles in action. In Japan, people doing business together often exchange gifts—sometimes expensive ones—in keeping with long-standing Japanese tradition. When US and European companies started doing a lot of business in Japan, many Western business people thought that the practice of gift giving might be wrong rather than simply different. To them, accepting a gift felt like accepting a bribe. As Western companies have become more familiar with Japanese traditions, however, most have come to tolerate the practice and to set different limits on gift giving in Japan than they do elsewhere.

Respecting differences is a crucial ethical practice. Research shows that management ethics differ among cultures; respecting those differences means recognizing that some cultures have obvious weaknesses—as well as hidden strengths. Managers in Hong Kong, for example, have a higher tolerance for some forms of bribery than their Western counterparts, but they have a much lower tolerance for the failure to acknowledge a subordinate's work. In some parts of the Far East, stealing credit from a subordinate is nearly an unpardonable sin.

People often equate respect for local traditions with cultural relativism. That is incorrect. Some practices are clearly wrong. Union Carbide's tragic experience in Bhopal, India, provides one example. The company's executives seriously underestimated how much on-site management involvement was needed at the Bhopal plant to compensate for the country's poor infrastructure and regulatory capabilities. In the aftermath of the disastrous gas leak, the lesson is clear: companies using sophisticated technology in a developing country must evaluate that country's ability to oversee its safe use. Since the incident at Bhopal, Union Carbide has become a leader in advising companies on using hazardous technologies safely in developing countries.

Some activities are wrong no matter where they take place. But some practices that are unethical in one setting may be acceptable in another. For instance, the chemical EDB, a soil fungicide, is banned for use in the United States. In hot climates, however, it quickly becomes harmless through exposure to intense solar radiation and high soil temperatures. As long as the chemical is monitored, companies may be able to use EDB ethically in certain parts of the world.

DEFINING THE ETHICAL THRESHOLD: CORE VALUES

Few ethical questions are easy for managers to answer. But there are some hard truths that must guide managers' actions, a set of what I call "core human values," which define minimum ethical standards for all companies.[1] The right to good health and the right to economic advancement and an improved standard of living are two core human values. Another is what Westerners call the Golden Rule, which is recognizable in every major religious and ethical tradition around the world. In Book 15 of his *Analects*, for instance, Confucius counsels people to maintain reciprocity, or not to do to others what they do not want done to themselves.

Although no single list would satisfy every scholar, I believe that it is possible to articulate three core values that incorporate the work of scores of theologians and philosophers around the world. To be broadly relevant, these values must include

---

EXHIBIT 2. What do these values have in common?

Non-Western	Western
Kyosei (Japanese): Living and working together for the common good.	Individual liberty
Dharma (Hindu): The fulfillment of inherited duty.	Egalitarianism
Santutthi (Buddhist): The importance of limited desires.	Political participation
Zakat (Muslim): The duty to give alms to the Muslim poor.	Human rights

---

elements found in both Western and non-Western cultural and religious traditions. Consider the examples of values in Exhibit 2.

At first glance, the values expressed in the two lists seem quite different. Nonetheless, in the spirit of what philosopher John Rawls calls "overlapping consensus," one can see that the seemingly divergent values converge at key points. Despite important differences between Western and non-Western cultural and religious traditions, both express shared attitudes about what it means to be human. First, individuals must not treat others simply as tools; in other words, they must recognize a person's value as a human being. Next, individuals and communities must treat people in ways that respect people's basic rights. Finally, members of a community must work together to support and improve the institutions on which the community depends. I call these three values "respect for human dignity," "respect for basic rights," and "good citizenship."

Those values must be the starting point for all companies as they formulate and evaluate standards of ethical conduct at home and abroad. But they are only a starting point. Companies need much more specific guidelines, and the first step to developing those is to translate the core human values into core values for business. What does it mean, for example, for a company to respect human dignity? How can a company be a good citizen?

I believe that companies can respect human dignity by creating and sustaining a corporate culture in which employees, customers, and suppliers are treated not as means to an end but as people whose intrinsic value must be acknowledged, and by producing safe products and services in a safe workplace. Companies can respect basic rights by acting in ways that support and protect the individual rights of employees, customers, and surrounding communities, and by avoiding relationships that violate human beings' rights to health, education, safety, and an adequate standard of living. And companies can be good citizens by supporting essential social institutions, such as the economic system and the education system, and by working with host governments and other organizations to protect the environment.

The core values establish a moral compass for business practice. They can help companies identify practices that are acceptable and those that are intolerable—even if the practices are compatible with a host country's norms and laws. Dumping pollutants near people's homes and accepting inadequate standards for handling hazardous materials are two examples of actions that violate core values.

Similarly, if employing children prevents them from receiving a basic education, then the practice is intolerable. Lying about product specifications in the act of selling may not affect human lives directly, but it too is intolerable because it violates the trust that is needed to sustain a corporate culture in which customers are respected.

Sometimes it is not a company's actions but those of a supplier or customer that pose problems. Take the case of the Tan family, a large supplier for Levi Strauss. The Tans were alleged to have forced 1,200 Chinese and Filipino women to work 74 hours per week in guarded compounds on the Mariana Islands. In 1992, after repeated warnings to the Tans, Levi Strauss broke off business relations with them.

CREATING AN ETHICAL CORPORATE CULTURE

The core values for business that I have enumerated can help companies begin to exercise ethical judgment and think about how to operate ethically in foreign cultures, but they are not specific enough to guide managers through actual ethical dilemmas. Levi Strauss relied on a written code of conduct when figuring out how to deal with the Tan family. The company's Global Sourcing and Operating Guidelines, formerly called the Business Partner Terms of Engagement, state that Levi Strauss will "seek to identify and utilize business partners who aspire as individuals and in the conduct of all their businesses to a set of ethical standards not incompatible with our own." Whenever intolerable business situations arise, managers should be guided by precise statements that spell out the behavior and operating practices that the company demands.

Some 90 percent of all *Fortune* 500 companies have codes of conduct, and 70% have statements of vision and values. In Europe and the Far East, the percentages are lower but are increasing rapidly. Does that mean that most companies have what they need? Hardly. Even though most large US companies have both statements of values and codes of conduct, many might be better off if they did not. Too many companies do not do anything with the documents; they simply paste them on the wall to impress employees, customers, suppliers, and the public. As a result, the senior managers who drafted the statements lose credibility by proclaiming values and not living up to them. Companies such as Johnson & Johnson, Levi Strauss, Motorola, Texas Instruments, and Lockheed Martin, however, do a great deal to make the words meaningful. Johnson & Johnson, for example, has become well known for its Credo Challenge sessions, in which managers discuss ethics in the context of their current business problems and are invited to criticize the company's credo and make suggestions for changes. The participants' ideas are passed on to the company's senior managers. Lockheed Martin has created an innovative site on the World Wide Web and on its local network that gives employees, customers, and suppliers access to the company's ethical code and the chance to voice complaints.

Codes of conduct must provide clear direction about ethical behavior when the temptation to behave unethically is strongest. The pronouncement in a code of conduct that bribery is unacceptable is useless unless accompanied by guidelines for gift giving, payments to get goods through customs, and "requests" from intermediaries who are hired to ask for bribes.

Motorola's values are stated very simply as "How we will always act: [with] constant respect for people [and] uncompromising integrity." The company's code of conduct, however, is explicit about actual business practice. With respect to bribery, for example, the code states that the "funds and assets of Motorola shall not be used, directly or indirectly, for illegal payments of any kind." It is unambiguous about what sort of payment is illegal: "the payment of a bribe to a public official or the kickback of funds to an employee of a customer ...." The code goes on to prescribe specific procedures for handling commissions to intermediaries, issuing sales invoices, and disclosing confidential information in a sales transaction—all situations in which employees might have an opportunity to accept or offer bribes.

Codes of conduct must be explicit to be useful, but they must also leave room for a manager to use his or her judgment in situations requiring cultural sensitivity. Host-country employees should not be forced to adopt all home-country values and renounce their own. Again, Motorola's code is exemplary. First, it gives clear direction:

> Employees of Motorola will respect the laws, customs, and traditions of each country in which they operate, but will, at the same time, engage in no course of conduct which, even if legal, customary, and accepted in any such country, could be deemed to be in violation of the accepted business ethics of Motorola or the laws of the United States relating to business ethics.

After laying down such absolutes, Motorola's code then makes clear when individual judgment will be necessary. For example, employees may sometimes accept certain kinds of small gifts "in rare circumstances, where the refusal to accept a gift" would injure Motorola's "legitimate business interests." Under certain circumstances, such gifts "may be accepted so long as the gift inures to the benefit of Motorola" and not "to the benefit of the Motorola employee."

Striking the appropriate balance between providing clear direction and leaving room for individual judgment makes crafting corporate values statements and ethics codes one of the hardest tasks that executives confront. The words are only a start. A company's leaders need to refer often to their organization's credo and code, and must themselves be credible, committed, and consistent. If senior managers act as though ethics do not matter, then the rest of the company's employees will not think they do either.

CONFLICTS OF DEVELOPMENT AND CONFLICTS OF TRADITION

Managers living and working abroad who are not prepared to grapple with moral ambiguity and tension should pack their bags and come home. The view that all business practices can be categorized as either ethical or unethical is too simple. As Einstein is reported to have said, "Things should be as simple as possible – but no simpler." Many business practices that are considered unethical in one setting may be ethical in another. Such activities are neither black nor white, but exist in what

Thomas Dunfee and I have called "moral free space."[2] In this gray zone, there are no tight prescriptions for a company's behavior. Managers must chart their own courses—as long as they do not violate core human values.

Consider the following example. Some successful Indian companies offer employees the opportunity for one of their children to gain a job with the company once the child has completed a certain level in school. The companies honor this commitment even when other applicants are more qualified than an employee's child. The perk is extremely valuable in a country where jobs are hard to find, and it reflects the Indian cultural belief that the West has gone too far in allowing economic opportunities to break up families. Not surprisingly, the perk is among the most cherished by employees, but in most Western countries it would be branded unacceptable nepotism. In the United States, for example, the ethical principle of equal opportunity holds that jobs should go to the applicants with the best qualifications. If a US company made such promises to its employees, it would violate regulations established by the Equal Employment Opportunity Commission. Given this difference in ethical attitudes, how should US managers react to Indian nepotism? Should they condemn the Indian companies? Refuse to accept them as partners or suppliers until they agree to clean up their act?

Despite the obvious tension between nepotism and principles of equal opportunity, I cannot condemn the practice for Indians. In a country, such as India, that emphasizes clan and family relationships and has catastrophic levels of unemployment, the practice must be viewed in a moral free space. The decision to allow a special perk for employees and their children is not necessarily wrong—at least for members of that country.

How can managers discover the limits of moral free space? That is, how can they learn to distinguish a value in tension with their own from one that is intolerable? Helping managers develop good ethical judgment requires companies to be clear about their core values and codes of conduct. But even the most explicit set of guidelines cannot always provide answers. This is especially true in the thorniest ethical dilemmas, in which the host country's ethical standards not only are different but also seem lower than the home country's. Managers must recognize that when countries have different ethical standards, there are two types of conflict that commonly arise. Each type requires its own line of reasoning.

In the first type of conflict, which I call a "conflict of relative development," ethical standards conflict because of the countries' different levels of economic development. As mentioned before, developing countries may accept wage rates that seem inhumane to more advanced countries in order to attract investment. As economic conditions in a developing country improve, the incidence of that sort of conflict usually decreases. The second type of conflict is a "conflict of cultural tradition." For example, Saudi Arabia, unlike most other countries, does not allow women to serve as corporate managers. Instead, women may work in only a few professions, such as education and health care. The prohibition stems from strongly held religious and cultural beliefs; any increase in the country's level of economic development, which is already quite high, is not likely to change the rules.

To resolve a conflict of relative development, a manager must ask the following question: Would the practice be acceptable at home if my country were in a similar stage of economic development? Consider the difference between wage and safety standards in the United States and in Angola, where citizens accept lower standards on both counts. If a US oil company is hiring Angolans to work on an offshore Angolan oil rig, can the company pay them lower wages than it pays US workers in the Gulf of Mexico? Reasonable people have to answer yes if the alternative for Angola is the loss of both the foreign investment and the jobs.

Consider, too, differences in regulatory environments. In the 1980s, the government of India fought hard to be able to import Ciba-Geigy's Entero Vioform, a drug known to be enormously effective in fighting dysentery but one that had been banned in the United States because some users experienced side effects. Although dysentery was not a big problem in the United States, in India poor public sanitation was contributing to epidemic levels of the disease. Was it unethical to make the drug available in India after it had been banned in the United States? On the contrary, rational people should consider it unethical not to do so. Apply our test: Would the United States, at an earlier stage of development, have used this drug despite its side effects? The answer is clearly yes.

But there are many instances in which the answer to similar questions is no. Sometimes a host country's standards are inadequate at any level of economic development. If a country's pollution standards are so low that working on an oil rig would considerably increase a person's risk of developing cancer, then foreign oil companies must refuse to do business there. Likewise, if the dangerous side effects of a drug treatment outweigh its benefits, then managers should not accept health standards that ignore the risks.

When relative economic conditions do not drive tensions, there is a more objective test for resolving ethical problems. Managers should deem a practice permissible only if they can answer no to both of the following questions: Is it possible to conduct business successfully in the host country without undertaking the practice? And, is the practice a violation of a core human value? Japanese gift giving is a perfect example of a conflict of cultural tradition. Most experienced business people, Japanese and non-Japanese alike, would agree that doing business in Japan would be virtually impossible without adopting the practice. Does gift giving violate a core human value? I cannot identify one that it violates. As a result, gift giving may be permissible for foreign companies in Japan even if it conflicts with ethical attitudes at home. In fact, that conclusion is widely accepted, even by companies such as Texas Instruments and IBM, which are outspoken against bribery.

Does it follow that all non-monetary gifts are acceptable or that bribes are generally acceptable in countries where they are common? Not at all. (See Exhibit 3.) What makes the routine practice of gift giving acceptable in Japan are the limits in its scope and intention. When gift giving moves outside those limits, it soon collides with core human values. For example, when Carl Kotchian, president of Lockheed in the 1970s, carried suitcases full of cash to Japanese politicians, he went beyond the norms established by Japanese tradition. That incident galvanized opinion in the US Congress and helped lead to passage of the Foreign Corrupt Practices Act of 1977. Likewise, Roh Tae Woo went beyond the norms established by Korean cultural tradition when he accepted $635.4 million in bribes as president of the Republic of Korea between 1988 and 1993.

EXHIBIT 3. The problem with bribery

Bribery is widespread and insidious. Managers in transnational companies routinely confront bribery even though most countries have laws against it. The fact is that officials in many developing countries wink at the practice, and the salaries of local bureaucrats are so low that many consider bribes a form of remuneration. The US Foreign Corrupt Practices Act of 1977 defines allowable limits on petty bribery in the form of routine payments required to move goods through customs. But demands for bribes often exceed those limits, and there is seldom a good solution.

Bribery disrupts distribution channels when goods languish on docks until local handlers are paid off, and it destroys incentives to compete on quality and cost when purchasing decisions are based on who pays what under the table. Refusing to acquiesce is often tantamount to giving business to unscrupulous companies.

I believe that even routine bribery is intolerable. Bribery undermines market efficiency and predictability, thus ultimately denying people their right to a minimal standard of living. Some degree of ethical commitment—some sense that everyone will play by the rules—is necessary for a sound economy. Without an ability to predict outcomes, who would be willing to invest?

There was a US company whose shipping crates were regularly pilfered by handlers on the docks of Rio de Janeiro. The handlers would take about 10% of the contents of the crates, but the company was never sure which 10% it would be. In a partial solution, the company began sending two crates—the first with 90% of the merchandise, the second with 10%. The handlers learned to take the second crate and leave the first untouched. From the company's perspective, at least knowing which goods it would lose was an improvement.

Bribery does more than destroy predictability; it undermines essential social and economic systems. That truth is not lost on business people in countries where the practice is woven into the social fabric. CEOs in India admit that their companies engage constantly in bribery, and they say that they have considerable disgust for the practice. They blame government policies in part, but Indian executives also know that their country's business practices perpetuate corrupt behavior. Anyone walking the streets of Calcutta, where it is clear that even a dramatic redistribution of wealth would still leave most of India's inhabitants in dire poverty, comes face-to-face with the devastating effects of corruption.

GUIDELINES FOR ETHICAL LEADERSHIP

Learning to spot intolerable practices and to exercise good judgment when ethical conflicts arise requires practice. Creating a company culture that rewards ethical behavior is essential. The following guidelines for developing a global ethical perspective among managers can help.

Treat Corporate Values and Formal Standards of Conduct as Absolutes

Whatever ethical standards a company chooses, it cannot waver on its principles either at home or abroad. Consider what has become part of company lore at Motorola. Around 1950, a senior executive was negotiating with officials of a South American government on a $10 million sale that would have increased the company's annual net profits by nearly 25%. As the negotiations neared completion, however, the executive walked away from the deal because the officials were asking for $1 million for "fees." CEO Robert Galvin not only supported the executive's decision but also made it clear that Motorola would neither accept the sale on any terms nor do business with those government officials again. Retold over the decades, this story demonstrating Galvin's resolve has helped cement a culture of ethics for thousands of employees at Motorola.

Design and Implement Conditions of Engagement for Suppliers and Customers

Will your company do business with any customer or supplier? What if a customer or supplier uses child labor? What if it has strong links with organized crime? What if it pressures your company to break a host country's laws? Such issues are best not left for spur-of-the-moment decisions. Some companies have realized that. Sears, for instance, has developed a policy of not contracting production to companies that use prison labor or infringe on workers' rights to health and safety. And BankAmerica has specified as a condition for many of its loans to developing countries that environmental standards and human rights must be observed.

Allow Foreign Business Units to Help Formulate Ethical Standards and Interpret Ethical Issues

The French pharmaceutical company Rhône-Poulenc Rorer has allowed foreign subsidiaries to augment lists of corporate ethical principles with their own suggestions. Texas Instruments has paid special attention to issues of international business ethics by creating the Global Business Practices Council, which is made up of managers from countries in which the company operates. With the overarching intent to create a "global ethics strategy, locally deployed," the council's mandate is to provide ethics education and create local processes that will help managers in the company's foreign business units resolve ethical conflicts.

In Host Countries, Support Efforts to Decrease Institutional Corruption

Individual managers will not be able to wipe out corruption in a host country, no matter how many bribes they turn down. When a host country's tax system, import and export procedures, and procurement practices favor unethical players, companies must take action.

Many companies have begun to participate in reforming host-country institutions. General Electric, for example, has taken a strong stand in India, using the media to make repeated condemnations of bribery in business and government. General Electric and others have found, however, that a single company usually cannot drive out entrenched corruption. Transparency International, an organization based in Germany, has been effective in helping coalitions of companies, government officials, and others work to reform bribery-ridden bureaucracies in Russia, Bangladesh, and elsewhere.

Exercise Moral Imagination

Using moral imagination means resolving tensions responsibly and creatively. Coca-Cola, for instance, has consistently turned down requests for bribes from Egyptian officials but has managed to gain political support and public trust by sponsoring a project to plant fruit trees. And take the example of Levi Strauss, which discovered in the early 1990s that two of its suppliers in Bangladesh were employing children under the age of 14 — a practice that violated the company's principles but was tolerated in Bangladesh. Forcing the suppliers to fire the children would not have ensured that the children received an education, and it would have caused serious hardship for the families depending on the children's wages. In a creative arrangement, the suppliers agreed to pay the children's regular wages while they attended school and to offer each child a job at age 14. Levi Strauss, in turn, agreed to pay the children's tuition and provide books and uniforms. That arrangement allowed Levi Strauss to uphold its principles and provide long-term benefits to its host country.

Many people think of values as soft; to some they are usually unspoken. A South Seas island society uses the word "mokita," which means, "the truth that everybody knows but nobody speaks." However difficult they are to articulate, values affect how we all behave. In a global business environment, values in tension are the rule rather than the exception. Without a company's commitment, statements of values and codes of ethics end up as empty platitudes that provide managers with no foundation for behaving ethically. Employees need and deserve more, and responsible members of the global business community can set examples for others to follow. The dark consequences of incidents such as Union Carbide's disaster in Bhopal remind us how high the stakes can be.

NOTES

1.   In other writings, Thomas W. Dunfee and I have used the term "hypernorm" instead of "core human value."

2.   T. Donaldson and T. W. Dunfee (1994). Toward a Unified Conception of Business Ethics: Integrative Social Contracts Theory. *Academy of Management Review*, 19(2): 252–284; T. Donaldson and T. W. Dunfee (1995). Integrative Social Contracts Theory: A Communitarian Conception of Economic Ethics. *Economics and Philosophy*, 110(1): 85–112.

Günter K. Stahl, Christof Miska, Laura J. Noval, and Verena J. Patock*

THE CHALLENGE OF RESPONSIBLE GLOBAL LEADERSHIP

I N THE WAKE OF A MAJOR ECONOMIC CRISIS and highly publicized corporate scandals, calls for more responsible corporate governance and leadership continue to grow (e.g. Pearce & Stahl, 2015; Waldman & Galvin, 2008). Ethical breaches have become front-page news, such as: Enron and Arthur Andersen's questionable accounting practices, misuse of company funds at Merrill Lynch and Elf in France, the collapse of Lehman Brothers, improper payments to government officials by Xerox managers in India, Nike's use of child labor in Pakistan, the corruption scandal involving Siemens, Shell's handling of human rights violations in Nigeria and BP's massive oil spill in the Gulf of Mexico, inappropriate trading and other illegal activities at Credit Suisse, Deutsche Bank, Citigroup and Goldman Sachs, the scandal surrounding Volkswagen's emissions-cheating program—the list is seemingly endless.

Not only Western leaders but also top-level executives in non-Western countries have been exposed for illegal activities and unethical business practices. Managerial malpractice, exacerbated by cultural factors, has been blamed for corporate scandals in South Korea (Choi & Aguilera, 2009) and for inadequate responses to environmental disasters in Japan (Tabucchi, 2012). Similarly, the recent dismissals, life prison terms and even executions of top managers on charges of corruption have shaken up the economic stability in China (Schneider, Barsoux, & Stahl, 2014).

These highly visible instances of managerial misconduct have eroded public faith worldwide and brought to the forefront the recognition that business leaders may engage in irresponsible behavior more frequently than previously assumed. As a result, trust in business is at one of the lowest levels on record. According to the 2013 Edelman Trust Barometer, less than 20 percent of the general public believes that business (or government) leaders can be trusted to tell the truth and make ethical decisions when confronted with a difficult issue. The Edelman Trust Barometer has been gathering data on trust, around the world, for more than a decade. In 2013, Edelman declared the "crisis of leadership" as the most important issue regarding worldwide economic development.

The calls for more responsible leadership are not only a reaction to recent business scandals and subsequent concerns with more ethical managerial conduct but they are also a result of increased stakeholder activism and scrutiny (e.g. Aguilera et al., 2007; Voegtlin, Patzer, & Scherer, 2012). In light of growing economic, social and environmental challenges around the world, there is increasing pressure from stakeholders—among them, governments, local communities, non-government organizations (NGOs), and consumers—for corporations and their leaders to engage in self-regulation, take more active roles as citizens in society, and "contribute to the creation of economic and societal progress in a globally responsible and sustainable way" (EFMD, 2005: 3). At the supranational level, since its official launch on July 26, 2000, the UN Global Compact has grown to more than 10,000 participants, including over 7,000 businesses in 145 countries around the world as of 2013 (UN Global Compact, 2013). As the growing membership of companies in the UN Global Compact along with booming corporate social responsibility (CSR) initiatives and social innovations indicate, more and more business leaders seek to actively contribute to the "triple bottom line" (Elkington, 1997), which simultaneously considers social, environmental, and economic sustainability (i.e. "people, planet, profits").

Responsible leadership thus includes decisions and actions taken by corporations and their leaders to both enhance societal welfare and avoid harmful consequences for stakeholders and society at large (Crilly, Schneider, & Zollo, 2008; Stahl & de Luque, 2014). These dual goals correspond with two major themes in the CSR, sustainability, and business ethics literature; namely, concerns about the detrimental impact of business on society (avoiding "negatives") and the objective of contributing to society (creating "positives"). As we will show in this reading, the trend of more and more companies operating in cross-border contexts dramatically increases the demands on managers in these two key aspects of social responsibility.

Today's executives are often confronted with environments characterized by wider-ranging diversity, with more stakeholders to understand and consider when making decisions, and with a need to engage in more frequent boundary-spanning activities within and across national borders. They face challenging and competing tensions both on and off the job, heightened ambiguity surrounding decisions and related outcomes, and thornier ethical dilemmas related to globalization (e.g. Bird & Osland, 2004; Lane et al., 2009). Stahl, Pless, and Maak (2013), in analyzing these issues, have identified four major areas in which global executives confront significant challenges. These include:

1. Diversity: The need to address the legitimate claims, rights, and expectations of a diverse group of stakeholders, both within and outside the organization.
2. Ethics: The need to ensure principle-driven, legally sound, and ethically acceptable behavior.

3. Sustainability: The need to contribute to protecting, preserving, and restoring the resources of the environment while improving human well-being and social equity.
4. Citizenship: The need to recognize, understand and effectively address human rights issues in the countries where the firm operates.

Effectively responding to these challenges requires executives to consider the needs of a diverse set of stakeholders, with sometimes conflicting values, perspectives, and interests, when making decisions. The increasing importance of doing business in emerging economies has greatly exacerbated this dilemma not only for leaders from Western multinational companies (MNCs) but also for those from emerging economies (see Stahl et al. 2016). As a result of these complexities, executives will often find it difficult, if not impossible, to determine when different is different and when different is wrong (Donaldson, 1996). One example of this is bribery, as in the recent corruption scandals at Alstom, Halliburton, Siemens, and GSK, which illustrate that MNCs from developed economies continue to participate in bribery, especially when operating in countries where law enforcement is weak and ineffective.

Global managers may engage in unethical or unlawful behavior because they think that it is acceptable in the host country, or that it will not be discovered due to inadequate control systems and lax enforcement practices (Donaldson & Dunfee, 1999; Puffer & McCarthy, 2008). Such environments, combined with an incomplete and inaccurate understanding of the local context, may tempt executives to adopt a "when in Rome, do as the Romans do" attitude of cultural relativism towards CSR, sustainability, citizenship, and ethics. On the other side of the spectrum, managers may be induced by factors such as company policies, codes of conduct, training programs, and even incentive systems to act everywhere in the world the same way as "things are done at headquarters," which can lead to neglect of the local stakeholders' needs. These examples illustrate that MNCs and their managers face a perennial dilemma: how to balance the need for global consistency in CSR approaches and ethical standards with the need to be sensitive to local stakeholder demands.

Next, we explore the foundations of responsible global leadership at multiple levels, from the micro (i.e. ethical decision-making processes and managerial behavior) through the meso (i.e. characteristics of the team and organizational context within which global executives operate), to the macro (i.e. aspects of the broader institutional and cultural environments that may affect executive decision making and responsible behavior). The multilevel framework guiding our discussion is depicted in Figure 1. We start our analysis with a broad overview of the growing body of research on ethical decision making and its implications for managerial behavior. We will then identify the individual and situational antecedents of managerial ethical choices and look at the different processes that hinder and promote managerial ethical decision making in a global context, with a particular focus on moral disengagement mechanisms, the role of intuition and emotions, and the influence of a key situational factor: moral intensity.

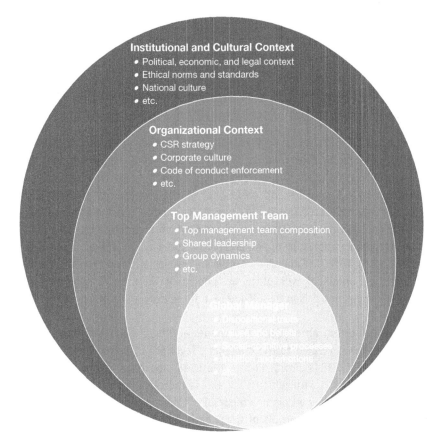

Institutional and Cultural Context
- Political, economic, and legal context
- Ethical norms and standards
- National culture
- etc.

Organizational Context
- CSR strategy
- Corporate culture
- Code of conduct enforcement
- etc.

Top Management Team
- Top management team composition
- Shared leadership
- Group dynamics
- etc.

Global Manager
- Dispositional traits
- Values and beliefs
- Social-cognitive processes
- Intuition and emotions

Figure 1. Multiple levels and factors influencing responsible global leadership

MANAGERIAL ETHICAL DECISION MAKING AND BEHAVIOR

A growing body of research that falls under the term "behavioral business ethics" or "managerial ethical decision making" (see O'Fallon & Butterfield, 2005; Tenbrunsel & Smith-Crowe, 2008, for reviews) studies the antecedents of managerial unethical behavior—such as cheating, lying, stealing, and discriminating practices—as well as the antecedents of managerial behavior that exceed moral minimums, such as engaging in philanthropy, contributing to environmental causes, supporting community development, and whistle-blowing (Crilly, Schneider, & Zollo, 2008; Treviño, Weaver, & Reynolds, 2006). The majority of the work in this field to date has focused on unethical behavior; however, research on what motivates managers to go beyond moral minimums and behave prosocially is on the rise (Mayer, 2010). For organizations, it is important to understand both sides of moral behavior: what motivates managers to avoid unethical or harmful behavior ("avoid harm"), and what motivates managers to proactively contribute to society ("do good").

In order to understand why managers avoid harm or do good, we review four different aspects of individuals' ethical decision making and behavior: their individual dispositions (including personality, philosophies, and identity), moral disengagement and motivated reasoning processes, the role of intuition and emotions, and the characteristics inherent to the ethical issue (i.e. moral intensity) (Jones, 1991).

Individual Differences: Traits, Moral Development, Moral Philosophies, and Moral Identity

Addressing all of the dispositional traits and individual variables that have been associated with unethical behavior at workplace is beyond the scope of this review; therefore, we focus on those that have received the most extensive empirical support according to recent reviews and meta-analyses of the literature (Kish-Gephart, Harrison, & Treviño, 2010; Treviño, Weaver, & Reynolds, 2006). Machiavellianism is a well-studied example of a dispositional trait, which characterizes individuals who use interpersonal relationships opportunistically and deceive others for personal gain (Christie & Geis, 1970). Similarly, narcissism and locus of control are personality traits linked to unethical workplace behavior that describes individuals with an excessive self-focus and driven by self-interest at the expense of others (Kish-Gephart et al., 2010).

Another important antecedent of managerial ethical behavior (less stable than personality traits) is related to the manager's level of cognitive moral development (CMD) (Kohlberg, 1984). According to the CMD approach, people have different levels of sophistication with which they assess moral dilemmas, and according to which they decide whether a certain course of action is morally right or wrong. Managers who are at the higher levels of CMD consider societal good in their decisions and are less likely to engage in unethical behavior (Blasi, 1980; Treviño, Weaver, & Reynolds, 2006; Kish-Gephart et al. 2010). Importantly, scholars find that most people operate at the "conventional" (middle) level of CMD, largely influenced by the environment, including social norms and organizational characteristics, in which they operate (Kish-Gephart et al. 2010).

In addition to personality traits and level of CMD, managerial ethical decision making is highly influenced by moral philosophies, which refers to managers' "stated beliefs or personal preferences for particular normative frameworks" (Kish-Gephart et al. 2010: 3). For example, a relativistic moral philosophy refers to the inherent belief that moral principles are situationally determined rather than universal, whereas an idealistic moral philosophy refers to the inherent belief that moral principles are universal (Kish-Gephart et al. 2010). Global managers who endorse a relativistic moral philosophy are more likely to adopt a "when-in-Rome-do-as-the-Romans-do" approach, embracing ethical norms that operate in the local context. Such an approach can be dangerous when working in countries with ethical standards that differ from international ones, such as where the employment of under-aged children is allowed, where security standards are very low, or where bribery is common practice (Donaldson, 1996). On the other hand, global managers who endorse an idealistic moral philosophy need to be wary of engaging in what is often referred to as ethical imperialism; that is, imposing international ethical standards onto local contexts when it is not warranted (Donaldson, 1996).

Finally, managerial ethical decision making is also influenced by the importance that managers attribute to their moral identity (Aquino & Reed, 2002). According to the moral identity approach, individuals are motivated to behave morally because of what they believe in terms of "who they are" (Blasi, 2004). The importance that people attribute to their moral identity has been linked to a number of positive ethical behaviors in organizations and other social contexts (e.g. Reed & Aquino, 2003; Reynolds & Ceranic, 2007). Interestingly, the self-importance of moral identity has been found to expand individuals' circles of moral regard by making them consider the welfare of those considered as "out-group" members (i.e. those who are different from the decision maker) (Reed & Aquino, 2003). Given that the ethical decisions reached by global managers are likely to have an impact on out-group members, such as employees or customers of different nationality or ethnic background, the importance that global managers attribute to their moral identity should facilitate ethical decision making in international contexts.

Social Cognitive Processes: Moral Disengagement and Motivated Reasoning

The traditional approach to address ethical decision making in organizations is based on the notion that there are certain managers who are "bad apples" and who can be clearly identified and avoided in organizations. More recent approaches in the field of behavioral business ethics, however, are based on the notion that the ethicality of individuals is malleable rather than stable (Monin & Jordan, 2009; Moore & Gino, 2013), and that many failures of ethical behavior result from individuals' unconscious and automatic biases rather than from their stable dispositions (Bazerman & Tenbrunsel, 2011). Such a recent approach echoes Hannah Arendt's (1963) exploration of the "banality of evil," in which she argued that much of what we call evil does not arise from the deliberate intention to do harm but arises from the failure to think about what we are doing (cited in Werhane et al., 2014: 2). The social cognitive approach to ethical decision making argues that feelings of discomfort (e.g. guilt, shame, or dissonance) arise when individuals consider behaving contrary to their own moral standards, prompting individuals to behave ethically (Bandura et al., 1996). People are capable, however, of engaging in several cognitive mechanisms that reframe an unethical or harmful act so as to make it appear right, which in turn enables them to engage in such behavior without feelings of guilt or dissonance (Bandura et al., 1996).

This process is referred to as "moral disengagement" and it has been found to be an important predictor of unethical behavior in organizations (Moore, 2008; Moore et al., 2012). Next, we review some mechanisms of moral disengagement, grouped into three types of cognitive restructuring, and provide examples of how these mechanisms can affect global managers. Table 1 provides an overview of all of the moral disengagement mechanisms.

- The first group of mechanisms consists in reframing the *harmful act* by employing moral justification (e.g. justifying the means with the ends), advantageous comparison (e.g. thinking that "others do worse things"), or disregarding/

Table 1. Examples of moral disengagement

Mechanism	Example
Moral justification	"We answered to a more important cause"; "My arm is twisted, I couldn't have done anything else"
Advantageous comparison	"Others do worse things"
Euphemistic language	"Being a team player" "Rightsizing" "Creative accounting"
Displacement of responsibility	"My boss told me to do it"
Diffusion of responsibility	"Everyone else in my group was doing it"
Distortion of consequences	"Nobody was really harmed" "it could have been worse"
Dehumanization	"They do not deserve better"
Attribution of blame	"They brought it upon themselves"

minimizing the consequences (e.g. thinking that "it is not a big deal"). Global managers may, for example, seek to reframe a harmful and/or unethical act by arguing that such behavior is in line with local standards, and that inculcating his or her home values onto other cultures would instead be ethically wrong, even if the act in question clearly results in harm to others (e.g. bribery, poor security measures, etc.). Likewise, global managers may be able to use advantageous comparison if they work in countries with poor reinforcement of ethical norms and where worse atrocities or violations of human rights occur compared to the ones perpetrated by the manager and his or her organization.

- The second group of mechanisms of moral disengagement consists in reframing *the role of the decision maker* in the ethical decision, for example by displacing responsibility (e.g. "my boss told me to do it") or diffusing responsibility (e.g. "it was a group decision"). As we will see in the next section, managers often take decisions in groups (top management teams and shared leadership), which can facilitate diffusion of responsibility. In addition, global managers may displace responsibility to the government(s) or to a weak institutional context for questionable ethical practices, as discussed in more detail later in this reading. If the manager is able to displace or diffuse responsibility, then he or she may feel relieved from his or her responsibility to address or improve the situation, under the excuse that "someone else" has made the decision.

- The third group of mechanisms of moral disengagement consists in reframing the *role of the victims* of the harmful behavior by either blaming (e.g. "they deserved it") or dehumanizing the victim (e.g. perceiving the victim as less than human and thus as unworthy of consideration). Scholars argue that dehumanization and blame processes are evident in "accounts of Wall Street traders who viewed clients not as unique individuals but as suckers asking to be conned" (Ashforth & Anand, 2003: 20). Perceiving the victims of harmful behavior as belonging to the "out-group" can facilitate dehumanization processes (Bandura, 2002; Moore & Gino, 2013). This suggests that global managers may find it easier to dehumanize or blame those affected by their decisions when the latter are psychologically and culturally different from themselves, as is likely to be the case in a global environment.

In addition to moral disengagement, scholars have found several instances of motivated reasoning in ethical situations; that is, reasoning that allows people to reach the conclusions they want to reach (Kunda, 1990; Ditto et al., 2009). For example, a recent study by Paharia, Vohs, and Deshpandé (2013) illustrates that individuals are likely to justify the use of sweatshop labor if they want to acquire the products elaborated with that type of labor, while such justification does not take place if those products are not desirable. Other scholars have also shown that people engage in motivated moral reasoning by selecting the moral principles and ideologies that best fit their desired conclusions (Ditto et al., 2009). In an international context, this suggests that global managers could make selective use of moral philosophies (e.g. relativistic vs. idealistic) that best justify harmful local practices if they have sufficient motivation for engaging in such behavior (e.g. monetary incentives, career advancement, etc.). To sum up, the research on motivated moral reasoning and moral disengagement demonstrates that even when managers have ethical predispositions and want to act in line with those predispositions, they may still act unethically, and re-interpret their unethical behavior in several ways so as to make it appear morally acceptable.

The Social Intuitionist Approach: The Role of Intuition and Emotions

Parallel to the findings on the limitations and biases of moral reasoning in facilitating ethical decision making, researchers have recently discovered that ethical judgment and behavior are often the result of automatic and intuitive affective processes rather than of deliberate and analytical reasoning (Haidt, 2001; Greene & Haidt, 2002; Sonenshein, 2007). This line of research was inspired by a seminal study that discovered that patients with damage to the brain areas responsible for the processing of emotions (but with intact analytical brain functioning) were incapable of reaching moral decisions (Damasio, 1994). Further neuroscientific evidence has provided evidence that when individuals contemplate moral dilemmas, the brain areas responsible for the processing of emotions are more likely to be activated than the brain areas responsible for analytical and deliberate reasoning (Greene et al., 2001). Partly based on these discoveries, the social intuitionist model to ethical decision making proposes that moral decisions result from "a sudden appearance in consciousness of a moral judgment, including an affective valence (good–bad)" (Haidt, 2001: 818), and that deliberate reasoning serves as a post-hoc rationalization of those initial intuitive/affective reactions to the moral dilemma. Empirical evidence in the social sciences has found that such affective-laden intuitions, often in the form of moral emotions such as empathy and guilt, are essential in promoting ethical and prosocial behaviors, and in inhibiting harmful and unethical behaviors (Eisenberg, 2000; Zhong, 2011).

The prevalence of intuition and emotions in determining ethical decision making presents some additional challenges for global managers. For instance, moral emotions are more likely to be aroused in moral dilemmas when the people affected by the decision maker are in his or her proximity (Greene et al., 2001). Given that global managers often reach decisions with ethical implications for others who are not only physically (in other countries) but also psychologically (out-group members) distant from themselves, they may be less likely to experience the moral emotions that would facilitate ethical behavior. Indeed, neuroscientific research has demonstrated that moral emotions that facilitate helping, such as empathic concern, are more often activated in the presence of in-group members (Mathur et al., 2010), and that individuals experience less emotional distress when they contemplate harming out-group members (Cikara et al., 2010). Fortunately, scholars have also identified interventions that help individuals draw "out-group" members into their circle of moral regard (Reed & Aquino, 2003), including intergroup contact (Pettigrew & Tropp, 2006), emphasis on shared identity (Gaertner & Dovidio, 2000), and re-categorization of out-group individuals into a superordinate, common group (Dovidio et al., 2009).

Characteristics of the Ethical Issue: Moral Intensity

In his seminal paper in the field of behavioral business ethics, Thomas M. Jones (1991) argues that managerial ethical choices are determined by the immediate characteristics inherent to the ethical issue, which the author terms the "moral intensity" of the issue. Although not an individual characteristic per se, the moral intensity of the issue has been consistently found to determine individual ethical choices (see Kish-Gephart et al. 2010, for a review). In the following, we review how different features of the ethical issue may relate to moral disengagement and emotional processes. The moral intensity of the ethical issue is defined by six main characteristics, which are illustrated in Table 2.

Two aspects related to the moral intensity of the ethical issue are particularly likely to pose challenges for global managers: proximity and social consensus. As previously mentioned, global managers are likely to experience low proximity (either physical, cultural, or psychological) to those who are affected by their behavior (both harmful and prosocial). Such low proximity inherent to the ethical issue may in turn facilitate dehumanization and blame processes towards others affected by the ethical behavior, as reviewed in the section on moral disengagement. At the same time, low proximity may decrease feelings of concern and empathy for those others, as we reviewed in the section on intuition and emotions.

In addition to low proximity, social consensus about the rightness or wrongness of an ethical act is likely to be low for managers who operate in global environments. For instance, employment of under-age children, bribery, poor security standards, and other business practices may have high social consensus in certain local societies, whereas the social consensus about these same practices in an international context may be low. In the face of such ambiguous social consensus, the manager has no clear indication of what the "right" course of action to follow is, and may thus be more likely to find justifications for engaging in harmful behavior (or for refusing prosocial behavior). Indeed, several managers who have engaged in unethical behavior have claimed that if something is not labeled as illegal, then it must be "OK" (Gellerman, 1986: 88; cited in Ashforth & Anand, 2003), and that practices are justified as long as they are standard industrial practice (Elsbach, 1994; Ashforth & Anand, 2003).

Table 2. Components of the moral intensity of the ethical issue

Mechanism	Definition/ Example
Magnitude of consequences (MC)	Sum of the harms and/or benefits of the action. *E.g.: an act that causes the death of a human being has greater MC than an act that causes a person to suffer a minor injury.*
Probability of effect (PE)	Likelihood that the action will take place and that it will result in the predicted outcome. *E.g.: selling a gun to a known armed robber has more PE than selling a gun to a law abiding citizen.*
Social consensus (SC)	To what extent the issue is approved by society. *E.g.: the wrongness of bribing an official in Texas has greater SC than the wrongness of bribing an official in Mexico.*
Proximity (PR)	Feeling of closeness to the objects/individuals affected. *E.g.: layoffs in a manager's work unit have greater PR than layoffs in a remote plant.*
Temporal immediacy (TI)	Time period before the onset of consequences. *E.g.: reducing the retirement benefits of old employees has greater TI than reducing the retirement benefits of young employees.*
Concentration of effect (CE)	Number of people affected by an act of given magnitude. *E.g.: cheating an individual or small group of individuals out of a given sum has a more concentrated effect than cheating an institutional entity.*

Source: Adapted from Jones (1991)

As already mentioned, such beliefs are problematic in a global environment, in which standard practices and illegality are different and conflicting between and within local and global contexts (Donaldson, 1996).

ROLE OF THE TOP MANAGEMENT TEAM AND SHARED LEADERSHIP

After having reviewed the micro level explanations as to why individual managers may behave in an ethical or unethical manner, we will now consider important aspects at the meso level of our framework and explore the immediate organizational context of those managers who operate at the top of MNCs. In the following, we discuss the idiosyncratic characteristics of the top management team (TMT); mainly, team diversity and the role of shared leadership. We also address the ways in which these characteristics may promote or impede TMT ethical decision making and, consequently, corporate social performance.

The decisions and actions of a company's top executives are key to its social performance and long-term viability. As Waldman (2011: 81) put it succinctly, "firms do not make decisions pertaining to responsibility or CSR; leaders do". Next to the day-to-day routine administration planning, organizing, coordinating, and controlling tasks (Finkelstein, Hambrick, & Cannella, 2009), top managers are in charge of setting a company's strategic direction (Cohen & Bailey, 1997), designing CSR and sustainability strategies (Waldman, Siegel, & Javidan, 2006), and promoting the integration of CSR principles and ethical norms within the company's structure, policies, and corporate culture (Desai & Rittenburg, 1997; Quinn & Dalton, 2009). Yet executive managers are often not the only decision-makers in a corporate setting. They are part of a team, the TMT, in which the decision making power and control are distributed and shared among a range of senior executives, such as the chief operations officer or the chief financial officer (Aggarwal & Samwick, 2003).

When investigating the influence of the TMT on corporate social performance, a range of team- or group-related factors need to be considered. These include: group composition design variables (e.g. demographics, diversity, size, and tenure), organizational context variables (e.g. corporate culture, reward system, supervision, training and resources), group processes (e.g. communication and conflict among internal group members or external parties), and group psychological traits (e.g. group norms, cohesiveness, team mental models, and group affect) (Cohen & Bailey, 1997). Mirroring the trend towards globalization, diversity as a group composition design variable has gained particular attention (Van Knippenberg & Schippers, 2007) because today's global managers are confronted not only with differing institutional and international contexts, and more diverse sets of stakeholders (Arthaud-Day, 2005), but also with more heterogeneous TMTs.

Diversity in a group context is known to pose both opportunities and challenges (Horwitz & Horwitz, 2007; Milliken & Martins, 1996), which can be explained by means of several mechanisms. Diversity can lead to social categorization, which may provoke stereotyping, polarization, and anxiety among group members (Williams & O'Reilly, 1998). In groups, individuals often classify themselves and others into social categories on the basis of visible attributes such as sex, age, or status (Tajfel, 1982; Tajfel & Turner, 1986). Through such classification processes individuals create a favorable self-identity and perceive others as less trustworthy, honest, and collegial. In particular, in diverse groups this can lead to dissatisfaction, incoherence, conflicts and as a result, poor performance outcomes. Similarly, influences on performance can arise from the degree to which group members perceive themselves to be similar to or different from others within the group (Pfeffer, 1983). Similarity based on characteristics stemming from attitudes or demographic variables enhances interpersonal liking, yet may make diverse groups, including their communication, cohesion, and integration less effective (Williams & O'Reilly, 1998). In a TMT context this means that teams whose members share certain characteristics, e.g. who are in the same age group or have the same nationality, values, or hobbies, may yield better results than heterogeneous teams, since lower levels of diversity would seem to promise harmonious social interactions and unity. However, cases such as Enron illustrate vividly how too much unity in the boardroom can bring about disastrous outcomes (Skapinker, 2003). With very few exceptions, Enron's board mainly consisted of white male US Americans, who uniformly described internal board relations as harmonious (US Government, 2002).

Although there were a multitude of factors that had contributed to Enron's collapse (McLean & Elkind, 2013), psychological phenomena such as "groupthink" may explain why the company's board members did not call a halt to the scandalous corporate malpractices in the first place. Next to the persuasion of doing something truly innovative, the tendency to mindlessly favor consensus and harmony over disagreement and conflict has likely provoked the unreasonable decisions that resulted in one of the largest corporate bankruptcies in US history. Irving Janis (1972), in his now classic study of the processes that lead to disastrous policy decisions, such as the Bay of Pigs or Watergate, describes how individuals in groups are more likely to thoughtlessly conform to collective judgments, without voicing their reservations out of the fear of being seen as disloyal or being ostracized. Groupthink predominantly occurs in groups that are highly cohesive and homogeneous, and it has been argued that the presence of diversity can reduce the probability of its occurrence (Cox & Blake, 1991; Stahl et al., 2010). From this perspective, diversity may be regarded as a potential measure to facilitate healthy dissent and critical evaluation among TMT members, thereby promoting responsible leadership.

In addition to reducing peer pressure, diversity is further recognized to contribute to higher sensitivity towards social issues (Hafsi & Turgut, 2013), to enhance a team's ability to handle differing environmental conditions, and to better respond to stakeholder needs around the world (Wong, Ormiston, & Tetlock, 2011). Moreover, diverse TMTs are considered to be more creative and innovative in solving CSR issues because they have access to larger and more diverse informational networks (Ancona & Caldwell, 1992). In this context, not only diversity in general but also distinct types of diversity may be of importance when composing TMTs. Researchers have found that educational diversity, similarly to national diversity, allows for a broader array of relevant information (Dahlin, Weingart, & Hinds 2005), while age diversity has been found to positively influence philanthropic decisions (Post, Rahman, & Rubow, 2011), and gender diversity has been linked to positive CSR outcomes (Hafsi & Turgut, 2013). These findings illustrate that there are several different ways of boosting diversity in a TMT.

Apart from the diversity aspect, the concept of shared leadership is the second crucial factor that may influence ethical decision making in TMTs and corporate social performance. Shared leadership reflects the idea that "leadership is not merely the influential act of an individual or individuals but rather is embedded in a complex interplay of numerous interacting forces" (Uhl-Bien, Marion, & McKelvey, 2007: 302). In other words, process towards productive outcomes is shaped not by a single manager or TMT member but rather by multiple social actors in the organization (Carson, Tesluk, & Marrone, 2007; Pearce, Wassenaar, & Manz, 2014). Shared leadership contributes to the idea that every member of the organization is an important part of a "checks and balances system" that ensures responsible managerial behavior and eventually prevents corruptive tendencies (Pearce & Manz, 2011). The lack of shared leadership has been identified as a major cause of irresponsible decisions and behaviors (Christensen, Mackey, & Whetten, 2014; Pearce et al. 2014). Hence, raising awareness and implementing the notion of shared leadership into the minds and business cultures of global managers and their organizations may not only create a common sense of responsibility but will also be an important measure to evoke critical thinking and to avoid corporate fraud in the future.

THE ORGANIZATIONAL CONTEXT

Continuing with the meso level of analysis, further influences on responsible managerial behavior lie within the organizational context. This is supported by a large body of research in social psychology: classic experiments such as Asch's (1951) conformity studies, Milgram's (1974) work on obedience to authority, and Zimbardo's (1972) prison experiment have demonstrated that the social context in which individuals are embedded can influence their revealed good and bad characteristics. The previously discussed research on ethical decision making also points to the importance of the organizational context (e.g. Craft, 2013; Lehnert, Park, & Singh, 2015; Treviño, den Nieuwenboer, & Kish-Gephart, 2014) and its ethical infrastructure—such as the ethical climate in the organization, the existence and enforcement of a

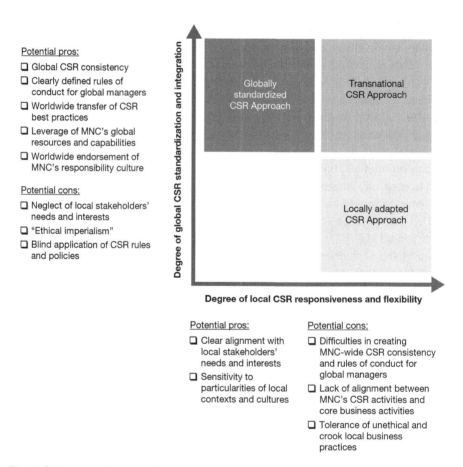

Figure 2. Three prototypical CSR approaches

Source: Adapted from Stahl et al. (2013).

code of conduct, and reward and sanctioning mechanisms—in influencing ethical and unethical choices.

Another important feature of the organizational context is the CSR strategy that a company adopts. As discussed earlier, MNCs operating across different countries and societies are confronted with the dual needs of globally integrating and standardizing their various CSR activities for consistency reasons and, at the same time, of adapting these activities locally in order to meet the demands of local stakeholders. Building on Bartlett and Ghoshal's (1998) global–local framework, a growing number of scholars (e.g. Arthaud-Day, 2005; Filatotchev & Stahl, 2015; Miska, Witt, & Stahl, 2016) have studied MNCs' approaches to CSR by focusing on three prototypical strategies: globally standardized, locally adapted, and transnational CSR approaches. Figure 2 provides an overview of the three prototypical CSR approaches.

The *globally standardized CSR approach* implies global CSR consistency and standardization regardless of the country in which a company operates. It relies on universal principles comparable to "hypernorms" (Donaldson & Dunfee, 1994), embodied in corporate codes of conduct that are assumed to apply across societies. While this strategy ensures clear global rules and consistency, employee awareness of ethical dilemmas, and the importance of responsible conduct worldwide, it may lead to ethical imperialism and arrogance. The mirror opposite of this strategy—the *locally adapted CSR approach*—aims at counterbalancing such risks because it emphasizes the need for sensitivity and responsiveness to local conditions when business is conducted in multiple countries. However, this approach poses the risk of decreasing the credibility of company-wide and universally accepted codes of conduct. The third approach—the *transnational CSR approach*—can be seen as a hybrid strategy, which aims to balance global and local demands. This approach provides a global template to guide managerial decision making and behavior regarding CSR, sustainability, and business ethics, while offering the flexibility required in specific situations and by particular local stakeholders.

Filatotchev and Stahl (2015), based on extensive case study research, concluded that the transnational CSR approach is the most effective in helping MNCs to coordinate their worldwide CSR activities. Israel-based Teva Pharmaceuticals, the world's largest generic drug company, provides an example of a company that has adopted a transnational CSR approach. At Teva, a global code of conduct applies to all managers and employees in the company's countries of operation. However, there are four specific areas in which subsidiaries have a high degree of flexibility when enacting the code: the protection of the natural environment, workplace safety, access to global health care, and the support of regions affected by natural disasters through medical help (Filatotchev & Stahl, 2015).

The three CSR approaches have far-reaching implications for global managers' decision making because they define the space for maneuver in terms of managers' ability (and opportunity) to engage in "do good" and "avoid harm" behaviors. Each approach requires specific skills and competencies to support it, at both the individual and organizational levels. The various key competencies required on the part of global managers to successfully implement the three approaches are summarized in Table 3. Based on this analysis, the transnational CSR approach is the most demanding because

Table 3. Competencies required to support different CSR approaches

Globally Standardized CSR Approach	Locally Adapted CSR Approach	Transnational CSR Approach
• Strong commitment to head office • Understanding of global stakeholders' needs • Big-picture thinking • "Helicopter" view • Understanding of universal ethical standards • Integrity and behavioral consistency	• Strong commitment to local stakeholders • Non-judgmental and open to different views • Local knowledge and experience • Intercultural sensitivity and perspective-taking skills • Adaptability and behavioral flexibility	Competencies required for globally standardized and locally adapted CSR approaches, plus: • Dual citizenship • Global mindset • Ability to balance paradoxes and contradictions • Tolerance of uncertainty • Multicultural identity • Long-term orientation • Moral imagination

Source: Stahl et al. (2013).

it requires that global managers balance various, often contradictory expectations, demands, and interests on the part of both global and local stakeholders. To successfully perform this balancing act, managers need to possess the capacity to integrate multiple cultural and strategic realities, as well as the ability to recognize, understand, and identify with both global and local perspectives, and to reconcile potential conflicts between them (Javidan & Bowen, 2013; Miska, Stahl, & Mendenhall, 2013).

THE INSTITUTIONAL AND CULTURAL CONTEXT

At the macro level of analysis, the institutional and cultural environments within which MNCs operate pose major constraints on the implementation of the previously discussed CSR approaches and on the enactment of responsible leadership (e.g. Aguilera et al., 2007; Waldman et al., 2006). The recent scandal over IKEA catalogues printed for the Saudi market is a case in point. In 2012, IKEA systematically removed women from the Saudi Arabian version of its catalogue. This step was followed by considerable criticism from global media as well as by Swedish politicians, seriously damaging IKEA's reputation as a socially responsible company and an employer of choice for women and minorities. It appears that in Saudi Arabia IKEA was leaning towards Saudi sensibilities, rather than promoting its own values such as "daring to be different" and promoting human rights universally through a global CSR approach (Miska & Pleskova, 2016). In the end, IKEA took full responsibility and apologized— in accordance with what the public in the Western world and respective institutional influences required.

Institutional factors include cultural norms and values, and they can constrain responsible managerial behavior in the global context because they embody societies' and nations' formal and informal rules (North, 1990). Hall and Soskice's (2001) "varieties of capitalism" is an approach intended to systematically capture the variations in companies' approaches to adhere to institutional rules as they strategically coordinate among their various stakeholders. These variations can be classified into two types of political economy: liberal market economics (LMEs) prevalent in Anglo-Saxon countries and characterized by companies coordinating their activities by means of competitive market arrangements and formal contracting; and coordinated market economies (CMEs), prevalent in Continental Europe, where companies depend on non-market relationships resulting in need for relational networks rather than competitive activities. This distinction assumes relatively strong institutional environments as established in many Western, developed economies. In contrast, the institutional environments in many emerging economies tend to be comparably weaker and less clearly graspable because they are frequently characterized by arbitrary law enforcement, bureaucratic irregularities, and corruption practices (Dobers & Halme, 2009).

Considering that emerging economies, such as the BRIC countries (Brazil, Russia, India, and China), have significantly increased their stakes in the world economy, global managers need to reconsider the numerous institutional variations in order to carefully navigate the differences with regard to responsible managerial behavior. In China, for example, one unique dimension of CSR relates to social stability and progress (Xu & Yang, 2010), which does not necessarily correspond to the Western understanding of CSR. Also, as Miska, Witt, and Stahl (2016) found in a study on Chinese MNCs, the Chinese government via the State-owned Assets Supervision and Administration Commission (SASAC) affects the global CSR-integration of state-influenced Chinese MNCs. Such governance structures concerning global CSR enactment are rather exceptional compared to other emerging economies, as well as contrasted to advanced economies.

Institutional environments not only shape CSR requirements and expectations on the part of various stakeholders but they also influence global managers' values, attitudes, and assumptions. Waldman et al.'s (2006) study, for example, demonstrated that several cultural dimensions have an impact on managers' CSR values. Of these dimensions, institutional collectivism—which is the extent to which institutional practices reward and encourage collective, rather than individual, action (Javidan et al. 2006)—was found to be associated with stakeholder and community welfare values. Thus, managers in these societies are likely to espouse these values.

When it comes to navigating cultural differences relevant for responsible managerial behavior in the global context, culture can be a particular asset in understanding the idiosyncrasies of specific institutional environments in which global managers operate. Culture can also pose a constraint on managers' ability to engage in responsible behavior, especially if they are unaware of the informal rules of specific contexts, lack cultural understanding, or have a "cultural imperialism" attitude. In this sense, Fitzsimmons, Miska, and Stahl (2011) pointed to the potential of multicultural managers who have acquired experience in multiple cultural settings. Due to their insights into different cultural contexts and their attendant perspective-taking abilities, multicultural managers might be better at reconciling conflicting cultural values and norms. Consequently, global managers who possess extensive experience in various cultural settings are likely to deal more efficiently with institutional and cultural variations in the global context.

Institutional and cultural differences can result in tough choices for global managers. Based on their own cultural values and ethical norms, they frequently need to decide when different is different and when different is ethically wrong. For example, the 2013 collapse of the Savar building in Bangladesh caused more than 1,000 deaths, making it one of the most lethal garment-factory accidents at that time. At first, the factory owners and government officials were considered the main culprits, since they had failed to enforce proper safety standards. However, soon after the disaster, international brands and retailers such as Walmart, Mango, Primark, and Matalan (Mail Online, 2013; *The Economist*, 2013) were criticized because they had garments produced in the factory. In most of the international brands' and retailers' countries of origin, labor safety standards are considerably higher. However, these companies relied on the less stringent institutional environment in Bangladesh—leading to fatal consequences.

CONCLUSION: THE CHALLENGE OF RESPONSIBLE GLOBAL LEADERSHIP

There is increasing pressure on corporations and their managers to act in a globally responsible, sustainable, and ethically sound manner. In this reading we provided an overview of existing and emerging research relevant to responsible global leadership—including work on ethical decision making, shared leadership, and corporate social responsibility—highlighting the multiple influences on responsible managerial behavior and the conditions under which global executives may engage in responsible or irresponsible conduct. We argued that global executives need to address the diverse, and often conflicting, demands of multiple cross-boundary stakeholders. The complexities of leading responsibly in a global environment span multiple layers comprising characteristics of the individual manager, aspects of the organizational context, including TMT decision making and corporate CSR strategies, as well as the broader institutional and cultural environments in which global corporations are embedded. In navigating these complexities, executives need to be aware of their own perspectives, orientations, and biases in situations of ethical decision making. Global managers need to possess a specific skillset and mindset to implement corporate CSR strategies. In particular, they must be able to balance global integration and local responsiveness with respect to CSR, sustainability, and ethics. While responsible leadership in a cross-border and culturally diverse context is highly demanding, it offers vast opportunities for global executives to make a difference for their companies and society.

NOTE

* This is an adapted and expanded version of the chapter entitled "Responsible Global Leadership: A Multi-level Framework", published in the "*Handbook of Research in Global Leadership: Making a Difference*" (Edward Elgar).

REFERENCES

Aggarwal, R. K., & Samwick, A. A. (2003). Why do managers diversify their firms? Agency reconsidered. *The Journal of Finance*, 58(1), 71–118.

Aguilera, R., Rupp, D. E., Williams, C. A., & Ganapathi, J. (2007). Putting these back in corporate social responsibility: a multilevel theory of social change in organizations. *Academy of Management Review*, 3, 836–863.

Ancona, D. G., & Caldwell, D. F. (1992). Bridging the boundary: external activity and performance in organizational teams. *Administrative Science Quarterly*, 37(4), 634–665.

Aquino, K., & Reed, A. (2002). The self-importance of moral identity. *Journal of Personality and Social Psychology*, 83(6), 1423–1440.

Arendt, H. (1963). *Eichmann in Jerusalem*. New York: Penguin.

Arthaud-Day, M. L. (2005). Transnational corporate social responsibility: a tri-dimensional approach to international CSR research. *Business Ethics Quarterly*, 15(1), 1–22.

Asch, S. E. (1951). Effects of group pressure on the modification and distortion of judgments. In H. Guetzkow (Ed.), *Groups, Leadership and Men*. (177–190) Pittsburgh, PA: Carnegie Press.

Ashforth, B. E., & Anand, V. (2003). The normalization of corruption in organizations. *Research in Organizational Behavior*, 25, (1–52).

Bandura, A. (2002). Selective moral disengagement in the exercise of moral agency. *Journal of Moral Education*, 31(2), 101–119.

Bandura, A., Barbaranelli, C., Caprara, G. V., & Pastorelli, C. (1996). Mechanisms of moral disengagement in the exercise of moral agency. *Journal of Personality and Social Psychology*, 71, 364–374.

Bartlett, C. A., & Ghoshal, S. (1998). *Managing Across Borders: The Transnational Solution* (2nd edn). Boston, MA: Harvard Business School Press.

Bazerman, M. H., & Tenbrunsel, A. E. (2011). Good people often let bad things happen – Ethical breakdowns. *Harvard Business Review*, 89(4), 58–65.

Bird, A., & Osland, J.S. (2004). Global competencies. In H.L. Lane, M.L. Maznevski, M.E. Mendenhall & J. McNett (Eds.), *The Blackwell Handbook of Global Management—A Guide to Managing Complexity*. (57–81) Malden, MA: Blackwell.

Blasi, A. (1980). Bridging moral cognition and moral action: A critical review of the literature. *Psychological Bulletin*, 88, 1–45.

Blasi, A. (2004). Moral functioning: Moral understanding and personality. In D. K. Lapsley, & D. Narvaez (Eds.), *Moral Development, Self and Identity*. (335–348). Mahwah, NJ: Lawrence Erlbaum.

Carson, J. B., Tesluk, P. E., & Marrone, J. A. (2007). Shared leadership in teams: an investigation of antecedent conditions and performance. *Academy of Management Journal*, 50(5), 1217–1234.

Choi, S., & Aguilera, R. V. (2009). CSR dynamics in South Korea and Japan: a comparative analysis. *Corporate Social Responsibility: A Case Study Approach*. (123–147) Cheltenham: Edward Elgar.

Christensen, L. J., Mackey, A., & Whetten, D. (2014). Taking responsibility for corporate social responsibility: the role of leaders in creating, implementing, sustaining, or avoiding socially responsible firm behaviors. *The Academy of Management Perspectives*, 28(2), 164–178.

Christie, R., & Geis, F. (1970). *Studies in Machiavellianism*. New York: Academic Press.

Cikara, M., Farnsworth, R. A., Harris, L. T., & Fiske, S. T. (2010). On the wrong side of the trolley track: neural correlates of relative social valuation. *Social Cognitive and Affective Neuroscience*, 5, 404–413.

Craft, J. L. (2013). A review of the empirical ethical decision making literature: 2004–2011. *Journal of Business Ethics*, 117(2), 221–259.

Crilly, D., Schneider, S. C., & Zollo, M. (2008). Psychological antecedents to socially responsible behavior. *European Management Review*, 5(3): 175–190.

Cohen, S. G., & Bailey, D. E. (1997). What makes teams work: group effectiveness research from the shop floor to the executive suite. *Journal of Management*, 23(3), 239–290.

Cox, T. H., & Blake, S. (1991). Managing cultural diversity: implications for organizational competitiveness. . *Academy of Management Perspectives*, 5(3), 45–56.

Dahlin, K. B., Weingart, L. R., & Hinds, P. J. (2005). Team diversity and information use. *Academy of Management Journal*, 48(6), 1107–1123.

Damasio, A. R. (1994). *Descartes' Error: Emotion, Reason, and the Human Brain*. New York: Free Press.

Desai, A. B., & Rittenburg, T. (1997). Global ethics: an integrative framework for MNEs. *Journal of Business Ethics*, 16(8), 791–800.

Ditto, P. H., Pizarro, D. A., & Tannenbaum, D. (2009). Motivated moral reasoning. In B. H. Ross, D. M. Bartels, C. W. Bauman, L. J. Skitka, & D. L. Medin, *Moral Judgment and Decision Making*. (307–338) San Diego, CA: Academic Press.

Dobers, P., & Halme, M. (2009). Corporate social responsibility and developing countries. *Corporate Social Responsibility and Environmental Management*, 16(5), 237–249.

Donaldson, T. (1996). Values in tension: ethics away from home. *Harvard Business Review*, 74(5), 48–62.

Donaldson, T., & Dunfee, T. W. (1994). Toward a unified conception of business ethics: integrative social contracts theory. *The Academy of Management Review*, 19(2), 252–284.

Donaldson, T., & Dunfee, T. W. (1999). When ethics travel: the promise and peril of global business ethics. *California Management Review*, 41(4), 45–63.

Dovidio, J. F., Gaertner, S. L., Schnabel, N., Saguy, T., & Johnson, J. (2009). Recategorization and prosocial behavior: common in-group identity and a dual identity. In S. Stürmer, & M. Snyder (Eds.), *The Psychology of Prosocial Behavior: Group Processes, Intergroup Relations, and Helping*. (191–207) Oxford: Wiley-Blackwell.

The Economist. (2013). Battle of the brands. *The Economist*, May 16. Retrieved from www.economist.com/blogs/schumpeter/2013/05/factory-safety [accessed May 19, 2016].

Edelman. (2013). Executive summary: 2013 Edelman Trust Barometer. Retrieved from http://de.scribd.com/doc/121501475/Executive-Summary-2013-Edelman-Trust-Barometer [accessed December 3, 2016].

EFMD. (2005). Globally responsible leadership—a call for engagement. Retrieved from www.grli.org/wp-content/uploads/2015/03/GRLI-Call-for-Engagement_English-2005.pdf [accessed February 20, 2016].

Eisenberg, N. (2000). Emotion, regulation, and moral development. *Annual Review of Psychology*, 51, 665–697.

Elkington, J. B. (1997). *Cannibals with Forks: The Triple Bottom Line of 21st Century Business*. Oxford: Capstone.

Elsbach, K. D. (1994). Managing organizational legitimacy in the California cattle industry: the construction and effectiveness of verbal accounts. *Administrative Science Quarterly*, 39, 57–88.

Filatotchev, I., & Stahl, G. K. (2015). Towards transnational CSR: corporate social responsibility approaches and governance solutions for multinational corporations. *Organizational Dynamics*, 44(2), 121–129.

Finkelstein, S., Hambrick, D. C., & Cannella, A. A. (2009). *Strategic Leadership: Theory and Research on Executives, Top Management Teams, and Boards*. New York: Oxford University Press.

Fitzsimmons, S. R., Miska, C., & Stahl, G. K. (2011). Multicultural employees: global business' untapped resource. *Organizational Dynamics*, 40, 199–206.

Gaertner, S. L., & Dovidio, J. F. (2000). *Reducing Intergroup Bias: The Common Ingroup Identity Model*. Philadelphia, PA: The Psychology Press.

Gellerman, S. W. (1986). Why "good" managers make bad ethical choices. *Harvard Business Review*, 86(4), 85–90.

Greene, J., & Haidt, J. (2002). How (and where) does moral judgment work? *Trends in Cognitive Science*, 6(12), 517–523.

Greene, J. D., Sommerville, R. B., Nystrom, L. E., Darley, J. M., & Cohen, J. D. (2001). An fMRI investigation of emotional engagement in moral judgment. *Science*, 293, 2105–2108.

Hafsi, T., & Turgut, G. (2013). Boardroom diversity and its effect on social performance: conceptualization and empirical evidence. *Journal of Business Ethics*, 112(3), 1–17.

Haidt, J. (2001). The emotional dog and its rational tail: a social intuitionist approach to moral judgment. *Psychological Review*, 108(4), 814–834.

Hall, P. A., & Soskice, D. (2001). An introduction to varieties of capitalism. In P. A. Hall & D. W. Soskice (Eds.), *Varieties of Capitalism: The Institutional Foundations of Comparative Advantage*. (1–70) Oxford: Oxford University Press.

Horwitz, S. K., & Horwitz, I. B. (2007). The effects of team diversity on team outcomes: a meta-analytic review of team demography. *Journal of Management*, 33(6), 987–1015.

Janis, I. L. (1972). *Victims of Groupthink: A Psychological Study of Foreign-Policy Decisions and Fiascoes*. Boston, MA: Houghton Mifflin.

Javidan, M., & Bowen, D. (2013). The 'global mindset' of managers. *Organizational Dynamics*, 42, 145–155.

Javidan, M., Dorfman, P. W., De Luque, M. S., & House, R. J. (2006). In the eye of the beholder: cross cultural lessons in leadership from Project GLOBE. *The Academy of Management Perspectives*, 20(1), 67–90.

Jones, T. M. (1991). Ethical decision making by individuals in organizations: an issue-contingent model. *Academy of Management Review*, 16(2), 366–395.

Kish-Gephart, J. J., Harrison, D. A., & Treviño, L. K. (2010). Bad apples, bad cases, and bad barrels: meta-analytic evidence about sources of unethical decisions at work. *Journal of Applied Psychology*, 95(1), 1–31.

Kohlberg, L. (1984). *The Psychology of Moral Development: Essays on Moral Development*. San Francisco: Harper & Row.

Kunda, Z. (1990). The case for motivated reasoning. *Psychological Bulleting*, 108(3), 480–498.

Lane, H. L., Maznevski, M. L., Mendenhall, M. E., & McNett, J. (Eds.). (2009). *The Blackwell Handbook of Global Management—A guide to Managing Complexity*. Malden, MA: Blackwell.

Lehnert, K., Park, Y. H., & Singh, N. (2015). Research note and review of the empirical ethical decision-making literature: boundary conditions and extensions. *Journal of Business Ethics*, 129(1), 195–219.

Mail Online. (2013). Miracle survivor of Bangladesh factory collapse changed into clothes of her dead colleague before being rescued: 19-year-old who lived off water from dripping pipe for 17 days emerged from ruins in a mauve wrap and pink scarf. *Mail Online*, May 10. Retrieved from www.dailymail.co.uk/news/article-2322391/Bangladesh-survivor-Reshma-Akhter-changed-dead-colleagues-clothes-trapped-rubble.html [accessed June 11, 2016].

Mathur, V. A., Harada, T., Lipke, T., Chiao, J. Y. (2010). Neural basis of extraordinary empathy and altruistic motivation. *Neuroimage*, 51, 1468–1475.

Mayer, D. M. (2010). From proscriptions to prescriptions: a call for including prosocial behavior in behavioral ethics. In: Schminke, M (ed.), *Managerial Ethics: Managing the Psychology of Morality*. (257–271) New York: Taylor & Francis.

McLean, B., & Elkind, P. (2013). *The Smartest Guys in the Room: The Amazing Rise and Scandalous Fall of Enron*. New York: Portfolio.

Milgram, S. (1974). *Obedience to Authority: An Experimental View*. New York: Harper & Row.

Milliken, F. J., & Martins, L. L. (1996). Searching for common threads: understanding the multiple effects of diversity in organizational groups. *The Academy of Management Review*, 21(2), 402–433.

Miska, C. & Pleskova, M. (2016). IKEA's ethical controversies in Saudi Arabia. In C. Barmeyer & P. Franklin (Eds.), *Case Studies in Intercultural Management: Achieving Synergy from Diversity*. (120–133) London: Palgrave Macmillan.

Miska, C., Stahl, G. K., & Mendenhall, M. E. (2013). Intercultural competencies as antecedents of responsible global leadership. *European Journal of International Management*, 7(5), 550–569.

Miska, C., Witt, M. A., & Stahl, G. K. (2016). Drivers of global CSR integration and local CSR responsiveness: Evidence from Chinese MNEs. *Business Ethics Quarterly*, DOI: http://dx.doi.org/10.1017/beq.2016.13.

Monin, B., & Jordan, A. H. (2009). The dynamic moral self: a social psychological perspective. In D. Narvaez & D. Lapsley (Eds.), *Personality, Identity, and Character*. (341–354). Cambridge: Cambridge University Press.

Moore, C. (2008). Moral disengagement in processes of organizational corruption. *Journal of Business Ethics*, 80, 129–139.

Moore, C., & Gino, F. (2013). Ethically adrift: how others pull our moral compass from true north, and how we can fix it. *Research in Organizational Behavior*, 33, 53–77.

Moore, C., Detert, J. R., Treviño, L. K., Baker, V. L., & Mayer, D. M. (2012). Why employees do bad things: moral disengagement and unethical organizational behavior. *Personnel Psychology*, 65, 1–48.

North, D. C. (1990). *Institutions, Institutional Change and Economic Performance*. Cambridge: Cambridge University Press.

O'Fallon, M. J., & Butterfield, K. D. (2005). A review of the empirical ethical decision-making literature: 1996–2003. *Journal of Business Ethics*, 59, 375–413.

Paharia, N., Vohs, K. D., & Deshpandé, R. (2013). Sweatshop labor is wrong unless the shoes are cute: cognition can both help and hurt motivated reasoning. *Organizational Behavior and Human Decision Processes*, 121, 81–88.

Pearce, C. L., & Manz, C. C. (2011). Leadership centrality and corporate social ir-responsibility (CSIR): The potential ameliorating effects of self and shared leadership on CSIR. *Journal of Business Ethics*, 102(4), 563–579.

Pearce, C. L., & Stahl, G. K. (2015). Introduction to the special issue: The leadership imperative for sustainability and corporate social responsibility. *Organizational Dynamics*, 44(2), 83–86

Pearce, C., Wassenaar, C., & Manz, C. (2014). Is shared leadership the key to responsible leadership? *The Academy of Management Perspectives*, 28(3), 275–288.

Pettigrew, T. F., & Tropp, L. R. (2006). A meta-analytic test of intergroup contact theory. *Journal of Personality and Social Psychology*, 90, 751–783.

Pfeffer, J. (1983). Organizational demography. In B. Staw and L. Cummings (Eds.), *Research in Organizational Behavior* (Vol. 5), (299–357), Greenwich, CT: JAI Press.

Post, C., Rahman, N., & Rubow, E. (2011). Green governance: boards of directors' composition and environmental corporate social responsibility. *Business & Society*, 50(1), 189–223.

Puffer, S. M., & McCarthy, D. J. (2008). Ethical turnarounds and transformational leadership: a global imperative for corporate social responsibility. *Thunderbird International Business Review*, 50(5), 303–314.

Quinn, L., & Dalton, M. (2009). Leading for sustainability: implementing the tasks of leadership. *Corporate Governance*, 9(1), 21–38.

Reed, A. I., & Aquino, K. (2003). Moral identity and the expanding circle of moral regard towards out-groups. *Journal of Personality and Social Psychology*, 84(6), 1270–1286.

Reynolds, S. J., & Ceranic, T. L. (2007). The effects of moral judgment and moral identity on moral behavior: an empirical examination of the moral individual. *Journal of Applied Psychology*, 92(6), 1610–1624.

Schneider, S., Barsoux, J.-L., & Stahl, G. K. (2014). *Managing Across Cultures*. London: Prentice Hall.

Skapinker, M. (2003). Too much unity in the boardroom. *The Financial Times*, January 25, p. 26.

Sonenshein, S. (2007). The role of construction, intuition, and justification in responding to ethical issues at work: the sensemaking-intuition model. *Academy of Management Review*, 32(4), 1022–1040.

Stahl, G. K., & de Luque, M. S. (2014). Antecedents of responsible leader behavior: a research synthesis, conceptual framework, and agenda for future research. *Academy of Management Perspectives*, 28(3), 235–254.

Stahl, G. K., Maznevski, M. L., Voigt, A., & Jonsen, K. (2010). Unraveling the effects of cultural diversity in teams: a meta-analysis of research on multicultural work groups. *Journal of International Business Studies*, 41(4), 690–709.

Stahl, G. K., Miska, C, Puffer, S. M., & McCarthy, D J. (2016, forthcoming). Responsible global leadership in emerging markets. *Advances in Global Leadership*, 9.

Stahl, G. K., Pless, N. M., & Maak, T. (2013). Responsible global leadership. In M. E. Mendenhall, J. Osland, A. Bird, G. R. Oddou, M. L. Maznevski, M. Stevens, & G. K. Stahl (Edn), *Global Leadership: Research, Practice, and Development* (2nd edn), (240–259). New York: Routledge.

Tabucchi. (2012). Japan. *International Herald Tribune*, July 6, p. 1.

Tajfel, H. (1982). Social psychology of intergroup relations. *Annual Review of Psychology*, 33(1), 1–39.

Tajfel, H., & Turner, J. (1986). The social identity of intergroup behavior. In S. Worchel and W. Austin (Eds.), *Psychology and Intergroup Relations*. (7–24). Chicago, IL: Nelson-Hall.

Tenbrunsel, A. E., & Smith-Crowe, K. (2008). Ethical decision making: where we've been and where we're going. *Academy of Management Annals*, 2, 545607.

Treviño, L. K., den Nieuwenboer, N. A., & Kish-Gephart, J. J. (2014). (Un) ethical behavior in organizations. *Annual Review of Psychology*, 65, 635–660.

Treviño, L. K., Weaver, G. K., & Reynolds, S.J. (2006). Behavioral ethics in organizations: a review. *Journal of Management*, 32(6), 951–990.

Uhl-Bien, M., Marion, R., & McKelvey, B. (2007). Complexity leadership theory: Shifting leadership from the industrial age to the knowledge era. *The Leadership Quarterly*, 18(4), 298–318.

UN Global Compact (2013). Global Corporate Sustainability Report 2013. *UN Global Compact Reports*, 5(1), 1–28.

US Government. (2002). *The Role of the Board of Directors in Enron's Collapse*. Washington, D.C.: US Government Printing Office.

Van Knippenberg, D., & Schippers, M. C. (2007). Work group diversity. *Annual Review of Psychology*, 58, 515–541.

Voegtlin, C., Patzer, M., & Scherer, A. G. (2012). Responsible leadership in global business: a new approach to leadership and its multi-level outcomes, *Journal of Business Ethics*, 105, 1–16.

Waldman, D. A. (2011). Moving forward with the concept of responsible leadership: Three caveats to guide theory and research. *Journal of Business Ethics*, 98(1), 75–83.

Waldman, D. A., & Galvin, B. M. (2008). Alternative perspectives of responsible leadership. *Organizational Dynamics*, 37(4), 327–341.

Waldman, D. A., de Luque, M. S. de, Washburn, N., House, R. J., Adetoun, B., Barrasa, A., & Wilderom, C. P. M. (2006). Cultural and leadership predictors of corporate social responsibility values of top management: a GLOBE study of 15 countries. *Journal of International Business Studies*, 37(6), 823–837.

Waldman, D. A., Siegel, D. S., & Javidan, M. (2006). Components of CEO transformational leadership and corporate social responsibility. *Journal of Management Studies*, 43(8), 1703–1725.

Werhane, P. H., Hartman, L. P., Archer, C., Englehardt, E. E., & Pritchard, M. S. (2014). *Obstacles to Ethical Decision-Making Mental Models, Milgram and the Problem of Obedience*. Cambridge: Cambridge University Press.

Williams, K. Y., & O'Reilly, C. A. (1998). Demography and diversity in organizations: A review of 40 years of research. *Research in Organizational Behavior*, 20, 77–140.

Wong, E. M., Ormiston, M. E., & Tetlock, P. E. (2011). The effects of top management team integrative complexity and decentralized decision making on corporate social performance. *Academy of Management Journal*, 54(6), 1207–1228.

Xu, S., & Yang, R. (2010). Indigenous characteristics of Chinese corporate social responsibility conceptual paradigm. *Journal of Business Ethics*, 93(2), 321–333.

Zhong, C. B. (2011). The ethical dangers of deliberative decision making. *Administrative Science Quarterly*, 56(1), 1–25.

Zimbardo, P. G. (1972). *Stanford Prison Experiment: A Simulation Study of the Psychology of Imprisonment*. Retrieved from www.prisonexp.org (accessed July 11, 2016).

Ina Aust and Marie-Thérèse Claes

GLOBAL LEADERSHIP FOR SUSTAINABLE DEVELOPMENT

THERE IS AN EMERGING GLOBAL trend in leadership that reflects upon 'leading with wisdom', 'spiritual leadership', mindfulness and responsibility. Otto Scharmer (2010) talks about the importance of conscience and the changing nature of capitalism—transforming business, society and self. Leaders are under inspired by what their company wants them to do, resulting in tensions, burnouts and depressions. Leaders talk about creating islands of sanity in the organization, about creating moments of authenticity and creating conditions for moments of authenticity. The leadership challenge is to move from 'egosystem' awareness towards an ecosystem of awareness.

READING OUTLINE

Opening case Unilever's Sustainable Living Plan

- Challenges for global leadership in the twenty-first century
- Global leadership initiatives for the twenty-first century
  - The sustainability challenge: The global leader as an implementer of ecological and social progress
  - The ethics challenge: The global leader as an 'architect of corporate conscience'
  - The citizenship challenge: The global leader as a statesman
  - The diversity challenge: The global leader as cosmopolitan
- Self-development for global leadership and sustainability
  - Embracing paradoxes, tensions and dilemmas
  - Leadership self-development through mindfulness
- Conclusion

FEATURES

Exhibit 1.   Global leaders' challenges
Activity 1.   Understanding global ecological challenges
Exhibit 2.   Millennium development goals
Activity 2.   Understanding global social challenges
Activity 3.   Reflect on global responsible leadership initiatives
Activity 4.   Extending the 'purpose'
Exhibit 3.   The Enron case
Exhibit 4.   The Ogoni versus Shell
Exhibit 5.   Good leadership in Thailand
Exhibit 6.   Pepsi bottling champions diversity despite hard times
Activity 5.   Case analysis: Oxfam and diversity
Exhibit 7.   Mindfulness
Activity 6.   Discussion questions
Activity 7.   How do managers embrace paradoxes?

UNILEVER'S SUSTAINABLE LIVING PLAN

In November 2010, Paul Polman, CEO of Unilever, announced the Unilever Sustainable Living Plan. With this ten-year plan, the company commited itself to 'sustainable growth' and the following key targets:

Health and hygiene: By 2020 we will help more than a billion people to improve their hygiene habits and we will bring safe drinking water to 500 million people. This will help reduce the incidence of life-threatening diseases like diarrhoea.

Improving nutrition: We will continually work to improve the taste and nutritional quality of all our products. By 2020 we will double the proportion of our portfolio that meets the highest nutritional standards, based on globally recognized dietary guidelines. This will help hundreds of millions of people to achieve a healthier diet.

Greenhouse gases: Halve the greenhouse gas impact of our products across the lifecycle by 2020.

Water: Halve the water associated with the consumer use of our products by 2020.

Sustainable sourcing: By 2020 we will source 100% of our agricultural raw materials sustainably.

Better livelihoods: By 2020 we will engage with at least 500,000 smallholder farmers and 75,000 small-scale distributors in our supply network.

Our people: Healthy employees and better workplaces.

> **Double sales:** We have ambitious plans to grow our company. In fact, we intend to double our sales ... But growth at any cost is not viable. We have to develop new ways of doing business which will increase the positive social benefits arising from Unilever's activities while at the same time reducing our environmental impacts.
>
> What makes our Plan different is that it applies right across the value chain. We are taking responsibility not just for our own direct operations but for our suppliers, distributors and – crucially – for how our consumers use our brands.
>
> Source: http://www.unilever.com/sustainable-living/ [accessed 22 February 2013].

CHALLENGES FOR GLOBAL LEADERSHIP IN THE TWENTY-FIRST CENTURY

The introductory case is an example of a response to the extended challenges for global leadership in the twenty-first century. Urgent ecological and social problems include climate change, ocean acidification, loss of biodiversity and environmental pollution, alongside a simultaneous increase in world population and the need to supply people with food, medicine, energy and education (see Ehnert et al., 2013). Climate change is one of three earth-system processes with a global dimension that are critical for sustaining the life on this planet as we know it (Rockström et al., 2009; WCED, 1987; Whiteman et al., 2013). The United Nations' World Commission on Environment and Development (WCED, or 'Brundtland Commission') has proposed that global problems cannot be solved by governmental institutions alone and that companies are key actors (WCED, 1987). Many companies have followed this call and have started caring for the environment, human rights, transparency and dialogue with civil society. Initiatives have been launched such as the UN Global Compact, the Globally Responsible Leadership Initiative (GRLI), the World Business Council for Sustainable Development (WBCSD) or CSR Europe. But the environment is only one of the issues leaders face in the twenty-first century. In their book, Stahl et al. (2013) identified four key areas in which global leaders face challenges (Exhibit 1).

EXHIBIT 1. Global leaders' challenges

- **Sustainability**—that is, to balance today's ecological, social and economic requirements with those of future generations
- **Ethics**—that is, to respond effectively to complex ethical issues and moral dilemmas
- **Citizenship**—that is, political co-responsibility of global MNCs for sociopolitical issues such as human rights, social justice and environmental protection
- **Diversity**—that is, to respond effectively to and 'to balance multiple and often competing stakeholder interests'

It is clear that exchanging 'good practices' is not enough to embrace these leadership challenges. The reason for this lies in the traditional logics that businesses usually follow: the logics of efficiency and effectiveness. While these logics have been very successful in bringing wealth to industrialized countries, they have also fostered exploitive, instead of regenerative and nourishing, behaviour (Wilkinson et al., 2001).

As illustrated in the introductory case of Unilever, global leadership in the twenty-first century does involve reflecting on the global and local ecological, social and economic impacts an organization has, and the social and ecological value it creates; it also involves developing action plans ways of doing business that are not only economically viable, but also ecologically and socially sustainable. This is not an easy task considering the different interests of actors involved, the inertia in international negotiations, the need for fast solutions (Whiteman et al., 2013), and the interdependency and complexity of leadership challenges in a global context because of 'pressures to adapt or fit in often combine with incomplete and inaccurate understanding of the local operating contexts' (Stahl et al., 2013: 449–450).

This reading examines the importance of global leaders in guiding and advancing the transformation from resource-intensive, unsustainable and sometimes even unethical business activities towards global sustainable, ethical and inclusive development. The questions guiding our analysis are what kind of global leadership roles arise for leaders in the twenty-first century and how leaders' self-development can be triggered to prepare for these roles. One answer to these questions that has emerged both in academia and practice is a stronger connection of global leadership to ethics (e.g. de Woot, 2005, 2009; Maak, 2007; Pless, 2007; Pless et al., 2012) and to ecological thinking (e.g. Ferdig, 2007; Quinn and Dalton, 2009). First, we will describe existing leadership initiatives at political and corporate levels. Next, we will explore the four global challenges in more depth by outlining the key roles of global leaders for the twenty-first century. Finally, we propose embracing paradoxes and mindfulness-based leadership as first steps towards self-development for sustainable global leadership.

GLOBAL LEADERSHIP INITIATIVES FOR THE TWENTY-FIRST CENTURY

Sustainable development at the societal level has been defined by the Brundtland Commission as a 'development that meets the needs of the present without compromising the ability of future generations to meet their own needs' (WCED, 1987: 43). In this vein, sustainable development is a normative approach to achieve intra- and intergenerational (with in and between generations) justice with regard to access to global resources and human development. Sustainable development can be described as developing and implementing ecological, economic, and social standards by respecting the boundaries of the global ecosystems called 'planetary boundaries' (see Rockström et al., 2009; Whiteman et al., 2013). Recent research has identified three critical earth-system processes with a global dimension: climate change, ocean acidification and stratospheric ozone depletion (e.g. Rockström et al., 2009).

PAUSE FOR REFLECTION

Think about what you know about the causes and consequences of climate change, ocean acidification and stratospheric ozone depletion.

ACTIVITY 1. UNDERSTANDING GLOBAL ECOLOGICAL CHALLENGES

1. Watch video no. 3, 'Climate change and climate impact' on 'World in Transition', http://www.va-bne.de/, and also check http://www.stockholmresilience. org/research/researchnews/tippingtowardstheunknown/thenineplanetary boundaries.4.1fe8f33123572b59ab80007039.html [accessed February 20, 2013].
    What do you learn about the planetary boundaries and about why it is important to maintain a global 'safe operating space'?
2. How about your personal impact? You can measure your ecological footprint online at http://www.myfootprint.org/ [accessed February 20, 2013].
    Check the website's advice on 'how to reduce your ecological footprint'. What would you be able and willing to change in your life for a more ecologically sustainable future?
    What would have to happen for you to be *more* willing or able to change? Why?
    Do you think the responsibility is personal, societal, political or economic?

Important milestones in the societal and political processes towards a sustainable development have been the UN conferences in 1987 (Rio de Janeiro), the adoption of Agenda 21 in Rio de Janeiro 1992, the acceptance of the Kyoto Protocol (linked to the UN Framework Convention on Climate Change) in 1997 in Kyoto and the last big world conference 2012 'Rio+20', again in Rio de Janeiro, as well as the Doha amendment to the Kyoto Protocol in 2012 in Qatar. Many political and private institutions worldwide have integrated sustainable development into their agendas as a core goal at national, regional and community levels. However, global progress is still too slow to compensate for the speed of ecological destruction and resource depletion. Beyond the ecological challenges, there is political agreement that the ecological challenges cannot be understood and resolved if disconnected from social human development (WCED, 1987).

With the role of business organizations, and especially multinational enterprises (MNEs), in global sustainable development more broadly accepted, former UN Secretary-General Kofi Annan founded the United Nations' Global Compact (UNGC) (http://www.unglobalcompact.org) in Davos, Switzerland, in 1999. This has become today's largest voluntary agreement between the United Nations and MNEs with the objective of global sustainable development. The UNGC includes ten universal, non-compulsory and not easily verifiable principles on the topics 'human rights', 'labour', 'environment' and 'anti-corruption'. In particular, the ten UNGC principles are assumed to contribute to reaching the eight Millennium Development Goals (Exhibit 2).

EXHIBIT 2. Millennium development goals

- To eradicate extreme poverty and hunger
- To achieve universal primary education
- To promote gender equality and empowering women
- To reduce child mortality rates
- To improve maternal health
- To combat HIV/AIDS, malaria and other diseases
- To ensure environmental sustainability
- To develop a global partnership for development

Source: http://www.un.org/millenniumgoals/ [accessed February 20, 2013].

Despite huge efforts and progress in some countries or regions made by MNEs, it has to be noted critically that the global challenges remain and that there is also considerable resistance to change in some business lobbies, opposing the emergence of a more responsible and sustainable development model.

PAUSE FOR REFLECTION

Think about what you know about the causes and consequences of global social challenges such as population growth, hunger, disease, etc.

ACTIVITY 2. UNDERSTANDING GLOBAL SOCIAL CHALLENGES

Check some of the following sources for further information:

- UN Global Compact Principles
- UN Universal Declaration of Human Rights
- International Labour Organization's (ILO) Core Labour Conventions
- UN Convention Against Corruption
- Caux Principles
- Global Sullivan Principles

1. What do you learn about the key global social challenges?
2. Where do you see the link between global ecological challenges and social challenges in your home country?

In 2003, the UNGC signed an agreement with the board of directors of the European Foundation for Management Development (EFMD), and the EFMD founded the GRLI. Today, the GRLI has become a pioneering group of 60 business schools/learning institutions and companies over five continents, with over 300,000 students and 1 million employees who are engaged in developing the next generation of globally responsible leaders (http://www.grli.org/).

ACTIVITY 3. REFLECT ON GLOBAL RESPONSIBLE LEADERSHIP INITIATIVES

Check whether your home country and/or institution is a member of the GRLI or similar initiatives, such as:

- Academy of Business in Society (ABIS, formerly EABIS)
- Business for Social Responsibility (BSR)
- CSR Europe
- CERES (Coalition for Environmentally Responsible Economies)
- European Alliance for CSR
- Global Reporting Initiative (GRI)
- International Business Leaders Forum (IBLF)
- World Business Council for Sustainable Development (WBCSD)

1. How has your country/institution been affected by this membership?
2. Do you think that this goes far enough to advance the global ecological and social agenda or that initiatives are needed in addition? Why? Which initiatives?

The GRLI suggests formulating the purpose of the globally responsible business as 'Creat[ing] economic and societal progress in a globally responsible and sustainable way' (GRLI, 2008). According to GRLI and de Woot (2005, 2009), this requires a new type of leadership and new corporate cultures. Businesses will have to face the four challenges we mentioned earlier: sustainability, ethics, citizenship and diversity. Let us have a closer look at these challenges.

The Sustainability Challenge: The Global Leader as an Implementer of Ecological and Social Progress

One response to the sustainability challenge seems to be a growing awareness among corporate leaders that pursuing economic goals is not sufficient if an organization is interested in managing for the long term and if we, as a human species, want to survive on this planet with a 'good' quality of life. However, the question of *how* sustainability can be achieved at the corporate level in different contexts is hotly debated. One major point of discussion is the purpose of business organizations. 'The social responsibility of the firm is to maximize profit for the shareholder' is a famous statement made by Milton Friedman (1970) that has profoundly influenced neoliberal thought. However, according to Chang (2011), shareholders often do not care about the long-term future of the company; they just want to maximize short-term profits. Shareholder value maximization squeezes suppliers, workers and the government—and in the long term investment falls.

Criticism of neoliberal thinking is based on the assumption that unlimited economic growth is not possible in a world of limited resources, that it is necessary to define a new understanding of sustainable growth and of the purpose of the organization (e.g. Dunphy and Griffiths, 2008; Gladwin et al., 1995; Porter and Kramer, 2006, 2011). The motivations for this can be rooted in an instrumental (e.g. legitimizing capitalism—Porter and Kramer, 2011), but also an ethical and political, stance (de Woot, 2005).

It has been suggested that the (neo)classical purpose of the company needs to be redefined 'from a short-term profit focus to an enlarged vision' (Swaen et al., 2011: 179), including economic, social and environmental progress (de Woot, 2005). The social, societal and ecological impacts of management decisions need to be understood and controlled, and active corporate investments are needed to sustain the corporate resource base for the future (e.g. Ehnert, 2009; Gladwin et al., 1995). Porter and Kramer (2011: 64) propose a 'shared value' approach that 'involves creating economic value in a way that also creates value for society by addressing its needs and challenges. Businesses must reconnect company success with social progress.'

ACTIVITY 4. EXTENDING THE 'PURPOSE'

The Unilever Sustainable Living Plan could be interpreted as an example of how an MNE can extend its purpose to become ecologically and socially more sustainable.

On global100.org, you will find a list of the 100 most sustainable corporations in the world. Choose one company, go to its website and its sustainability/CSR reports.

1. How do these organizations communicate their 'purpose'? Find out for one organization what it *really* does.
2. Come up with an example from a pioneering MNE or an SME (such as Umicore, Belgium) and find out how it has made the change towards becoming a more sustainable business.

Key tensions for leaders can be expected between present and future (or short- and long-term effects), and between dealing efficiently and sustainably (in the sense of regeneration, reproduction) with resources (Ehnert, 2009; Ehnert et al., 2013). The first tension refers to the challenge of anticipating future ecological, social and economic developments and integrating them into present decision making. The second tension refers to the challenge of using resources efficiently and at the same time investing in their reproduction (as in sustainable forestry or fishing industries). For example, saving costs by reducing energy consumption is insufficient and can be complemented by investments in regenerative energies. Collaborations such as partnerships with NGOs, with social activist movements, with governmental organizations or with local communities (Ehnert et al., 2013; Stahl et al., 2013) can inspire leaders.

The Ethics Challenge: The Global Leader as an 'Architect of Corporate Conscience'

The ethical global leadership challenge is to respond effectively to complex ethical issues and moral dilemmas (Stahl et al., 2013: 244). Although multiple competing conceptualizations on leadership exist, leadership is always about influence, power and impact on others (Yukl, 2010). Because of this influence, the relationship between the leader and followers can be misused to advance personal careers or the self-interest of the organization at the expense of organization members and a broader public, and it can be misused to support 'crimes of obedience' (Hinrichs, 2007), suggesting that unethical or even illegal behaviour is right, as we have learned from the Enron case (Exhibit 3).

EXHIBIT 3. The Enron case

At Enron, nobody was asking the right questions. The environment was such that control was less important than numbers. When there is such pressure to make the numbers, tight control is required, but it was completely lacking at corporate level. If you were a new employee and to notice that your boss was fudging, you would not question his or her behaviour for fear of losing your job, and you would think: 'If everybody else is doing it, including my boss, maybe it is not that bad.' You might be scared, but you would not stick out your neck. The climate was ripe for abuse.

Responsible leadership means that the leader has the task of building and being the 'architect of corporate conscience' (Goodpaster, 2007), of being a sense-maker and sense-giver. The role of 'sense-maker' and 'storyteller' is to create 'a shared sense of meaning and purpose through which they raise one another to higher levels of motivation and commitment for achieving sustainable value creation and responsible change' (Maak and Pless, 2009: 539). Leaders and companies can become *ethically fit* if they acknowledge that:

- people in organizations are more than economic resources and they are not owned by the company (Ehnert, 2009; Greenwood, 2002); and
- ecological, social and economic environments are not 'resource pools' that can be endlessly exploited by those having economic or political power.

Ethical or responsible leadership can be achieved by focusing on communication, by caring for people and by developing new corporate cultures, based on values and moral convictions that determine what we perceive as good or bad and which actions and consequences we deduce from this (de Woot, 2005). Typical tensions are created between economic rationality (efficiency) and relational rationality (social legitimacy) or justice, and between cultural relativism and ethical imperialism.

On the one hand, leaders run into the danger of producing unethical or unsustainable behaviour because of overly adapting to local cultural values (*cultural relativism*) when 'global corporations operate in nations where bribery, sexual harassment, racial discrimination, and a variety of other issues are not uniformly viewed as illegal or even unethical' (Vickers, quoted in Stahl et al., 2013: 244). Cultural relativism is morally blind (Donaldson, 1996; Stahl et al., 2013). On the other hand, global managers can use (ethical) and universal guidelines in a rigid way, which could lead to what Stahl and colleagues (2013) call *ethical imperialism* – for example in situations in which cultural and situational appropriateness of universal guidelines is neglected. The authors conclude that, 'in the global arena, both cultural relativism and ethical imperialism are likely to lead instead to inappropriate, irresponsible leadership behaviour' (Stahl et al., 2013: 250).

Cultural differences on ethics exist (White and Taft, 2004) and require awareness, tact and subtlety. The challenge for global leadership is to decide when cultural differences are 'just different' or when they are wrong (Donaldson, 1996), and to avoid extreme positions of ethical universalism and cultural relativism. In balancing culturally relativist with ethically universalist positions, leaders may again have to deal with paradoxes, tensions, ambiguities and dilemmas (Stahl et al., 2013; Ehnert, 2009). By definition, a dilemma is a situation in which a choice between two equally (un)desirable alternatives is required and cannot be avoided. Dealing with ethical dilemmas is a challenge familiar to many of those operating in culturally diverse environments—in particular, how to cope with and reconcile ethical differences and emotions that might be involved and which might hinder developing trustful cross-cultural relationships. This reconciliation is something that can take time and in many cases needs a respectful step-by-step approach.

The Citizenship Challenge: The Global Leader as a Statesman

The global leadership challenge of becoming a 'good' citizen refers to the political co-responsibility of global MNCs for sociopolitical issues such as human rights, social justice and environmental protection. The new global leader's role is that of a 'statesman' not only pursuing local interests, but also recognizing that the main political question for our time concerns the theme of what kind of world we want to build together with the immense resources we master (de Woot, 2005). New global leaders seem to believe that this responsibility becomes all the greater as their creativity and power grows.

By enlarging their political culture, responsible leaders accept a debate whenever their actions can have major social consequences (de Woot, 2005). New types of dialogue, which include new representatives of civil society, such as NGOs, universities, religions and international institutions, will be added to the old type of discussion with social partners and governments (see UN Global Compact or the EU Multi-Stakeholder Forum on Corporate Responsibility).

However, leaders are not waiting for political actors to set the 'right' institutional frameworks (Ehnert et al., 2013). Instead, particular global leaders have become active, as in the example of Unilever and many other companies, and participate proactively in preparing and implementing new global rules (see Exhibit 4).

EXHIBIT 4. The Ogoni versus Shell

Royal Dutch Shell plc (Shell) began oil production in the Niger Delta region of Nigeria in 1958 and has a long history of working closely with the Nigerian government.

In the 1970s and 1980s, the company extracted tens of millions of barrels of oil a year from Ogoniland while allowing the people to slide into destitution because it was destroying their environment. In the early 1990s, the Nigerian government brutally repressed the growing Ogoni movement against the oil company.

On 10 November 1995, Ken Saro-Wiwa, an acclaimed writer and leader of the Movement for the Survival of the Ogoni People (MOSOP), was hanged, along with eight other Ogoni leaders, after a trial before a military tribunal that was condemned around the world as a sham.

One month after the executions of the Ogoni Nine, Shell signed an agreement to invest US$4 billion in a liquefied natural gas project in Nigeria. The Center for Constitutional Rights (CCR), Earth Rights International (ERI) and other human rights attorneys sued Shell for human rights violations against the Ogoni (see also *The Guardian*, 10 June 2009).

The Diversity Challenge: The Global Leader as Cosmopolitan

Different facets of the global leadership diversity challenge are described and analysed throughout Part V. Diversity can be more than cultural diversity; it refers also to gender, age, educational background, etc. (Danowitz et al., 2012), or to the meaning of leadership (see Exhibit 5).

EXHIBIT 5. Good leadership in Thailand

A leader has to touch the heart (*kao jai*); everything is about the heart: being kind, being generous, listening, forgiving. Giving is very important in Thailand: *hai apai* (to have compassion) is one of the precepts. It is the basis of the *mai pben rai* (it does not matter) expression that Thai people will use in any situation where they were wronged. Its source is religious, based on Buddhist precepts. Young managers get ideas from the West, and they try to use them. When they get older and have more responsibilities, when they get to the top positions, they encounter serious problems and they find that ideas from the West maybe don't work so well. The solutions given by the consultants don't always work. Then they turn to the Asian sentiment, the local wisdom. Many of the Thai leaders go to their master (mostly a monk): they go to the temple to do charity, to pray, to meditate. They may have problems and frustrations; they go to their master to get relief, a clear mind, more consciousness, to get rid of something that makes them suffer. When you are in trouble, you cannot see anything. The monk cannot give you the solution, but can comfort you, show you the right way of thinking so that you can see the solution yourself.

Hai apai is the most important: to give forgiveness, to pardon. As in the story of Saladin (1137–1193), who fought the Crusaders but at the same time was seen as a chivalrous knight in Europe. He was fighting Richard I of England, but when Richard was wounded, Saladin sent him his personal doctor; and when Richard lost his horse, Saladin sent him two new horses. Students will not understand life if you don't give them the concept of *hai apai*.

Source: Dr Nirundon, Kasetsart University Bangkok, personal communication to Marie-Thérèse Claes, 15 February 2013.

The role of a global leader is to embrace diversity as a cosmopolitan leader and to bridge cross-cultural differences in leadership styles and roles. Cosmopolitan thinking with a global mindset refers to the 'ability to view the world from different angles' (Pless et al., 2012: 245) and to reconcile global versus local tensions, the willingness to be open to and to learn from other cultural systems (see Exhibit 6).

EXHIBIT 6. Pepsi bottling champions diversity despite hard times

Among boards of US Fortune 500 companies, one of the most diverse is that of Pepsi Bottling Group. The company has four women among its ten board members. Eric J. Foss, chairman and chief executive of Pepsi Bottling, considers a diverse board necessary because:

It's difficult, if not impossible, for homogeneous boards to challenge and offer different perspectives, unique experiences and the broad-based wisdom that makes the board, and therefore the company, as effective as they can be.

Part of the strategic rationale for this is that our employee base needs to be reflective of our customer base. As our customers continue to become more diverse, it's important that organizationally we look like them. It's not a fad. It's not an idea of the month. It's central and it's linked very directly to the business strategy. That is the case in great times and in more challenging times.

> Our approach to diversity is a fully integrated program ... It runs boardroom to backroom, as we like to say. It plays across all levels of the organization.

Source: Based on the *New York Times* interview, 13 February 2009, available at www.nytimes.com/2009/02/14/business/14interview.html?_r=2& [accessed February 20, 2013].

ACTIVITY 5. CASE ANALYSIS: OXFAM AND DIVERSITY

Oxfam is an international aid organization, operating in over 70 countries worldwide (http://www.oxfam.org.uk). The NGO is based on voluntary workers' input and its headquarters are situated in the UK.

Oxfam operates in four official languages: English, French, Spanish and Portuguese. However, in reality, management operates almost exclusively in English and key reports are expected in English. At the managerial level, English is the main working language. In particular, leadership team communications, key reports and publications are all in English. The pre-eminence of English and the lack of clear policy concerning the language(s) result in barriers for a great majority of non-native English speakers. They face hurdles in developing within the organization and even in accessing relevant information. Additionally, there is the burdensome work of translation, which, due to the lack of homogeneously implemented translation policies, results in poor-quality documents.

Western historical influence is seen in the upper management levels of the organization, which are dominated by British and other Western nationalities. The current board of directors also illustrates the influence of the donating organizations within Oxfam, since they are well represented.

This clearly contrasts with the NGO's commitment to become a more diverse organization. To fully deliver the mandate of fighting poverty and inequality, values of equality and inclusion are embedded in the HR practices of the company, and it aims to recruit more people from the developing world for leadership positions. The challenge is how to do this while English is, practically, a requirement for advancement and some potential leader candidates from developing countries do not possess the adequate language skills.

A survey conducted in Oxfam Latin America and Caribbean (LAC), West Africa (WAF) and South Africa (SAF) investigated the role of languages in the internal communication (Lehtovaara, 2009). A closer look at the results shows that, in all regions examined, some people can speak fairly good English and the sufficient level of English language knowledge needed for the top management work could be reached by some people fairly easily. Indeed, 97 per cent of the informants said they had some to fluent English, 42 per cent spoke fluent to native English and 73 per cent used English daily at work. The employees also agreed that English is seen as the official language in the NGO, and 94 per cent agreed that English is necessary in their work. Especially in African regions, knowledge and use of English are very high.

In other words, English skills should not be a barrier to advancement in the career of a majority of employees; only 36 per cent agreed that English skills are a barrier to advancement (mainly in the LAC region). A huge majority of 94 per cent were eager to improve their English skills and participate in language training if it were offered. Moreover, a majority of these employees have a good education, with Bachelor and Master's degrees. This is why a cultural change in favour of awareness and appreciation of language skills and tolerance towards imperfect language proficiency and varieties of English is needed in the NGO.

Oxfam has the diversity in-house—enough employees with a good education and a good knowledge of English—but the NGO seems to have a blind spot that prevents it from seeing this.

1. What could Oxfam do to achieve the goal of including diversity at head-quarters?
2. What should happen at the local levels and at headquarters?

SELF-DEVELOPMENT FOR GLOBAL LEADERSHIP AND SUSTAINABILITY

Against the background of these key global challenges, the question arises how leaders can trigger their self-development, perhaps even before they have come into powerful positions that allow them to act as globally responsible and sustainable leaders. First, it seems that a global leader who wishes to make a real contribution to sustainable development needs to master the 'management' of the paradoxes, dilemmas and potential tensions involved. Table 1 provides a summary of the key global leadership challenges, the leadership roles discussed and examples of tensions to be expected in this area, as well as suggests how to deal with these challenges.

One overarching competence for global leaders is to learn how to embrace paradoxes, tensions and dilemmas by becoming aware how they respond emotionally, cognitively and perhaps even physically to these tensions, changing this response if it creates inertia, stress and conflict instead of creativity and joy.

Embracing Paradoxes and Tensions

Reconciling ecological, social/human and ecological challenges at global and local levels can create multiple paradoxes and tensions (e.g. Ehnert et al., 2013; Stahl et al., 2013). Paradoxes can be defined as 'contradictory yet interrelated elements that exist simultaneously and persist over time' (Smith and Lewis, 2011: 382). The difference between paradox and dilemma is that, in a paradox, 'no choice need be made between two or more contradictions. Both contradictions in a paradox are accepted and present. Both operate simultaneously' (Cameron, 1986: 545). It is assumed that corporate success and performance depend on the ability to deal with paradoxes and tensions successfully at individual and organizational levels (see Smith and Lewis, 2011; see also Activity 7).

Table 1. Global leadership challenges, roles, and competences

Challenge	Sustainability	Ethics	Citizenship	Diversity
Themes	Ecological, social issues	Ethical dilemmas	Sociopolitical issues	Cross-cultural, diversity issues
Leadership roles	Extending the purpose—the global leader as the implementer of ecological and social process	Ethical fitness—the global leader as an 'architect of corporate conscience'	Good citizenship—the global leader as a statesman	Embracing diversity—the global leader as cosmopolitian; inclusiveness
Key tensions (examples)	Present vs future; efficiency vs substance	Efficiency vs responsibility; cultural relativism vs ethical imperialism	Global co-responsibility vs local legal obligation	Global vs local; universal vs cultural
Leadership competencies	Knowledge on planetary boundaries, global and local ecological and social challenges	Responsibility mindset; ethical fitness	Political consciousness	Cultural intelligence; global mindset

Sources: Stahl et al. (2013); Ehnert et al. (2013).

In paradox research, several answers are provided on how organizations can respond to tensions using a 'both/and' perspective (Poole and van de Ven, 1989; Jarzabkowski et al., 2013; Smith and Lewis, 2011). Ignoring or denying paradoxes is dangerous because it can lead to dysfunctional effects on a long-term basis. Even though paradoxes cannot be 'resolved', defensive or active strategies can be used as a response (Jarzabkowski et al., 2013). The objective of *defensive* strategies is to reduce the tensions (and emotional reactions to them) by splitting the contradictory positions and then dealing with them at different times or in different locations. In contrast, *active* strategies aim at dealing with a paradox constructively and on a long-term basis (Jarzabkowski et al., 2013; Smith and Lewis, 2011). In a world of complex, paradoxical demands, individual managers need a much higher capacity of finding contextually adequate responses to paradoxes, as well as individual awareness of situations creating tensions that can be emotionally difficult to bear.

PAUSE FOR REFLECTION

Go back to the description of the Unilever Sustainable Living Plan and check the company's performance indicators.

Find examples for potential paradoxes and tensions that the 'new purpose' could create.

What are the responses the company suggests?

Leadership Self-Development through Mindfulness

We have seen that embracing paradoxes and tensions requires individual managers to have a much higher capacity for reflection. The GRLI proposes Taylor's (2006) 'whole-person learning', which refers to reconnecting the *brain, heart* and *mind*. Actually, in the perception of Eastern philosophy, the mind and heart have never been disconnected. In Western leadership studies, the relationship between mindful practice and ethical decision making has been made in recent years only. Mindfulness (see Exhibit 7) considers observations arising from 'the inside out' as an approach to engage in thoughtful awareness, to shift perspective and to achieve creative learning. Mindfulness is considered as *one* possible path for self-development and self-discovery (Kabat-Zinn, 1990). Mindful meditation can help us to gain a better control over paradoxical demands and to achieve better solutions. The 'Ulysses program', a leadership development programme at PricewaterhouseCoopers (PwC), for example, includes meditation, yoga and reflective exercises (Pless et al., 2012).

EXHIBIT 7. Mindfulness

Mindfulness, as defined by Kabat-Zinn (1990), means paying attention in a particular kind, benevolent and non-judgemental way to the present moment and to what thoughts, emotions, or voluntary or involuntary physiological reactions are arising inside a person.

Mindfulness is an attitude that can be learned through continuous, often year-long and disciplined practice, and promotes the mind's ability to be focused and to become aware of the 'auto-pilot' way in which we often use our brain, of our health, well-being, emotional balance, stress resistance, resilience (Kabat-Zinn, 2009; Walach et al., 2007), job satisfaction (Hülsheger et al., 2013), and of ethical decision making (Ruedy and Schweitzer, 2010), developing conscious and relationships with others. Although inspired by Eastern, Buddhist philosophy, mindfulness in Kabat-Zinn's (1990) interpretation is not a religion or ideology. Mindfulness practice includes exercises in breathing, meditation and yoga.

According to Tom Clark, executive coach, mindfulness-based leadership supports leaders as '[a]dvocates for a better future: this is something that goes beyond emotional intelligence. It involves a tremendous human capacity to ignite hope and passion in self and others, respond appropriately to challenges and create sustainable practices and organizations' (personal communication). We assume that mindful leadership has the potential to make contributions to organizational sustainability and global sustainable development.

CONCLUSION

In this reading, we explored the importance of global leaders in guiding and advancing the transformation from resource-intensive and irresponsible business activities to globally sustainable development. We further invited the reader to actively reflect on the personal impact and to think about how to respond to global sustainability challenges. Corporate global leadership development programmes, as well as business schools, have started addressing this need.

Yet the impact of many business activities on the planetary boundaries is still highly problematic. Unilever offers an example of how to decouple economic growth from resource consumption, to control the impact of businesses on societies throughout the whole supply chain, and to think in a systemic and responsible way about the purpose of business.

ACTIVITY 6. DISCUSSION QUESTIONS

1. Think about yourself and how you treat your individual resources and relationships. What are your personal economic, social and, perhaps, ecological resources?
2. Where do your inner and outer resources come from? (Parents, friends, a scholarship, training, etc.)
3. What do you do to regenerate, nourish or renew your physical, psychological, social, economic, etc. resources and relationships? Why do you (not) do it?
4. What do you think will happen if you continue doing this for the next ten years?
5. What could you do to start nourishing your personal resources and relationships today?
6. Do you see paradoxical choice situations and dilemmas if you look at your individual sustainability?
7. How could these be dealt with by applying 'both/and' instead of 'either/or' thinking?

ACTIVITY 7. HOW DO MANAGERS EMBRACE PARADOXES?

'A truly visionary company embraces both ends of a continuum: continuity *and* change, conservatism *and* progressiveness, stability *and* revolution, predictability *and* chaos, heritage *and* renewal, fundamentals *and* craziness. *And, and, and'* (Collins, 1995).

Talk to expatriates or global managers by using the following questions and reflect on the usefulness of their responses for you.

1. Can you provide an example of a tension that is vital to achieving both high performance at your company and to contributing to organizational and/or societal sustainability?
    *   How do you help others move from an *either/or mentality* (decisions as trade-offs or compromises) towards more paradoxical *both/and* thinking – what Collins calls the 'genius of the and'?

- How do you encourage paradoxical thinking—even deliberately stressing tensions during decision making—to encourage both better, more creative results and contributions to sustainability?
- One risk when dealing with tensions is that they can raise anxiety, cause defensiveness and frustrate effective decision making. How do you help others work through such discomfort so that they can manage paradoxes?
- At your company, how do your strategy, values and/or vision encompass sustainability and paradoxes?
2. How do you provide a strategy that is clear, yet recognizes competing demands?
3. How does your culture further support both/and thinking?

Source: Lewis et al. (2014).

REFERENCES

Cameron, K. (1986) 'Effectiveness as Paradox: Consensus and Conflict in Conceptions of Organizational Effectiveness', *Management Science*, 32(5): 539–553.

Chang, H.-J. (2011) *23 Things They Don't Tell You about Capitalism*, London: Penguin.

Collins, J. (1995) '*Building Companies to Last*'. Retrieved from http://www.jimcollins.com/article_topics/articles/building-companies.html (accessed July 11, 2016).

Danowitz, M. A., Hanappi-Egger, E., and Mensi-Klarbach, H. (eds) (2012) *Diversity in Organizations: Concepts and Practices*, London: Palgrave.

de Woot, P. (2005) *Should Prometheus Be Bound? Corporate Global Responsibility*, Basingstoke: Palgrave Macmillan and EFMD.

de Woot, P. (2009) *Lettre ouverte aux dirigeants chrétiens en temps d'urgence*, Paris: Desclée de Brouwer.

Donaldson, T. (1996) 'Values in Tension: When is Different Just Different, and When is Different Wrong', *Harvard Business Review*, September–October: 48–62.

Dunphy, D., and Griffiths, A. (2008) *The Sustainable Corporation: Organisational Renewal in Australia*, Sydney: Allen & Unwin.

Ehnert, I. (2009) *Sustainable Human Resource Management: A Conceptual and Exploratory Analysis from a Paradox Perspective*, Heidelberg: Physica-Verlag.

Ehnert, I., Harry, W., and Zink, K. J. (eds) (2013) *Sustainability and Human Resource Management: Developing Sustainable Business Organisations*, Heidelberg: Springer.

Ferdig, M. A. (2007) 'Sustainability Leadership: Co-Creating a Sustainable Future', *Journal of Change Management*, 7(1): 25–35.

Friedman, M. (1970) 'The Social Responsibility of Business is to Increase Profits', *The New York Times Magazine*, 13 September, 32–33, 122–126.

Gladwin, T. N., Kennelly, J. J., and Krause, T.-S. (1995) 'Shifting Paradigms for Sustainable Development: Implications for Management Theory and Research', *Academy of Management Review*, 20(4): 874–907.

Globally Responsible Leadership Initiative (GRLI) (2008) *A Call to Action*, Brussels: GRLI.

Goodpaster, K. E. (2007) *Conscience and Corporate Culture*, Oxford: Maxwell.

Greenwood, M. (2002) 'Ethics and HRM: A Review and Conceptual Analysis', *Journal of Business Ethics*, 36(3): 261–278.

Hinrichs, K. T. (2007) 'Follower Propensity to Commit Crimes of Obedience: The Role of Leadership Beliefs', *Journal of Leadership and Organizational Studies*, 14(1): 69–76.

Hülsheger, U. R., Alberts, H. J. E. M., Feinholdt, A., and Lang, J. W. B. (2013) 'Benefits of Mindfulness at Work: The Role of Mindfulness in Emotion Regulation, Emotional Exhaustion, and Job Satisfaction', *Journal of Applied Psychology*, 98(2): 310–25.

Jarzabkowski, P., Lê, J., and van de Ven, A. H. (2013) 'Responding to Competing Strategic Demands: How Organizing, Belonging, and Performing Paradoxes Coevolve', *Strategic Organization*, 10 April, 1–36.

Kabat-Zinn, J. (1990) *Full Catastrophe Living: Using the Wisdom of Your Body and Mind to Face Stress, Pain, and Illness*, New York: Bantam Dell.

Kabat-Zinn, J. (2009) *Letting Everything Become Your Teacher: 100 Lessons in Mindfulness*, New York: Dell.

Lehtovaara, H. (2009) 'Working in Four Official Languages: The Perceptions of OGB Employees on the Role of Language in Internal Communication', Master's thesis, Helsinki School of Economics, Helsinki.

Lewis, M. W., Andriopoulos, C., and Smith, W. (2014) 'Paradoxical Leadership to Enable Strategic Agility', *California Management Review*, 56(3): 58–77.

Maak, T. (2007) 'Responsible Leadership, Stakeholder Engagement, and the Emergence of Social Capital', *Journal of Business Ethics*, 74(4): 329–343.

Maak, T., and Pless, N. M. (2009) 'Business Leaders as Citizens of the World: Advancing Humanism on a Global Scale', *Journal of Business Ethics*, 88(3): 537–550.

Pless, N. M. (2007) 'Understanding Responsible Leadership', *Role Identity and Motivational Drivers*, 74(4): 437–56.

Pless, N. M., Maak, T., and Stahl, G. K. (2012) 'Promoting Corporate Social Responsibility and Sustainable Development through Management Development: What Can Be Learned from International Service Learning Programs?', *Human Resource Management*, 51(6): 873–903.

Poole, M. S., and van de Ven, A. H. (1989) 'Using Paradox to Build Management and Organization Theories', *The Academy of Management Review*, 14(4): 562–578.

Porter, M. E., and Kramer, M. R. (2006) 'Strategy and Society: The Link between Competitive Advantage and Corporate Social Responsibility', *Harvard Business Review*, 84(12): 78–92.

Porter, M. E., and Kramer, M. R. (2011) 'Creating Shared Value: How to Reinvent Capitalism – and Unleash a Wave of Innovation and Growth', *Harvard Business Review*, January–February: 62–77.

Quinn, L., and Dalton, M. (2009) 'Leading for Sustainability: Implementing the Tasks of Leadership', *Corporate Governance*, 9(1): 21–38.

Rockström, J., Steffen, W., Noone, K., Persson, A., Chapin, F. S. I., and Lambin, E. F. (2009) 'A Safe Operating Space for Humanity', *Nature*, 461: 472–475.

Ruedy, N., and Schweitzer, M. (2010) 'In the Moment: The Effect of Mindfulness on Ethical Decision Making', *Journal of Business Ethics*, 95(Suppl. 1): 73–87.

Scharmer, C. O. (2010) 'The Blind Spot of Institutional Leadership: How to Create Deep Innovation Through Moving from Egosystem to Ecosystem Awareness', Paper prepared for the World Economic Forum, Annual Meeting of the New Champions, Tianjin, People's Republic of China, September.

Smith, W., and Lewis, M. (2011) 'Toward a Theory of Paradox: A Dynamic Equilibrium Model of Organizing', *Academy of Management Review*, 36(2): 381–403.

Stahl, G. K., Pless, N. M., and Maak, T. (2013) 'Responsible Global Leadership', in M. E. Mendenhall, J. S. Osland, A. Bird, G. R. Oddou, M. L. Maznevski, M. J. Stevens, and G. K. Stahl (eds), *Global Leadership* (2nd edn), New York and London: Routledge, 240–259.

Swaen, V., de Woot, P., and de Callataÿ, D. (2011) 'The Business School of the Twenty-First Century: Educating Citizens to Address the New World Challenges', in M. Morsing and Sauquet-Rovira, A. (eds), *Shaping and Transforming Ethical Business Conduct*, London: Sage, 165–92.

Taylor, B. (2006) *Learning for Tomorrow: Whole Person Learning—The Oasis School of Human Relations*, Boston Spa: Oasis.

Walach, H., Nord, E., Zier, C., Dietz-Waschkowski, B., Kersig, S., and Schüpbach, H. (2007) 'Mindfulness-Based Stress Reduction as a Method for Personnel Development: A Pilot Evaluation', *International Journal of Stress Management*, 14(2): 188–198.

White, J., and Taft, S. (2004) 'Frameworks for Teaching and Learning Business Ethics within the Global Context: Background of Ethical Theories', *Journal of Management Education*, 28(4): 463–77.

Whiteman, G., Walker, B., and Perego, P. (2013) 'Planetary Boundaries: Ecological Foundations for Corporate Sustainability', *Journal of Management Studies*, 50(2): 307–336.

Wilkinson, A., Hill, M., and Gollan, P. (2001) 'The Sustainability Debate', *International Journal of Operations & Production Management*, 21(12): 1492–1502.

World Commission on Environment and Development (WCED) (1987) *Our Common Future*, Oxford: Oxford University Press.

Yukl, G. (2010) *Leadership in Organizations* (7th edn), New Jersey: Pearson Prentice Hall.

Websites

www.ceres.org [accessed 20 February 2013]

www.csreurope.org [accessed 22 August 2016]

www.grli.org/ [accessed 20 February 2013]

www.unilever.com/sustainable-living/ [accessed 22 February 2013]

www.unglobalcompact.org/AboutTheGC/TheTenPrinciples/index.html [accessed 20 February 2013]

www.un.org/millenniumgoals/ [accessed 20 February 2013]

www.unglobalcompact.org/AboutTheGC/index.html [accessed 20 February 2013]

The World's Most Ethical Enterprises (WME): https://ethisphere.com/ethisphere-announces-the-2016-worlds-most-ethical-companies-celebrating-10-years-of-measuring-corporate-integrity-and-recognizing-those-that-excel/ [accessed 22 August 2016]

The world's most sustainable companies: www.forbes.com/sites/kathryndill/2016/01/22/the-worlds-most-sustainable-companies-2016/#46a96e49965f [accessed 22 August 2016]

Tom Clark, mindfulness-based leadership training: www.mindfulnet.org [accessed 22 August 2016]

www.wbcsd.org/home.aspx [accessed 22 August 2016]

www.va-bne.de/ [accessed 22 August 2016]

www.myfootprint.org/ [accessed 22 August 2016]

Charlotte Butler and
Henri-Claude de Bettignies

CHANGMAI CORPORATION[1]

DAVID MCLEOD HAD BEEN GENERAL MANAGER of the All-
Asia Paper Co. (AAP), part of Changmai Corporation, for just two months. Previously, he had spent four years running a large and long-established pulp mill in South Africa. Bored by a job that had fallen into well-ordered routine, McLeod had eagerly responded to the challenge presented to him by Changmai's director of personnel, Barney Li, to take over as head of the five-year-old AAP pulp mill, one of the biggest in South East Asia, and double production within a year.

As Li explained, the ethnic Chinese owner of the Changmai group, Tommy Goh, was dissatisfied by the performance of the mill, then headed by a Malaysian expatriate and producing on average 21,500 tons of pulp per month. The mill contained state-of-the-art equipment that, Goh felt, was not being used to full capacity. He was therefore looking for an experienced Western manager to introduce a more professional approach and increase production. Time was of the essence as Goh's instinct, which had never failed him yet, told him that the volatile paper industry was about to undergo one of its periodic surges. When this happened, Goh wanted to be able to take full advantage of the rise in pulp prices. Currently, the mill's production costs ran at US$250 per ton of kraft pulp, and if, as Goh anticipated, the price were to climb again beyond a previous high of US$700 per ton, he stood to make a real killing.

McLeod, a highly qualified engineer, had a wide experience gained in some of the most sophisticated pulp mills in the world. Scottish by birth, he had begun his career in Scandinavia before moving on to Canada, the United States, and finally South Africa. For him, the opportunity to work in Asia was an added attraction. When he finally met Goh, in a hotel room in Hong Kong, he was impressed both by the man and by his knowledge of the industry.

At age 45, the entrepreneurial Goh was head of a diversified empire. Building new businesses was his life's blood, so although rich and successful, he remained restless, always searching for the next big opportunity. Closest to him, apart from two family members working in the Changmai group, were those dating from his early days in the tough world of street trading, where he made his first million by the age of 24. These people bore Goh unstinting loyalty.

Goh was a forceful personality, whose enthusiasm for what the mill could achieve made McLeod eager to get to work. His new boss, McLeod decided, was a man of some vision, clearly used to making fast decisions and seeing them implemented immediately. In meetings, Goh's impatience was signaled by the way in which he constantly checked his Rolex wrist watch and barked orders to the young, smartly suited aide, who relayed his chief's commands into a mobile phone. McLeod was surprised, therefore, when Goh invited him to lunch and then took him to a small, back-street restaurant that looked only one level up from a street stall, even though the food was excellent. The incongruity of Goh, his aide, and himself in such a setting, whilst outside Roni, the waiting driver, leaned against the BMW eating a bowl of noodles, had struck McLeod forcefully. It was a memorable introduction to the cultural dissonances of this new world.

Goh's latest project was to build a rayon mill on the AAP site. Although the latter chemical processes were different, pulp and rayon used the same wood and shared the initial production stages, so the synergies were obvious. To build the rayon mill, Goh had entered into a 50:50 joint venture with a Chicago-based US company whose representative, Dan Bailey, was permanently on site. McLeod was pleased to learn that he would find a fellow Westerner at AAP. Most of the workers on the site, said Li, were locals led by expatriate managers, mainly from the region.

Fired by his meeting with Goh, McLeod had gone to AAP full of energy and enthusiasm. His first sight of the mill was a rude shock. To his experienced eye, the five-year-old infant looked more like a battered old lady. On closer inspection, it was clear that although the mill was indeed equipped with the most modern technology, its maintenance had been dangerously neglected. A dozen urgent repairs leapt to McLeod's eye following his first tour of the mill, and every succeeding day he discovered more. In the first few months, McLeod worked 18 hours a day, often being called out in the middle of the night to deal with some urgent breakdown. The local employees he found willing, but completely untrained. Safety precautions were rudimentary, and McLeod was undecided about whether or not to try and impose Western standards. However, in a preliminary effort to raise standards, he had regularly toured the site and pointed out the most glaring breaches of safety regulations to the offending superintendents.

Until today, McLeod had felt that, with effort and organization, he could get the mill into shape and reach Goh's target. Then, at 10 o'clock that morning, he had received a visit from Mr. Lai, a government official from the Ministry of Safety and Environmental Control. McLeod knew that Lai had been inspecting the site for the past three days and had anticipated a reprimand from him as, judged by Western environmental standards, the mill had several defects. On the other hand, thought McLeod, no accidents had occurred whilst Lai was on site, which was a good sign and perhaps an indication that his emphasis on obeying safety rules was having an effect. So he was relieved when a beaming Mr Lai said how pleased he was with his inspection and invited McLeod to walk with him down to the river into which waste water from the mill was emptied after passing through the two-level treatment plant. Goh had been very proud of this feature of the mill, which, he had told McLeod, made environmental standards at AAP "the equal of those prevailing in Oregon." After primary treatment in a settling basin, the water passed through to a lagoon for secondary, bacteriological treatment in accordance with government standards. Only after two days of treatment in the lagoon was the water let out into the river.

As they walked along the muddy bank and discussed Lai's findings, only minor infringements were mentioned, from which McLeod inferred that local enforcement of environmental regulations was indeed less stringent than in the West.

"So, all in all," Lai concluded, "I would say that I could put in a favourable A1 report on environmental standards at the mill—except," he paused, "for two small problems that I am sure can be easily resolved given goodwill on both sides. The first concerns the broken filter in the waste water unit which, I understand from your foreman, should be fixed in the near future. However, in the meantime, as I saw for myself, the water coming through the outlet pipe is quite polluted. Such a pity for the villagers who live on the other bank and fish in the river, especially coming after the unfortunate incident last year when, as I understand it, the lagoon dam collapsed and untreated waste water poured into the river, just at this very bend. I hear that several shacks were washed away and that the river was poisoned. The villagers have told me how angry they were when they found dead fish floating in the river. They say the compensation they received was very small—hardly anything in fact—and now, seeing the brown water coming out of the outlet pipe, they greatly fear a repeat of this shocking incident.

"Just imagine, Mr. McLeod, if one of the local newspapers decided to write about their fears, about how the poor villagers and their simple fishing life were threatened by a rich and powerful company. Such publicity would be most unwelcome to AAP, not to mention Mr. Goh. It might even harm his plans for future projects involving government concessions. How angry he would be in such a case—and I hear that his anger can be terrible indeed for those around him. You would have my very great sympathy." And the smooth brown face of Mr. Lai had looked anxiously up at McLeod, apparently in genuine concern.

"My other small concern," continued Mr. Lai, "is the mill's long-term safety record. Really, I am sorry to see that so many grave accidents have occurred; two deaths by falling from a height, and another from being caught and mangled by machinery in motion. Then there are several reports of serious burns and blisters to people working in the lime kiln, an operator blinded in one eye after iron chips flew out of the spinning tank, and another who lost an arm when he slipped onto the roller conveyor. Plus many other small accidents such as people being struck by falling objects or stepping onto nails with their bare feet. When you add up the number, Mr. McLeod, the safety record does not look very harmonious.

"But do not look so worried, Mr. McLeod," continued Lai. "I am sure we can find a solution if we put our heads together. I am returning to my hotel room in the village now, to write my report. It is my last task before I go on leave for a week. My wife has won money on a lottery ticket and is going to use it to make a pilgrimage to Lourdes. As Christians, it has always been our dearest wish to visit Lourdes together one day. It would have meant so much to us. But sad to say this will not be. I cannot accompany her, as the lottery money will only pay for one person. So I must stay at home and look after our children." Lai sighed. "For someone like me on the salary of a humble government official, to visit Lourdes with my wife must remain just a dream. I was only just thinking to myself how wonderful it would be if I had a fairy godfather who could wave his wand and make my dream come true."

McLeod felt sweat trickle down his back, not wholly because of the humid heat of the morning. The collapse of the lagoon dam, which had happened long before his arrival, he knew about. According to Goh, the contractors building the dam had cheated by using poor-quality cement. As a result, the dam had burst after a season of exceptionally heavy rains, with the consequences as recounted by Lai. However, Goh had assured McLeod that, since then, the lagoon had been rebuilt using the best quality materials and had been thoroughly tested. There was absolutely no possibility of such an incident being repeated. As for the filter, although it had been faulty for some time, the pollution that resulted from it was very really minor, as proved by the fact that the daily effluent readings of the water passing through the pipe still fell within the safety range specified by the Ministry. A new filter had been ordered, but unfortunately had not yet arrived. With so many other things on his mind, it had not occurred to McLeod to associate the past lagoon collapse with the present fault in the waste unit and Lai's official inspection. Now, he cursed himself for not having seen the potential danger of their being connected. As he was only too well aware, if the incident were resurrected by Lai and the gossip that he had picked up, exaggerated by stories of the present pollution, were repeated into the wrong ears, then the effects could be catastrophic both for AAP and for the Changmai group. Inevitably, Goh had business rivals who would be only too pleased to have ammunition with which to attack him.

As for the safety record, McLeod wondered where Lai had got his information, because not all the examples he gave were familiar to him. McLeod had been strictly monitoring the accident figures since his arrival and, although there had been the usual crop of minor injuries inevitably associated with high-tech machinery and an unskilled workforce, nothing major had occurred. Again, Lai must be using past history, for, as McLeod knew, in the early years of operations, the mill's safety record had been very poor. As he tried vainly to think of a suitable reply, Lai turned to leave.

"You know where to find me," said Lai. "I will return to the Ministry tomorrow at 9:30 with my report, which I am sure will be positive now that we have had this little chat. I must say, I will be glad to get back to my family. We are quite worried about my eldest son. He has recently graduated from a small technical college in the south of England. It was a great sacrifice to send him, but we hoped that it would open up many opportunities for him. He is now a qualified mechanical engineer, but so far has not been able to find a job that suited his talents. You know, it has occurred to me while touring this mill that here would be an ideal opening for my son. He would be very interested to work with your control distribution system. Computers have always fascinated him, and I am sure he could very quickly learn to manage the system. What a good start it would be for him. Perhaps you have a suitable vacancy? If so, let me know tomorrow. Good day, Mr. McLeod."

With a final beaming smile, Lai got into the company car that had been arranged for his use during his stay and was driven off. His mind whirling, McLeod drove back to the office. This was the last thing he had expected. As he thought about what had passed, his shock was replaced by anger. How dare Lai try to blackmail him in this way? He would never give in to such demands. The thought of an inexperienced, unqualified person meddling in the computerized Control Distribution Center, one of the mills's most advanced features, made his hair stand on end. It was AAP's nerve centre, monitoring operations in all parts of the mill. Any breakdown there would be disastrous. Then he remembered Lai's comments about the damage that would be caused by a negative report that dug up the old scandal of the lagoon and hinted that history might repeat itself, or which highlighted AAP's early safety record, and the effects of all this on the villagers and on Goh. What was he going to do?

Just then, his thoughts were interrupted by a knock and his secretary, Anna, rushed into the room. "Quick," she said, "accident in the chemical area. Many people hurt." Grabbing his hard hat, McLeod rushed from the room and drove over to the plant, where a crowd was gathering. He cursed. The chemical plant had been one of the worst maintained areas and he had been renovating it as fast as he could.

The supervisor, Mr. Budi, met him. "It is not as bad as we first thought," said Budi, "there was a loose valve and some of the chlorine leaked. But one of the workers panicked and started shouting, and then everyone began rushing about yelling it was 'another Bhopal.' Only one person has been hurt because of the leak—he inhaled the gas and so burned his throat. His hands and eyes also need medical attention. Two others were trampled in the rush to get out, but I think that the guards are getting things under control."

McLeod looked out of the window. The security guards were trying to disperse the crowd, with some success.

"Luckily, it is nearly lunch time," continued Budi. "That should help."

McLeod inspected the leak. As Budi said, it was minor. But given the lack of training among the staff and the reluctance to wear safety clothing, any incident could quickly become a full-scale disaster. "I will go and see the injured men in the clinic," said McLeod, "and then get back to the office. Let me know if you need me."

Back in his office, McLeod added "safety drill" to the long list of jobs he had to tackle in the very near future. He knew he should phone Goh and tell him what had happened, but he did not yet feel strong enough. On impulse, he decided to go over to see Dan Bailey on the rayon site. He needed to talk to someone, a fellow Westerner. As he drove up, however, he saw that Dan, too, was having problems. He was arguing with a man McLeod recognized as one of the local contractors, whose gang was part of the construction team. As McLeod arrived, the contractor shrugged and walked off.

"Whats up, Dan?" asked McLeod, seeing the anger in Dan's face.

"We have just had another man killed in a fall from the scaffolding," Bailey replied. "That makes ten since we started eight months ago. The man was not wearing boots, safety harness, or a hard hat. I have told the contractors over and over again that they must provide the right equipment; it is even written into their contract. But they say 'yes, boss' and do nothing. They say they cannot afford to because Goh has negotiated such a tight contract. I spoke to Goh about it, but he says the workers do not belong to him, and that he cannot be held responsible for what the contractors do in his plant. His main concern is to get the mill finished fast and start production. Everyone squeezes everyone else, corners get cut, and as usual it is the poor bastards at the bottom who pay for it. Have you seen the way they are living? There is no more room in the dormitories, so some containers have been temporarily converted by putting in wooden bunks. They have no running water, no electricity, they work up to their knees in mud in bare feet, and no one thinks anything of it. What a country!"

McLeod nodded in agreement. "The working conditions were the first thing that shocked me when I came to the site. I mentioned it to Goh, but he got really mad and told me the West had a nerve to try and interfere with other countries. He said to me, 'Look at your own history and see how you treated your workers in the past. Did any outsider tell you it was wicked? Look at conditions in your cities today—the drugs and violence, the crime, and the homelessness—and then decide if you have a right to preach to others. I cannot stand this Western pressure for labour rights in Asia, and your arguments about "social dumping." It is the same in China, where the Americans are always moaning about human rights. To us, trying to impose Western values seems just a dirty trick to protect your inefficient businesses. Do not condemn us before you take the beam out of your own eye.'" McLeod paused. "Goh must have learned that at mission school," he said with a smile. Then he went on to describe his encounter with Mr. Lai.

Dan's reply was not comforting. "Sounds like you have got no choice, old buddy," he said. "But it just shows you how the attitude towards the enforcement of environmental standards, which is being monitored by powerful pressure groups, differs from the way that safety legislation, which does not attract the same level of interest in the outside world, is more or less ignored. But if you think you have got problems, listen to this." Bailey lowered his voice. "You know that our CEO, Howard Hartford, is visiting from Chicago on his annual tour of our operations in the region? I spent yesterday morning with him in a meeting with Goh—it was quite a combat. Anyway, that evening, as I was leaving the office, Benny Burdiman, who is heading procurement for the rayon project, poked his head round the door, apologized for disturbing me, and asked me to sign a form so that he could go to town next day and clear the new power boiler we have been expecting through customs. The form, from accounts, was a bill for 'R.S. Tax: US$35,000.' I was puzzled, as I thought everything had been paid for. I remembered authorizing a cheque for the vendors a week ago. I had not a clue what this was for."

Bailey continued, "Well, you know what Benny is like. He has been with Goh from the beginning and is the sharpest negotiator in the region. He treated me like I was a backward child and explained that the boiler was now in a bonded warehouse at the port. To get it, he had to give the director of customs a little present. He said it was quite normal and that US$35,000 was the going rate. Apparently 'R.S. Tax' is a local joke—it stands for 'Reliable service tax.' Accounts keep a special budget to pay it. 'You will get used to it,' Benny said. "He wanted me to sign at once, but I said now hold on, I will have to think about this. Let me get back to you tomorrow."

"So what did you do?" asked McLeod.

"I dumped it straight in the CEO's lap," said Bailey, with some satisfaction. "You know how outspoken he has always been in the press about the decline of moral values in business. Well, I told him the whole story last night over dinner and said that obviously, in the light of the circular he sent round to all operations six months ago, stating the company's commitment to conducting business round the world in a totally clean way and in the best traditions of US ethical business practice, backed by the threat of legal prosecution and instant dismissal for anyone contravening these standards, etc., etc., there was no way I could do what Benny wanted. Then I also reminded Hartford how vital the boiler was for the plant and how far we already are behind schedule, and how there are half a dozen other important items to be delivered in the very near future. He looked quite dazed."

"So what did he decide?" asked McLeod.

"Have not heard from him yet," said Bailey. "But he promised to call me before he left this evening".

McLeod turned to go, "See you in the bar after work then, Dan. Cannot wait to hear how it ends."

McLeod returned to the office and, to his relief, the rest of the afternoon passed without incident. Standing at the guest house bar later, he reviewed his day: a near riot and an attempt to blackmail him. Not quite what he had anticipated on taking the job. Still pondering his problems, McLeod took to his drink over to a quiet corner, but within a few minutes he was joined by Hari Tung, financial director of the Changmai Corporation, and a Frenchman, Thierry Dupont.

Born locally, Harvard-trained Hari Tung was a very smart young man who worked closely with Goh. Thierry Dupont, who worked for a French multinational, was one of the many vendors to the rayon project; he was on site to check the machinery that his company had supplied. He was holding a bottle of champagne. "Come, my friends," said Thierry, "celebrate with me. I have just heard that I have won a very lucrative contract for my firm with, let us say, a large conglomerate in a country not far from here. And you know what? I got it because of my 'corruption skills.' I outbid and outdid German and United States, even Japanese competition to get it. It was hard work requiring a lot of creativity, but it was worth it and tonight, I am so proud."

"Proud!" exclaimed McLeod. "You cannot be serious! You are corrupt, and you have corrupted someone else. What is there to be proud of in that?"

"My friend," said Thierry, "thanks to this contract, my company back home will have work for the next two years. With 9% unemployment in France, anyone who creates jobs is a hero. In my opinion, corruption is a small price to pay to give work to Europeans. And, of course, there will be a nice little promotion in it for me. Now, stop making a fuss and have a drink."

"But David has a point," said Hari in his perfect English. "By your actions, you are corrupting others. And, if you think about it, that is not the only way that you in the West are helping to corrupt the people of this region. It is something that I and my friends, who are the fathers of young children, often argue about. Look at the Western values that the young are absorbing while watching your films, full of sex and violence. What sort of heroes are they going to copy? I have always been glad to be part of a culture with such a strong sense of family. Take Mr. Goh, whose family is extended to include all those who work for him. They know that the next generation will also find a place with him and so, secure in their 'iron rice bowl,' they work together for the good of the group, not for the individual as I have seen people do in the West. But this sense of community is beginning to break down, and we Asians are allowing it to happen."

Hari continued. "Although we welcome the transfer of Western technological progress, we do not feel the same about your moral standards. As we see it, Western values are poisoning the local people who in the end, we fear, will be as morally bankrupt as people in your part of the world. You cannot stop the poison spreading. In every hotel, there is CNN showing the same images, encouraging the same materialist attitudes of want, want, want. Global products for global consumers, they claim. But where will it all end? Imagine, if each and every one of the 1.2 billion Chinese were to consume as much as the Americans, it would mean 'good bye, planet Earth.' It could not support that degree of consumption and the pollution that would go with it. And we would all be responsible."

"What absolute rubbish," said Thierry. "It will never happen. Come on, let us talk about something more cheerful. Leave morality to the professors. While there is business to be done and a buck to be made, why should we worry?"

QUESTIONS TO CONSIDER

1. What reasoning should McLeod apply to try to handle the dilemmas he is facing?
2. How do you think Bailey's CEO, Mr. Hartford, should respond to Bailey's predicament?
3. What is your reaction to the debate presented in the final paragraphs?

NOTE

1   This case was written by Charlotte Butler, Research Associate, and Henri-Claude de Bettignies, Professor at INSEAD. It is intended to be used as a basis for class discussion rather than to illustrate effective or ineffective handling of a situation.

Nicola Pless and Thomas Maak

LEVI STRAUSS & CO.: ADDRESSING CHILD LABOUR IN BANGLADESH

MATT WILSON[1] WAS DRIVING BACK from a factory close to Mymensingh in the administrative division of Dhaka. It was a September afternoon and the Jeep trip had been long and arduous. It was monsoon season in Bangladesh, the dirt tracks were muddy and Matt's vehicle got stuck several times. This was not the first time during the past weeks of travel when tropical downpours made driving quite difficult in Asia. Yet, as operations manager, he had to visit the ten suppliers in Chittagong and Dhaka. The purpose of the visits was to carry out the annual supplier assessments together with Kamir Rao, the regional advisor for South Asia. To get to the production sites, he had to drive through rural areas, where rice, mustard and tea are grown. From the jeep, he could see the workers in the paddy fields. Two-thirds of the Bangladeshi population of some 150 million work in the agricultural sector.[2] According to UNICEF, about 36 per cent of the population lives on less than a dollar a day.[3] He also thought he saw children working in the fields but then he could have been wrong. It is often difficult to tell a person's age in Bangladesh because people look younger due to malnutrition.

Matt had worked for Levi Strauss & Co. (LS&Co.) for eight years before moving to South East Asia. He had worked at the company headquarters in San Francisco, where he joined LS&Co. in 1997 after graduating from a top ten US business school. He joined LS&Co. because of the company's reputation as a good "corporate citizen" with a commitment to best business practices and its international presence (see Appendices 1 and 2). He soon got the opportunity to spread his wings in South Asia. With five years as operations manager in Bangladesh, he had built long-term relationships with most of LS&Co.'s suppliers in the garment industry. Since the 1980s, the garment industry had become the mainstay of Bangladesh's economy thanks to the country's rock-bottom labour costs. In fact, the industry contributes 75 per cent to the country's export earnings and employs over 3 million people, most of them women (90 per cent).[4] Back in the '80s, LS&Co. decided to expand its business internationally, both in sales markets and for sourcing its products.[5] Today they work with over 600 suppliers in 50 countries. It is these firms that produce LS&Co.'s branded garments.

This shift towards international suppliers has raised many thorny issues: Do suppliers meet LS&Co.'s' standards? What about child labour, environmental protection, health and safety, and human rights? These considerations led LS&Co. to draw up and introduce *Global Sourcing and Operating Guidelines* (see Appendix 3) in 1991, which were implemented the following year. These guidelines comprised two parts: the "Country Assessment Guidelines" and the "Business Partner Terms of Engagement" (TOE), which set specific standards for suppliers in areas such as: freedom of association; fair employment practices; workers' health and safety; and environmental management. In fact, LS&Co. was the first company to institute such a supplier code of conduct, thereby setting a standard for multinational companies.[6]

The company has conducted regular assessments since 1992 to ensure suppliers meet LS&Co.'s standards (TOE). The firm employs 20 factory assessors around the world. These staff are specially trained to assess and monitor compliance with the TOE code. This year, Matt had accompanied Kamir on most of the assessment visits to suppliers' factories in Bangladesh. It came as a shock when they discovered that two of the new suppliers were employing children under the minimum working age of 15. The two suppliers were actually offering very good working conditions by Bangladeshi standards: new factory buildings; safe machines and production equipment; a healthy, clean and safe environment for workers; and a staff canteen. Matt was also very pleased with the quality of products they delivered. Finding out that the two new suppliers were employing young children therefore came as a major disappointment.

However, he knew that the issue of underage labour is a complicated one in the country. While child labour violates International Labour Standards (ILO) as well as company guidelines, it is rife in Bangladesh and does not infringe local laws. According to UNICEF statistics, 13 per cent of children between the ages of 5 and 14 are involved in child labor activities.[7] Furthermore, many children born in the country are not issued birth certificates, a fact that makes it hard to determine their real age. In Bangladesh, whole families depend on a child's income. This places a great burden on kids. Not only are they deprived of schooling (which is often the only way out of the poverty trap) but they also have no say when it comes to where they work, the kind of jobs they do and their working conditions. Moreover, many of these children are cruelly exploited, run serious health risks and are paid a pittance (which is one of the reasons why employers prefer hiring children to adults). Put baldly, they have no rights. In fact, a great many children in Bangladesh grow up under conditions that can all too easily lead to exploitation and even prostitution (see Appendix 4).

Shortly after returning from the trip, Matt arranged a meeting with Kamir and the management team to address the suppliers' violations of ILO and TOE standards and to reach a decision on how best to deal with the situation. During the meeting, they discussed the situation in depth and identified the various stakeholders that would be affected by their decision. They also brainstormed different options for dealing with underage employees. Then they considered the challenge of reaching a solution that complied with international labour standards, reflected LS&Co.'s corporate values and met stakeholders' needs.

CASE DISCUSSION QUESTIONS

1. Who are the stakeholders that are affected by the management team's decision?
2. What are the management team's options?
3. Which solution would best suit Levi Strauss & Co.?

APPENDIX 1: MEMO BY THE PRESIDENT AND CEO JOHN ANDERSON ACCOMPANYING THE WORLDWIDE CODE OF BUSINESS CONDUCT[8]

TO: **Levi Strauss & Co. Employees Worldwide**

FROM: **John Anderson**

SUBJECT: **Worldwide Code of Business Conduct**

LS&CO. has a long and distinguished history of corporate citizenship, including our unwavering commitment to responsible business practices. Our values and strong belief in "doing the right thing" are the foundation of our success.

To ensure we provide our employees with a clear set of standards and guidance for conducting our business with integrity and the highest degree of compliance with the law, we established LS&CO.'s **Worldwide Code of Business Conduct**.

This code certainly does not cover every ethical or legal situation we may encounter in our business operations, but it does provide an excellent summary of important guidelines that define the way we choose to do business.

Our Worldwide Code of Business Conduct applies to all employees around the world; however, with a global footprint of more than 110 countries, we and our affiliates apply the code as appropriate in individual countries, consistent with local laws.

If you have any questions about the Worldwide Code of Business Conduct or how it should be applied in your location, please consult with your manager, Human Resources representative, the Legal department or the Chief Compliance Officer in San Francisco.

The integrity of our employees makes LS&CO. a great place to work. I encourage you to familiarize yourself with our Worldwide Code of Business Conduct and apply these standards to your work every day.

John Anderson
President and
Chief Executive Officer
Levi Strauss & Co.

APPENDIX 2: LEVI STRAUSS & CO. FACT SHEET[9]

Levi Strauss & Co. Fact Sheet

Founded in 1853 by Bavarian immigrant Levi Strauss, Levi Strauss & Co. (LS&CO.) is one of the world's largest brand-name apparel marketers with sales in more than 110 countries around the world. There is no other company with a comparable global presence in the jeans and casual pants markets. Our market-leading apparel products are sold under the **Levi's®, Dockers® and Signature by Levi Strauss & Co.™ brands**.

Company Profile

- FY 2008 Net Revenues: $4.4 billion
- Global presence: Three geographic divisions: Levi Strauss Americas (LSA), Levi Strauss Europe, Middle East and North Africa (LSEMA) and Asia Pacific Division (APD).
    - Regional headquarters located in San Francisco, Brussels and Singapore
    - Global sourcing headquarters in Singapore.
    - More than 5,000 registered trademarks in approximately 180 countries.
    - We derive approximately 40 percent of our net revenues and regional operating income from our European and Asia Pacific businesses.
- Retail distribution: LS&CO. products are sold through approximately 60,000 retail locations worldwide, including 260 company-operated stores and approximately 1,500 franchised stores around the world.
- Licensing: LS&CO. trademarks are licensed for products and accessories complementary to our core branded products and extend our brands into product categories that broaden the product range available to consumers and create compelling and distinctive brand looks, including:
    - Tops, sweaters, jackets, and outerwear
    - Kidswear
    - Footwear and hosiery
    - Loungewear and sleepwear
    - Belts, bags and wallets
    - Eyewear
    - Luggage and home bedding products
- Sourcing: We source our products primarily from independent manufacturers located throughout the world.
    - Contractors are located in approximately 45 countries around the world
    - No single country represents more than 20 percent of our production
- Employees: More than 11,400 worldwide
    - 4,700 in the Americas
    - 4,400 in Europe
    - 2,300 in Asia Pacific
- Ownership: The company is privately held by descendants of the family of Levi Strauss. Shares of company stock are not publicly traded. Shares of Levi Strauss Japan K.K., the company's Japanese affiliate, are publicly traded in Japan.

APPENDIX 2—*continued*

A Unique History

LS&CO.'s history and longevity are unique in the apparel industry: Levi's® jeans are the original, authentic and definitive jeans. In 1853, during the California Gold Rush, our founder, Levi Strauss, opened a wholesale dry goods business in San Francisco. That business became known as "Levi Strauss & Co." In 1873, Levi Strauss and Jacob Davis, a tailor, saw a consumer need for work pants that could hold up under rough conditions. They worked together and received a U.S. patent to make "waist overalls" with metal rivets at points of strain on the pants – and in so doing created the world's first jean. Levi Strauss & Co. brought these new workpants to market that year, and, in 1890, began using the lot number "501" to identify the product.

In 1986, we introduced the Dockers® brand of casual apparel, which was at the forefront of the business casual trend in the United States. In 2003, in response to the emergence and success of the mass channel, we launched the Levi Strauss Signature® brand of jeans and casual apparel for consumers who shop in the channel.

LS&CO.'s commitment to quality, innovation and corporate citizenship, manifested in many ways throughout our history, began with Levi Strauss and continues today.

Values and Vision

Four core values are at the heart of Levi Strauss & Co.:

- Empathy
- Originality
- Integrity
- Courage

These four values are linked. Our history demonstrates how these core values work together and are the source of our success. Generations of people have worn our products as a symbol of freedom and self-expression in the face of adversity, challenge and social change. The special relationship between our values, our consumers and our brands is the basis of our success and drives our core purpose. It is the foundation of who we are and what we want to become:

People love our clothes and trust our company.

We will market and distribute the most appealing and widely worn apparel brands.

Our products define quality, style and function.

We will clothe the world.

Corporate Citizenship

We believe that commercial success and corporate citizenship are closely linked. This principle is embedded in our 156-year experience and continues to anchor how we operate today. For us, corporate citizenship includes a strong belief that we can help shape society through civic engagement and community involvement, responsible labor and workplace practices, philanthropy, ethical conduct, environmental stewardship and transparency. Our "profits through principles" business approach manifests itself in how we develop our business strategies and policies and make everyday decisions. Our history reflects our approach to corporate citizenship:

- In 1991, we were the first multinational apparel company to develop a comprehensive supplier code of conduct targeted toward ensuring that individuals making our products anywhere in the world would do so in safe and healthy working conditions and be treated with dignity and respect. For more information, see "Sourcing and Logistics – Sourcing Practices."

APPENDIX 2—*continued*

- Our commitment to equal opportunity and diversity predated the U.S. civil rights movement and federally mandated desegregation by two decades. We opened integrated factories in California in the 1940s. In 1960, we integrated our newly opened plants in the American South.

- In 1992, we became the first <u>Fortune 500</u> company to extend full medical benefits to domestic partners of employees, a practice now followed by many corporations and public agencies.

- We participate in public advocacy relating to trade policy. We believe that worker rights protections and enforcement measures should be an integral part of all bilateral, regional or multilateral trade negotiations. Since 2000, we have been a leader in publicly advocating this position.

- The Levi Strauss Foundation, a charitable foundation supported by us, focuses its core grantmaking primarily in three areas: AIDS/HIV prevention, building assets, and workers' rights in countries where we have a business presence.

- We support and encourage employee community involvement through volunteer activities, paid time off and grants by the Levi Strauss Foundation to nonprofit organizations we assist through our community activities.

- The Red Tab Foundation, a nonprofit organization created and largely funded by our employees, offers financial assistance to our employees and retirees who are unable to afford life's basic necessities.

APPENDIX 3: GLOBAL SOURCING AND OPERATING GUIDELINES[10]

Levi Strauss & Co. Global Sourcing and Operating Guidelines

Levi Strauss & Co.'s (LS&CO.) commitment to responsible business practices — embodied in our Global Sourcing and Operating Guidelines — guides our decisions and behavior as a company everywhere we do business. Since becoming the first multinational to establish such guidelines in 1991, LS&CO. has used them to help improve the lives of workers manufacturing our products, make responsible sourcing decisions and protect our commercial interests. They are a cornerstone of our sourcing strategy and of our business relationships with hundreds of contractors worldwide.

The Levi Strauss & Co. Global Sourcing and Operating Guidelines include two parts:

The Country Assessment Guidelines, which address large, external issues beyond the control of LS&CO.'s individual business partners. These help us assess the opportunities and risks of doing business in a particular country.

The Business Partner Terms of Engagement (TOE), which deal with issues that are substantially controllable by individual business partners. These TOE are an integral part of our business relationships. Our employees and our business partners understand that complying with our TOE is no less important than meeting our quality standards or delivery times.

Country Assessment Guidelines

The numerous countries where LS&CO. has existing or future business interests present a variety of cultural, political, social and economic circumstances.

The Country Assessment Guidelines help us assess any issues that might present concern in light of the ethical principles we have set for ourselves. The Guidelines assist us in making practical and principled business decisions as we balance the potential risks and opportunities associated with conducting business in specific countries. Specifically, we assess the following:

Health and Safety Conditions — must meet the expectations we have for employees and their families or our company representatives;

Human Rights Environment — must allow us to conduct business activities in a manner that is consistent with our Global Sourcing and Operating Guidelines and other company policies

Legal System — must provide the necessary support to adequately protect our trademarks, investments or other commercial interests, or to implement the Global Sourcing and Operating Guidelines and other company policies; and

Political, Economic and Social Environment — must protect the company's commercial interests and brand/corporate image. We do not conduct business in countries prohibited by U.S. laws.

Terms of Engagement

Our TOE help us to select business partners who follow workplace standards and business practices that are consistent with LS&CO.'s values and policies. These requirements are applied to every contractor who manufactures or finishes products for LS&CO. Trained assessors closely monitor compliance among our manufacturing and finishing contractors in more than 50 countries. The TOE include:

APPENDIX 3 — *continued*

Levi Strauss & Co.

Ethical Standards
We will seek to identify and utilize business partners who aspire as individuals and in the conduct of all their businesses to a set of ethical standards not incompatible with our own.

Legal Requirements
We expect our business partners to be law abiding as individuals and to comply with legal requirements relevant to the conduct of all their businesses.

Environmental Requirements
We will only do business with partners who share our commitment to the environment and who conduct their business in a way that is consistent with LS&CO.'s Environmental Philosophy and Guiding Principles (See TOE Guidebook p.68).

Community Involvement
We will favor business partners who share our commitment to improving community conditions.

Employment Standards
We will only do business with partners who adhere to the following guidelines:

Child Labor
Use of child labor is not permissible. Workers can be no less than 15 years of age and not younger than the compulsory age to be in school. We will not utilize partners who use child labor in any of their facilities. We support the development of legitimate workplace apprenticeship programs for the educational benefit of younger people.

Prison Labor/Forced Labor
We will not utilize prison or forced labor in contracting relationships in the manufacture and finishing of our products. We will not utilize or purchase materials from a business partner utilizing prison or forced labor.

Disciplinary Practices
We will not utilize business partners who use corporal or other forms of mental or physical coercion.

Working Hours
While permitting flexibility in scheduling, we will identify local legal limits on work hours and seek business partners who do not exceed them except for appropriately compensated overtime. While we favor partners who utilize less than sixty-hour work weeks, we will not use contractors who, on a regular basis, require in excess of a sixty-hour week. Employees should be allowed at least one day off in seven.

Wages and Benefits
We will only do business with partners who provide wages and benefits that comply with any applicable law and match the prevailing local manufacturing or finishing industry practices.

Freedom of Association
We respect workers' rights to form and join organizations of their choice and to bargain collectively. We expect our suppliers to respect the right to free association and the right to organize and bargain collectively without unlawful interference. Business partners should ensure that workers who make such decisions or participate in such organizations are not the object of discrimination or punitive disciplinary actions and that the representatives of such organizations have access to their members under conditions established either by local laws or mutual agreement between the employer and the worker organizations.

Discrimination
While we recognize and respect cultural differences, we believe that workers should be employed on the basis of their ability to do the job, rather than on the basis of personal characteristics or beliefs. We will favor business partners who share this value.

APPENDIX 3—*continued*

Levi Strauss & Co.

Health and Safety

We will only utilize business partners who provide workers with a safe and healthy work environment. Business partners who provide residential facilities for their workers must provide safe and healthy facilities.

Evaluation and Compliance

All new and existing factories involved in the manufacturing or finishing of products for LS&CO. are regularly evaluated to ensure compliance with our TOE. Our goal is to achieve positive results and effect change by working with our business partners to find long-term solutions that will benefit the individuals who make our products and will improve the quality of life in local communities. We work on-site with our contractors to develop strong alliances dedicated to responsible business practices and continuous improvement.

If LS&CO. determines that a contractor is not complying with our TOE, we require that the contractor implement a corrective action plan within a specified time period. If a contractor fails to meet the corrective action plan commitment, Levi Strauss & Co. will terminate the business relationship.

APPENDIX 4: BANGLADESH: SHETRA'S STORY[11]: THE LIFE OF A SEXUALLY EXPLOITED CHILD IN BANGLADESH

The World Congress III against the Sexual Exploitation of Children, set for 25–28 November 2008 in Brazil, aims to promote international cooperation for more effective action on sexual exploitation. Here is one in a series of related stories.

BARISAL, Bangladesh, 19 November 2008 – a recent survey by UNICEF Bangladesh found the average age at which children became involved in commercial sexual exploitation was 13.

Although sexual abuse affects all strata of society, it remains a taboo that is not talked about in Bangladesh. As a result, many children who are being exploited as part of the commercial sex industry do not tell anyone.

The non-governmental organization Association of Voluntary Action for Society (AVAS) runs a drop-in centre here that is supported by UNICEF's HIV/AIDS programme. Through the drop-in centre, sex workers have access to condoms to prevent HIV infection, as well as other basic health services, counselling and HIV education.

Shetra's Story

Recently, a sexually exploited 13-year-old named Shetra was found in a hotel by a peer educator from AVAS. Here is her story, as told to UNICEF's Kathryn Seymour:

"My father died when I was six or seven, so my mother has always had to work to support us. When my mother goes to work, I look after my smallest sister, who is only 11 months old. My middle sister is eight.

"All four of us live in a rented house in Barisal, but the rent is very expensive. My mother often can't earn enough as a maid, and things are very difficult. Sometimes, we can't manage food or the rent for our house. Recently, I began to think that I really needed to earn some money to help us out, so I decided to go look for a job.

"For a short while, I got a job as a maid. My employer beat me and only gave me one meal a day, so I quit. Two months ago, I started as a sex worker.

"My mother doesn't know where I go when I leave to meet men. I tell her that I am going to visit a friend. When I give her the money afterwards and she asks me where it came from, I tell her that I got a job on the roads chipping bricks. This is the story I tell everyone.

How it Started

"I started as a sex worker because of one of our neighbours. He is close friends with my family, so I call him 'uncle', even though he is not my relative. One day, he called me and said that he had someone for me to meet at his house. When I got to his house, he introduced me to another man who he said I should also call 'uncle'.

"We went to a hotel together and that was my first time. It hurt a lot. Since then, two or three days a week I go to the hotel with this uncle. One time, he took me to his home when no one else was there. I've been to other hotels and sometimes to houses when the wives are away.

"Normally, the oldest men come to me. I think that they are mostly over 40 years old. My neighbour usually calls me when there is a man for me. I don't know if there are other girls that he calls, but there might be.

"I want to stop doing this, but I don't know how because my mother needs the money. I don't want to continue because then I know that I won't have an education, but I need to help feed my family."

NOTES

1. This case is a real-life example. However, names of places, people and biographical information are fictional. The number of assessors and suppliers contracted reflect an estimation. Bangladesh. (http://en.wikipedia.org/wiki/Bangladesh) Retrieved April 15, 2009.
2. UNICEF – Bangladesh – The big picture. (www.unicef.org/infobycountry/bangladesh_bangladesh_background.html) Retrieved April 15, 2009.
3. Bangladesh. (http://en.wikipedia.org/wiki/Bangladesh) Retrieved April 15, 2009.
4. Baron, D.P. 2003. *Business and its Environment,* 4th ed., New Jersey: Prentice Hall, p. 761.
5. Product Sourcing Practices (www.levistrauss.com/Citizenship/) Retrieved April 15, 2009.
6. Baron, D.P. 2003.
7. In their statistics, UNICEF defines child labour as the "Percentage of children aged 5 to 14 years of age involved in child labor activities at the moment of the survey [1999–2007]. A child is considered to be involved in child labor activities under the following classification: (a) children 5 to 11 years of age that during the week preceding the survey did at least one hour of economic activity or at least 28 hours of domestic work, and (b) children 12 to 14 years of age that during the week preceding the survey did at least 14 hours of economic activity or at least 42 hours of economic activity and domestic work combined." (www.unicef.org/infobycountry/stats_popup9.html) Retrieved April 15, 2009.
8. www.levistrauss.com/sites/default/files/librarydocument/2010/5/wwcoc-english_0.pdf.
9. www.levistrauss.com/library/levi-strauss-co-fact-sheet.
10. www.levistrauss.com/sites/default/files/librarydocument/2010/4/CitizenshipCodeOf Conduct.pdf.
11. www.unicef.org/infobycountry/bangladesh_46449.html.

LITERATURE AND SUGGESTED READINGS

Baron, D.P. 2003. *Business and its environment,* 4th ed., Upper Saddle River, NJ: Prentice Hall.

Donaldson, T. & Dunfee, T. (1999). *Ties that bind.* Boston, MA: Harvard Business School Press.

Freeman, R.E. 1984. *Strategic management: A stakeholder approach.* Boston, MA: Pitman Publishing.

Johnson, M. 1993. *Moral imagination: Implications of cognitive science for ethics.* Chicago, London: The University of Chicago Press.

Maak, T. & Pless, N.M. 2006a. Responsible leadership: A relational approach. In T. Maak & N. M. Pless (Eds.), *Responsible leadership.* London, New York: Routledge, 33–53.

Maak, T. & Pless, N.M. 2006b. Responsible leadership in a stakeholder society. A relational perspective. *Journal of Business Ethics,* 66(1), 99–115.

Pless, N.M. 2007. Understanding responsible leadership: Roles identity and motivational drivers. *Journal of Business Ethics,* 74(4), 437–456.

Pless, N.M. & Maak, T. 2005. Relational intelligence for leading responsibly in a connected world. In K.M. Weaver (Ed.), *Proceedings of the Sixty-fifth Annual Meeting of the Academy of Management,* Honolulu.

Werhane, P. 1999. *Moral imagination and management decision making.* New York, Oxford: Oxford University Press.

Barbara Coudenhove-Kalergi and Christian Seelos

EVN IN BULGARIA: ENGAGING THE ROMA COMMUNITY[1]

As an energy and environmental services provider, we fulfil the daily needs of our customers. Through our reliable and high quality services, we make a sustainable contribution to their quality of life.

EVN corporate policy statement

I want to live like a normal human being and not like in the dark age.

Mehmet Denev, a Stolipinovo resident who won a court case against EVN on the grounds of ethnical discrimination of the prevailing electricity regime

STEFAN SZYSZKOWITZ, MANAGING DIRECTOR of EVN Bulgaria, a subsidiary of the Austrian energy provider EVN, was nervous. He was walking to the office building of EVN close to the historic center of Plovdiv, Bulgaria's second-largest city, when a horse cart passed by. Horse carts are still the typical vehicles of the Roma minority in Bulgaria and quite a common sight in Plovdiv, which is home to Europe's biggest Roma ghetto, Stolipinovo. This afternoon, Szyszkowitz would meet some of the most influential Roma leaders in this settlement. He wanted to discuss EVN's plans on how to improve the supply of electricity to the inhabitants of Stolipinovo after long years of a tight electricity regime that only supplied electricity during the night—leaving an estimated 70,000 people without the ability to cook, heat their homes, or switch the lights on during the day.

It was early July in 2007 and the air was stuffy. Szyszkowitz did not like the idea of going to Stolipinovo. He knew the quarter only from the outside, but he had heard the stories from his technicians about angry mobs, broken sewage systems, inadequate water supply, and garbage that piled up on the streets because the municipal waste collections had stopped servicing Stolipinovo. However, Szyszkowitz knew that EVN had arrived at a turning point, a crucial moment for the success or failure of its plans on how to deal with this complex and emotional situation.

EVN had inherited this problem from the old energy distribution company (EDC) of Plovdiv as part of its acquisition of two distribution companies in southeastern Bulgaria in 2004. Now, Stolipinovo was EVN's problem. It was not the only challenge that EVN faced in Bulgaria. Already, after a few years of operating, the company was cornered on all sides, with every step being watched very closely. EVN could not afford to lose any more credibility. Municipal elections were scheduled later that year, which usually meant that rival political parties would readily exploit any opportunity to frame a foreign company as a scapegoat for all kinds of local problems. Stefan Szyszkowitz knew this meeting had to be successful, but he wondered whether he could reason with the Roma. This was a discriminated-against population group that had been displaced, segregated, and oppressed for centuries. They were the poorest of the poor in Bulgaria. Would they be willing and able to pay if EVN were to decide to improve the much-needed electricity supply? If the situation were left unresolved, would EVN be judged as an accomplice to a growing humanitarian disaster in one of the youngest member states of the European Union? And how would this affect EVN's business strategy in the country and the region?

BULGARIA'S ELECTRICITY SUPPLY CHALLENGES

In many countries of the former Eastern bloc, the energy industry played an important role in the national ideology. Electricity was seen as a symbol of the social compact between state and citizen, as well as a practical necessity for industrialization and thus progress. Electricity presented "the good life."[2] This attitude was also true for Bulgaria. During the Communist regime and under Russian influence, Bulgarian engineers were trained in the Soviet Union, and the utilities were state-owned and promoted as a point of national pride. "Each year in June, the day of the electrical engineer was celebrated. The Bulgarians took great pride in their electro-technical competence and were very self-confident," observed Stefan Szyszkowitz. In addition, Bulgaria has traditionally been a significant net exporter of power to the neighboring countries.

However, due to rapid industrialization, irrational energy use, energy waste, and the fragile transmission network, the electricity supply was highly unreliable. This saw a growing sense of disillusionment with the Communist Party rise in the mid-1980s. In most large towns, an electricity regime of three hours on and three hours off for at least six days a week was introduced, but even these supplies could not be guaranteed, and the power was frequently suspended without warning. "The dark nights played a prominent role in the demoralization of society and in the draining away of faith in a system, which, after forty years of socialism, was not able to guarantee a normal daily life."[3] The socialist economy responded to the emerging shortages in the way typical of that system—by building new capability. The construction and commission of four additional reactors in Kozloduy, Bulgaria's biggest nuclear power plant, also strengthened Bulgaria's role as a net exporter of energy.[4] Kozloduy later became one of the critical issues of Bulgaria's negotiations when the EU made the shutdown of the nuclear power plant a precondition to the country's EU membership. The government agreed reluctantly to the closure of the two oldest reactors by 2002 and of reactors three and four in 2006.

Power Sector Reform[5]

Due to the gradual disruption of the relationship with Russia, reform of the power sector became essential. This was to pave the way to effective privatization of the state-owned utilities. Part of the appeal of privatization was the money to be earned by the state, as well as the desperately needed investment in the network infrastructure, mainly to reduce commercial and technical losses and to bring effective management into Bulgarian companies. This meant breaking up the state monopoly represented by the National Electric Utility NEC, which owned almost all nuclear, hydro, and pumped hydro power plants in Bulgaria and controlled 87.9% of total capacity.

In April 2000, the seven state-owned power distributors and the independent power generation companies, including Kozloduy and the thermal power plants Maritsa East, were separated from the NEC and registered as legal enterprises. In autumn of the same year, a State Commission on Energy Regulation was set up with responsibility for the electricity prices charged by the energy carriers, and for licensing and permits for energy facilities. The NEC was transformed into the national power transmission company, acting as a so-called single buyer—that is, it would purchase electricity from the independent producers and sell it to the utilities, which, in their function as distributors, would sell the power to the end-users.

Even though the reform of the power sector was deemed to be a success in general, several issues were insufficiently tackled.

1. *Economic Issues*

   A transparent and independent pricing policy, as one of the most important objectives of the reform, was overlooked. In fact, the State Commission on Energy Regulation remained largely financially dependent on the state budget. Moreover, the reform started with the freezing of electricity prices for final customers, not allowing the market mechanism to form competitive and cost-covering prices. In addition, the NEC continued to export energy to neighboring countries such as Greece or Turkey at cheaper rates than it provided it to domestic customers, thus undermining the market mechanism.

   At the same time, the independent power distributors could not procure the necessary collection rates of electricity bills. Generally, 30–35% of electricity was lost in the frail transmission network or to theft. A large portion of the outstanding payments belonged to the municipalities financed by the state budget, which in turn relied in part on the revenue of the NEC operations.

2. *Environmental Issues*

   The environmental issues posed a substantial challenge to the reform efforts—mostly in relation to projected high costs in dealing with environmental destruction rooted in the transition period. The Communist five-year plans had not been geared towards making production cleaner or repairing the ravages already caused. Sofia and the surrounding areas remain today one of the most polluted regions in the country. According to a World Bank study published in 2000, the Bulgarian energy industry was the biggest source of air pollution; the total investment costs of meeting the EU requirements for the rehabilitation of the thermal power plants up to 2010 were estimated to be US$1.6 billion, at a minimum. As is so often the case, there were to be intrinsic trade-offs between Bulgaria's objectives to ensure least-cost energy supply to the country and to remain a dominant energy supplier in the region, while at the same time minimizing its dependence on energy imports and meeting national and international environmental commitments.

3. *Social Issues*
    The social impact of the sectoral reform was never subject to any specific studies and seemed not to be considered. However, the social challenges were critical. The Bulgarian end-users were not only faced with relative high costs of energy, but at the same time were burdened with low household incomes. Low-income households accounted for 38% of the total in 2000. They spent 14% of their income on energy. In terms of international benchmarks such as the UK energy poverty threshold of 10%, a large share of the Bulgarian population were thus categorized as energy-poor.[6] In the same year, 20% of the households relied on social assistance to cover energy costs.

4. *Non-Payments and Electric Power Theft*[7]
    According to the World Bank, the electricity market in Bulgaria has one of the highest levels of hidden cost among EU member states. These hidden costs include poor bill collection rates or excessive technical losses and losses resulting from theft. The amount of unpaid bills is a result of both household and business indebtedness. In 2005, the EDCs lost between 20% and 23% of distributed electric power as a result of technical losses or thefts.

    Theft of electricity in Bulgaria is generally carried out by companies and by households at an approximate rate of 1:5. In 2003, about €50 million losses from electricity thefts were registered, with average losses accounting for 6–7% of distributed energy.[8] Reportedly, small energy-intensive companies or production facilities, restaurants, and hotels are among the most frequent violators. Anton Gramatikov, director of the metering department, said that:

> After the privatization the technical losses were discussed in one of the working groups set up for the integration process. The Austrians could not grasp that the majority of the technical losses was due to energy theft. They couldn't believe that this was even possible. For them it was a completely new problem and they had no ready solution.

A particular problem faced by the EDCs in Bulgaria was the non-payment en masse of electricity bills in neighborhoods populated by the Roma ethnic minority, such as Stolipinovo in Bulgaria's second-largest city Plovdiv (see Exhibit 1).

EXHIBIT 1. Hidden costs in the energy sector

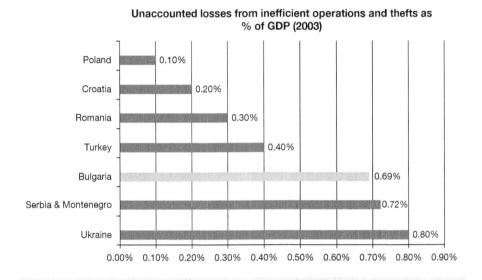

Unaccounted losses from inefficient operations and thefts as % of GDP (2003)

Poland	0.10%
Croatia	0.20%
Romania	0.30%
Turkey	0.40%
Bulgaria	0.69%
Serbia & Montenegro	0.72%
Ukraine	0.80%

Source: Ebinger, J. (2006). *Measuring Financial Performance and Infrastructure: An Application to Europe and Central Asia,* Washington, DC: *World Bank.*

ROMA "THE PEOPLE"[9]

The Roma are considered to be the European Union's largest and most vulnerable ethnic minority group. Although precise figures are unavailable, it is estimated that about 10 million Roma live in Europe as a whole—a population size higher than that of a number of EU member states. However, Roma-related issues remained overwhelmingly absent from the political agenda in most of the EU member states until the beginning of the twenty-first century, when the rights and living conditions of Roma were incorporated into the EU accession process of the new member states of Eastern Europe, such as Bulgaria.

As an endogamous culture with a tendency to self-segregation, the Roma have generally resisted assimilation into other communities in whichever countries they have moved to—the positive aspect being that they have managed to successfully preserve their distinctive and unique culture. The price of this cultural persistence, however, has been isolation from the surrounding population, and this has made them vulnerable to being stereotyped. Discrimination against and stereotyping of Roma is still widely spread, and it permeates many aspects of life, including education, employment, and housing.[10] The poverty of many Roma communities, which is even more obvious in ghettos, contributes to general resentment because the Roma are perceived as parasites living off state welfare payments, thieves, and so on. In summary, the persistent disadvantages in education, which limit future opportunities and access to the labor market, the poor health service, and the inadequate housing and marginalization of settlements characterize the situation of the Roma population in Europe.

Roma, in general, are not an homogeneous group. The diversity among the Roma populations is ranges from the various dialects of the Romany language to the proportions living in cities, integrated neighborhoods, or segregated rural settlements. Also, the Roma are not a united community, but rather are divided into many groups—depending, for example, on their exact descent or language and religious affiliation. This diversity creates significant challenges regarding research and the collection of quantitative and qualitative data on the Roma population. Information or reliable and exact data on true Roma living conditions and poverty is often scarce and fragmented, making it extremely hard to develop policies for this community.

The Roma of Bulgaria: The Socio Economic Context[11]

It is estimated that about 800,000 Roma live in Bulgaria—although the official census of 2001 reported only 370,000, or 4.68% of the total population. The difference is attributed to a large number of Roma self-identifying as Bulgarians or Turks. The Bulgarian Roma were primarily nomadic or semi-sedentary until 1958, when the Communist regime launched a campaign of forced assimilation, restricting their traditional customs and forcing them to settle down. The Communist government also banned the public use of the Romany language.[12] The so-called process of revival in the mid-1980s during which Turks and the Muslim Roma were forced to adopt Bulgarian names was followed by a period during which the official position more or less denied the very existence of Roma in Bulgaria. During the socialist era policies of resettlement, assimilation programs, or employment provision, Roma communities became heavily reliant on state social support. Despite extensive involvement in the shadow economy, Roma households are still heavily dependent on welfare payments today (see Table 1 and Exhibit 2).

In Bulgaria, the long and painful transition from a planned state economy to a free market has hit the Roma the hardest. When subsidies of state-owned enterprises

Table 1. Source of income

Source of income that provides the most money for a Roma household in %				
	BG	CZ	HUN	RO
Regular wage jobs	25.9	40.3	14.8	10.6
Occasional jobs	2.5	2.8	3	0.5
Salary/payment for work at a civil organization	1.1	0.4	0.2	0
Self-employment/own business	2.1	2.8	0.4	1.1
Pensions	26	15.5	23.6	13.3
Unemployment benefits	15.2	23.2	22.4	9.1
Scholarship	0.3	0.6	0.3	0.4
Child support (including paid maternity leave)	15.3	10.6	27.2	25.4
Other	11.6	3.8	8	38.7

Source: UNDP survey 2004.

EXHIBIT 2. Formal and informal sector employment

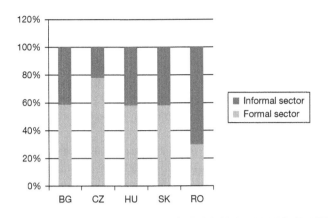

Source: UNDP (2002).

were slashed, it was often Roma who were the first to be dismissed. Many have never recovered from the economic restructuring. The community's geographical isolation increased, resulting in negative effects on the Roma's ability to find jobs. Many Roma neighborhoods turned into ghettos, which were abandoned by most state institutions, making access to administrative, medical, and other services very difficult. A large number of young Roma dropped out of school, causing functional illiteracy that again hampered labor market integration and led to more poverty.[13]

In 1992, the term "Bulgarian Ethnic Model" (BEM) emerged, and it soon became part of the political rhetoric. This coincided with the signing of the association agreement of Bulgaria with the EU, which insisted on including an article safeguarding the human rights of ethnic minorities.[14] Even if it is true that many positive steps have been taken to protect the Roma's ethnic and cultural identity—also under the watchful eye of the EU—the Roma have largely remained at the very bottom of Bulgarian society.

No Voice—No Power

The Roma population is poorly represented in the Bulgarian political system. The Roma community has never managed to unify behind one Roma party to attend and participate at the National Assembly, despite potentially having more than enough votes to do so.[15] This damages the situation of the Roma on both national and local levels even further, because they have almost no political power to voice their concerns. The non-Roma parties have generally ignored Roma issues, even though Roma-dominated organizations have supported the election of municipal councilors in many municipal elections. Every post-Communist election has also seen the open buying of Roma votes by competing non-Roma politicians offering cash handouts, food, jobs, and promises of other post-election services and benefits to Roma voters, for example the cancellation of their electricity bills.

The Roma Housing Situation[16]

The Roma never were landowners and therefore possessed limited economic resources. They continued to be poor under the era of central planning, and they had no property to reclaim when post-Communist restitution began. As a result, Roma migration to urban and suburban areas intensified, leading to the expansion of ghettos, with all the corresponding social consequences.[17]

A relatively high percentage of the Roma population lives in inadequate housing conditions, such as sub standard housing or shanty towns. Bulgaria particularly stands out in comparison with other CEE countries with a large Roma population. According to the Bulgarian National Statistical Institute, almost half of the Roma population in Bulgaria still lacked running water in their homes in 2001 and were forced to use water from street pipes or wells. Most Roma neighborhoods have damaged sewage systems or none at all, and this increases the risk of infectious diseases and epidemics such as hepatitis. Overpopulation in Roma neighborhoods and homes is the norm. Often, more than three generations live under the same roof. As most municipal authorities have left Roma neighborhoods, there is no control over illegal construction, and sidewalks and streets are used for building.[18] The majority of the buildings in Roma ghettos are built illegally, making it very difficult for the utility services to reach customers. Some housing projects aimed specifically at Roma actually maintain the isolation and segregation of these communities.[19]

In 2007, 64% of the Bulgarian Roma population lived in neighborhoods with poor health conditions, and 34% lived in areas separate from surrounding cities or in the cities themselves,[20] where they are concentrated in ghettoized neighborhoods, such as Fakulteta in Sofia, Nadejda in Sliven, Komluka and Meden Rudnik in Burgas, and Stolipinovo and Sheker Mahala in Plovdiv.

Energy Supply and Bad Debts in Roma Neighborhoods[21]

Many people in Bulgaria fail to pay their electric bills, and many of them are Roma. Bad debts in terms of electricity or water bills have existed for years in Roma neighborhoods. The accumulating debts posed a growing economic problem for the utilities that serve Roma settlements all around the country. The roots of the problem are multi dimensional. Since the fall of the Communist regime, there had been almost no new investments in the communal infrastructure. Technical connection to electricity or heating networks was particularly difficult, if not impossible, in the settlements mainly inhabited by Roma or Turks. This structural situation, combined with the existing bad socio-economic situation, led many Roma to steal electricity by illegally tapping the grid. This again led to frequent blackouts because of the instability of the grid, and this subsequently led to an unreliable supply. At the same time, because bills remained unpaid, the utilities had no capital to invest in the upgrading or renovation of the electricity infrastructure, which led to a further downgrading in service quality.

There are two quick answers one hears when asking why the Roma in Bulgaria do not pay their electricity bills: first, they are too poor; and second, they are manipulated by political forces. However, it is not that simple. Failure to pay is not only due to factors like affordability, the general income situation, or a household's budgeting and management skills; the reasons also lie in the dynamics within the community, and a general feeling of being treated unfairly by general society and its institutions.

Bad Debts—A Sociological Phenomenon[22]

> The Roma people in Stolipinovo feel very powerful because they are large in numbers. They live in a city within a city. When they are isolated like this, they only follow their own rules. Even the police haven't dared to go into this ghetto. But if they live in smaller settlements or if they live in mixed districts with non-Roma families, then they abide the rules of society.
>
> Anton Gramatikov, director of the metering
> department of EVN Bulgaria

Some Roma simply refuse to pay, for example, when they know that many of their neighbors are refusing to pay or because their electricity lines have been tapped by neighbors who run up their bills. Some Roma do not pay because they believe that they are being unfairly overcharged by the electrical utility company or by its corrupt employees.

The endemic non-payment reveals a complex process of social, economic, and psychological factors leading to the refusal to pay. A research study by the Open Society Institute (OSI) reveals how a vicious circle is kicked off: deprivation and prejudice lead to the segregation of the already marginalized Roma minority. As a result, they effectively lose most of their links and bridges to other segments within society. At the same time, they are deprived of effective access to institutions and authorities. The only thing that holds the community together is its close internal links. When the payment of utility bills appears against such a background and in the context of poverty, the absence of immediate punishment for non-payment can lead to a process that normalizes non-payment as accepted behavior and even a group norm.[23]

Ineffective Responses and Growing Tensions

> The Roma were blamed for stealing the electricity. The truth is, the stealing happened everywhere, the Bulgarians did it, too! But the electricity company decided to install the meters on poles 15 meters high in special boxes, which are secured and locked. The consumers were actually prevented from tracking their consumption; they did not know how much energy they were using. In the end it's a matter of trust. If you don't trust, you don't pay.
>
> Daniela Michalova, a lawyer working for the
> Open Society Institute

The electrical utilities responded in a variety of ineffective ways to the Roma failure in paying their bills. In districts where the companies were technically able to cut off electricity to individual customers, Roma had illegally reconnected their houses, bypassing electric meters. Therefore, the electricity meters, some of which were more than 30 years old and very easy to manipulate, were installed on exterior boards that were fixed on poles at about 15 meters above the ground. "The Roma destroyed the boards and the meters, and illegally connected themselves to the electricity lines," remembered Anton Gramatikov. "They are very creative. The high poles were no real obstacles for them, but it made them angry. They attacked the electricians, for whom it became dangerous to go into Stolipinovo or other Roma ghettos." However, the installation of the electric meters on high poles became common practice in Roma neighborhoods in all Bulgarian cities, and the meters turned into a much-contested symbol of discrimination and distrust among the Roma.

For self-protection, the electricity distributors eventually started to collectively cut off electricity supply in whole districts or blocks without distinguishing between residents who paid their bills and those who failed to pay. This led to more unrest, as regularly paying households were also "punished," among them ethnic Bulgarian families. "We pay our bills regularly, but we get no electricity because of the Roma. They have brought us back to the eighteenth century," said Diana Ilieva, furious after the power cuts in 2002 that affected about 300 households of non-Roma families living in Stolipinovo.[24]

STOLIPINOVO—A SPECIAL CONFLICT AREA

"During 2002, the Roma ghettos in Bulgaria began to resemble enclaves of the third world in a country that dreams of joining the first world."[25]

The majority of Roma living in the southeastern territory of Bulgaria, the operating area of EVN, are concentrated in the towns of Plovdiv and Sliven. According to the official census, around 27,000 Roma live in the Plovdiv region, with a total population of over 700,000 people. However, the real number of Roma in Plovdiv is estimated to be much higher and is considered to be close to 80,000. This figure represents 11% of the population of the Plovdiv region and around 20% of the population of the town of Plovdiv. Plovdiv is home to four districts that are mainly inhabited by Roma: Stolipinovo, Sheker Mahala, Hadji Hassan Mahala, and Arman Mahala—the biggest being Stolipinovo. The number of its inhabitants is estimated to be around 35,000 during summer, with almost double the figure in winter due to migration patterns. "Even though Stolipinovo is a desperate place to live, many people move there during the winter months," explained a Bulgarian consultant for EVN. "Some Roma even use it as a resource and make a business out of it. They 'collect' and charge other Roma for using the water and the electricity."

Stolipinovo is considered the most problematic Roma district in Plovdiv, partly because of its sheer size, but also because of the particularly depressed socio-economic situation of its residents. It is estimated that the unemployment rates in Stolipinovo reach up to 90%, according to information of the Employment Agency Plovdiv, and 97% of those 90% do not qualify for welfare subsidies.

Moreover, the housing situation in Stolipinovo is acute. People live either in run-down blocks built in the Communist era or houses, many of which are illegally built with no connection to water, sewage, electricity, or gas for heating. Illegal construction presents a potential danger for inhabitants because of bad construction materials and static stability, and of streets obstructing emergency services and exits, as well as the provision of utilities. Garbage is not collected in Stolipinovo by the city, resulting — together with an inappropriate and patchy sewage system — in bad water quality and the danger of infection and epidemics[26].

The Political Game

Yet another dimension is added to the complexity of the situation in Stolipinovo. During Bulgaria's transition from the Communist regime to democracy and conse-quent democratic elections, the votes of the Roma and Turkish minorities became valuable, particularly on a municipal level. Because of their weak socio-economic situation, the Roma are easy to manipulate. Many observers claim that parties of all political camps have paid for Gypsy votes with cash and food supplies, or by bribing Roma with festivals and conferences. Various political forces have lured in the Roma population with promises to improve their living conditions.

In Stolipinovo, the major bait was the cancellation of accumulating debts for electricity bills. This created and fostered a sense of immunity from punishment among the irregular payers. In addition, the exertion of political pressure of the political decision maker on the EDCs to play along was well established, origi-nating in the culture of dominant political influence in the former state-owned enterprises.

The Genesis of the Electricity Regime

On February 21, 2002, the long-lasting conflict between the state-owned electricity supplier in Plovdiv and the Roma in Stolipinovo finally erupted into violence. When the utility disconnected the whole neighborhood after unpaid bills dating back several years reached a multi-million leva (the Bulgarian currency) mark, riots broke out. Outraged Roma erected roadblocks with garbage cans and started to throw stones at cars passing by.[27] The regional coordinator of the Internal Macedonian Revolutionary Organization (IMRO) commentated on the events in Stolipinovo:

> What happened is a sad epilogue of a policy of manipulation, demagogy and compromise that had been conducted over the past four, five years. The debts of the Roma residents were not collected so that the ruling political force in Plovdiv could win the votes of the people living in the Roma residential areas. The problem of paying the money was being settled by a telephone call by the former district governor and of ex-mayor.[28]

The disturbances went beyond any previous incidents in terms of numbers of demonstrators and readiness for violence. "The Bulgarians will regard the Taliban in

Afghanistan as angels if they leave us in darkness," threatened an angry Roma resident in connection with cut-off electric power supply of the residential areas of Stolipinovo and Sheker Mahala. This eruption of violence and the fear of repeats forced the public authorities to seek a way out of the dilemma.

Local authorities, executives of EDC Plovdiv, and representatives of the protesting Roma reached an agreement whereby the power supply debtors in the Roma suburbs were to pay 10% of the amount due for January, accounting for 299,000 leva (US$ 134,000). According to EDC Plovdiv's executive director, the company was prepared to restore the power supply if the agreement was honored and the sum agreed was paid.[29] The agreement seemed of little value. Only a few weeks later, five power supply posts were destroyed in the residential areas Hadzhi Hassan, Arman Mahala, and Stolipinovo.

Finally, as a last sanction, the neighborhood was put on a regime—electricity supply was cut off from 8 am until 7 pm—in order to protect the EDC from more excessive losses. Stolipinovo was soon regarded as a lost cause.

Stolipinovo—Looking for a Way out

"We have inherited a disaster," said Stefan Szyszkowitz as he recalled events. "We became aware of the importance of Stolipinovo when the media began to hunt us and we didn't know how to react properly to their accusations. Facts just did not count anymore." Suddenly, Stolipinovo emerged as the most important question of economic future for the company, its image, and its long-term strategy in Bulgaria, inseparably linked to the question of social responsibility.

After bad press regarding the court decision on the discrimination issue was reported in one of the leading Austrian newspapers in December 2006—triggering even more bad press in Austria—Rudolf Gruber, EVN's chairman of the supervisory board, urged Szyszkowitz to take action and assured the full backing of the board.

Risky Customers

The issue of "risky customers," as the non-paying customers mainly living in Roma ghettos were called, was not new to the Bulgarians who worked for EVN's predecessor. To learn about the dimension of the risky customers on EVN's territory, the customer service center organization KEZ carried out an analysis of the neighborhoods regarding their risk potential. The analysis included questions about topics such as safety, the height at which the meters were installed, and an assessment by KEZ regarding the level of tension and the risk of escalation.

KEZ reported that, in 147 neighborhoods with 99,000 customers, 50,500 could be classified as risky customers—corresponding to 51%. In 85 neighborhoods, the quota of risky customers was over 50%, and in 76 neighborhoods, the meters were installed higher than 2 meters off the ground. Some 41 neighborhoods were classified as having a "very high" risk of social tension and escalation regarding maintenance of the electric installations, and 70 neighborhoods were classified to have a "high" risk (see Exhibit 3).

EXHIBIT 3. Risky customers/potentials

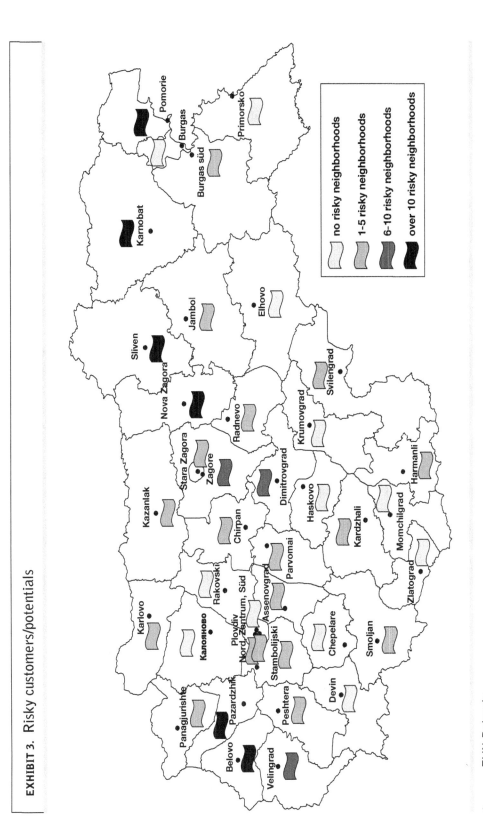

Source: EVN Bulgaria.

The data found for Stolipinovo was the most disturbing.

- Of the 5,500 electronic meters installed in an area of 1.7 quare meters, 3,400 were sabotaged or destroyed.
- Some 2,000 houses were not connected to the grid at all.
- The electric infrastructure consisting of 17 transformer substations and 112 km of electricity lines was found to be in a bad and neglected state.
- The transformer substations were easy targets for continuous vandalism. Maintenance was impossible without police protection.
- The accumulated bad debts amounted to €6 million with a collection rate of only 3%.
- EVN estimated that it had to invest around €34,000 in the maintenance of the electricity supply and around €17,000 in the security measures.
- Yearly energy consumption was estimated to be 50 GWh. Technical losses in Stolipinovo amounted to 41%.

A Technical Approach

Even though the Bulgarians were well aware of the high-risk customer problem, a solution had never been prioritized or promoted either due to political pressure and/ or lack of leadership. Nevertheless, in 2003, one of the predecessor companies of EVN, EDC Stara Zagora, installed electronic meters with distant meter reading and built-in relays to turn on or cut off the electricity to reduce the presence of employees and prevent social conflicts and attacks in Roma neighborhoods. The new meters were installed at eye level to make maintenance more convenient. In order to prevent tampering or vandalism, a security firm was recruited. It turned out that this concept unintentionally also led to a higher collection rate.

This important lesson provided a strong argument for the technical approach EVN developed to replace the old meters and repair the grid, as well as transmission substations. In May 2006, a proposal on how EVN could proceed in the seven riskiest Roma neighborhoods was submitted to the management board (see Exhibit 4).

To build a sustainable economic model, five targets were set for the investment to pay off. The new technical solution should lead to:

- an increase of collectability of the electricity bills up to 100%;
- a reduction of energy consumption between 30% and 50%;
- a reduction of technical losses to 10%;
- a payback rate of the old debts of about 15%; and
- the acquisition of new customers by preventing illegal tapping.

Moreover, in its proposal, the technical working group listed the following "non-economic" reasons to justify the investments.[30]

- Legal requirements: We do not have the right to cut off customers who are paying their bills regularly.

EXHIBIT 4. Risky neighborhoods: opportunity overview

No	Data/ Indicators	Units	ERP Plovdiv-WV Stolipinovo	Plovdiv-WV Shekera	Stara Zagora-WV Makedomski	Stara Zagora-WV Zora	Burgas-WV Pobeda	Sliven WV Komluka	Yambol-WV D.Sjuleimezova	Total
1	Number of customers	Number	5,330	810	950	850	790	1,010	990	10,730
	BEFORE ACTION									
2	Delivered Energy per Transformer Station per Year	KWh	54,300,000	8,840,000	8,100,000	7,300,000	10,350,000	10,200,000	4,300,000	103,390,000
		Leva	3,118,449	507,681	465,183	419,239	594,401	585,786	246,949	5,937,688
3	Sales Quantity per Year	KWh	34,600,00	6,800,000	5,500,000	5,500,000	3,800,000	4,850,000	1,600,000	62,650,000
		Leva	3,820,532	750,856	673,750	673,750	465,500	594,125	196,000	7,174,513
4	Collection Rate per Year	Leva	38,205	7,509	640,063	579,425	148,960	404,005	7,840	1,826,006
		% of Sales	1,00%	1,00%	95,00%	86,00%	32,00%	68,00%	4,00%	25,45%
5	Balance of Receivables per March 1, 2006	Leva	9,707,000	2,067,000	17,000	10,700	143,000	145,000	1,890,000	13,979,700
6	Grid Losses per Year	KWh	19,700,000	2,040,000	2,600,000	1,800,000	6,550,000	5,350,000	2,700,000	40,740,000
		% of energy to be distributed	36,28%	23,08%	32,10%	24,66%	63,29%	52,45%	62,79%	39,40%
	OUTCOMES AFTER IMPLEMENTATION OF MEASURES									
7	Delivered Energy per Transformer Station per Year	KWh	38,010,000	6,188,000	6,885,000	5,840,000	7,245,000	7,140,000	3,010,000	74,318,000
		Leva	2,182,914	355,377	395,406	335,391	416,080	410,050	172,864	4,268,083
8	Sales Quantity per Year	KWh	34,209,000	5,569,200	6,196,500	5,256,000	6,520,500	6,426,000	2,709,000	66,886,200
		Leva	3,777,358	614,951	759,071	643,860	798,761	787,185	331,853	7,713,039
9	Collection Rate per Year incl. Old Debts	Leva	3,966,226	676,446	759,071	643,860	878,637	865,904	381,630	8,171,774
		% of Sales	105,00%	110,00%	100,00%	100,00%	110,00%	110,00%	115,00%	105,95%
10	Grid Losses per Year	KWh	3,801,000	618,800	688,500	584,000	724,500	714,000	301,000	7,431,800
		% of distributed energy	10,00%	10,00%	10,00%	10,00%	10,00%	10,00%	10,00%	10,00%
	OUTCOMES AFTER IMPLEMENTATION OF PROJECT									
11	Economic Effectiveness of Electricity Sales	KWh	0	0	696,500	0	2,720,500	1,576,000	1,109,000	6,102,000
	Economic Effectiveness of Electricity Distribution	KWh	16,290,000	2,652,200	1,215,000	1,460,000	3,105,000	3,060,000	1,290,000	29,072,000
		Leva	935,535	152,304	146,685	83,848	478,718	349,758	196,540	2,343,388

Source: EVN Bulgaria.

- We have to create conditions for the equal treatment of customers. Special rules or exemptions for non-paying customers will lead to the assumption that some customer groups are privileged. This will undermine the payment practices of paying customers.
- The current situation of differing customer treatment leads to political speculations and social tensions.
- The current situation has a negative impact on the image of our company.

Getting in Contact with the Roma—A Viral Approach

"It is a legend that all Roma have tribal leaders. In Stolipinovo, they are totally unstructured. The only thing that holds them together is their belief that they cannot leave Stolipinovo."

Stefan Abadjiev, EVN consultant

At the same time, Stefan Szyszkowitz still had no idea with whom to negotiate in the Roma community in Stolipinovo. "Their claim to leadership is built on mutual dependencies, economic power and rivalry. The biggest risk for EVN was to step into an unknown situation and get involved in any of the ongoing political, religious or internal fights," said Szyszkowitz. Several attempts to find influential, but trusted, personalities failed, as political groups tried to influence any discussion in their interest.

According to an insider, there are three influential groups within Stolipinovo.

- *The "bandits"*—families or groups who have become relatively rich by trafficking drugs, alcohol or humans. Some of them are busy in the scrap-metal business, stealing cables and metal parts for resale.
- *The "rich families"*—families who draw their power from setting up NGOs and benefit from the huge sums of European or US institutions that are flowing into projects labeled "support for Roma." Critical voices say that the funds are mainly used to build power networks and benefit family members more than the needy persons.
- *The religious communities*—mainly the Protestant and the Muslim faiths have influence in Stolipinovo.

None of these was an acceptable partner for EVN, especially because one of the most influential powers—the Muslim community—is closely related to the political party MRF, which was already infamous for manipulation during election campaigns.

Finally, with the help of Daniela Michalova, a lawyer working with the Open Society Institute and the Helsinki Committee for Human Rights, who was experienced in working with Roma, EVN was able to identify a handful of Roma leaders who assured in a credible way that their agenda was the improvement of the living conditions in Stolipinovo and who were prepared to lobby for this issue in community meetings. Daniela Michalova spoke Romany, and managed to convince them to be at least prepared to meet with EVN representatives and discuss their proposition regarding the technical approach. "It took us a couple of months to find partners who were willing to talk but in the end, it is essential to have the Roma leaders on your side," explained Daniela Michalova. "In Stolipinovo, we have identified nine leaders for 35,000 people. Also, the leaders only talk to other leaders." Therefore the meeting had to be arranged as senior-level events.

INVEST IN A "LOST CAUSE"?

Stefan Szyszkowitz took a deep breath. It was time to go. He checked again the "dos and don'ts" that Daniela Michalova had written down for the meeting: show respect, do not refuse anything that is offered, do not put a drinking glass on the floor, do not whisper. He would meet her at the periphery to Stolipinovo where the car could not pass because the illegal building activities left only narrow streets. It was not advisable to leave a company car in Stolipinovo without protection anyway. When he rode through the busy streets of Plovdiv, it was hard to believe that a neighborhood like Stolipinovo even existed. However, now he had to deal with it. Many questions arose.

- *How should he proceed given that the local authorities were not prepared jointly to tackle the problems in Stolipinovo?* Should EVN try to go ahead and push the technical solution right away? Or should it continue the electricity regime for the time being and try to get support from other stakeholders? There were indications that the public were starting to understand the complex situation better and acknowledging a period of grace for EVN to deal with the problem.
- *Was the technical approach developed by his technicians enough to tackle the complex problem of Stolipinovo?* Evidence showed that the new digital meters facilitated the targeting of defaulters and made mass cut-offs needless. The big hope was that the collection rates would go up as a result—but by how much and for how long?
- *Could he afford to put a huge investment in the grid-renovation of a neighborhood that was seen as "lost cause"?* Or should he focus on the modernization of the infrastructure elsewhere in its service area? Would EVN ever be able to earn back these investments? The investment would only pay off if the Roma (1) were willing and (2) could afford to pay their bills. Could he even trust them if an agreement were reached?
- *How could EVN ensure a sustainable solution in Stolipinovo?* Is it even EVN's role to deal with a long-standing local problem like this? What is EVN's responsibility in this conflict?
- *How would EVN's shareholders react?*

NOTES

1. C. Seelos (2011). *EVN in Bulgaria – Making it work.* These two cases can be used as standalone cases or together with the following case which is available from IESE Business School Publications (www.iesep.com/en/): *EVN in Bulgaria: "Eastern Fantasy" Meets Eastern Reality* (SM-1565-E).

2. World Bank (2006). *Reforming Power Markets in Developing Countries,* Washington, DC: World Bank.

3. Crampton, R.J. (2007). *The Oxford History of Modern Europe: Bulgaria,* Oxford: Oxford University Press, 374.

4. Business Insights (2009). *The Eastern European Electricity Market Outlook,* London: Business Insights Inc.

5. Main sources:
    a. Doukov, D. (2001). Bulgaria Power Sector Reform: Case Studies of Power Sector Reform in Developing Countries, Center for Energy Efficiency EnEffect, Sofia.
    b. Austrian Energy Agency, at http://enercee.net [accessed January 2011].

6. See www.poverty.org.uk [accessed January 2011].

7. See Center for the Study of Democracy (2010). *The Energy Sector in Bulgaria, Major Governance Issues,* Sofia: Center for the Study of Democracy.

8. Novonite.com (2004). BGN 100 M Annual Losses of Power Theft in Bulgaria, 8 January. Retrieved from www.novinite.com/articles/29689/BGN+100+M+Annual+Losses+of+Power+Theft+in+Bulgaria [accessed March 2011].

9. Main sources:
    a. Center for Liberal Strategies, Bulgarian National Television, Alpha Research Polling Agency, Open Society Institute – Sofia, NGO Links, (2007). *The National Deliberative Poll: Policies towards the Roma in Bulgaria, Briefing Materials.*
    b. European Commission (2004). *The Situation of Roma in an Enlarged European Union,* Luxembourg: Office for Official Publications of the European Communities.
    c. Crampton (2007).
    d. Petrova, D. (2004). The Roma: Between a Myth and the Future. Retrieved from www.errc.org/article/the-roma-between-a-myth-and-the-future%3Clabjegyzet1%3E/1844 [accessed March 2011].

10. Ringold D., Orenstein M., & Wilkens E. (2005). *Roma in an Expanding Europe, Breaking the Poverty Cycle,* Washington DC: Worldbank, 13.

11. Main sources:
    a. EURoma (2010). *EURoma Report: Roma and the Structural Funds,* Madrid: Fundacion Secredariado Gitano.
    b. Ringold et al. (2005).
    c. Revenga A., Ringold D., & Tracy W.M. (2002). *Poverty and Ethnicity: A Cross-Country Study of Roma Poverty in Central Europe,* Washington, DC: World Bank.

12. Crampton (2007), 440.

13. EDIS S.A. (2007). European Survey on Health and the Roma Community. In (2009) *Health and the Roma Community: Analysis of the Situation in Europe Bulgaria, Czech Republic, Greece, Portugal, Romania, Slovakia, Spain,* Madrid: FSG–Fundación Secretariado Gitan, 97.

14. Crampton (2007), 438.

15. Hajdinjak M. (2008). Political Participation of Minorities in Bulgaria, IMIR Research Paper, Sofia: International Center for Minority Studies and Intercultural Relations, 17.

16. Main sources:
    a. European Union Agency for Fundamental Rights (FRA) (2009). *Housing Conditions of Roma and Travellers in the European Union,* Vienna: FRA.
    b. EDIS S.A. (2007), 97.

17. United Nations Development Programme (UNDP) (2002). *Roma in Central and Eastern Europe: Avoiding the Dependency Trap,* Bratislava: UNDP, 15.

18. EDIS S.A. (2007), 98.

19. FRA (2009). *Housing Discrimination against Roma in Selected EU Member States—An Analysis of EU-MIDIS Data,* Vienna: FRA, 19.

20. EDIS S.A. (2007), 25.

21. If not stated otherwise, sourced from Report PR Agency ICONA [EVN internal document].

22. Pallai, K. (2009). *Who Decides? Development, Planning, Services and Vulnerable Groups*, Budapest: Open Society Institute.

23. Pallai (2009), 8.

24. *The Sofia Echo* (2002). *Power Cuts Spark Roma Riot*, 21 February. Retrieved from http://sofiaecho.com/2002/02/21/630763_power-cuts-spark-roma-riot [accessed March 2011].

25. Bulgarian Helsinki Committee (2002). *Human Rights in Bulgaria in 2002–Annual Report*, Sofia: Bulgarian Helsinki Committee, *24*.

26. Nahabedian, M. (2002). *The Roma in Plovdiv*, Gdańsk: European Center for Democracy and Solidarity. Retrieved from: www.europeanforum.net/news/13/roma_in_plovdiv [accessed March 2011].

27. *The Sofia Echo* (2002).

28. Research PR Agency ICONA [EVN internal document].

29. *The Sofia Echo* (2002).

30. EVN Bulgaria (2006). Implementation Strategy of the Technical Concept in the Risky Quarters [EVN internal document].

Index

Page numbers in *italics* denote a figure/table

ABB (Asea Brown Boveri) 3–4, 10, 19,
  19–21, 290
absolutism 404, 406
absorption strategy: and international
  mergers and acquisitions 326, 331–2
Accenture 32
adaptation strategy: and multicultural
  teams 336
administrative heritage 15
African workers: rewarding of at
  Socometal 70–1
alliances *see* cross-border alliances
Amelio, William 373, *374*
Aquinas, St Thomas 84
Arthur Andersen 8, 416
assertiveness: cultural dimension of 122,
  124, 133, 143, *148*
assignments, international *see* international
  assignments
Aviva 35

baby boomers 28, 112
Bailey, Fred 236–42
balance-sheet approach: and expatriate
  compensation 192, 221–2, *225*
Banai, M. 36, 47, 49
Bangladesh: addressing child labour in by
  Levi Strauss 409, 466, 468, *469*
BankAmerica 414
Barnevik, Percy 3–4, 10
Barsoux, J. 163, 416
Bartlett, C.A. 14–16, 44, 429
basic rights, respecting 408
Bennett, D.R. 51

Bernard, Olivier 70–2
Berry, J.W. 165, 335
Björkman, I. 3, 61, 266, 316, 388
Black, J.S. 47, 189, 219, 229, 236
Boeing 273
Boisot, M. 48
Bonache, J. 192–3, 218, 222, 223, 228–9,
  232
BP 273, 416
Brannen, M.Y. 29, 159, 339
Braun, W.H. 55
Brazil 12, 19, 30, 32, 119, 121, 123, 160,
  191, 431, 476; *see also* cross-cultural
  differences in leadership
Bretton Woods Agreement (1944) 8
Brewster, C. 46, 49, 195, 198, 201
Bribery 161–2, 403–4, 418, 420, 422, 424,
  447; *see also* ethics
BRIC countries 27, 191, 386, 431
'Bridging Cultures' program 145
Briscoe, D.R. 49, 52, 125, 193
BT 27
Buddhism 406, *408*, 448, 453
Bulgaria 244, 477–90, *491*
Burger King 52

Caligiuri, P. 243
capabilities: as sources of competitiveness
  17–18
career: international xviii, 191–4, 200–2,
  223, 249–53; manager career paths and
  alliance learning 304; and multiculturals
  177–84
Carl, D. 126

Cartels 7
categorical imperative 161
Caterpillar 27–8
Caux Principles *443*
CEMEX 19
CERES (Coalition for Environmentally
    Responsible Economies) Principles *444*
Changmai Corporation (case study) 458–65
Child, J. 48, 320, 339
child labour *see* addressing of in Bangladesh
    by Levi Strauss
Chile 210, 216
China 6, 14, 18, 29, 32–3, 61, 158, 232,
    244, 263, 268, 270, 294, 303, 316,
    373–9, 382–3, 388–9, 392–6, 406, 416,
    463; cross-cultural differences in
    leadership 119, 121, 128, 131, 141–3,
    141, *147–51*; Cultural Revolution 357,
    360; establishment of Product
    Development Centre for Hi Tech Systems
    63–9; 'Guanxi' 46, 53, 68, 142–3; Haier
    356–72; and localisation/local employees
    46, 52–3; shortage of talented managers
    29, 30, 51, 290
'China plus one strategy' 36
Ching, P.-S. 46, 49
Chrysler: merger with Daimler 162
Cisco 30, 324
Citigroup 146, 416
citizenship, good 408
coaching: and Hi Tech Systems PDC in
    China 67
Coca-Cola 415
codes of conduct 403, 409–11, 418, 429
Collings, D.G. 44, 189, 191–2, 195–7, 201–2
colonialism 46
communication: and cultural diversity within
    cross-border alliances 278–9, 288,
    301–4, 384; and language 261; and
    post-merger integration 324, 328–9; and
    virtual work 264–5
communism, fall of 14
commuter assignments 195, 197, *203*, 228
compensation: balance-sheet approach 192;
    cost of living allowance (COLA) *224*; and
    expatriates 226–32; and global talent
    management 36, *224*, 228; and Hi Tech
    Systems PDC in China 67; link to
    strategy 225–7; and local employees
    231–2; satisfaction with 228–9
compensatory justice 231–2
competence development: and Hi Tech
    Systems PDC in China 67–8

competition: and global talent
    challenges 26–7
competitive advantage 17–18, 26–7, 32, 38,
    95, 217, 227, 273, 297, 342, 379;
    capabilities and knowledge as sources
    of 17–18; and corporate culture 73
computers 8
conflict of cultural tradition 411
conflict of relative development 411
Confucianism/Confucius 67, 141–2,
    360, 405–7
Coopers & Lybrand 8
Corinthios, Antoine 77–8, 83, 89–91
corporate culture 73; components of 74;
    creating an ethical 409–10; 'exporting'
    of to other countries 75; flexibility
    versus consistency issue 75; French
    differences 81–8; *see also* organizational
    culture(s)
corporate social responsibility (CSR)
    417–19, 426–7; prototypical CSR
    approaches *428–9*
corruption; *see also* bribery
cosmopolitans 165
cross-border acquisitions *see* IM&As
    (international mergers and acquisitions)
cross-border alliances 266; alliance
    manager 279–81; archetypes of 272;
    benefits of cultural diversity 324;
    cultural audit 278; developing
    capabilities 291–2; Human Resource
    policies 285–6; impact of multicultural
    employees on 162–3; implementing
    286–96; knowledge exchange 300; and
    national cultures 340–2; and negotiation
    team 281–2; network boundaries 306–7;
    obstacles to learning in 297–8; and
    organizational cultures 334–9; and
    organizational development and change
    activities 291; and partner selection
    277–9; and performance management
    305–6; and rewards 274, 287; principles
    of effective learning in 301–6; shared
    culture 296; staffing 288–9; strategic
    intent 298; success 269; and teams 331;
    training and development 282; and
    transnationalism 307–8; venture
    champions 285
cross-cultural differences; attitudes towards
    hierarchy and authority 385; Brazil
    131–5, *132*, 145, *147–51*; China 140–3,
    141, *143–7*; and communication 384;
    dimensions 121–3, *124*;

Egypt 137–40, *138*, 145, *147–51*; and ethics 405, 407, 412–13; France 135–7, *136*, 145, 147–51; and international mergers and acquisitions 334; and leadership qualities 126–8, 129–30; management practices 125–6; and negotiations 158–9; steps towards understanding and adapting to 143–4; *see also* cross-border alliances

cross-cultural similarities; global leadership 426

cultural adaptability 144–5

cultural artifacts 74, 80, 94–5

cultural audits 278, 375

cultural differences *see* cross-cultural differences

cultural dimensions, common 121

cultural diversity: in cross-border alliances *see* cross-border alliances

cultural due diligence 163

cultural relativism 403–5, 407, 418, 447, *452*

culture; *see also* corporate culture; cross-cultural differences; organizational culture 119

culture clusters 122–3, 128

CultureGrams 145

customers: and global talent challenges 27

Daimler-Chrysler 162

Deloitte 37

Delta Beverages India case study 243

demographics: and global talent challenges 28; and localisation 45

deregulation 14

developing economies 27

Di Stefano, Joe 168, 175

Dickman, M. 27, 193, 196

differentiated approach: and talent attraction and selection 35

distributive justice 220, 232

diversity: and cosmopolitanism 449; integrated with management practices 115; leadership 113; management of 116; strategies 105

domestic cultural diversity: and cross-border alliances 335

Donaldson, T. 161, 403, 418, 420

downsizing 11

Doz, Y. 14, 15, 44

dual-career couples 191, 212

due diligence 77, 86, 163, 278, 339, 343

Dunfee, Thomas 161, 411, 418, 429

Eastern Europe 14, 27, 51–3, 123, 125, 195, 481

EDB 407

Edström, A. 12, 289, 190, 222, 225

education: and localization 50–1

Egypt: cross-cultural differences in leadership 122–3, 137, 140, 143–5, *147–51*

Ehnert, I. 438, 440, 445, 448

emotions: and cultural diversity within cross-border alliances 336–8

employee-of-the-year/month 90, 96

employees, multicultural *see* multicultural employees

employment relations, early 6–7

enacted values 74

Enron 416, 426–7, 446

Entero Vioform drug 412

Equal Employment Opportunity Commission 411

equity theory 231–2

espoused values 74

ethical imperialism 404, 420, 423, 428–9, 447, *452*

ethics 403–16; and absolutism 405, 406; and bribery 407, 409–10, 412, 413, 415; and Caux Principles 443; and CERES Principles 444; and Changmai Corporation case study 458–66; and codes of conduct 403, 409–11, 418, 429; conflicts of development and conflicts of tradition 410; and core values 407–8, *408*; creating an ethical corporate culture 409–12; and cross-cultural differences 405, 407, 412, 447, 449; cultural relativist approach 403–5, 407, 418, 447; Eastern and Western approaches 453; and ethical imperialism 404, 420, *428*, 429, 447, *452*; and Global Sullivan Principles *443*; guidelines for ethical leadership 413–14; and ILO's Labor Conventions *443*; and multicultural employees 161–2, 168; and nepotism 411; philosophical traditions of 403; principles guiding 406; and software piracy 405; and UN Universal Declaration of Human Rights 406, 443; universalist and relativist perspectives 161

ethnic minority 105, 481–2

European Union (EU) 478, 481

Evans, P. 3, 44, 45, 56, 194, 266

EVN in Bulgaria (case study) 477–93

expatriate performance appraisal 208–17; adjustment to a new culture 212–13; by home office management 209–11, 215; by local management 209, 215; factors affecting 211–13; guidelines 213–17; performance criteria 215–16; and technical job know-how 212; trying to objectify the evaluation 214–15

expatriates/expatriate assignments 8–9, 11, 12, 13, 18, 45–7, 49, 50; case studies 236–43, 276–82, 249–55; compensation 218; and cost 230; and failure 192, 229; impact of multicultural employees on 159–61; performance of 209–14; recruitment and selection 191, 197, 199, *203*, 220; relationship between local employees and 56–8, 220, 231–2; retention of 192; and return on investment (ROI) 200; self-initiated 194, 228; skills developed as result of assignment 208, 209, 213; and training 198, 201, 213; turnover rate 217

FedEx 17

feedback: and cross-border alliances 293, 300

flexpatriate assignment 198, 201–2

Ford 273, 286, 295

Foreign Corrupt Practices Act (US) 412–13

foreign direct investment 6, 14, 26, *34*, 268

Four Seasons Hotel and Resorts; approach to international growth 77; choice of Le Calvez as general manager in France 86; contribution of corporate culture to success 75; cultural challenges in operating in France 75; entering Paris and becoming a French employer 81; globally uniform standards 79; goals, beliefs and principles 98; Golden Rule of human resources and implementation of at F.S. George V hotel 80; implementation of 35-hour work week 88; international structure 76; management discipline at F.S. George V 95; overview and features of 75; performance 76; results at the F.S. George V hotel 93; running the F.S. George V 89

France 12, 70–1, 75, 121–3, 131; cross-cultural differences in leadership 135–7, *136*, 145, *147–51*; cultural challenges of operating in 83–5; operating in by Four Seasons *see* Four Seasons Hotels and Resorts

Francis, Olivia 172

frequent flyer assignments 228

Friedman, Thomas 27, 120

Fryxell, G.E. 55–7

Fuji Photo Film 7

Furst, B. 57

future-oriented behaviors: cultural dimension of 122

Gabrielli, Jose Sergio 30

Galbraith, J.R. 12, 189–90, 222, 225

Galinsky, A.D. 159

Galvin, Robert 414, 416

Gamble 52, 54, 57

GCC (Gulf Cooperation Council) 51–4,

GE Capital 327, 331

GE (General Electric) 279, 376, 415

gender egalitarianism: cultural dimension of 123, *124*, *150*

General Agreement on Tariffs and Trade (GATT) 8

General Electric *see* GE

General Motors (GM) 273, 304

geocentric organization 14

Germany 28, 32, 122, 214, 222, 329, 359, 365, 415

Gerstner, Louis (Lou) 105–7, 114–16, 118, 377–8

Ghettos 481, 483–6, 488

Ghoshal, S. 14–16, 44, 429

Ghosn, Carlos 155–60, 162–5

global leadership/leaders 119–55, 416–59; attributes of 144; challenges to 423–4, 440–1; characteristic traits 420; and citizenship 447, *452*; and cross-cultural differences 125–8, *129–30*; cross-cultural differences in Brazil 131–5, *132*, 145, *147–51*; cross-cultural differences in China 140–3, *141*, 143, 145–9; cross-cultural differences in Egypt 137–40, *138*, 145, *147–51*; cross-cultural differences in France 135–7, *136*, 145, *147–51*; cross-cultural similarities 128, 131, 144; development of 145–6; and diversity 417, 426–7; and ethics 419–25; and GLOBE project 119–55; handling cross-cultural challenges 120–1; impact of globalization 119–21; as implementer or ecological and social progress 444–6; shortage 145–6; steps towards cross-cultural understanding and adaptability 143; and sustainability

444–6; *see also* responsible global leadership/leaders
global managers: shortages of 120, 284
global mindset 145–6; definition 450
global staffing *see* staffing
Global Sullivan Principles *443*
global talent challenges 24, 25–32, 26, 40–1; and competition 26–7; and customer demands 27; definition 25; and demand and supply for workers with competencies 28–30; and demographics 28; and expansion of world trade 25–6; and globalization 25–8; and individuals entering the labor market 27–8
global talent management 24, 26–8, 32–8; attraction and selection 35; barriers to 29–40; and compensation 37; definition 25; integrated and flexible systems of HR actions for 38–9; location planning and management 32–5; and organizational linkages 32; and performance assessment 36; reduction and removal 38; results of effective 26, 39; and retention 37–8; training and development 36
global teams 257; and language 261–2; and leadership 265; and modes of communication 264; obstacles created by cultural differences; and perception of power 258–60; process 260–1; rules of engagement *262*; social distance 257–61, 263–5; and virtual work 228; *see also* multicultural teams
globalization 13–18; factors increasing 14; and global talent challenges 25–8; impact of on global leadership 119–21; road map for managing 14–16
GLOBE (Global Leadership and Organizational Behavior Effectiveness) 119
Godfrey, M. 47
Govindarajan, V. 27, 225–6
Great Depression 6
Guangdong Electronics (case study) 388
Gulf Cooperation Council *see* GCC 45, 51, *54*
Guthridge, M. 35, 37, 39

Hai apai *448–9*
Haier: Haier in Japan (case study) 356–72
Haier Asia International (HAI) 356, 365
Hailey, J. 49, 50
Hanson, Peter 61, 63
Harry, W.E. 30, 37, 44, 47, 53
Harvey, M. 197, 218, 219, 220

Harzing, A.-W. 189, 192
headquarters-coordination route 10
health and safety *see* occupational health and safety
Hedlund, G. 14
Hengst, Wolf 79–80
Heterarchy 14
Hi Tech Systems: establishment of Product Development Centres in China 61–9
hierarchy: and cross-cultural differences 141
Hitch, Stephen 28
Hofstede, Geert 11, 121, 335, 340; Culture's Consequences 83
Hong Kong 50, 374, 383, 405, 407, 458
human dignity, respecting 408
Human Resource Management Journal 120
human rights 49, 359, *408*, 414, 416, 418, 422, 430, 440, 442, 447, 463, 467
Huselid, M.A. 35
Hutchings, K. 53

IBM: and diversity 105–18; merger with Lenovo *see* Lenovo–IBM merger 373
IBTs (international business travellers) 194–6, 199, 201
IJVs (international joint ventures): Guangdong Electronics case study 388; Haier in Japan case study 356; negotiation challenges 282; *see also* cross-border alliances
IKEA 430
IM&As (international mergers and acquisitions) 316; absorption strategy 326, 331–2; attitudes towards 319–20; and communications 328–9; cultural clash 334–7; and due diligence 278, 339; employee reactions 319–20; holding strategy 326, 332; impact of multicultural employees on 162–3; importance of speed and timing 327–8; integration approach 323–5; integration process 292, 321, 324, 325–6; key human resource issues 288–9, *345*; and leadership 284, 320; Lenovo-IBM case study 373; management of cultural change 334–9; people challenges *344*; performance and success rate of 269, 292–3, 336; post-merger integration 381–2; preservation strategy 326, 331–2; reasons for failure 270; responsibilities of transition team *280*; retaining talent 333; role of integration manager *280*; symbiosis strategy 326;

trust 320–5; types of *272; see also* cross-border alliances
implicit leadership theory (ILT) 126
in-group collectivism: cultural dimension of 123
India 19, 27, 29, 32, 36, 158, 161, 191, 109, 211, 212, 216, 217, 263, 316, 359, 407; bribery in 413; Delta Beverages case study 243; and Entero Vioform drug 412; and nepotism 411; shortage of talented managers 30; software industry 14
Industrial Revolution 5
industrialization: impact of 5
inpatriation 197
institutional collectivism; cultural dimension of 123
integration managers 163, 330, 331, 333, *344,* 345
Intel 275
intellectual property rights: and localization 48
international assignments 189–90; case studies 236–55, 243–8, 249–53; commuter and rotational 195–7; and expatriates *see* expatriates/expatriate assignments; and family issues 212, 219; flexpatriate 198, 201–2; frequent flyer 228; global virtual teams 228; occupational health and safety 198; permanent transfer 196–7, *203*; policies surrounding alternative 195–6; recruitment and selection 197; and reward 200–1; short-term 197–9, 201; and training 198
international business travellers *see* IBTs
international human resource management (IHRM): evolution of 18
international joint ventures *see* IJVs
International Labour Organization (ILO); Core Labor Conventions *443*
international mergers and acquisitions *see* IM&As
internationalization 4–7; birth of multinationals 7–8; of HRM 11–13; impact of advances in transport and communications on 8; impact of industrialization on 5–6; impact of war and economic depression on 6–7; paths to 15; pioneers of early 5; staffing for 8–9
inverted triangle 360–3, 366–8, 370–1
ISO 9000 series *394*
Israel/Israelis 263, 429
ITT 15

Jackson, S.E. 24, 25, 29, 167
Japan/Japanese 14–16, 28, 32, 156, 159, 213, 222, 237–42, 266–8, 273–4, 286–7, 290–7, 302–6, 339, 405; early employment practices 6–7; gift giving tradition 407, 412; Haier in Japan case study 356; headquarters-coordination route 10–11; HRM practices 12
Javidan, M. 119, 126, 426, 430, 431
Johnson & Johnson 409
joint ventures *see* IJVs (international joint ventures)
Jonsson, Anders 62
justice approach: and ethics 440–1

Kant, Immanuel 161
Kanter, Rosabeth Moss 329
Kao 16
Kindle, Fred 4
Kiriazov, D. 51–3
knowledge: as sources of competitiveness 17
knowledge workers: increase in demand of 29
Koreans 359, 412
Kotchian, Carl 412
Kyoto Protocol 442

labor market, expansion of 26
Lane, H.W. 243
language: and multiculturals 156–7, 178
Lasserre, P. 46, 49
Latin America 27, 112, 123, *124*, 215, 297
Laurent, A. 125
Le Calvez, Didier 84, 86–8, 90–2
leadership: global *see* global leadership; and international mergers and acquisitions 284–5, 320, 330–1; and Lenovo–IBM merger 386
Legend 373–7
Legendre, Phillippe 92
Lenovo–IBM merger; background 373–7; cultural differences and ways to overcome 384; and leadership 386; post-merger integration 381–2; restructuring 382–3; timeline *374*
Levi Strauss; addressing child labor in Bangladesh 466
Lind, Johan 62
Litvin, D. 49, 50
Liu Chuanzhi 373–4
local employees/localisation 12, 18, 44–58; barriers to and disadvantages of utilizing 48–9, 51–5; benefits of utilizing 47–8,

50–1; as better off than other groups of employees; change in competence compared with expatriates; compensation discrepancies between expatriate and 218; costs and demographics of 46, 55; definition 46; education and the workplace 52–3; emphasizing corporate identity to; and ethics 50; HR practices that discourage the socializing role of; importance of; key stages in designing a strategy 55–7; and nonattractiveness of jobs on offer 53–4; and Oman 56; and pay differentials 232; resentment towards expatriates; rewarding of; role of expatriates in 57–9; and selection 54; as source of help and support for expatriates 197; and training 54–5

location planning and management 32–3

Lockheed Martin 409, 412

Lokananta, Titus 125

MBA 51, 63, 172, 177, 181, 183–4, 237–8, 246–7

McDonald's 52, 78, 120

McKinsey 8, 30

McNulty, Y. 199

Maljers, Floris 18

management practices: cross-cultural differences 125–6

marginals 164–65

Marwaha, Ravi 382, 383

matrix structures 3, 9–11

Matson, Bill 384

Matsushita 15–16

Mayrhofer, W. 195, 221, 228 339–41

Maznevski, M. 157–8, 168

meganational firm 15–16

Mendenhall, M. 169, 172, 208, 249, 316, 341, 430

mentoring 55, 57, 110, 111, 115, 169

mergers and acquisitions (M&As) see IM&As (international mergers and acquisitions)

Mexico/Mexicans 12, 19, 125, 158, 175–6, 246, 412, 416, 425

Michaels, E. et al.: The War for Talent 38

Michelin 94, 160

Micklethwait, J. 51

Microsoft 30, 33, 36, 377

mindfulness 438, 441, 453

Mitsubishi 357, 366

moral free space 411

Motorola 280–81, 286, 305, 409–10, 414

multi-focal organization 14

multicultural employees 155–69; attributes of 156; cosmopolitans 164–6; dividend and baggage of 181–2; and ethics 161–2; impact on cross-border alliances, mergers and acquisitions 162–3; impact on ethics and leadership 161–2; impact on expatriation 159–62; impact on intercultural negotiations 158–9; impact on teams 156–8; integrated 165, 166; managing 166–8; marginals 164, 165, 166; and organizational culture development 167–8; recruitment and staffing 167; separated 165, 166; training and development 167, 168–9; types of 164–6, 165

multicultural teams 157, 181; see also global teams

multidomestic approach 4, 15–16

multinationals 5–8, 11–12, 14, 17–19, 29–30, 35–6, 38, 44–5, 195, 226, 232, 238, 268, 342, 359

National Commission on Adult Literacy 28, 30

national cultures: and cross-border alliances 334–42

NEC 15

Neeley, T. 257, 261,

negotiations: impact of multicultural employees on intercultural 156

nepotism 52–3, 411

Nigeria 47, 177–80, 182–184, 185, 404, 416, 448

Nike 17, 49, 416

Nokia 27, 32–3, 146, 272

Nooyi, Indra 155–9, 161

Novartis 36–7, 40, 321

NUMMI 273, 304

Oddou, G. 208

Ode, Uwa 177

'old school tie' network 53

Oman: and localisation 45, 54

O'Neill, Curtis 63–4

Open University 51

organizational culture(s) 73–96; and crossborder alliances 334–9, 341; and multicultural employees 185–6

Osland, J. 417

Owen, Robert 6

Oxfam 450–1

P&G (Procter & Gamble) 7, 40, 290
Palmisano, Sam 27–8, 31, 40 105–6, 112, 114, 116, *374*, 378
Panasonic 16, 365–7
pay-for-performance 37
PepsiCo 155, 157–8, 161, *450*
performance appraisal, expatriate *see* expatriate performance appraisal
performance assessment: and global talent management 36
performance evaluation: organizational culture differences 83–4
performance management: and expatriates 201; and Hi Tech Systems PDC in China 67–8
performance orientation, cultural dimension of 122, *124*
Perlmutter, H.V. 14
permanent transfer 196–7, 203
Peterson, M.F. 125
Philips 15–16
Pless, N. 168, 417, 441, 449, 453, 466
polychronic cultures *101*
population shrinkage 28
power distance: cultural dimension of 123, *124*
Prahalad, C.K. 14–15, 44
PriceWaterhouseCoopers 168, 453
privatization 14, 480–1
Procter & Gamble *see* P&G
Product Development Centre (High Tech Systems) 61
psychological testing 7
Pucik, V. 3, 190, 226, *298*,

Rank Organisation 7
recruitment: of country manager 243; and expatriates 230; and Four Seasons' F.S. George V hotel 89–90; and international assignments 191, 197, 199, *203*, 220, 222; and multicultural employees *167*, 168
reduction and removal: and global talent management 37
Reiche, B.S. 177, 192, 356
Renault 156–7, 162, *164*
Renault-Nissan alliance 156–7, 162, *164*
repatriation 12, 56–7, 192, 197, 200, 218, 220, 231, 290, 300, *301*
resource allocation: within cross-border alliances 281, 288
resource-based perspective 18, 227

responsible global leaders/leadership 416–37; and cultural and institutional context 430–2; and diversity 417, 425–7; and ethical decision-making 418, 419–25; Globally Responsible Leadership Initiative (GRLI) 440, 444, 453; and moral disengagement 418, 421, 423, 424; and moral intensity 418, 420, 424, 425; and organizational context 418, *419*, 428–30; role of multicultural managers 431; *see also* global leadership/ leaders retention: and expatriate employees 192; and global talent management *203*; and High Tec Systems PDC in China 69; and localisation 50
retirement 28, 33, 83, 88, 91, 370, *425*
return on investment (ROI): and expatriates 200
rewards: and cross-border alliances 288, 293, 294, *298*, 300, 343, *344*; and international assignment 201, 232
Rhône-Poulenc Rorer 414
Richey, David 78–80, 93–4
Rochon, Pierre 82
Roh Tae Woo 412
Roma Community 478
Rome, Treaty of (1957) 8
rotational assignments 195–7, *203*
Ruhs, M. 47
Russia 27, 51, 122–23, 191, 415, 478, 479

Samsung 359
Sanyo 356–7, 360, 365–72
Saudi Arabia 45, 51, 54, 359, 404, 411, 430
Schlumberger 36, 40
Schneider, S.C. 163
Schuler, R.S. 24, 49, 125, 193, 221, 320
Schweitzer, L. 454
Scullion, H. 35, 40, 49, 192, 194–5
Sears 414
Selmer, J. 45–8, 55–7, 193, 202
selection: criteria 11, 53; and Delta Beverages India *245*; expatriates 201; and Four Seasons' F.S. George V hotel 89–90, 95; and Hi Tech Systems PDC in China 66–7; and international assignments 191, 197–9, 201, *203*; and local employees 53; of talent 35–6
Shell 9, 13, 47, 49, 66–7, 69, 84, 146, 416, *448*
Siemens 5, 17, 146, *386*, 416
Smith, P.B. 125
social identity theory 323

Socometal 70
software piracy *405*
South America 13, 121, 210, 215, 377, 414
South Korea 19, 123, 246, 416
Southwest Airlines 73
Spanish siesta 47
Sparrow, P. 45–6, 50, 52
Stahl, G.K. 155, 163, 169, 193, 249, 316, 373, 416
staffing 8, 29, 50, 168; cross-border alliances 275, 277–8, 288–9; Delta Beverages India case study 244; and expatriates *see* expatriates; for internationalization 8–9
Stanford Professional Education, Executive Programs
succession planning *110*, 189, 246
Sugiura, Hideo 44
Suutari, V. 202, 219–20, 223 228

tacit knowledge 17–18, 227, *289*, 297
Tahvanainen, M. 196–8
Taiwan 19, 66
talent *see* global talent challenges; global talent management
Tata Steel 19
Taylor, Kathleen 81
teams: and cross-border alliances 281, 290, 303; impact of multicultural employees on 156–8; transition 163, 333, *374*
telecom industry 27
Teerikangas, S. 316, 319, 326, 328, 329, 331, 332, 335, 338, 339, 340, 344, 346
Tesco 35
Teva Pharmaceuticals 249
Texas Instruments 409, 412, 414
Thailand 123, 365, *448–9*
Thomas, D.A. 105
Thomas, D.C. 158, 159, 193, 341
ThyssenKrupp 40
Toyota 40, 273, 276, 304–5
training and development: cross-border alliances 267, *277*, 282, 291, *298*, 302–3; and expatriates 198, *203*, 213, *224*, *245*; global talent management 36; and international assignments 201; and local employees 53–4, 56; multicultural employees *167*, 168–9
transition team 163, 333, *374*
transnational organization 4, 14, 275

Transparency International 415
Trompenaars, F. 121, 125
Tung, R. 192, 199
turnover rates: factors contributing to 318

UN Global Compact 417
UN Universal Declaration of Human Rights *443*
uncertainty avoidance: cultural dimension of 123
unemployment 37, 83, 411
Unilever 12, 15–16, 18, *438*, 445, 448, *452*, 454
Union Carbide 47, 407, 415
USAA 73
Uwa Ode (case study) 177–85

values: and corporate culture 409; ethics and core 407
van den Bosch, Johannes 175
virtual teams 125

Wal-Mart 73
Wall, Jim 37
Walt Disney Company 73
Walzer, Michael 406
Ward, Steve 373, 381, 383, *386*
Warner, M. 51, 55
Watson, Sir Thomas 377
Weber, Andreas 249
Weir, D. 53
Welch, D.E. 222
Whirlpool *285*
White, J. 161, 447
women: participation in international management 191
world trade: expansion of and global talent challenges 25–6
World War I and II 6
Worm, V. 194–5, 197

Xerox 7, 297, 416

Yamani 51
Yang Yuanqing 373–6, 381–3, 386
Young, John 81

Zaibatsu 7
Zhang Ruimin 356–8, 360–2, 364, 366–7
ZZJYT (self-managed unit) 360